Windows 2000:
The Complete Reference

About the Authors

Kathy Ivens has been a computer consultant and author since 1985. She has written and contributed to more than forty books, and hundreds of magazine articles. She also writes the Reader Challenge for *Windows 2000 Magazine* (formerly known as *Windows NT Magazine*).

Kenton Gardinier, MCSE, is a Sr. Enterprise Systems Engineer specializing in performance analysis and optimization of Windows NT/2000 networks. Gardinier also lectures on various NT/Win2K issues, such as capacity planning, performance optimization, fault tolerant management and enterprise management, and frequently contributes to various magazines. In addition, he is the author of *Windows NT Performance Tuning & Optimization* (Osborne/McGraw-Hill,1998). He is the vice president for the Triangle NT User Group and serves on the board of the Worldwide Association of NT User Groups.

Our Thanks to Contributing Authors

The authors are extremely grateful for the expertise of the following contributing authors.

Larry Seltzer is a freelance writer and contract programmer who has worked in the personal computer industry since 1983. He has written commercial and in-house corporate software, and directed testing labs at *PC Week, Windows Sources*, and *PC Magazine.*

Jim Boyce is a former Contributing Editor and monthly columnist for *Windows Magazine*. He has authored and co-authored over 40 books about computer software and hardware. Jim has been involved with computers since the late seventies as a programmer and systems manager in a variety of capacities. He has a wide range of experience in the DOS, Windows, Windows NT, and UNIX environments. In addition to a full-time writing career, Jim is a founding partner and Vice President of Minnesota Webworks, a Midwest-based Web development firm (http://www.mnww.com).

Bill Wolff is the founder and president of Wolff Data Systems, a collective of senior level Microsoft Certified Professionals working primarily with Microsoft Back Office applications for a wide variety of client companies. Bill also runs the Philadelphia Back Office Users Group.

Windows 2000:
The Complete Reference

Kathy Ivens
Kenton Gardinier

Osborne/**McGraw-Hill**

Berkeley   New York   St. Louis   San Francisco
Auckland   Bogotá   Hamburg   London   Madrid
Mexico City   Milan   Montreal   New Delhi   Panama City
Paris   São Paulo   Singapore   Sydney
Tokyo   Toronto

Osborne/**McGraw-Hill**
2600 Tenth Street
Berkeley, California 94710
U.S.A.

For information on translations or book distributors outside the U.S.A., or to arrange bulk purchase discounts for sales promotions, premiums, or fund-raisers, please contact Osborne/**McGraw-Hill** at the above address.

Windows 2000: The Complete Reference

1234567890 DOC DOC 019876543210

ISBN 0-07-211920-9

Publisher
  Brandon A. Nordin

Associate Publisher and Editor-in-Chief
  Scott Rogers

Acquisitions Editor
  Wendy Rinaldi

Project Editor
  Betsy Manini
  Lisa Theobald
  Patty Mon

Acquisitions Coordinator
  Monika Faltiss

Technical Editor
  Chris Branson

Copy Editor
  Gary Morris

Proofreader
  Rhonda Holmes

Indexer
  Valerie Perry

Computer Designers
  Jani Beckwith
  Elizabeth Jang
  Dick Schwartz

Illustrators
  Robert Hansen
  Brian Wells
  Beth Young

Series Design
  Peter Hancik

This book was composed with Corel VENTURA™ Publisher.

For Sarah,
the best and brightest and funniest,
who has proven it's much more fun,
and so much easier,
to be a grandma than a mom.
Kathy Ivens

This book is dedicated to the three most cherished women in my life,
my lovely fiancée Amy,
my mom, and my sister
for their encouragement, patience, and love.
I'd also like to dedicate this book to my dad,
who is no longer with us,
for instilling in me values that I will always carry with me.
Kenton Gardinier

Contents at a Glance

Part III   Connecting with Windows 2000

Part IV   Inside Windows 2000

Part V   Internet and Intranet Functionality

Part VI   Enterprise Components

Part VII   Appendix

Contents

Part I

Understanding Windows 2000

Part II

Learning the Basics

Part III

Connecting with Windows 2000

Part IV

Inside Windows 2000

Part V

Internet and Intranet Functionality

Part VI

Enterprise Components

Part VII

Appendix

Acknowledgments

The authors would like to thank all those wonderful, incredibly talented, folks at Osborne/McGraw-Hill who worked so hard to bring this book to you. Wendy Rinaldi is a dream of an Acquisitions Editor, with an amazing depth of knowledge about publishing, writing, and even the technical stuff. Monika Faltiss performed with an incredible level of efficiency as she kept us organized and on track. Betsy Manini used her considerable skills to make sure the manuscript matched our hopes for it, and Gary Morris saved all of us from embarrassment by making sure we followed the rules we were supposed to learn in high school English classes.

In addition, the authors owe a round of applause and very special thanks to our technical editor, Chris Branson (MCSE, CNE) for his expertise and assistance. Chris is a senior support engineer for Microsoft Corporation. He has been a systems engineer and network administrator, and he currently leads one of Microsoft's Corporate Preview Support teams.

Introduction

Windows 2000 represents a major shift in the Windows network paradigm, with features that include concepts that are new to the Windows network structure. This can be disconcerting because these features aren't "extras," they're at the core of this operating system.

Learning the Active Directory, the Microsoft Management Console, and the other new management features may seem overwhelming at first, and in fact, the time you'll spend in the learning curve can be quite consuming. We wrote this book to help you put the concepts and tasks you need to understand into an orderly pattern, which will shorten your own learning curve.

What's in This Book?

This book covers all the important concepts, features and functions that are built into Windows 2000. You'll find both technical discussions and step-by-step instructions throughout the pages.

In **Part I,** Understanding Windows 2000, we present an overview of the operating system. Then we spend a lot of time (and pages) on the deployment issues. Moving to this operating system isn't just a matter of installing the files, there are a lot of tasks to attend to before you reach that step.

Part II, Learning the Basics, is filled with information about the concepts and tools that users see and interact with. There are plenty of explanations of what's new (which is almost everything) and how it all works.

Part III, Connecting with Windows 2000, covers the parts of the operating system that you'll work with to keep networking functions running smoothly. Protocols, management tools, and user issues are discussed in depth and with great detail.

Part IV, Inside Windows 2000, is a thorough discussion of the file systems, subsystems, and functions you'll use to administer your network.

Part V, Internet and Intranet Functionality, covers the management issues you'll face in these areas. You'll find plenty of features to take advantage of, because Windows 2000 offers a lot of management features that use a Web-based paradigm.

Part VI, Enterprise Components, is a guide to getting the most out of the enterprise functions built into the operating system. These features add power to your network environment.

Part VII is the Appendix. All computer books have at least one appendix, because that's the logical place to put lists and other important information about the book's subject matter. In this case, the Appendix is filled with detailed information about the various versions of Windows 2000. There's also important information about upgrade paths, so you know which previous versions of Windows can be upgraded to Windows 2000.

Is This Book for You?

This book is written for network administrators, IT Professionals, and power users. The authors have made an assumption that the reader is familiar with basic networking issues.

We wrote this book for the people who bear the responsibilities for managing Windows 2000 networks. You can translate "managing" to include deployment, configuration, and day to day administration.

The Complete Reference

Part I

Understanding Windows 2000

Chapter 1

What's New in Windows 2000

When Microsoft changed the name of Windows NT 5 to Windows 2000, they were making a point: There are many profound new features and improvements in Windows 2000.

Some of the features, such as improvements in the NTFS file system, have been on the Microsoft drawing board since the early 1990s. Some, like the reassignment of tasks from various program folders to the Control Panel, bring Windows 2000 more in line with the user interface of Windows 98. But spend a few minutes with Windows 2000 and there's no mistaking that much has changed.

Improvements in Installing NT

The installation of Windows 2000 has been improved for both upgrades and new installations. Administrators of large networks will find powerful tools for flexible remote installations across the LAN. Users of Windows NT 3.51, Windows NT 4, Windows 95, and Windows 98 will be able to upgrade their installations and preserve system settings.

Windows NT 4 was able to upgrade existing installations of earlier Windows NT versions, but could only overwrite or avoid existing Windows 95 or Windows 98 installations. And Windows 2000 now recognizes FAT32 partitions, which Windows 98 and some versions of Windows 95 support for large and more efficient partitions.

Some Windows 95 and Windows 98 applications require modifications or upgrades in order to operate under Windows NT or Windows 2000. During the upgrade to Windows 2000 you will have the option of providing "upgrade packs" for these applications. You can get these from the application vendor.

Windows 2000 supports dual-boot with Windows 95, Windows 98, and other operating systems, but there are numerous problems with specific configurations, and the considerations in planning such a setup are complex. See Chapters 2 and 3 for a complete explanation of installing Windows 2000.

Installation Service

When Microsoft designed the Win32 programming model many years ago, it failed to provide a standardized software installation facility. This error has finally been rectified in Windows 2000 with the new Windows Installer service. According to Microsoft, the Installer service will eventually be provided as a service pack to Windows 95, Windows 98, and Windows NT 4.

Prior to Windows Installer, applications needed to manage all aspects of installation on their own. Microsoft has always provided guidelines for software installation, such as using the Program Files directory and checking file versions for common files, but these guidelines couldn't account for all system configurations, and not everyone (including Microsoft) followed them consistently.

With the Windows Installer service, program installations all follow a consistent set of rules implemented in the service. Old setup programs will continue to work as they did before. New programs, in order to use the Installer service, need to write a program description file in Windows Installer format. Windows Installer takes this file and does the rest of the work.

Windows Update Manager

Users of Windows 95 and 98 with Internet Explorer 4 are able to update individual components of the operating system over the Internet, directly from Microsoft's Web site, using the Windows Update process. Windows NT users have had to check for service packs and the numerous "hot fixes" on Microsoft's FTP site.

Now Windows 2000 has the same Windows Update process, run through the Windows Update Manager. A Web-based interface lists all the components for which new versions are available and lets you choose which you want to perform. These can include Microsoft components, such as updates to Internet Explorer, and third-party components.

Windows Update (see Figure 1-1) is also available as part of the Plug and Play process: When you install a new device, you can select a number of locations from which to install device support software that includes Windows Update.

User Interface

The Windows 2000 user interface is very similar to the Windows NT 4 user interface with Internet Explorer 5.0 installed, but there are some differences. There are reorganizations of items and enhancements in the behavior of the software. Windows users shouldn't have much trouble finding their way around, although the behavior of the software has changed enough that you may find it confusing at times.

Things Have Moved

For years Windows NT has spread administrative features across a number of locations, including the Control Panel, the Administrative programs, and the Accessories program groups. Microsoft has consolidated most of these in the Control Panel, partly for consolidation's sake itself, and partly to make the interface more consistent with that of Windows 98.

As with earlier versions of Windows, there's usually more than one way to access a program; for instance, you can access the System Properties program in the Control Panel or by right-clicking on My Computer and selecting Properties. Other things are slightly different, too. Network Neighborhood, for example, has been replaced by "My Network Places." And there are some new programs, such as the new Disk Defragmenter, and new tasks such as Quota management for disks, which allow

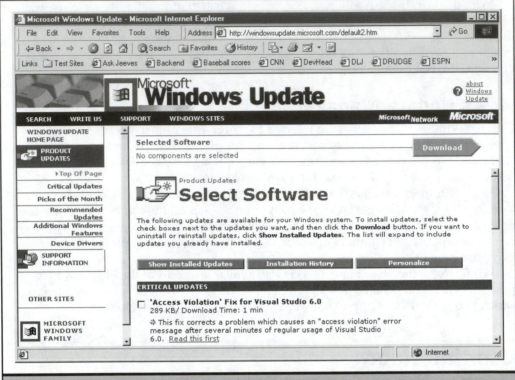

Figure 1-1.   *The Windows Update Manager can be invoked directly or as an optional location from which to install components*

you to limit the amount of disk space available to particular users. The behavior of Windows Explorer has changed, too (see Figure 1-2).

After playing around with Windows 2000, you'll also notice some minor features not available in other versions of Windows. For example, you can now drag most of the special folders from your desktop to the Start Menu, and their contents will cascade off the Start Menu for easy access. This works for My Computer, My Network Places, My Documents, and the Control Panel, as well as some third-party products.

See Chapters 5, 6, and 9 for further discussion of the Windows 2000 desktop.

Internet Explorer 5

Windows NT 4 *still* comes out of the box with Internet Explorer 2.0, although service packs will upgrade it to more modern versions. Windows 2000 comes with Internet Explorer 5, freeing applications to assume the availability of rich and modern Web-based capabilities.

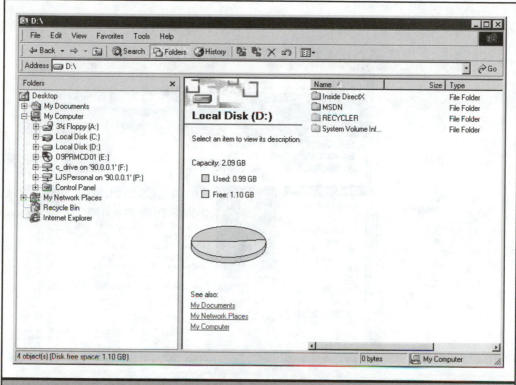

Figure 1-2.   *Windows Explorer's setup has changed. All the same locations are there, but you have to open up My Computer yourself*

Internet Explorer 5 improves many aspects of browsing (see Figure 1-3). You now have the ability to Show Related Links, improve management of the Favorites and Links features, and the management of relevant network parameters (such as proxy server settings) integrated into the browser. Internet Explorer 5 also upgrades the Outlook Express mail program to version 5.0 and adds some enhancements to the Windows user interface, such as the Quick Launch bar (to the right of the Start button).

Note   *See Chapter 11 for a complete explanation of Internet Explorer 5 in Windows 2000.*

Content Indexing Service

Microsoft Index Server has been extended into a system-wide service for indexing content. It works with Active Directory (see the "Networking" section) and other services to index data in file systems and Web sites, and then find, use, and exchange that information. Windows 2000 Index Services are useful for end users to be able to

Figure 1-3. *Internet Explorer 5, the foundation for much of Windows 2000's user interface, also adds new browser features, such as lists of links related to the ones you are viewing*

find data on their own computers and for administrators, Webmasters, and programmers to help users find data on large networks and intranets.

Hardware Support

Hardware support in Windows NT has always lagged behind that of Windows 95 and Windows 98, but this too has been addressed in Windows 2000. Not only does substantially more hardware work in Windows 2000, but it is easier to install and easier to manage. In most ways, hardware support in Windows 2000 is on par with that of Windows 98. The addition of the Windows Driver Model (WDM) to Windows 2000 means that device drivers for many classes of hardware are interchangeable between Windows 98 and Windows 2000. Note that Microsoft will not ship a version of Windows 2000 for the Alpha processor.

There are still many issues specific to Windows 2000 for device support: for example, many devices come with software that requires the use of a Windows 9x-specific VxD, or virtual device driver. On the other hand, many devices designed for servers and high-end workstations, such as RAID drives, are available only for Windows NT and Windows 2000. So don't assume that devices supported on one platform will be available on the other.

Plug and Play

Plug and Play is more than the automatic recognition of hardware by the operating system. It is a philosophy that pervades the operating system, and provides for the dynamic recognition of a changed environment and the ability to adapt to it. Plug and Play must assure that devices are not only properly recognized but also configured so it does not conflict with other devices in the system. Windows 95 was the first Windows to have this ability. It has been improved over the years with the development of device driver models and the steady disappearance, through attrition, of hardware, such as the old IBM AT architecture known as ISA (Industry Standard Architecture), which was not conducive to Plug and Play. Making Windows 2000 support Plug and Play was one of the more difficult tasks that its development team faced.

Making Plug and Play practical in Windows 2000 required new hardware standards designed to facilitate cooperative configuration. In Windows 2000 this is achieved through ACPI (Advanced Configuration and Power Interface), which supplants Windows 95's reliance on APM (Advanced Power Management) and the Plug and Play BIOS standards for similar capabilities. APM support exists in Windows 2000 for legacy power management, but the standard access to these functions is through ACPI.

Devices with WDM support also have Plug and Play driver support. Legacy Windows NT device drivers are supported in Windows 2000, but they have no Plug and Play capabilities. As with Windows 95 and Windows 98, a system with all Plug and Play enabled hardware and device drivers is far easier to manage than one still containing legacy devices, due to the added management burden on the user for those devices.

The inclusion of Plug and Play in Windows 2000 makes it architecturally even more removed from Windows NT 4. Bus drivers, such as support for PCI and PCMCIA, are now separate from the Windows Hardware Abstraction Layer (HAL). This allows them to adapt dynamically with changes to other system components, including device drivers. There are many new ways to install devices and the software that enables them, such as the Spooler and Control Panel applications. There are also new Plug and Play APIs for reading and writing information to and from the registry, and the corresponding modifications made to the registry structure.

For the purposes of Plug and Play, ACPI defines the interface between the operating system and hardware Plug and Play management features. Other standards are also involved, including the Universal Serial Bus specification, the PCI Local Bus specification, and PCMCIA standards.

Windows 2000 can recognize and adapt to Plug and Play hardware events at both run time and boot time. When it does so, the Plug and Play Manager in Windows 2000 retrieves the requirements for the device—which it can do because devices are self-describing—and determines which available system resources, such as Interrupt Request Lines (IRQs), it will assign to the device. If necessary, it will reassign resources belonging to other devices in order to make a best fit for the overall system needs. Then the Plug and Play Manager loads the appropriate device drivers for the new device.

Add/Remove Hardware Wizard

Much like Windows 98, Windows 2000 has a wizard to walk the user through the process of adding new non-Plug and Play hardware (see Figure 1-4). This same wizard can be used to remove drivers from a particular device. You will find the wizard in the Control Panel, just like in Windows 98.

 See Chapters 3 and 6 for further discussion of hardware configuration and the Add/Remove Hardware Wizard.

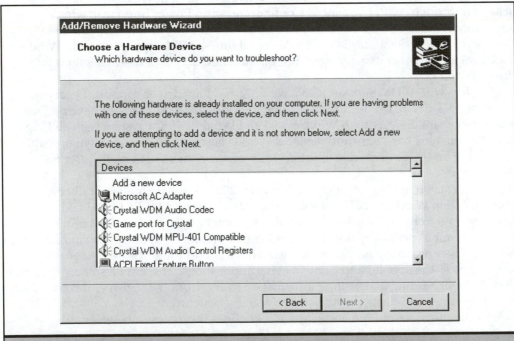

Figure 1-4. *Plug and Play and the new Hardware Wizard make hardware configuration in Windows 2000 far simpler than in Windows NT 4*

Windows Driver Model

The Windows Driver Model is a new, layered device driver model supported in Windows 98 and Windows 2000. It is designed to facilitate Plug and Play in Windows 2000. From the perspective of Plug and Play, WDM has three types of drivers:

- **Bus drivers** control buses like PCI, and PCMCIA, which themselves have child devices. Not all devices rely on bus drivers, which are usually provided by Microsoft as part of the operating system.

- **Function drivers** are the main drivers that service the device functionality. Function drivers are usually implemented as a pair of drivers, the class driver (usually written by Microsoft) and the minidriver (usually written by the device vendor). The Plug and Play Manager loads one function driver for each device.

- **The filter driver** is an optional driver that monitors and potentially modifies the input or output of the device. For example, a filter driver could compress or decompress certain data heading to a device.

Because of the paired function driver structure, device vendors need only write the minidriver, which is the device-specific portion of the driver. Functions that are generic to the class of driver are in the class driver, and therefore come "for free" to the device.

KERNEL MODE STREAMING   WDM is also the means through which Kernel Mode Streaming is implemented in Windows 98 and Windows 2000. Kernel Mode Streaming extends the data streaming techniques from Microsoft's DirectShow (formerly ActiveMovie) into the operating system kernel in order to provide for the most efficient and highest performance data stream possible.

NEW TYPES OF DEVICES   Mostly because of WDM, whole new classes of devices are supported on Windows 2000 that weren't available on Windows NT 4. These include:

- **WDM Video Capture**   Windows 2000 provides a class driver for video capture devices. The new video capture facilities improve on the old Video for Windows system while providing a mapping layer to provide compatibility with it. It works with DirectShow and Kernel Mode Streaming and supports television tuner and input selection.

- **Digital Cameras**   Digital cameras are popular items that require the Plug and Play capabilities of WDM, because most are designed to be easily connected to and disconnected from the computer.

- **USB**   Universal Serial Bus (USB) is a peripheral device bus that supports the dynamic connection and removal of devices, such as cameras and scanners, transferring data at medium speed. USB support is typical in new computer systems, but Windows NT lacked driver support for it.

- **IEEE 1394 (Firewire)**   IEEE 1394, also known as Firewire, is a high-speed device connection designed for motion cameras and high-speed scanners, which need to transfer large amounts of data quickly.

- **AGP**   AGP (Accelerated Graphics Port) is a dedicated graphics card slot in your computer that offers more than double the speed of a normal PCI card. Windows 2000 has built-in support for AGP.

- **DVD**   DVD players are super CD-ROM players and much more. DVD-ROM disks can hold many times the data that CD-ROMs can, and DVD movies and games have richer action.

- **Multiple Monitor Support**   With Windows 2000, as with Windows 98, you can install up to nine video adapters and monitors and lay them out in a logical design so that they form a large virtual screen to build an inexpensive and powerful video wall.

DirectX 7

Windows 2000 is now a top-notch gaming platform because it supports DirectX 7, which allows games and other programs to take direct advantage of the hardware for fast graphics, 3-D, input, and multiplayer support.

The new version 7 improves the level of detail and clarity in 3-D games and simulations, provides for hardware acceleration of the DirectMusic interface for quality soundtracks, and improves performance (see Figure 1-5).

Networking

Windows 2000 contains many significant enhancements in the networking area. The new Active Directory allows better management of large distributed networks, and most other components of Windows 2000 integrate with the AD to improve the usability and manageability of the network. The historical distinction between LAN-oriented computing and Internet computing breaks down in Windows 2000 as users can now perform Internet operations on NT shares and conventional file operations on Internet resources. Support for the new WebDAV protocol is at the heart of it.

The intelligent design of a complex network often mandates that the logical storage structure differ from the physical structure. The new Distributed File System allows Windows 2000 users to create a directory hierarchy consisting of file shares from across the network, including non-Windows systems. Partly because of the flexibility and power of the AD, the new IntelliMirror service lets users and administrators keep the contents of files and folders consistent across the network.

Windows 2000 has improved support for use in Virtual Private Networking, a growing technique for creating secure encrypted connections over public networks, principally the Internet. The improved hardware support in Windows 2000 allows

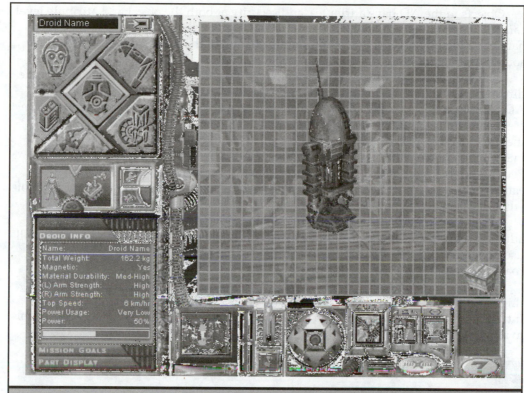

Figure 1-5.   *DirectX 7 support means that Windows 2000 is a first-class game system that is on par with Windows 98*

systems to use power management to put the system to sleep until a network or communications connection, such as a LAN request or FAX, must be serviced.

Other hardware enhancements address the need to support enterprise-scale servers. Thus Windows 2000 support Hierarchical Storage Management and clustering.

Active Directory

After years of claiming to have one, Windows finally has a true directory service. Active Directory (AD) allows administrators to organize a logical hierarchy of resources on the network, such as servers, files, printers and users, so that they can be managed intelligently. AD is more than an organizational tool. Applications and network services can use it to distribute their resources to appropriate locations. For example, users may be in physically distant locations and log on to different servers, but need access to common documents and applications.

Objects in the AD have attributes, and security at both the object and attribute level can be managed individually. For example, a user may be able to view another user's name and e-mail address, but not other information in the directory such as phone or social security numbers.

In a large and distributed network managed by a directory, the performance of the directory service can be a limiting factor on the usefulness of almost any application. AD addresses this by replicating the directory across the network. Administrators can create multiple copies of the directory, and the AD service will replicate changes in the directory across the network to keep them synchronized. There is no central master copy of the directory in this scheme, which is called multimaster replication. Because of AD, administrators can manage the network in a logical fashion. Rights can be delegated for the administration of logical groups of users and resources, not of whole servers.

In conjunction with IntelliMirror and the Windows Installer service, AD lets administrators distribute applications to users regardless of their physical location. All users assigned the specific application will have it installed on demand even if they roam to a remote office.

Programmers can use AD with standards-based protocols, including LDAP (Lightweight Directory Access Protocol) and ADSI (Active Directory Services Interface). Microsoft Exchange is an example of an application that uses these protocols to allow AD to manage users.

| Note | *See Chapter 15 for a complete explanation of AD.* |

Different Domain Structure from NT 4

AD represents a significant change in the administrative structure of Windows networks, and switching to it is a major endeavor. Taking full advantage of AD means abandoning your existing NTLM domain structure, at least in the long term.

VPN Enhancements

Virtual Private Networks (VPNs) allow users to connect over a public Internet service to a private network by encrypting the public portions of the communication. The Windows NT 4 Option Pack lets users connect to VPNs using PPTP (Point to Point Tunneling Protocol), which is a more generalized service for encoding one network protocol inside another. VPNs free organizations from managing remote access servers and phone access to their network, shifting the burden to low-cost and ubiquitous Internet Service Provider accounts.

Windows 2000 adds new options for VPN access. L2TP (Level 2 Tunneling Protocol) is an IETF (Internet Engineering Task Force) standard. (See http://search.ietf.org/internet-drafts/draft-ietf-pppext-l2tp-16.txt) It improves on PPTP and adds features of L2F (Level 2 Forwarding) to standardize and improve the tunneling process. Unlike PPTP, L2TP supports protocols other than IP, can create and manage multiple simultaneous tunnels between endpoints, and provides for tunnel authentication.

Windows 2000 also supports IPSec, a secure encrypted version of IP also designed by the IETF. IPSec authenticates and encrypts each packet. IPSec is designed for server-to-server tunneling, so it complements the use of PPTP and L2TP without changes on the client.

IntelliMirror

IntelliMirror is a Windows 2000 service that manages the replication of data across networks. When intelligently managed, IntelliMirror improves performance and data consistency and provides users with a consistent and appropriate experience no matter where on the network they connect. Users can roam to any system on the network and have access to their desktop preferences and settings, data, folders and applications. They can also take certain data offline, such as on a notebook computer on the road, edit it, and have IntelliMirror replicate the changes back to the network.

Working with the Windows Installer service and AD, IntelliMirror can be set to install applications on demand when users require them. Access to these applications can be set on a user or group basis. Administrators can use IntelliMirror and AD to centrally set and lock user Windows desktop preferences. Users can utilize the Windows 2000 Synchronization Manager (see Figure 1-6) to control the timing and extent of synchronization performed by IntelliMirror between the workstation and server.

Server Management

Windows 2000 is designed for use in larger, more complex networks than previous versions of Windows NT. The following features have been optimized for large networks:

- Administrators can intelligently manage storage through integrated support for Hierarchical Storage Management. User access to storage can be further controlled through support for Disk Quotas.

- Windows 2000's Distributed File System (Dfs) allows disparate file systems to be tied together into a single integrated storage hierarchy.

- An improved Backup facility replaces the inadequate feature in Windows NT 4, although many organizations will still be better served by a third-party product.

HIERARCHICAL STORAGE MANAGEMENT   Managing online and offline storage gives headaches to managers and users on a network. HSM eases this task by letting administrators automatically move data between high-cost storage, such as disks, and low-cost storage, such as tape. The applications don't see the difference; when they

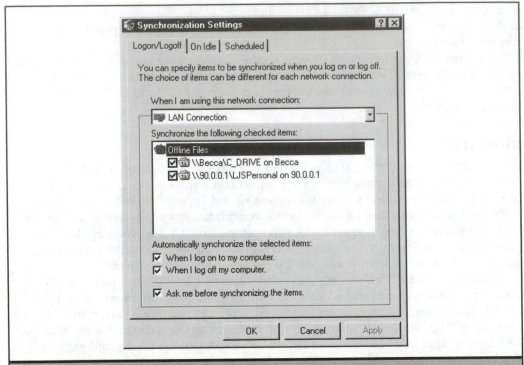

Figure 1-6.   *The Synchronization Manager controls the Windows 2000 IntelliMirror feature, which lets you use and manage network data even while offline*

request data on tape, Windows 2000 automatically moves it to disk for user access. New HSM APIs allow developers to manage this process themselves.

DISK QUOTAS   For many years, Netware administrators have had the ability to limit the amount of disk space allocated on a share to a user. Now Windows networks have the same capability through Disk Quotas, integrated with the AD. These limits can be set and monitored on a user or group basis.

DISTRIBUTED FILE SYSTEM   One of the organizational strengths of UNIX has been its ability to present all storage in a single unified namespace. Windows 2000's Distributed File System (Dfs) presents the same vision of file systems on the network. Under the control of the administrator, files from different servers can be presented in a single root. This makes complex network easier to use and manage. Dfs Load Balancing allows the creation and management of Dfs replicas, and the dynamic assignment of users to the nearest or most available replica.

BETTER MICROSOFT BACKUP   It's still not a full enterprise backup system, but the Backup program bundled with Windows 2000 (see Figure 1-7) has many more features than the inadequate Windows NT 4 version. Like the Windows NT 4 version, the new NTBACKUP is a version of Seagate Software's backup program that supports the core Windows 2000 distributed services, such as AD, Dfs, and the Certificate Server. NTBACKUP can run on schedule and, when run on a domain controller, can back up core Windows 2000 services without intervention. But there are advanced features of Windows 2000, such as HSM, that NTBACKUP cannot manage.

Note   *See Chapter 10 for a complete explanation of Microsoft Backup.*

Figure 1-7.   *Windows 2000 has a new and improved Backup program, including wizards for common backup tasks*

HIGH-END HARDWARE   Windows 2000 adds the following support for very high end storage systems based on new interfaces:

- **I2O** is a standard developed by Intel and numerous storage companies to create intelligent high-speed storage management hardware. I2O adapters relieve the CPU of much of the processing work involved with storage management and speed throughput accordingly.

- **Fibre Channel** is a 1GB/sec data transfer standard that blurs the line between high-speed networking and high-speed data storage. It maps common protocols, such as SCSI and IP, onto a common physical interface.

- **IEEE 1394,** also known as FireWire, is a new standard for high-speed peripheral devices such as motion cameras and scanners.

OTHER SERVICES

- **Remote Storage Services**   Seagate also provides Windows 2000's new Remote Storage Services, which automatically monitor the amount of free space on disks. When free space drops below a set threshold level, RSS works with HSM to move data to remote storage.

- **Link Tracking**   Windows 2000 has improved support for link tracking. In previous versions, even though Windows attempted to track the target of a shortcut if it moved, it was possible for the link to be broken. Windows 2000 uses a volume-wide indexed ID for each resource that may be so tracked, assisting in the tracking of items that may have been moved or renamed.

- **Internet Print Protocol (IPP)**   The new Internet Print Protocol allows users to share and utilize printers across the Internet via standard Internet protocols. Users can browse print queues over the Internet and find new printers and install drivers for them, all over the Internet.

- **Printer Load Balancing**   In conjunction with the clustering services in Windows 2000 Advanced Server and DataCenter Server, Administrators can set up print servers to automatically fail over or load-balance in order to improve availability of printing services.

Internet Information Server 5

Internet Information Server version 5 adds several new features, most prominently support for the new WebDAV (Web Distributed Authoring and Versioning) protocol for file share access over Web URLs.

We are accustomed to dealing with Internet resources using specific limited protocols. Our interaction with Web resources is mostly read-only, although we can send data using HTML forms and potentially even send a whole file with the HTTP PUT method. Windows 2000 uses WebDAV to leap beyond these restrictions.

On a Web server that supports WebDAV, such as IIS5, you can share folders for programs to access as file stores. You can then treat those files and folders as if they were shared on a local area network. When you set up a new network share in My Network Places, you can specify an http or ftp URL to the share, and Web server administrators can manage rights on these servers. This is how Office 2000 manages Web-based document development.

WebDAV also addresses network concerns such as file access permissions, file integrity and, once again through AD, offline editing. By using WebDAV, an organization can perform true file sharing over the Internet.

Internet Information Server 5 also integrates with the rest of Windows 2000 to support Dfs as a store for the Web server. You can also manage Internet Information Server 5 through AD. Security in Internet Information Server 5 is integrated with AD and the rest of Windows 2000. Kerberos is available for Web client authentication, and several new encryption protocols are supported.

Because security management of a Web server is complex, several security wizards have been included in Windows 2000 for common tasks. The Certificate Wizard allows you to create and manage digital certificates for users and servers to enable SSL encryption for secure communications over the Web. The Permission Wizard makes it easy to set up and manage access restrictions on a Web site. The Certificate Trust Lists (CTL) Wizard lets you configure lists of trusted certificate authorities for a particular directory.

Network Protocol Enhancements

Network management at the protocol layer has been enhanced in Windows 2000. Differentiated Quality of Service (Diffserv) allows administrators to designate certain applications as requiring greater or lesser priority for network bandwidth. For example, we might assign a greater priority to streaming multimedia services or IP Telephony. Administrators can also use this feature to manage the impact of various applications on network resources. A similar service is available for 802.1p LANs, which is a standardized way to assign prioritized service for a specific network.

The Admission Control Service (ACS) allows administrators to manage the reserved bandwidth for these applications using the AD. All of these Quality-of-Service features are accessible through generic QoS and Traffic Control APIs, which applications can use without reference to the specifics of the network's implementation.

Terminal Server Enhancements

Windows 2000 includes several enhancements to the Windows Terminal Services. There is a new remote administration mode in which connections can be used to administer a Windows 2000 Server via a thin client connection. Applications can now be installed on such a remote session.

Mobile Computing

Support for mobile computing in Windows NT was always spotty and vendor specific. Windows 2000 builds mobile computing support into the operating system and enhances it in ways that bring it beyond even Windows 98. This support requires hardware support for the most modern mobile computing standards, most importantly Advanced Configuration and Power Interface (ACPI). Combined with AD and the rest of the operating system, mobile computing support in Windows 2000 is state of the art (see Figure 1-8).

ACPI

ACPI is the new standard for hardware and power management in both notebook and desktop systems. It enables sophisticated power management capabilities beyond those of the old Advanced Power Management (APM). ACPI makes it easier to support features like the hibernation of a notebook and insertion and removal of PC cards. ACPI allows Windows 2000 to manage the power state of individual components of hardware and software in the system. For example, it is ACPI that enables Windows 2000 to wake up a sleeping computer in response to a ringing phone line on a fax card.

OnNow Power Management

OnNow is a series of efforts designed to enhance the usability of computers through better hardware and power management. The basic idea is that PCs should be ready to use in seconds, like televisions, instead of having to go through a long and complex power-up process. OnNow is based on ACPI as a foundation. OnNow also dictates automatic management of power and the ability to handle appropriate events, even while "asleep."

Windows 2000 notebook users will notice new options on their Shut Down dialog box. In Stand By mode, which consumes less power than the normal on state but keeps enough state alive to return the computer quickly to a powered-up state. When enabled Hibernate writes the state of all data to the hard disk and shuts the computer down. The next time it is powered up, the state is read from disk and the computer is restored rather than booting up again.

Users can control the power management policies of the computer in the Power Options Control Panel applet.

Roaming Users

Thanks to AD and IntelliMirror, Windows 2000 has extensive support for mobile users, helping them access their documents while on the road and to keep work accessible and up to date for other users on the network.

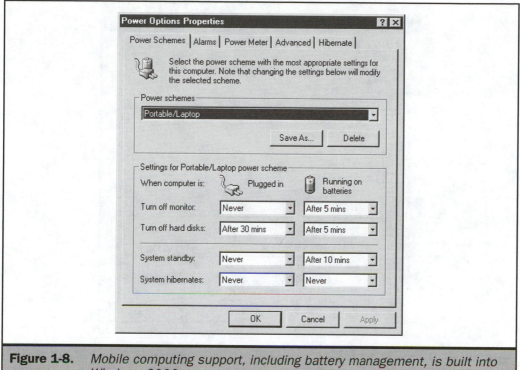

Figure 1-8.   *Mobile computing support, including battery management, is built into Windows 2000*

Users make network folders available offline, and then use the Synchronization Manager to replicate copies to the notebook. The user can edit the contents of the folder offline and, when they synchronize again, the changes will be replicated back to the network. Users can take Web documents or conventional Office documents offline. The ability to do this is subject to other capabilities of Windows 2000, such as security management.

Security

Windows 2000 has a series of new security systems, including both public key and private key encryption, to support a variety of security needs. In fact, the security infrastructure of Windows 2000 is radically improved over that of Windows NT 4, and administrators will need to study it to make effective use of the system (see Figure 1-9).

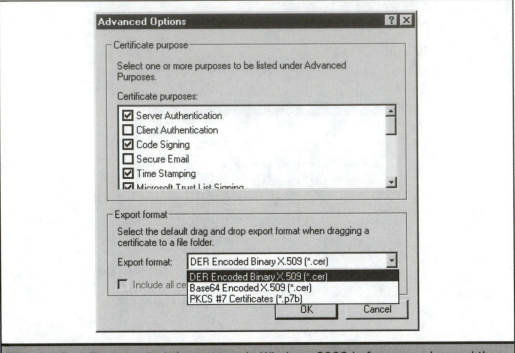

Figure 1-9.   *The security infrastructure in Windows 2000 is far more advanced than in Windows NT 4. For example, administrators can use digital certificates to positively identify users across the LAN or Internet*

Note   *See Chapter 21 for a discussion of Windows 2000 security features.*

KERBEROS   Network security in Windows NT 4 is based on the NTLM (NT Lan Manager) protocol, which has its roots in Microsoft's DOS-based networking from the 1980s. Windows 2000 network security is based on version 5 of Kerberos, a protocol developed at MIT, that is now defined by the Internet Engineering Task Force (IETF) as RFC 1510.

Kerberos provides:

- **authentication services**   to prove to services and other users on the network that you are who you are
- **data integrity**   to guarantee that data is not modified in transit on the network
- **data privacy**   to guarantee that data is not intercepted and read by an unauthorized party

Windows NT 4 has authentication through NTLM, but not in as robust or standard a form as Kerberos.

TRANSPORT LAYER SECURITY SUPPORT   Like Kerberos, Transport Layer Security (TLS) is a distributed Internet security protocol. It supports different pluggable encryption algorithms, depending on what the client requests and what the administrator allows.

SECURITY SUPPORT PROVIDER INTERFACE   Security Support Provider Interface (SSPI) is an API for application protocol developers to use for common access to security features, such as encryption, authentication, and message privacy.

SMART CARD SUPPORT   Smart cards—credit card-sized intelligent devices that can protect a password, a private key, or a certificate—improve the security of user authentication in a number of scenarios, such as client authentication, single sign-on, secure storage, and system administration. Smart cards are a key component of the public-key infrastructure that Microsoft integrates into the Windows platform.

DIGITALLY SIGNED DRIVERS   Because device drivers have to be trusted by the operating system and a buggy driver can make the entire system unstable, Microsoft has instituted a quality control procedure for drivers distributed with the operating system and through the Windows Update process. Drivers distributed by Microsoft must be tested by Microsoft's Windows Hardware Quality Labs and digitally signed to identify the author (see Figure 1-10). Much as with a Java applet or an ActiveX control encountered on the Internet, a user attempting to install a new device driver is informed whether the driver is signed and, if so, who the author is. The user can then decide whether that author is trustworthy.

ENCRYPTED FILE SYSTEM   Windows 2000 supports a new file system format called Encrypted File System (EFS) in which the data itself is encrypted. This creates a new element of physical security: even if the hard disk is physically compromised, the data on it will be difficult to obtain. Because EFS is supported as part of the file system services, it is transparent to the user and easy to manage.

Improved OS Core

The core operating system features of Windows 2000 have been enhanced to improve performance and reliability. Some of the changes are seamless and apply to all situations, and some present new capabilities for users and programmers.

Note   *See Appendix A for further discussion of these issues.*

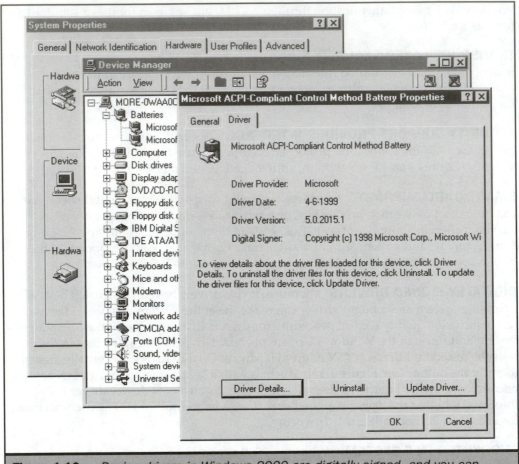

Figure 1-10.   *Device drivers in Windows 2000 are digitally signed, and you can confirm the author's identity*

Job Objects

Windows NT's process model has always had a weakness when it comes to certain sophisticated applications, especially server applications. Such programs often need to launch other processes and control their execution, possibly terminating them before they quit on their own. Windows doesn't have this capability.

But in Windows 2000, programmers can use the new Job Object not only to group child processes together and treat them as a group, but to create a sandbox, or set of restrictions within which those child processes must run. Among the restrictions a programmer can set for a child process are limits on its working set size, restrictions on access to the clipboard, limits on ability to access the user interface, limits on time executing, and limits on creating or accessing other jobs.

Thread Pooling

Windows NT has always had a rich thread management capability, but thread programming is easier and quicker in Windows 2000 with the new Thread Pooling functions. These functions address several common programming scenarios typically found in server applications. By incorporating them into the Windows 2000 API, robust server applications will be easier to write and debug.

Fewer Reboots

The need to reboot systems, especially servers, has been an embarrassing problem for Windows NT since its first appearance. Windows 2000 makes rebooting a much less frequent event. Numerous operations that previously required reboots may now be performed live without interrupting service to users. These operations include:

- Windows NT Services can now stop and restart more consistently with rebooting. Services can even be installed or removed without a reboot.

- Administrators can manage disks and volumes dynamically without a reboot.

- Plug and Play allows the addition of many types of hardware without restarting the server.

- IP addresses can be changed to resolve a conflict.

Improved Reliability

Windows 2000 reduces the number of blue-screen crashes with a number of safety features, including:

- **Kernel-mode write-protection** uses hardware protection and the Windows 2000 memory manager to write protect code and certain read-only data areas of the kernel and device drivers.

- **Pool Tagging** improves the safety and efficiency of memory management in device drivers.

- **Device drivers and other system files in Windows 2000** can be digitally signed, authenticating their origin and allowing the user to make a decision about whether that author can be trusted. This decision can be established as a policy in the system.

■ **All operating system files** are protected from modification by the System File Protection feature. This feature, which protects against malicious and accidental modification of files, as well as version mismatches, checks all files and catalogs them. Changes to these files, including deletion, will cause the SFP service to retrieve a known-good version of the file from the dllcache directory or, failing that, from the install media.

In fact, even in the event of a kernel crash, a new kernel-only dump speeds up reboots on systems with large amounts of physical memory. Such dumps only occur after a stop error, meaning only when absolutely necessary.

COM/COM+

Modern Windows programs are written using objects in the Component Object Model (COM). COM is a standard by which binary objects can, at run time, query each other's capabilities and invoke them. Most new Windows services, such as AD and DirectX, are accessible only through COM interfaces. Windows 2000 continues the definition of Windows in COM terms and extends it with COM+.

COM+ is a set of runtime services for COM objects to use that make COM-based applications easier to write. All the services are self-describing, so applications can adapt at run time to available facilities. For example, the publish and subscribe events service allows multiple COM+ client applications to subscribe to a published event. When the event fires, the COM+ service searches the subscription database and notifies all subscribed clients.

Utilizing Microsoft Message Queuing Services (MSMQ), COM+ provides for queued components, so that an application can use a COM+ component asynchronously over a network.

COM+ also provides integrated Microsoft Transaction Server support for all COM+ operations and interoperability with other transaction environments, such as Transaction Internet Protocol (TIP).

64-Bit Extensions

Windows NT has run on the 64-bit Alpha processor for years, but only in a 32-bit mode. It's been one thing to avoid 64-bit operation on the Alpha, but Intel is on the verge of shipping their 64-bit Merced processors, which have a native operating mode of 64-bits. Windows 2000 isn't a 64-bit operating system, but it does include extensions for using 64-bit addressing.

Note *Mircosoft will not ship a version of Windows 2000 for the Alpha processor.*

These extensions are known by a variety of names in Microsoft literature, including Enterprise Memory Architecture (EMA) or Address Windowing Extensions (AWE). They are not to be confused with Windows NT Server Enterprise Edition's ability to extend the amount of memory available to an application to 3GB on an Intel processor and 6GB on an Alpha processor. They are also separate from the Alpha-specific VLM APIs.

AWEs allow a program to access up to 63GB of memory space on a Pentium Xeon processor. The extensions are designed to allow regular Win32 programs to add the capability to access and manage data beyond the normal 32-bit limitations. Special APIs allow the program to open a Window to the 64-bit memory.

Many applications today can benefit from access to these enormous amounts of physical memory, including large database servers, applications that manage complex models for financial systems, weather, and CAD. In such applications, the ability to use physical memory easily compensates for the added development work of specially managing this memory.

Management

Large distributed network environments of the type enabled by Windows 2000 require robust management facilities. Windows 2000 integrates management of its resources, the security of access to them, and other systems on the network.

Most Windows NT 4 administrators are already used to the Microsoft Management Console (MMC) from its application in the Windows NT Option Pack (see Figure 1-11). Windows 2000 administrators, and even end users, will confront the MMC in nearly every administration task.

Server Configuration Wizard

Most servers fit into a set of standard server types, such as file server, print server, Web server, and so on. The new Server Configuration Wizard walks the administrator through the process of setting up the appropriate type of server, and only installs those services appropriate to the task. For example, setting up a Web server will install Web services, but not necessarily telephony services. Setting up an AD Server will install AD and Domain Name Services, and make the server a domain controller.

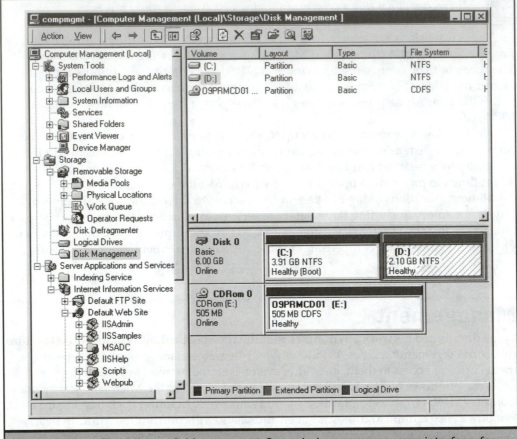

Figure 1-11. *The Microsoft Management Console is a common user interface for the numerous management tasks in Windows 2000*

Web-Based Enterprise Management and Windows Management Instrumentation

Web-Based Enterprise Management (WBEM) is an Internet-based initiative of the Desktop Management Task Force (DMTF) for a set of management and standard technologies designed to unify the management of enterprise computing environments. WBEM provides for using Internet standards such as CIM and XML to create interoperable, independently developed management applications.

Windows Management Instrumentation (WMI) is Microsoft's implementation of WBEM for Windows 2000. Using the Common Information Model (CIM), the Managed Object Format (MOF), and a new standard Windows programming interface based on

COM, developers can create standard applications for Windows 2000. Using the WMI scripting interface, administrators can create scripts to manage tasks.

Disaster Management

When things go wrong on a Windows NT 4 NTFS partition, or during the boot process of Windows NT 4, they *really* go wrong. You can't access the partition from a DOS boot floppy, and booting the operating system can make it difficult to work on the damaged system.

Windows 2000 adds diagnostic and recovery features to address this. The System Recovery Console allows users to boot off floppies or the Windows 2000 CD-ROM into a text mode setup program that can access NTFS partitions without having to boot the operating system installed on the computer. From this mode, you can run tools to repair a damaged file system or Master Boot Record. You can change your boot.ini file to make this mode a boot-time option by running winnt32/cmdcons.

Windows 2000 also has a new Safe Mode boot option that you can select at boot time by pressing F8, just as with Windows 95 or Windows 98.

The
Complete
Reference

Chapter 2

Planning for Installation

After you begin seeing what Windows 2000 is all about and learn fundamental differences between it and previous NT versions, you'll start to realize that this isn't simply another software upgrade. It's much more than simply popping in the CD and running the setup program. The process of migrating to Windows 2000 can be extremely complex and intimidating. There's no reason to be intimidated, but you must be aware that the new OS will affect almost every facet of your environment, from how you manage users to the way your infrastructure is organized.

To overcome or minimize the challenges of migrating to Windows 2000's radical new design, it is recommended that you spend a considerable amount of time planning and designing for it. These are crucial phases that help you iron out any kinks before you actually migrate to the new platform. Although this chapter is not all-inclusive, it is intended to bring insight into the migration of Windows 2000. The process comprises three distinct phases: preparing your current infrastructure, designing Windows 2000 into your environment, and finally, the actually migration procedures.

Preparing Your Current Infrastructure

Your first step toward Windows 2000 migration is preparing your network environment. The more preparation you do, the smoother the transition will be. Preparation can be interpreted in many ways, but basically you are gaining an understanding of your environment to find out if you have what it takes to perform the upgrade. The larger and more complex your network environment is, the more crucial and valuable this stage will be. Preparing your environment includes, but is not limited to, documenting network intricacies, inventorying hardware and software, installing and/or configuring TCP/IP, restructuring the NT domain model, standardizing software versions, and training. For those of you working with small NT networks or well-documented environments, you are ahead of many, but don't take this preparation lightly.

Understand Your Environment

One of the most important aspects of preparing for Windows 2000 is understanding your environment. It may seem difficult enough keeping up with daily administrative and maintenance tasks without also taking the time to understand the roles of servers, client configurations, TCP/IP subnet configurations, site connectivity, and much more. However daunting a task this may seem, it is imperative that you have at least a basic understanding of each network component and how they interact. For example, knowing that a remote site is built upon a separate NT domain with a dedicated 256Kb connection to the main office and to the Internet can help you design the Active Directory (AD).

Understanding your environment not only helps with migration planning, it also provides insight into how your system is functioning now and where it is heading. As you gain knowledge, you begin determining the baseline values of performance levels, finding potential problem areas, and reducing the number of variables that you have to deal with during the migration to Windows 2000.

Perform a Site Survey

A site survey can easily become a large project all by itself. Performing a site survey involves inventorying all hardware and software components in your environment. The following sections give examples of some of the items you will want to include in your inventory.

Inventories can easily become meaningless unless you also document how the machines, network devices, and so on relate to one another. For example, it is extremely useful to know that all client machines use the Dynamic Host Configuration Protocol (DHCP) to get needed TCP/IP information. Another piece of useful information might be that the five client machines located in the small branch office across town have a 64Kb point-to-point connection with the main office.

 There are several utilities available to make your life easier when inventorying your environment. For example, Microsoft's Systems Management Server (SMS) automates the procedure by gathering computer information (amount of RAM, types of software installed, etc.) at specified intervals or when a user logs onto the network.

DOCUMENT CURRENT SERVICES   Be sure you have detailed information about the following existing services:

- DNS servers
- WINS servers
- DHCP servers
- Static IP addresses
- Subnets
- Gateways
- RAS servers
- VPNs
- Web servers

You may have other services I don't have (or haven't thought of).

DOCUMENT THE CONFIGURATION OF EVERY COMPUTER   Get as much detailed information as possible about each computer, including the following:

- Computer name
- Host name
- Role of the machine (PDC, BDC, messaging, client, etc.)

- Physical location (Raleigh, New York office, etc.)
- Hardware vendor
- BIOS version
- Operating system and release/service pack level
- RAM
- NIC and driver info
- IRQ and I/O assignments
- Hard drive type and size (add SCSI adapter information if the drive is SCSI)
- Disk subsystem configuration (e.g., hardware RAID 5)
- CD-ROM type and speed
- Other peripherals (internal tape, internal modem, CDR, internal removable media drives, etc.)
- Information about unusual hardware configurations (I have one workstation that contains two parallel ports and four serial ports, because I use it as a server for printers, modems, a digital camera, and anything else I want to play with)
- Drivers and Web addresses or telephone number for the vendors
- Network subsystem configuration
- Installed applications
- Topology
- NT domain model(s)
- TCP/IP information
- DNS zones
- DHCP scopes and options
- WINS information
- Network devices (routers, switches, hubs, etc.)
- Network device locations
- Connectivity type and speed
- ISP information

MAP THE COMPUTERS IN YOUR ORGANIZATION   In addition to creating an inventory of what you have, you may consider producing a relational mapping diagram. As shown in Figure 2-1, this is a visual representation of your network that serves as a high-level overview of how devices relate to one another without bogging you down with details. Use the information you have gathered during the inventory to perfect the diagram.

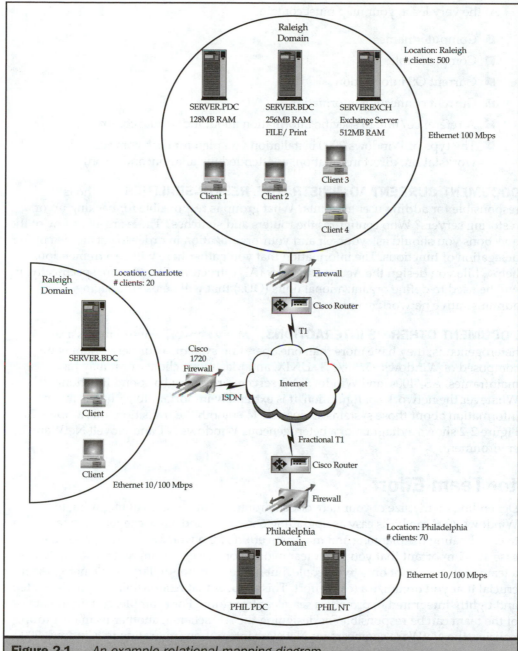

Figure 2-1.   *An example relational mapping diagram*

At the very least, your map must contain

- Computer names
- Computer roles
- Current OS information
- Current connection information
- A reference/link to specific information about individual computers
- The type of Windows 2000 installation you plan for each computer (server, workstation, direct installation, unattended installation, and so on)

DOCUMENT CURRENT ADMINISTRATIVE RESPONSIBILITIES   Who is responsible for adding user accounts? What group is responsible for backing up or restoring servers? Who configures the routers and switches? These are just a few of the questions you should ask yourself and your organization in order to get an idea of the delegation of functions. The information that you gather here will be a tremendous help while you design the Active Directory (AD) structure. Stated more specifically, it will be used to define organizational units (OUs) that will be used to segment administrative network maintenance.

DOCUMENT OTHER OS INTERACTIONS   Many network environments are heterogeneous; they have more than one operating system. Your network may be composed of Windows 95/98/NT, UNIX, and Macintosh clients, or it may have mainframes, AS/400s, and Windows NT servers providing back-end functionality. Whatever the network configuration, it is extremely important to gather as much information about those systems as possible to smooth the transition to Windows 2000. Figure 2-2 shows a diagram of a heterogeneous Windows NT and Novell NetWare 3.12 environment.

Foster Team Effort

Depending on the size of your network environment, the process of migrating to Windows 2000 can be as easy as upgrading one server and a few clients in a small office to coordinating the planning and migration efforts for a worldwide enterprise. In either case, it is important that you foster teamwork. For those working with small networks, a team may consist of only two people, but in the medium- to large-scale networks it is crucial that you organize a team effort. This ensures that responsibilities are delegated and tightly integrated to provide a seamless transition. For example, certain members of the team can be responsible for designing the AD schema, another team for group policies, the NetWare engineers for NetWare integration/migration to Windows 2000 issues, and so on. Groups or teams are responsible for two things: they must deal with their compartmentalized issues, and they must also work with the other teams to flesh out any integration challenges.

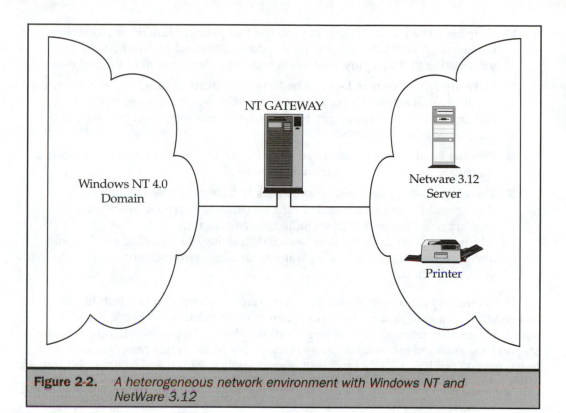

Figure 2-2. *A heterogeneous network environment with Windows NT and NetWare 3.12*

Note   *Although it may be premature to assign responsibilities for certain aspects of the migration, it is a good idea to begin thinking about the individuals or groups you may want to head these areas. This is useful for scheduling training as well as coordinating the design phase.*

Microsoft has had the opportunity to work with many enterprises throughout the Windows 2000 beta phases and has found through observation that successful implementations include team leads. Some of the team leads that Microsoft recommends using are the following:

■ **Deployment Team Lead**   An individual who has an overall knowledge of the network infrastructure and Windows 2000 services. This person is responsible for organizing the deployment of Windows 2000 into the production environment.

■ **Deployment Site Lead**   The Deployment Site Lead's responsibilities are similar to the Deployment Team Lead but narrower in scope. The individual manages deployment issues for a specific site and communicates directly with the Deployment Team Lead.

- **Helpdesk Lead**   The Helpdesk Lead has two primary functions: managing the helpdesk staff while deploying Windows 2000, and providing valuable information to the Deployment Team regarding deployment to the end users.

- **Network Infrastructure Lead**   The Network Infrastructure Lead is responsible for the overall network infrastructure, including but not limited to topology, AD infrastructure, throughput, traffic patterns, and integrating new network services with existing ones.

- **Product Lead**   The Product Lead organizes all server-related components and is actively involved in the deployment phase.

- **Training Lead**   This person coordinates all training-related activities throughout the organization. Training is critical to everyone involved in the migration to Windows 2000 including the end user. In addition to organizing the Windows 2000 training, the Training Lead should also plan training on internal operations for administrators, engineers, helpdesk staff, and others.

The teams and team leads mentioned above are not a requirement, but they should be used only as a guideline for your particular environment. For instance, some enterprise environments may be so large and complex that the network infrastructure should be segmented into smaller, more manageable parts. In this case, you may want to have an AD architect, a DNS architect, a group policy leader, and so on. Don't forget other important areas, such as hardware compatibility issues and vendor/ Windows 2000 compatibility, for which you may want someone to take responsibility.

Use TCP/IP

Windows 2000 is heavily dependent on TCP/IP and related services. As a result, it is imperative that you install and configure TCP/IP in your environment before you make the transition to Windows 2000.

 Readers who have and are familiar with TCP/IP can jump ahead to the next section on standardizing DNS.

Why should you install TCP/IP when Windows 2000 will install it during the upgrade? The reasoning is rather straightforward. If you haven't installed it by now, chances are that you aren't too familiar with some of its intricacies such as subnetting. Installing TCP/IP now will give you hands-on experience and allow you to find out how it will integrate into your environment.

Installing TCP/IP on Windows NT 4

Installing a protocol, such as TCP/IP, on Windows NT 4 is a simple procedure on both clients and servers. However, configuring it is not trivial because of the dependencies that may or may not exist in your environment. For example, your company or organization may be contemplating jumping on the Internet, which would require a valid IP address(s) and/or IP address translation.

To install TCP/IP on Windows NT 4, do the following:

1. Open the Network applet located in the Control Panel, and select the Protocol tab as shown below.

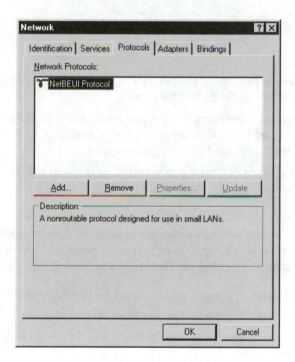

2. Click the Add button to display a list of protocols.

3. Select the TCP/IP Protocol and click OK.

4. You are then asked if you want to use DHCP as shown in the following illustration. Choose No if you want to statically assign an IP address; otherwise, click Yes.

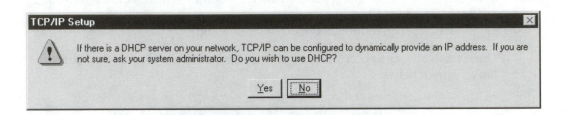

5. You may then be prompted to specify the location of the NT distribution files. If so, specify the full path of their location.

6. Click Close to close the Network properties dialog box. If you are statically assigning an IP address, Windows NT asks you to supply that information (IP address, subnet mask, and default gateway).

7. Click OK, and when NT asks you whether or not you want to restart your machine, choose Yes.

IP ADDRESSING   If you have never before used TCP/IP in your environment, you will need to consider the IP address range to use for your internal network. To help you decide which range to use, answer the following questions:

1. How many machines (clients and servers) do you have on the network?

2. When, if ever, will your company get Internet connectivity?

3. If you're getting connected to the Internet, will a firewall or router perform address translations?

It's no problem if you can only answer the first question. You can use the Request for Comments (RFC) 1918-compliant private IP addresses listed in Table 2-1 for the

TCP/IP Subnet Class	Private IP Address Range	Number of Hosts
Class A	10.0.0.0-10.255.255.255	16,777,214
Class B	172.16.0.0-172.31.255.255	65,534
Class C	192.168.0.0-192.168.255.255	254

Table 2-1. *Private IP Address Ranges That Can Be Used to Configure TCP/IP*

internal network. Once you do get connected to the Internet, it will get a little more complicated because these IP addresses aren't allowed on the Internet.

Use DHCP and WINS

Start using DHCP and WINS immediately. The DHCP service saves you a tremendous amount of time when configuring client machines to use TCP/IP. The service allows you to pass TCP/IP parameters, such as an IP address, WINS server, and default gateway to the client without having to visit each station (as shown in Figure 2-3). On the other hand, WINS greatly reduces the amount of traffic on the network by providing NetBIOS name resolution. Installing WINS is strictly meant to provide legacy support for those down-level clients that have yet to be upgraded to support AD.

 Windows 2000 in native mode doesn't rely on NetBIOS for name resolution. Instead, it is heavily dependent on the Domain Name System (DNS) or Dynamic DNS (DDNS) and therefore will not need WINS.

Standardize DNS

Windows 2000 in native mode uses DNS for name resolution. At this stage in the process, it is best to leave your DNS service as is, but you should standardize on the DNS naming conventions in order to make life easier once you make the switch to Windows 2000. However, you need to begin interacting with those people or groups in your organization that are responsible for DNS and gather as much information as possible about the current implementation.

Start implementing DNS names now. Windows 2000 supports standard RFC 1123 DNS characters (letters A–Z, numbers 0–9, and the dash [-]) as well as RFC 2044 Unicode Character Support based on UTF-8 encoding. Keeping domain and machine names short and simple lessens the chance that you will run into problems with your naming conventions.

Except for very small companies, renaming NT domains can easily become an administrative nightmare. As long as they are DNS compliant, leave them alone.

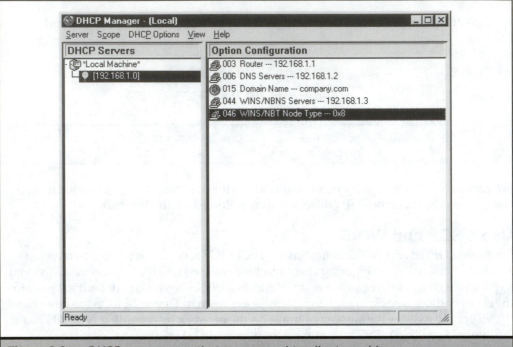

Figure 2-3. *DHCP parameters that are passed to client machines*

Naming Conflicts

Another issue that should get your attention with regard to naming conventions is duplicate computer or host names. It is a tedious but easy problem to fix. Taking the time to find those duplicate names now will save you from troubleshooting during Windows 2000 implementation.

Consolidate NT Domains

If you don't use a single-domain model, it is important to start consolidating account domains and collapsing unneeded resource domains. The fewer domains you migrate to Windows 2000, the fewer problems you will encounter. For instance, if you keep your current Windows NT 4 domain architecture and migrate that over to the new OS, you may find it more difficult to manage the AD because of the unnecessary number of trees, domains, or organizational units you now have to deal with. For more information on AD, refer to Chapter 15.

There are a couple of ways to consolidate your NT domain structure before switching to Windows 2000. The first and recommended approach is to use third-party utilities (mentioned in the "Third-Party Domain Consolidation Utilities" section). The second and more time-consuming approach is to manually move users, groups, and so on to another domain. There is one other option. You can wait until you install Windows 2000 and use its built-in domain consolidation utility. This is recommended only as an absolute last resort because you're not adequately preparing yourself for the upgrade and you're more likely to run into snags where you may have to restructure AD in the midst of building the infrastructure.

New and Improved Domains

The domain concept is not entirely a dead issue, as you will see in the explanation of AD in Chapter 15. However, the limitations present in NT 4 domains are nonexistent in Windows 2000. The older domain models (single, single master, multiple master, and complete trust) have many limitations (that don't require discussion here), but certainly of concern is the domain's size limit. Windows NT 4's limitation centered on the 40MB recommended limit for the Security Accounts Manager (SAM), which houses the user, group, and machine accounts. For example, assume that a domain will have 26,000 users, 250 group accounts, and 26,000 machine accounts. Multiply these numbers by the respective space requirements for each account and then add the products—$(26,000 \times 1K) + (250 \times 4K) + (26,000 \times 0.5K)$. What you'll see is that the SAM reaches the maximum recommended limit.

AD simply doesn't have this size limitation. The directory service can store upwards of 17 million objects such as users, groups, and machine accounts. In fact, Compaq (http://www.compaq.com/) reports that it has successfully tested AD with over 16 million objects.

The only impeding factor that you may encounter when consolidating domains is NT 4's size limitation.

Third-Party Domain Consolidation Utilities

The two most notable domain consolidation/management utilities available for Windows NT 4 are Mission Critical's OnePoint Domain Administrator (http://www.missioncritical.com/) and FastLane Technologies' (http://www. fastlanetech.com/) DM/Manager. Both products are designed to simplify the transition to Windows 2000 by automating domain consolidation and reconfiguration.

The Built-in Consolidation Utility

Microsoft has licensed Mission Critical Software's Domain Administrator to assist in the NT domain consolidation. This utility, bundled within Windows 2000, automates the challenges you face, even with large account domains. It automates the process of migrating user, group, and machine accounts from other domains and even migrates directory service information from Novell NetWare.

Standardize Software Releases

Almost every organization is guilty to some degree of having multiple versions of the same application in use. A simple yet powerful example is the use of Web browsers. Some people may be using Internet Explorer 3, 4, or 5; some are using Netscape Navigator/Communicator 4.3 or 4.6; and others may be using both Internet Explorer and Netscape. There may be very good reasons for running different versions of the same application. For instance, ApplicationX version 1 may only run reliably on Windows 95, and ApplicationX version 1.4 requires Windows NT 4. The point is that it's important to standardize software releases to reduce the chances of problems during migration. In the example above, ApplicationX version 1.4 may be supported under Windows 2000 but version 1 may not be. Besides, administratively supporting one version is much easier than keeping up with the intricacies of many different versions.

Find out which version or software release(s) makes sense for your environment and thoroughly test it. The versions that are test worthy should be used throughout the organization, and the other versions should be put to rest.

 As with any upgrade, you should safeguard yourself from disaster by backing up the system before you make changes. This goes without saying on servers, but you should also take precautions on client machines, too.

Service Packs

Windows NT service packs and hotfixes are far from exempt from problems. Use Service Pack 4 or higher (Service Pack 5 works extremely well), and test it thoroughly. If you are comfortable that everything appears to be working smoothly, install and test it some more on the other NT machines in your environment. Your goal is to run the same service pack and hotfixes on each Windows NT machine on your network. Remember to back up the machine before installing a service pack or hotfix.

Application Compatibility Issues

The list of Windows 2000 compatible/AD Aware applications is exploding. Support from Microsoft and application vendors has been extremely encouraging. And this has been going on since early beta stages. You can keep up-to-date on application compatibility issues from Microsoft's Windows 2000 Readiness Web site at http://www.microsoft.com/windows2000/ready/, or you can check with the specific vendor. Despite all the efforts that have been made, there may be a chance that a particular application is incompatible with Windows 2000, and it can be a result of many different things.

Part of your responsibility in the Windows 2000 upgrade process is to ensure that those applications and services that you have decided to keep supporting will be supported under the new operating system. The best way to find out whether or not your applications will work properly and be supported is to check both with Microsoft and the third-party vendor. Most application vendors are already touting that their product will be Windows 2000 ready, or they can reassure you that their product will be ready once Windows 2000 ships. If they can't provide you with that type of information, then constantly stay in touch with them until the compatibility issues are resolved.

Migrating from NT 3.51

Although the migration path from Windows NT 3.51 to Windows 2000 is supported, Microsoft recommends that you upgrade to Windows NT 4 first. This is intended to ease your migration pains and permit a smoother transition. I personally had experienced a few problems upgrading from NT 3.51 to 4, and the OS differences in that case are small in comparison to an upgrade to Windows 2000. Every environment is different, so you may not have the same luck that I did, but you'll be much safer taking the incremental upgrade path instead. With Windows NT 3.51 upgraded to 4, you'll have one less variable to be concerned about. This will give those working with the NT 3.51 interface more time to interact with the NT 4 interface if they haven't already acquainted themselves with it.

Training

Start training on Windows 2000 as soon as possible. Don't wait and expect that when it's time to migrate you'll be ready. You won't unless you start training now. Microsoft is admitting that this is one of the biggest upgrades since Windows 95. Even if the actual migration is planned a year from now, you won't want to wait until the last minute to get up to speed on the many new features and enhancements Windows 2000 has to offer.

Organize Training Efforts

As you read earlier in the "Foster Team Effort" section, there are many facets of the migration process that individuals or groups need to take responsibility for. Some may be responsible for AD, while others need to be concerned about the end user or DNS. Training should therefore parallel these needs and responsibilities. In other words, it isn't necessary to have everyone involved in the migration effort training on every aspect of Windows 2000. Give them training that's pertinent to their responsibilities, and their strength in those areas will be solid.

Important Training Topics

The following list of Windows 2000 topics should only be used as a reference point. I highly recommend that you get training on these topics. However, you may feel that your organization needs training on other topics as well.

- Active Directory
- TCP/IP

- DNS
- Windows 2000 Administration
- Security
- Clustering
- Deployment
- Internet Information Server (IIS)
- Proxy

Training Options

Because of the importance of this upgrade, available training options for the new OS are growing at unbelievable speeds. Here are just a few:

- Instructor-led courses
- Video-based training
- Self-based training
- Online training

Table 2-2 expands on what is available in these areas of training. Choosing the most appropriate method for learning is strictly a personal preference. Some people need a classroom environment, while others learn more by studying by themselves. Reading magazines and Web sites can familiarize you with the issues at hand, and then if necessary you can consider using instructor-led courses. Of course, hands-on experience is one of the best training methods you can ask for.

Preparation Checklist

Use the following list as a quick reference guide for preparing your current network for Windows 2000:

1. Inventory all hardware and software.
2. Document computer roles and interactions within your environment.
3. Install TCP/IP, DHCP, and WINS.
4. Standardize DNS naming conventions and clean up duplicate names.
5. Begin Windows 2000 training immediately.
6. Collapse the NT domain structure into larger and fewer domains.
7. Standardize the software versions, service packs, and more across your entire network.

Instruction Category	Instruction Type	Web Site
Instructor-Led Authorized Training Centers	Cedalion Education	http://www.cedalion.com/
	Productivity Point International	http://www.propoint.com/
	New Horizons	http://www.newhorizons.com/
Video-Based Training	KeyStone Learning Systems	http://www.keystonetraining.com/
	Transcender Corp.	http://www.transcender.com/
	Wave Technology, Int'l.	http://www.wavetech.com/
Self-Based Training Techniques	ENT Magazine	http://www.entmag.com/
	Microsoft Certified Professional magazine	http://www.mcpmag.com/
	Windows NT magazine	http://www.winntmag.com/
	Windows NT Systems magazine	http://www.ntsystems.com/
	Microsoft's Web site	http://www.microsoft.com/windows/server/
	Compaq's Web site	http://www.compaq.com/partners/microsoft/windows2000/
	User groups	http://www.ntpro.org/wantug/memberlist.asp
Online Training	Drake Training	http://www.drakeintl.com/training/
	Ziff-Davis Education	http://www.zdeducation.com/zdu/
	McGraw-Hill Online Learning	http://www.mhonlinelearning.com/

Table 2-2.   *Training Resource Information*

Designing a Windows 2000 Environment

At this stage in the process, you have stabilized your current environment by standardizing DNS and software release levels, and have done your best to consolidate NT domains. In addition, you should have everyone on a training schedule, whether it's instructor-led, online training, or some form of self-based training. The training you receive will be a tremendous help as you begin designing Windows 2000 into your environment.

Team Effort

In the preparation stage I recommended that you begin organizing a team that is responsible for the move to Windows 2000. Now is the time to really push toward teamwork. Each individual and each group is part of a team that works together for the successful completion of Windows 2000 migration. Delegate responsibilities, communicate goals, and give direction so that everyone can plan their work with the big picture in mind.

Create a Lab/Test Environment

Set up a lab before deploying Windows 2000 throughout your company; the advantages it provides are enormous. This OS is quite different from previous incarnations of Windows NT, and even if you had a smooth transition from NT 3.x to NT 4, you can't count that experience, because the differences between whatever OS you're running and Windows 2000 are great and can be confusing.

Create an independent, detached network that consists of at least one domain controller and one workstation. Use this network to install and configure the operating system (change the hardware and reinstall to overcome any compatibility problems).

Learn how to configure and manipulate groups and users. Add a member server for file and print services, and install the important software applications. Add a Windows 9x workstation if you have those legacy clients on your system.

Mirror as many hardware and software configurations as possible from your environment in the lab. Experience tells me that it's difficult, if not impossible, to completely replicate a production environment in a lab (unless you have an unlimited budget and lots of time). However, the more you can mimic, the smoother your transition will be. Time spent in the lab testing configurations is the most opportune for finding problems that may arise in your production environment. If you do find problems, you can probably head them off before they impact your environment.

Experiment and keep notes.

DNS and AD Design Considerations

As mentioned before, Windows 2000 is completely dependent on DNS for name resolution. DNS affects how you will design the organizational layout including the forests, trees, domains, and even sites. For this reason, DNS should be the first concept you design. Pay close attention to details when you are designing DNS because you won't be able to change your naming conventions in the initial release without destroying what you have already created. For example, if you decide to change the root domain's namespace, you'll have to reconstruct not only the root domain but also any child domains (subdomains) attached to it.

If you aren't currently providing DNS services internally (you're essentially shut off from the outside world), some of you are relying on an Internet Service Provider (ISP), and some of you are providing an internal and external DNS resource to the company (split DNS) as shown in Figure 2-4. In the first two scenarios you don't have as much to contend with as those who are currently providing DNS services internally.

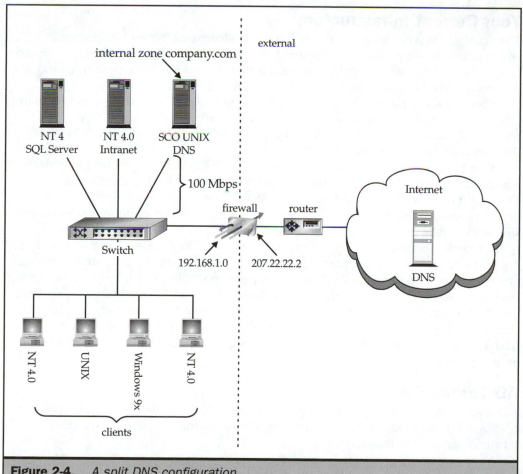

Figure 2-4. *A split DNS configuration*

This may even be the first time that you have to work closely with DNS. Whatever scenario you're dealing with, you still are forced to work closely with DNS issues and determine how they relate to the AD structural foundations of your IT infrastructure.

If you're already using DNS, you should have followed my previous recommendations and begun interacting with those who are currently responsible for the DNS implementation, and found out the implementation details. You should now be comfortable answering the following questions:

- Which namespaces is the DNS implementation serving?
- Which OS platform and server software is handling DNS?
- If a non-Microsoft OS is hosting the company's DNS, does it support RFC 2136 dynamic updates?

Your Current Infrastructure

The number of combinations that you can use to structure DNS and AD in your environment is astounding. If I attempted to describe every single possibility it would give us both a migraine. A better approach is to narrow down the possibilities and concentrate on the issues that will be most pertinent to you.

What are those issues? To name a few: creating basic AD structures (trees, domains, OUs, etc.), assembling AD structures with DNS, security, and so on. I'll cover those topics and more in this section so that you can familiarize yourself enough to tailor them to your own environment.

It isn't necessary to plan a structure around your current network building blocks because DNS and AD are meant to break away from the old NT domain model. Designing DNS and AD should instead be focused on using appropriate namespaces and the various objects within AD to better accommodate users, administrative tasks, site and intersite communication, and much more.

If you are designing for large enterprises, you don't have to assume that you'll need one or more forests, a large number of trees, or many domains to adequately represent your environment. Keep the structure as simple as possible, especially in the beginning design phases. Unlike the old NT domain model, DNS and AD are built to be scalable.

The most basic concept that you should always strive for when designing is simplicity. Figure 2-5 is an example of a simplistic design approach. Keeping the design as simple as possible, especially in the beginning design phases, allows for easier growth and change.

AD Terminology

Although this book has an entire chapter (Chapter 15) dedicated to AD, it is useful to review AD terminology before proceeding. The following is a short list of AD terminology used in this chapter:

■ **Domain**   Similar to the domain concept in previous versions, domains are administrative boundaries. They contain user, group, and/or computer accounts.

■ **Forest**   A group of trees such as the one illustrated in the following illustration.

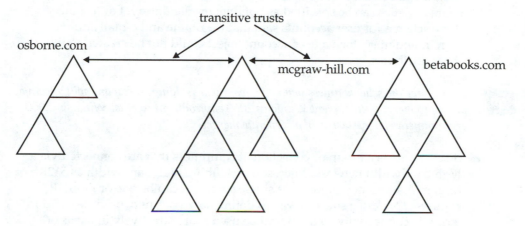

■ **Global Catalog**   A collection of information that is replicated across domains. The information contained in the GC is a subset of object characteristics that has been specifically specified.

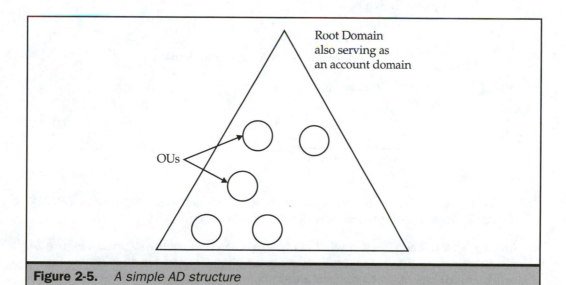

Figure 2-5.   *A simple AD structure*

■ **Organizational units (OUs)**   OUs are similar to domains in that they provide additional administrative boundaries. They hold AD objects and can be created in such a way as to organize the company's structure. For example, you can create OUs to reflect different remote sites or departments.

■ **Schema**   A schema is the definition for which object attributes or characteristics can be specified as optional or mandatory. For instance, if the schema for user accounts said that username and e-mail address were mandatory, then a user account object could not be created without these attributes.

Caution   *Don't alter the schema unless you know what you're doing. It can and will affect your ability to merge your current Windows 2000 environment to other Windows 2000 environments later, such as in a corporate merger.*

■ **Site**   A site is a group or collection of computers that are connected via a high bandwidth network. Microsoft is defining high bandwidth as 512Kb or higher. A site is not limited to a single subnet; it can be one or more IP subnets. Think of a site as a way to define how your network is laid out in terms of connectivity so that it can be used more effectively in terms of network performance.

■ **Structural Domain**   These are domains without user, group, and/or computer accounts. They serve as placeholders for future expansion. The epitome of a structural domain is a root domain in a large, enterprise-level organization, such as the one shown here.

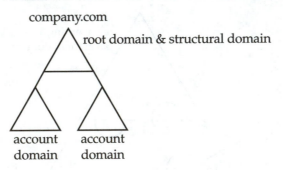

■ **Tree**   A tree is a collection of one or more domains that share the same DNS configuration information as well as a global catalog.

An easy way to keep track of what fits where is to visualize the structure. Figure 2-6 is a visual representation of the terminology listed above. For instance, everyone (in their right mind) knows that a forest is a group of trees. The rest is a bit harder to grasp but nonetheless easier than trying to remember how everything fits by memorizing

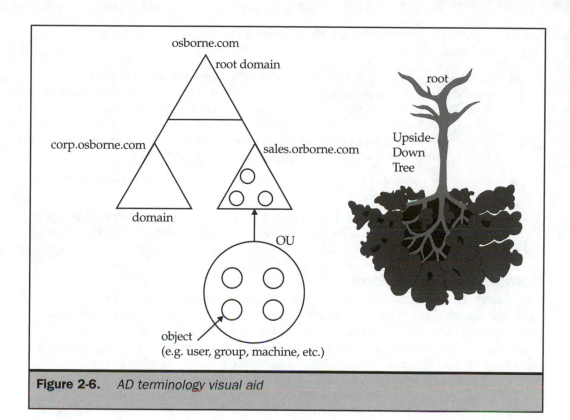

Figure 2-6.   *AD terminology visual aid*

definitions. Visualize hierarchically the following: a tree's leaves are domains; a domain is made up of one or more OUs; and finally, an OU is comprised of objects.

Implementation Decisions

The question you should be asking yourself right now is "What is the best way I can provide DNS name resolution to all clients in the organization?" If you're running in a pure Windows-based environment, then many battles have already been won. It is so much easier from an IT and political point of view to replace/upgrade existing DNS servers and define namespaces. For instance, if a Windows NT 4 server hosts DNS services, it wouldn't be technically and politically problematic to upgrade it to Windows 2000.

Reality and experience, however, tell me that many administrators currently use some flavor of UNIX to serve their DNS needs. If you fit this description you'll also need to prepare yourself for some battles.

The choices you have for designing and integrating DNS for Windows 2000 with non-Microsoft systems are somewhat limited, and some of them definitely won't make you a UNIX hack's best friend. Here are the simplest options for easing migration efforts:

- Use Windows 2000 DNS servers alongside the current DNS servers. Don't create separate namespaces for them, but rather use the current namespace and set the Windows 2000 DNS servers as primaries while the others are secondary. This approach allows both parties to service DNS requests. Be sure to update the legacy DNS servers to support the Service Location resource record (SRV RR - RFC 2052) and the Dynamic Update protocol (RFC 2136).

- Completely remove existing, non-Microsoft DNS servers and replace them with Windows 2000 DNS servers.

- Do not use Microsoft DNS. In this case, you must update current non-Microsoft DNS servers to comply with SRV RR and Dynamic Update standards. For example, BIND 8.1.2 for UNIX is compliant.

Domain Considerations

DNS and domain structural designs are meant to be accommodating, but the combination can quickly become complex and unwieldy if not analyzed closely. The design decisions that you make now can and will affect later decisions. You may already have a DNS naming convention in place that you can use, but you also need to consider how this affects child domains, replication traffic, the number of domain controllers needed, and more.

The best place to start discussing the DNS and AD relationships is at the top. The root domain is the underlying foundation of a tree, which also represents a contiguous namespace. It is the top of *your* tree in the Internet namespace. It's easy to confuse this with what is the authoritative root domain, which is ".". Therefore, company.com or .com aren't root domains but are more of what's called a Fully Qualified Domain Name (FQDN). It is authoritative for company.com, but that doesn't make it a root server. Root servers reside in the .edu, .com, .org, and .mil namespaces and are the final authorities for their respective domains. Consequently, they're root servers. When I use the term "root" or "root domain," I'm referring to the top of your AD structure.

The only exception that I can think of when a root domain would also be a root server would be where the network isn't connected to the Internet. In this case, DNS is used for internal purposes only.

All other domains that are tied to this tree from the root have the same extension (contiguous namespace). For example, corporate.company.com and development.company.com are child domains of company.com. Subdomains of the previously mentioned child domains would be in the format similar to os.development.company.com. In most instances, using the current root domain is probably the best stance to take because it more than likely properly represents or distinguishes the company.

With this basic structure in mind, use these recommendations for designing the DNS and AD structure:

- Keep the number of trees to a minimum. Remember that every tree you create requires another namespace. Usually creating more than one tree would only apply to large international companies. A good alternative would be to create more domains.

- Use geographical naming conventions when you begin considering what to name your root and child domains. These names should rarely, if ever, change, so name them carefully.

- Domains bind replication traffic. Domain controllers (DCs) only replicate with each other in their domain. Communication with the other domains is done through the GC. If you feel compelled to create another domain because of a slow WAN link, consider redefining your site to replicate traffic during off-hours first. If this still doesn't satisfy the traffic congestion problem, create another domain.

- Keep the number of domains to a minimum. Yes, I realize that I just told you that creating more domains would be a better alternative than creating another tree and I'm sticking to that recommendation. However, fewer domains equate to less cost (fewer DCs), fewer trust relationships, and less complicated replication schematics. For small or even mid-size environments, your root domain may be the only domain you need for user accounts, groups, and machine accounts.

DOMAIN AND SECURITY CONSIDERATIONS   In general, it is never advised to create domains for security purposes alone. Instead, use OUs to enforce separate security policies or administrative boundaries. Then, of course, for every rule there is an exception. For example, if a company has autonomous relations with a parent company, then a separate domain (and in rare cases a tree) would best fit the model of the organization.

OUs allow you to delegate administrative responsibility at various levels. As you design OUs into the domain structure, create a common group of OUs that can be contained in all domains. Don't get too carried away, though, and create numerous OUs, because too much of a good thing can be just as harmful. In particular, as the number of OUs in your environment grow, so will your administration needs.

OUS AND GROUP POLICY OBJECTS   OUs combined with Group Policy Objects (GPOs) can also tighten security. Both OUs and GPOs can be nested within themselves to match just about any security policy you can imagine. GPOs can not only be applied to OUs, but to domains and sites as well. Part of the design process is defining how and where GPOs will be applied. Be extremely cautious when applying GPOs, because they can wreak havoc on the system as a whole. They can easily lock out users or render security useless. As a result, I would highly recommend that you designate someone to be responsible for designing and managing GPOs.

For more information regarding security, see Chapter 21.

Site Construction

Sites help define the physical network infrastructure. As mentioned earlier, a site is a group or collection of computers that are connected via a high-bandwidth network. The basic design principles behind the concept of a site are AD authentication and replication control. A sample site configuration is shown in Figure 2-7.

AD authentication is based on Kerberos instead of NT LAN Manager (NTLM). One of Kerberos's improvements over NTLM is that client machines will try contacting the closest DC. This does not mean the closest in terms of physical location but rather performance (high bandwidth and availability). A site then influences which DC the client machine communicates with first. More information on Kerberos can be found in Chapter 21.

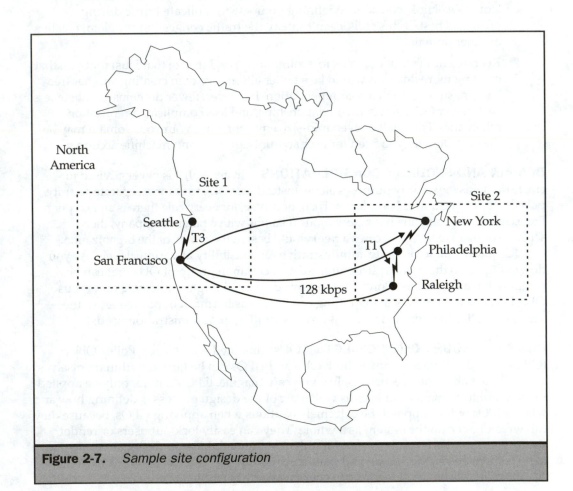

Figure 2-7. *Sample site configuration*

The other principal concept behind sites is that they define areas of high bandwidth, which is extremely useful in reducing the amount of replication traffic and hence network traffic in general.

So what factors should be considered when designing sites? Here are a few recommendations:

- Minimize the number of sites you use because you can always add more (i.e., start with a single site).

- Place at least one DC at each site to handle authentication and replication traffic.

- Use a 1:1 ratio with sites and domains whenever possible.

Administrative Centralization/Decentralization

As you probably have already guessed from the discussion on OUs and GPOs, system administration can be centralized, decentralized, or a combination of the two. I recommend the latter. That way you'll have control over all objects without being bogged down with daily administrative duties such as adding user accounts or granting privileges to someone so that they can print to a particular printer.

Hardware Design

The first thing you must do for every computer that will become a Windows 2000 Server is ensure that the machine conforms to the Hardware Compatibility List (HCL). I assure you the HCL takes no prisoners, and Microsoft is quite serious and firm about compatibility.

I've experienced several installations in which a warning was displayed saying that a component might not be compatible (even though I'd checked the HCL). Each time this occurred, the device was a PCI NIC, but there may be other devices that generate the same warning. Setup did not stop or hang; the installation program merely flashed the warning. Each time, the component installed flawlessly. If you see such a message, don't panic.

Minimum vs. Recommended

Microsoft often states the absolute minimum hardware requirements needed to run their operating systems. Sure, you can run Windows 2000 on a Pentium 166 with 64MB of RAM, but can it run applications without trying your patience or service users efficiently? Always begin hardware design specifications with the recommended as your minimum. Also, consider checking Microsoft's Web site to get the latest information on configuration recommendations.

Machine Roles Determine Hardware

A machine's role(s) greatly influence the type of hardware it will need. The best way to illustrate this is through an example. Suppose you're designing the configuration of your domain controllers, and you have made plans for two separate domains. One domain may have thousands of users, while the other only will handle a couple of hundred. One of the many issues that you'll design for is the disk subsystem. More specifically, you'll have to gauge the OS partition size. For the large domain, I would recommend mirroring two 9.1GB drives; while the domain with a couple of hundred users should only require 4.3GB drives. The requirements in this case have fluctuated because of the roles each of the machines play in your environment.

Out with the Old, In with the New

Is it necessary to swap out the vast majority of hardware and replace it with newer, faster technology? Generally, no. What you may consider doing is looking at how well the server currently performs with Windows NT 4. Also, check your site survey (from the preparation section of this chapter) to see how much disk space on the OS partition is available, the type and speed of the NIC card, and so on, to see if they at least meet the recommended hardware configuration. If the server or client machine is at or below expectations, strongly consider upgrading the components that would make a difference. In most cases, adding memory will improve performance and better prepare the machine for the new OS.

Create a Deployment Plan

You need to commit some information to paper and share it with all the folks in your organization who are involved in the migration to Windows 2000. This includes members of the IT team, the executive team (especially the people who sign the checks), and the users. Not everyone will see the same paperwork, because the executive team and users need only know what to expect and how to handle events. The technical details are distributed to the IT team.

Choose a Plan and Stick to It

Some environments are small enough and are so familiar with Windows 2000 that it's possible to consider an "all or nothing" approach. What this means is upgrading to Windows 2000 in a short timeframe and going native immediately afterwards. However, for all practical purposes, if your environment has any size to it (e.g., many users, several domains), the only practical approach is to migrate gradually into Windows 2000—what Microsoft calls the Incremental In-Phase Upgrade. In fact, I strongly recommend phasing into Windows 2000, especially for companies that have a regional or international presence.

Document Your Installation Plan

You also need to create a list of upgrade dates for each site, department, and computer. There's a logical pecking order:

- Domain controllers
- File and print servers
- Workstations

Let users know what to expect both in terms of dates and what to do to get their work done after the new OS is installed. Remember that you may have to set dates for reinstalling software, too.

Schedule a time period to analyze your new AD environment. This should include any restructuring to make your environment more effective and efficient.

Create a Contingency Plan

Create contingency plans for those users who may not be able to log on, or who may not be able to find the software or the data files they need. I've learned that the best way to implement a contingency plan is to convert a couple of workstations for myself under different user names. After I test these workstations and can access the company software and data, I can let other people use those workstations until the problems on their own workstations are resolved.

Integration with Other Systems

I have already touched on one issue regarding integration of other systems (Windows 2000 DNS and your current DNS services), and there may be many more depending on your environment. Unfortunately, there are simply too many to possibly cover them all.

The best way to overcome any issues that may arise is to meet with those parties involved in the design phase. Explain to them your migration plans so that you both may uncover and carefully examine any issues before you begin implementation.

Migrating Novell NetWare

It goes without saying that Novell NetWare has been a big competitor of Microsoft. In Windows NT 4 and earlier, Microsoft provided a utility that migrated bindery-based users and groups from various NetWare OS versions, but it didn't migrate NetWare Domain Services (NDS).

Now, Microsoft has entirely replaced that utility (NetWare Convert) and licensed Mission Critical Software's Domain Administrator, which enables Windows 2000 to migrate both bindery and directory services information into an offline database. From there, administrators can model the migrated information before committing it to AD.

Design Checklist

To help remind you of some of the key concepts in the design phase, here is a list you can check against:

1. Give individuals or teams direction in the design phase.

2. Create a lab environment to test various configurations and migration scenarios.

3. Structure DNS and AD with the business focus, current topology, and administrative issues in mind.

4. Work with your current DNS implementation team.

5. Design group policies.

6. Focus on security-related issues.

7. Work with vendors on any application issues that you foresee.

Implementation

At this stage you have done all the planning and designing you'll ever care to do. You're ready to install and configure your site. Pay close attention to design phase documents such as deployment plans, DNS and AD design plans, notes from the lab, and so on. Documentation will keep you focused and on track throughout the migration to Windows 2000.

Be Safe, Not Sorry

Anytime that you are about to make changes to a production environment server or client machine, you should always proceed with caution. The Windows 2000 migration is no exception.

Document

Yes, there's more documentation to do. Don't get swamped with documentation efforts, but keep notes as you proceed. Take notes on the actual implementation process so that you can continue to improve upon it. Who knows, you may even find shortcuts to your goals or solutions to problems you didn't expect.

Back Up, Back Up, Back Up!

Back up all servers right before you migrate them to Windows 2000. This includes backing up the registry. The more fall-back plans you have, the less downtime you will experience, and you'll look like a hero in the process.

Client machines are an entirely different issue. Backing up client machines can take too much time and may even be impossible for some of the larger organizations. Can you imagine trying to back up 500, much less 1,000 machines? However, there may be certain machines that catch your attention—namely, those of the executives of the company, your boss, or developers. An alternative for other client machines is to make sure that users are storing all their important data on a server so that the data is backed up.

Installation Scenarios

The permutations and combinations that exist to describe the environments that are migrating to Windows 2000 are so extensive it's not possible to cover more than the most common. You may be upgrading from NT 3.x or NT 4 (with a variety of service pack levels installed). Perhaps you're migrating from NetWare or UNIX. Maybe this is your first network. Even if you're working with a unique set of circumstances, you should still be able to find the guidance you need within the scenarios covered in this chapter.

Installing Servers

There are several common scenarios for installing servers, and it's possible that you're dealing with more than one of the following scenarios:

- Upgrading PDCs to Windows 2000 DCs
- Upgrading BDCs to Windows 2000 DCs
- Upgrading member servers to Windows 2000
- Installing Windows 2000 Server as a new OS (called a *fresh install* or *fresh copy*) on a domain controller
- Installing a fresh copy of Windows 2000 Server on a member server

 Windows 2000 does not distinguish between a PDC and a BDC; there are only domain controllers.

For this discussion, the term "member server" encompasses a wide range of server roles, including:

- Certificate servers
- Database servers
- E-mail servers
- File and Print servers
- Proxy servers
- Routing and Remote Access servers
- Terminal servers
- Web servers

Your installation may have member servers with roles not mentioned, but the concepts discussed in this chapter for member servers will apply.

Remember to check whether the machine conforms to the HCL to avoid any unnecessary hassles or surprises.

Upgrading Servers

You can install Windows 2000 Server onto a disk partition that currently contains Windows NT 3.51 Server, Windows NT 4 Server, or Windows NT 4 Terminal Server. Upgrading installs Windows 2000 Server into the same directory as the current operating system.

If you are currently running Windows NT 4 Server Enterprise Edition, you can only upgrade to Windows 2000 Advanced Server; you cannot upgrade to Windows 2000 Server.

Note   *See Appendix A for all the rules about upgrading.*

You cannot upgrade or install Windows 2000 on a drive that is compressed with any utility except the NTFS file system compression utility. If you're using DriveSpace or DoubleSpace, uncompress the volume before running Windows 2000 Setup.

Upgrading Domain Controllers

When you upgrade a domain controller, the information on the existing computer is retained. A successful upgrade results in the usual smooth user logons, authentication, and other domain controller functions.

Before you upgrade a domain controller, you must have a way to roll back your changes if something goes amiss. The best way to accomplish this is to make sure you have a viable BDC before upgrading your PDC. If you don't have a BDC, create one. Test your BDC to make sure it will perform properly as a PDC (just in case your existing PDC doesn't turn into a Windows 2000 DC smoothly).

- Synchronize all BDCs with the PDC.
- Take the PDC off line.
- Promote a BDC to a PDC and make sure it performs its tasks correctly.
- Demote the computer back to a BDC, take it offline, and bring the PDC back online.
- Track any changes to the domain (new users or password changes) that will have to be entered if you roll back your upgrade.

Keep the tested BDC as an NT 4 server until you're confident your PDC upgrade to Windows 2000 is working properly.

If you're migrating from Windows NT 4, don't worry about running a mixed environment of domain controllers. Windows 2000 and Windows NT 4 work well together. For instance, using a Windows 2000 domain controller as if it were a Windows NT 4 BDC, and receiving domain account replication from a Windows NT 4 PDC, works quite well.

Upgrading Member Servers

You can upgrade your member servers on a schedule that's independent of your domain controller upgrades. In fact, you can upgrade your member servers before you upgrade your domain controllers (although you won't be able to use Active Directory until you've put your Windows 2000 domain controllers online).

Be sure to back up each member server before beginning the upgrade. It's a good idea to have a spare computer around that can act as a replacement for the original computer if the upgrade takes longer than expected, or you encounter a problem. You can move it around the network to act as the backup for each member server you're upgrading. This can be time-consuming (changing a file and print server to a BackOffice server isn't accomplished in ten minutes), but the continuity this scheme provides can be important.

If you're planning to operate for a while with a mixed environment, consider upgrading DNS and DHCP servers quickly in order to gain the additional benefits available in Windows 2000:

- Windows 2000 DNS provides dynamic synchronization for DHCP servers and clients. Older versions of DNS do not synchronize dynamically with DHCP.

- Windows 2000 DHCP provides a number of enhanced features, including the ability to take advantage of clustering and load balancing. Clustering and load balancing features are available in Windows 2000 Advanced Server and Datacenter Server.

Detailed information about DNS and DHCP can be found throughout this book.

| Note | *If your mixed environment includes legacy UNIX systems, Windows 2000 DNS has enhanced functions for BIND version 4.9.4 and higher. You might want to consider upgrading your version of BIND to gain this advantage. (You don't have to update BIND for compatibility because Windows 2000 supports earlier versions.)* |

Installing Windows 2000

Whether you're performing a clean installation or upgrading an existing computer, you'll find that the installation process is more user-friendly than its predecessor. I would go so far as to say that it's more refined than the intuitive Windows 98 install.

The install is essentially performed in just a few steps. The setup program invokes the setup wizard, which guides you through a series of questions; then you install the networking portion; and finally, it completes the setup by copying the necessary files and restarts the computer. The following sections describe this process in detail.

Installing from Scratch

Installing from scratch means that you have either blown away any existing OS and reformatted the drive or you have brand new hardware. The procedure described here also applies to installing a fresh copy (installing to a different directory than the current OS) of Windows 2000. Note that I'm assuming that you have thoroughly checked for any hardware incompatibilities.

To install Windows 2000, do the following:

1. Insert Disk 1 from the Setup boot disks, and turn on or restart the computer. If you have a system that supports booting from a CD-ROM, you can use it instead of the diskettes. We'll proceed as if you were installing from a bootable CD-ROM.

2. Setup prompts you to read and accept the licensing agreement (you have to agree) and then asks you to select an existing partition or create a new one. Unless you plan to install to a different directory, create a new partition. Doing so also causes Setup to ask you to specify the size of the partition.

3. Next you choose the file system format of the partition. If this machine is intended to be a DC, you are required to use NTFS 5.

4. Once the formatting (you may have used the same file system or converted file systems) is complete, Setup copies the necessary files to the hard disk and then restarts the machine.

5. Remove the Windows 2000 CD-ROM and any diskettes from the drives.

6. After the machine has restarted, place the Windows 2000 CD-ROM back into the drive so that Setup can copy additional files. The machine will be restarted once again before the Windows 2000 Setup Wizard is started.

7. Click Next on the Windows 2000 Setup Wizard screen so that it can gather information about your machine. If Windows 2000 detects a possible conflict, it will display a dialog box listing the conflicts. If you've done your homework, those conflicts have already been resolved.

8. Make any needed changes on the Regional Settings page and click Next.

9. On the Personalize Your Software screen, type your name in the Name box and your company or organization name in the Organization box. Click Next when you've entered the information.

10. Choose a licensing mode and enter the number of licenses you have purchased. This depends on the type of license you purchased. It can either be Per Seat or Per Server. Click Next to proceed.

11. On the Computer Name And Administrator Password screen, type in your DNS-compliant computer name in the Computer Name box. Then type the administrator password in the Password and Confirm Password box.

12. Click Next to advance to display configuration options. If you change the default settings, you are forced to test the change.

13. Once you have configured the display settings, set date and time zone options. Click Next when done.

14. The next few screens are related to network configuration options. The only thing you should configure at this point is TCP/IP. Choosing Typical Settings configures TCP/IP to use DHCP. This is sufficient for client machines, but if you are installing a server, you don't want to use this setting because you'll have to use a statically assigned IP address.

15. Still within the network configuration phase, you'll be asked if you want to join a domain. Specify a domain only when you have already created a Windows 2000 domain, of which this machine should be a part.

16. Click Finish, and the Setup program restarts the computer.

Installing DNS and AD Services

Before you can begin building your Windows 2000 infrastructure from your design specifications, you must install and configure the DNS and AD services. For more information on DNS and AD, refer to Chapters 14 and 15, respectively. Since each environment differs in configuration, the following sections only will step you through the installation procedures.

You must be logged on with administrative privileges in order to install DNS and AD components. It is also assumed that the machine's network configuration settings are properly configured and that you have statically assigned an IP address to the machines.

INSTALLING DNS   To install Microsoft's DNS Server, perform the following steps:

1. Double-click the Add/Remove Programs applet within the Control Panel.

2. Click on Add/Remove Windows Components to invoke the Windows Components Wizard.

3. Highlight the Networking Services option and click Details.

4. Check the box beside Dynamic Name Service (DNS) as shown in the following illustration, and then click OK.

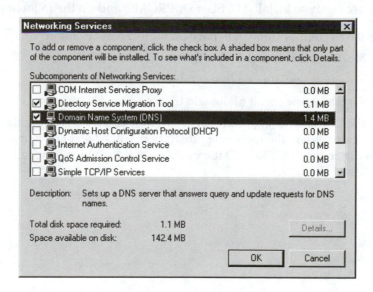

5. Click Next to begin installing DNS. If Windows 2000 can't find the system files needed, you will be prompted to insert the CD or specify their location.

6. If you have another DNS server on your network, specify the Primary DNS server's IP address in the Primary DNS Server box. Otherwise, click OK twice and then select Finish to complete the installation.

7. Close the Add/Remove Programs window and you're done.

Why would you want to do any of the installation procedures for DNS when DCPROMO takes care of all this for you? There are several reasons, including that you may want to have a stand-alone server handling DNS related queries, or you may not want to integrate DNS and AD.

Using DDNS requires you to integrate DNS and AD. Therefore, you must promote the server to a DC. In addition, the integration of the two services passes DNS replication responsibilities from DNS to AD.

INSTALLING AD   There are two possible scenarios for installing AD. The first is upgrading a Windows NT 4 PDC or BDC, and the second is installing AD on a stand-alone server. If you are upgrading a PDC or BDC, DCPROMO will run automatically. Otherwise, you need to manually invoke DCPROMO.

DCPROMO is a wizard that promotes a Windows 2000 member server to a DC. The new version of NTFS, NTFS 5, is required in order to install AD. If you haven't already converted to NTFS 5, do so now. See Chapter 20 for more information on NTFS 5 and other file systems. To manually start DCPROMO, click Run from the Start menu, enter **dcpromo**, and click OK.

Now you are ready to install AD. Start DCPROMO and do the following:

1. Go to the System Volume path page and select New domain.

2. Click Next and then select Create new domain tree.

3. Select Create a new domain tree and then click Next.

4. Select Create a new forest of domain trees and then click Next.

5. Enter the DNS name (e.g., company.com) that you chose during the design phase, as shown in the following illustration. Click Next again to advance to the following screen. DCPROMO then verifies that the name is not already in use.

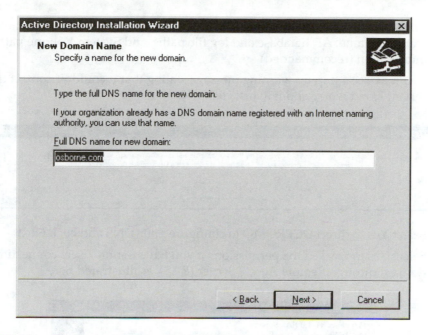

6. Windows 2000 then suggests a NetBIOS name based on the domain name you
   specified. It also gives you the opportunity to specify a NetBIOS name like the
   one shown in the following illustration.

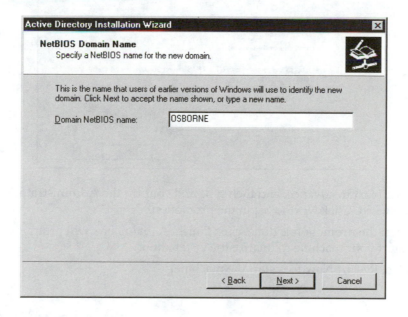

7. Click Next for the next three screens to accept the defaults for comparable NetBIOS name, AD database and log file paths, and System Volume path information (recommended).

8. You may see a pop-up warning message stating that it couldn't contact the DNS server. Don't worry about it; just click OK.

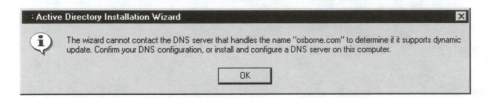

9. Select Yes to direct DCPROMO to configure your DNS and click Next.

10. Select Yes to weaken the permissions if you have remote users connecting to the domain through Remote Access Server (RAS), as illustrated here.

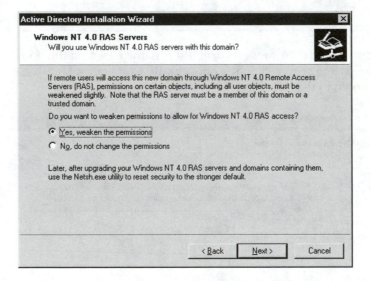

11. Click Next to advance, and then type and confirm the Administrator's password. Click Next to begin the promotion.

12. When the promotion is done, click Finish. A dialog box will prompt you to restart your machine to finalize the installation.

13. Select Restart Now to restart the machine.

UNDERSTANDING WINDOWS 2000

ADDING ANOTHER DC TO A DOMAIN   To provide better response time to users, add fault tolerance, or to add availability to the domain, you can add an additional DC. You'll once again use DCPROMO, but the options you select will be slightly different.

To add another DC to a domain, do the following:

1. Click Run from the Start menu and type DCPROMO. After you have finished typing, click OK.

2. Click Next to advance to the next screen, and then select Replica domain controller in existing domain.

3. Click Next and then type the DNS name of the domain you wish to replicate.

4. Click Next and then enter the name and password, with administrative privileges, in that domain.

5. Click Finish and allow the machine to restart.

Once the machine is back online, it will serve as a DC for the domain you specified.

Conclusion

Migrating to Windows 2000 can be categorized as a three-step process. You first take necessary precautions by preparing your network for the upgrade. This first step should also include getting everyone familiar with the new OS by giving them a substantial amount of training. The training will be especially beneficial to you in the second phase, when designing your environment of Windows 2000. In the third stage, you're ready to take the plunge and begin the upgrades. By following the steps outlined in this chapter, you should have a smooth transition to the enhanced features and radical new design of Windows 2000.

The Complete Reference

Chapter 3

Unattended Installations

Nobody ever accused Windows 2000 of being a simple product to install, even on one isolated system. Installing it on a large number of systems in a complex enterprise network is inconceivable without a strategy and automation tools.

Fortunately, Windows 2000 administrators have at their disposal powerful tools for scripting the automation of Windows 2000 deployment across the network. You also have many different methods of performing remote installations, and many ways to automate those installations. Some methods allow you to "push" the entire installation to a client without even visiting the computer.

Windows NT 4 administrators will recognize most of their familiar tools for automating installations, such as Sysprep, which is a tool for cloning installations of Windows 2000 in a safe way. They will also recognize answer files, which are a settings file you pass to the winnt32 setup program in order to automate it.

If you've used conventional automated installations with answer files, you'll be impressed by the new Setup Manager in the Windows 2000 Resource Kit, a wizard that walks you through the process of creating answer files. In the past this was a manual, error-prone process. The Resource Kit includes a variety of other essential tools for administrators, such as the SIDwalker Security Administration Tools, which manage the individual security identities in Windows 2000 Access Control Lists.

Also new in Windows 2000 automated installation is the ability to control networking configuration (including controlling multiple network cards and different protocols), and to change the binding order. You can now tell the system to log on automatically as administrator one or more times after setup is complete. You have many ways to specify commands that will be executed after setup is complete.

If you have implemented Windows 2000's Active Directory, DHCP, and DNS on your network, then you are most of the way toward using Windows 2000's Remote Installation Services (RIS). RIS utilizes these features of Windows 2000 networking to automate installations of clients across the network in a highly efficient and customizable manner. In some cases, you will not even need to visit the system in order to perform an installation of Windows 2000 Professional on it.

Upgrade or New Installation?

Before you begin the installation process, you need to decide whether you are performing a new, clean installation of Windows 2000 or upgrading a previous operating system. This concern is enhanced in Windows 2000, which can upgrade Windows 98 systems as well as Windows NT. The different automated installation methods may or may not support the different methods:

Installation Method	Windows 2000 Version	Upgrade Supported?	Clean Installation Supported?
Sysprep	Server and Professional	No	Yes

Installation Method	Windows 2000 Version	Upgrade Supported?	Clean Installation Supported?
Syspart	Server and Professional	No	Yes
SMS	Server and Professional	Yes	Yes
Bootable CD-ROM	Server and Professional	No	Yes
Remote Installation Services	Professional	No	Yes

Microsoft Systems Management Server

If you are using Microsoft's SMS or some other management software, such as Computer Associates' Unicenter, to manage software on your network, you can take advantage of it to deploy Windows 2000 as well. Microsoft's SMS can deploy Windows 2000 to clients and servers, even, in some cases, pushing the installation to the new system without physically visiting it. SMS is especially valuable in deploying to geographically distributed systems. If you are using third-party management software, check with the vendor for its support of Windows 2000 installations.

Winnt32—the Setup Command

Most Windows NT administrators have worked with the winnt32 command, which is the command-line utility that runs Windows NT and Windows 2000 installation. The syntax for the winnt32 command is

```
winnt32 [/s:sourcepath] [/tempdrive:drive_letter]
[/unattend[num][:answer_file]] [/copydir:folder_name]
[/copysource:folder_name] [/cmd:command_line]
[/debug[level][:filename]] [/udf:id[,UDB_file]]
[/syspart:drive_letter] [/noreboot] [/makelocalsource]
[/checkupgradeonly]
```

where

- **/checkupgradeonly**   This option does not actually install Windows 2000, but checks the system for compatibility with Windows 2000.

- **/cmd:command_line**   This option specifies a command line to execute after the GUI portion of setup and after the system reboots. It's a good opportunity to start installation of applications. As an alternative, you can specify such a command in the answer file using the UserExecute key in the [SetupParams] section. Only the first such switch or key will be executed. If there are embedded spaces in the command—for example, between the command and its parameters—enclose the entire command following the colon in quotes. Network drives may not exist at this point in setup, so the command and any data it references should be on locally available drives. See also the cmdlines.txt section below.

■ **/cmdcons**   This option adds a recovery console option for repairing a failed installation.

■ **/copydir:folder_name**   This option creates a subfolder within the folder that contains Windows 2000 (e.g., c:\winnt). You can use this option several times.

■ **/copysource:folder_name**   This option is similar to /copydir, but the target folder is temporary and removed by setup before it completes. This might be useful as a source folder for device drivers needed in setup, for example.

■ **/debug[level][:file_name]**   This option creates a debug log (the default name is %windir%\Winnt32.log) during installation. The level setting specifies the amount of information that is logged: 0 = severe errors, 1=errors, 2 = warnings, 3 = information, and 4 = detailed information for debugging.

■ **/m:folder_name**   This option instructs Setup to copy replacement files from an alternate location. It directs Setup to look at the alternate location first and to copy the files from that location (if files are present) instead of from the default location.

■ **/makelocalsource**   This option instructs setup to copy all the Windows 2000 source files to a temporary location on the hard disk before installation, and to install them from there. This can be useful if you are installing from a CD or network location that may become unavailable at some point during installation.

■ **/noreboot**   This option instructs setup not to reboot the computer during installation. This gives you the opportunity to examine the system and execute other commands.

■ **/s:sourcepath**   This option tells setup to copy files from an alternate folder instead of the current directory. You can specify multiple /s: parameters, which can speed up the file copy phase of setup and provide some fault tolerance to the process.

■ **/syspart:drive_letter**   The syspart option lets you place a partial Windows 2000 installation on the primary partition of a secondary hard drive in the system. You can then put that hard disk in a different system and, when it boots, setup will continue and complete on the new system. You must also use the /tempdrive option and point it and the /syspart option to the same partition. You can only run the /syspart option from a system running Windows NT or Windows 2000.

- **/tempdrive:drive_letter**   Used in conjunction with /syspart, /tempdrive directs setup to place its temporary files on the specified drive.

- **/udf:ID[,UDB_file]**   This option is used to specify a UDB (uniqueness database) file and an ID to fill in values in that file. UDB files are used with the /unattend option and can specify per-computer values that override defaults in the answer file.

Note   *If you specify an ID but not an answer file, setup prompts you to insert a disc that contains the $Unique$.udb file. Answer files and UDB files are a complex topic, and are discussed in more detail in the section "Answer Files and UDB Files."*

- **/unattend**   Upgrades the system with no new settings.

- **/unattend[seconds][:answer_file]**   This switch is the heart of unattended installation. The first form, with no options, specified that setup should upgrade the previous version of Windows, taking all existing user settings, and complete without user intervention.

  The second form allows you to specify the name of the answer file (see the section "Answer Files and UDF Files," later in this chapter). The seconds option specifies the amount of time Windows 2000 spends at the boot menu before continuing. This can be useful on computers with other operating systems, such as Windows NT 4, installed.

Note   *This parameter has changed from its form in Windows NT 4. The full "/unattend" must now be used instead of just "/u."*

If you want to install from a DOS or Win16 environment and need a 16-bit setup, you can still do so with the 16-bit winnt command:

```
WINNT [/S[:sourcepath]][/T[:tempdrive]]/U[:answer_file]]
[/R[x]:folder][/E:command]
```

where

- **/E:command**   Like the /cmd: option for winnt32, this option specifies a command line to execute after the GUI portion of setup and after the system reboots. It's a good opportunity to start installation of applications. As an alternative, you can specify such a command in the answer file using the UserExecute key in the [SetupParams] section. Only the first such switch or key is executed. If there are embedded spaces in the command—for example, between the command and its parameters—enclose the entire command following the colon in quotes. Network drives may not exist at this point in setup, so the command and any data it references should be on locally available drives.

- **/R:folder_name**   Like /copydir option on winnt32, this option creates a subfolder within the folder that contains Windows 2000 (e.g., c:\winnt). You can use this option several times.

- **/Rx:folder_name**   Like /copysource option on winnt32, this option is similar to /R, but the target folder is temporary and removed by setup before it completes. This is useful as a source folder for device drivers needed during setup.

- **/S:sourcepath**   Exactly like the /s: in winnt32, this option tells setup to copy files from an alternate folder instead of the current directory. Unlike the /s: in winnt32, you can only specify one sourcepath.

- **/T:tempdrive**   Like /tempdrive for winnt32, this option specifies a drive onto which setup places temporary files. If you don't specify a drive, setup finds one for you.

- **/U:answer_file**   This option tells setup to perform an unattended installation using the specified answer file. This option requires an /s parameter as well.

Answer Files and UDF files

The normal setup process asks the user numerous questions about how to configure the system. Fortunately, in most cases you can create an answer file, which contains settings that are the answers to the questions setup will ask. Thus, if you know what settings you want to use in advance, you can tell setup to read its answers from the answer file and setup will proceed "unattended." Setup files are at the heart of unattended installation of Windows 2000.

Some of the questions in setup are specific to individual computers, so the answer file cannot be correct for more than one computer. This is where uniqueness database (UDB) files come in. These are files that you define for each computer. They contain settings that override those in the answer files.

Answer Files

Windows administrators should be familiar with the general file type of answer files, which are similar to other types of Windows configuration files:

```
; lines in answer files which begin with a
; semi-colon are comments and are ignored by setup.
[section name]
key1=value
key2="value with embedded spaces"
```

Answer files have many sections corresponding to different categories of information, and individual keys within each section.

In earlier versions of Windows NT, you needed to create answer files manually, or by modifying sample files to your own needs. This required knowledge of all the potential settings and was error prone and time-consuming. Recently, Microsoft introduced a utility with the Windows NT Resource Kit called Setup Manager, and this utility has been improved in the Windows 2000 Resource Kit. It is a wizard that asks you questions about the installation you wish to create and then uses your answers to create an answer file, a UDF file, and a batch file that invokes the Windows 2000 setup (winnt32.exe) using these files. Setup Manager is a considerable time-saver for administrators, who should view it as the preferred method for creating these files.

Even though Setup Manager can also modify existing answer files, you may still wish to edit these files. There are tasks that you may need to perform that cannot be performed in an unattended installation, as follows:

- Installing applications that run as Windows 2000 services. There is a workaround for this, which is described later in the "Using the Cmdlines.txt file" section.

- Creating multiple hardware profiles.

- Installing multiple language versions of Windows 2000. You must do this manually with the appropriate Multilanguage pack.

- Installing Plug and Play ISA drivers.

UDF Files

The Uniqueness Database (UDF) File is in the format of an answer file, and it contains settings that override those in the answer file. The idea of the UDF file is to provide information particular to a computer, such as the computer name, while allowing the answer file itself to be useful for a large number of systems.

The Setup Manager creates UDF files in addition to answer files, and is the preferred method of creating them. But if you need to edit UDF files, it's a simple process. The UDF file has two basic sections: one for the Unique IDs for each computer, and one for the parameters for each Unique ID. For example:

```
[UniqueIds]
    COMPUTER1=UserData,GuiUnattended
    COMPUTER2=UserData,GuiUnattended
    COMPUTER3=UserData,GuiUnattended
[COMPUTER1:UserData]
    ComputerName=COMPUTER1
[COMPUTER1:GuiUnattended]
    TimeZone=" (GMT-5:00) Eastern Time (US & Canada)"
[COMPUTER2:UserData]
    ComputerName=COMPUTER2
[COMPUTER2:GuiUnattended]
```

```
    TimeZone=" (GMT-5:00) Eastern Time (US & Canada)"
[COMPUTER3:UserData]
    ComputerName=COMPUTER3
[COMPUTER3:GuiUnattended]
    TimeZone=" (GMT-5:00) Eastern Time (US & Canada)"
```

In the above example, COMPUTER1, COMPUTER2, and COMPUTER3 are Unique IDs; UserData and TimeZone are parameters. When the setup is performed with this UDF file, these values will substitute for those in the answer file.

Using the Cmdlines.txt file

Sometimes you need or want to execute other commands after setup. The /E and /cmd parameters to setup provide a way to run one program. The cmdlines.txt file provides a way to run multiple commands during the GUI mode of setup. These commands need to have a "silent" mode that does not require user interaction, and possibly their own scripting facility.

The answer file (usually unattend.txt) needs to have an "OEMPreinstall=Yes" entry in the [Unattended] section. If the command executables themselves are not in the setup directory, you must specify a complete path. These commands are executed at the end of setup, prior to the reboot for first logon, so network drives will not be available at this point. If you need to execute commands after setup but with access to network facilities, use the "RunOnce" facility described later in the section "Setup Manager."

Place the cmdlines.txt file in the OEM folder in the distribution folder (see "Distribution Folders" later in this chapter). Here is the syntax for the cmdlines.txt file:

```
[Commands]
"command1 p1 p2 p3"
"command2 p4 p5 p6"
```

The individual commands must be surrounded by quotes.

Running Programs Once as the New System Logs On

In addition to cmdlines.txt, which runs programs during Setup, you can have programs run once after the newly set up system has rebooted. By listing the command lines to execute as entries in the [GuiRunOnce] section of the answer file, the programs run after the system starts up but before the user logs on. These entries correspond to those created by the Run Once facility in Setup Manager, and show up on the new system as entries in HKEY_LOCAL_MACHINE\Software\Microsoft\Windows\CurrentVersion\RunOnce.

```
[GuiRunOnce]
"%systemdrive%\appfolder\appinstall -quiet"
```

Like programs listed in cmdlines.txt, you should ensure that the program suppresses any user interface. Search its documentation for parameters, such as "-quiet", that may perform this function. If the application forces a reboot, see if that too can be suppressed. Also, because the shell is not loaded at the time Run and RunOnce keys execute, any programs that require an instance of Windows Explorer (usually "shell extensions") will not work in this scenario.

Installing New Applications

One of the most common reasons to run programs once after installing Windows 2000 is to install applications on the system. As stated above, you should make sure that the installation program has a "quiet" mode.

If you want to create a batch file that initiates the setup programs for many applications, you should serialize the installations, so that each waits for the previous one to finish before beginning. Use the "start /wait" command to do this:

```
Start /wait <path to 1st application>\Setup <command line parameters>
Start /wait <path to 2nd application>\Setup <command line parameters>
Exit
```

Setup Manager

If you've installed Windows 2000 or Windows NT manually, you know that there are a very large number of potential questions for you to answer. The answer files that script unattended installations have to answer almost all these questions, so they are necessarily complex. In the past, writing answer files was a difficult combination of modifying sample files and scrambling for inadequate documentation. All that ends in Windows 2000, where Microsoft has finally supplied a tool, the Setup Manager (see Figure 3-1), that generates answer files, as well as UDF files and a batch file to invoke the unattended installation.

Invoke the Setup Manager from the Windows 2000 Resource Kit, or extract it from the \support\tools\deploy.cab file on your Windows 2000 CD. Setup Manager is a long and complex wizard. At the outset, decide whether to create a new answer file, edit an existing one, or create one based on the configuration of the computer on which Setup Manager is running.

The decisions you make at any one point in Setup Manager can take you down a completely different path of questioning. For example, if you choose to do a Sysprep installation, you will not be asked to create a distribution folder. This chapter does not discuss all permutations of running Setup Manager, instead it presents an overview of the types of questions you will be asked to give you a sense of the power of the tool.

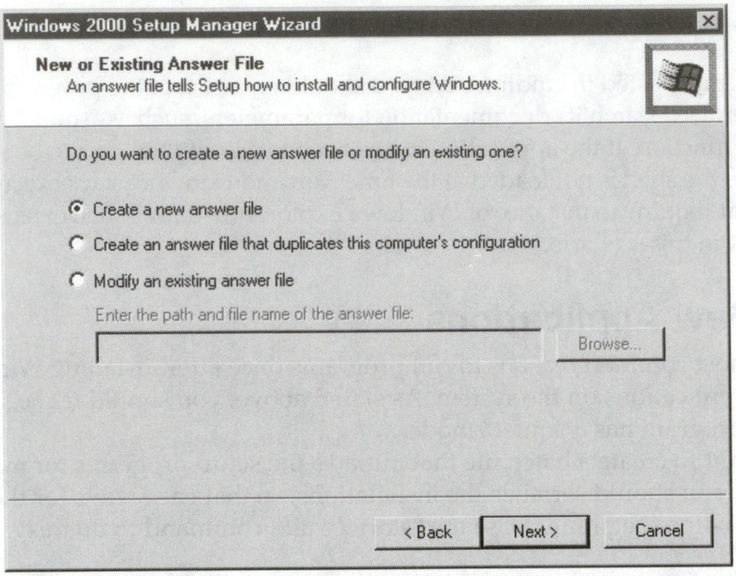

Figure 3-1. *The Setup Manager is a wizard that asks you questions and creates an answer file, other supporting files, and a distribution folder using your answers. It can also create one based on the computer on which you run it, or modify an existing answer file*

You should not have great trouble understanding the questions and answering them as it suits your organization.

If you are using Setup Manager to create a Sysprep installation, and you are running it on the system to be prepared for duplication by Sysprep, then it is easiest to let Setup Manager create the Sysprep directory and copy the Sysprep files. Otherwise, you will have to copy these files to the Sysprep master system yourself. Remember that you can do this by extracting the contents of the \support\tools\deploy.cab file from your Windows 2000 CD.

Your next major decision is whether you are creating an answer file to install Windows 2000 Professional, Windows 2000 Server, or to do a Remote Installation Services install or a Sysprep install. The latter two have some differences in their answer file settings.

Then you need to decide just how automated the installation will be. In the User Interaction Level dialog box (see Figure 3-2), you choose between the following options for your unattended install:

- **Provide Defaults** The answers you provide to the questions in the wizard will be defaults to questions the user sees, but the setup will not be automated.

- **Fully Automated** The setup is completely automated using the settings you provide in the wizard. The user is asked no questions.

- **Hide Pages** If you answer the question in the wizard, the user does not see the corresponding page during setup.

- **Read Only** If a page is not hidden from the user, it is locked so that the user cannot modify settings.

- **GUI Attended** Only the text mode portion of setup is automated; the GUI portion runs interactively.

Depending on your decision at the User Interaction Level dialog, you may or may not be asked certain questions. For example if you choose *GUI Attended*, you won't be asked for a Time Zone, but the user will be. After this, you will be asked for your name and the Organization name, followed by the CD key.

Next you are asked for the names of the computers on which this unattended installation will be performed (see Figure 3-3). You can add several names to the list or import a list of names from a text file. This information is used in part to create a UDF file so you can customize information for each computer.

After this, you have the option of creating an administrator password. If you have set the installation to be fully automatic, you will have to provide a password or set it to be blank. It's best not to use a real password here, because the one you enter into

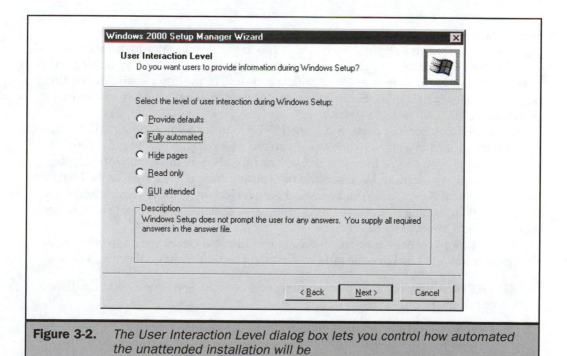

Figure 3-2. *The User Interaction Level dialog box lets you control how automated the unattended installation will be*

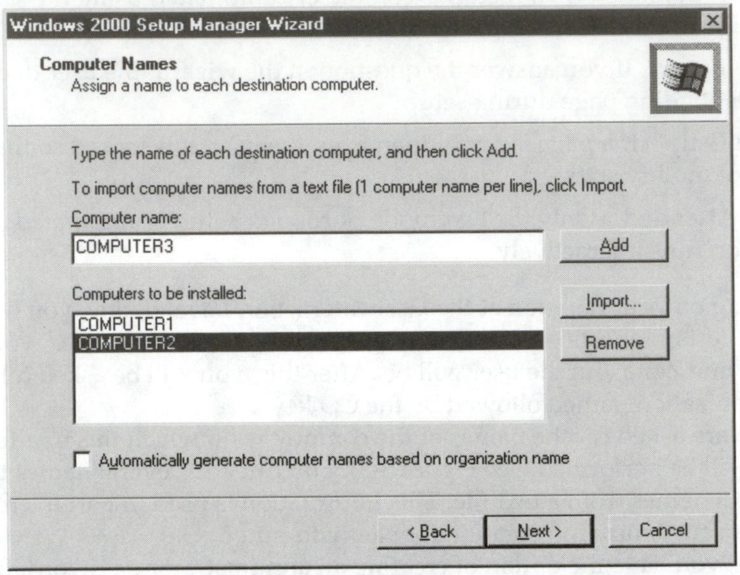

Figure 3-3.   *The list of computer names you provide to Setup Manager will be used to create a UDF file for customizing the install to each computer*

Setup Manager will be written in clear text into the answer file. Choose a temporary password and change it the first time you log on to the system after installation.

Next come the display settings on the target system. You can specify resolution, color depth, and refresh frequency, or make no choice. In the latter event, depending on your choices earlier in the Setup Manager, the user may have a chance to specify, or Windows 2000 will select a default.

In the Network Settings page, you can tell setup to make default settings (TCP/IP, DHCP, client for Microsoft Networking) or you can make detailed settings for network configuration. If you choose to customize, you can specify how many network adapters are in each target system, and you can add networking components, such as the NetWare client and IPX/SPX protocol. Whether you choose typical or custom network settings, you then move on to joining a domain or workgroup and, optionally, to creating an account in a domain. Next you specify time zone.

At this point you have created a basic answer file, and can move on to creating a distribution folder. You have the option of making certain additional settings first:

- **TAPI settings,** such as your Country, area code and an access code for dialing out of the phone system
- **Regional settings,** which define the primary language and internationalization rules to use on the target system

- **Which folder** (\winnt by default) should receive the Windows 2000 program files
- **Printers,** including local and network printers, and their drivers
- **Programs** you specify to run once as setup finishes (if you install printers in the previous step, you will see that Setup Manager uses this "Run Once" capability to add the printers)

Now Setup Manager asks you whether you want to create a distribution folder or if this answer file will be used to install from the CD. If you are going to install from CD, save the answer file and exit. If you are creating a distribution folder, you are asked for its location. Fortunately, Setup Manager includes a Browse button here for you to find a good spot on the network. You can also create a new network share at this point.

If you have to load mass storage drivers or Hardware Abstraction Layers (HALs) that aren't part of the standard Windows 2000 distribution, Setup Manager can load them into the distribution folder at this point. You also are given an option to define a cmdlines.txt file (see "Using the Cmdlines.txt File" earlier), which is a list of commands to execute at the end of Setup. Then OEMs get the option of defining a logo and background to use during setup. Lastly, you can specify additional files to be copied to the system.

At the end of Setup Manager, you have three files: an answer file (unattend.txt by default; if you specified Remote Installation Service, the file is named winnt.sif), unattend.udf, and a batch file named unattend.bat.

Note   *The batch file is written to assume the saved location you specified in Setup Manager. If you move the files to another location, edit the batch file to change the folder references.*

Distribution Folders

Most of the automated installation methods, including Remote Installation Service, require that you create a distribution folder. A *distribution folder* is a directory containing all the files needed to set up Windows 2000. This includes not only the actual install files from the setup disk, but third-party device drivers, other files you may wish to have on the installed system, and configuration files which instruct the installation program how to configure the system.

Depending on the configuration of your network, you may be best off creating several distribution folders. Doing so simplifies deployment if you have several types of systems that have different installation characteristics. Furthermore, installation over a network consumes great deals of network bandwidth, albeit for relatively brief periods of time. You may do everyone a favor by isolating that traffic, especially keeping it off of crucial routing points on the network.

The Windows 2000 Remote Installation Service (RIS) requires that the distribution folder be on an isolated volume. Microsoft is unclear as to the reasons for this requirement, but it appears to be due to the considerable performance burden installation places on the I/O subsystem of the server. Microsoft also recommends using SCSI drives rather than IDE drives, which would also be explained by performance concerns. Some Microsoft documentation on this service says that the distribution folder must be on its own "drive," but all that is required is a logical volume such as a partition on another drive. Of course, if the performance concerns are all they are supposed to be, putting the distribution on a partition of another functioning drive would probably be even worse than if it shared space with another in-use drive, because head movement between the partitions would tax the drive considerably. The bottom line should be that if you have any performance concerns at all for the server doing the installation, follow Microsoft's recommendation.

Here are some guidelines for creating distribution folders:

- The easy way to create a distribution folder is to use the Setup Manager Wizard from the Windows 2000 Resource Kit.

- To create a distribution folder manually, first create a network share on the target drive and create a \i386 folder in that share. Then copy the contents of the \i386 folder from the Windows 2000 CD-ROM to the \i386 folder you just created.

- In the \i386 folder, create a subfolder named \$OEM$. If you use the OEMFILESPATH key in your answer file you can store the \$OEM$ folder outside the distribution folder. This could be useful if more than one of your distribution folders share common contents in the \$OEM$.

- \OEM can optionally contain a file named cmdlines.txt which contains commands to execute during the GUI portion of setup.

- In the \OEM\textmode folder, place hardware-specific files, such as device drivers and third-party HALs. You should also have a file here named txtsetup.oem, which controls which of these files are loaded.

- The \$OEM$\$$ folder should be structurally identical to the %windir% folder (usually c:\winnt); in other words, it should contain a system32 subfolder, and so on. Setup copies any files in this subtree to the corresponding folders on the target system.

- You can also include any number of subfolders named \$OEM$\drive_letter, where drive_letter is the letter of a drive in the target system. For example, setup copies files in \$OEM$\C to the C: drive, \$OEM$\D\DATA to the D:\DATA folder, and so on.

There is a special case, \$OEM$\$1, which is the drive specified by the %systemdrive% variable, which is the drive onto which the operating system is installed. Depending on how your different systems are to be configured, it may be advantageous to specify the system drive abstractly rather than to hard-code it to drive C.

Plug and Play Mass Storage Devices

Windows 2000's Plug and Play support usually finds and installs support for devices without your having to specify them. But this process doesn't occur until the GUI stage of the installation. It may be necessary or convenient for you to manually install a device, most likely a SCSI drive, before Windows 2000 autodetects it. This is one of the purposes of the \$OEM$\textmode\txtsetup.oem file. Vendors ship a txtsetup.oem file with their drivers, and you can copy the appropriate entries to yours from their file. Make sure that these drivers are signed, or Windows 2000's setup program will fail. For each device, include the driver.sys, driver.dll, and driver.inf file to the \$OEM$\ textmode folder, where *driver* is the actual driver filename. Add the same filenames to the [OEMBootFiles] section of the answer file.

| Note | *Some drivers, such as SCSI miniport drivers, may not include a .dll file.* |

Further information on the format of txtsetup.oem may be obtained from the Microsoft Windows 2000 Device Driver Kit. The most current Windows 2000 DDK documentation can be read at http://www.microsoft.com/ddk/ddkdocs/win2k/default.htm.

In the answer file, you need to create a [MassStorageDrivers] section with one entry for each device; for example:

```
EMSCSI = "OEM SCSI for Adaptec 154x/164x", oemscsi
```

HALs

You may need to install a third-party HAL for some systems, especially multiprocessor systems. If so, copy all the HAL files provided by the vendor to the OEM\textmode folder. Edit the [Unattend] section of the answer file, and add any entries from the [Computer] section of the vendor's Txtsetup.oem file. As you did with any boot devices, add the driver names to the [OEMBootFiles] section of the answer file.

Plug and Play Non-Mass Storage Devices

Plug and Play devices that are not mass storage can also be installed manually. It's usually not necessary to preinstall these devices rather than to let Windows 2000 find and configure them, but you can do so if you want to prevent users from seeing the automated detection and installation process.

Create a folder in the Distribution Folder subtree into which you will put all the Plug and Play device drivers and their .inf files. For example, you might call the folder OEM\$1\PnPDrvs. In this example, add the following line to the unattend.txt file:

```
OEMPnPDriversPath = "PnPDrvs"
```

The OEMPnPDriversPath key can specify several folder paths relative to OEM\$1\. For example, you could specify:

```
OEMPnPDriversPath = "PnPDrvs\audio; PnPDrvs\video; PnPDrvs\net;"
```

Converting Short Filenames to Long Filenames

It's probably rare these days, but in building a distribution folder tree you may need to use tools that cannot manage long filenames. More commonly, you may encounter situations where the filename in addition to the full folder path exceeds the length limit (frequently 64 characters) that your applications can manage.

If you need to use short filenames in the distribution folder but want the files renamed to long names by the setup program, create a $$Rename.txt file in the folder. You must create a $$Rename.txt for each folder that contains filenames you want to convert.

The file should be in this format:

```
[section_name_1]
shortname_1 = "long name 1"
shortname_2 = "long name 2"
```

For example:

```
[\data\larry]
ddata1.foo = "First Data File.mdb"
ddata2.foo = "Second Data File.mdb.bak"
```

Notice that the section name is the folder on the source drive in which the files are located. If the long filename has embedded spaces or commas, it must be surrounded by quotes.

Bootable CD-ROM

Windows 2000 introduces a new method of simple automated installs. If you can configure the BIOS on your system to boot from the CD-ROM before the floppy drive, then you can have Windows 2000 install directly from the CD-ROM with the procedure controlled by a simple answer file on the floppy drive.

The advantage of this method is that it requires very little preparatory work. Most of the other methods require that you be able to boot an operating system on the target system, and many require extensive preparation of distribution folders on the network. But if you want a fairly straightforward default installation on the system, the bootable CD-ROM can make Windows 2000 installation easy.

The system must specifically support the El Torito specification for bootable CD-ROM images. This is common nowadays but not universal. Check with your system vendor if you are not sure if your system supports El Torito.

This installation method only supports a single partition, and you cannot specify third-party drivers. If you need to set up other partitions or install drivers for hardware not inherently supported by Windows 2000, you will have to do so manually after installation. Depending on the extent of such work, you may be better off choosing another installation method. Fortunately, you can easily experiment on one system with this method and see how far it goes in fulfilling your needs.

Preparing for Bootable CD-ROM Installation

You need very little to prepare for a bootable CD-ROM install. Make sure that the BIOS knows to boot the system from the CD-ROM and not the floppy.

You will need a floppy disk with an unattended answer file named Winnt.sif. The best way to create the answer file is to use the Setup Manager wizard from the Windows 2000 Resource Kit. The answer file is, by default, named unattend.txt, so you'll have to rename it.

Once you have created the file, edit it and add a [Data] section with the following entries:

```
[Data]
UnattendedInstall=yes
MSDosInitiated=no
AutoPartition=1
```

The last entry controls whether the setup program partitions the hard disk automatically. If you change the setting:

```
AutoPartition=0
```

then setup will stop during the text mode portion and let you manually partition the hard disk.

Save the file as winnt.sif on the floppy disk. Place the floppy disk in the primary floppy drive and the CD-ROM in the boot CD-ROM drive, and restart the system. It boots into the setup program and proceeds automatically, according to the answer file you created. Setup completes without intervention, unless you instructed it to do otherwise.

Sysprep

Sysprep is a tool that allows you to create an image of one Windows 2000 installation and clone it to other systems with identical hardware, using a third-party disk duplication system. The main advantage of this method is speed. Installing a new system is as simple as transferring the disk image to the target hard disk, and you may be able to place the disk image on a CD-ROM that you can carry from system to system or physically ship to remote locations.

You can get Sysprep from the Windows 2000 Resource Kit, or from the Windows 2000 CD-ROM. Use the Expand utility or Windows Explorer to expand \support\ tools\deploy.cab, in which you will find sysprep.exe, setupcl.exe, and a sample sysprep.inf file.

Sysprep is a bit of a hack though; the hardware has to be identical on every system, so in a normal environment you probably need to maintain multiple images for different hardware configurations. But if you have many systems with identical hardware configurations, Sysprep can be a good choice for you.

All Windows 2000 systems need a unique security identifier (SID), which is used by Windows 2000 to validate systems and users. If you merely clone a system on a network, the two identical SIDs will cause conflicts. For this reason, Sysprep sets the system up to generate a new, unique SID the next time you boot up. You can disable the sidgen process, although there is rarely reason to do so.

1. First, install Windows 2000 and any applications you want onto the master system. Do not make the computer a member of a domain, and leave the administrator password blank.

2. Confirm that the image is what you intended it to be. You should also delete any temporary files, including logs from Windows 2000 and applications. If necessary, defragment the disk.

3. Prepare the system image for duplication by running Sysprep with the appropriate parameters and, optionally, a sysprep.inf file, which is a partial answer file (discussed in the section "Sysprep.inf").

4. Duplicate the disk using a third-party duplication product, such as Symantec's Ghost, or a hardware duplicator.

5. Boot the new, duplicated hard disk in the other system; Windows 2000 generates a unique security identity (SID) for the system, and a Mini-Setup wizard launches to complete any unanswered questions on the setup (such as computer name).

NT4 administrators should note that sysprep syntax has changed in Windows 2000.

```
sysprep [-quiet] [-nosidgen] [-reboot] [-noreboot] [-pnp]
```

where

- **-quiet**   Silent mode, no dialogs
- **-nosidgen**   Don't generate a unique SID (security ID) on next restart
- **-reboot**   Reboots the system after sysprep finishes
- **-noreboot**   Does not reboot the system after sysprep finishes
- **-pnp**   Forces Plug and Play enumeration on next reboot

Sysprep.inf

If you use a sysprep.inf answer file, you can stop the Mini-Setup wizard from starting the next time the cloned copy of Windows 2000 boots. The Sysprep answer file must be named Sysprep.inf, and must be in the %system%\Sysprep folder. It's a subset of the conventional answer file, and only certain switches and parameters are accepted:

```
[Unattended]
OemSkipEula
OemPnPDriversPath
ExtendOEMPartition
[GuiUnattended]
AdminPassword
Autologon
TimeZone
OemDuplicatorString
[UserData]
all keys accepted
[LicenseFilePrintData]
all keys accepted
[GuiRunOnce]
[Display]
all keys accepted
[RegionalSettings]
all keys accepted
[Networking]
only InstallDefaultComponents
[Identification]
all keys accepted
[NetClients]
```

```
all Microsoft Client for Networking and Netware keys only
[TapiLocation]
all keys accepted
[Fax]
all keys accepted
```

The Mini-Setup Wizard

If you don't include a sysprep.inf, then the next time the cloned system boots up, it enters what is called the Mini-Setup wizard, which is a partial setup program with which the user can answer any remaining questions about the installation. This wizard should take only 5 or 6 minutes to run instead of the 45 to 60 minutes that the normal installation requires.

The wizard asks the user to do the following:

- View the End-User Licensing Agreement
- Set Regional Settings
- Enter User Name and Company
- Enter Computer Name
- Enter Administrator Password
- Configure TAPI Settings
- Configure a Server Licensing Scheme (for installations of Windows 2000 Server and Advanced Server only)
- Configure Time Zone
- Select Finish/Restart

Using Cmdlines.txt with Sysprep

You can run a cmdlines.txt file at the end of the GUI portion of the Mini-Setup Wizard, but it will require some extra setup.

You need to have a sysprep.inf file. In the [Unattended] section, create a key:

```
InstallFilesPath=drive:\path
```

where

drive:\path is any folder you wish, but it must exist during the Mini-Setup Wizard. Create the folder if need be. In the folder, create a subfolder named *OEM* and place the cmdlines.txt file in it.

Changing NTFS Partition Sizes and Sysprep

Some third-party disk duplication systems allow you to shrink partitions from their original allocated size. You might want to do this if you had an image created on a 6GB hard drive and wanted to apply it to a 4GB hard drive (presuming, of course, that there is 4GB or less of data).

Microsoft advises against doing this, as it may compromise metadata that NTFS stores about the size of the volume. Microsoft has some guidelines and workarounds that should allow you to use Sysprep in cases where the drive sizes may differ.

■ Make your images on the smallest volume or partition that will be used on a target system.

■ Modify the sysprep.inf file to include the ExtendOEMPartition key in the [Unattended] section with the appropriate value:

```
ExtendOEMPartition=0   ; do not extend partition
ExtendOEMPartition=1   ; extend partition to the end of the disk
ExtendOEMPartition=n   ; extend the partition n megabytes
```

When you use the third-party tool to transfer the disk image to the new disk, prevent it from extending the partition to the length of the disk. You may need to consult the product's documentation for this. When you boot the duplicated disk after this procedure, the Mini-Setup Wizard extends the partition according to your instructions in sysprep.inf.

Remote Installation Services

Remote Installation Services (RIS) is an optional service that comes with Windows NT Server and it's designed to make it easy to deploy Windows 2000 Professional to a variety of clients throughout an enterprise. It is built on and requires Active Directory, as well as Windows 2000's DNS and DHCP.

With RIS, you can define which systems will be configured with specific, customized parameters, stored in the Active Directory, without the need for you to visit each computer. When the user logs on, the new installation is pushed to the client system. With the Automatic Setup option, the installation can be completely automated. By default, users have only the option of automatic setup, but you can configure the Active Directory's default domain account policy object so that users have additional system installation options.

RIS works by booting installation images, similar to Sysprep images, over the network. Because boot images are used, clients that share an image need to have compatible hardware. Clients also need to have either a bootable network adapter or use a special boot floppy that connects to the RIS server and boots the system image.

When the system boots, it makes a request for DHCP services from a DHCP server, and then for an operating system using "Pre-boot eXecution Environment" (PXE) remote boot technology. PXE is an Intel Specification for remote operating system booting, part of their "Wired for Management" initiative. See http://www.intel.com/ial/wfm/tools/pxepdk20/index.htm for more information.

To know if you have a RIS-compatible network adapter, examine the boot messages of your client system when it turns on. A PXE boot ROM message should appear on the screen and display the PXE ROM version number. RIS supports PXE ROM version .99c or greater. If you have an earlier version, check with your hardware vendor to see if an upgrade is available.

Currently, RIS does not support remote installation of Windows 2000 Server. Support for portable computers is spotty: you cannot boot via RIS using PCMCIA or PC Card-based network adapters, although there are some notebook docking stations that support PXE-based booting through integrated network adapters. Such a system needs a PXE boot ROM version .99L or greater. Check with the manufacturers to see if they support PXE and RIS.

Microsoft has noteworthy hardware requirements for RIS servers. RIS servers need to be dedicated Windows 2000 servers, which in itself poses a nontrivial cost. Furthermore, the distribution folder for RIS needs to be stored on a different volume than the Windows 2000 system. Microsoft recommends that this be a separate hard drive and that you use SCSI. Clearly, the performance demands of RIS are considerable.

Because of the potentially large performance burden installation places on the network, it may be a good idea to create several RIS Servers distributed so that installations don't occur across slow links or crucial routing points on the network. Fortunately, RIS and Active Directory provide management features that allow you to control which systems receive boot images from which RIS Servers.

In some simple environments, it may make sense to run DHCP and RIS on the same physical server. This increases the efficiency of the process, because if the DHCP server replies to a client request, a RIS server on the same box will necessarily respond to a PXE request.

But this is not likely to be a practical setup in a normal complex environment. DHCP servers are not heavily taxed, and are likely to be low-power systems that serve a large number of clients. RIS servers need to be carefully placed and allocated so that they don't overburden the network. An overburdened RIS server can also result in timeout errors on the clients. If you already have software installation servers, they may be good points on which to install RIS. You have probably planned their location with the same sort of considerations you would use for a RIS server.

Every RIS Server must be authorized in the Active Directory, in order to prevent unauthorized servers from servicing clients. Use the Windows 2000 Server DHCP snap-in to authorize a server for RIS and DHCP. You don't need to install the DHCP service on a particular server in order to use the DHCP snap-in to manage RIS.

The RIS boot sequence is entirely insecure, and open to address spoofing or examination by wire sniffing. You should use other network security mechanisms to ensure the security of installations.

To help you manage which servers will service which clients, RIS has two mechanisms, prestaging and server referral.

In the Active Directory you can specify which RIS server a client computer uses. This is *prestaging*, and can be applied to groups. If groups are physically close, this can be a good scheme. But this server is not necessarily the one that first responds when the client requests RIS service. Whenever any RIS server replies to a client request for service, it checks that client against the Active Directory to see if the client is registered, as explained above, to accept service from a specific RIS server. It does so by means of a GUID that is provided as part of the request. You can usually obtain the GUID by reading the system's BIOS settings. The system vendor may also ship a floppy disk with the system that contains a mapping of the system's serial number to the GUID. If you have the ability to sniff network packets, the GUID can be found inside the DHCP Discover packet.

If the client is registered in the Active Directory as being serviced by a different RIS server, the responding server forwards the request on to that server. This is known as *server referral.* Each RIS server has two settings: "Respond to client computers requesting service" and "Do not respond to unknown client computers." By appropriate use of these settings and by prestaging all accounts, you can set up some servers to respond to client requests and make appropriate referrals and others to actually provide service. If your DHCP and RIS requests are made across routers, then you must make sure that the routers forward the requests. If the router forwards DHCP requests, it will also forward RIS requests, but you must make sure that the RIS requests are forwarded to the proper RIS server.

It is possible to have other Remote Boot/Installation servers on the same physical network. As you can learn from the Intel site mentioned above, PXE support is available for other operating systems, such as Linux. But you should know that the PXE client has no way of knowing which server it should respond to. You should use a combination of prestaging and physical network segmentation to manage this problem.

Installing RIS

To install RIS during Windows 2000 Server installation, select Remote Installation Services from the Optional Components list. To install it after Windows 2000 Server installation, select Add/Remove Programs from Control Panel, then Add/Remove Windows Components, and click Next to start the wizard. Select Remote Installation Services from the components list, and continue the wizard to install the software. Windows 2000 DNS and DHCP services are also required for RIS, so you may also need to select these from the Optional Components list. You may need to restart your server at this point.

 If you do not already have a Windows 2000 Server domain controller on this network, your RIS server will need to act as one. You can promote it to domain controller status using the DCPROMO application.

You have now added the RIS software to the server, but you must still set it up.

Use Run to start the Remote Installation Services Setup wizard, with the command **risetup.exe**. After the welcome screen, you're asked for a folder name in which your images, other distribution files, and RIS itself are located (see Figure 3-4). This folder needs to be on a different volume than that on which Windows 2000 itself is installed. Microsoft advises that, for performance purposes, it should be on a separate drive, preferably SCSI.

On the next page of the wizard, you can make two basic settings for the RIS server: whether it should respond to client requests, and whether it should respond to requests from unknown clients. Ultimately, the server will be useless unless you enable the first setting, although you may want to forgo enabling the server until you are finished configuring it. You can enable the server later through the MMC (see Figure 3-5). The second setting is advisable if you want to exert careful control over which systems can be serviced by this RIS server.

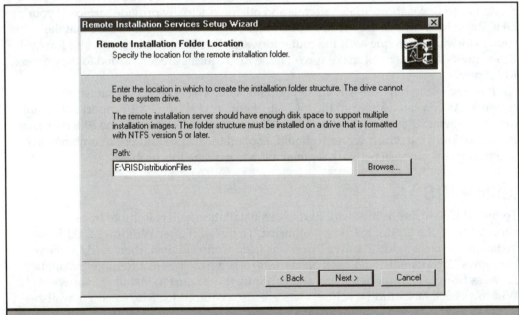

Figure 3-4.   *The distribution folder for Remote Installation Services needs to be on a different volume, and probably different drive, than Windows 2000*

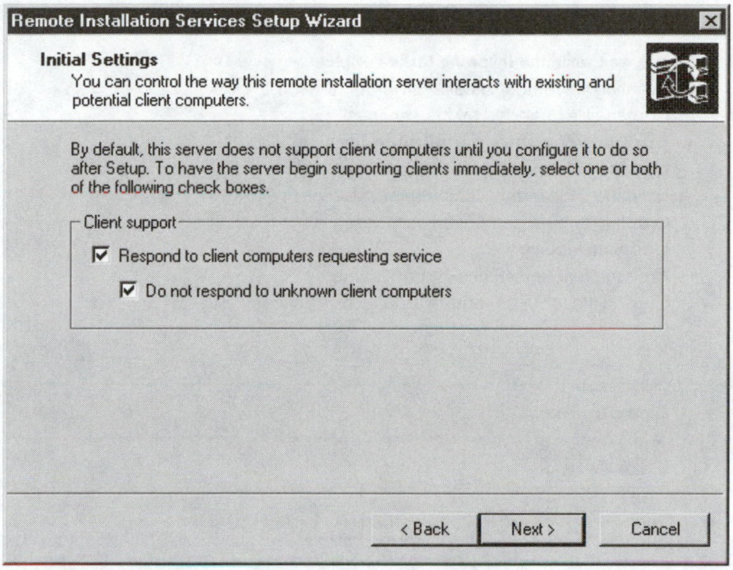

Figure 3-5.   *You can enable the RIS server during its initial configuration or wait until later*

Next, you are asked for the path of your source files. At this stage, what the wizard is asking for is the path to the root of your Windows 2000 Professional CD-ROM, and it will probably guess the same path from which Windows 2000 Server was installed. If you are planning to use image files created with the RIPrep utility with RIS, you will be able to do so at a later stage, but you need to include your Windows 2000 Professional files at this stage. Make sure the CD-ROM or a copy of the appropriate files is in the correct location, and press Next to continue.

Provide a name for the folder, beneath the folder you specified above, that will contain the installation image for RIS to use. Choose whatever name you wish, or take the default, and continue. You also need to create a "Friendly Description" for this Windows 2000 installation image. When clients boot, they will see this name, so something explanatory (such as the default value) is helpful.

The wizard displays your settings for confirmation (see Figure 3-6). You can click Back to fix any errors or click Finish to proceed with the installation. The installation takes several minutes at least, because a large number of files are copied from the CD-ROM to the hard disk.

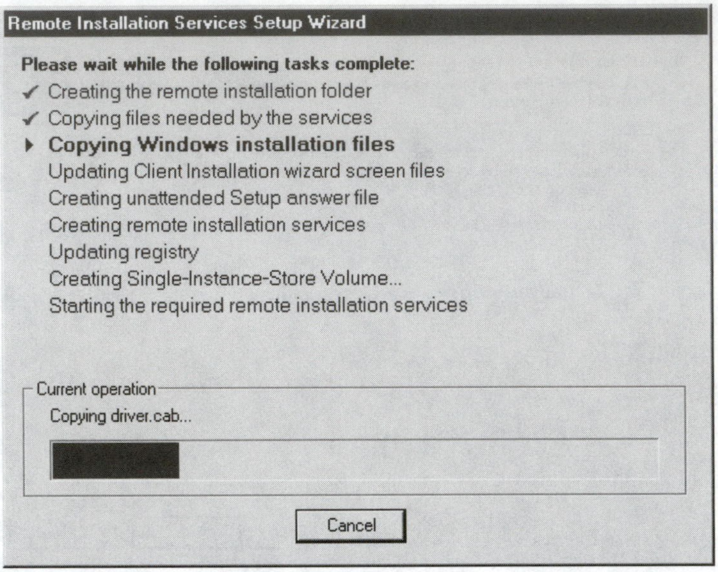

Figure 3-6. *When you finish the RIS Setup Wizard, it performs all the tasks you described*

Managing RIS Clients and Servers

Now, you need to configure the server appropriately for your installation and clients. Some management of the RIS server is done using the DHCP Manager, which you can start by clicking on Start, Programs, Administrative Tools, and then DHCP Manager. You should see a window similar to that in Figure 3-7.

You must authorize the server to run on the domain. This is a security precaution to allow administrators absolute control over who is providing critical services such as remote boot and installation. Right-click on the name of your server in the DHCP Manager window and select "Authorize". It may take several minutes for authorization to complete. Press F5 to refresh the display periodically until the server's status changes from "Not authorized" to "** Active **", and the light on the server icon changes from red to green.

To configure the RIS options you use a different Microsoft Management Console (MMC) snap-in. Click Start, Programs, Administrative Tools, and then Active Directory Users and Computers. Since your RIS server is necessarily a domain controller, it's listed in the right pane when you select Domain Controllers in the left pane. Right-click on the line containing the RIS server, and select Properties. On the Properties dialog that appears, select the Remote Install tab. The dialog box resembles that shown in Figure 3-8.

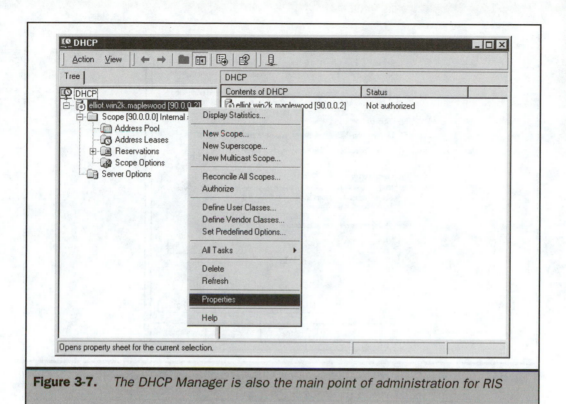

Figure 3-7.   *The DHCP Manager is also the main point of administration for RIS*

Tip   *You can perform most, but not all RIS server management remotely from another
system on the network. You must be logged in as a domain administrator, and have
installed the Administrator Tools MSI package. An example of a function that cannot be
performed remotely is adding an additional OS image to the RIS server.*

In the upper "Client support" section of the Properties page, you see the two
options you had during RIS installation: whether the server responds to client requests
and whether it responds to unknown computers (those that have not been prestaged).
If you wish to change either of these settings in the future, this is the place to do so.

You also have an option here to verify the server, which simply tests to see if the
service is running. Press the Show Clients button to see a special custom Active
Directory search request for Remote Installation Clients. What this query actually finds
are clients that have already been serviced by this server, sorted by the GUID of the
client. Of course, when you're performing the first install, the window is empty.

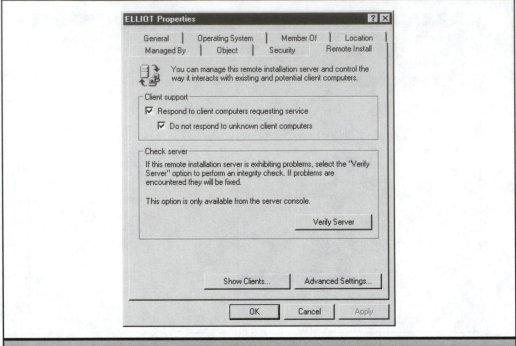

Figure 3-8.   *The Remote Install Properties page is where most RIS server management is performed*

Clicking on Advanced Settings reveals a variety of settings that really should be more plainly accessible (see Figure 3-9). Any nontrivial use of RIS will involve these "Advanced Settings."

Each computer on your network needs a unique computer name. RIS lets you define an algorithm for naming the computers you install, using a particular server. In the New Clients tab of the Advanced Settings dialog box (see Figure 3-10), you can key the computer name off the different variations of the user's real name, username, the unique address in the network adapter, or some custom value.

The fields you can use for formatting names are

User's First Name	%First
User's Last Name	%Last
User's logon name	%Username
MAC address of computer's network card	%MAC
Incremental Number	%#

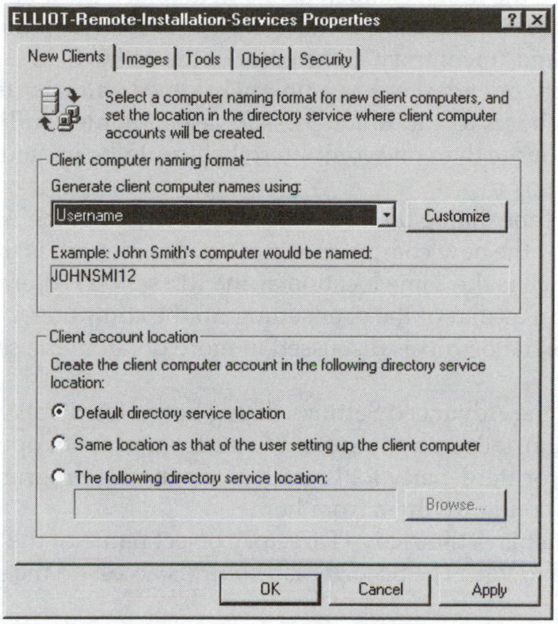

Figure 3-9. *The Advanced Settings dialog box contains many crucial pages for accessing the full power of RIS*

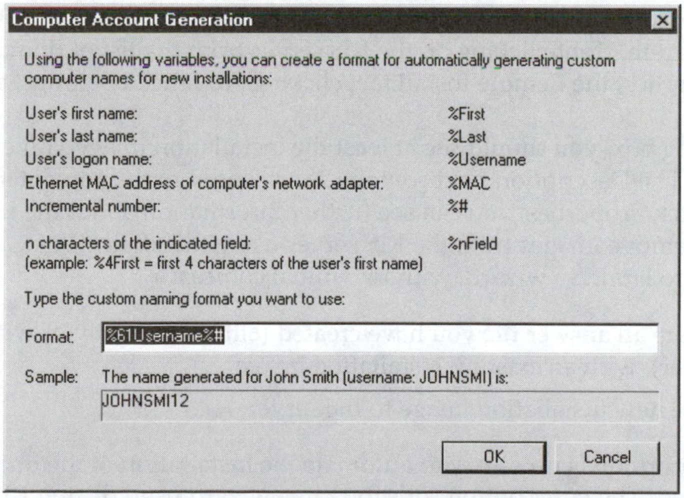

Figure 3-10. *You can create unique computer names for each computer based on some portion of the user's username, first name, last name, or other personal values, and add incrementing numbers to increase the variability*

If you want to use the first *n* characters of a field, place the *n* between the "%" and the name. For instance, *%5Username* is the first five characters in the username field, or "mcontr" for username "mcontrary". The point of the MAC field is to make a random number, as every network adapter has a uniquely keyed value in its ROM. The point of the incremental number is to add uniqueness in case of name conflict. For instance, if "John Smith" set up more than one computer, they could be named JOHNSMITH1, JOHNSMITH2, and so on.

The lower part of the dialog box lets you control where in the Active Directory the computer account for the new computer is created. The default is the default directory service location, which is the same location as the RIS server. Alternately, you can place it in the same location as that of the user setting up the computer, or some arbitrary location. The Images dialog box is discussed in more detail in the section "Creating and Managing Images."

The Tools tab of the Advanced Settings dialog box is for displaying third-party tools that have been installed on the system to perform preboot operations. RIS has interfaces available for third-party tools, such as diagnostic programs, to plug in. You can remove tools or configure them from here.

The Object tab displays the Active Directory object name of the RIS server. This is unlikely to be of use to you. The Security tab controls access to the service.

Creating and Managing Images

You perform most image management using two features: the Images tab of the RIS Advanced Settings dialog box, and the RIPrep utility (discussed in the section "The RIPrep Utility," later in this chapter).

You can get to the Images manager by entering the Active Directory Users and Computers snap-in, right-clicking on the RIS server from the list of domain controllers, selecting properties, the Remote Install tab, clicking Advanced Settings, and then the Images tab.

In the dialog box, you should see at least the installation image you created while installing RIS. The Description field contains the friendly name you entered. If you select it and click Properties, you can see further information about the install image. You can also remove images from the RIS server using this dialog box.

Click Add to launch a wizard, with two initial choices:

- Associate an answer file you have created (either manually or with the Setup Manager), with an existing installation image
- Install a new installation image to the server.

The former option is necessary to automate the installation of the images you have already installed. The latter option runs the same wizard used during RIS installation to install the initial image.

If you click Add to associate an answer file with your installation image, you're asked the location of the answer file. You can select the sample, another RIS server, or some arbitrary location. Select the image with which you will associate the answer file, select the friendly name, review your settings, and you're done. Now you have an additional image entry in your images dialog box (see Figure 3-11).

SIF Files

SIF files are just another type of unattended answer file, and like other types, the preferred method of creating them is the Windows 2000 Setup Manager. See the section "Setup Manager" for detailed information on its operation.

Security Considerations

The user account that performs the unattended OS installation needs to have Logon As A Batch Job rights. To add this, on the RIS server click Start, Programs, Administrative Tools, and then Domain Controller Security Policy. Expand Local Policies and select User Rights Assignment. Double-click on Log On As A Batch Job on the right pane, and if the appropriate user is not listed, click Add and select the user from the resulting dialog box.

Note   *Security settings on groups can sometimes take time to apply fully.*

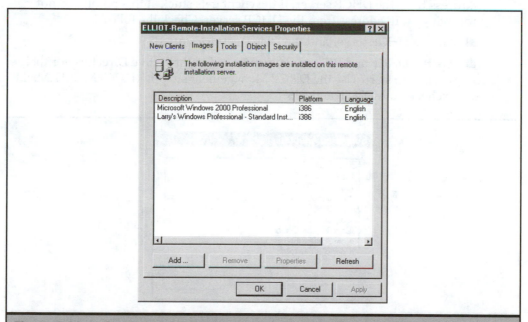

Figure 3-11.   *The Images dialog box lists the operating system images that clients can boot and install from*

Creating a Boot Floppy

If your clients do not have PXE-compatible network adapters, you still may be able to use RIS. Run the rbfg.exe utility, located in the \\RISservername\Reminst\Admin\ i386 folder. This utility creates a boot floppy that will find the RIS server and boot the system using an image. The list of supported network adapters for this floppy is not comprehensive, though. Click the Adapter List button to see if yours is supported (see Figure 3-12).

Insert a blank, formatted floppy disk in the appropriate drive, and click on the Create Disk button to make the boot floppy.

The RIPrep boot floppy contains a utility named RBFG.EXE, which is hard-coded to the list of network adapters supported by Windows 2000 RIS at the time of product shipment. You cannot add new adapter support to the floppy disk. Microsoft will add new adapter support over time, and will make an updated RBFG.EXE available through Windows Update and other normal channels.

The Boot-Time Experience

When the client computer boots, the PXE boot ROM initializes and follows this procedure:

1. The client displays the message "BootP," indicating that it is requesting an IP address from the DHCP server. If the client gets stuck at this point, it is not receiving an IP address from the DHCP server. Check the following:

   ■ Are the DHCP server and the DHCP service started?

   ■ Are the DHCP and RIS servers authorized in the Active Directory for their services to start? Use the DHCP Management snap-in (DHCPMGMT.MSC) to check both DHCP and RIS.

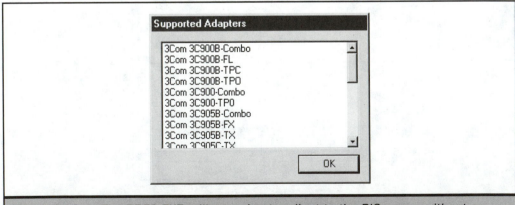

Figure 3-12.   *The RBFG.EXE utility can boot a client to the RIS server without a PXE-compatible adapter, but it has its own restricted list of network adapters*

- Are other DHCP clients on this segment receiving addresses?
- Is the DHCP server properly configured? For example, does it have a proper address scope?
- Is there a router between the client and server, and is it allowing DHCP requests to pass?
- Are there any DHCP error messages in the system log in Event Viewer?

2. When the client receives an IP address from the server, the client message changes to "DHCP." If the client gets stuck with the DHCP message on, then it is not receiving a proper response from the RIS server. Check the following:

- Are the RIS server and the RIS service (BINLSVC) started?
- Is the RIS server authorized in the Active Directory for its service to start? Use the DHCP Management snap-in (DHCPMGMT.MSC) to check.
- Are other remote boot clients of this RIS server moving beyond the DHCP message? If so, reconfirm that this system's boot ROM is supported.
- Are there any DHCP, DNS, or Active Directory error messages in the system log in Event Viewer?

3. The client displays the message "BINL" and prompts the user to press F12. This confirms that the client has contacted the RIS server and is waiting to transfer the first image file, named OSChooser. It's possible that this process will occur so quickly that you will not see the BINL message or the TFTP transfer of the image. If some portion of this process fails, investigate the following:

- There may be a timeout occurring on the transfer of the image because of contention on the network. Retry the boot attempt.
- To see whether there is a problem on the server, stop and restart the RIS service by entering these commands at the command line: Net Stop BINLSVC and Net Start BINLSVC.
- If the client is still failing at the same point, check the RIS object properties in the DHCP manager of the Active Directory. Also check the Event Viewer for any relevant errors in the System Log.

4. The client boots into the Client Installation Wizard. Select the appropriate installation image and continue with installation.

The RIPrep Utility

The RIPrep utility is located on the RIS server in \\RISservername\Reminst\Admin\ i386\Riprep.exe.

You use the RIPrep utility to install the image of a client computer onto the RIS server so that it can be installed on other clients. RIPrep currently only supports a single disk partition (C: Drive). Therefore, all the applications and operating system software that make up the C: Drive must be installed before you run the RIPrep

Wizard. In fact, if you even have a second partition on the system, RIPrep will express regret that the system is not supported and exit.

When the wizard starts, enter the name of the RIS server (there is no browse button, so you must know it). Then enter the name of a folder into which the image of this computer will be installed. Once again, there is no way to browse, so plan ahead to avoid a conflict. Then enter friendly name information to describe this entry in the Active Directory and for the client when they select an image from which to boot.

In some cases, it is possible to use RIPrep to prepare images for installation on different target hardware. The source and target systems must use the same HAL. RIPrep-based images cannot be replicated to storage mechanisms such as DVDs, CDs or ZIP drives, nor does RIS provide a mechanism for replicating images across the network to other RIS servers. It is possible to perform such replication using Microsoft's SMS or some third-party replication mechanisms, as long as these products maintain the file attributes and security settings of the replicated images.

Changing Partition Sizes

By default, RIPrep instructs setup to format the target drive to its full size as NTFS. To override this default, prepare a system to clone with the right size volume, i.e., the size you want the target system to have. The target system must have a drive at least that size.

Connect to the servername\reminst share. Run admin\i386\riprep.exe. This creates a template file on the RIS server named remoteinstall\setup\languages\ image\folder_name\i386\templates\riprep.sif. Find the line in the file: "UseWholeDisk=yes" and change it to "UseWholeDisk=no". This stops the setup program from extending the volume to the end of the disk

The
Complete
Reference

Chapter 4

Migrating Windows NT 4
Environments
to Windows 2000

Planning and designing for your transition from an NT 4 environment to a native Windows 2000 environment is not a process to be taken lightly. You are faced with many choices and challenges even when coming from a homogeneous Windows NT 4 network infrastructure. The specific challenges you'll find will be unique to your organization, but the more you understand your environment and the concepts behind the upgrade paths you develop, the smoother your experience will be.

Why dedicate an entire chapter to migrating from Windows NT 4 when Chapters 2 and 3 examined many issues of preparation, design, and implementation? For starters, this chapter heightens your awareness of the underlying issues for this particular type of migration effort. It is a logical continuation, an elaboration, of the previous chapters. It's important that you not substitute one for the other because this chapter explores in depth many decision factors with which you'll have to come to terms.

A View from Afar

While there may be variations within them, there are really two options available to you for migrating to Windows 2000 from Windows NT 4:

- **Upgrade your current domain infrastructure.** A domain upgrade, also known as an *in-place upgrade*, focuses on the design of your existing domain. For small or some medium-size organizations with very few domains, this may be sufficient. As you will see later, the larger your environment, the more difficult this option may be. After implementing an in-place upgrade, you can set out to restructure your environment with Windows 2000 in mind. Note that the domain restructure can come before or after the in-place upgrade and is sometimes looked upon as a second migration option.

- **Start from scratch and create a Windows 2000 domain structure (tree or forest) alongside your current Windows NT 4 design.** As you can imagine, this requires additional hardware and political support. Don't forget about this option just yet. It may be the best alternative for some.

Before going further in describing the details of these options for migrating, I strongly recommend that you revisit Chapter 2's section on what you need to do to prepare your environment as well as consider taking the preparatory measures discussed in the next section, "Preparing Windows NT 4 Server."

Preparing Windows NT 4 Server

Preparing your Windows NT 4 environment can seem a complicated and never-ending task. The intention or goal behind this is to make the transition as smooth as possible. Moreover, it drastically reduces the amount of time you spend firefighting issues such as users being unable to log on or connect to the domain, users not being able to use resources that they once used, security issues surrounding trust relationships and file resources, and much more.

The majority of the recommendations in this section should be considered in addition to the ones that you performed in Chapter 2, but some also serve as a reminder because of their importance.

Training

Training is crucial. Simply put, without training of some sort (self-based, online, instructor led, and so on), your designing will be a wasted effort and the resulting implementation could be disastrous.

Some of the most important areas requiring training are TCP/IP, Active Directory (AD), and Domain Name (DNS). More information on these subjects can be found in Chapters 13, 15, and 14, respectively. In addition, these important technologies comprise so many different concepts that it would be to your advantage to have several people dedicated to learning each of them. Don't forget, though, that there are other areas that require training such as Windows 2000 administration, security, deployment, and so on. People can only be spread so thin in their responsibilities, so carefully choose who's going to support each aspect of Windows 2000.

Training usually means taking a class or reading material, but some of this training won't necessarily be geared to support staff or the end user. You may find yourself educating department heads and CFO/CEO types in an attempt to get the proper support, resources, and finances for what you need to make the transition a success.

Get DNS in Order

I'm going to assume that all DNS issues are in order and it won't be an inhibiting factor for your transition to Windows 2000. This assumption stems from the DNS recommendations given in Chapter 2.

If you or the person responsible for DNS is not comfortable with DNS in relation to Windows 2000, I'd suggest that you get training immediately before proceeding. I'd also suggest carefully reading Chapter 14 in order to get quickly acclimated to Windows 2000's DNS. Windows 2000's dependence on DNS is enormous, and you need to be prepared. It's important to know not just the technical details behind setting up and configuring DNS servers, but also about namespace design and the part it plays in the high-level infrastructure design.

Also, if you feel you know DNS, either because of your experience with previous Windows NT versions or because you come from a UNIX background, don't be overly confident that you'll know everything there is to know about Windows 2000's DNS. There are many changes and relatively new standards that it supports, such as Dynamic DNS (DDNS), that may challenge your knowledge and may require additional training in order to successfully plan, design, and support the Windows 2000 infrastructure.

Define a Backup Strategy

Safeguarding data is another one of those issues whose importance can't be overemphasized. The ramifications of an upgrade failing or mistakenly deleting important data are enough to make anyone cringe.

To spare yourself administrative nightmares, you must adequately prepare yourself for the worst. Don't fall victim to the "it only happens to other people" scenario. Devise a plan that incorporates anything that is valuable to you including domain servers, member servers, and even client machines.

Your backup strategy should include the following:

■ **Perform a full backup with verification on all servers.** Verification doesn't just mean that your backup program performs verification. It also means that you should test restoring the tape to another server or to unused disk space to make sure that data can be retrieved from tape.

■ **Back up the Registry.** (Most backup utilities support this option.)

■ **Take a BDC offline before you begin the migration.** First, force a full synchronization of the domain to ensure that you have the latest updates to the SAM. Once it's offline, promote it to a PDC and then prevent anyone from making changes to the domain's SAM. This ensures that your offline copy is up-to-date with the domain. If you can't prevent people from making changes to the SAM (i.e., adding/deleting users, adding groups, etc.), then make sure you document those changes.

NetBIOS-Related Issues

Let's face reality. NetBIOS has been around for quite some time, and it may stay around longer than you might like. All Windows-based machines rely on it for name resolution, and many Windows applications rely on it as well.

NetBIOS is a broadcast-based, application programming interface (API). This means that every time one computer wants to communicate with another, it broadcasts a query on the network. The more computers on the network, the more congested with broadcasts the network becomes. However, the real limitation (or savior, depending on how you look at it) is that NetBIOS is non-routable so it doesn't always affect or reach the entire network.

One of several ways to overcome the limitations inherent to NetBIOS is using the Windows Internet Naming Service (WINS). WINS helps prevent unnecessary NetBIOS broadcasts by dynamically storing computer names and corresponding IP addresses to provide name resolution.

What does this have to do with Windows 2000 migration? If you haven't started using WINS, do so immediately. Also, if you have been using WINS, you'll want to perform routine maintenance before you upgrade to the new OS. You'll have to keep WINS around until no NetBIOS-based applications exist on your network and you have upgraded all down-level client machines to Windows 2000 Professional. As I said earlier, NetBIOS may be around longer than you'd like.

 Switching to native mode doesn't mean that NetBIOS magically vanishes. You will need it as long as you have down-level clients and applications that rely on NetBIOS.

WINS

Microsoft has published numerous articles on WINS maintenance issues; they can be found on the TechNet Web site (http://www.microsoft.com/technet/). The maintenance issues that you should be concerned with before migrating to Windows 2000 are compaction and defragmentation.

Compaction and defragmentation clean up the WINS database by removing old or stray entries. The utility that accomplishes this is JETPACK.EXE; it has the following syntax:

JETPACK.EXE <database name> <temp database name>

To compact and defragment a WINS database, you can create a batch file or type the following at the Command prompt:

```
CD %SYSTEMROOT%\SYSTEM32\WINS
NET STOP WINS
JETPACK WINS.MDB TEMP.MDB
NET START WINS
```

Other recommendations for WINS are as follows:

- Configure WINS node type to use H-node for name resolution. This tells WINS clients the order in which to resolve names: WINS, broadcast, DNS, and then LMHOSTS.

- Place WINS on a member server if you have a large number of users to segment responsibilities of authentication and WINS name registration.

DHCP Issues

Fortunately, Dynamic Host Configuration Protocol (DHCP) is not going away with Windows 2000. When you upgrade a server running DHCP, the new version automatically replaces the old (this is true for many other services as well). The new version is tightly integrated with DNS. In fact, the relationship between DHCP and DNS is so close that the two services will be passing a lot of information regarding client machines (names, IP addresses, registrations, etc.) to each other. For this reason, I highly recommend that you place the two services on the same machine and avoid placing them on DCs. Of course, there are exceptions to every rule, such as number of users in your environment and the power of the computer, but the recommendation generally makes sense.

Choosing a Migration Route to Windows 2000

There are several deciding factors that will logically guide you to the migration option that is best for you and your network environment. They include, but aren't limited to, the following:

- Number of domains in your current infrastructure
- Type of NT 4 domain model implemented
- Number of users
- Number of trust relationships
- Political hurdles
- Finances/budget
- Time

With these factors in mind, the decision you make should take the path of least resistance and should accomplish the following:

- Minimize the impact on users
- Reduce administration
- Improve manageability of the domain structure

In-Place Upgrade

In-place upgrades use your existing domain architecture to structure the AD model. Each current domain is incrementally upgraded to Windows 2000 until all domains in your new AD environment match the structure you previously had. Upgrading one domain at a time allows you to gradually work into AD. Any Windows NT 4 domains not yet converted will still remain connected to the upgraded domain through already established trust relationships, and users will continue to connect to any domains (upgraded or not) as if they are still NT 4 domains.

Say you have a single-master NT 4 domain structure with an account domain and two resource domains. The account domain is the first domain that will switch to AD, so you'll upgrade the PDC and any BDCs. The upgraded PDC in this case is also referred to as the *operations master* because it serves both as an AD DC and a PDC for down-level clients.

 Remember to follow the recommendations outlined in the previous sections before you attempt to upgrade any domain.

Next, test the functionality of the new domain and its interactions with any other domains (in this case the two resource domains). Once you're convinced that everything is running smoothly and as expected, proceed to upgrade the other two resource domains and test after every domain upgrade. Now, although Windows 2000 domains automatically establish two-way transitive trusts, when you perform an in-place upgrade, the existing trusts will be used instead. So, in this example, the resource domains still use a one-way trust relationship to the account domain. Figure 4-1 shows the logical progression for this in-place upgrade example.

At this stage in the process, you can either leave the domain structure as is or migrate the resource domains into the account/root domain. In Chapter 2, I recommended that you consolidate domains before you begin upgrading domains. The difference here is that you are choosing to consolidate after instead of before the process. The choice is up to you. It is advisable, however, that you consolidate your domains because the AD gives you greater flexibility for administration and management with OUs, group policies, and much more.

The following sections cover some important areas that you need to consider before deciding whether or not to use this option.

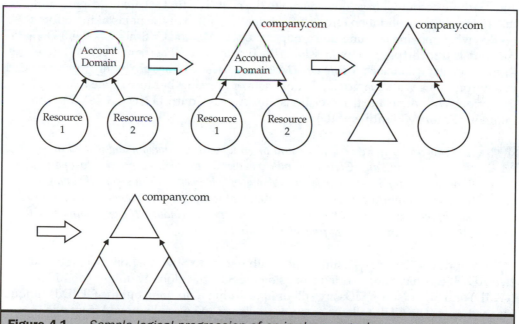

Figure 4-1.   *Sample logical progression of an in-place upgrade*

Timing Considerations

Probably one of the most important considerations for evaluating your migration strategy is timing with regard to completing the migration cycle. Timing when NT 4 domains, users, and so on are going to be migrated will affect not only you and your available resources but, more importantly, the end user. Some crucial questions to ask yourself are

- How large (or small) is your Windows NT network environment?
- How many domains need to be converted?
- How long do you estimate it would take you to migrate each domain?
- What spoken and nonspoken expectations exist? In other words, does the boss think you'll be able to do a quick conversion over the weekend or that it should take longer (months, a year, etc.)?
- Which strategy causes the least amount of disruption to the end user?
- Will some users be affected more than others?

Moving and Collapsing Domains

There are several utilities that can help you move objects (user accounts, groups, and machine accounts) from one domain to the next. The first set are third-party utilities that help with consolidation efforts by automating much of the painstaking effort needed when moving accounts and groups. They are Mission Critical's OnePoint Domain Administrator (http://www.missioncritical.com/) and FastLane Technologies' (http://www.fastlanetech.com/) DM/Manager. These utilities are highly recommended in environments with a large number of users or domains because of the many NT 4 limitations with regard to trust relationships, Access Control Lists (ACLs), and the infamous Security Identifier (SID).

 A SID is unique for each user account or group within a domain and is used in conjunction with an ACL to determine whether or not access is granted to a particular resource. In simple terms, when user A requests to open a file, his/her SID and group SIDs are contained within an access token that is compared to the file's ACL. If they match, the user can open the file. The limitation in a Windows NT environment is that SIDs can't be easily moved from one domain to another.

In Windows 2000, NT 4's limitations with regard to SIDs are nonexistent because two AD objects have been added alongside the SID: the globally unique identifier (GUID) and SID history. SIDs are still unique within a domain, but the GUID is unique for the forest. The GUID allows accounts or objects to be easily moved from one domain to the next. On the other hand, a SID history contains information on where the account has been. So, if you move user A to another domain, the SID history keeps track of the domains he/she belonged to. The GUID, SID, and SID history are all contained within the access token. For detailed information about security related issues, such as the ones mentioned here, see Chapter 21.

Other utilities that are useful when moving accounts between domains while in mixed mode are found within the Windows 2000 Resource Kit. These utilities are to be used only after the upgrade. They include:

- **MoveCleanup**   Cleans up accounts after moving from a domain
- **MoveSetup**   Moves groups
- **MoveTree**   MoveTree moves a large number of users at one time
- **NetDom5**   Moves computers accounts to a domain or a particular OU

After consolidating your domains, you can begin collapsing those domains that are no longer serving a purpose in your AD infrastructure by moving the DCs to another domain or removing them completely.

Trusting Relationships

If you're at all familiar with Windows NT 4 domain models (you should be familiar with at least your own environment by now), you may have already realized that NT 4 trust relationships can get confusing and cause trouble. For the in-place upgrade example above, the trust relationships aren't difficult to understand, but you can see as the domains increase, the number of trust relationships skyrocket. Refer to the following section, "Calculating the Number of Trusts," to get an accurate representation of the number of trusts your environment has. As a result, you need to either consolidate your domains to minimize the number of trusts and the traffic generated from them or consider the start from scratch method.

CALCULATING THE NUMBER OF TRUSTS   You can perform two different calculations to determine the number of trust relationships needed for a particular domain model. You can determine the number of trusts between master/account domains, and between master/account and resource domains. It is important to perform these calculations so you know exactly how many trust relationships you're dealing with. Trusts affect network performance, especially when WAN links are brought into the equation.

To calculate the number of trusts between master domains (T_m), use the formula

$$T_m = N_m(N_m - 1)$$

where N_m is the number of master domains.

To calculate the number of trusts between master and resource domains (T_r), use the formula

$$T_r = N_m N_r$$

where N_m is the number of master domains and N_r is the number of resource domains.

Table 4-1 shows the results of these formulas applied to different domain model scenarios.

Model	Number of Master Domains	Number of Resource Domains	Total Number of Trusts
Single	1	0	0
Single master	1	2	2
Multiple master	2	2	6
	2	3	8
	7	20	182
Complete trust	8	0	56

Table 4-1. *Calculating the Number of Trust Relationships*

The total number of trusts involved in a multiple-master domain implementation is computed by adding the total number of trusts between the master domains to the total number of trusts between master and resource domains.

$$T = T_m + T_r, \text{ or } T = N_m(N_m - 1) + N_m N_r$$

As Table 4-1 shows, with the multiple-master model, the number of trusts escalates with each domain addition. The more domains in your Windows NT environment, the more impact trust relationships have on performance and your migration efforts, especially on the network subsystem.

REPLICATION Trusts also play a key role in how domain replication will affect your environment. The more domains you have, the more information that will be passed among them, not to mention the more replication problems you may encounter. You'll have to consider providing higher bandwidth between domains (if needed) and beefing up domain controllers as well as Global Catalog servers.

Starting from Scratch

Starting from scratch means that you are creating your designed AD infrastructure from the ground up and alongside your current NT domain model. As soon as the design is implemented, you can migrate accounts.

Start by creating as much of the AD domain structure as possible. This includes creating the root domain, child domains, OUs, or other objects that you are planning to use in the new environment. I strongly suggest that you minimize the number of domains and even consider using a single-domain model. Then establish one-way trusts from each NT 4 domain to the appropriate AD structure as shown in Figure 4-2. The next step involves migrating accounts from the old domain structure to AD as

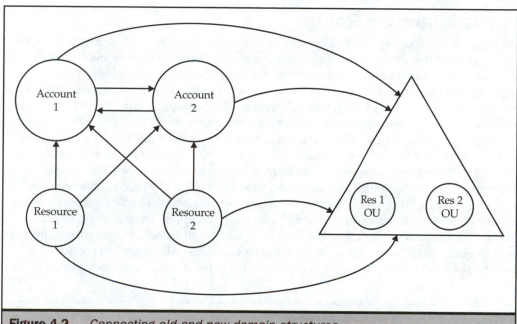

Figure 4-2.   *Connecting old and new domain structures*

explained earlier. Using the third-party utilities mentioned earlier in this case will save you a lot of time and trouble.

At first glance you may think that you'll have to deal with more trust relationships than if you performed an in-place upgrade. This is true only in the interim, because once you have migrated the accounts, you should have far fewer trusts than you started with because you aren't dependent on your old infrastructure. In fact, you'll be dealing with trusts only as long as it takes to migrate accounts from the old domain model. There also aren't as many intermediate steps involved as in the in-place upgrade.

The Catch

There are several challenges that you must address before implementing the start from scratch method:

- The initial costs can be enormous, especially for larger enterprises. Typically, the extra costs come from the extra hardware needed to support the AD shell.

- Moving accounts can be tedious and cumbersome without the use of third-party utilities. However, you'll deal with this issue in either option you choose.

- In most cases, the migration time is greatly shortened. The disadvantage to this is that you can't proceed at a leisurely pace and testing functionality has to be done more quickly.

The Best Migration Route

So, what domain models best fit either upgrade option? I'll be the first to admit that I don't have all the answers (I can't even come close). The migration option that you choose is dependent on you, your current NT 4 domain model, the size of your organization, and so on. What I hope you get out of this is that it opens your mind to the varied possibilities and helps you determine the advantages and disadvantages of going one way or the other for your particular environment.

In general, you can use Microsoft's recommended approach (the in-place option) for any NT 4 domain environment. Figures 4-3 and 4-4, respectively, show examples of multiple-master and complete-trust domains being migrated using the in-place option. However, I recommend using the in-place option for single and single-master domain models because of their relatively simple design and their ability to easily snap into AD.

Larger enterprises that have multiple-master or complete-trust domain models should seriously consider using the start from scratch approach. This approach permits you to more easily mold your current infrastructure into AD as well as reduces the number of trust relationships (with transitive trusts) and replication problems.

Client Considerations

Microsoft has gone to great lengths to ensure that down-level clients can still operate in a Windows 2000 AD environment. In fact, you don't have to upgrade them to Windows 2000 Professional in order to participate in the domain or take advantage of many Windows 2000 features.

There are several considerations that you should examine before selecting which operating system the client machines should use.

- In order to use AD services, Windows 9*x* and Windows NT computers need to use AD client software (see the "Using the AD Client Software" section).

- Windows 2000 member servers and workstations (Professional) can automatically use AD.

- Windows 2000 Group Policies aren't supported by DOS, Windows 3.1, Windows 9*x*, or Windows NT computers. They must resort to the System Policy Editor (POLEDIT.EXE).

- All down-level clients rely on NetBIOS for name resolution, while Windows 2000 computers don't. Therefore, you'll still want to keep WINS in the environment.

- Down-level clients rely on NetBIOS, and as a result they use broadcasts more frequently than a Windows 2000 computer would. Broadcasts chew up valuable network bandwidth.

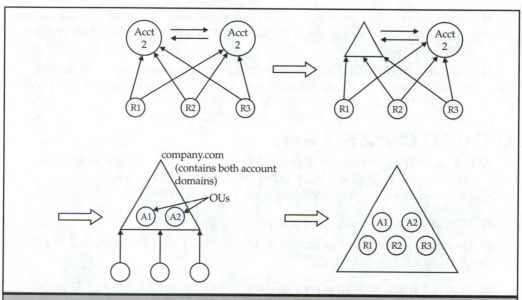

Figure 4-3.   *Multiple-master domain model migration using the in-place option*

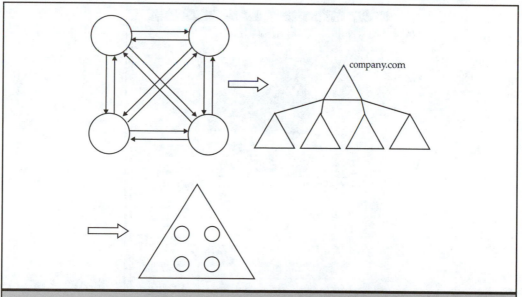

Figure 4-4.   *Complete trust switching to an AD model using the in-place option*

■ Intellimirror, which provides user data management, software installation and maintenance, and user settings management, is only supported with Windows 2000 computers.

■ Windows 2000 Professional requires more hardware resources, so you will probably need to upgrade. I would recommend a Pentium Pro or higher with at least 128MB of RAM for starters.

Using the AD Client Software

The AD client software is network client software for Windows 9x and Windows NT down-level computers. It allows them to log onto and use AD networks.

By definition, the following operating systems are AD aware:

■ Windows 2000 Server (member server) or Professional

■ Computers running Windows 9x or Windows NT that have installed the AD client software add-on

The Active Directory client is provided on the Windows 2000 Server CD-ROM. To install the AD client software on a Windows 9x computer, do the following:

1. Install Internet Explorer 5.0 or higher.

2. Enable the Active Desktop as shown in the following illustration.

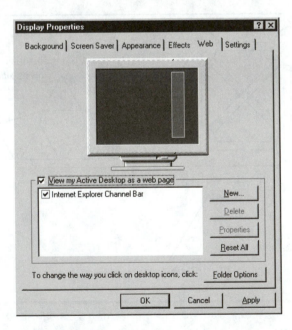

3. Double-click on the DSCLIENT.EXE file to initiate the Directory Service Client Setup Wizard.

4. Click Next twice and the wizard will begin installation.

5. Once the Directory Service Client Setup Wizard finishes, click the Finish button as shown in the following illustration to restart the computer.

6. Windows 9*x* then asks you if you want to restart your machine. Click Yes.

Upgrading Clients to Windows 2000 Professional

The intrinsic values that Windows 2000 Professional brings to a Windows 2000 environment are enormous. It combines the best features from Windows 98 and Windows NT to provide a secure, easily manageable, and more robust operating system. Some of the most notable features that it brings to your Windows 2000 environment include

- AD support
- Support for a larger range of hardware features (Plug and Play, power management, etc.)
- Internet Explorer 5 and DirectX7 included
- Greater manageability (Intellimirror support, Group Policy aware, etc.)
- More robustness (requires fewer reboots, greater protection against rogue applications, etc.)
- NetBIOS independent
- Greater file system support (EFS, NTFS 5, DFS, FAT32, etc.). For more information on file systems, refer to Chapter 20.

For these reasons, and many more, I strongly recommend that you consider upgrading your down-level clients to Windows 2000 Professional.

The basic installation process for Windows 2000 Professional is the same as for installing any other Windows 2000 operating system. For this reason I won't rehash information that I've already given. Instructions on installing Windows 2000 are located in Chapter 2, and you can also refer to Chapter 3 for information on unattended installations of Windows 2000 Professional.

Switching to Native Mode

You've chosen an upgrade option and implemented it. Then you worked out client issues such as adding the AD client software to Windows 9x and Windows NT computers and upgrading to Windows 2000 Professional. Now, you have to decide if and when you should switch to native mode.

Mixed Mode/Native Mode Differences

Your domain is running in a mixed mode under the following conditions:

- The PDC is upgraded, but you haven't upgraded all of the BDCs

- The PDC and all BDCs are upgraded, but the native mode switch has not been turned on

Note   *Even when you make the switch to native mode, your domain may still contain down-level client machines, but they will act as if they are functioning in a Windows NT 4 domain environment.*

Switching your domain to native mode causes the following effects:

- The operations master no longer performs NT LAN Manager (NTLM) replication (no more BDCs exist). Instead, the domain uses the AD replication protocol.

- You can no longer add BDCs to the domain without promoting them to AD.

- Down-level clients that aren't AD-aware use passthrough authentication because they can't use Kerberos-based authentication.

- Group management is greatly improved. You can now use universal groups, nested groups, and full, cross-domain administration.

Switching to native mode should be done as quickly as possible so that you can get the increased manageability, functionality, security, and much more.

Before making the switch to native mode, test your domain's functionality to ensure that everything is operating smoothly. The switch is irreversible so it is important that you are assured that everything is working properly. As soon as you are confident of this, make the switch.

Turning on Native Mode

Now, the moment that you've been waiting for: switching to native mode. The actual process of changing the domain mode is easy, but as you are well aware, the preparation to get to this phase has been at the least challenging.

Double-check to make sure that you have upgraded all BDCs and have performed all the necessary testing because the switch is irreversible. If you decide you want to back out after the mode change, you'll have to destroy everything that you worked on so diligently.

To change to native mode, do the following:

1. On a DC, run Active Directory Users and Computers, as shown in the following illustration, located in Start | Programs | Administrative Tools group.

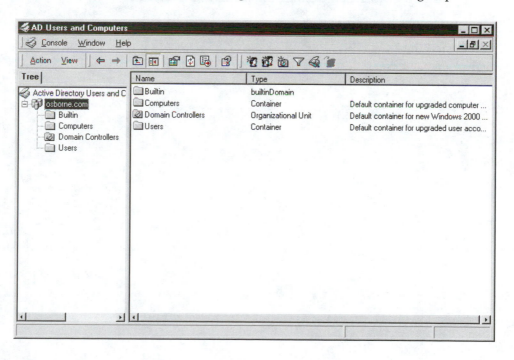

2. Right-click the domain object, and then click Properties to display the domain object properties like the one shown in the following illustration.

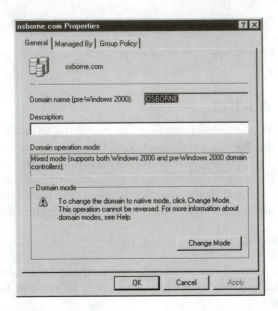

3. Click the Change Mode button.

4. Restart the DC.

The
Complete
Reference

Part II

Learning the Basics

The
Complete
Reference

Chapter 5

Booting

There are really two boot processes for your computer. The computer itself boots, and then the operating system boots. If you've configured your computer for dual booting, you can choose the operating system you want to load.

In the event of a problem, or a total failure, you can overcome operating system boot emergencies if you've planned ahead (or even if you haven't, but it's harder). This chapter covers the operating system boot process, along with information you can use to prepare for and troubleshoot problems.

The Boot Process

During installation, the Windows 2000 Setup program placed data on the first sector of your computer's primary partition (the boot sector). The data is the Master Boot Record (MBR), and it holds executable instructions on an *x86* computer. In addition to the executable instructions, the MBR has a table with up to four entries, defining the locations of the primary partitions on the disk. The installation program also copied the two files that initiate the Windows 2000 boot sequence (Ntldr and Ntdetect.com) to the root directory of the boot drive, and Boot.ini, the file that contains startup options, is placed on the root directory of the boot drive. (See the section "About Boot.ini" later in this chapter.)

> **Note**   *If the boot sector that's targeted by Windows 2000 was previously formatted for DOS (Windows 9x qualifies as DOS), Windows 2000 Setup copies the existing contents of the boot sector to a file named bootsect.dos, placing it in the root directory of the boot drive.*

MBR Code Executes

As the last step of the BIOS boot process, your computer reads the MBR into memory and then transfers control to that MBR code. The executable code searches the primary partition table for a flag on a partition that indicates that the partition is bootable. When the MBR finds the first bootable partition, it reads the first sector of the partition, which is the boot sector.

The Windows 2000 startup files are on the system partition, and the operating system files are on the boot partition, with the following details:

- The system partition holds hardware-specific files that are needed to boot Windows 2000, including the MBR. On *x86* machines this must be a primary partition that's marked active. It's always drive 0, because that's the drive the BIOS accesses to turn the boot process over to the MBR.

- The boot partition holds the operating system files, the %SystemRoot% directory. The support files (\%SystemRoot%\System) must also be on the boot partition.

> **Tip**   *It's not necessary to make the system partition and the boot partition the same partition, although that's the common approach.*

Windows 2000 Startup Files Execute

The boot-sector code reads Ntldr into memory to start the operating system boot process. Ntldr contains read-only NTFS and FAT code. It starts running in real mode, and its first job is to switch the system to a form of protected mode. This first instance of protected mode cannot perform physical-to-virtual translations for hardware protection—that feature becomes available when the operating system has finished booting. All the physical memory is available, and the computer is operating as a 32-bit machine. Then Ntldr enables paging and creates the page tables. Next, it reads Boot.ini from the root directory and displays the boot selection menu on the monitor.

If Ntldr is either missing or corrupt, you'll see this error message:

Ntldr is missing.

Press CTRL-ALT-DEL to restart.

Don't bother using the suggested sequence; it just restarts the cycle that results in the same error message. You must replace Ntldr.

Boot into Windows 2000 with your bootable floppy (see "Create a Bootable Floppy Disk" later in this chapter).

■ If Ntldr is missing, copy it from the floppy disk to the root directory of the boot drive (usually C:).

■ If Ntldr exists on the hard drive, it's probably corrupted. To replace it, you must first change the read-only attribute.

If you don't have a bootable floppy, you'll have to start with the Windows 2000 Setup Boot Disk Floppy disk and work your way through all four floppy disks to get to a repair feature (see the section "Repairing the Operating System" later in this chapter).

Boot Selection Menu Displays

The boot selection menu appears, displaying the operating system choices available on the computer. There may not be more than one choice (Windows 2000), depending on whether or not an operating system existed before Windows 2000 was installed on the computer.

 Unlike Windows NT, there is no menu choice to boot Windows 2000 into VGA mode in case of a problem. Instead, there is a way to display a variety of startup options when you're troubleshooting the boot process. Those options are discussed in the section "The Advanced Options Menu," later in this chapter.

■ If the user selects Windows 2000, the operating system boot continues.

■ If the user selects DOS (which usually means Windows 9x), Ntldr reads the contents of Bootsect.dos into memory and then forces a warm reboot followed by execution of the code in Bootsect.dos. This causes the computer to boot as if the code in Bootsect.dos were being executed from a DOS MBR.

■ If the user presses F8, more boot options display (discussed later in this chapter).

If the user doesn't make a selection before the specified time for choosing an operating system elapses, the default operating system (which is usually Windows 2000) starts.

 Using an arrow key to move through the selections stops the countdown clock, giving users plenty of time to make a decision.

Ntdetect Launches

When the user selects Windows 2000 from the onscreen menu (or the timeout duration forces the selection), Ntldr launches Ntdetect.com. Ntdetect queries the system's BIOS for device and configuration information. The information Ntdetect gathers is sent to the registry and placed in the subkeys under HKEY_LOCAL_MACHINE\Hardware\ Description.

If there's a problem with Ntdetect (e.g., it's missing or corrupt), you may not see an error message. Instead, the boot process may just stop. The cure for a missing or corrupt Ntdetect.com is to replace it. Use a bootable floppy disk to boot your computer, and copy Ntdetect from that floppy disk to the root directory of your hard drive. See the section "Create a Bootable Floppy Disk," later in this chapter.

Ntoskrnl Runs and HAL Is Loaded

After Ntdetect finishes its hardware-checking routines, it turns the operating system boot process back to Ntldr, which launches Ntoskrnl.exe and loads Hal.dll (both files are in the \%SystemRoot%\system32 directory).

Ntoskrnl.exe contains the kernel and executive subsystems. This is the core file for the kernel-mode component of Windows NT. It contains the Executive, the Kernel, the Cache Manager, the Memory Manager, the Scheduler, the Security Reference Monitor, and more. This is the file that really gets Windows 2000 running.

In order for hardware to interact with the operating system, Ntoskrnl.exe needs the Hal.dll, which has the code that permits that interaction (the filename stands for Hardware Abstraction Layer).

Sometimes you may see an error that indicates a problem with Ntoskrnl.exe, but the error is frequently spurious, and is caused by the fact that the directory referenced in Boot.ini doesn't match the name of the directory into which the Windows 2000 system files were installed. This generally means that someone renamed the %SystemRoot% directory, or created a new directory and moved the Windows 2000 files into it. Move the files back to the location specified in Boot.ini. (On the other hand, it could mean that someone edited Boot.ini, in which case you need to correct that error.)

How Ntldr Chooses Drivers

When you install Windows 2000, the drivers that match your equipment aren't the only drivers copied to your computer. Every driver known to any Microsoft programmer has an entry in the registry. Open the registry to HKEY_LOCAL_MACHINE\System\CurrentControlSet\Services to see a very long list of services for device drivers.

Select any subkey and look at the REG_DWORD data item named Start. The data is a hex entry and it ends with a number in parentheses. That number is the pecking order for Ntdlr, and the most important drivers have (0) in the data value. Drivers with a data value of (1) are the next most important, and so on up to the data value (4). I've found that drivers with a (3) or (4) are for devices that aren't installed in my computer

Drivers Load

Ntldr now loads the low-level system device drivers, but the services are not initialized—that occurs later. This is the end of the boot sequence, and the process that starts at this point is called the load sequence.

Operating System Loads

Ntoskrnl.exe begins to load the operating system. The Windows 2000 kernel is initialized and subsystems are loaded and initialized, providing the basic systems that are needed to complete the task of loading the operating system. The boot drivers that were loaded earlier by Ntldr are now initialized, followed by initialization of the rest of the drivers and services.

When the first-level drivers are initialized, you may encounter a problem, usually in the form of a STOP on a Blue Screen of Death. This almost always occurs during the first boot after you've updated a driver. Ntoskrnl initializes the driver, and the operating system balks. Use the Advanced Menu options to load the Last Known Good Configuration (see the section "The Advanced Options Menu" later in this chapter). Then either obtain a better driver from the manufacturer or stick with the previous driver.

Sans a driver error, the Windows 2000 kernel and executive systems are now operational. The Session Manager Subsystem (Smss.exe) sets up the user environment. Information in the registry is checked, and the remaining drivers and software that require loading are loaded. The kernel loads Kernel32.dll, Gdi32.dll, and User32.dll, which provide the Win32 API services that client programs require.

The Win32 subsystem then performs the following tasks:

- Launches Winlogon.exe, which sends the logon dialog box to the screen.
- Loads the Local Security Authority (Lsass.exe).

■ Launches Services.exe, which in turn loads the installed version of Windows 2000 (Professional, or one of the Server versions).

The logon process now begins, so go to work!

About Boot.ini

The contents of the onscreen menu are determined by Boot.ini. However, the role of Boot.ini extends beyond presenting a menu of choices for users. This file is an important element in the machinery that controls the operating system boot process.

Boot.ini Contents

Boot.ini is a text file that holds the information needed to complete the boot process. You can edit the file in any text editor (the file is read-only and hidden, so you must change the attributes before you can save your edits—don't forget to change the attributes back when you've finished editing).

Like any .ini file, each section of the file is headed by a section title enclosed in brackets. The information in the file is created during installation of the operating system, so it's specific to the computer. The file has two sections:

■ [boot loader]
■ [operating systems]

The [boot loader] section contains the timeout specification along with the path to the default operating system. The timeout specification is the amount of time, in seconds, during which the user can make a selection from the onscreen menu. By default, the timeout duration is 30 seconds, and the user sees a countdown to 0 on the screen. The default operating system loads if the user fails to make a choice within that time.

You can change the default operating system and the length of the countdown without editing Boot.ini:

1. Open the System applet in Control Panel (the quick method is to right-click My Computer and choose Properties).

2. Move to the Advanced tab.

3. Click Startup and Recovery to access the fields for changing the default OS or the time specification for the display of the onscreen menu (see Figure 5-1).

If there is only one operating system choice in Boot.ini, Windows 2000 doesn't wait the full time to load it, even if the timeout duration is specified for 30 seconds, 60 seconds, or more. Instead, after about 3 seconds, the operating system begins loading.

The [operating systems] section contains the path(s) to the operating system(s) installed on the computer. In *x*86-based computers, each path is entered on its own

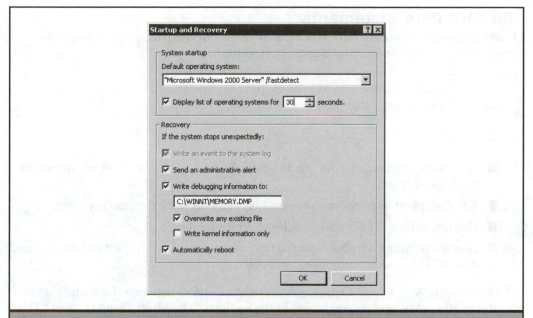

Figure 5-1. *If there are no real choices, there's no point in making the user wait 30 seconds*

line. The format of the information is based on the conventions in the Advanced RISC Computing (ARC) specifications.

Text strings enclosed by quotation marks are the strings that display in the onscreen menu. For example, here's the Boot.ini file that was automatically placed on the root of the boot drive during installation of Windows 2000 Server on a new drive.

```
[boot loader]
timeout=3
default=scsi(0)disk(0)rdisk(0)partition(1)\WINNT
[operating systems]
scsi(0)disk(0)rdisk(0)partition(1)\WINNT="Microsoft Windows 2000 Server" /fastdetect
A Windows 2000 Professional installation that previously held Windows 95,
and is dual-booting, has this Boot.ini file:
[boot loader]
timeout=30
default=multi(0)disk(0)rdisk(0)partition(1)\WINNT
[operating systems]
multi(0)disk(0)rdisk(0)partition(1)\WINNT="Microsoft Windows 2000 Professional"
C:\="Microsoft Windows"
```

*x*86 ARC Path Statements

On *x*86 computers there are two structures available for the ARC path: a line that begins with multi() or a line that begins with scsi():

```
multi(A)disk(B)rdisk(C)partition(D)\<%SystemRoot%>
scsi(A)disk(B)rdisk(C)partition(D)\<%SystemRoot%>
```

where:

- **A** is the ordinal number for the adapter (the first adapter is 0, which should be the boot adapter).

- **B** is disk parameter information, and is used only with the scsi() syntax.

- **C** is the ordinal for the disk attached to the adapter.

- **D** is the partition number, and the first number is 1 (as opposed to adapters and drives, which begin numbering with 0).

The way the A, B, C, and D parameters are used differs between the multi() syntax and the scsi() syntax, and are explained in the sections "The Multi() Syntax" and "The scsi() Syntax" later in this section.

The multi() Syntax

For *x*86 computers, the syntax differs between multi() and scsi(). The multi() syntax tells Windows 2000 to depend on the computer BIOS to load the system files. This means that the operating system uses INT 13 BIOS calls to find and load Ntoskrnl.exe and any other files needed to boot the operating system. In early versions of Windows NT, the multi() syntax was valid only for IDE and ESDI drives, but for Windows NT 3.5 and higher, the syntax can be used for SCSI drives also if the SCSI device is configured to use INT 13 BIOS calls.

You can invoke the multi() syntax to start Windows 2000 on any drive, as long as those drives are identified through the standard INT 13 interface. Because support for INT 13 calls varies among disk controllers, and also because most system BIOS can identify only one disk controller through INT 13, the reality is that it's only possible to use the multi() syntax to launch Windows 2000 from the first two drives attached to the primary disk controller (or the first four drives if you have a dual-channel EIDE controller).

- In an IDE system, the multi() syntax works for up to four drives (the maximum number of drives permitted on the primary and secondary channels of a dual-channel controller).

- In a SCSI-only system, the multi() syntax works for the first two drives on the SCSI controller that loads first during bootup.

- In a mixed system (SCSI and IDE), the multi() syntax works only for the IDE drives attached to the first IDE controller.

Using the explanations for the parameters given earlier in this chapter, the specifics for the ARC path statement using the multi() syntax are

- **A** is the ordinal number for the adapter (the first adapter is 0, which should be the boot adapter).

- **B** is always 0 because the multi() syntax invokes the INT 13 call and does not use the disk() parameter information.

- **C** is the ordinal for the disk attached to the adapter (a number between 0 and 3, depending on the number of drives on the adapter).

- **D** is the partition number, and the first number is 1 (as opposed to adapters and drives, which begin numbering with 0).

The scsi() Syntax

For *x*86-based computers, it's common to use the scsi() syntax if you boot Windows 2000 from a SCSI device. The scsi() syntax tells Windows 2000 to load and use a device driver to access the boot partition. For an *x*86-based computer, that driver is Ntbootdd.sys, placed on the root of the system partition during installation (it's a renamed copy of the device driver for the specific adapter). For a RISC-based computer, the driver is built into the firmware.

Here are the specifics for the parameters in the ARC path when you use the scsi() syntax on an *x*86 computer:

- **A** is the ordinal number for the adapter linked to the Ntbootdd.sys driver.

- **B** is the SCSI ID for the target disk.

- **C** is the SCSI logical unit (LUN). While this could be a separate disk, most SCSI setups have only one LUN per SCSI ID.

- **D** is the partition.

If you have multiple SCSI controllers, each of which uses a different device driver, the value of A is the controller linked to Ntbootdd.sys. During installation of Windows 2000, the drive attached to one of the controllers is determined to be the boot drive. Setup copies the driver for that controller to the root directory of the system partition, changing the driver filename to Ntbootdd.sys.

Technically, you don't have to use the scsi() syntax for SCSI drives, unless either one of the following conditions exists (both of these prevent INT 13 BIOS calls from working):

- The BIOS is disabled on the controller that has the disk on which Windows 2000 is installed.

- The boot partition starts or extends beyond the 1024th cylinder of the drive.

However, even if your SCSI drive is able to work with INT 13 BIOS calls, it's preferable to use the scsi() syntax, which forces the use of Ntbootdd.sys to continue the operating system startup.

The signature( ) Syntax

In Windows 2000, the signature() syntax is supported in the ARC path entry in Boot.ini. This syntax may be used if either one of the following conditions exists:

- The partition on which Windows 2000 is installed larger than 7.8GB, or the ending cylinder number is greater than 1024 for the partition.

- The drive on which you installed Windows 2000 is connected to a SCSI controller in which the BIOS is disabled (INT13 BIOS calls cannot be used during bootup).

The signature() syntax is technically the same as the scsi() syntax, but is used to support the Plug and Play architecture available in Windows 2000. Using the signature() syntax forces Ntldr to locate the drive whose disk signature matches the value in the parentheses, even if the drive is connected to a different SCSI controller number. This is important if you add SCSI controllers.

The value that's placed in the parentheses is derived from the physical disk's MBR, and is a unique hexadecimal number. The value is written to the MBR during the text-mode portion of Setup.

As with the scsi() syntax, the signature() syntax requires the specific SCSI driver, renamed to Ntbootdd.sys, on the root of your drive.

Tweaking Boot.ini

You can enhance the operating system boot process by tweaking the entries in the Boot.ini file.

The most common alteration made to Boot.ini is to change the timeout duration from 30 seconds to some smaller number. (You can also make this change in the System applet in the Control Panel, as explained earlier in this chapter.)

Sometimes users set the timeout duration to 0, so the computer automatically boots into the default operating system. This is not recommended, not just because it eliminates the opportunity to load the previous operating system (if one exists), but because it inhibits the ability to press F8 to display the troubleshooting menu.

Unlike in Windows NT, you cannot eliminate the timeout duration and leave the onscreen menu up until the user makes a choice (even if it takes forever). If you edit Boot.ini and change the timeout duration to –1, it's ignored. During the next boot, the duration is reset to its previous state.

However, you can force the menu to stay on the screen until you're ready to make a decision by pressing any key except the ENTER key, or by using an arrow to highlight a different choice. Because it requires user intervention, this does not help if your goal is to have the menu remain on the screen until the user is available (perhaps he or she is at the coffee machine).

You can add switches to the lines in Boot.ini, and some of the commonly used parameters include the following:

- **/BASEVIDEO,** which forces the system into 640 × 480, 16-color VGA mode.

- **/BAUDRATE=NNNN,** which sets the baud rate of the debug port. The default baud rate for the port is 19,200, but 9,600 is the preferable rate for remote debugging via modem. Using the /BAUDRATE switch automatically uses the /DEBUG switch.

- **/BOOTLOG,** which writes a log of the boot process to %SystemRoot%\Ntbtlog.txt. The log file contains a list of drivers that load or do not load during boot.

- **/CRASHDEBUG,** which enables the debug COM port for debugging if Windows 2000 crashes (has a STOP error), but allows you to continue to use the COM port for regular modem operations.

- **/DEBUG,** which enables the kernel debugger to perform live remote debugging through the COM port.

- **/DEBUGPORT=COMX,** which chooses a COM port for the debug port. By default, the debug port is COM2 if it exists. If COM2 doesn't exist, the default changes to COM1.

- **/FASTDETECT,** which tells Ntdetect not to check parallel and serial ports, instead letting the Plug and Play drivers perform that task. Microsoft says that the switch is added automatically to the Boot.ini line that references Windows 2000 if you are dual booting with a previous version of Windows NT. However, the switch is frequently added to computers that did not contain a previous version of any operating system and do not dual boot.

- **/INTAFFINITY,** which forces the multiprocessor HAL (Halmps.dll) to set interrupt affinities so that only the highest numbered processor in an SMP receives interrupts. By default, the multiprocessor HAL permits all processors to receive interrupts.

- **/NODEBUG,** which disables the kernel debugger. This speeds up the boot process, but if you run code that has a hard-coded debug breakpoint, a blue screen results.

- **/NOGUIBOOT,** which stops initialization of the VGA video driver that's responsible for presenting bitmapped graphics during the boot process. The driver is used to display progress information during bootup, and, more importantly, displays the "blue screen of death," so disabling it will disable Win2K's ability to do those things as well.

- **/NOSERIALMICE:COMX,** which disables the mouse port check for the specified COM port. This is useful if you have a UPS on COM1 and don't want the operating system to check the port for a mouse (the UPS sometimes interprets the communication signal as a warning and starts shutting down).

- **/PAE,** which has NTLDR load ntkrnlpa.exe. This program supports the version of the *x*86 kernel that is able to take advantage of Intel Physical Address Extensions (PAE) even when a system doesn't have more than 4GB of physical memory. (PAE permits an *x*86 system to have up to 64GB of physical memory, but the operating system must be specially coded to use memory beyond 4GB, which is the standard *x*86 limit.) The PAE version of the Win2K kernel presents 64-bit physical addresses to device drivers, so this switch is useful for testing device driver support for large-memory systems.

- **/NOPAE,** which forces NTLDR to load the non-PAE version of the Win2K kernel, even if the system contains more than 4GB of RAM and can support PAE.

- **/NOLOWMEM,** which only works if the /PAE switch is used and the system has more than 4GB of physical memory. Using the /NOLOWMEM switch tells the PAE-enabled version of the Win2K kernel, ntkrnlpa.exe, not to use the first 4GB of physical memory. Instead, it will load all applications and device drivers and allocate all memory pools from above that boundary. Use this switch only when you are testing device driver compatibility with large-memory systems.

- **/SOS,** which forces the loader to display the names of modules that are loaded instead of displaying dots.

Hide Menu Choices

You can hide items on the onscreen menu. For example, if a computer has Windows 9*x* installed in addition to Windows 2000, you may not want a user to launch the previous operating system, but you also don't want to remove it (in case you have a need in the future to let the user access Windows 9*x* for some reason). This is also a way to hide a Windows 2000 server installation and permit the user to access the Windows 2000 Professional installation, or vice versa.

To make menu items inaccessible, add the entry [any text] to the Boot.ini file at the point where you want the onscreen menu to end. Everything below that entry is invisible and inaccessible. For example, here's a Boot.ini file that prevents users from accessing Windows 95:

```
[boot loader]
timeout=30
default=multi(0)disk(0)rdisk(0)partition(1)\WINNT
[operating systems]
multi(0)disk(0)rdisk(0)partition(1)\WINNT="Windows 2000 Professional"
[any text]
C:\="Microsoft Windows"
```

If you want to permit access to the lines below the [any text] entry, just remove the entry.

■ The Advanced Options Menu

If there's a problem booting the operating system, start your computer again, and this time use the Advanced Options menu. When the usual menu appears, notice the line at the bottom of your screen:

"For troubleshooting and advanced startup options for Windows 2000, press F8"

Pressing F8 brings up a menu with these choices that are designed to help you repair the problem that prevented a good boot:

- Safe Mode
- Safe Mode with Networking
- Safe Mode with Command Prompt
- Enable Boot Logging
- Enable VGA Mode
- Last Known Good Configuration
- Directory Services Restore Mode (domain controllers only)
- Debugging Mode

 If you used Remote Install Services to install Windows 2000, the advanced startup options may include additional options related to RIS.

Use the arrow keys to select the advanced startup option you want to use, and press ENTER to return to the original Boot menu. Then select the operating system you want to start with the advanced option you chose.

 If you select an advanced option, you must choose a version of Windows 2000 in the original Boot menu. Do not try to use any of the advanced options with a previous version of Windows.

If you want to return to the original Boot menu without selecting an advanced option, press the ESC key.

Safe Mode

The best part of Safe Mode is that it allows access to all your drives, regardless of the file system. If it works, you can make configuration changes to correct the problem. For instance, it's common to need Safe Mode to remove a newly installed driver that doesn't work properly, or to undo some configuration scheme you've experimented with.

- **Safe Mode** loads only the basic files and drivers needed to get the operating system up and running: mouse, monitor, keyboard, storage, base video, and default system services.

- **Safe Mode with Networking** adds network support (NIC drivers), although this won't work with PCMCIA NICs.

- **Safe Mode with Command Prompt** is the same as Safe Mode, except the boot process ends with a command window instead of the GUI.

 Using any of the Safe Mode options causes a log file to be written to %SystemRoot%\ Ntbtlog.txt. See "Enable Boot Logging" in this section.

Enable Boot Logging

This option instructs Windows 2000 to create a log file (%SystemRoot%\ Ntbtlog.txt). The file displays a list of all the drivers that are loaded, or not loaded. Here's a small section of a typical Ntbtlog.txt file (this is a Unicode file, by the way):

```
Loaded driver \SystemRoot\System32\DRIVERS\parport.sys
Loaded driver \SystemRoot\System32\DRIVERS\serial.sys
Loaded driver \SystemRoot\System32\DRIVERS\serenum.sys
Loaded driver \SystemRoot\System32\DRIVERS\fdc.sys
Loaded driver \SystemRoot\System32\DRIVERS\mouclass.sys
Loaded driver \SystemRoot\System32\Drivers\NDProxy.SYS
Loaded driver \SystemRoot\System32\Drivers\EFS.SYS
Did not load driver \SystemRoot\System32\Drivers\NDProxy.SYS
Loaded driver \SystemRoot\System32\DRIVERS\usbhub.sys
Loaded driver \SystemRoot\System32\DRIVERS\flpydisk.sys
Did not load driver \SystemRoot\System32\Drivers\Sfloppy.SYS
Did not load driver \SystemRoot\System32\Drivers\Scsiscan.SYS
Did not load driver \SystemRoot\System32\Drivers\Changer.SYS
Did not load driver \SystemRoot\System32\Drivers\Cdaudio.SYS
```

Enable VGA Mode

Familiar to Windows NT 4 users, this option starts Windows 2000 using the basic VGA driver. Use this choice after you install a new video driver for your video card that doesn't work (which is quite apparent when the operating system GUI mounts the next time you boot). The basic video driver is the same driver used when you start Windows 2000 with any of the Safe Mode choices.

Last Known Good Configuration

Use this option to start Windows 2000 with the registry settings that were saved at the last shutdown. This option doesn't solve problems caused by missing or corrupt drivers, but it's useful in overcoming problems caused by configuration changes you made in your last session. Those changes are lost, which is usually a good thing.

Directory Services Restore Mode

This option is only available for domain controllers, and it restores the %SystemRoot%\Sysvol directory and the Active Directory. The Sysvol directory stores the domain's public files, which are replicated among the domain controllers.

Debugging Mode

Use this option to start Windows 2000 and send debugging information to another computer through a serial cable.

Creating a Bootable Floppy Disk

If one of the files that load early in the operating system boot process (Ntldr, Ntdetect.com, or Boot.ini) is missing or corrupted, you never get to the Advanced Options menu to repair your system. You can remedy this by using a boot disk that's created specifically for your Windows 2000 installation.

Creating a Bootable Floppy Disk from Your Own System

If you're smart, you'll create a bootable floppy disk as soon as your Windows 2000 installation is up and running (without error). Unfortunately, users rarely heed this advice and don't think about the need for a bootable floppy disk until there's a problem booting. However, if you're a resourceful person who plans ahead, here's how to accomplish this task:

1. Put a floppy disk in the drive.

2. Open My Computer or Windows Explorer and right-click on the floppy drive object.

3. Choose Format from the shortcut menu and format the disk using the default options.

4. Copy the following files from the root directory of your hard drive to the floppy disk:

   ■ Ntdetect.com
   ■ Ntldr
   ■ Boot.ini
   ■ Ntbootdd.sys (if it exists)

Test the disk by restarting the operating system.

Ntbootdds.sys only exists if you have a SCSI system. It's your SCSI driver, renamed.

Creating a Bootable Floppy Disk on Another Windows 2000 Computer

If it's too late, and you need a bootable floppy disk to start a broken system, you can create one from another Windows 2000 computer that's running the same version (Professional or one of the Server versions) and the same file system (NTFS, FAT, or FAT32).

1. Follow the steps described for creating a boot floppy from your own computer.

2. Open Boot.ini and examine it to make sure it matches your own configuration. If it doesn't, use the information in the section "About Boot.ini" to adjust the settings.

3. If you have a different SCSI controller, find the correct driver file and copy it to the floppy disk. Delete the Ntbootdd.sys file you copied from the computer you used to create the disk, and then rename your SCSI driver to Ntbootdd.sys.

4. If the source computer uses an IDE controller, and your system has a SCSI controller, use Notepad to adjust the setting in Boot.ini and then copy the correct SCSI driver to the floppy disk and rename it Ntbootdd.sys.

5. If the source computer uses a SCSI controller, and your system has an IDE controller, use Notepad to adjust the setting in Boot.ini and delete Ntbootdd.sys if you copied it from the source computer.

Test the bootable floppy disk on your computer.

Creating a Bootable Floppy Disk on a Computer Running a Different Version of Windows

If you cannot find another computer that's running the same version of Windows 2000 and using the same file system, you may still be able to create a bootable floppy that works on your own computer. You'll need the following supplies:

■ A blank floppy disk.

■ Setup Boot Disk 1 (one of the floppy disks included in your Windows 2000 package).

■ The Windows 2000 original media on CD-ROM. (If the original files are on a network server, you don't need the CD-ROM.)

■ The driver file for your SCSI controller (if your computer has a SCSI controller).

If you can't locate the floppy disks for your Windows 2000 media, you can create them, using the instructions in the section "Creating Windows 2000 Floppy Disks" later in this chapter.

You can perform this task at any computer that has a CD-ROM drive (into which you'll insert the Windows 2000 CD-ROM) or that has access to the network share that holds a copy of the files from the Windows 2000 CD-ROM.

1. With the first Windows 2000 Setup disk in the floppy drive, open My Computer and right-click on the Floppy Drive object.

2. Choose Copy Disk from the shortcut menu.

3. Follow the prompts to insert the source disk (Setup Boot Disk 1) and the target disk (your blank floppy disk) until the copy process is completed.

4. Delete all the files on the new disk.

5. Copy Ntdetect.com and Ntldr from the i386 directory on the CD-ROM or the network sharepoint to the new floppy disk.

6. Rename Ntldr to Setupldr.bin.

7. Open Notepad and create a Boot.ini file and save it to the new floppy disk (see the next section, "Creating a Quick Boot.ini File").

8. If your computer has a SCSI controller, copy the correct driver to the new floppy disk and rename the file to Ntbootdd.sys.

9. Return to your computer, boot up with this floppy disk, and log on.

10. Place the Windows 2000 CD-ROM in the CD-ROM drive, or access the network share where the Windows 2000 files are stored.

11. Copy Ntldr from the \i386 directory to the root directory of your hard drive.

I have no explanation for the fact that you can't simply copy Ntldr to your new floppy disk and use it (without renaming it), when you create a bootable floppy disk on a computer that isn't running Windows 2000. I tried to, and received an error message about Ntldr immediately after the floppy was accessed during the boot process. However, following the steps I've outlined here worked fine.

Creating a Quick Boot.ini File

Your emergency Boot.ini file only has to load Windows 2000, so there's no need to worry about any lines in the Boot.ini file that refer to another operating system, even if your computer is configured for dual booting. Here's an example:

```
[boot loader]
timeout=30
```

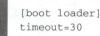

```
Default= scsi(0)disk(0)rdisk(0)partition(1)\Winnt
[operating systems]
scsi(0)disk(0)rdisk(0)partition(1)\winnt="Microsoft Windows 2000 Server"
```

■ If your computer boots from an IDE or EIDE hard drive, replace scsi(0) with multi(0).

■ If your Windows 2000 system files are not in a directory named Winnt, replace both instances of the reference with the correct directory name.

■ Read the section "About Boot.ini" earlier in this chapter if you have multiple controllers, drives, or partitions to make sure you're referencing the right hardware.

Creating Windows 2000 Floppy Disks

If you don't have a copy of the floppy disks that ship with Windows 2000, you need to create them, because you might need them to repair your system. To accomplish this, get your hands on four blank, formatted floppy disks and then follow these steps:

1. Insert the Windows 2000 CD-ROM in the CD-ROM drive, or map a drive to the network share that holds the Windows 2000 files.

2. Open the Run command on the Start menu and enter **x:\bootdisk\makeboot.exe a:**, substituting the appropriate drive letter for x.

3. Follow the instructions to complete the process.

 Disks created from Windows 2000 Professional cannot be used for Windows 2000 Server, and vice versa.

Creating and Using an Emergency Repair Disk (ERD)

Windows 2000 handles the creation and use of the ERD in a far different manner than previous versions of Windows NT. You'll find it less powerful than earlier incarnations (but on the other hand, there are additional repair and recovery procedures available in Windows 2000 that didn't exist in Windows NT).

ERD Functions

The ERD can help repair problems with the following elements:

- System files
- Partition boot sector
- Startup environment settings for dual-boot systems

You cannot use the ERD to repair registry problems.

Creating an ERD

If you used previous versions of Windows NT, you'll be disappointed by the ERD feature in Windows 2000. Rdisk.exe is gone, and instead you get to travel through layers of menu items to create the ERD.

The ERD is part of the Backup feature set, and to get started, click the following menu commands:

1. Start

2. Programs

3. Accessories

4. System Tools

5. Backup

When the Backup program window opens, click Tools | Create an Emergency Repair Disk from the menu bar. A dialog box opens to tell you to insert a blank, formatted diskette in Drive A:. Do so, then click OK. After a short time, a dialog box appears to tell you that the repair data was successfully saved. Label the disk ERD and put it in a safe place.

The following files are placed on the ERD:

- autoexec.nt
- config.nt
- setup.log

Setup.log is a list of loaded files and drivers, along with other configuration information about your computer. Figure 5-2 displays a portion of this file.

 You should re-create the ERD when you change the configuration of your system.

Using the ERD

If your operating system won't boot, you can try to repair the installation with the ERD. This is usually successful if the problem is caused by missing or corrupt system files or dual-boot settings. The ERD cannot repair the registry.

You actually begin another installation of the Windows 2000 when you want to repair your system.

Figure 5-2. *The setup.log file on the ERD has configuration information about your system*

- If your computer cannot boot from the CD drive, boot with Setup Disk 1 of the Windows 2000 floppy disks.

- If your computer is capable of booting from the CD drive, use either the Windows 2000 CD or Setup Disk 1.

- Alpha-based computers must use the CD.

Windows 2000 goes through the Setup program. At the end of the process, the Setup program realizes that Windows 2000 is already installed and offers you the options you need to perform a repair. A Welcome to Setup message appears on your screen, displaying these three choices:

- To set up Windows 2000 now, press ENTER.

- To repair a Windows 2000 installation, press R.

- To quit Setup without installing Windows 2000, press F3.

Press R to display the Repair menu, which offers two choices:

- To repair a Windows 2000 installation by using the recovery console, press C.
- To repair a Windows 2000 installation by using the emergency repair process, press R.

Press R to use the emergency repair process. The next screen contains a message that essentially warns you that this is an iffy procedure. In addition, you're asked to choose either a Manual Repair (by pressing M) or a Fast Repair (by pressing F).

Manual Repair lets you make the decisions about the repair process—you can replace system files, the partition boot sector, or the startup environment. The registry is not repaired. Setup will ask you to put the ERD into drive A.

Fast Repair turns the repair process over to the Setup program. Setup will attempt to repair system files, the partition boot sector, the startup environment, and the registry. (The registry repair procedure restores the registry that was created when you first installed Windows 2000.) After you've selected the tasks you want Setup to perform, you're prompted to insert the ERD.

Note *You can use either of these repair options even if you don't have an ERD. If you press L, Setup will search for the Windows 2000 installation files.*

After the tasks are completed, restart your computer. If the operating system still doesn't boot, you'll have to reinstall Windows 2000.

The Recovery Console

The Recovery Console is a command-line program you can use to fix system problems. Although the feature offers a limited set of commands, you can repair the MBR, copy system files that are missing or corrupted, and reconfigure services that are not working properly (or at all).

There are two ways to use the Recovery Console:

- Use the Windows 2000 Setup disks or the bootable Windows 2000 CD to reach the Recovery Console option.
- Install the Recovery Console and make it available on the Windows 2000 boot menu.

Using Setup to Access the Recovery Console

This method is the commonly used lifesaver when your operating system either doesn't boot at all, or boots with so many error messages that it's clear you have a problem.

Start by booting your computer with Setup Boot Disk 1 and follow the prompts to insert the other three disks while Windows 2000 gets ready to install itself. When the last floppy disk has completed its work, a Welcome to Setup message appears on your screen. The message displays three options:

■ To set up Windows 2000 now, press ENTER.

■ To repair a Windows 2000 installation, press R.

■ To quit Setup without installing Windows 2000, press F3.

Press R to display the Repair menu, which offers two choices:

■ To repair a Windows 2000 installation by using the recovery console, press C.

■ To repair a Windows 2000 installation by using the emergency repair process, press R.

Press C to start the Windows 2000 Recovery Console (don't panic if you experience several seconds of black before anything happens).

The Recovery Console operates in text mode, and the screen displays a numbered list of operating system directories. Usually, there's only one (C:\Winnt), unless you're dual booting between two versions of Windows 2000.

1. Enter the number next to the Windows 2000 installation you want to log on to in order to make repairs, and press ENTER.

2. The administrator is automatically logged on, so type the administrator's password and press ENTER.

3. You're at a command prompt in the %SystemRoot% directory, usually C:\Winnt.

You can now enter the Recovery Console commands required to perform the repair tasks.

 Because you log on to the Recovery Console, you cannot use this feature if the Security Accounts Manager (SAM) hive is corrupt or missing.

Recovery Console Commands

The following commands are available in the Recovery Console:

```
CD/CHDIR
CHKDSK
CLS
COPY
DEL/DELETE
DIR
```

```
DISABLE
ENABLE
DISKPART
FIXBOOT
FIXMBR
FORMAT
LISTSVC
LOGON
MAP
MD/MKDIR
MORE
RD
REN/RENAME
RMDIR
SYSTEMROOT
TYPE
ATTRIB
EXTRACT
```

Most of these are very common MS-DOS commands, but some may not be familiar to you (enter **Help /*commandname*** for information about any command). Using these commands can be dangerous, so the Recovery Console is no place for computer newbies. Type **Exit** to leave the Recovery Console and restart your computer.

Recovery Console Restrictions

The following restrictions are in effect when you're working in the Recovery Console:

- You can access and view only the %SystemRootr% directory (and subdirectories) for the Windows 2000 installation you selected on the opening screen (usually C:\Winnt). If you try to view another %SystemRoot% directory, you'll see an "Access Denied" error.

- You can copy a file from a floppy disk to a hard disk.

- You can copy a file from one location on a hard disk to another location on a hard disk.

- You cannot copy a file from the local hard disk to a floppy disk.

Installing the Recovery Console

You can install the Recovery Console so it's permanently available when you want to tweak configuration settings and drivers (or perform repairs when necessary).

Installation is accomplished with the Winnt32 command, which is on the Windows 2000 CD-ROM in the \i386 folder. Enter the following command to install the Recovery Console:

```
x:\foldername\Winnt32 /cmdcons
```

where

```
x: is the drive letter for the Windows 2000 CD-ROM or the mapped
drive letter for the network share location of the Windows 2000
installation files.
```

■ *foldername* is \alpha or \i386.

A Setup dialog box appears to confirm the installation of the Recovery Console as a startup option. Click Yes to continue and a Setup Wizard takes over to install the necessary files automatically. You must restart your computer to complete the installation.

When the operating system boots, a new option appears on your menu: "Microsoft Windows 2000 Command Console." Its entry in Boot.ini is

```
C:\CMDCONS\BOOTSECT.DAT="Microsoft Windows 2000 Command Console" /cmdcons
```

Uninstalling the Recovery Console

You can remove the Recovery Console and its menu entry by taking these steps:

1. Edit Boot.ini to delete the Recovery Console line.

2. Delete the \Cmdcons directory from the root of the boot partition.

3. Delete the file named Cmldr from the root directory of the boot partition.

Uninstalling the Recovery Console makes sense if multiple users have access to a computer, and any of them fall into that "knows enough to be dangerous" category that all administrators dread.

Chapter 6

The User Interface

The user interface begins with the desktop that appears when the operating system loads. The desktop contains icons, the menu system, and a taskbar to provide the navigation tools you need when working in Windows 2000.

If you've used Windows NT 4 or Windows *9x*, a great deal of the Windows 2000 UI will be familiar, but you're going to find some differences that will have an impact on your navigation habits.

The Desktop

The desktop is a folder that contains folders and shortcuts, just like the other folders in your system. The difference between the desktop and all the other folders is that the desktop can't be closed.

The desktop folder is at the top of your computer's hierarchy, which is obvious when you open Explorer, but less obvious when you open My Computer, which defaults to the My Computer object at the top of the hierarchy. However, if you open the drop-down list on the toolbar, you find Desktop at the top of the hierarchy (see Figure 6-1).

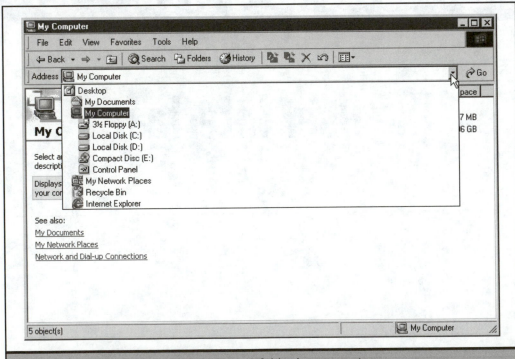

Figure 6-1. *The desktop is the topmost folder in your system*

Configuring the Desktop

If you're migrating to Windows 2000 from a non-Windows operating system, read this section to learn how to configure your desktop and its elements. If you're upgrading to Windows 2000 from Windows NT or Windows 9x, the desktop configuration procedures are almost exactly what you're used to (you can skip this section).

The basic configuration options for the desktop are in the Display Properties dialog box, which you access with one of the following methods:

- Right-click a blank area on the desktop, and choose Properties from the shortcut menu.
- Open the Display applet in the Control Panel.

You can individualize your desktop with wallpaper or pattern decorations, using the Background tab of the Display Properties dialog box (see Figure 6-2). Windows 2000 installs wallpaper and pattern files you can use, or you can provide your own.

All the configuration changes you make to your desktop are yours, and are loaded whenever you log on. If you share your computer with other users, their own desktop settings are loaded when they log on.

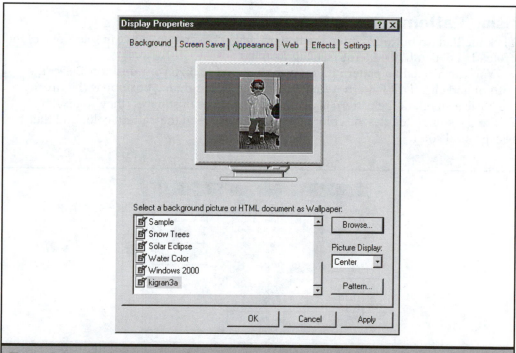

Figure 6-2. *Customize your desktop with designs, decorative elements, or family pictures*

Using Wallpaper on Your Desktop

Any file with the extension .bmp, .htm, or .html can be used for wallpaper (if you enable Web content display, you can also use .jpg files). Use the Browse button to locate files on your system.

While you're on the Internet, if you see a graphic you'd like to use for wallpaper, right-click the graphic image and choose Set as Wallpaper from the shortcut menu. To use an .htm (or .html) document as wallpaper, save the document and use the Browse button on the Background tab of the Display Properties dialog box to locate it.

By default, wallpaper is centered on your desktop, but you can use the choices in the Picture Display box to change the way wallpaper displays:

- Tile repeats the image to fill the desktop.

- Stretch expands the image to fill the desktop (which usually distorts the image).

 You cannot tile or stretch .htm/.html documents.

Many of the preinstalled wallpaper files require you to enable the Active Desktop to use the picture. If you select one of those files, you're asked if you wish to enable Active Desktop in order to use the wallpaper.

Using Patterns on the Desktop

Click the Pattern button to open the Pattern dialog box, where you can select one of the preloaded decorative patterns (see Figure 6-3).

You can also edit a pattern if you want to individualize your desktop. Select the pattern and click Edit Pattern. When the Pattern Editor dialog box opens (Figure 6-4), the basic element of the pattern is displayed as a series of squares (they're pixels). Clicking a square toggles the color of the square between the pattern color and the background color.

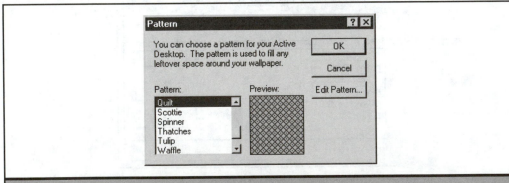

Figure 6-3.   *Decorate the desktop background with a pattern*

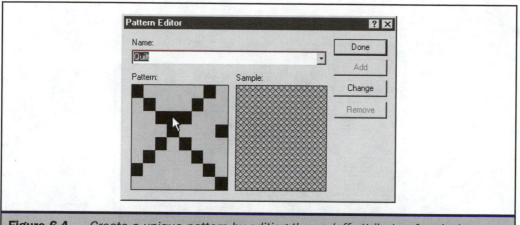

Figure 6-4. *Create a unique pattern by editing the on/off attribute of a pixel*

Tip   *You should change the name of the pattern after you alter it.*

When you install a pattern on the desktop, the desktop icons and their titles float on top of the pattern so you can see both the icon and the title clearly.

Using Screen Savers

The design of modern monitors has precluded the original need for screen savers, which was to prevent images from burning into the display. Today there are two reasons for using a screen saver:

- It adds security to an unattended computer, through the use of a password.
- It's cool.

To choose a screen saver, go to the Screen Saver tab of the Display Properties dialog box (Figure 6-5) and select a file from the list in the Screen Saver box. As you choose a screen saver, you can see a miniature preview of its graphics and animation in the preview monitor on the dialog box. To see a real preview, click the Preview button. The screen saver fills your screen and remains there until you move your mouse, click a mouse button, or press any key on the keyboard.

Specify the number of minutes you want to elapse before the screen saver kicks in by entering a number in the Wait box. You can use the up and down arrows to change the existing number or enter a number directly.

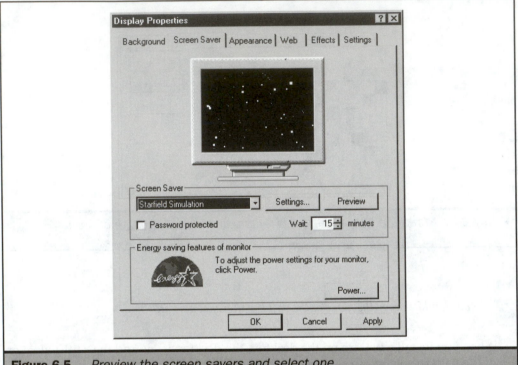

Figure 6-5. *Preview the screen savers and select one*

Click the Settings button to change the options that control the screen saver's appearance and onscreen behavior. The options are specific to the screen saver, and therefore vary. For some screen savers you can change colors and texture, others have settings for the shape of the elements in the graphic, and some permit changes to the animation effects.

Password-Protecting Screen Savers

When you password-protect a screen saver, using the mouse or keyboard to remove the screen saver produces a password dialog box instead of the desktop. If the correct password isn't entered, the screen saver doesn't leave. This not only protects the data that's currently on your screen from prying eyes, it also prevents anyone from using your computer at all.

To turn on password protection, select the Password Protected check box. To unlock your desktop when the screen server is active, use your logon password.

If you're administering Windows 9x workstations, note that you must set a discrete password for the screen saver by clicking the Change button. You can use the logon password if you wish; you just have to enter it because it's not automatically assigned.

On Demand Screen Savers

The elapsed time you specify for having the screen saver kick in shouldn't be too short because it's annoying to have to clear it when you just stop working for a couple of minutes. On the other hand, if you specify a long interval, leaving your desk means your computer could be exposed to prying users for a significant length of time.

The solution is to launch your password-protected screen saver at will, which can be accomplished through the use of a shortcut. Look in %SystemRoot%\System32 for your screen saver file. The format of the filename is ss*Name*.scr, where *Name* is a form of the screen saver name you choose. For example, if you chose the 3D Pipes screen saver, look for sspipes.scr.

Right-drag the screen saver file to the desktop and choose Create Shortcut(s) Here from the shortcut menu. When you leave your desk, open the shortcut to launch the screen saver.

You can eliminate the need to get to the desktop in order to launch the screen saver in either of two ways:

- Put the screen saver shortcut on the QuickLaunch toolbar on your taskbar (just drag it there to install it).
- Create a CTRL-ALT keyboard shortcut to launch the screen saver.

To create a keyboard shortcut, right-click the screen saver shortcut icon and choose Properties from the shortcut menu. Go to the Shortcut tab and place your mouse pointer in the text box labeled Shortcut key. Enter the letter you want to use for your shortcut key. Just enter the letter; you don't have to press CTRL and ALT. (You can't delete the word "none" that appears in the text box, but as soon as you enter a character it disappears.) The shortcut key text box displays CTRL-ALT-*yourletter*.

Forcing the Use of Password-Protected Screen Savers

Administrators can and should force the use of password-protected screen savers on certain desktops. Consider doing this for any workstations in which the logged-on user has access to sensitive files (payroll, financial information) or has high-level permissions for server-based files. You can enforce screen saver usage via the registry. Go to HKEY_CURRENT_USER\Control Panel\Desktop and make the following changes:

- Change the data in the data item ScreenSaveActive to 1.
- Change the data in the data item ScreenSaverIsSecure to 1.
- Change the data in the data item ScreenSaverTimeOut to specify the number of seconds that should elapse before the screen saver kicks in (the registry uses seconds, even though the Display Properties dialog box uses minutes).
- Change the data in the data item Scrnsave.exe to the filename for the screen saver you want to use.

The password-protected screen saver is established at the next logon. To prevent users from overriding these settings by changing them in the Screen Saver tab of the Display Properties dialog box, eliminate that tab. Here's how:

1. Go to HKEY_CURRENT_USER\Software\Microsoft\Windows\CurrentVersion\Policies.
2. Create a subkey under this key named System.
3. Create a DWORD data item in the new System subkey named NoDispScrSavPage.
4. Change the data value of this new data item to 1.

The Screen Saver tab disappears immediately; you do not have to reboot.

Changing the Appearance of Windows

You can use the Appearance tab of the Display Properties dialog box to change the look of all the elements that appear on your desktop, including software windows, dialog boxes, and so on.

You can choose a predesigned scheme from the Scheme text box and apply it, or choose one that comes close to what you like and change individual elements by choosing those elements from the Items text box. Depending on the item you choose, you can change colors, fonts, or both. If you design your own scheme, click the Save As button to name it.

Configuring the Web Elements on Your Desktop

The Web tab, seen in Figure 6-6, is the place to add Web content to your desktop, including active pages such as news headlines or stock tickers.

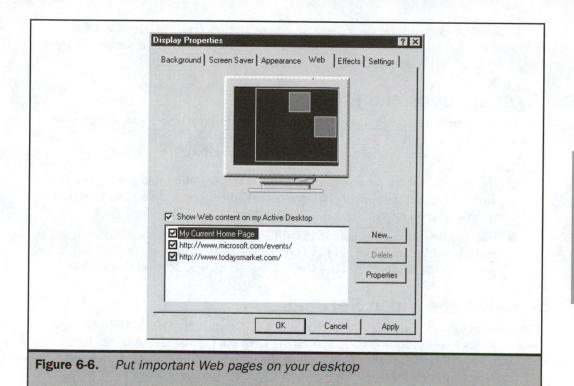

Figure 6-6.   *Put important Web pages on your desktop*

LEARNING
THE BASICS

Click New to connect to the Microsoft Active Desktop Gallery or add a URL for a Web page you already know you want to display. You can also use the Browse button to load a locally stored picture or HTML document.

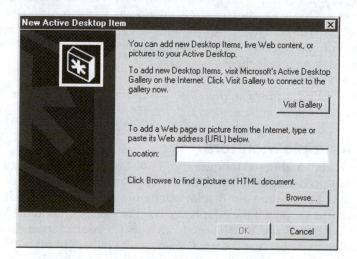

To use Web elements on your desktop, you must turn on the Active Desktop feature. Detailed information on setting up an active desktop is in the section "Active Desktop" later in this chapter.

Configuring Icons and Effects

Use the Effects tab to change the icon for the default desktop object and to turn special visual effects on and off.

Two of the items on this tab are new as of Windows 2000:

■ *Use transition effects for menus and tooltips.*   This selection determines the way menus and tooltips appear. The default is Fade effect, and you can turn it off by selecting Scroll effect.

■ *Hide keyboard navigation indicators until I use the* ALT *key.*   This selection hides the underlined letters of the hot keys on menus unless you press the ALT key before you open the menu. If you use the ALT-key shortcuts, deselect this option.

Configuring the Video Settings

The Settings tab is for setting colors, resolution, and monitors. The Troubleshooting button opens the Windows 2000 Help system, with the Display Troubleshooter selected. The Advanced button opens a new dialog box with a full set of tabs and configuration options for your video controller, your monitor, and other display options (see Figure 6-7).

Multiple Monitors

Windows 2000 supports the use of multiple monitors. You can use this feature to create a desktop that contains multiple programs or windows. As you work, you can move items from one monitor to another, or stretch windows across multiple monitors. You can keep an eye on Web activity on one monitor while you edit data on another. You can even open multiple pages of a single document across monitors, or view sets of columns from the same spreadsheet.

   If you've installed and used multiple monitors in Windows 98, be aware that the technology for multimonitor systems is different for Windows 2000.

Installing Multiple Monitors

Before you can install additional monitors, you must be sure your current video settings are configured properly. Open the Display Properties dialog box and move to the Settings tab. Make sure your display adapter is specifically named; you cannot install multimonitor support if the adapter is listed as VGA or Standard VGA. If that's the case, you must obtain and install specific drivers for your adapter. In addition, be sure your color configuration is set for 256 colors or better (16-bit high color is recommended).

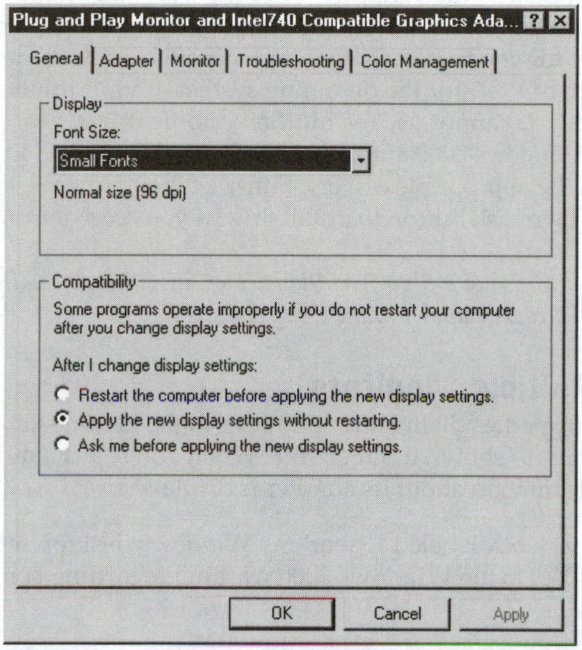

Figure 6-7. *Tweak your video system with the options available on the tabs in the Advanced dialog box*

To install an additional monitor, insert the additional video adapter (PCI or AGP) and plug the monitor into the card. You must make sure the VGA Disabled switch is activated on the adapter (check the documentation or call the manufacturer; it's almost always a jumper or a dip switch). Windows 2000 requires a VGA device, and it must be the primary adapter, so additional adapters that do not have the ability to disable VGA are not compatible with the multimonitor feature in Windows 2000.

Note *The reason you can only have one VGA device, and must disable VGA on all other adapters, is that your Power On Self Test (POST) locates a VGA device and passes the information to the operating system. POST can only handle one VGA device.*

Locate your primary display adapter in PCI slot 1, which is the PCI slot nearest to the outside edge of the motherboard and furthest away from the ISA slots. Usually, the computer's BIOS detects the VGA device based on slot order. If your BIOS has an option for selecting the device that is to be treated as the VGA device, you don't have to use slot 1 (but you do have to configure the BIOS).

If you have an adapter that's designed to connect to multiple monitors, merely connect the cable for the additional monitor.

If you have an onboard video adapter, inserting a second adapter usually disables it. In order to be certified as Windows 2000 compatible, the motherboard and BIOS must provide a way for you to have both adapters active, with the primary adapter becoming the source of VGA for the operating system. If your motherboard doesn't provide this feature, you cannot use the multimonitor features.

Reboot to have Windows 2000 automatically detect the new video adapter and monitor, and install the appropriate drivers. Either let the hardware wizard find the right drivers, or use the Have Disk button to install drivers you receive from the manufacturer.

 If the new monitor is not a Plug And Play device, install it manually with the Add/Remove Hardware applet in the Control Panel.

Configuring Multiple Monitors

Open the Display Properties dialog box and move to the Settings tab, where you see two monitor icons, as shown in Figure 6-8. When you select a monitor icon, it's highlighted and information about its adapter is displayed.

1. Select the check box labeled Extend my Windows desktop into this monitor, and answer Yes to the Windows 2000 warning regarding compatibility.

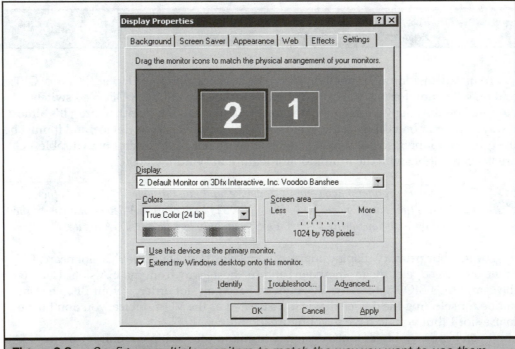

Figure 6-8. *Configure multiple monitors to match the way you want to use them*

2. To avoid a migraine, drag the monitor icons so they represent the way your physical monitors are arranged. If you have icon 2 on the left, but monitor 2 is on the right side of your desk, you'll drive yourself crazy. If you've stacked the monitors on your desk, stack the icons, too. The edge at which the icons meet is the point at which your mouse passes from one monitor to the other.

Tip   *The icons automatically lock together by matching the connected edge. If you want a separation between the icons, hold down the CTRL key while you drag. However, this action may interfere with the system's ability to map coordinates (see "Monitor Coordinates" later in this section).*

3. You can set the color depth and resolution for each monitor; they do not have to be the same.

4. If you have a third monitor, repeat all these steps. When the monitor icons are in their proper positions in the dialog box, click OK to close the dialog box and restart the computer.

Using Multiple Monitors

Your primary monitor displays the Logon dialog box when you boot your computer, and when you launch software applications, the opening window will usually appear in the primary monitor. After that, it's up to you. Use the Settings tab of the Display Properties dialog box to drag windows between monitors or stretch windows across monitors.

Note   *Not all screen savers are designed to work with multiple monitors.*

Monitor Coordinates

If a software application uses the primary monitor for dialog boxes and message boxes, even after you've moved the program to another monitor, it means the coordinates for the placement of dialog boxes are programmed into the software code.

The coordinates for the primary monitor (and for single monitor systems) start at 0,0 in the upper left corner and continue to X,Y coordinates based on resolution. For instance, if my monitor (primary or sole) is running at 1024×768, the coordinates are 0,0 through 1023,767. The coordinates for my second monitor start at 1024,768 and end at the X,Y resolution. If my second monitor is also 1024×768, the X,Y coordinates are 2047,767. A third monitor would have coordinates that began at 2048,768 and continue to the appropriate X,Y for the monitor's resolution.

Locking the Computer

If you don't want to use a password-protected screen saver, you can secure your computer with the Windows lockdown feature. The advantage of this method is that it doesn't use system resources the way a screen saver does. (The screen saver polls to determine whether or not the input devices are idle, which uses resources.)

Locking your computer when you leave your desk eliminates the chance that anyone else can see your screen or access files. You don't have to close application windows or stop processes to lock down your machine. To use the lockdown function, press CTRL-ALT-DEL to bring up the Windows Security dialog box shown in the following illustration.

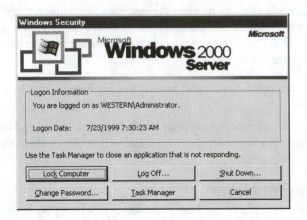

Click Lock Computer to hide your screen and prevent access. The only thing displayed on your monitor is a message indicating the computer is locked

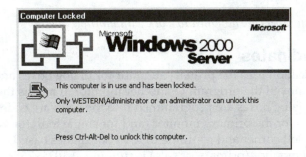

For computers that contain sensitive material and should therefore be locked whenever the user leaves, create a desktop shortcut to the Lock Computer feature. To accomplish this, create a desktop shortcut to %SystemRoot%\System32\ Rundll32.exe. Open the Properties for the shortcut and add parameters to the path in the Target text box so that the text matches the following string:

C:\WINNT\system32\rundll32.exe user32.dll,LockWorkStation

substituting your own drive and folder if your system files are not in C:\WINNT.

My Computer and Windows Explorer

Windows 2000 has both My Computer and Windows Explorer, continuing the interface paradigm that started with Windows 95. However, Windows 2000 clearly favors the use of My Computer over Explorer. Here's the evidence.

- My Computer is a default desktop icon.

- Windows Explorer has moved out of the Programs menu and onto the Accessories submenu.

- My Computer has a link to My Network Places (Network Neighborhood was not available in previous incarnations of My Computer).

- My Computer has a command named Explorer Bar in the View menu. Use the Folders submenu option to change the display of My Computer so it looks and acts exactly like Explorer.

- Windows Explorer contains a link to My Computer.

Look and Feel

My Computer uses a Web-like interface (see Figure 6-9) to display all the drives in your computer, including any mapped drives. There's also a folder for the Control Panel, and links to other system folders.

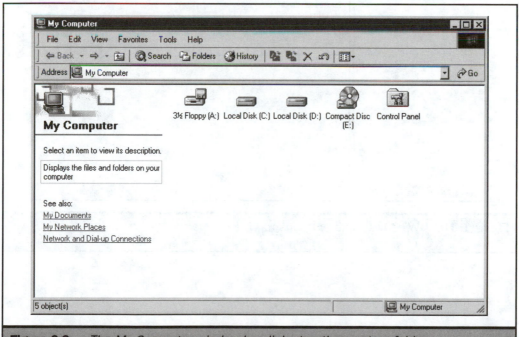

Figure 6-9. *The My Computer window has links to other system folders*

The look of Windows Explorer has changed in Windows 2000 (see Figure 6-10). Previous versions of Windows opened Explorer with drive C selected and expanded, but now the top of the desktop hierarchy, My Documents, is the default selected object (it's expanded to include its subfolders). You must expand the My Computer object to see your drives, and then expand each drive to see its folders and files. See the "Interface Tips and Tricks" section at the end of this chapter for a workaround.

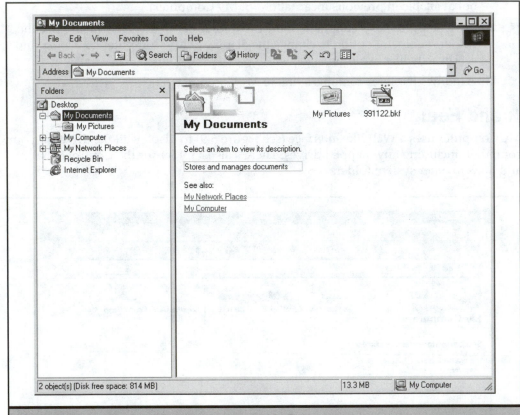

Figure 6-10.   *Windows Explorer opens to My Documents*

Windows Explorer and My Computer have menus and toolbars for manipulating your Windows 2000 system. Most of the commands are self-explanatory, but a few are new, or work differently than previous versions of Windows, so they bear some discussion.

The Explorer Bar command on the View menu offers a variety of submenu choices: Search, Favorites, History, and Folders. The toolbar has icons for each of these commands. Choosing an option opens the appropriate display in the left pane (see Figure 6-11). By default, no option is selected in My Computer, and the Folders option is preselected in Windows Explorer. The Tip of the Day submenu item displays elementary-level tips for navigating the Web.

Use the close buttons on the left pane and the Tip of The Day window to return to the standard My Computer display.

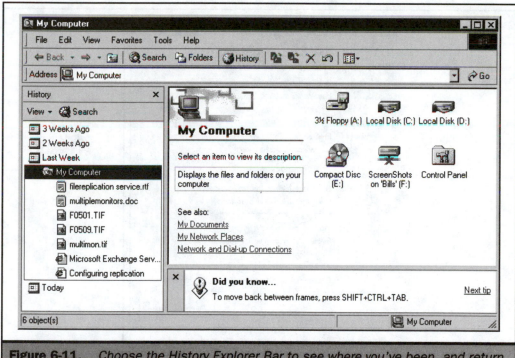

Figure 6-11. *Choose the History Explorer Bar to see where you've been, and return there with a single click*

Folder Options

The command for customizing folder views in My Computer and Explorer has moved to the Tools menu—the command is Folder Options. The dialog box that displays when you choose the command is shown in Figure 6-12.

USING ACTIVE DESKTOP   You can turn on the Active Desktop feature, which is explained in the section "Active Desktop" later in this chapter.

WEB VS. CLASSIC FOLDER VIEWS   You can set folders to display content as Web content or in the classic Windows folder style. By default, folders are set for Web content, but you can change that on the General tab of the Folder Options dialog box.

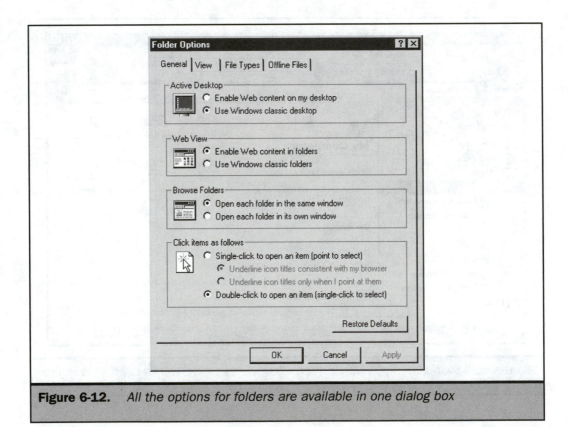

Figure 6-12.   *All the options for folders are available in one dialog box*

OPENING FOLDERS   The Browse Folders options control the way windows open as you drill down through your system. Whether you opt for replacing or adding windows, you can always hold down the CTRL key to use the opposite effect.

SINGLE-CLICK VS. DOUBLE-CLICK   You can open items with a single-click instead of the traditional double-click if you wish (handy for people who spend a lot of time on the Web). If you select the single-click option, choose whether you want all titles underlined (like the Web) or you'd prefer to have an underline appear when you point to an item.

HIDING AND SHOWING FILES   Use the options in the View tab to change the way files and folders display (see Figure 6-13). Notice that the View tab has a button named Like Current Folder, which you can use to tell Windows 2000 to use the configuration options you set here on all Windows folders.

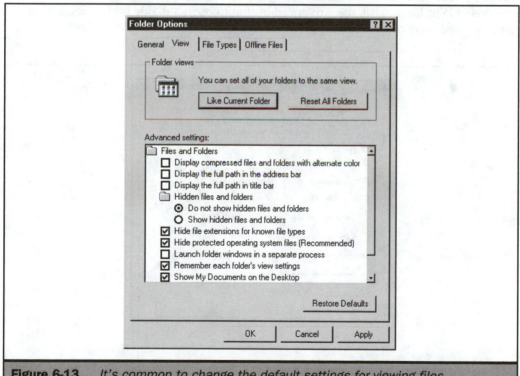

Figure 6-13.   *It's common to change the default settings for viewing files and folders*

The same dialog box is available in Control Panel, in the Folders applet. See Chapter 7 for more information about configuring your system with Control Panel applets.

Notice that there is an option to show or hide hidden files, and a separate option to hide protected operating system files. Some system files have a new security designation, *super hidden* (not to be confused with the normal hidden attribute). You can configure your system to hide those files while showing standard hidden files (or show both file types).

FILE TYPES   Add, modify, and remove file associations with the File Types tab. The functions are the same as in previous versions of Windows.

OFFLINE ACCESS   Offline access for network files is a way to make sure you can continue to work when you're not connected to the network. The configuration options are available on the Offline Files tab (see Figure 6-14). This is a far more robust and logical system than the offline access features offered in My Briefcase, in previous versions of Windows. Click the Advanced button to open a dialog box in which you can configure your computer's behavior when the network connection is lost.

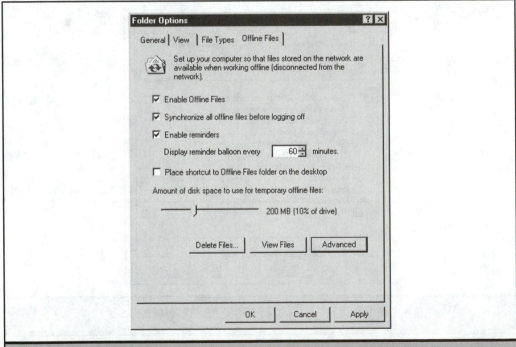

Figure 6-14.   *Configure your system so you can work on network files even when you're not connected to the network*

The definition of *network* does not necessarily mean a network file server, it can mean any shared resource you access on any computer on the network.

Customizing Individual Folders

In addition to setting general folder options, you can customize the way an individual folder displays its contents. On the View menu, the command named Customize this Folder opens a wizard that walks you through the changes (you cannot bypass the wizard and instead make changes in a dialog box). Specify the type of change you want to make (see Figure 6-15).

Switching and Editing Templates

You can switch to a new template for this folder, or modify a template to insert your own customized options. The wizard displays the list of available templates (see Figure 6-16), each of which provides a specific type of interface.

 After you customize a folder, an additional template named Current displays in the template list. This template reflects your previous customization efforts. You cannot edit this template.

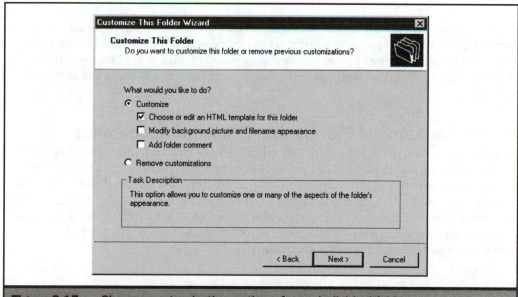

Figure 6-15. *Choose customization options for an individual folder*

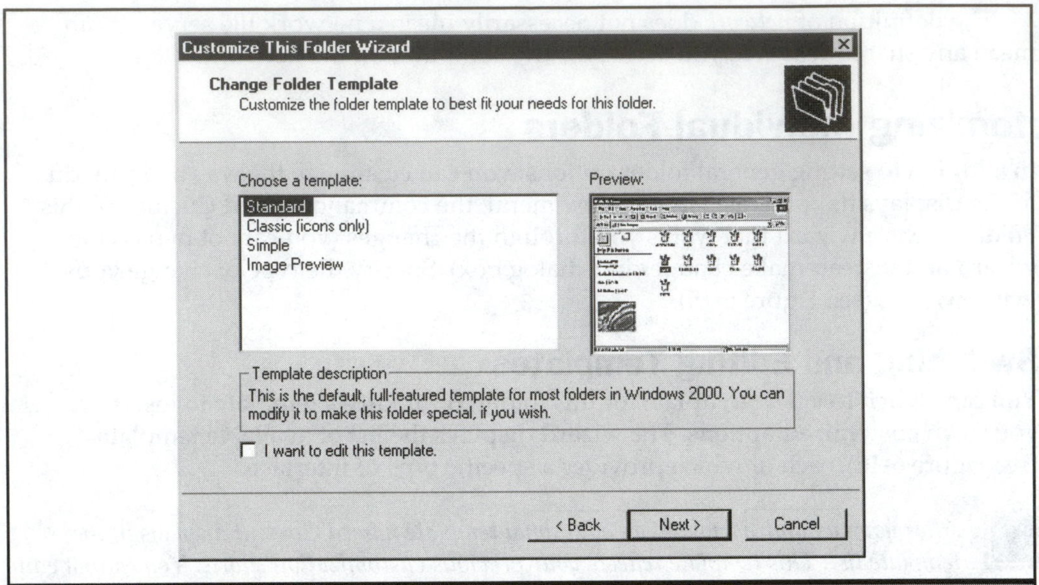

Figure 6-16. *Select a template to see its description in the wizard window*

You can edit the template, but you should be aware that I mean the word "edit" quite literally. No easy-to-use graphical window opens to offer choices—instead, the folder's HTML file, named Folder.htt, opens in Notepad. Figure 6-17 shows a part of the file for the Standard template. Edit the appropriate lines to make the changes you need.

Modify Background Picture and Filename Appearance

You can change the design of a folder by adding a background picture or changing the color scheme for the display of filenames. The background picture acts as wallpaper for the folder, and in fact the wallpaper files that are available for the desktop are also available for any folder. The filename appearance colors that can be changed include the color of the text and the background color of the box in which the filename appears.

If you add a background picture, you frequently must change the display of filenames in order to be able to see them clearly.

Folder Comments

You can add a comment about a folder to explain its use. The comment appears when you select the folder in a parent folder.

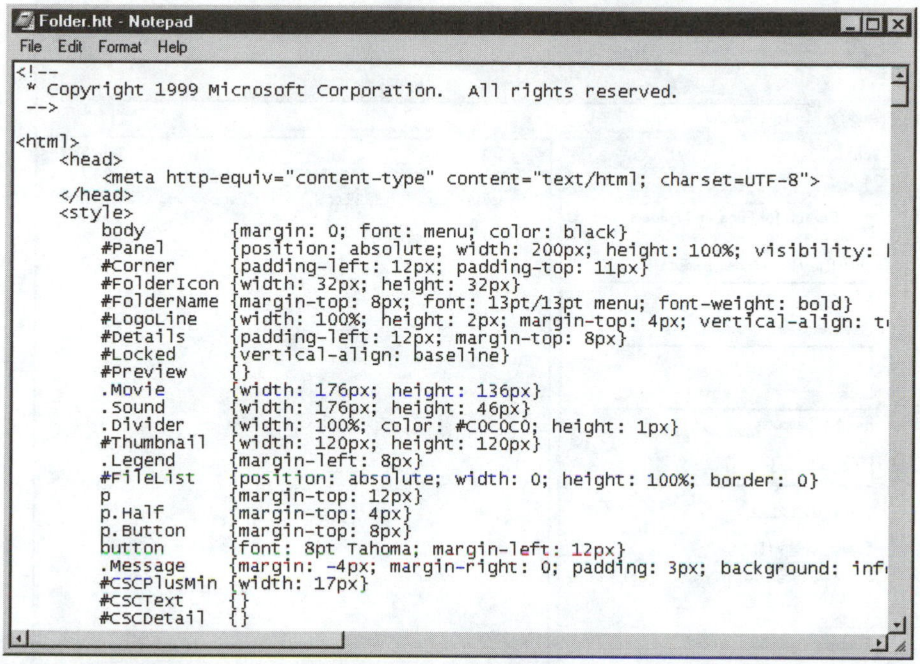

Figure 6-17.   *Edit the folder by making changes to Folder.htt*

System Folders

When you select the \%SystemRoot folder, the \%SystemRoot\System32 folder, or the \Program Files folder, neither My Computer nor Explorer automatically displays the folder's files. Instead, you see a message reminding you that there's probably no reason to be modifying the files in this folder. If you insist, there's a Show Files link you can click to display the folder contents.

Administrators and power users who don't want to bother with the extra work to access these system folders can change that behavior by renaming (or deleting) the files named Folder.htt, and Desktop.ini. These files exist in each of those folders, and you have to make sure you've enabled the display of hidden and system files in order to find them.

> **Tip**   *After you rename the files, renaming again to restore the original filenames doesn't restore the function.*

Search

You can search for files, folders, and other items from My Computer and Explorer by clicking the Search icon on the toolbar, or by pressing F3. Either action produces the Search pane shown in Figure 6-18.

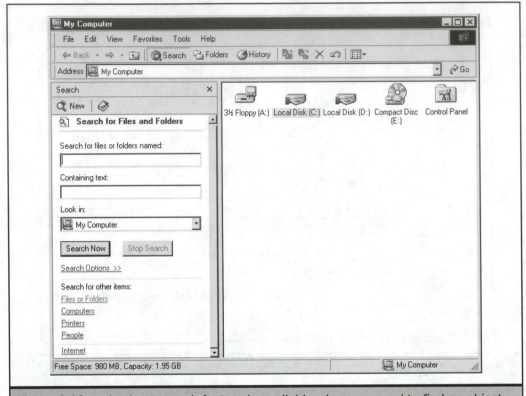

Figure 6-18. *A robust search feature is available when you need to find an object*

Note *The Search command replaces the Find command of previous versions of Windows (even on the Start menu).*

The Search feature works inconsistently, depending on the way you invoke it:

■ If you're working in My Computer mode (meaning you don't have a left pane displaying the hierarchy), the Search pane opens with My Computer as the default location for the Search. This occurs even if you select a drive in My Computer before clicking the icon on pressing F3.

■ If you're working in Explorer mode (the left pane displays the hierarchy), selecting a drive before invoking Search changes the default search location to all your local hard drive(s). Selecting another object in the hierarchy changes the default search location to the matching location.

My Network Places

My Network Places, which displays the computers and shared resources you can access, is a more robust incarnation of the Network Neighborhood folder in previous versions of Windows. The folder opens with two icons: Add Network Place and Entire Network.

Add Network Place

Use Add Network Place to create a link (to which you attach your own friendly name) to a folder on another computer, the Web, or an FTP site. This task is accomplished with the help of a wizard, which starts by asking you to enter the location of the folder you want to attach, using one of the following formats:

- \\server\share
- http://webserver/share
- ftp://ftpsite

You can also click Browse and expand the network objects to find the location you need.

When you're finished, the new location is added to My Network Places, saving you the trouble of drilling down through network objects to find it. It also appears in the hierarchy in the left pane of Explorer. All the locations you add to My Network Places are connected to your personalized settings; they do not appear to other users of your computer.

  Front Page extensions are required for adding Web folders.

Entire Network

Open the Entire Network icon to see the window shown in Figure 6-19. You'll notice immediately that you're not looking at objects representing the members of the network. You must select a link to specify what you're looking for when you browse the network.

  If your computer is part of a workgroup instead of a domain, an icon named Computers Near Me is also available. Open it to see the computers in your workgroup.

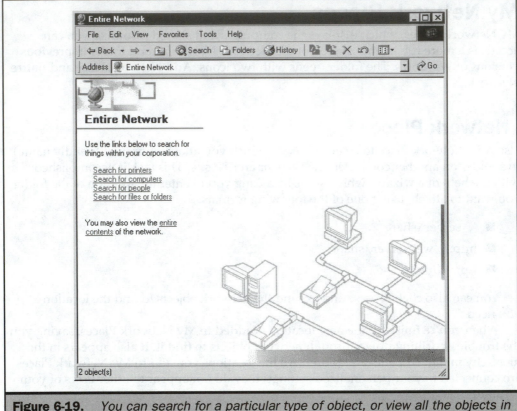

Figure 6-19.   *You can search for a particular type of object, or view all the objects in the network*

Use the search links to locate a particular type of network object, or use the entire contents link to move to the Entire Network window, seen in Figure 6-20.

If you are also connected to another network type, such as NetWare, an icon for that network is in the Entire Network Window.

■ Open the Directory object and then choose a domain to display the Active Directory.

■ Open the Network object and then choose a domain to display the computers.

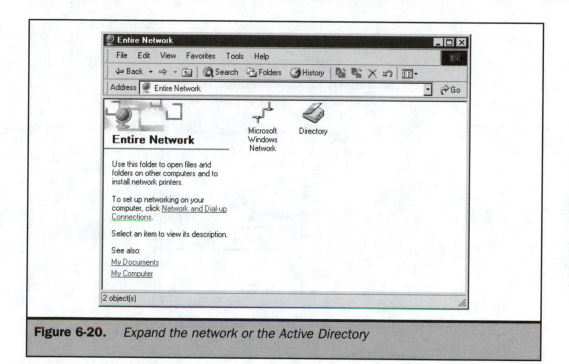

Figure 6-20.   *Expand the network or the Active Directory*

My Documents

The desktop folder My Documents is the default repository of all documents you save for software applications that are written for Windows 2000. The applications included with the operating system, such as Notepad and Wordpad, use My Documents as the default location when saving.

The folder itself is a shortcut, and the actual location is %BootDrive%:\Documents and Settings\%UserName%\My Documents. Therefore, each user who logs on to the computer has his or her own My Documents folder.

You can create subfolders under My Documents if you prefer to save documents by file type, by project, or by any other scheme you like.

Change the My Documents Target Folder

You can change the target location of the My Documents folder, which is useful if you prefer to save documents on a network server. Right-click the My Documents folder and choose Properties from the shortcut menu. The current location of the folder displays on the Target tab. Click the Move button to open the Browse for Folder dialog box, and expand the hierarchy as needed to find the target location you want (see Figure 6-21)

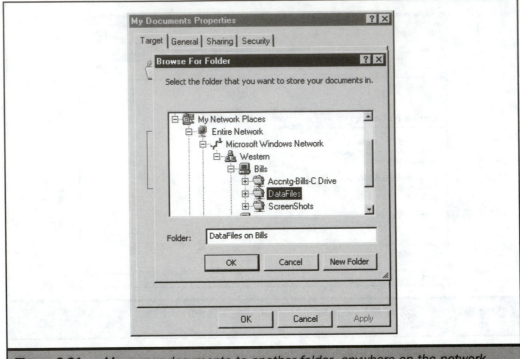

Figure 6-21. *Move your documents to another folder, anywhere on the network*

  You can also create a folder as you browse the hierarchy by clicking the New Folder button.

When you click OK, you're offered the opportunity to move all the contents of the current My Documents Folder to the new location. Most of the time, that's exactly what you need to do. You're also asked to confirm the movement of the system file, Desktop.ini. If you've customized the display of the My Documents folder, your customized options are in Desktop.ini, so you should move it, otherwise, it doesn't really matter.

  If you relocate My Documents to a remote computer, when you right-click on the folder the Make Available Offline command appears on the shortcut menu. It's a good idea to make sure the files in this folder are always available.

Remove the My Documents Folder

If you prefer to save documents in specific folders, not in My Documents, you can remove the My Documents folder from the desktop. Open My Computer or Explorer and choose Folder Options from the Tools menu (or open the Folders applet in Control Panel), and then move to the View tab. Scroll through the options, and deselect Show My Documents on the Desktop.

My Pictures

The My Documents desktop folder has a subfolder named My Pictures, designed to hold the pictures you create or edit with your digital camera (or any other picture files). This folder offers viewing technology that makes it possible to display thumbnail pictures instead of file icons (the View menu has a Thumbnails command, and it's selected by default for this folder). In addition, selecting a picture file displays that file in the built-in preview pane, where you can zoom, pan, or switch to a full-screen preview (see Figure 6-22).

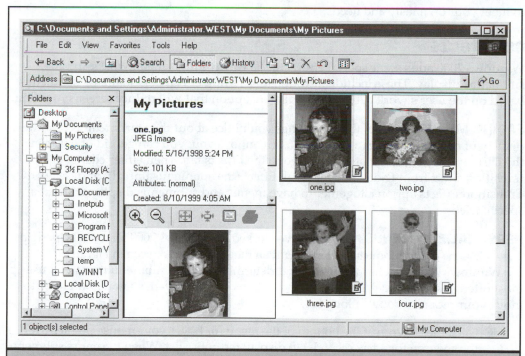

Figure 6-22. *Zoom and pan as you preview your picture files in the My Pictures folder*

You can add the same graphic functions to any folder, so you're not locked into using the My Pictures folder for full-featured storage of picture files. Instead, you can use or create a folder anywhere in your system hierarchy and then add the graphical features by opening the folder and choosing Customize This Folder. This launches the Customize This Folder wizard, described in the "Customizing Individual Folders" section earlier in this chapter.

On the second wizard window, select Choose or Edit an HTML template for this folder. When the templates display, select Image Preview. Click Finish and the new folder is imbued with the graphic functions. Choose Thumbnails from the View menu to complete your task.

Start Menu

The items on the Start menu and its submenus are slightly different from those found in previous versions of Windows NT and Windows 9*x*. Beyond that, they behave differently. The Windows 2000 Start Menu user interface has several new wrinkles, but if you don't care for them you can customize the Start menu's behavior to meet your own taste and needs.

Menu Effects

Windows 2000 adds some special effects to the way the Start menu works and the submenus display. These include introducing a fading effect, personalizing submenus based on the user's work habits, and a display option that will reduce screen crowding.

FADING MENUS   One of the first things you notice about the Start menu is that the display of menu items uses a fade effect. If it annoys you, you can get rid of it. Open the Display Properties dialog box and go to the Effects tab. Then either change the transition effect from Fade Effect to Scroll Effect (the submenus unfurl), or deselect the Transition Effects option altogether to have menus and submenus display without any special tricks.

PERSONALIZED MENUS   After you've worked in Windows 2000 for a while (perhaps a week), some of the submenus are shorter than they had been, as seen in Figure 6-23.

Windows 2000 watches you work and determines which submenu items you use most often. As a helpful gesture, only those items are displayed, so you don't have to move your mouse through a long list.

- Click the chevron at the bottom of the menu (or hover your mouse pointer over the chevron for a few seconds) to display the entire list. When the entire submenu displays, the most-used items are highlighted to make it easy to see them.

- If you want to turn off this feature, open the Taskbar and Start Menu Properties dialog box and deselect the Use Personalized Menus option (it's on the General tab).

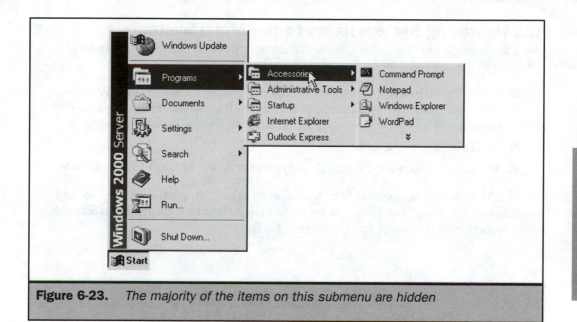

Figure 6-23.   *The majority of the items on this submenu are hidden*

SCROLLING PROGRAM MENU   By default, as your Programs menu gets crowded enough to fill the length of the column, a new column appears to continue the listings. Eventually, multiple columns can fill your screen. In the Taskbar and Start Menu Properties dialog box, select the option Scroll the Programs Menu to change this behavior so that all your programs are displayed on one column, which is scrollable.

Menu Items

By default, the following menu items are on the Start menu (from the bottom up):

- Shut Down
- Run
- Help
- Search
- Settings
- Documents
- Programs
- Windows Update

As you install software, the applications are added to your Start menu.

Add Operating System Items to the Menu System

There are some operating system items that do not appear on the Start menu by default, but you can add them:

- The Administrative Tools submenu under the Programs Menu for Windows 2000 Professional (it is on the Start menu for all versions of Windows 2000 Server).

- The Favorites menu item.

- The Logoff menu item, which displays on the menu as Logoff <username>.

To add these items, open the Start Menu and Taskbar Properties dialog box and move to the Advanced tab. Select the menu items you want to add from the Start Menu Settings section of the dialog box (see Figure 6-24).

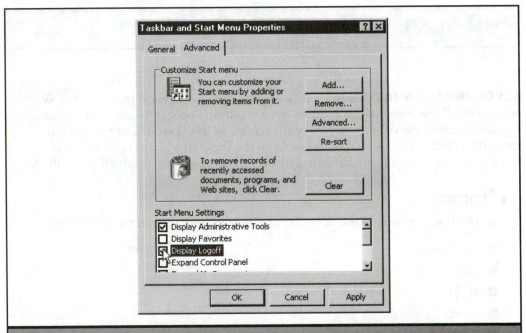

Figure 6-24. *Not all the available system items are included on your Start menu, but you can add those you want to use*

Expand Menu Items

You can also expand some of the existing Start menu items. "Expand" means you can add submenus to menu items that formerly opened folder windows, such as Control Panel or Printers. For example, if you select the option to expand Control Panel, the Control Panel submenu item under Settings displays a list of Control Panel programs instead of opening the Control Panel folder window. As seen in Figure 6-25, you can select the specific Control Panel applet you want to work with. The applet appears as a discrete window on your screen; you don't have to open Control Panel.

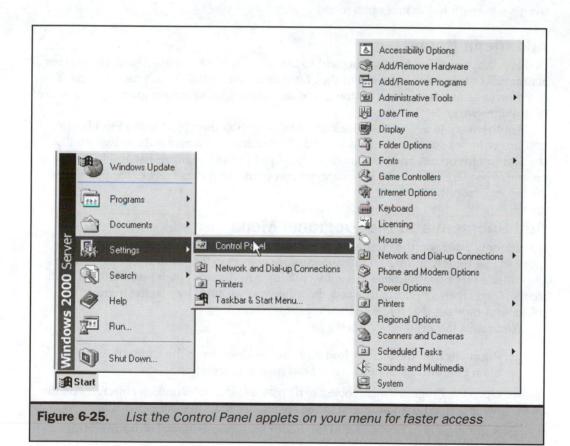

Figure 6-25. *List the Control Panel applets on your menu for faster access*

Explorer and Command Prompt Have Moved

One of the most important changes in the menu system for Windows 2000 is the fact that two oft-used programs, Windows Explorer and Command Prompt, have been moved from the Programs menu to the Accessories submenu.

Move Menu Items

You can rearrange the items on your Programs menu or any of its submenus. Just drag a listing to another position on the menu, from the Programs menu to a submenu, or from a submenu to the Programs menu.

Add Menu Items

You can drag any file object or shortcut to the Start button to create a menu item. This action places that item at the top of the Start menu, above the default menu items. You can then drag any item that's on the top of the Start menu to the Programs menu or any of its submenus.

Another way to accomplish the same goal is to drag the object to the Start button and hover for a couple of seconds instead of releasing the mouse button. Eventually the Start menu opens, and you can drag the object to the Programs list and hover for a couple of seconds. When the Programs menu opens, drag the object to the position you prefer and drop it.

Add Submenus to the Programs Menu

A submenu listing on the Programs menu (distinguished by an arrow) is nothing more than a folder, and the submenu items are objects in that folder. You can create a submenu on your Programs menu by creating a folder, and then populating it with items. You can also perform this task the other way around, by placing items in a folder and moving that folder to the Programs menu.

To create a folder, follow these steps:

1. Right-click on the Start button and choose Open from the shortcut menu to open the folder that holds your Start menu information.

2. Open the Programs menu object to display a folder that contains objects for all the items on the Programs menu (some are folders and some are individual items).

3. Right-click on a blank spot in the folder and choose New, Folder from the shortcut menu.

4. Name the new folder appropriately (it will be a listing for a submenu on the Programs menu).

5. Open the new folder as a window instead of a full screen.

6. Open Explorer or My Computer as a window instead of full screen.

7. Right-drag items from Explorer or My Computer to the new folder, choosing Create Shortcut(s) Here from the menu that appears when you release the right mouse button.

Alternatively, you can create a folder (in Explorer, My Computer, or on the desktop) and populate it with items. Then drag the folder to the Start button and follow the instructions described earlier to add it directly to the Programs menu.

 Folders and their accompanying submenus aren't restricted to the Programs menu; you can nest submenus. Just drag the object (folder or item) to the appropriate submenu.

Remove Menu Items

To remove a menu item, right-click the Start button and choose Open from the shortcut menu. Move to the folder that holds the item and delete it.

Share Menu Items with Other Users

When you install software, or manually place an item on the Programs menu (or submenu), the menu item exists only when you log on to the computer. Other users won't see it. You can provide access to menu items (and therefore to software) for all the other users who access this computer, or to specific users.

You need administrative rights to perform these tasks.

To share a menu item with all users, right-click the Start button and choose Open All Users from the shortcut menu. When the All Users folder opens, drill down to the appropriate folder and right-drag files from Explorer or My Computer into the folder (choose Create Shortcut(s) Here from the menu that appears when you release the right mouse button).

To share a menu item with specific users, open Explorer and expand the Documents and Settings folder (see Figure 6-26). Then expand the appropriate user folders and drill down to the Programs menu or submenu folder you need. Right-drag files from Explorer or My Computer into the target folder (choose Create Shortcut(s) Here from the menu that appears when you release the right mouse button).

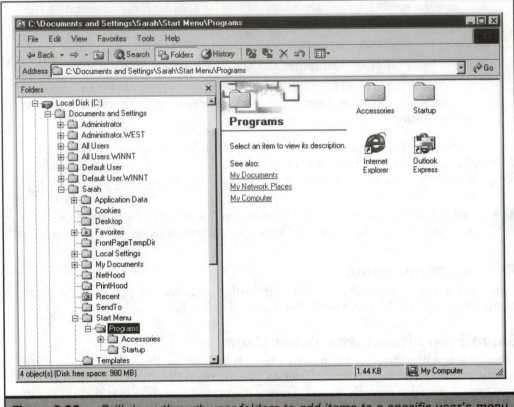

Figure 6-26.   *Drill down through user folders to add items to a specific user's menu*

The Taskbar

In addition to availing yourself of the tools built into the taskbar, you can customize the taskbar and its behavior to increase its usefulness.

Default Taskbar Tools

The taskbar holds the Start button, as well as buttons for every open window and dialog box. You can switch between windows by clicking the appropriate taskbar buttons.

The taskbar tray, which is located on the right side of the taskbar, displays the system time by default. You can enable the display of other icons on the taskbar tray by using the configuration options available for various features. For example, your sound card, your LAN connection, and other features have options to display icons on the tray. These icons give you one-click access to information and configuration options.

In addition, right-clicking on a blank spot on the taskbar displays the taskbar menu seen in Figure 6-27.

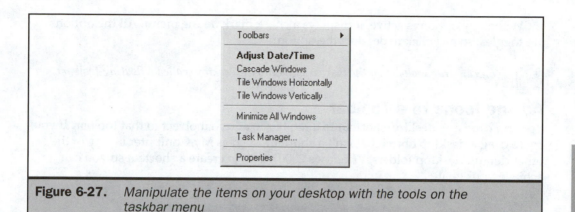

Figure 6-27.   *Manipulate the items on your desktop with the tools on the taskbar menu*

Taskbar Toolbars

You can put toolbars on your taskbar, grouping similar tools into their own toolbar set. The toolbars can be those provided with the operating system, or those you create yourself from scratch.

Built-in Toolbars

Windows 2000 provides four taskbar toolbars:

- **Quick Launch toolbar** contains icons for the desktop, Internet Explorer, and Outlook Express. By default, this toolbar is placed on your taskbar.

- **Address toolbar** has a replica of the Address toolbar in Internet Explorer. You can enter a URL without the need to open IE.

- **Links toolbar** contains icons for Web sites that Microsoft thinks you want to (or should) visit. Clicking an icon opens your browser, which travels to the appropriate Web site.

- **Desktop toolbar** contains icons for all the shortcuts on your desktop.

Displaying and Modifying Toolbars

To display a toolbar on the taskbar, or remove it, right-click a blank area on the taskbar and point to Toolbars. Select or deselect the toolbar of interest (it's a toggle).

Right-click on a blank spot on a toolbar to display a menu that lets you make the following changes to the toolbar's appearance:

- **View, Large** displays large icons (and enlarges the toolbar and taskbar to accommodate the new size).

- **View, Small** displays small icons (the default).

- **Show Text** displays the title of each icon in addition to the icon.

- **Show Title** displays the name of the toolbar.

When any option is active, it displays a check mark on the menu. All the options are toggles, so just click to deselect the option.

 You can drag toolbars off the taskbar and onto the desktop (called a floating toolbar).

Adding Icons to a Toolbar

You can drag any desktop shortcut to a toolbar to add that object to that toolbar. If you try to drag a desktop object that isn't a shortcut, such as My Computer or any of the other default desktop folders, Windows 2000 offers to create a shortcut so you can achieve your goal.

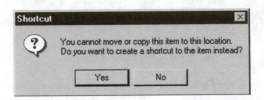

If you right-drag a desktop object that isn't a shortcut to a toolbar, the shortcut menu that appears when you release the mouse button has two choices: Create Shortcut(s) Here and Cancel.

When you left-drag a desktop shortcut to a toolbar, it isn't moved, it's copied. The shortcut remains on the desktop as well as the toolbar. On the other hand, using a right-drag on a desktop shortcut produces the usual right-drag menu when you release the mouse button (Copy Here, Move Here, Create Shortcut(s) Here, Cancel).

 You can move folders and data files to a toolbar in the same manner that you move icons.

If you want to resize a toolbar, point to the vertical bar at the left edge of the toolbar and drag it in the appropriate direction.

Removing Icons from a Toolbar

You can remove an icon from a toolbar by deleting it or by moving it to the desktop.

■ Delete a toolbar icon by right-clicking and choosing DELETE.

■ Drag a toolbar icon to the desktop to turn it into a desktop shortcut instead of a taskbar shortcut.

Creating Your Own Toolbars

It's frequently handy to have a toolbar that's dedicated to a collection of tools, a project you're working on, or some other set of related objects. To create a personalized toolbar, right-click on a blank spot on the taskbar and choose Toolbars, New Toolbar. This opens the New Toolbar dialog box.

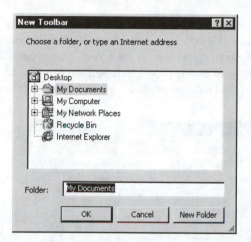

- Browse your system to find the folder you want to use for the toolbar.

- Enter a URL to create a new Address toolbar with a specific address.

- Create a new folder for the toolbar (first, expand drives and folders to reach the parent folder).

Active Desktop

You can opt to use the Windows 2000 Active Desktop interface, which lets you display Web pages on your desktop and have their contents updated automatically (hence the term "active"). For example, you could add a page that provides stock market prices, or weather conditions.

 There's no point in enabling this feature if you're not connected to the Internet.

Enable Active Desktop

There are several ways to turn your desktop into an active desktop.

- Open the Display Properties dialog box and move to the Web tab. Select the option to show Web content on the desktop; then select or deselect the Web pages you want to display. (You may find preselected Web sites on that page; the contents seem to vary, especially for Windows 2000 Server).

- Open the Folder Options applet in Control Panel (or from the Tools menu of a folder) and select Enable Web Content on My Desktop.

- Right-click a blank spot on the desktop and choose Active Desktop, Show Web Content.

The change is immediate; your browser opens and puts your selections on your desktop. On a side note, unless you used the Display Properties dialog box, where you could make your own selections, you may find Web pages you didn't expect. In fact, you may find error messages about pages that couldn't be found. Right-click a blank spot on the desktop and deselect the problem page from the menu.

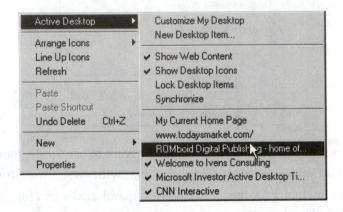

The desktop shortcut menu only includes the active desktop Web sites when the active desktop is enabled.

Choose Active Desktop Web Sites

To select Web sites for your active desktop, open the Web tab of the Display Properties dialog box. (The active desktop functions are not enabled unless the active desktop is enabled.)

Select and Deselect Existing Active Desktop Sites

You can select and deselect existing sites by clicking the check box (when you select and deselect sites with the desktop shortcut menu, those changes are reflected in this dialog box).

Remove Active Desktop Sites

To remove a site, select it and click Delete. If you want to reestablish this site you'll have to add it back from scratch, because removing a site is not the same as deselecting it.

Add New Active Desktop Sites

If you want to add more sites to your active desktop, click New to open the New Active Desktop Item dialog box seen in Figure 6-28.

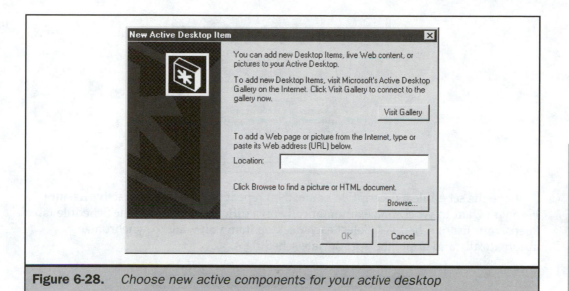

Figure 6-28. *Choose new active components for your active desktop*

- Click Visit Gallery to travel to Microsoft's Active Desktop Gallery, which features a wide choice of active desktop items.

- Enter the URL for Web site in the Location text box.

- Click Browse to search your system for graphic files or HTML documents.

 If you enter a URL, a dialog box appears to confirm the site address and offer the opportunity to enter a password, if one is necessary.

Your selection is downloaded (a process called *synchronizing*), and its entry is added to the list of active Web sites on the Display Properties dialog box, as well as the list that appears on the desktop shortcut menu.

Configure Synchronization

By default, active desktop items are synchronized (the display is updated) manually. To perform this task, place your pointer along the top of the active desktop item until a gray bar appears above the display window. Then click the arrow on the left side of the bar and choose Synchronize from the menu.

To establish a synchronization schedule, select the item on the Web tab of the Display Properties dialog box and choose Properties. Move to the Schedule tab and select the option to synchronize on a schedule. Click New to create a new synchronization schedule.

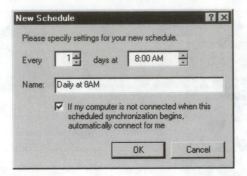

Give the schedule a descriptive name; then repeat this task for any active desktop item you want to synchronize automatically on a different schedule. The Schedule tab keeps your list of schedules. Select each desktop item you want to synchronize automatically and apply the appropriate schedule.

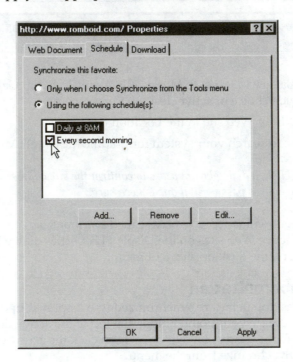

A constantly changing Web site, such as a stock ticker (shown in the illustration) or a hurricane watch, is far more useful if it is updated very frequently.

Most such sites provide a customization option (usually a button) on the desktop item so you can set a synchronization schedule that keeps you abreast of the news.

Recover a Broken Active Desktop

If Windows 2000 has a problem updating or loading your active desktop, the feature is turned off and the Active Desktop Recovery window seen in Figure 6-29 appears.

Most of the time this problem occurs immediately after you've added a new active item to your desktop, usually caused by an unavailable Web page (although a system crash will frequently cause the same problem). You can use the options on the Recovery window to fix the URL, deselect the new item, or turn off the active desktop feature.

LEARNING
THE BASICS

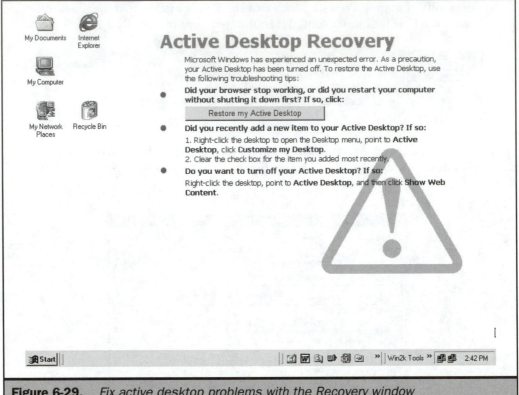

Figure 6-29.   *Fix active desktop problems with the Recovery window*

Interface Tips and Tricks

Here are some shortcuts and tips that make life easier as you navigate your system. These represent my own discoveries as I played with Windows 2000; you'll find plenty of your own to add to this list.

Open With on Shortcut Menus

Even when a data file is associated with a program, you can easily use another application to open the file. The Windows 2000 shortcut menu for data files includes an Open With command in addition to the Open Command. You no longer have to select the file, then hold down the SHIFT key while you right-click, to find this command.

RunAs Command

Suppose you're logged onto a computer as a user with standard user permissions, or you're accessing files on a remote computer. You need to perform a task that requires administrative permissions levels. If you know the logon name and password of an administrator, you no longer have to log off and then log back on. Instead, you can use the RunAs command. This command lets you start any program, the MMC, or Control Panel item as long as you provide the appropriate user account and password information.

The syntax for RunAs is

```
RUNAS [/profile] [/env] [/netonly] /user:<UserName> program
```

where:

- **/profile** tells the system that the user's profile must be loaded
- **/env** tells the system to use the current environment
- **/netonly** is used if the credentials are only used for remote access
- **/user** *<UserName>* should be in the form user@domain (do not use with /netonly) or domain\user
- **program** is the path and command line for the executable file

The system prompts for the password connected to the username you enter in the command line.

Change the Way Explorer Opens

If you want Explorer to behave the way it did in previous versions of Windows, you can change its configuration. First, create a desktop shortcut to \%SystemRoot%\Explorer.exe. Right-click the shortcut icon and choose Properties from the shortcut menu. Move to the Shortcut tab and add the following parameter to the path in the Target text box: **/e,c:** (be sure there's a space between the filename and this new parameter). Hereafter, when you use the shortcut to open Explorer, Drive C is selected and expanded. You can create multiple shortcuts that are configured to open and expand other drives, or to select specific folders. Be sure to name each shortcut with a descriptive title.

Change Regedit's Memory

Regedit has changed its behavior so that the key you are working in when you close the editor is displayed when you next launch Regedit. If you've been working deep down in the subkey structure, this can be extremely annoying, because it can take quite some time to scroll to the top of the hierarchy.

**LEARNING
THE BASICS**

You can remember to close all the expanded keys and return to the top of the hierarchy before exiting Regedit, or you can edit the registry to stop this annoying behavior.

Regedit stores the last key you used in the registry, so you have to delete that information and then stop any subsequent efforts to write the information. Because the latter step involves security and permissions, you must use Regedt32 to perform this task. To do this, go to

HKEY_CURRENT_USER\Software\Microsoft\Windows\CurrentVersion\ Applets\Regedit

Then open the LastKey item and delete the value, creating an empty string. Click OK to close the String Editor. Then follow these steps:

1. Select the Regedit key in the left pane again, and choose Security, Permissions.

2. When the Permissions for Regedit dialog box opens, click Advanced to open the Access Control Settings dialog box.

3. Select your user account and click View/Edit.
   For the Set Value item, select the Deny check box and click OK to return to the Access Control Settings dialog box. A new item of the type Deny now exists for the user account.

4. Select the new Deny <user account> item and click View/Edit.
   Select the option at the bottom of the dialog box to apply the permisions only within this container (this confines the Set Value denial to the Regedit subkey, and prevents it from affecting the Favorites subkey).

5. Close Regedt32.

| Note | *This is a per user setting, not a computer setting.* |

The Regedit key does not exist if you haven't run Regedit on this machine. If the key isn't there, don't add it to the registry manually-instead open and close Regedit to create the key.

Quick Access to My Computer

If you're not using the Quick Launch toolbar on the taskbar (or even if you are), you can put a shortcut to My Computer on the Start menu. In fact, you have two options for performing this task, and each has a different result.

Drag the My Computer icon to the Start button to place My Computer on the top portion of the Start menu. When you point to it, a submenu appears listing all the contents of the My Computer folder. This is a quick way to get to any of those items via the Start menu.

Right-drag the My Computer icon to a blank spot on the desktop, and choose Create Shortcut(s) Here from the menu that appears when you release the right mouse button. Then drag that shortcut to the Start button to add My Computer as a menu item (with no submenu for the individual elements in the My Computer folder). Selecting this menu item opens the My Computer folder.

Copy and Paste into DOS Windows

If you want to copy text from a DOS window to the clipboard, select the text with the left mouse button, and then click the right mouse button to copy it to the clipboard. To paste the contents of the clipboard into a DOS window, merely right-click in the DOS window at the appropriate point.

LEARNING
THE BASICS

Chapter 7

The Control Panel Applets

Most of the installation and configuration chores you attend to in Windows 2000 are performed in one of the Control Panel applets. This chapter offers an overview of some of those applets, omitting those that are covered in other chapters throughout this book. For convenience, the applets are presented here in alphabetical order, just as they are in the Control Panel.

 While it may not be specifically stated in the discussion of each applet, Windows 2000 offers the ability to put an icon on the taskbar for many of the Control Panel utilities.

Accessibility Options

The Accessibility applet contains a variety of options for users whose vision, hearing, or mobility is impaired. Its Properties dialog box has tabs for configuring Keyboard, Sound, Display, Mouse, and General options.

Keyboard Options

The Keyboard tab offers utilities that make using the keyboard easier by requiring less input from the user. A new option named Show Extra Keyboard Help In Programs is useful for applications that provide extra help for keyboard actions.

StickyKeys, when enabled, permit the user to press the SHIFT, CTRL, ALT, and Windows keys without simultaneously pressing the second key when using a key combination shortcut (such as CTRL-C). The second key is pressed separately. You can configure StickyKeys to toggle on and off with a keyboard shortcut, instead of opening the Accessibility applet. To display an icon in the taskbar system tray when StickyKeys is activated, select the Show StickyKeys Status On Screen check box.

FilterKeys lets you adjust the sensitivity of the keyboard to insure that unintentional keystrokes are ignored. This is accomplished by setting the length of time a key must be held down before registering as a keystroke. Once FilterKeys is enabled, click the Settings button to open the Settings For FilterKeys dialog box. Here you can elect to use a single-key shortcut to enable FilterKeys without having to use the Accessibility applet. In addition, you can set options to ignore repeated and quick keystrokes, as well as set the timing intervals for such keystrokes. To make sure you're aware that FilterKeys is enabled, you can also set notification options that will add an icon to the taskbar system tray and produce a beep when keys are pressed or accepted.

The ToggleKeys feature alerts you when you're working with the CAPS LOCK, NUM LOCK, and SCROLL LOCK keys enabled (a really annoying circumstance). The utility uses beeps to let you know when you've inadvertently pressed one of those keys.

Sound Options

The Sound tab has options for users who are hearing impaired, or who work in a noisy environment. Two features, SoundSentry and ShowSounds, are available to provide visual clues whenever your computer produces a sound. With SoundSentry enabled, you'll see a visual clue every time your computer produces a sound. The visual indication is, by default, a flashing caption (title) bar in the active window. However, the flash is momentary and easy to miss if you're not paying attention, so you might want to change the default. To use a different visual indicator, click Settings and make your selection from the drop-down list. ShowSounds requires applications that support this feature, which displays descriptive text or icons when a sound is produced.

Display Options

The Display tab contains a single option, Use High Contrast, which can be quite useful to a visually impaired user. This feature overrides application-specific colors in favor of a color scheme designated by the user.

In addition, a magnifier is available (see "Utility Manager" later in this section).

Mouse Options

Anyone who has a hard time getting the mouse to behave properly should consider turning on the MouseKeys feature found in the Mouse tab. You can control the mouse using the keys on the keyboard's number pad. To adjust the speed and acceleration of the mouse pointer when using the number keys, click Settings to open the Settings for MouseKeys dialog box. Here you enable a keyboard shortcut for MouseKeys, set the speed and acceleration, and designate the NUM LOCK position that turns MouseKeys on and off. You can use the CTRL and SHIFT keys to temporarily speed up or slow down the pointer.

General Options

The General tab, seen in Figure 7-1, provides a number of miscellaneous options. You can automatically turn on accessibility features, activate warning messages, enable support for alternative serial input devices, and apply the selected accessibility features to the logged-on user or to all users.

Additional Accessibility Options

There are some additional utilities that qualify as accessibility options, even though they're not available through the Control Panel applet. To access them, choose Programs | Accessories | Accessibility from the Start menu. The following sections show what you'll find.

Accessibility Wizard

The wizard walks you through the steps of setting accessibility options for users who are visually, hearing, or touch impaired.

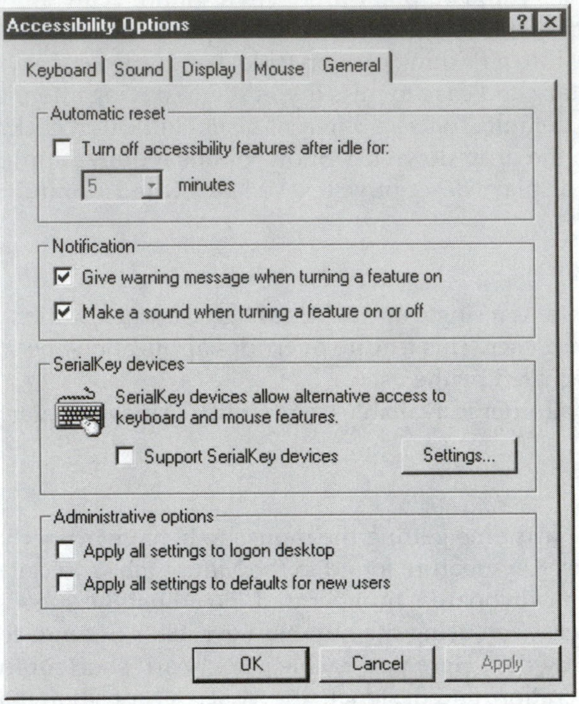

Figure 7-1. *Manage option behavior on the General tab*

Magnifier

The Magnifier is a handy tool that splits your screen and displays an enlarged view of the area around the mouse pointer in the top half of the screen. As you move your mouse pointer, the Magnifier changes the display to reflect the new location. When the Magnifier starts, it automatically opens the Magnifier Settings dialog box. Here you can set the magnification level, as well as change the tracking, color, and presentation options. You can minimize the Magnifier Settings dialog box to get it out of your way. However, closing (as opposed to minimizing) it also closes the Magnifier. You can also close the Magnifier by right-clicking on the Magnifier portion of the screen (the top half) and choosing Exit from the shortcut menu. If you elect to hide (as opposed to close) the Magnifier, the only way to bring it back is by enabling Show Magnifier in the Magnifier Settings dialog box.

Narrator

For the visually impaired, the Narrator provides a text-to-speech utility that reads the data displayed on the active window, including the contents, menu options, and any text you may have entered. It works with the Windows 2000 desktop, as well as Internet Explorer, Wordpad, Notepad, the Control Panel, and Windows 2000 setup. It may or may not work with other programs.

On-Screen Keyboard

The On-Screen Keyboard is a graphical representation of a standard keyboard that floats onscreen when activated. It is extremely handy for anyone with limited mobility who may have trouble using the keyboard but can adequately manipulate the mouse. Click a key to simulate typing that key. Actually, this is great for all the closet hunt-and-peck typists out there. You can tell everyone that your carpal tunnel syndrome prevents you from using the keyboard and you're forced to use the mouse instead.

Utility Manager

In addition to providing access to the Magnifier and the Narrator, the Utility Manager also offers a couple of options for automating the startup of both utilities. You can elect to have either or both start automatically each time you start Windows, or each time you start the Utility Manager. Other than setting these options, its use is rather limited. It's easier to create a shortcut to the utilities or even access them directly from the Accessibility menu.

Add/Remove Hardware

If your computer BIOS, all the internal components, and all the hardware devices connected to ports are compatible with Advanced Configuration and Power Interface (ACPI) and Plug and Play, you'll probably never have to use the Add/Remove Hardware applet. Adding a new device will result in Plug and Play recognition during the next startup, and the device will be installed automatically.

Alas, unless every computer in your enterprise is fairly new, you won't achieve this state of automated network administration. As a result, you need to know how to use the Add/Remove Hardware applet. Typically, Add/Remove Hardware is launched to perform the following tasks:

- Install hardware that was not detected by Plug and Play during startup
- Uninstall hardware
- Unplug (or eject) hardware

LEARNING
THE BASICS

Install Hardware Devices

If the device you add to a computer isn't detected and installed automatically, open the Add/Remove Hardware applet to install the device drivers manually. There are too many device types to discuss the specific steps for installation for each, so this section is an overview of the manual device installation procedure.

Open the Add/Remove Hardware applet, click Next to move past the opening window (a welcome screen), and select Add/Troubleshoot a device in the next window. Windows 2000 launches a search for a new Plug and Play device (which will most certainly fail, or it would have detected the device during startup). The wizard next presents a list of devices that are already installed, which you can use for troubleshooting installed devices (covered later in this section).

Select Add A New Device and then click Next to move to the Find New Hardware Wizard window. Windows 2000 can detect some non-Plug and Play devices and you can opt to let the wizard search for the new device, or skip the search to install the device manually. If the search succeeds, follow the prompts to complete the installation of the drivers. If the search fails, the wizard automatically presents the device list you see if you choose a manual installation. Select the appropriate device, and follow the prompts to complete the installation.

If the device driver has a Microsoft digital signature, installation is automatic. If the driver does not have a digital signature, you'll see a Digital Signature Not Found message and you're asked if you wish to continue. Click Yes to complete the installation.

Troubleshoot Hardware Devices

To troubleshoot a device, follow the same steps for installing a new device. After the wizard fails to locate new hardware, the list of installed devices is displayed. Select the device you want to diagnose and click Next. Then follow the prompts (which differ by device). Most of the time, you're instructed to click Finish on the wizard window, which automatically launches the Windows 2000 hardware troubleshooter.

Troubleshooters work by asking users to select an option. The first set of options on the hardware troubleshooter are problem descriptions, as seen in Figure 7-2.

The troubleshooter makes a suggestion and asks if it worked. This continues until you solve the problem or the troubleshooter gives up and recommends you call a support desk.

If you're comfortable with hardware issues, you can use the Device Manager to troubleshoot hardware problems with more flexibility than the troubleshooter offers. See the discussion in the "Device Manager" section later in this chapter.

Uninstall Hardware

If you're going to remove a hardware device from the computer, you should tell Windows 2000 so it doesn't load the device drivers and look for the device during startup. The correct order of tasks is

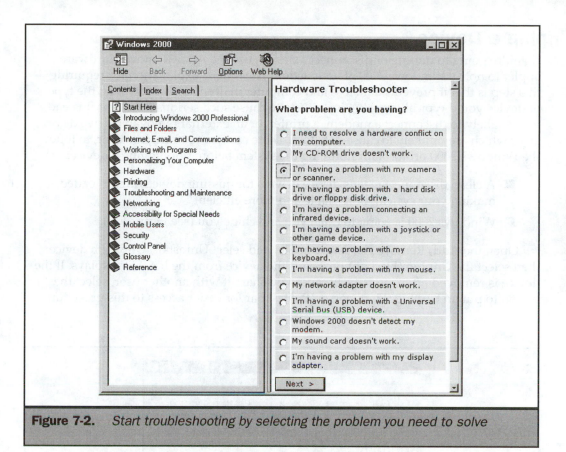

Figure 7-2.   *Start troubleshooting by selecting the problem you need to solve*

1. Use the Add/Remove Hardware applet to uninstall the device.

2. Physically remove the device.

Open the Add/Remove Hardware applet and select Uninstall/Unplug a device; then choose Uninstall. Select the device, and confirm the decision to uninstall it. Then shut down and remove the device.

Windows 2000 does not remove device drivers when you uninstall a device. If you think this might present a problem when you install a new device of the same type, check the documentation for the device or contact the manufacturer to learn the names and locations of installed device drivers so you can remove them manually.

If you don't remove the drivers and you reinstall the device in the future, Windows 2000 finds it during the search for devices, even if it was not found automatically during its original installation.

Unplug a Device

If you're going to unplug or disconnect a device, use the Add/Remove Hardware applet to notify Windows 2000 of your action. The official explanation for requiring this step is that it prevents data loss and computer malfunctions. However, the type of device you'd typically unplug isn't likely to cause such serious problems. Instead, you're likely to disconnect a modem, a printer, or an external removable drive device, all of which are unlikely to cause data loss. There are two reasons, however, to follow the Windows 2000 protocol for notifying the system before unplugging a device:

■ A clean disconnect means device drivers for missing devices aren't loaded, making your system more stable and more efficient.

■ Windows 2000 is going to catch you and chide you (see Figure 7-3).

Open the Add/Remove Hardware applet and select Uninstall/Unplug a device; then select the Unplug/Eject option. Select the device from the list that displays. If the device is removed often, perhaps because you share it with another user, select the option to put an Unplug/Eject icon on the taskbar for easier access to this procedure.

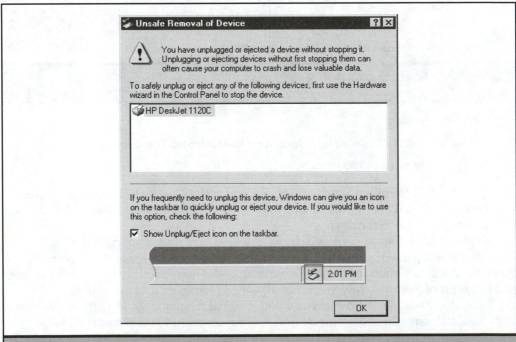

Figure 7-3.   *Oops, I moved the printer to another computer and forgot to tell the operating system*

Add/Remove Programs

The Add/Remove Programs applet has received a facelift from previous versions of Windows, as you can see in Figure 7-4. New features have been added and existing ones modified. The Sort By text box at the top of the window lets you sort the list of installed applications by Name, Size, Frequency Of Use, and Date Last Used.

Change/Remove Programs

By default, the applet opens to the Change/Remove Programs window, which lists all the Windows programs currently installed on your computer. Select a listing to gain additional information about the application. The selected listing displays Change and/or Remove buttons as follows:

■ If the listing displays separate Change and Remove buttons, you can use the Change button to restart the installation and make changes to the setup configuration. You may need to reinsert the original CD to access files not copied to your hard drive the first time.

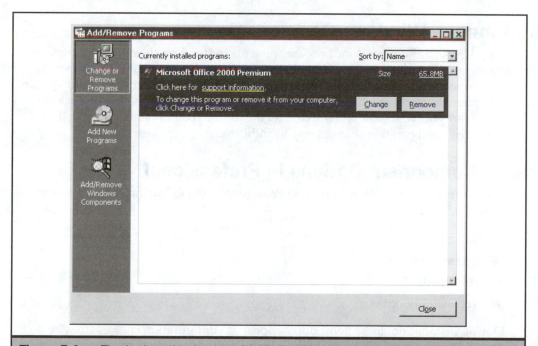

Figure 7-4.   *The look and behavior of Add/Remove programs has changed*

■ If the listing presents a Change/Remove button, probably your only option is to remove it.

Add New Programs

Use the Add New Programs button to install an application. Three options appear in the Add/Remove Programs window:

■ **Add a program from CD-ROM or floppy disk**   Clicking the button named CD or Floppy launches the wizard that walks you through the installation. The wizard searches the floppy and CD-ROM drives for a setup program. As soon as it finds one, it provides the path and filename. Click Finish to install the program, or click Browse to locate another file.

■ **Add programs from Microsoft**   This option launches your browser and takes you directly to the Microsoft update Web site, where you can find and download updates, patches, and drivers.

■ **Add programs from your network**   If applications are available for installation from a network share, a list of those programs appears in the Add Programs From Your Network list. If the administrator has categorized applications, you can filter the list by using the Category drop-down list.

Add/Remove Windows Components

Clicking the Add/Remove Windows Components button launches the Windows Components Wizard, which displays a list of available Windows 2000 components. Select components to add and deselect components to remove them from your system. If a component has choices of subcomponents, you can view the choices by clicking Details. After you've selected/deselected all the desired components, click Next to complete the configuration changes you've indicated.

Missing Component Options in Professional

During the installation of Windows 2000 Professional, the following components are installed by default:

■ Games
■ Accessories
■ Multimedia
■ Accessibility options

During installation, these items don't appear as configuration choices (they're hidden), so there's no opportunity to omit them. After installation, the items don't appear in the Windows Components section of the Add/Remove Programs applet in the Control Panel, and therefore can't be removed in order to gain back disk space.

You can change Setup to provide the option to skip the installation of one or more of these components, or you can change the Windows Components display so you can remove these components after installation.

Display Hidden Items During Installation

You can display the hidden items during Setup by making changes to the installation procedure, but because you can't make changes to files on a CD-ROM, you'll have to use a network share as the installation source drive.

Copy the \i386 folder of your Windows 2000 Professional CD-ROM to a network share. Then open a command prompt and expand the file named Sysoc.in_ (the command is **expand -r sysoc.in_**). Open Sysoc.inf (the file that results from expanding with the –r switch) in Notepad or another text editor.

Locate the "old base components" line and find the lines for the components you want to appear in the component list. Remove the word HIDE and the comma that follows it.

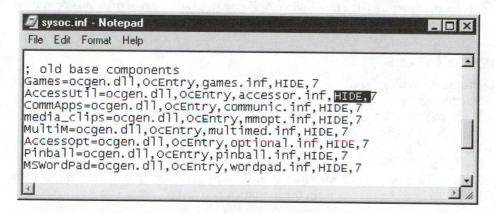

Some of the entries are interdependent on other entries: for example, if you want to display Games, you must display Accessutil. Check the Windows Components display in the Add/Remove Programs applet for Windows 2000 Server to see which components are nested. When you've finished making changes, save and close the file.

 Rename Sysoc.in_ to Sysoc.bak so it isn't expanded in the future.

Display Hidden Items in Add/Remove Programs

After installation, Sysoc.inf in the %SystemRoot%\Inf directory controls the display of components in the Add/Remove Programs applet in the Control Panel. Make the changes described above to the file to add components to the displayed list.

 You can use the same technology in reverse, hiding components you don't want users to change.

LEARNING THE BASICS

Date/Time

The Date/Time applet has survived unchanged from Windows NT 4. The Date & Time tab contains, appropriately enough, a calendar and a clock. To change the system date, select the month from the drop-down list and select the day in the calendar. Changing the time is simply a matter of resetting the clock by using the up and down arrows or by typing in the correct time.

To change your time zone, click the Time Zone tab and select the correct time zone from the drop-down list. If your time zone supports Daylight Savings Time, you can have the computer automatically adjust the clock for you by enabling the daylight savings option at the bottom of the tab.

Fax

The Fax applet is not part of the Control Panel when you first install Windows 2000. It appears after you install a fax device (or if you upgrade from a previous operating system in which fax services had been installed).

Configure Faxes

The Properties dialog box for the Fax applet, seen in Figure 7-5, provides everything you need to set up and manage faxing services.

The data you enter is automatically transferred to the cover page you select when sending a fax. On the Cover Pages tab, you can select a preloaded cover page and use it as is, modify it, or create your own.

Use the Status Monitor tab to turn the Fax Status Monitor on and off, and to adjust its settings. The monitor provides information during the sending or receiving of faxes (you can also cancel a fax call from the monitor). You can place an icon on the taskbar for quick access to the Status Monitor tab, the Fax Queue, and the My Faxes folder.

Configure Faxing Properties

The Advanced Options tab provides access to additional features:

- **Fax Service Management Console**   This displays your installed fax devices and provides configuration options for logging fax events.
- **Fax Service Management Help**   This set of help files is specifically focused on managing fax services.
- **Add a Fax Printer**   This adds a fax printer to your Printers folder. You can create multiple fax printers (they're virtual printers) to accommodate a variety of configuration options.

Use the Fax Service Management Console to change the faxing properties for a device. Right-click the device listing and choose Properties to open the device's

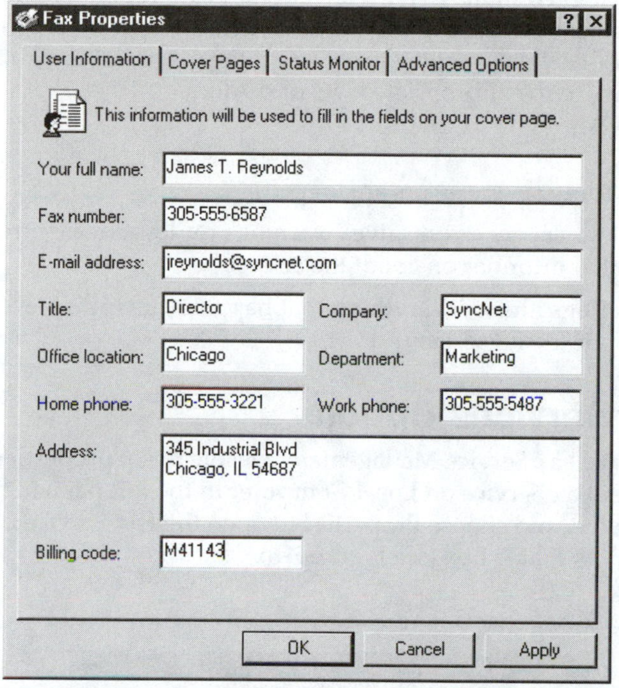

Figure 7-5.   *Add the information you want to attach to the faxes you send*

Properties dialog box. You can enable or disable the send/receive functions, and manage incoming faxes by opting for one of the following actions:

■ Print the fax to a designated printer.

■ Save the fax to a file.

■ Send the fax to a designated local e-mail address via Microsoft Exchange Server.

You can also configure the level of detail you want to log for each fax event. Logged events include the following:

■ **Inbound**   Records events while receiving faxes

■ **Initialization/Termination**   Records events while starting and stopping faxes

■ **Outbound**   Records events while sending faxes

■ **Unknown**   Records all other fax events

The events are logged in the Event Viewer Application Log. Within the Fax Service Management Console you can select the level of detail you want recorded in the Application Log for each fax event. Simply select the event in the right pane, right-click, and choose the appropriate level of detail:

- None
- Minimum (only severe errors are logged)
- Medium (logs severe errors, gives warnings for less severe errors, and provides some detailed information about the session)
- Maximum (logs almost everything that happens, including every attempt to fax and every successful session)

Configure Fax Services Options

You can also use the Fax Service Management console to set properties for the fax service. Right-click Fax Service on Local Computer in the left pane of the Fax Service Management console, and choose Properties to open the Fax Service on Local Computer Properties dialog box (see Figure 7-6).

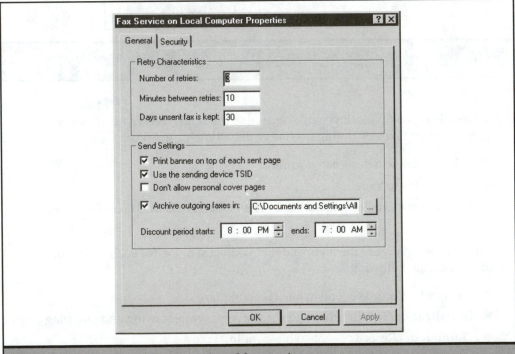

Figure 7-6.   *Configure the behavior of fax services*

The General tab provides options to configure the retry parameters. You can also customize the settings for sending faxes:

- **Print Banner on top of each sent page.**   The banner contains the date, time, and page number. If used in conjunction with the TSID option, the banner will also include the TSID (Transmitting Station Identifier).

- **Use the sending device TSID.**   The TSID typically includes the sending fax number and business name. If you disable this option, the fax number entered in the User Information tab of the Fax Properties sheet is used.

- **Don't allow personal cover pages.**   Enable this option to insure consistency in all faxes, which means that only the default cover page can be used on outgoing faxes.

- **Archive outgoing faxes in.**   Stores a copy of all outgoing faxes in the specified location.

- **Discount period starts.**   To take advantage of discount rates based on the calling time, specify the time range during which discounts are available from your local phone company. When a user sends a fax configured to be sent using discount rates, the fax is held until the time specified here.

The Security tab (Figure 7-7) lets you set faxing permissions for users and groups.

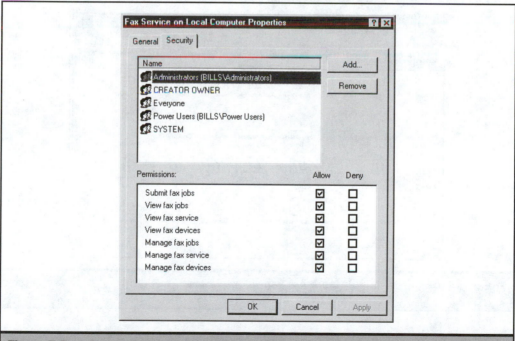

Figure 7-7.   *Select a user or group to specify permissions*

LEARNING THE BASICS

Fonts

You can use the Fonts applet to install, view, and delete fonts on your system. As you can see in Figure 7-8, all the fonts installed on your computer appear in the Fonts folder. To see what a font looks like, double-click its listing to display a window with examples of various sizes of the font.

Supported Fonts

Windows 2000 comes with built-in support for outline, vector, and raster font-types.

Outline Fonts

Outline fonts are rendered from line and curve commands, and can be scaled and rotated without losing readability. The outline fonts supported by Windows 2000 include

- TrueType (the icon is two overlapped capital *T*'s)
- OpenType (the icon is an italic capital *O*)
- Type 1 (from Adobe Systems—the icon is a capital *A*)

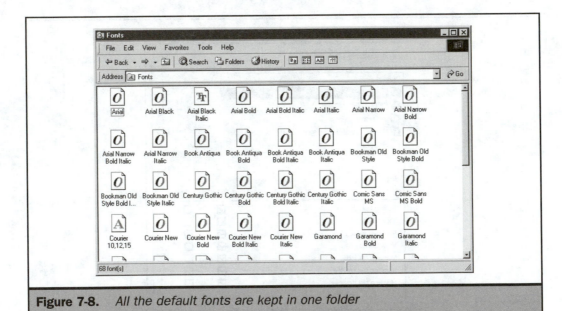

Figure 7-8.   *All the default fonts are kept in one folder*

Vector Fonts

Vector fonts are rendered mathematically and are used for plotters. Windows 2000 supports the following vector fonts:

- Modern
- Roman
- Script

Raster Fonts

Raster fonts are stored and printed as bitmap images. Windows 2000 includes support for raster fonts for backward compatibility, and the following fonts are supported:

- Courier
- MS Sans Serif
- MS Serif
- Small
- Symbol

Installing Fonts

To install a new font, choose File | Install New Font, which opens the Add Fonts dialog box. Move to the appropriate drive and folder, and select the font you want to add to your system. Then click OK to add the font. The new font now appears in the Fonts folder and is available to applications and for printing.

Configure the Fonts Folder

You can alter the way you view fonts to make it easier to find what you're looking for. Use the View menu to choose to display fonts grouped by similarity, or to hide the listings for variations of the same font (bold, italic, etc.).

If you use TrueType fonts exclusively, choose Tools | Folder options and move to the TrueType Fonts tab to select the option to display only TrueType fonts in your applications.

Keyboard

Use the Keyboard applet to set the response rate of your keyboard and/or to change the input languages and keyboard layouts.

Configure Response Rates

The Speed tab includes Character Repeat and Cursor Blink Rate options, which you can adjust to match your own preferences.

■ To adjust the delay between the appearance of the first instance and the second instance of a character when you hold a key down, use the Repeat Delay slider bar. Move it toward Long to increase the time it takes for a second character to appear, or toward Short to decrease the time.

■ To retard the speed at which a character repeats when you hold a key down, use the Repeat Rate slider bar.

■ If the cursor drives you nuts because it blinks too quickly or too slowly, here's your chance to have it your way. Just move the Cursor Blink Rate slider to Slow or Fast.

Configure Language and Layout

The Input Locales tab is the place to change the language and keyboard layout. (This tab is identical to the Input Locales tab found on the Regional Options applet.) If the software application you're running supports other languages or layouts, you can change the defaults by clicking Add to open the Add Input Locale dialog box and selecting the appropriate locale or layout. You can assign a shortcut key for switching between input locales if you have more than one locale installed. Click Change Key Sequence to set the shortcut key.

You can also change the key used to turn off CAPS LOCK. The default key is the CAPS LOCK key, but some of us have a tendency to hit the TAB key when we think we're getting rid of solid, all-capital letters when we're typing. If you prefer to use the SHIFT key to turn off CAPS LOCK, select that option.

Configure Hardware Properties

The Hardware tab provides a list of installed devices along with basic information about each device. Use the Troubleshooting button that starts the Windows 2000 Keyboard Troubleshooter if you're having problems with the installed keyboard. To view and change the keyboard driver and resource settings, click the Properties buttons.

Mouse

The Mouse applet contains a variety of options for calibrating your mouse and customizing the way it works. The mouse is such an important tool that it's important to make sure it operates efficiently and comfortably.

Configure Mouse Button Actions

The Buttons tab contains the basic, most important configuration options. If you're a southpaw, you can switch the actions attached to the left and right buttons. Of course, changing that configuration means that all the help files and books you refer to will be wrong, and you'll have to mentally substitute "left-click" every time you see the phrase "right-click." Many left-handed people find it's not difficult to use the mouse buttons in their default configuration, as long as the mousepad and the rodent are placed on the left side of the keyboard. It's certainly easy to switch back and forth, so test each configuration option for at least several hours (or days) before deciding whether you want to change the default actions.

You can also configure your mouse actions so that a single click opens files and folders (consequently, pointing to an object selects it). Adjust the sensitivity to a double click by moving the slider bar and testing the results on the jack-in-the-box.

Modify Mouse Pointers

Move to the Pointers tab if you have difficulty spotting or keeping track of the mouse pointer. You can opt to use a different pointer scheme, customize pointers, or create your own schemes. To create a custom scheme:

1. Select a scheme from the drop-down list.

2. Move to the Customize box and double-click the first pointer you want to change.

3. The %SystemRoot%\Cursors folder opens. Scroll through the available cursors and double-click the one you want to use to replace your selection.

4. When you've finished modifying cursors, click Save As to open the Save Scheme dialog box.

5. Enter a new name and click OK to save the customized scheme.

If at any time you decide you prefer the original cursor, highlight the listing and click Use Default to restore it.

 You can turn the pointer shadow off or on using the Enable Pointer Shadow option.

Configure Pointer Movements

The Motion tab provides options to set the speed, acceleration, and snap properties of your mouse. To change the speed at which your pointer moves, adjust the Speed slider bar to the left (decrease the speed) or right (increase the speed).

The Acceleration option enables you to set the pointer to move ahead of the mouse when you increase the speed with which you move the mouse. The higher the acceleration, the more quickly the pointer reaches its top speed. Therefore, with high acceleration and a quick mouse movement, the pointer travels a greater distance than it would with a lower acceleration setting.

The last option, Snap To Default, is one you'll either love or hate. When it's enabled, the mouse pointer moves automatically to the default button in all dialog boxes (e.g., it rushes to the OK button instead of the Cancel button if OK is the default option). While it sounds great, some people find it annoying and confusing when a pointer has a will of its own and moves without an accompanying mouse movement from the user.

Configure Hardware Properties

Use the Hardware tab to configure your mouse's hardware properties, where the installed pointing devices are listed in the Devices box. To view a device's Properties dialog box, double-click the listing (or select the listing and click Properties). In addition to providing information about the mouse and its drivers, the Properties dialog box has an Advanced Settings tab where you can fine-tune your mouse.

> **Note** *This is the same Properties dialog box you see when you select the mouse from the Device Manager.*

Phone and Modem Options

The Phone and Modem Options applet configures telephony services. The first time you open this applet, you must specify your country, area code, and whether you must dial a number to access an outside line. This establishes your default location, which Windows 2000 names My Location. Thereafter, opening the applet displays the Phone and Modem Options dialog box, which contains three tabs: Dialing Rules, Modems, and Advanced.

Configure Dialing Rules

The dialing rules you configure for telephony services affect all TAPI-supported programs and utilities. Rules are configured on a location basis, because the actions needed at one location frequently differ from those needed at other locations. For example, in your office you may need to dial 9 for an outside line, but if you travel, your hotel may require you to dial 8 instead of 9. You may need different dialing rules even if you never leave your desk. For example, dialing out to accomplish work for a client may require a specific credit card account.

To create a new location, click New on the Dialing Rules tab to open the New Location dialog box seen in Figure 7-9. Name the location and fill in the fields with the appropriate information.

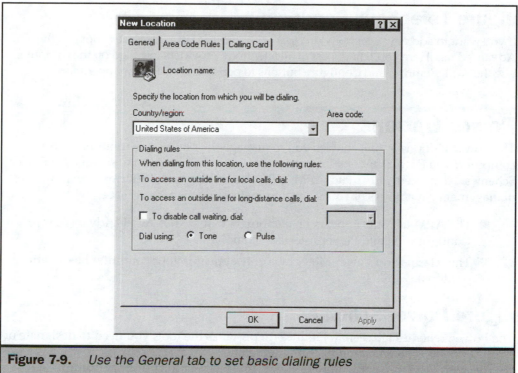

Figure 7-9. *Use the General tab to set basic dialing rules*

- Use the Area Code Rules tab to configure the rules for each area code you dial.
- Use the Calling Card tab to select and configure the credit cards you use for dialing long distance.

Configure Modems

Adding, removing, and configuring modems is a snap with the Modem tab options. To remove or configure a currently installed modem, select the device and click Remove to eliminate the modem or Properties to reconfigure it (enable the modem speaker, or set initialization strings).

To install a new modem, click the Add button to launch the Add/Remove Hardware Wizard. This is the same wizard that installs all hardware, but when you launch it from this applet, it starts at the Install New Modem window.

Configure Telephony Services

If you want to add new telephony services or configure existing services, move to the Advanced tab. Here you'll find a list of all telephony providers installed on the computer. Use the Add, Remove, and Configure buttons to perform the necessary operations.

Power Options

The Power Options applet enables you to manage the power consumption of your computer. The Power Options Properties dialog box can have up to seven tabs: Power Schemes, Advanced, Hibernate, APM, UPS, Power Meter, and Alarms. The power management capabilities of your computer determine the tabs you see.

- The APM tab only appears on computers that are not ACPI (Advanced Configuration and Power Interface) compliant.
- The Alarms and Power Meter tabs only appear if your computer has a battery (laptops).

Configure Power Schemes

The Power Schemes tab seen in Figure 7-10 provides the tools you need to designate or create a power scheme, or modify an existing one.

A *power scheme* is a collection of settings for reducing the power consumption of devices on your computer when you're not working. When the power scheme kicks in after a period of idle time, your computer goes into Standby mode by shutting down the disk, monitor, or both (depending on your selections). Moving or clicking the mouse, or pressing a key, brings the computer out of Standby mode and you can resume working. It's always safest to move the mouse instead of clicking or pressing a key, because you could be writing to an active window. Table 7-1 describes the available power schemes and their default settings.

Note *Idle time is defined as a lack of keyboard or mouse action.*

You can select a power scheme from the Power Schemes drop-down list and use it as configured, or you can edit the scheme to change one or more items. After you modify the scheme, you can save it under a new name with the Save As button.

Note *If you enable hibernate support (on the Hibernate tab) for Windows 2000 Professional (not Server), a System hibernate scheme is added to the Power Schemes tab.*

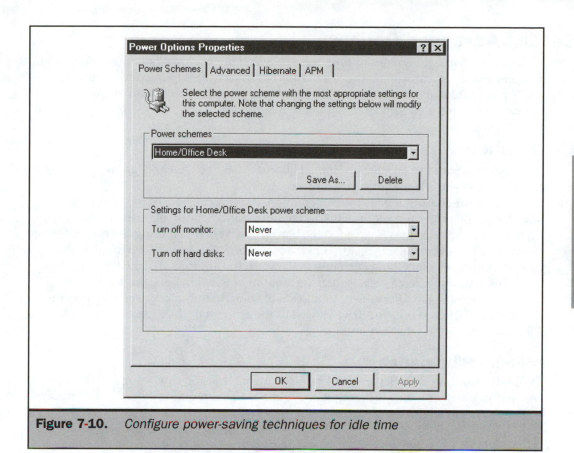

Figure 7-10.   *Configure power-saving techniques for idle time*

Power Scheme	Turn off monitor	Turn off hard disks
Home/Office Desk	Never	Never
Portable/Laptop	After 15 minutes	After 30 minutes
Presentation	Never	Never
Always On	After 20 minutes	Never
Minimal Power Management	After 15 minutes	Never
Max Battery	After 15 minutes	Never

Table 7-1.   *Default Power Scheme Settings*

Setting Advanced Options

Unless you enable hibernate support, the Advanced tab contains only the option to put a power management icon on the taskbar for one-click access to the power options.

If you enable hibernate support, the Advanced tab offers an option to require a password when the computer comes out of hibernation.

Hibernation

Hibernation is Standby on steroids. If the Hibernate tab does not appear on the dialog box, your computer does not support hibernation.

When your computer goes into hibernation, the current state of the computer is saved, and then the computer is shut down. Information about all open applications, documents, and windows is saved to the hard drive. When you bring the computer out of hibernation, everything is restored to the prehibernation state. Keep in mind that hibernation saves everything currently in RAM, so the amount of available hard disk space must be equal to or greater than the amount of RAM in your machine.

The Hibernate tab offers the option to enable hibernation mode, and displays the amount of free space on your drive as well as the amount of disk space required to hibernate (based on what's running).

Manual Hibernation

For both Windows 2000 Server and Professional, hibernation can be implemented manually. When you enable hibernation, your Shut Down dialog box adds Hibernate to the choices available for shutdown.

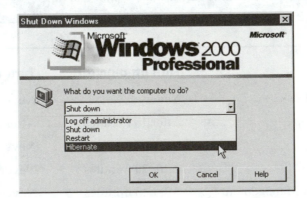

When you select the Hibernate option from the Shut Down dialog box, it takes a few seconds to save the contents of RAM to hard disk (the system displays a Hibernating message window with a progress bar). The message "It is now safe to turn off your computer" appears, and you can hit the power switch knowing that when you turn the computer on again, it will boot into the same state it was in when you put it into hibernation.

At the next power up, after the POST, the following message appears: "The system is being restarted from its previous location. Press the spacebar to interrupt." A progress bar displays as the data that was saved is loaded into RAM. If you enabled password protection for Standby procedures, the computer boots in "locked" mode and you must press CTRL-ALT-DEL and log on. If you didn't enable password protection, the computer boots and everything on your screen is exactly the same as it was before you manually hibernated the computer.

If you press the spacebar during startup, the following message displays:

System restart has been paused:

Continue with system restart.
Delete restoration data and proceed to system boot menu.

Use the cursor key to select the option you require.

Automatic Hibernation

Only Windows 2000 Professional supports automatic hibernation. After you've enabled hibernation (on the Hibernate tab), the Power Schemes tab displays a new power scheme list labeled System Hibernates. Use the drop-down list to select a time period for inactivity, after which the system hibernates instead of going into Standby. Be sure the hibernation period is longer than your Standby choices.

You must have administrator permissions to enable hibernation. In addition, network policy settings must permit you to enable hibernation support.

If the Power Options dialog box has an APM tab, check the settings on the tab to make sure the Advanced Power Management functions are enabled.

Hibernation as a Shutdown Technique

There is one important difference between starting up after manually effecting hibernation and starting up normally: the post-hibernation startup is incredibly faster than the normal startup. "Faster" doesn't do justice to the difference—this is the speed of light compared to the speed of a snail. I'm tempted to tell you that you should shut down all open software (just to be on the safe side) and hibernate instead of shutting down every time you need to turn off your computer. However, hibernation instead of shutting down doesn't work if the reason you're shutting down is to install new hardware devices, or refresh the computer to compensate for memory leakage. It is, however, an option to think about if you always shut down your workstation when you leave the office.

Configure Power Alarms

The Alarms tab appears only if your computer has a battery (see Figure 7-11). You can set a Low battery alarm to warn you that you need to start thinking about saving your work and preparing for a loss of power. You can also set a second alarm (the Critical Battery alarm) to warn you when a power loss is imminent.

The way each alarm functions is identical—click the Alarm Action button to set the power level that triggers the alarm, and configure notifications and actions in the event of a near-dead battery.

Configure UPS Devices

The capabilities of UPS units may differ by manufacturer and model, but the typical configuration options include the following:

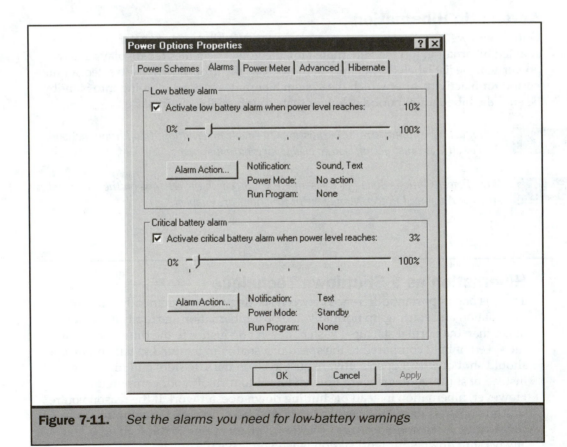

Figure 7-11.   *Set the alarms you need for low-battery warnings*

- The serial port used for communication between the device and the computer.

- The conditions that kick off a "danger" message from the UPS to the computer (low voltage, low battery power remaining, etc.).

- The actions initiated by a power emergency (notify the user, run a program, etc.).

If you launch a program, be sure it can execute fully within about 20 seconds, and don't use any code that displays dialog boxes or otherwise asks for user input. After you've configured the UPS, pull the UPS plug out of its electrical socket. Make sure everything works the way you expect it to, and if not, reconfigure the UPS service.

Regional Options

Use the Regional Options applet to modify the manner in which dates, numbers, and currency are displayed. You can make sweeping changes by selecting a different locale, which in turn resets currency, date, time, and number formats in accordance with the standards of the selected locale. If, on the other hand, you only want to make minor changes, you can customize your own locale. The dialog box has six tabs: General, Numbers, Currency, Time, Date, and Input Locales.

The General tab provides the means to change the input locale and add other languages. Changing the locale does not change the language, merely the formatting and keyboard layout for those special characters used in the language of the locale. If the language you want to switch to doesn't appear on the locale drop-down list, you can add it from the list at the bottom of the General tab.

You can even use a different locale for each program you work in. Merely add the various locales by moving to the Input Locales tab and clicking the Add button. This opens the Add Input Locale dialog box, and you can choose a locale to add from the Input Locale drop-down list.

Use the Keyboard layout/IME drop-down list to choose a keyboard layout for the locale. Then click OK to return to the Regional Options Properties dialog box. Add as many locales as you want, and then click OK.

Now, when you're using software and you would prefer a different locale/keyboard layout, press ALT-SHIFT to switch between locales (you can change the hot key combination in the Input Locales tab). You can tell which locale is active by the icon in the taskbar system tray.

The Numbers, Currency, Time, and Date tabs contain common formatting settings. You can determine which of those items you want to change.

| Note | *One item of recent and timely interest is the way that the Calendar option in the Date tab dealt with the Y2K issue. Windows 2000 was designed to let you decide which two-digit dates would revert to the 1900's and which would roll over to the new millennium.* |

Scanners and Cameras

Use the Scanners And Cameras applet to install, remove, and modify scanners and cameras.

- The Add button takes you directly to the Scanner And Camera Installation Wizard.
- The Properties button opens the Properties dialog box for the selected device (the properties differ by device type).

The Properties dialog box has an Events tab if the device supports event activation. Events enable you to trigger an action when you use the device. For example, you can set an event to open a supported program and send a picture to that program when you scan an image. However, only software that supports imaging-device linking can accept scanner or camera events. All software installed on your machine that supports device linking appears in the Send To This Application list. To enable a link, select the desired event from the Scanner (or Camera) Events drop-down list. Use the Send To This Application list to select the target program, then click OK.

 Applications that support picture insertion from scanners and cameras, but do not support linking, do not appear on the list.

If you want to apply rigid color control across all your publishing devices, you'll love the Color Management tab. By default, the RGB Color Space Profile is selected, but you can install other profiles by clicking Add and selecting a different profile from the Add Profile Association dialog box. To insure the colors your imaging devices use are the same as those you see onscreen, set the Color Management profile for your monitor by using the Settings tab in the Display applet. Click the Advanced button, open the Color Management tab, and make the appropriate changes.

Sounds and Multimedia

In previous versions of Windows, the Control Panel had both a Sounds applet and a Multimedia applet, but Windows 2000 has combined them. You can use this applet to control event sounds, configure multimedia devices (both input and output), and configure a speech engine.

Configure Sounds

Use the Sounds tab to assign sounds to events, customize sound schemes, and control speaker volume.

By default, some system events are assigned sounds, but you can remove or modify those sounds. To view the events capable of producing sounds, and the sounds associated with them, scroll through the Sound Events list. In addition to the events that occur in the operating system, the applications you install may add their own events to the list.

To add or change an assigned sound, select the event and choose a different sound file from the Name drop-down list or use the Browse button to locate a sound file. If you want to sample the sound, click the Play arrow next to the Name text box.

You can create your own sound scheme, a group of similar sounds in which specific sounds are assigned to specific events. Simply make all the sound assignment changes to an existing scheme and click the Save As button. Enter a name for the new scheme and click OK.

To control speaker volume, use the slider bar. You can opt to place an icon on the taskbar for volume control, which means you don't have to open the Sounds And Multimedia applet when you want to change the volume. The taskbar icon volume control is linked to the volume control on the Sounds tab, and changing one changes the other.

Configure Audio Properties

Use the Audio tab to set the properties for recording and playback devices.

Select the Sound playback device you want to use from the drop-down list, which contains the known sound playback devices in your system. You can set the volume and then click Advanced to tweak the sound playback device performance. The advanced options available depend on the device.

The sound recording device section of this tab is for selecting and configuring a recording device, typically a microphone. You can set the volume and tweak the properties (which differ depending on the device).

The MIDI Music Playback section of the tab is for selecting and configuring the device that delivers MIDI output (frequently the sounds in games).

Configure Hardware

The Hardware tab provides a list of installed multimedia devices. You can modify properties by selecting a device and clicking the Properties button. This is not a place to mess around haphazardly; be sure you have documentation from the manufacturer.

Configure Speech Recognition Engines

If you install a speech recognition engine, the Sounds And Multimedia Properties dialog box sports a fourth tab, Speech. This tab offers configuration options for both input and output speech engines. You can set the options for the installed engine(s), which differ from product to product.

- Click Pronunciation to edit the way the engine interprets your words (if it's an input engine), or pronounces words (if it's an output engine).

- Click Training to work with an input engine so your voice and pronunciation is understood.
- Click Special Handling to specify the way you want an output engine to pronounce numbers, abbreviations, currency, and symbols.
- The Microphone Settings Wizard will help you fine-tune the microphone for an input engine.

System

The System applet in the Control Panel provides a wealth of tools and shortcuts for a large variety of system maintenance requirements. The System Properties dialog box has five tabs, each dealing with a different facet of your computer. The General tab is informational only, providing information about the computer and the operating system.

Network Identification

The Network Identification tab displays information about the computer name and the domain in which it exists (if the computer is a member of a domain). If the computer is a domain controller, you cannot make changes to the name or the domain. If the computer is not a domain controller, you can use the tools on this tab to join a domain, change the name of the computer, or change the domain.

Set Up the Computer on a Domain

The Network ID button opens the Computer Identification Wizard, which walks you through the steps required to join a domain. Use this tool if you have just installed the operating system without setting up the configuration for joining a domain. The wizard creates the computer name (which must be unique on the domain), a user account, and all the other information required for domain authentication. You must have administrator permissions to create a computer on the domain; otherwise you must have a network administrator create the computer on the domain.

 You can also use the Computer Identification Wizard to join a workgroup.

Change Computer Identification Information

To modify the identification settings for the computer, click Properties to open the Identification Changes dialog box seen in Figure 7-12.

To change the name of the computer, enter a new name in the Computer name text box. If the computer is a member of a domain, you will be asked to provide a user name and password in order to complete the name change operation. You must be an administrator on the local computer to change its name.

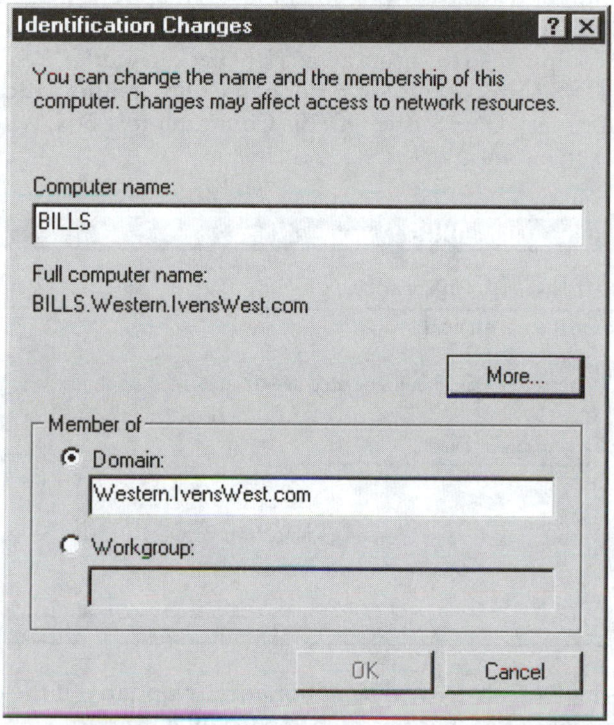

Figure 7-12. *Change the identification of a computer by changing its properties*

- For TCP/IP networks, the computer name can contain up to 63 characters, using only the numbers 0–9, the letters A–Z and a–z, and hyphens.

- If you're using any protocol except TCP/IP, the computer name can contain up to 15 characters.

- If your network is using Microsoft DNS, you can use any characters except periods.

To change the domain membership for this computer, enter a new, valid domain name in the Domain text box. If the computer was a member of a workgroup, select the Domain radio button, and then enter the name of the domain you want this computer to join. You must be an administrator of the local computer to make either change.

The rule of thumb for changing a computer name is "Don't do it." There's almost never a good reason. In fact, the only reason I can think of is when the following circumstance occurs: A computer crashes and instead of buying a new computer, or waiting for a repair, you replace the computer with an existing computer (perhaps one that's in storage or is being used by someone with less urgent work to complete). You should change the name of the replacement computer so the user can go right back to work.

To change the DNS suffix of the computer name (either automatically or manually), click More. In the Primary DNS Suffix Of This Computer text box, type the DNS suffix you want to use for this computer.

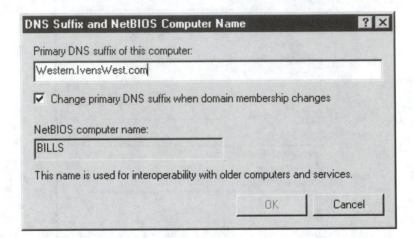

To make sure the DNS suffix will be automatically updated if the computer joins a different domain, select the check box labeled Change Primary DNS Suffix When Domain Membership Changes. Changing the DNS suffix does not affect domain membership. The suffix may contain up to 155 characters, including periods and hyphens.

Hardware

The Hardware tab provides access to a number of hardware-related features, including the Add/Remove Hardware Wizard, the Device Manager, Driver Signing options, and Hardware Profiles.

For more information on the Hardware Wizard, see the section "Add/Remove Hardware" earlier in this chapter.

Driver Signing

The Driver Signing options let you set the permission level for installing software, including drivers. You can choose to allow the installation of all drivers regardless of their digital signatures, display a warning for unsigned files, or block the installation of unsigned files altogether. Because you may be installing files from a wide variety of vendors, it's not a good idea to restrict installation.

These settings are user specific, not computer specific. However, if you are an administrator for the computer, you can make your choices the default for all users signing on to this machine by enabling the Apply Setting As System Default Option.

Whenever you want to check your system for unsigned system files, run the File Signature Verification utility by choosing Start | Run. Then enter **sigverif** and click OK. When the File Signature Verification dialog box appears, click Start to run the utility or Advanced to set search and logging options.

Device Manager

The Device Manager is an indispensable tool for troubleshooting hardware problems, updating drivers, and changing the configuration of installed hardware devices. Here are some guidelines to keep in mind when using Device Manager:

■ You must have administrative privileges on the computer.

■ You can only manage local devices

■ Network policy settings may prevent you from making changes to devices.

VIEWING SYSTEM DEVICES   The first and most obvious service the Device Manager provides is a quick view of your system and all the hardware devices installed. It lets you know, at a glance, if there are any immediate hardware problems or conflicts by flagging those devices that are not working properly (yellow exclamation point) or that it does not recognize (yellow question mark). In addition to providing an overview of your system hardware, the Device Manager also offers a variety of ways to view the information. The available views include

■ **Devices by type**   The default view, which lists the installed devices alphabetically by type.

■ **Devices by connection**   Lists the connection types with all devices on the connection appearing as a subset of the connection type.

■ **Resources by type**   Displays devices as subsets of the resources they are using. Resources include DMA, I/O, IRQ, and memory address.

■ **Resources by connection**   Similar to the Resources By Type view, this view displays the resource list with connection types as the subset.

■ **Show hidden devices**   Handy for locating devices that have been disconnected but not uninstalled from the computer. It also displays non-Plug and Play devices that are installed.

PRINTING REPORTS ON SYSTEM DEVICES   In addition to viewing the device information, you can print reports by selecting Print from the View menu to open the Print dialog box shown in Figure 7-13.

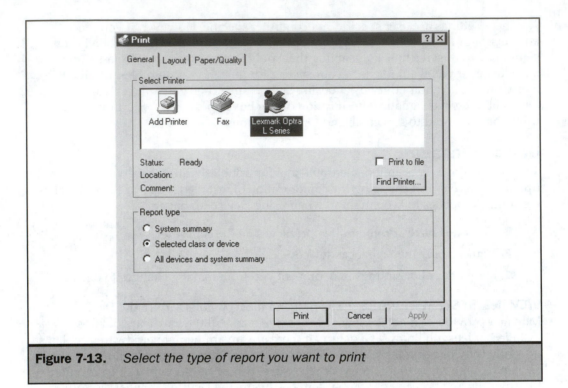

Figure 7-13. *Select the type of report you want to print*

There are three reports available:

- **System summary** Contains basic system information such as operating system, processor, and installed memory. In addition, the report contains summaries of disk drive information, IRQ usage, DMA usage, Memory usage, and I/O ports usage.

- **Selected class or device** Contains details about the selected device(s). Included in the report are the device's class, description or name, the resources it's using, and information about device drivers.

- **All devices and system summary** Prints the same information as the System Summary Report, then the information in the Selected class or device report for every installed device.

It's a good idea to print the All Devices And System Summary report for each computer and keep the printout either in the desk on which the computer sits or in an accessible file folder. Alternatively, you can print all the reports to a file and amass the information in one large "our network computers" document.

MANIPULATING DEVICES   You can also manage devices in the Device Manager. You can modify settings, change drivers, enable and disable devices, and uninstall devices. To access the properties of a device, double-click its listing, or right-click the listing and choose Properties from the shortcut menu. Because every device requires a device driver, each Properties dialog box contains at least two tabs: General and Driver.

- The **General tab** provides basic information, such as device name, type, and manufacturer, as well as its current status (working or not), a troubleshooter in case the device isn't working, and a Device Usage option to enable or disable the device.

- The **Driver tab**, as you might expect, provides information about the driver currently installed for the device. This includes the driver name, provider, date, version, and digital signature, if any.

Click Driver Details to open the Driver File Details dialog box, which displays the path and name(s) of installed driver(s). You can use the buttons on the dialog box to uninstall the current driver, or update it.

If the device uses system resources, there's a Resources tab that lists the resources being used, and provides an option for manually changing them. Don't perform this action unless you're very comfortable with hardware issues. The Resources tab also contains a conflicting device list that alerts you to any resource conflicts between the selected device and any other installed devices.

An Advanced tab appears for devices that have additional options that can be set by the user. You may find other devices with special tabs of their own. For example, installed ports contain a Port Settings tab, modems have Modem and Diagnostics tabs, and the USB Root Hub contains a Power tab.

REMOVE DEVICES   In addition to viewing installed devices and modifying their properties, you can also use the Device Manager to remove devices. To remove a device, right-click its listing and select Uninstall from the shortcut menu. You can also remove a device by opening its properties dialog box, selecting the Driver tab, and clicking the Uninstall button.

CUSTOMIZE THE DEVICE MANAGER WINDOW   Like all Microsoft Management Consoles, you can customize the Device Manager window. Simply choose Customize from the View menu to open the Customize View dialog box seen in Figure 7-14.

As you can see, there are a number of options for customizing the Device Manager console. Although the console tree is hidden in the Device Manager window by default, it is enabled (by default) in the Customize View dialog box, and can be displayed by clicking the Show/Hide Console Tree button on the Standard toolbar. The remaining options let you hide or display the menu bar, the toolbar, the status bar, and the description bar. You can also elect to hide or display snap-in menus and toolbars.

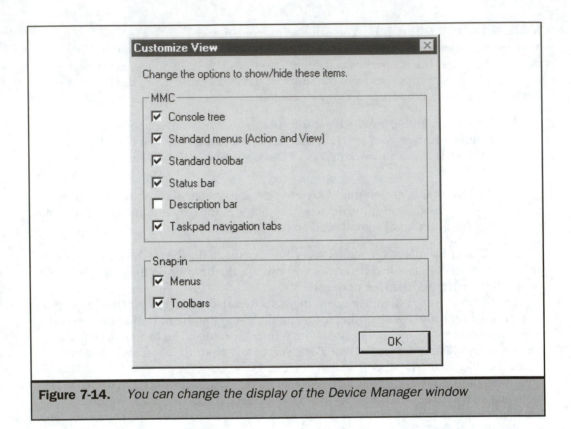

Figure 7-14.   *You can change the display of the Device Manager window*

Hardware Profiles

Hardware profiles are useful for computers that frequently change hardware, particularly laptops. A hardware profile provides Windows with the all the information it needs to load the correct drivers and settings during startup. If you're using a laptop and plug into a variety of different hardware scenarios, you can create a different profile for each scenario. This way, when you arrive at a new location, you don't have to reset each affected device; you simply enable the appropriate hardware profile and you're ready to go to work.

    You can also use hardware profiles when different users share the same desktop computer. Each user may require different peripherals, such as printers and scanners, or even have a particular mouse preference.

CREATE A HARDWARE PROFILE   To create a hardware profile, click Hardware Profiles to open the Hardware Profiles dialog box (see Figure 7-15).

Create a new profile by copying an existing profile, giving it a new name, and selecting the options for choosing a profile when the computer boots. You can opt to

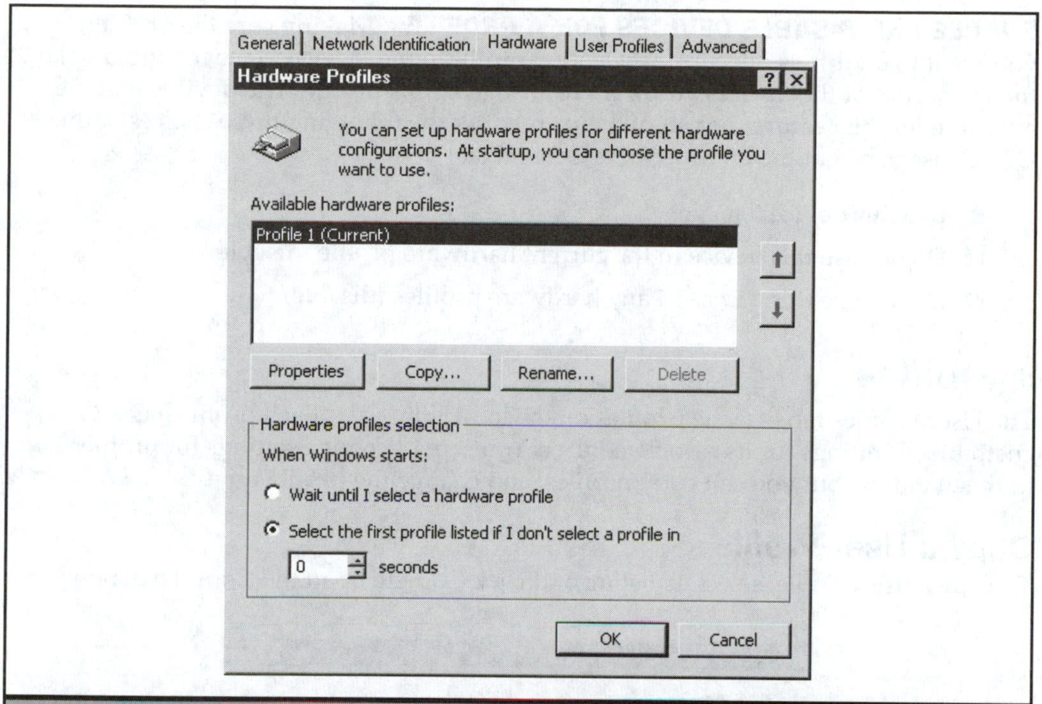

Figure 7-15. *Create a unique hardware profile to match each permutation and combination of devices the computer may contain*

make the system wait until you choose a profile, even if it takes forever, or load the first profile in the list after a specified number of seconds. If you choose to autoload a profile, use the Up and Down arrows in the dialog box to put the appropriate profile at the top of the list.

Now you can enable and disable devices for the profile. This operation is performed in the Device manager, which applies the changes to the currently loaded hardware profile. This means you have two methods for changing the devices in a profile:

- Reboot and select your new profile; then go into Device Manager and make the changes.

- Use the new profile as your regular profile (after all, it's a copy of your regular profile), and make the changes in Device Manager immediately. They are applied against the currently loaded profile (the one you copied from) instead of the new profile (the one you copied to).

If you use the second option, you may want to rename the profiles to make it clear which is which. You may also want to change the order of the listing.

ENABLE AND DISABLE DEVICES FOR A PROFILE Making sure the profile you want to modify is the currently loaded profile, open Device Manager and display the Properties of the devices you want to change in this profile. The devices that are available for this feature (not all of them are) offer the following three choices in the Device usage box at the bottom of the General tab:

- Use this device (enable)
- Do not use this device in the current hardware profile (disable)
- Do not use this device in any hardware profiles (disable)

User Profiles

The User Profiles tab lists the profiles on the local computer. Each profile has customized settings for its associated user. You cannot change settings for profiles in this window, but you can copy profiles, and change the profile type.

Copy a User Profile

To copy a user profile, select its listing and click Copy to open the Copy To dialog box.

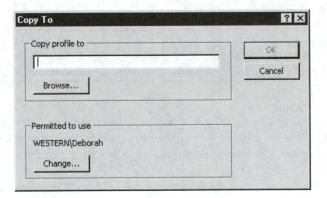

Select another location, which is typically another computer. You can use the UNC for the target computer or click Browse and expand the network to locate the appropriate target. Copying a user profile to another location is useful when a user is changing projects or offices and uses a locally cached profile.

You can also use the Permitted To Use function instead of (or in addition to) copying the profile to a new location. If you don't copy the profile, and use the Change button to select a user name from the list of users in the domain, you've effectively created a profile for a new user on this computer. This is a quick way to add a user profile if a new user is going to be accessing this computer.

Change to a Roaming Profile

If the domain administrator has created a configuration for a roaming profile for a user, you can switch the local profile to a roaming profile. If this option isn't available for the selected user, when you select Change Type, the Roaming Profile option is grayed out and inaccessible.

Advanced

The Advanced tab provides access to those options that enable you to tweak your system's performance, modify the environment variables, and designate some startup and recovery settings. Some settings can be modified by any user; others require administrator privileges. In addition, some of the settings are specific to the logged-on user and others are systemwide settings.

Performance Options

The performance options include processor resource allocation and virtual memory settings. Click the Performance Options button to view the Performance Options dialog box, which has two sections: Application Response and Virtual Memory.

In the Application Response section, you can direct processor resources to the activities you consider most important. (By default, Windows 2000 allocates processor resources in variable time slices to applications, giving the foreground application the larger slices. This ensures that the application will run as smoothly as possible. However, it also means that background tasks get less processor time, and therefore run slower.

- Select Applications to provide more processor resources to the application running in the foreground.
- Select Background Services to distribute processor resources equally between tasks running in the foreground and background.

In the Virtual Memory section, click the Change button to display the Virtual Memory dialog box shown in Figure 7-16. Changing virtual memory settings, which requires administrator privileges, enables you to size and locate the paging file.

In addition to changing the size of the paging file, you can also change the size of the Windows 2000 registry. While the 8MB default should be adequate for most scenarios, you may find that adding a large number of users requires increasing its size. Or perhaps on a single-user machine you may decide to reduce the size to improve system performance. Either way, you can limit the registry size by setting the Maximum Registry Size (MB) option in the Virtual Memory dialog box.

Environment Variables

Click Environment variables to view the environment for the currently logged-on user and for the system. You can add, remove, or modify the environment variables (you must have administrator permissions to change system variables).

To create a new variable, click New and enter a name and value for the variable; then click OK. To modify an existing variable, select it and click Edit. Deleting a variable is even easier—select the variable and click Delete.

In addition to creating variables in the System applet, you can also add them to the Autoexec.bat file. Keep in mind that Windows sets the environment variables in order,

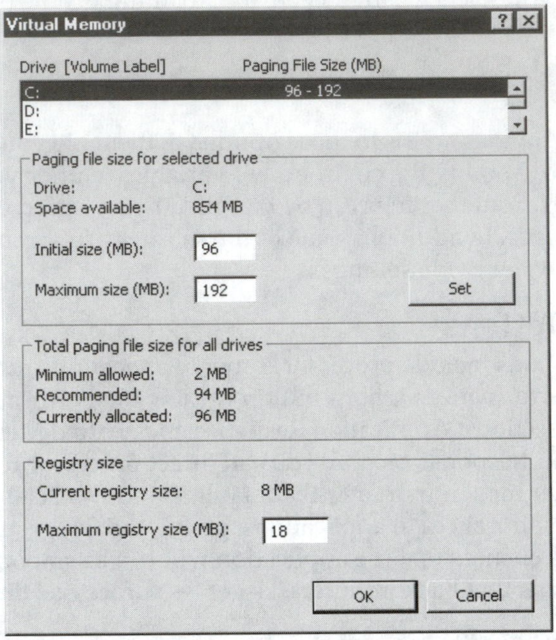

Figure 7-16. *Tweak the virtual memory settings for the computer*

starting with the Autoexec.bat file, then system variables, and finally user variables. Therefore, a user variable will override a similar variable in the Autoexec.bat file.

Startup and Recovery

The Startup and Recover options include setting the default operating system as well as determining what actions take place when a fatal system error occurs. If you dual boot, you can use the System startup option to indicate which is the default operating system and specify the amount of time you want the startup menu displayed before the default operating system is launched.

The Recovery options let you create information about a system crash that may be helpful in determining (and hopefully fixing) the problem. The Recovery options:

■ **Write an event to the system log.** Enabling this option causes an event to be recorded in the system log when a fatal error occurs. (This is a default action on Windows 2000 Server).

■ **Send an administrative alert.** This automatically generates an alert and sends it to the system administrator.

■ **Write debugging information to:**   This option can be very useful in determining the cause of the problem. It writes the contents of system memory, at the time of the crash, to a file on the hard disk. Therefore, it requires an amount of disk space equal to the amount of RAM plus an additional megabyte. The default dump file is %SystemRoot%\Memory.dmp. You can opt to overwrite this file each time a stop error occurs. However, you must rename the last-written file after rebooting to make sure you have a copy of its contents (I use the date of the dump as the filename). You can also choose to record only kernel information, rather than the entire contents of RAM.

■ **Automatically reboot.**   If you want the system to automatically reboot after a stop error occurs, enable this option.

Chapter 8

Microsoft Management
Console (MMC)

239

Microsoft Management Console (MMC) is a generalized framework for administration and management of computer system configurations. It is designed to replace the dozens of proprietary interfaces used to manage Windows NT, Back Office, and third-party offerings. The architecture is well documented, and Microsoft is committed to moving all of its management tools to this platform in the near future. Broad use and acceptance of MMC and the availability of development tools and templates will encourage the Windows marketplace to follow this initiative.

MMC is a display tool for hosting management components called snap-ins. The console itself offers no management capabilities, but instead coordinates seamless integration between numerous snap-ins. MMC is shipped as a multiple document interface (MDI) application, similar to Windows Explorer, that heavily leverages Internet technologies and ActiveX controls for rendering. It runs on any Win32 platform including Windows 2000, Windows NT 4, and Windows 95/98.

Snap-ins are shipped with the operating system and various add-on and third-party applications. Administrators construct comprehensive management tools by assembling snap-ins and other components into a series of MDI windows. Most snap-ins are remote-enabled so the tools can manage local computers or servers and workstations anywhere in the Enterprise. The tools are saved in shell-aware files that can be added to the desktop as shortcuts, inserted in the Start menu structure, e-mailed to other administrators, posted to Web pages, copied to floppies, and so on. These tools simplify administration through interface integration, task orientation, and project delegation.

A user can run multiple MMC tools at the same time, each in its own process, with its own particular views. These can run alongside other non-MMC management tools. Standard operating system techniques for task switching are used to jump from one tool to another. MMC can also host Web links, shortcuts to other tools, scripts, and other capabilities.

MMC, code-named Slate, was first released as version 1.0 in the NT Option Pack. Internet information Server and Transaction Server introduced administrators to the new interfaces and techniques. Subsequent NT service packs and Back Office 4.5 introduced MMC version 1.1 featuring taskpads and HTML help integration. Small Business Server (SBS) was the first product to feature a comprehensive administrator console based on MMC taskpads. The success of SBS emphasized the need for simpler task-oriented management interfaces. Windows 2000 combines all of these enhancements and is based on MMC release 1.2, which adds list view exporting, Microsoft Installer integration, System Policy integration, and filtered views.

There are several benefits to this new technology that apply to various skill levels. Users focus on Control Panel applets and wizards to configure their machines. Novice administrators are assigned taskpads with limited visibility and control. Power administrators utilize the full suite of MMC components. Enterprise administrators create custom tools from snap-in palettes and distribute or assign them to peers throughout the organization. This management hierarchy promotes consistent interfaces by reusing snap-ins and taskpads, reduces overall training time, documents processes using Web page snap-ins, and controls access using policies and delegation.

MMC does not replace Enterprise management tools. It works in conjunction with them and can call or be called from their consoles. It is not a replacement for the Web Based Enterprise Management (WBEM) initiative, although it can be used to build WBEM tools. It does not replace Systems Management Server; in fact, SMS 2.0 uses MMC as the required administrative interface. It is not a complete Web-based management tool written for Internet Explorer (IE), but it does host Web pages and other document objects. The flexibility and performance of the Win32-based MDI interface in MMC provide a solid framework for Windows 2000 administrators to complete projects quickly and efficiently.

MMC User Interface

The MMC console has several personalities. It can host multiple snap-ins at one time in one or several MDI windows. It can also limit the view to a single window for less experienced users. Taskpads offer an HTML display solution to the management technology underneath. Various interface features like menus, toolbars, and status bands can be toggled on or off. Authoring can be controlled through switches, dialogs, and policies.

Novice administrators will find the single view easiest to learn and use. Several of the options in the Administrative Tools menu use this approach. Figure 8-1 shows the Event Viewer for the local computer.

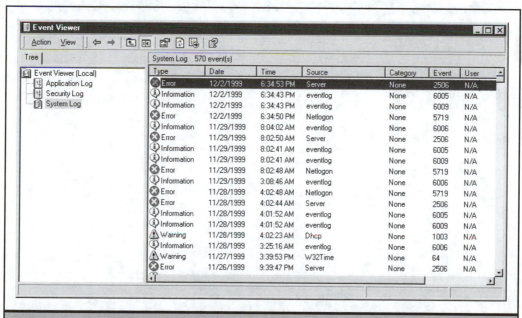

Figure 8-1.   *Single view of the Event Viewer snap-in*

Taskpads are a clever combination of DHTML and scripting that call COM management components and display the results in the familiar Web paradigm. This view is best for part-time administrators and users more comfortable with a Web browser than the Windows Explorer interface. Wizards are provided to build simple taskpad interfaces. Even though taskpads are Web enabled, they do not work directly in a browser and cannot be used for remote Web administration. Figure 8-2 shows the Event Viewer in a taskpad without a menu or toolbar.

Multiple Document Interface (MDI)

Expert-level administrators primarily work in multiple windows targeting multiple servers and services. The Win32 MDI interface is well suited for this application and is the windowing technology behind MMC. Each child window can sport its own menu and toolbar, include namespace trees, render Web pages, interact with ActiveX controls, or display taskpads. Several of these options are depicted in Figure 8-3.

Window selection is made from the main console menu at the top of the parent window. Standard MDI keystroke combinations also work:

- CTRL-W   Opens a new Window
- CTRL-F6   Cycles between windows

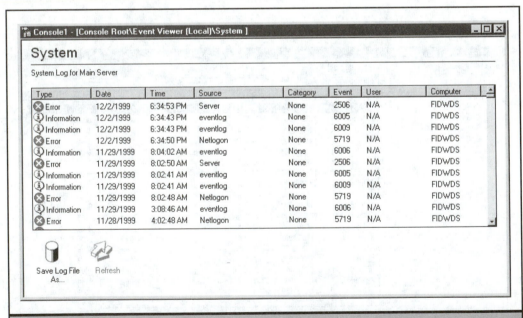

Figure 8-2.   *Taskpad view of the Event Viewer snap-in*

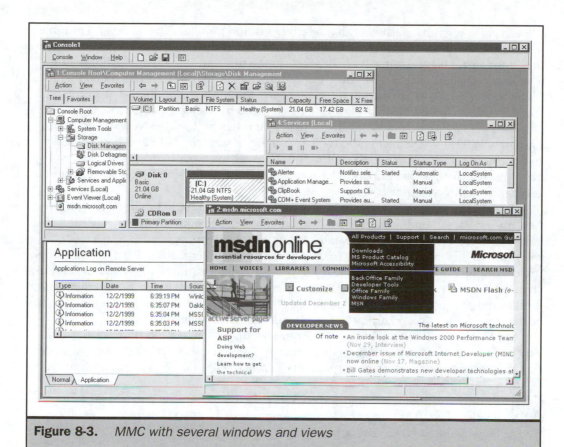

Figure 8-3. *MMC with several windows and views*

- CTRL-F10   Maximizes the child window
- CTRL-F5   Restores the child window to normal size
- CTRL-F4   Closes the active child window
- F5   Refreshes the contents of the current window
- CTRL-P   Prints the current page

Menus, Toolbars, and Bands

The parent window has a permanent menu that includes the Console, Window, and Help options. *Console* is used to create new consoles, open and save console files, add/remove snap-ins, set authoring and security options, and select the four most recently used consoles. The *Window* menu lists child windows and controls their behavior. Children can be cascaded, tiled, or arranged as minimized icons. The name of each child window is listed with a relative position number. The name and number appear in the title bar of each child window until that window is maximized. The name and number then appear in square brackets in the title bar of the parent MDI window. The number is not visible when only one child window exists. The *Help* menu includes Help Topics, a link to Microsoft on the Web, and the MMC About box. The permanent menu is controlled by MMC and cannot be changed by a snap-in or extension.

The permanent toolbar is not customizable and has buttons for New, Open, Save, and New Window. The menu and toolbar use the rebar style that has a handle bar to control the position. When the mouse hovers over the rebar handle, the pointer changes to a two-headed horizontal arrow. Slide this handle bar to move or size the toolbar or menu component.

Each child window has its own menu and toolbar. The Action menu dynamically lists options based on the current snap-in and namespace node. Snap-ins and extensions can customize this menu to add or remove items as needed. Pay close attention to this menu to find key management tasks. For consistency, snap-in authors are encouraged to place common tasks in the All Tasks cascading menu and new object items in the New menu. Important items often appear directly in the Action menu as well as the All Tasks menu. The Action menu doubles as the context menu for each namespace node. Access this by right-clicking the node name.

The View menu offers selections to control list display mode, filtering, sorting, and other options provided per snap-in or extension. The console tree, description bar, status bar, menus, and toolbars can be toggled on or off in the Customize View… option.

Tip	*Be careful toggling these features, especially the menus, because you need the menu to get them back. The Customize View… option also appears on the window menu when the MMC icon is clicked. The menus and toolbars can be restored there.*

The Favorites menu item works like Favorites in a Web browser. In a complex console tree, there are many snap-ins displayed in order of appearance. It is useful for frequent administrative tasks to be isolated in a convenient set of folders. Add often-used namespace nodes to the Favorites list by selecting the node and clicking the Favorites menu Add to Favorites… option. A friendly name can replace the formal namespace description. The Organize Favorites… menu option and Folders provide a method to categorize and organize the favorites. Favorites are then displayed in the Favorites menu with submenus representing the folder hierarchy. They also appear in the console tree Favorites page accessed by clicking the Favorites tab at the top of the tree.

Several snap-ins also add a child window menu called Tools. This provides a launching pad for external utilities, wizards, and configuration property pages. The Tools menu will be significant for complex products like the Microsoft Back Office suite.

The child window toolbars are configurable by the applicable snap-in and extensions. Multiple toolbars can appear dynamically. Use the rebar handle to move toolbars to the desired position. The Properties, Refresh, and Help buttons are common and useful. Use the following keystrokes to access these features from the keyboard:

- ALT-ENTER   Display the properties box for the selected item
- F5   Refresh
- F1   Help

Two interesting features are new to version 1.2 of MMC. The View menu has a Choose Columns… option that can selectively display and reorder columnar lists. This is extremely useful for complex management tasks that involve dozens of informational columns. Unfortunately, you can only have one list displayed at a time. Fortunately, the column presentation is stored when you save the console file in author mode. The Event Viewer column selection list is displayed in Figure 8-4.

The other interesting feature appears in the Action menu. Export List… opens a file Save As dialog box and prompts for a filename, type, and selection. Any standard snap-in list can be saved to text (TXT) or comma-separated values (CSV). The entire list is saved unless the Save Only Selected Rows box is checked. The output file can be imported into other tools for reporting and archiving. This solves a long-time dilemma for NT administrators: the lack of a print command. Export lists to CSV files, import them into Excel, and format to your heart's content!

The final pieces of the interface puzzle are the description and status bars. These are toggled on and off in the Customize View… menu option and work independently for each child window. The description bar appears above the list view on the right side of the window and displays summary information for lists and queries. The status bar runs the width of the child window along the bottom edge and displays process status and information like menu text. Figure 8-5 shows the Event Viewer with the number of events in the description bar and the menu text in the status bar.

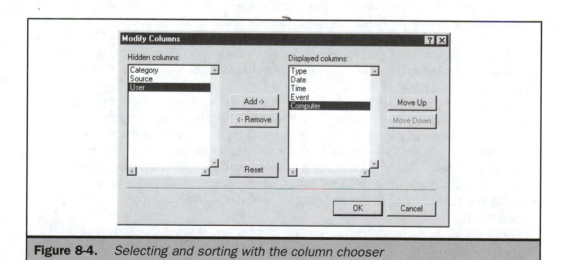

Figure 8-4. *Selecting and sorting with the column chooser*

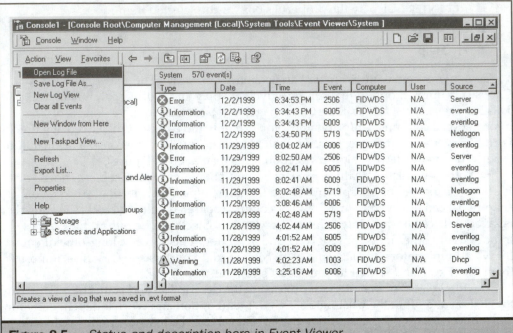

Figure 8-5.   *Status and description bars in Event Viewer*

Scope Pane

A typical MMC console tool can host multiple snap-ins at one time. The snap-in capabilities are categorized and placed in named containers. Multiple snap-ins and containers are listed in the console tree on the left side of a child window. This tree can be toggled on or off using the Customize View… menu option in each child window. The hierarchical collection of names, resembling the Windows Explorer file interface, is called the *namespace.*

The tree and namespace are often referred to as the *scope pane.* The tree has node points that can expand and collapse as needed to allow concise control over screen real estate and administrator focus. Each node is provided by the parent snap-in for the child window or one of its extensions. Each node has a name and an optional set of properties, accessible from the Properties menu item or a toolbar button. Selecting a Container node displays the child nodes for that container on the pane to the right. Selecting a child or leaf node displays the list, Web page, ActiveX control, or taskpad associated with that node.

Navigate the namespace by scrolling the tree up and down to find the desired node. The arrow, home, end, and page keys all work here. Closed container nodes save screen space and have a small box with a plus sign in them. Click on the box or press the plus sign to expand the node. Click or press minus to close the node once again. When a node is opened and has child nodes, press the first letter of the child names to jump from one item to another. Other useful keystrokes for the namespace include

- F2   Rename the selected node
- +   Expand the selected node
- −   Collapse the selected node

Contents Pane

The right side of a child window is referred to as the contents or results pane. The information displayed here changes based on the current node selected in the namespace. Some child windows have the console tree hidden or disabled. In this case, only the contents pane is visible and the selected node cannot be changed.

The contents pane may include a standard list, a taskpad, an ActiveX control, a Web page, or a custom combination of the four. The keystrokes and navigation techniques vary with the type of content. Standard lists are very common and usually have several columns of output. The Choose Columns… option in the View menu controls which columns are visible and in which order. The mouse can also be used to drag column headers left and right to affect the display order. Clicking column headers sorts by that column, and clicking again sorts descending. A small arrow appears in the column header indicating the sort status. The column width, order, visibility, sorted column, and sort direction information persist in memory. This column configuration data is saved when an MSC file is created.

Note   *The Export List… option mentioned earlier depends on the currently selected column list, column order, and sort column. Use this as a simple report writer. Yes, printing selected lists of user accounts works quite well with this technique!*

Some standard lists offer the four basic Explorer views for their objects. This is configured per snap-in. Figure 8-6 shows the Users folder in two different windows, one with Large icon view and the other with Detail view.

MMC Component Architecture

MMC is a customizable framework comprised of snap-ins, extensions, property sheets, wizards, HTML help, taskpads, Web pages, and ActiveX controls. There are well-documented specifications for developing snap-ins that fit seamlessly into this architecture. The following section explores the parameters and design issues that must be considered when building a well-behaved snap-in. This process will help administrators understand MMC capabilities and limitations.

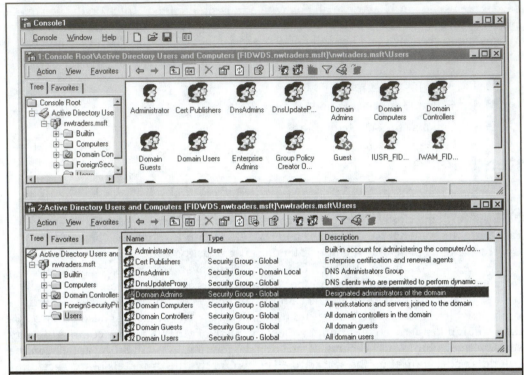

Figure 8-6. *Two standard list view options for the Users container in Active Directory*

Snap-Ins and Extensions

Snap-ins are the atomic units of management behavior in MMC. They work as OLE in-process servers that run in the context of the MMC console window. Snap-ins are typically stored in a Dynamic Link Library (DLL), and several snap-ins can exist inside one DLL. Snap-ins may call on other supporting controls and DLLs to accomplish their tasks. They are written using standard COM interfaces and render traditional list and tree views, DHTML, Java™, and ActiveX controls. The Win32 programming environment provides advanced MDI window management, a customizable user interface, multiselect lists, and advanced drag and drop. Microsoft and independent software vendors save valuable development time and resources by building snap-ins instead of full-blown products. They also gain the flexibility to ship snap-ins on their own, bundled with other products, or as extensions to existing products.

There are several types of snap-ins:

- **Standalone**   Snap-ins that can work on their own, providing namespace, menus, toolbars, and contents pane results

- **Extensions**   Helper code that extends or complements other snap-ins, optionally providing new nodes, additional menu, toolbars, and enhanced contents pane results

- **Required Extensions**   Like extension above, but automatically added to the primary snap-in for every node in the namespace; cannot be removed programmatically

- **Dual-mode**   Can operate as either a standalone or extension snap-in

Snap-ins are COM objects and as such must be registered on each machine. Snap-ins and extensions that can be added to an MMC console file must be listed at HKEY_LOCAL_MACHINE\Software\Microsoft\MMC\Snapins. They are listed by Globally Unique IDentifier (GUID), a 128-bit number assigned to each COM component. There are several optional keys for each of the registered items. Standalone snap-ins have an empty key named Standalone. The descriptive name displayed in the Add Standalone Snap-In dialog box is stored in the NameString value. Entries can also register About boxes, providers, version numbers, and one or mode node types.

Nodes are the folders that appear in the namespace in the scope pane. Each node has a GUID and is listed in HKEY_LOCAL_MACHINE\Software\Microsoft\MMC\ NodeTypes. Node types have name values and optional extension keys. The extensions are PropertySheet, ContextMenu, Task, and NameSpace keys. Each key has a GUID that points to a COM component registered in HKEY_CLASSES_ROOT\CLSID and HKEY_LOCAL_MACHINE\Software\Classes\CLSID. This is where the name of the DLL actually lives in a key called *InprocServer32*. Standalone components also list a program identifier, or ProgID, that programmers use to refer to the object in source code. The ProgID is also registered in HKEY_CLASSES_ROOT.

This registry detail is difficult to follow but does promote an understanding of the snap-in architecture and how nodes and extensions are registered and reused. When a snap-in is loaded, calls to the registry deliver a list of extension GUIDs and their actual DLL locations on the disk. MMC then calls the extensions, which in turn programmatically modify the console tree namespace nodes, menus, property sheets, and wizards.

Extensibility Mechanisms

Snap-ins create the namespace, or ordered collection of nodes, from registered node types and extensions. They also create optional Tasks and New menu items as shown in Figure 8-7. The All Tasks menu is for actions that do not create new objects like

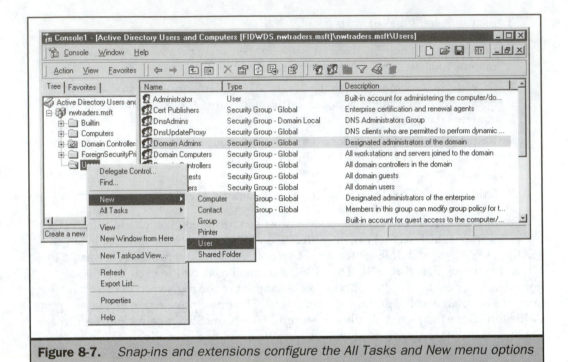

Figure 8-7.   *Snap-ins and extensions configure the All Tasks and New menu options*

reports and wizards. Nodes are owned by a particular snap-in or extension. Only the node owner can place menu items on the first-level menu (the Action menu in the child window, also available when right-clicking). Extensions can add items to the second-level Tasks and New menus. Menu items are added in the order the extensions are loaded, and menu separators are controlled by MMC. The user cannot adjust the menu order or position. Snap-ins can also create their own toolbars that can dock anywhere the user wishes. Table 8-1 shows a list of extensibility mechanisms.

Property Sheets

Snap-ins are good for listing information, but many administrative tasks require data input. In some cases, the number of columns is so great that the list view is not practical for review or input. The developer can build either modal dialogs or nonmodal property pages for these situations. Standard-size property pages are recommended and display standard Windows controls on tabbed dialog pages. Each control could map to a column in the list view and display in an appropriate format: text, label, list box, combo box, check box, radio button, or custom controls. Snap-ins can extend the property sheet dialog by adding tabbed pages as shown in Figure 8-8:

Mechanism	Description
Namespace Enumeration	Determines which nodes appear in a container
Context Menu Extension	Adds items to the context menu
Create New Menu Extension	Adds items to the New menu
Tasks Menu Extension	Adds items to the Tasks menu
Toolbar and Toolbar Buttons Extension	Adds a toolbar or button to the host window
Property Page Extension	Adds one or more property pages
View Menu Extension	Adds views (primary snap-in only)
Wizard Chaining	Adds one or more wizard pages to a frame
Help Extension	Adds HTML Help to the console help

Table 8-1.   *Extensibility Mechanisms*

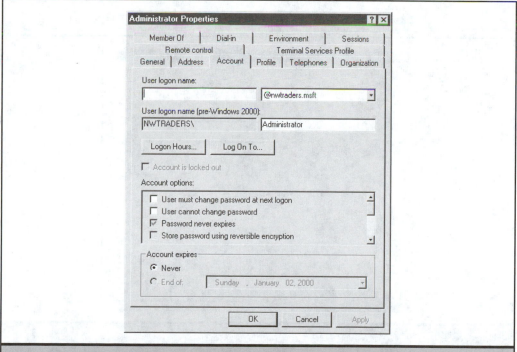

Figure 8-8.   *Active Directory User property tabs*

Wizards

Wizards are dialog pages that chain together and lead the user through a series of tasks. Wizards are common in Windows technology and are best recognized by the Back and Next buttons on the bottom of the page. They provide instruction and progress status. Snap-ins can create and extend wizards by chaining standard large pages, much like a script or set of instructions. A sample wizard is shown in Figure 8-9:

MMC 1.2 uses the Wizard97 style and allows snap-ins and extensions to modify the wizard chain. As third parties learn to extend MMC, wizards could get quite interesting. The new user wizard might have additional pages for faxing services, security cards, cube assignment, and other personnel-related issues.

Integrated HTML Help

MMC uses the HTML Help system that stores help topics as Web content in compressed files with the CHM extension. Snap-ins provide their own CHM files that are combined into a single collection file. The actual help presented to the user is a compilation of the various CHM files with single table of contents, index, and search pages. This can be a little confusing because the Contents topics appear in a somewhat random order and each extension can provide one or more topic areas. However, the Action/context menu for each node has a Help item that is linked directly to the help pages for that node. The Contents page can be hidden from view by default, making

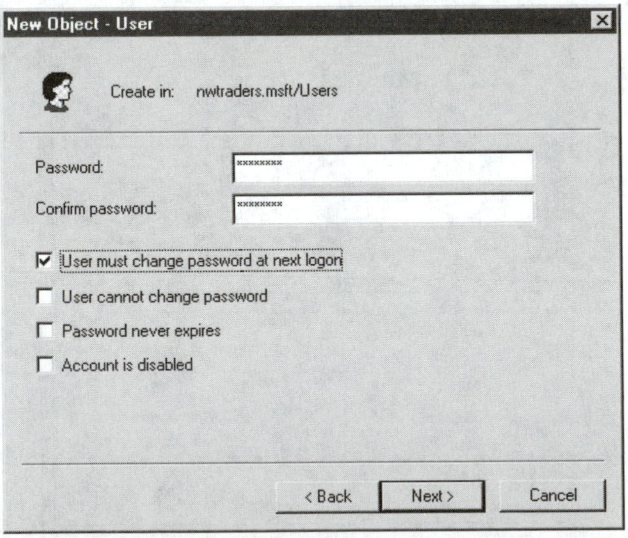

Figure 8-9. *The Create New Object—(User) Wizard*

this more approachable for novice administrators. Figure 8-10 shows a console with several snap-ins and the resulting help file, with the Contents page displayed.

Taskpads

Taskpads are Web-based graphical views of selected nodes in the scope pane. DHTML and scripting combine with standard HTML and ActiveX controls to provide a rich user display in the contents pane. This display is a combination of columnar lists, hyperlink tasks, and custom content. Not all node types in the namespace support taskpads. If they do, the New Taskpad View… option appears in the Action menu. Selecting this option runs a wizard that configures the taskpad. Each node can have multiple taskpads. The Taskpad title appears in a tab at the bottom of the contents pane. Toggle between the normal and taskpad views by clicking these title tabs.

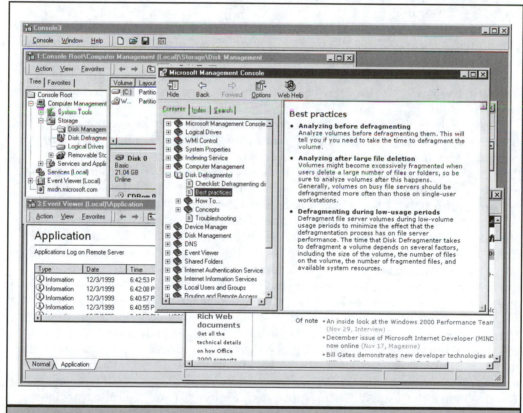

Figure 8-10.   *Multiple console Snap-Ins integrate Help*

Edit the selected taskpad with the Edit Taskpad View… option in the Action menu. Delete the selected taskpad with the Delete Taskpad View menu option.

There are standard, standard list, and custom taskpads. The default or standard taskpad displays tasks and a taskpad title. Create this by selecting No List in the Taskpad Display wizard page. The Taskpad Target wizard page determines the focus. A taskpad designated for the Selected tree item will only display for this particular node. If the node type is repeated several times like the logs in Event Viewer, the taskpad can work for all nodes of this type. If the latter is selected, the taskpad can be set as the default display. This makes the taskpad display first whenever the node is selected. You can still access the normal view and other taskpads by clicking the tabs at the bottom of the contents pane. Complete the wizard by adding tasks.

The standard list view variant adds an ActiveX list control showing the content normally displayed in the contents pane list view. The list can be horizontal or vertical, which also determines the placement of the tasks below or to the right of the list. The list size can be small, medium, or large. Horizontal works best for lists with many columns, and vertical is favored for long lists with fewer columns. Several taskpad variations appear in Figure 8-11.

Custom taskpads provide their own DHTML page, which displays tasks and other graphical items using Web-authoring technology. These are popular in Microsoft Back Office products like SQL Server. As developers learn the nuances of custom taskpads, this approach should predominate since they offer a richer display environment than standard list views. Also expect to see authoring tools specifically oriented to MMC taskpad creation.

Tasks are hyperlinks (graphical buttons) configured to open or execute a specific action. A user clicking on a task button sends a notification message to the underlying snap-in that in turn performs the task action. The task links are HTML image tags (IMG) and have a description (ALT attribute) that displays when the user moves the mouse over the link. Tasks are created as the final step in the New Taskpad View Wizard, or through the Tasks property pages in the Edit Taskpad View dialog.

The three task Command Types include Menu command, Shell command, and Navigation. Each command has a Task, Description, and lightweight black-on-white icon. The order of the tasks is configured in the Edit Taskpad View dialog, on the Tasks property page. Unfortunately for MMC authors, there is no simple drag-and-drop interface to rearrange the tasks, tools to import them from other taskpads, or even copy and paste. This is indeed a tedious task, but the benefits to novice users are many.

Menu commands associate an Action menu item supported in the list view with an icon and description. These commands can apply to the list in details pane or the entire tree item. For instance, the list-based Properties task will display the Properties dialog for the currently selected list item. This is beneficial to new users that may not know how to press ALT-ENTER for the Properties dialog or right-click for the Action menu. The tree item task Clear All Events applies to the entire list and typically associates with an Action menu item provided by the snap-in that works at the node level.

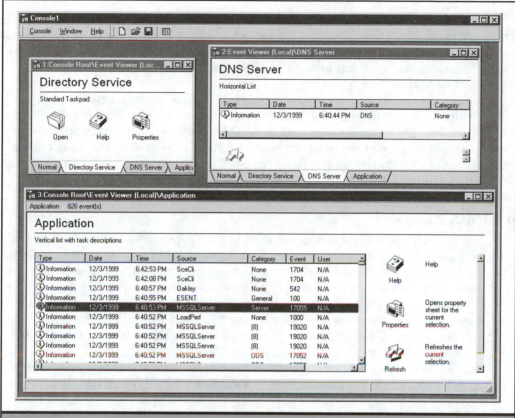

Figure 8-11. *Event Viewer has three taskpads (standard, horizontal list, and vertical list) with various tasks*

Shell commands interact with the operating system and scripting environments. They are basically shortcuts that call any executable, script, batch file, or associated file type. The commands open in another window outside of MMC. Optionally select parameters that pull information from the currently selected list item. The Start In folder and window style are other configurable options.

Navigation tasks are links to views saved to the MMC Favorites folder. Creating favorites is an extra step that organizes selected nodes into the Favorites tab in the scope pane. For accomplished users, the Favorites tab is handy and fast. For novice users, the console tree including the favorites may be hidden from view. Associating a Favorite with a taskpad task makes a simple navigation structure for multiple taskpads. You can literally hyperlink from one to the other. Note that the same result is provided by menu commands that open other nodes.

Folders

There is a special snap-in called New Folder. Several New Folders can be added to each console. The folders act as containers for other nodes and snap-in objects. Once the new Folder is added, you can select Rename from the Action/context menu to give the Folder a meaningful name.

Use folders to logically organize tools and tasks. When adding snap-ins to the Add/Remove Snap-In dialog, select the desired folder in the Snap-Ins Added To combo box. This places the desired snap-in into that container in the namespace. Once done, you cannot reorganize the parent container for a node by drag and drop or even using a simple wizard. You must instead remove the snap-in from one folder and then re-add it to another folder.

Web Links

The Link To Web Address snap-in is used to add Web pages to your console. This is a useful but awkward process. Selecting the Link To Web Address snap-in from the Add /Remove Snap-in dialog opens a wizard that prompts for an URL and descriptive name. When the user selects the descriptive name from the namespace, MMC acts as an OLE document container and loads Internet Explorer into the contents pane. It passes the URL to IE, which navigates the Web and returns the desired page. Scripting, DHTML, embedded objects, and other goodies all work as advertised. In fact, any IE5 compliant page works, including XML, and XSL.

Once the link is added to the namespace, the Action/context menu allows for node rename. Selecting properties from this menu also allows the target URL to change. However, you cannot browse from this property page, add links from your favorites, or search the Web. You can, of course, copy and paste links from the IE address bar.

The steps involved in creating a single link are time-consuming. It would be much easier to provide a copy-and-paste feature so multiple Web links could be created quickly. The inability to drag and drop links from one folder to another is also inefficient.

On the positive side, coupling custom Web development with the MMC console namespace provides an excellent platform for internal documentation, interactive administrative tools, facility maps, and vendor support links. Figure 8-12 shows an example of vendor links:

ActiveX Controls

The ActiveX snap-in adds any registered ActiveX control to the scope namespace. The Insert ActiveX Control Wizard guides the user through the control selection process. There is a drop-down box listing several control categories. Most of the controls listed have no application and may not even display in the MMC contents pane. If the control is written to OLE Control Extensions (OCX) '94 standards, the interface appears in the

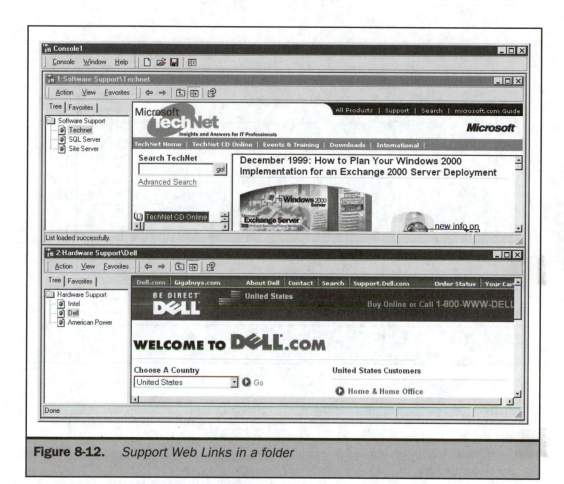

Figure 8-12. *Support Web Links in a folder*

contents pane. The Calendar Control from Microsoft Office, found in the Embeddable Objects category, is pictured in Figure 8-13.

Software developers create Win32 DLL components using specific interface guidelines. The components are compiled and registered as ActiveX controls. Other products like Visual Studio make use of these controls for user forms, reports, development tools, and other custom tasks. A control that is useful in Visual Studio may have no meaning and may not display in MMC. The control registration process flags a component with the intended use. That is how MMC can categorize them. But there is no specific flag for MMC compatibility, so the user is left to trial and error in selecting console-safe controls. A well-written control can be very useful; a good example of this would be a complex network topology map. Interactive maps would be hard to build with the DHTML taskpad architecture, but work very well with

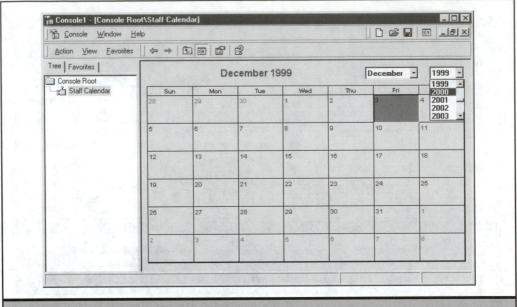

Figure 8-13. *Calendar ActiveX control in the contents pane*

Win32 graphic APIs. This approach provides an upgrade path for existing custom management applications. They can be recompiled as ActiveX controls and made to seamlessly fit into the namespace and contents pane style of MMC.

Corporate developers should be familiar with ActiveX Control technology in Visual Studio. A control created in Visual Basic can incorporate rich interface elements, ActiveX Data Objects (ADO) connecting to legacy databases, Collaborative Data Objects (CDO) interfacing to Exchange e-mail, and dozens of other COM references. This means that MMC can host complete data entry and reporting applications.

You can also host ActiveX controls inside of Web pages if your browser is Internet Explorer. Windows 2000 includes IE5 and MMC hosts IE as a document object. That is how the Link To Web Address snap-in works. Wrapping ActiveX Controls in DHTML Web content provides a synergy that incorporates the best aspects of each technology. In fact, this is the basic idea behind taskpads, which use wizards to build DHTML pages combining tasks (Web links) and the list view (ActiveX control).

Tool Files

Tools are saved instances of MMC console configurations with the Management Saved Console (MSC) file extension. The saved information includes the console tree namespace determined by the selected snap-ins, the extension snap-ins applied to each snap-in, list column settings, taskpads and tasks, favorites, views, and the display configuration. Any time a tool file is opened, it will display exactly the same state in which it was saved. The MSC file type is registered with the Windows Explorer shell. It can be used as a shortcut on the desktop, in menus, on the taskbar, and via scripting routines. The simple file structure can be copied to disk folders, e-mailed to a colleague, or posted to a Web site.

The MSC tool is a definition of a console configuration. It does not include the snap-in DLL files, the ActiveX OCX files, or the HTML Web links. These files must be installed and registered on the target machine with the exception of the Web links. An Active Directory administrator can collect valuable snap-ins and publish them to administrative users. Groups of snap-ins are added to a package. MSC tools published in the directory are configured to auto-download the required DLL and OCX files as needed. This is a clever method of distributing administrative consoles. The roaming admin can access the tools from any desktop knowing the necessary components will come along for the ride.

A quick inspection of an MSC file with Notepad suggests the use of OLE-structured storage with the various snap-ins, taskpads, and views stored in a proprietary format. There is no indication of HTML tags in these documents, so the actual taskpad Web pages are probably manufactured on the fly. Much of the data is stored in Unicode, which is expected given the international flavor of Windows 2000.

Selecting Save or Save As creates MSC consoles from the Console menu in the parent MDI menu. The default save folder is the Administrative Tools menu for the current user. Save the files to the Default User Administrative Tools menu folder so all users on that machine have access. The Options item in the Console menu configures the icon, console mode, and optional user mode settings. The Console mode has four choices, as displayed in Figure 8-14:

- **Author mode**   Full access with modify rights, add snap-ins, create taskpads, view the console tree, create windows

- **User mode**   Full access: complete access to window management, view the console tree, cannot add snap-ins or change properties, create windows

- **User mode**   Limited access, multiple window: view only the console tree items visible when the file was saved, create windows

- **User mode**   Limited access, single window: view only the console tree items visible when the file was saved

The three user mode choices have three additional settings at the bottom of the Options dialog. The right-click context menu can be removed from taskpad lists. This further simplifies operation for novice users by restricting them to predefined tasks. Changes to the console configuration can be restricted. This maintains the console layout carefully planned by the tool author. View creation can also be restricted. This

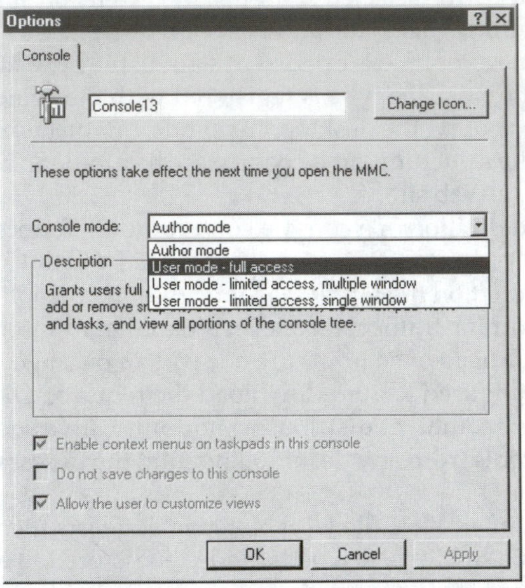

Figure 8-14. *Setting user options for a saved console file*

keeps a user from adding windows rooted at any node in the console tree. Again, the novice user might be confused by this advanced technique.

MMC consoles are very powerful administrative tools, and their use should be judicially controlled. Setting basic NTFS or network permissions on the MSC files can limit access to authorized users. Adding the Group Policy snap-in provides a finer level of detail. The Group Policy\User Configuration\Administrative Templates\ Windows Components\Microsoft Management Console folder controls various settings for the current tool, as seen in Figure 8-15. The list of available snap-ins comes from a configurable registry key. There are various settings that also apply to the Group Policy snap-in itself that, of course, can be used to change the group policy.

Working with Tools

The seasoned administrator's ability to author management tools for novice and casual users is a powerful MMC feature. There are several key steps to this process. We will build a sample tool consisting of popular snap-ins and save this as a Management Saved Console file. The tool has several child windows, taskpads, Web links, and favorites.

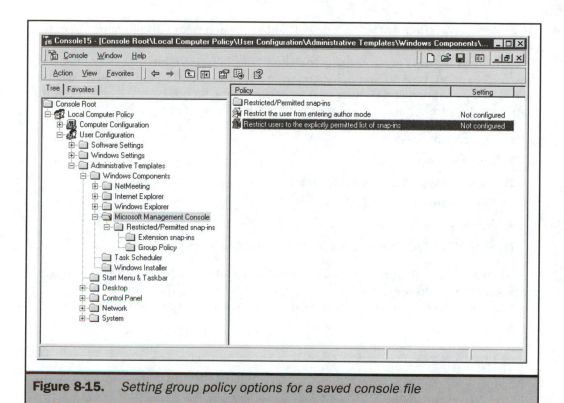

Figure 8-15.   *Setting group policy options for a saved console file*

This process starts from an existing console tool or an empty MMC window. The existing tool saves some time by skipping the Add/Remove Snap-In step. Use the Save As… option from the Console menu to give the tool a new filename and location. Typing **MMC** at the Windows 2000 Start menu Run… command opens the blank MMC window. Name the file with the Save or Save As… menu options.

Adding Snap-Ins

A console tool is the sum of its snap-ins. Click Add/Remove Snap-In… on the Console menu or press CTRL-M to open the snap-in dialog. There is a combo box at the top of the Standalone page. This entry defaults to Console Root, meaning that the target snap-in appears at the top level of the namespace hierarchy. Folder snap-ins with meaningful names are used to nest other snap-ins in a logical hierarchy.

Start with two Folder snap-ins. Click the Add… button to open the Add Standalone Snap-In dialog. Scroll to the Folder Snap-In and click Add twice. Click Close to return to the Add/Remove dialog. The New Folder names cannot be changed—yet.

Click OK to return to the MMC window. Right-click each folder and Rename them to **Local** and **Server**.

Return to the Add/Remove Snap-In dialog. Select Local in the drop-down list and click Add to open the Add Standalone Snap-In dialog pictured in Figure 8-16. Select the following snap-ins and choose local computer as the target. Notice that some of the snap-ins have additional configuration settings for the target computer.

- Device Manager
- Event Viewer
- Local Users and Groups (does not apply to domain controllers)
- Performance Logs and Alerts
- Services
- Shared Folders (has additional configuration settings)

When all items are added, click Close and OK to return to MMC. Browse through the new hierarchy to see the nodes, subnodes, and list views. This tool provides the basic administrative needs for a local workstation or stand-alone server.

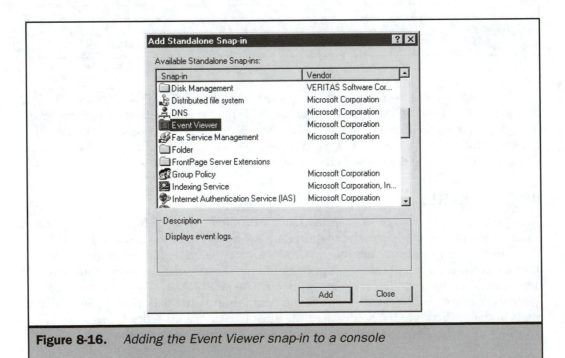

Figure 8-16. *Adding the Event Viewer snap-in to a console*

Snap-ins appear in the scope pane namespace in the order of selection. Carefully plan the layout of complex tools and organize with named folders.

The Server version will target a file server and use the convenient Computer Management snap-in with selected extensions. Start the Add/Remove process by clicking CTRL-M. Double-click Server in the Snap-Ins Added To list. This has the same effect as a selection from the drop-down box. Click the Add button, select Computer Management (actually a snap-in of snap-ins), and click Add. Click the Browse button to find the intended server as shown in Figure 8-17. Close the Add Standalone dialog. The DNS name of the selected server displays next to the snap-in name. Select the Computer Management snap-in and click About to see the vendor and version information. Close the About box.

Configuring Extensions

Some snap-ins like Computer Management are really collections of smaller snap-ins. Event Viewer is an example of a snap-in that can work on its own merit or act as an extension to another standalone snap-in. The Extension page on the Add/Remove Snap-In dialog configures the extensions and whether they apply in the current situation. Select this page to see that Computer Management includes over a dozen extensions. The default adds all extensions. Clear this box to enable detailed selection in the Available extensions list. Notice the description and About box at the bottom of

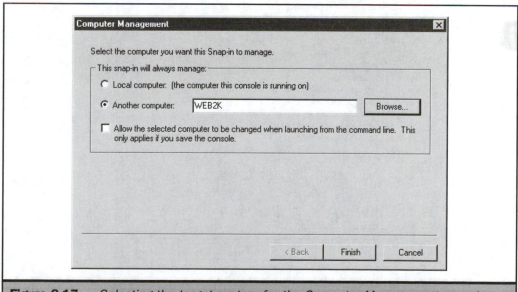

Figure 8-17. *Selecting the target system for the Computer Management snap-in*

the list. Add or remove the items of interest as pictured in Figure 8-18, and click OK to return to MMC.

Browse the namespace tree to see the difference between stand-alone snap-ins and the convenient Computer Management with extensions approach. The folder icons grouping the System Tools, Storage, and Services in the Server folder are only possible with custom programming. Also notice the ease of managing multiple machines with one tool.

Creating Favorites

The namespace is starting to get busy with dozens of nodes. There are certain nodes that are used constantly. Add the most popular nodes to the Favorites tab in the scope pane. Start with the System Log in Event Viewer. Select this node and click Add to Favorites… on the Favorites menu. Click the New Folder… button and create a folder called Local. Make another called **Server** to match the structure in the namespace tree. Make sure that the Local folder is selected before clicking OK in the Add to Favorites dialog. Repeat this process for the Services and Shares nodes on the local machine.

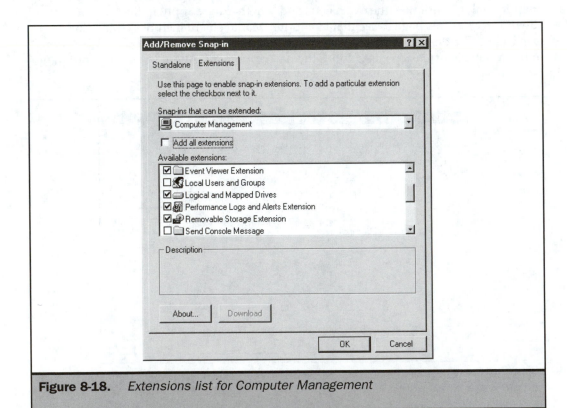

Figure 8-18. *Extensions list for Computer Management*

The Server folder in this example targets a domain controller. The same Favorites would be useful. Repeat the steps above to add the System Log, Services, and Shares for the remote server. Click on the Favorites tab in the scope pane to inspect your work. Notice that the folders work differently than in the namespace tree and the icons are replaced with generic document types. In fact, the items work like hypertext links in a Web browser and this is the technology used to display Favorites. Also notice that the context menu for a favorite item does not allow rename or property inspection.

Right-click a Favorite or click the Favorites menu to open the Organize Favorites dialog. Use this facility to Create Folders, Rename, Move, and Delete items. The Rename button works for the folders as well as Favorite items. The Move to Folder... button repositions items to a particular folder but does not affect the order within a folder. All Favorites appear sorted within their folder. Make plenty of folders to keep your Favorites organized and easy to find.

Open the Favorites menu to see that the folders created above now appear as submenu options. Select several of these Favorites to see the associated list appear in the contents pane. Switch back to the Tree tab in the scope pane and check if the namespace focus changes to match the selected Favorite.

Creating Taskpads

Taskpads provide a simpler, cleaner view of the management data. They are very useful for novice administrators and help integrate operating system commands and scripts into the console tool. There are three basic types of taskpads, so we will create one of each.

Open the Event Viewer node in the Local folder. Right-click the Application log and select New Taskpad View... to open the Taskpad View Wizard seen in Figure 8-19. Select the default horizontal view, InfoTip, and Large. In the Taskpad target page, select All tree items and Change default display. On the next page, set the name to My Event and the description to something about the local computer. Do not start the task wizard and click Finish. The My Events title appears in the contents pane with a list control displaying the event log. A set of tabs on the bottom of the contents pane lets you toggle between the standard list view and any taskpads that apply to this snap-in or node. Click on several of the Event Viewer nodes to see that the new taskpad applies to all nodes of type Event Viewer. This includes the event nodes for the remote server, which are working as an extension snap-in inside Computer Management.

Taskpads are associated with node types or a particular node. To demonstrate, make another taskpad for the local Services node. Right-click Services and select New Taskpad View.... Make this a medium size vertical list with text descriptions. Set the taskpad Target to Selected tree item and create a useful name and description. Start the new Task Wizard. Add a menu command that Starts a service by selecting List in details pane for the Command source and Start as the Available command. Accept the default name, description, and icon. Check the Run This Wizard Again box on the Completing The New Task Wizard page and select Finish. Add another menu command to stop services. Finally, add a Navigation command that selects the Services

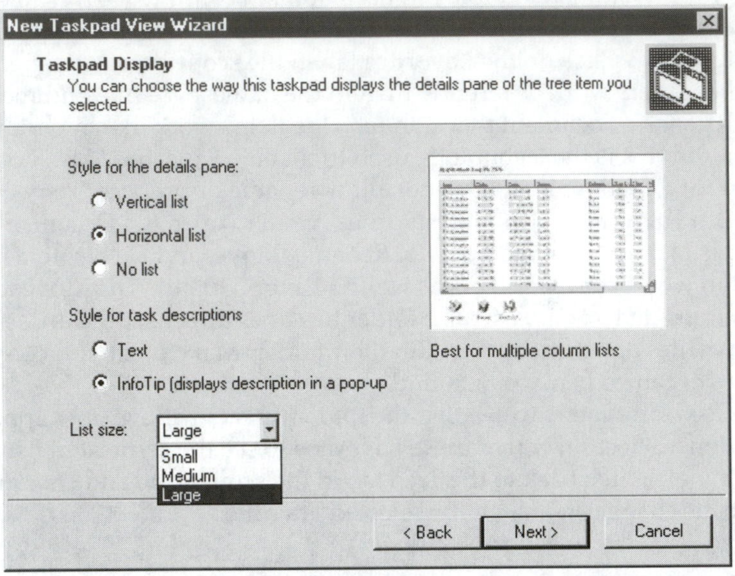

Figure 8-19.   Creating a taskpad with the wizard

in the Server folder. Notice that Navigation commands limit the choice to a predefined favorite. Complete this task and click Finish to see the result. The familiar Services list appears in a box in the taskpad with the tasks to the right side. The task names and descriptions display in table format. Moving the selection cursor through the list of services enables or disables the Start and Stop tasks appropriately. To make this clearer, select Choose Columns… from the View menu and hide the Description. This will show the Status column right next to the Service name. To test the third task, click on the link to navigate to the remote Server services node. Notice that the taskpad is not in effect because we limited its use to the node where it was created. To navigate back to the Services taskpad on the local computer, click the Back button on the toolbar.

Go back and add tasks to the Event Viewer taskpad by selecting any event node, displaying the taskpad view, and selecting Edit Taskpad View… in the Action menu. Select the Tasks page and click the New button. Create a menu command that performs a refresh. Select the default name, description, and icon. Run the wizard again by checking the box before clicking Finish. Add a shell command that opens a support Web site by typing www.microsoft.com/technet in the Command field. Click OK to close the taskpad Properties dialog. Notice that the descriptions do not appear next to the tasks. Gently move the mouse pointer over the tasks to see the descriptions as InfoTips in place of text blocks. Click the Refresh task to force the event list to redisplay. Also click the Technet task to open the Microsoft technical support page in a separate Internet Explorer window.

User Interface Management

So far, all work was completed in a single child window. Advanced administrators who are very comfortable with the Explorer-type interface will prefer this approach. Novice administrators benefit from a more focused view. Concentrate on the Services and Events for this exercise.

Create a separate window for the System Event Log on the local computer. Right-click the System node and select New Window from Here. This opens a child window. Use the toolbar's maximize, minimize, and restore buttons to make both child windows viewable. Open the MMC Window menu to see the window names and numbers. Notice that windows can be cascaded and tiled. Experiment with this to position the windows in a desirable arrangement.

The focused taskpad view of the System events is too busy for a novice. Select Customize… from the View menu and clear the following boxes:

- Console tree
- Standard menus
- Standard toolbar
- Taskpad navigational tabs

Check the description bar option to add a line at the top of the contents pane. This is useful for certain snap-ins like Event Viewer, which displays the number of events as a description. To finish the novice effect, slide the bar separating the scope and contents pane to the left. This will hide the Favorites page and limit the view to the custom taskpad.

Create a third window for technicians who only have access to the local server. Right-click on the Local folder in the console tree and select New Window from Here. Leave the tree, menus, and toolbars at their default settings. Add the description bar using the Customize option in the View menu. This view can be saved in a restricted form for local technicians to complete their work.

Saving Console Files

Once the tool is working to your satisfaction, save the result in one or more MSC files. Start with the advanced administrator version. Maximize the window that shows the entire namespace. Select Save As from the Console menu. The default Save In folder is the Administrative Tools section of the Start/Programs menu. This is stored in your local profile under Documents and Settings. To make the tool appear for all users of the local machine, save it in the Administrative Tools section of the All Users profile. Provide a useful name like "Admin console" and click Save as seen in Figure 8-20.

LEARNING THE BASICS

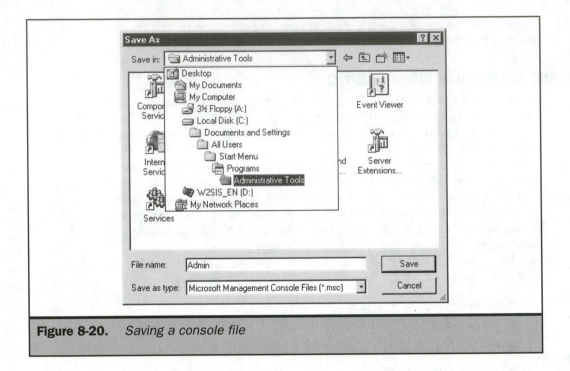

Figure 8-20.   *Saving a console file*

The technicians should only see the window that focuses on the local computer. Select that window in the Window menu. Select Options from the Console menu. Notice that the name and icon can be set here. Change the Console mode from the default of Author to User mode – limited access, multiple window. This prevents the technician from adding new snap-ins and limits their scope of work to the tree items provided. Select Save As from the Console menu and name the file **Technician console**.

The last step is the novice console that isolates a single taskpad. Select the System window from the Window menu. This already has a taskpad with several tasks and no confusing trees, menus, or toolbars. Select Options from the Console menu, and set the Console mode to User mode – limited access, single window. Check the Do Not Save Changes on the bottom of the dialog. Remove the Enable context menus and Allow the user to customize views. Save this version as Novice console. Ignore the warning message about multiple windows. The novice will only see the one window.

Note   *In practice, this method is less efficient than authoring separate files from scratch for each level of usage. The novice console will open several snap-ins that will not be used, which is a waste of processing cycles. It does save authoring time to use the same administration console as a template for more focused views. Experiment with both methods to determine your best solution.*

Quit MMC and open the Start/Programs/Administrative Tools menu. The three new consoles will appear in alphabetical order. Test each version to see that it provides the level of control that is needed. Secure the files in NTFS with appropriate user permissions. The MSC files can be copied, moved, or linked with shortcuts. Send them to coworkers via e-mail or a Web download. Make sure that custom or third-party snap-ins are installed on all administrator machines, or build an auto-download facility with Active Directory. Experiment and make your job easier.

Searching for Snap-Ins

The first place to look for snap-ins is the Administrative Tools menu. Commonly used standalone snap-ins are preconfigured as read-only MSC files and placed in the Documents and Settings\All Users\Start menu\Programs\Administrative Tools folder. Inspect these shortcuts to determine where the actual .MSC files are located.

Tip *Create your own MMC tool and place a shortcut in the folder for all users of a machine to see it in their Administrative Tools menu.*

MSC files are registered with the Explorer shell and can work anywhere a shortcut works. Copy them to the desktop, taskbar, menu folders, Web links, or any place convenient. The default behavior of the MSC file type is defined in the Folder Options File Types property page. Notice in the following illustration that the default action is to Author the file by calling MMC.EXE with the /a option.

Tip *One interesting place an MSC shortcut appears is the context menu for the desktop My Computer object. Right-click this object and select Manage to quickly access the MMC Computer Management console. You can do the same from the Computers container in Active Directory Users and Computers.*

Dozens of snap-ins ship with Windows 2000. The actual items available at any given time depend on installed options. Back Office and the Windows 2000 Resource kit already provide several snap-ins, and that list will grow as Microsoft evolves its management strategy. Third parties will catch on quickly and conform to this emerging standard. Many of these options are listed in the following sections. This is not meant to be a comprehensive list, but a snap-in sampler.

Windows 2000 Professional Snap-Ins

The most common Windows 2000 Professional snap-ins are combined into one container called Computer Management. The default configuration for Computer Management appears in Figure 8-21.

The nodes and extensions are separated into three main categories: System Tools, Storage, and Server Applications and Services. The latter container expands as various services are added to your configuration.

Table 8-2 describes the snap-ins available with a typical Windows 2000 Professional installation and the Windows NT 4 counterparts.

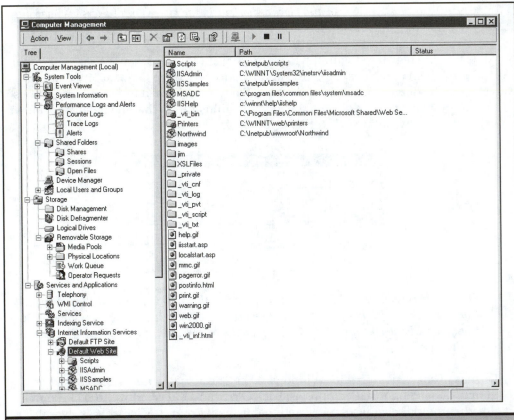

Figure 8-21.   *Computer Management consists of the several common snap-ins*

Win2000 Pro Snap-In	Description	Windows NT 4 Tool
ActiveX Control	Display OCX'94-compliant controls	
Certificates	Browse certificates for users, services, and computers	Internet Explorer
Component Services	COM+ management	NT Option Pack, Transaction Server, DCOMCnfg
Computer Management	Container node for other tools listed in bold	
Device Manager	List and configure hardware devices	Control Panel Devices
Disk Defragmenter	Disk defragmenter	Diskeeper
Disk Management	Dynamic disk and volume management	Disk Administrator
Event Viewer	Event logs	Event Viewer
Fax Service Management	Fax management	
Folder	Create node containers	
Front Page Extensions	FrontPage Web security	
Group Policy	Edit Group Policy Objects	System Policy Editor
Indexing Service	Index service	NT Option Pack
IP Security Policy Management	Manger Internet Protocol Security	
Link to Web Address	Display Web pages by URL	
Local Users and Groups	Manage local user and group accounts	User Manager
Performance Logs and Alerts	Performance data logs and alerts	Performance Monitor
Removable Storage Management	Hierarchical storage management	

Table 8-2. *Windows 2000 Professional Snap-Ins and Windows NT 4 Counterparts*

Win2000 Pro Snap-In	Description	Windows NT 4 Tool
Security Configuration and Analysis	Security analysis based on templates	
Security Templates	Edit security templates	User Manager Policies Menu
Services	Start, stop, and configure services	Control Panel Services, Server Manager
Shared Folders	Display shared folders, sessions, and files	Server Manager
System Information	Display system information for troubleshooting	Windows NT Diagnostics

Table 8-2.   *Windows 2000 Professional Snap-Ins and Windows NT 4 Counterparts* (continued)

Windows 2000 Server Snap-Ins

Any server promoted to a domain controller has three key snap-ins added to the Administrative Tools menu and the add snap-in list. Each deals with a specific facet of Active Directory. Administrators will spend much of their time in Active Directory User and Computers. This will also be the central directory for the next version of Exchange. The four major snap-ins for Active Directory are pictured in Figure 8-22.

The Domain Name Service (DNS) for the TCP/IP protocol is a critical requirement for Active Directory. This snap-in manages more than computer names and their corresponding IP addresses. Special <SRV> records are added to DNS that help Active Directory servers talk to each other. Table 8-3 shows the Windows 2000 Server snap-ins, descriptions, and their Windows NT 4 counterparts.

Resource Kit Snap-Ins

The Windows 2000 Resource Kit includes dozens of administrative utilities and advanced documentation. Two special snap-ins ship with the Resource Kit:

Resource Kit Snap-In	Description
ADSI Edit	Low-level object and attribute editor
SIDWalker Security Manager	Manage computer server resources moved between domains

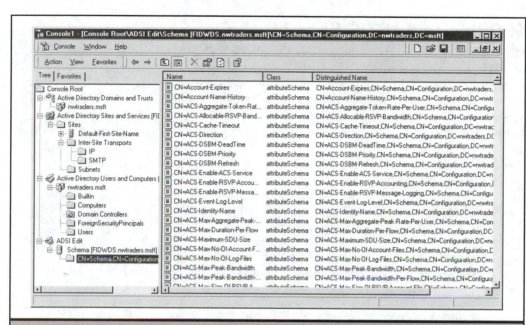

Figure 8-22.   *Several Active Directory snap-ins with the schema classes list*

Win2000 Server Snap-In	Description	Windows NT 4 Tool
Active Directory Domains and Trusts	Configure trusts to other domains	User Manager for Domains Trust menu
Active Directory Sites and Services	Configure directory replication and routing	
Active Directory Users and Computers	Manage domain computer, user, and group accounts	User Manager for Domains, Server Manager
DNS	Domain Naming Service	DNS Manager
QoS Admission Control	Network Quality of Service configuration	
Routing and Remote Access	Protocol routing configuration	

Table 8-3.   *Windows 2000 Server Snap-Ins and Windows NT 4 Counterparts*

Back Office and NTOP Snap-Ins

MMC first debuted in the Windows NT Option Pack (NTOP). The main components of NTOP are now part of the Windows 2000 operating system package. The Back Office products are migrating to MMC as new releases hit the streets. Small Business Server (SBS) is a subset of Back Office and includes Exchange, SQL, and Proxy servers. SBS is notable in that a clever administrator console is built using MMC taskpad technology. This is a good example of where Microsoft is heading with administrative tools in the future.

Here is summary of current Option Pack and Back Office components that currently use MMC:

- **NT Option Pack**
  - Internet Information Server 4.0
  - Transaction Server 2.0 (now part of Component Services)
  - Message Queue Server (now part of Component Services)
  - Certificate Server
  - Index Server
- **Back Office 4.5**
  - SQL Server 7.0 (Enterprise Manager and OLAP Services)
  - Systems Management Server 2.0
  - SNA Server 4.0
  - Proxy Server 2.0
  - Site Server 3.0 (Standard and Commerce Edition)
- **Other**
  - Small Business Server 4.5 (includes NTOP, SQL, Proxy, admin taskpads)
  - FrontPage Server Extensions 2000

Noticeably absent from this list is Exchange Server 5.5, which still uses a proprietary Win32 interface with the familiar scope and contents panes. Exchange Server 2000 integrates with Windows 2000 and relies on MMC for management and administration.

Custom-Built Snap-Ins

The Windows SDK includes technical documentation for commercial developers interested in writing snap-ins and extensions. Visual C++ templates and code samples aid in this effort. Visual Basic and Visual InterDev developers should wait for refreshes of those products or toolkits specific to MMC authoring. MMC hosts ActiveX controls natively and ActiveX documents via Internet Explorer, so explore those options.

Complex Web pages with the latest scripting technology are the best bet for the creative administrator. Internet Explorer is an integral part of the MMC framework, and Windows 2000 includes IE 5 as a minimum platform. Dynamic HTML (DHTML), Extensible Markup Language and StyleSheets (XML/XSL), Cascading Style Sheets (CSS), behaviors, HTML+Time, Windows Media Player, and other rich Web technologies can display most any piece of management information in any way imaginable. Add some scripting and COM components to create that special effect. What a great tool for internal documentation!

The Complete Reference

Chapter 9

The Command Prompt

W indows 2000 includes some changes (improvements) to the command-line interface and the commands. The Command Prompt menu item has moved to the Accessories submenu, so if you're a command junkie, you should move the item either to the Start menu or the Programs menu for easier access. In fact, you may want to create a desktop shortcut to the Command Prompt and put it on your Quick Launch toolbar. (Chapter 6 has instructions for performing these tasks.) You can also open a Command Prompt window by entering **cmd** in the Run text box.

The Command Prompt Window

Commands are executed from a Windows 2000 command prompt window, and there are a few to choose from, as follows:

■ If you open %SystemRoot%\System32\Command.com, the window's title bar says MS-DOS Prompt. The prompt reflects the directory, and above the prompt you can see a reference to Microsoft Windows DOS. This window is running an MS-DOS application (command.com).

■ If you choose the menu item Command Prompt (from the Accessories submenu), the window's title bar says Command Prompt. The prompt is C:\>, and the reference display above the prompt is Microsoft Windows 2000. This window is running the Windows 2000 application Cmd.exe.

■ If you open the Start menu, choose Run, and then enter **cmd** (or **cmd.exe**), the window's title bar displays the path to cmd.exe (%SystemRoot%\System32\cmd.exe). The prompt is C:\>, and the reference display above the prompt is Microsoft Windows 2000. This window is running the Windows 2000 application Cmd.exe.

Change the Properties of the Command Prompt Window

The Console applet that was available in the Control Panel in Windows NT 4 is gone, and customization of the Command Prompt window is accomplished from the window itself. Right-click on the title bar of the window to display the menu seen here.

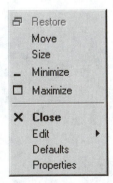

You can use either the Defaults command or the Properties command to customize the Command Prompt window—the same choices appear in the Properties dialog box that opens. There is a difference, however, in the way each command affects your system.

The Defaults command permanently changes the settings for all Command Prompt windows, including the window that opens when you invoke Cmd.exe from the Run command on the Start menu. The changes you make are not put into effect in the current window, but you'll see them in the Command Prompt windows you open hereafter. (If you right-click the shortcut on the Start menu system, you'll see the changes you made reflected in the tabs of the shortcut's Properties dialog box.)

The Properties command changes the settings for the current Command Prompt window. The changes take effect immediately. However, when you click OK, you have the opportunity to make the changes permanent (affecting all future windows) by changing the properties of the shortcut.

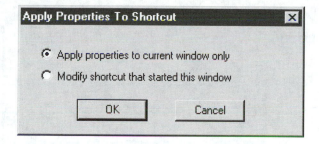

Command Prompt Window Options Tab

You can further configure the window by changing the settings in the Options tab (see Figure 9-1). The choices available here cover a variety of configuration options.

- **Cursor Size**   Change the size of the blinking cursor. Small is an underline, Medium is a small square, and Large is a square the same size as the font.

- **Command History**   The buffer size is the number of commands stored in the buffer. The number of buffers is really the number of processes that can maintain history buffers. Increasing either one of these options uses more memory. Enable the Discard Old Duplicates check box to have the system eliminate duplicate commands in the buffer history.

- **Display Options**   You can change the size of the window from Window (the default) to Full Screen on an x86 computer (RISC-based computers cannot display a full screen Command Prompt window). To toggle an x86 computer between Window and Full Screen while you're working in the Command Prompt window, press ALT-ENTER.

- **Edit Options**   Select Quick Edit Mode to drag the mouse for cutting, copying, and pasting text, instead of using the Edit menu. Select Insert Mode to insert text in the Command Prompt window instead of overwriting existing text.

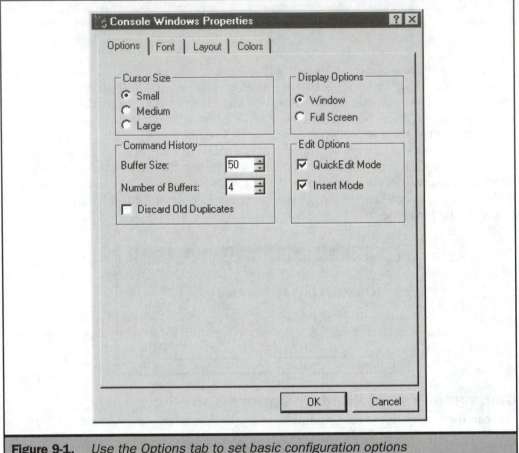

Figure 9-1.   *Use the Options tab to set basic configuration options*

| Tip | *Insert Mode is handy if you're not a terrific typist; it lets you back up through a command and parameters and correct typing errors.* |

Command Prompt Window Font Tab

Use the Font tab to select Raster Fonts (the default) or TrueType font. Change the size of the Raster font by selecting a different pixel measurement from the list of sizes. Change the size of the TrueType font by selecting a different point size (or enter a point size directly in the text box at the top of the list). Click the Bold Fonts check box to use bold fonts in the window.

Command Prompt Window Layout Tab

Use the Layout tab to size and position the Command Prompt window with the following options:

- **Screen Buffer Size**   Specify the width and height of the screen buffer. The width is the number of characters that display on a line. The height is the number of lines that display for text that's in the buffer. If the size of the window is smaller than the size of the buffer, scroll bars appear to let you view the contents of the buffer.

- **Window Size**   Specify the width (number of characters) and height (number of lines) for the window.

- **Window Position**   By default, the system positions the window, but you can deselect this option and specify the left and top settings for the window's position on your monitor.

Command Prompt Window Colors Tab

Use the Colors tab to set the color for each of the following elements:

- Screen Text
- Screen Background
- Popup Text
- Popup Background

Copy and Paste in the Command Prompt Window

To copy text from a Command Prompt window, select the text using one of these methods:

- If you've configured the Command Prompt window for Quick Edit Mode, drag your mouse across the text you want to copy and press ENTER to place it on the clipboard.

- If you haven't configured the Command Prompt window for Quick Edit Mode, right-click on the title bar and choose Edit | Mark. Then position your cursor at the beginning of the text you want to copy. Hold down the SHIFT key and click the end of the text you want to copy. Alternatively, drag your mouse to select the text after you choose Edit | Mark. With the text highlighted, press ENTER to place the text on the clipboard.

Note   *You cannot cut text from a Command Prompt window, you can only copy.*

To paste the text into a Windows application window, choose Edit | Paste or press CTRL-V. To paste the text into an MS-DOS program (or another Command Prompt window), right-click the title bar and choose Edit | Paste.

To Paste text from another application into a Command Prompt window, position your cursor at the point of insertion. Then use one of these methods to paste the text:

- If you have configured the Command Prompt window for Quick Edit Mode, right-click to paste the text automatically.

- If you haven't configured the Command Prompt window for Quick Edit Mode, right-click and choose Paste from the menu that appears.

- If you're truly a command-line freak and prefer to do everything at the keyboard instead of using a mouse, press ALT-SPACE and then enter **e**, **p**, which stands for Edit | Paste.

Command Extensions

The power of the Windows 2000 command line is augmented by command extensions, which add functionality to the following commands:

- ASSOC
- CALL
- CD or CHDIR
- DEL or ERASE
- ENDLOCAL
- FOR
- FTYPE
- GOTO
- IF
- MD or MKDIR
- POPD
- PROMPT
- PUSHD
- SET
- SETLOCAL
- SHIFT
- START

The extensions are particular to each command, and you can get specific information by entering *<command> /?* at the command line.

Extensions are enabled by default, but you can disable and reenable them by entering **cmd /e:on** or **cmd /e:off** at the command line. You can also use the registry to set the default option for turning extensions on or off, and for applying the configuration to the computer or to an individual user on a computer.

To enable or disable extensions for the computer, open a registry editor and go to HKEY_LOCAL_MACHINE\Software\Microsoft\Command Processor. To enable or disable extensions for the current user on a computer, go to HKEY_CURRENT_USER\Software\Microsoft\Command Processor. Open the data item named EnableExtensions, and enter **1** (on) or **0** (off) in the DWORD editor. In the illustration, the data type is Hex, so the entry is translated to 0x1 or 0x0.

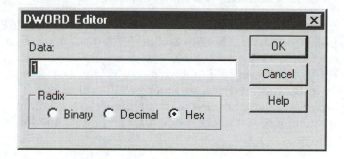

If the enabling configuration differs among the setting locations, there's a pecking order for extensions enabling, as follows:

1. Command-line entry (**cmd /e:X** where *X* is on or off)

2. Current User registry setting

3. Local Computer registry setting

Folder and Filename Completion

Folder and filename completion is a feature that lets you type a partial directory name or filename against a command with the system filling in the rest. The feature works by means of a control character you enter that invokes the feature. For example, you can enter **cd \pro** *<control character>* to get to the Programs Files directory, or enter **type myf** *<control character>* to display the contents of myfile.txt on the screen. If there are multiple directories or files that match the characters you enter, pressing the control character again moves you to the next instance. When you get to the correct target, press ENTER to complete the command. If no target matches your string, the system beeps.

Name completion is not turned on by default, but you can invoke it for a command session by entering **cmd /f:on** at the command line. Once invoked, you can use CTRL-D to complete a directory entry and CTRL-F to complete a filename entry.

If you want to make the feature permanent, a registry entry accomplishes the task. You can enable autocompletion either for the computer or for the current user. The process of entering the control characters in the registry turns on the feature.

To enable name completion for the computer, open a registry editor and go to HKEY_LOCAL_MACHINE\Software\Microsoft\Command Processor.

- For directory name completion, open the value item CompletionChar and enter, in Hex, the control character you want to use.

- For filename completion, open the value item PathCompletionChar and enter, in Hex, the control character you want to use.

To enable name completion for the current user, go to HKEY_CURRENT_USER\ Software\Microsoft\Command Processor and perform the same steps described for entering the characters in the local machine.

The control characters are entered in the registry as Hex. For example, if you want to use the TAB key as the control character, enter **9** as the value.

The PathCompletionChar value item may not appear in the Command Processor key, in which case you must add it. The method for accomplishing this depends on the registry editor you use.

If you're using Regedit:

1. Select the Command Processor subkey in the left pane.

2. Right-click on a blank spot in the right pane and choose New, DWORD value.

3. Name the value PathCompletionChar.

4. Open the new PathCompletionChar value and enter, in Hex, the character you want to use.

If you're using Regedt32:

1. Select the Command Processor subkey and choose Edit | Add Value from the menu bar.

2. Enter PathCompletionChar in the Value Name text box.

3. Specify REG_DWORD in the Data Type text box.

4. Open the new PathCompletionChar value and enter, in Hex, the character you want to use.

Here's a quick explanation of the differences between the filename and directory name completion functions:

- The filename completion feature works on directories, too, because it's actually searching for a complete path, matching against both file and directory names.

- If the file completion control character is used on a command that works only against directories (for example, CD or RD), only directory names are searched.

- The directory completion function matches only against directory names, which makes it faster for directory searching than the filename completion function when there are both files and directories with matching strings.

- You can use the same control character for both the directory name and filename autocompletion feature.

- If you use different control characters in the registry values, the current user settings take precedence over the local computer settings.

If you spend a lot of time at the command line (some of us are really command-line freaks and are comfortable and happy entering text), this function is extremely useful. Not only does it save typing, it also eliminates those frustrating moments when you either make a typo or forget the exact spelling of a directory or filename. To make all of this even easier, here are some tips on using the name completion feature:

- You must enter a space between directory commands, such as **cd** or **rd**, and the backslash.

- The completion function automatically places quotation marks around names that contain spaces.

- You can use the left arrow to back up and then enter the control character again. All text to the right of the cursor is discarded. This is handy if you want to widen the search by shortening the string.

- After searching, if you edit the string and press the control character again, the existing list of matches is ignored and a new list is generated.

Wildcard Shortcuts

Windows 2000 has a command-line wildcard shortcut feature. You can enter a command and a string representing a partial name (of a directory or a file, depending on the command) and end the string with a wildcard. Windows executes the command against every matching directory or folder. Most of us are aware of this feature and use it constantly, as in the command **dir *.txt** or **dir tr***.

The wildcard also works with other commands, such as cd. If you enter the command **cd \wi*** on a computer that has a directory named Winnt, the command executes properly. If you enter the same command on a computer that has a directory named Winnt and a directory named Wizards, the command executes against the first match (Winnt).

This feature does not offer the flexibility and user-control of the name completion feature, which displays each match as you continue to press the control character, and leaves it to the user to press the ENTER key when the appropriate command appears.

Commands

The command line is a favored tool for many administrators and power users, especially those of us whose computing roots go back to the DOS-only world. This section discusses commands that have disappeared or changed from previous versions of Windows (especially Windows 9x), in addition to commands for Terminal Services, with which you may not be familiar.

Unsupported MS-DOS Commands

A number of MS-DOS commands have disappeared from Windows 2000. In fact, some of them had already disappeared in earlier versions of Windows NT, but they're covered here in case you're migrating from a non-Windows environment and aren't familiar with the Windows NT commands.

Table 9-1 describes the obsolete commands, along with those explanations that could be found.

Unsupported Command	Explanation
Assign	No longer supported.
Backup	No longer supported.
Choice	No longer supported.
Ctty	No longer supported.
Dblspace	No longer supported.
Defrag	Disk optimization is automatic. If you want to manually defrag a disk, open My Computer, right-click on the drive and choose Properties. On the Tools tab, select Defragment Now.

Table 9-1.   *MS-DOS Commands That Are Not Available in Windows 2000*

Unsupported Command	Explanation
Deltree	Replaced by rmdir/s, which removes directories that contain files and/or subdirectories.
Diskperf	No longer supported.
Dosshell	Not needed.
Drvspace	No longer supported.
Emm386	Not needed.
Fasthelp	Not needed; use the help command instead.
Fdisk	Replaced by Disk Management.
Include	Multiple configurations of the MS-DOS subsystem are not supported.
Interlnk	No longer supported.
Intersrv	No longer supported.
Join	Not needed with the support for larger partitions.
Memmaker	Not needed; the operating system automatically optimizes the MS-DOS subsystem's use of memory.
Menucolor	Multiple configurations of the MS-DOS subsystem are not supported.
Menudefault	Multiple configurations of the MS-DOS subsystem are not supported.
Menuitem	Multiple configurations of the MS-DOS subsystem are not supported.
Mirror	No longer supported.
Msav	No longer supported.
Msbackup	Not needed; use the backup utility in the Administrative Tools applet in Control Panel.
Mscdex	Not needed; Windows 2000 provides CD-ROM access for the MS-DOS subsystem.
Msd	Not needed; use the System Information snap-in.

Table 9-1. *MS-DOS Commands That Are Not Available in Windows 2000* (continued)

Unsupported Command	Explanation
Numlock	No longer supported.
Power	No longer supported.
Restore	No longer supported.
Scandisk	No longer supported.
Smartdrv	Not needed; Windows 2000 provides caching for the MS-DOS subsystem automatically.
Submenu	Multiple configurations of the MS-DOS subsystem are not supported.
Sys	Windows 2000 system files will not fit on a floppy disk.
Undelete	No longer supported.
Unformat	No longer supported.
Vsafe	No longer supported.

Table 9-1.   *MS-DOS Commands That Are Not Available in Windows 2000* (continued)

MS-DOS Commands That Have Changed

Some of the MS-DOS commands that are available in Windows 2000 have changed since Windows *9x*, and for the most part the changes bring additional power.

CHCP

This command displays or configures the active code page number. It has changed in that it now only changes code pages for full-screen mode.

Use the command without parameters to display the active code page number; use the syntax

```
chcp nnn
```

to specify the code page number *nnn*.

DEL or ERASE

This command has a number of switches that are not available in Windows 9*x* (or earlier):

- **file or directory** (including wildcards) targets the named file or directory.
- **/P** prompts for confirmation before deleting each file (available in Windows 9*x*).
- **/F** forces deleting of read-only files.
- **/S** deletes specified files from all subdirectories in which they exist.
- **/Q** indicates quiet mode (do not ask for confirmation on global wildcard).
- **/A** selects files to delete based on attributes.

 Use the standard attribute abbreviations when selecting by attribute: R S H A (use the minus sign (–) to indicate "not").

DIR

The following parameters are available for DIR:

- **[drive:][path][filename]** specifies the drive, directory, and/or files to list.
- **/A**   Display files with specified attributes (available in Windows 9*x*)

  - **D**   Directories
  - **R**   Read-only files
  - **H**   Hidden files
  - **A**   Files ready for archiving
  - **S**   System files

- **/B**   Use bare format (no heading information or summary) (available in Windows 9*x*)
- **/C**   Display the thousand separator in file sizes
- **/D**   Same as W, but files are listed sorted by column
- **/L**   Display in lowercase (available in Windows 9*x*)
- **/N**   New long list format (filenames are on the far right)
- **/O**   Listed in sorted order (available in Windows 9*x*)

  - **N**   By name (alphabetic)
  - **S**   By size (smallest first)

- **E**   By extension (alphabetic)
- **D**   By date/time (oldest first)
- **G**   Group directories first (use: to reverse order)
- **/P**   Pause after each screenful of information (available in Windows 9x)
- **/Q**   Display file owner
- **/S**   Display files in specified directory and all subdirectories (available in Windows 9x)
- **/T**   Controls which time field is displayed or used for sorting
  - **C**   Creation
  - **A**   Last access (earliest first)
  - **W**   Last written
- **/W**   Display in wide list format (available in Windows 9x)
- **/X**   Display the short names generated for non-8.3 filenames (like /N with the short name inserted before the long name, but if no short name is present, blanks are displayed)
- **/4**   Display four-digit years (available in Windows 9x)

 Use a minus sign (–) as a prefix to indicate "not."

DISKCOPY

Diskcopy no longer supports the following parameters:

- **/1**   Copied only the first side of the disk
- **/M**   Used for multipass copy using memory

FORMAT

The Format command takes any of the following syntax forms:

```
FORMAT volume [/FS:file-system] [/V:label] [/Q] [/A:size] [/C] [/X]
```

```
FORMAT volume [/V:label] [/Q] [/F:size]
```

```
FORMAT volume [/V:label] [/Q] [/T:tracks /N:sectors]
```

```
FORMAT volume [/V:label] [/Q] [/1] [/4]
```

```
FORMAT volume [/Q] [/1] [/4] [/8]
```

where

- **volume**   The drive letter (must be followed by a colon), mount point, or volume name
- **/FS:*filesystem***   The type of the file system (FAT, FAT32, or NTFS)
- **/V:*label***   The volume label (the symbols ^ and & are permitted in the volume label)
- **/Q**   Quick format (available in Windows 9*x*)
- **/C**   Files created on the volume will be compressed by default
- **/X**   This volume to dismount first if necessary
- **/A:*size***   Override the default allocation unit size

    - NTFS supports 512, 1024, 2048, 4096, 8192, 16K, 32K, 64K
    - FAT supports 512, 1024, 2048, 4096, 8192, 16K, 32K, 64K, (128K, 256K for sector size > 512 bytes)
    - FAT32 supports 512, 1024, 2048, 4096, 8192, 16K, 32KK, 64K, (128K, 256K for sector size > 512 bytes)

- **/F:*size***   Size of the floppy disk to format (160, 180, 320, 360, 640, 720, 1.2, 1.23, 1.44, 2.88, or 20.8) (available in Windows 9*x*)
- **/T:*tracks***   Number of tracks per disk side (available in Windows 9*x*)
- **/N:*sectors***   Number of sectors per track (available in Windows 9*x*)
- **/1**   Format a single side of a floppy disk (available in Windows 9*x*)
- **/4**   Format a 5.25-inch 360K floppy disk in a high-density drive (available in Windows 9*x*)
- **/8**   Format eight sectors per track (available in Windows 9*x*)

The following switches are no longer supported:

- **/B**   Allocate space on the formatted disk for system files
- **S**   Copy system files to the disk
- **U**   Don't prepare disk for unformatting

MORE

Unlike its counterpart in Windows 9*x*, the Windows 2000 More command has parameters:

- /E   Enable extended features
- /C   Clear screen before displaying page
- /P   Expand FormFeed characters
- /S   Squeeze multiple blank lines into a single line
- /T*n*   Expand tabs to n spaces (default is 8)

The following switches can be present in the More environment variable:

- +*n*   Start displaying the first file at line n
- **files**   List of files to display (separate filenames with blanks)

If extended features are enabled, the following commands can be used at the "-- More --" prompt:

- **P** *n*   Display next n lines
- **S** *n*   Skip next n lines
- **F**   Display next file
- **Q**   Quit
- **=**   Show line number
- **?**   Show help line
- **<space>** Display next page
- **<ret>**   Display next line

PROMPT

You can add these new characters to your prompt:

- **$A**   Ampersand
- **$C**   Open parentheses
- **$F**   Close parentheses
- **$S**   Space

Terminal Services Commands

Windows 2000 Terminal Services are robust and reasonably easy to install and administer. In addition, the hardware savings for this paradigm are substantial, so it's quite possible that adoption of the thin client approach to networks will spread as companies migrate to Windows 2000. This section covers some of the commands commonly used to administer a Terminal Services system.

Change Logon

Use this command to enable or disable logons to the server from client sessions, or to ascertain the current logon status. You must have administrative permissions to use this command. The syntax is

```
change logon {/enable | /disable | /query}
```

where

- **/enable** enables logons from client sessions.
- **/disable** disables future logons from client sessions. Users who are currently logged on are not affected.
- **/query** displays the current logon status, whether enabled or disabled.

If you disable logons while you are connected to the Terminal server from a client session, you must reenable logons before logging off or you won't be able to reconnect. If you fail to do this, you (or another administrator) will have to log on at the console in order to reenable logons from client sessions.

Change Port

This command changes COM port mappings so they're compatible with MS-DOS applications. The syntax is

```
change port [portx=porty | /d portx | /query]
```

where

- *portx=porty* maps port *x* to port *y*.
- **/d** *portx* deletes the mapping for COM port *x*.
- **/query** displays the current port mappings.

This command is necessary if you use high port numbers, because most MS-DOS applications support only COM1 through COM4. For example, if you're using COM10 in your system, enter **change port com10=com1**.

Remapping works only for the current session; it does not survive a logoff (which is a quick way to reset the port to its original configuration).

LEARNING THE BASICS

Change User

Use this command to change settings for mapping .ini files. The syntax is

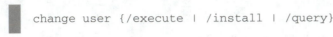

```
change user {/execute | /install | /query}
```

where

- **/execute** enables .ini file mapping to the home directory (the default setting).
- **/install** disables .ini file mapping to the home directory, using the system directory instead.
- **/query** displays the current setting for .ini file mapping.

Use the /install parameter before you install an application, so that.ini files for the application are created in the %SystemRoot% directory. You can use these .ini files as master copies for the user-specific .ini files. After you've installed the application, use /execute to change the configuration settings to support standard .ini file mapping.

Of course, after you invoke the /execute parameter and then run the application for the first time, the software searches the home directory for its .ini files. Whenever.ini files are found in the system directory rather than the home directory, Terminal Services copies the .ini files to the home directory. This gives each user a personal, unique copy of the .ini file you established as the master. Configuration options made by the user are saved for that user.

| Tip | *Software applications must be able to handle .ini files in this manner in order to work properly in a Terminal Services environment. Under Terminal Services, the Add/Remove Programs applet assumes and ensures a multiuser environment during software installation.* |

Cprofile

Use this command to clean profiles in order to get rid of wasted space. If any user-specific file associations are disabled, the process removes those associations from the registry. (Profiles that are currently in use are not modified.) You must have administrative permissions to run cprofile. The syntax is

```
cprofile [/l] [/i] [/v] [filelist]
```

or

```
cprofile [/i] [/v] filelist
```

Overview of Software Installation in Terminal Services

When a Terminal Services system is in install mode, all registry entries that are created by the installation program are shadowed in HKEY_LOCAL_MACHINE\ SOFTWARE\Microsoft\Windows NT\CurrentVersion\TerminalServer\Install. Those registry entries are usually made to keys in HKEY_CURRENT_USER because most .ini file items are related to user configuration options.

During software installation, if .ini file entries are added using system calls, they are added to the .ini files in the %SystemRoot% directory. When you return the system to execution mode (by entering **change user /execute**), and the application tries to read a registry entry under HKEY_CURRENT_USER that does not exist, Terminal Services checks for the shadow copy of the key in the \TerminalServer\Install subkey. If that copy exists, the keys are copied to the appropriate location under HKEY_CURRENT_USER.

When the application tries to read from an .ini file that doesn't exist (it searches the home directory), Terminal Services searches for the .ini file under the system root. If the .ini file exists in the system root, Terminal Services copies it to the \Windows subdirectory of the user's home directory.

When a user logs on, Terminal Services checks whether its system .ini files are newer than the .ini files on the user's computer. If the system version is newer, the user's .ini file is either replaced or merged with the newer version. (The replace vs. merge decision is based on whether or not the INISYNC bit, 0x40, is set for this .ini file). The existing version of the .ini file is renamed Inifile.ctx.

If the system registry values under the \TerminalServer\Install key are newer than the user's values under HKEY_CURRENT_USER, then the user's version of the key is deleted and replaced with the newer values from \TerminalServer\Install.

where

- **/l** cleans all local profiles. Additionally, you can specify a list of target profiles with the *filelist* parameter.

- **/i** interactively prompts the user.

- **/v** displays information about the tasks being performed.

- *filelist* is a list of filenames from which you want to remove user-specific file associations.

Note   *Use a space to separate each file in the list. Filenames can contain wildcard characters.*

Terminal Services supports the use of file associations on a per-user basis, so that one user can associate a file extension with a specific application and another user can associate the same file extension with a different application.

The user-specific file association feature can be enabled or disabled by the administrator. If user-specific file associations are enabled, cprofile removes the wasted space from the user's profile. If user-specific file associations are disabled, cprofile also removes the corresponding registry entries.

Flattemp

This command enables or disables flat temporary folders. You must have administrative permissions to use the command. The syntax is

```
flattemp {/query | /enable | /disable}
```

where

- **/query** displays the current setting.
- **/enable** enables flat temporary directories.
- **/disable** disables flat temporary directories.

By default, temporary folders are created for multiple users by creating subfolders in the \Temp folder, using *logonID* as the subfolder name. For instance, for the user with the logon ID 20, there is a temporary folder C:\Temp\20.

Use flattemp to change the default behavior and point directly to the user's \Temp folder instead of creating subfolders. This only works when each user has a separate temporary folder in the home directory. If an administrator disables using separate temporary folders per session (the option is set in the Configuration tool), flattemp settings are ignored.

 Tip *While theoretically you can store user temporary directories on a network share, this practice frequently causes problems. It's best to use the default Terminal Services protocol, which keeps temporary directories on the local hard disk.*

Logoff

This command logs a user off from a session and deletes the session from the server. The syntax is

```
logoff [sessionid | sessionname] [/server:servername] [/v]
```

where

- *sessionid* is the numeric ID by which the session is identified to the server.
- *sessionname* is the name of the session.

- **/server:***servername* is the name of the Terminal server containing the session whose user you want to log off. If this parameter is omitted, the current server is assumed.

- **/v** displays information about the tasks being performed.

Any user can log off from his or her own session. To log off users from other sessions, you must have Full Control permissions. When you log off a user, all processes are terminated and the session is deleted from the server. You cannot log off a user from a Console session.

 If you are logging off another user, send a warning message first (use the msg command) so the user has time to save data and close applications.

Msg

Use this handy command to send a message to a user. The syntax is

```
msg {username | sessionname | sessionid | @filename | *}
[/server:servername] [/time:seconds] [/v] [/w] [message]
```

where

- *username* is the name of the recipient.

- *sessionname* is the name of the session recipient.

- *sessionid* is the numeric session ID of the recipient.

- **@***filename* specifies a file containing a list of usernames, session names, and session IDs that you want to use as a recipient list.

- * sends the message to all user names on the system.

- **/server:***servername* is the name of the Terminal server whose session or user you want to receive the message. If omitted, the server where you are currently logged on is used.

- **/time:***seconds* is the amount of time the message you sent is displayed on the recipient's screen before disappearing. If omitted, the message remains on the recipient's screen until the user clicks OK.

- **/v** displays information about the tasks being performed.

- **/w** specifies that you want to wait for an acknowledgement from the user that the message has been received.

- *message* is the text of the message. If omitted, the system prompts for it.

If you use the /w parameter, also invoke the /time:*seconds* parameter to avoid a long delay if the user does not immediately respond.

You don't have to type the message text—you can send a message that's contained in a text file. To accomplish this, enter the less than symbol (<) followed by the filename.

Query Process

Use this command to display information about the processes currently running on a Terminal server. You can also determine which programs a specific user is running, and which users are running a specific program. The syntax is

```
query process [ * | processid | username | sessionname | /id:nn |
programname] [/server:servername] [/system]
```

where

- ***** lists the processes running in all sessions.

- *processid* is the numeric ID that identifies the process you want to query.

- *username* is the name of a user whose processes you want to list.

- *sessionname* is the name of the session whose processes you want to list.

- **/ID:*nn*** is the ID of the session whose processes you want to list.

- *programname* is the name of the program (full name, including the .exe extension) whose processes you want to list.

- **/server:*servername*** is the name of the Terminal server whose processes you want to list. If omitted, the server where you are currently logged on is assumed.

- **/system** asks for current information about system processes is displayed.

Query process returns the following information:

- The user who owns the process

- The session that owns the process

- The ID of the session

- The name of the process

- The state of the process

- The ID of the process

Query Session

This command provides information about sessions on a Terminal server. The list that's returned includes information about active sessions, and also about other sessions that the server runs. The syntax is

```
query session [sessionname | username | sessionid] [/server:servername]
[/mode] [/flow] [/connect] [/counter]
```

where

- *sessionname* is the name of the session you're querying.
- *username* is the name of a user whose session you're querying.
- *sessionid* is the ID of the session you're querying.
- **/server:***servername* specifies the Terminal server to query (the default is the current server).
- **/mode** displays the current line settings.
- **/flow** displays the current flow-control settings.
- **/connect** displays the current connect settings.
- **/counter** displays the current counters information, which includes the total number of sessions created, disconnected, and reconnected.

Query Termserver

This command searches the network and returns a list of all the Terminal servers on the network. The syntax is

```
query termserver [servername] [/domain:domain] [/address] [/continue]
```

where

- *servername* is the name that identifies the Terminal server.
- **/domain:***domain* names the domain to query for Terminal servers. If omitted, the current domain is assumed.
- **/address** asks for the network and node addresses for each server.
- **/continue** prevents pausing at the end of each screen of information.

Entering the command without any parameters returns a list of all Terminal servers on the network.

Query User

Use this command to get information about user sessions on a Terminal server. The syntax is

```
query user [username | sessionname | sessionid] [/server:servername]
```

where

- *username* is the logon name of the user you are querying.
- *sessionname* is the name of the session you are querying.
- *sessionID* is the ID of the session you are querying.
- **/server:***servername* names the Terminal server you want to query. If omitted, the current Terminal server is used.

Reset Session

Use this command to reset (remove) a session from the Terminal server. The syntax is

```
reset session {sessionname | sessionid} [/server:servername] [/v]
```

where

- *sessionname* is the name of the session you want to reset. (Use Query session to get this information.)
- *sessionid* is the ID of the session to reset.
- **/server:***servername* names the Terminal server containing the session you want to reset. If omitted, the current Terminal server is used.
- **/v** displays information about the tasks being performed.

Shadow

Use this command to establish a remote control connection to an active session of another user. You can either view the session or actively control it (which means you can input keyboard and mouse actions). The syntax is

```
shadow {sessionname | sessionid} [/server:servername] [/v]
```

where

- *sessionname* is the name of the session you want to control.

- *sessionid* is the ID of the session you want to remotely control. (You can use the query user command to display a list of sessions and their session IDs).

- **/server:***servername* names the Terminal server containing the session you want to control. Omitting this assumes the current Terminal server.

- **/v** displays information about the tasks being performed.

To end shadowing, press CTRL-* (* from the numeric keypad only). You can define a hot key to end shadowing in Terminal Services Manager.

Microsoft has given administrators the freedom to decide some of the "political" issues involved with shadowing. The debate about the expectations of user privacy will probably never end, but if your company has a policy on this issue, you can configure your system to match that policy (using Terminal Services Configuration). You can send a warning message to users before monitoring begins, or not. By default, user warnings are enabled.

- The Console session cannot remotely control another session, nor can it be remotely controlled by another session.

- The session of the person performing the remote control tasks must be able to support the video resolution used at the target session.

Tscon

This command connects to another session. The syntax is

```
tscon {sessionID | sessionname} [/server:servername]
[/dest:sessionname] [/password:password] [/v]
```

where

- *sessionID* is the ID of the session to which you want to connect.

- *sessionname* is the name of the session to which you want to connect.

- **/server:***servername* names the Terminal server containing the session to which you want to connect. If omitted, the current Terminal server is used.

- **/dest:***sessionname* is the name of the current session, which will be automatically disconnected when you connect to the new session.

- **/password:***password* is the password of the user who owns the session to which you want to connect. This password is required when you do not own the target session.

- **/v** displays information about the tasks being performed.

Tsdiscon

Use this command to disconnect a session from a Terminal server. The syntax is

```
tsdiscon [sessionid | sessionname] [/server:servername] [/v]
```

where

- *sessionid* is the ID of the session to disconnect.

- *sessionname* is the name of the session to disconnect.

- **/server:***servername* is the Terminal server containing the session you want to disconnect. If omitted, the current Terminal server is used.

- **/v** displays information about the tasks being performed.

Tskill

This command ends a process. The syntax is

```
tskill {processid | processname} [/server:servername]
[/id:sessionid | /a] [/v]
```

where

- *processid* is the ID of the process you want to end.

- *processname* is the name of the process you want to end (wildcards are permitted).

- **/server:***servername* is the Terminal server containing the process you want to end. If omitted, the current Terminal server is used.

- **/id:***sessionid* ends the process running in the specified session.

- **/a** ends the process running in all sessions.

- **/v** displays information about the tasks being performed.

- Administrators have full access to all tskill functions, including the ability to end processes that are running in other users' sessions.

- A user can end only the processes that belong to him or her.

- If all processes running in a session are ended, the session ends.

Tsshutdn

If you have administrative permissions, you can use this command to remotely shut down or reboot a Terminal server. In addition, you can power off the server if the computer supports the software control of AC power. The syntax is

```
tsshutdn [wait_time] [/server:servername] [/reboot] [/powerdown]
[/delay:logoffdelay] [/v]
```

where

- *wait_time* is the number of seconds to wait (the default is 60), after notifying users, before logging off all users from their sessions.

- **/server:***servername* names the Terminal server to shut down. If omitted, the current Terminal server is shut down.

- **/reboot** reboots the Terminal server after user sessions are ended.

- **/powerdown** turns off the Terminal server (the computer must support software control of AC power).

- **/delay:***logoffdelay* is the amount of time, in seconds (the default is 30), to wait after logging off users, before ending all processes and shutting down the Terminal server.

- **/v** displays information about the tasks being performed.

When you use this command, all connected sessions receive notification of the impending shutdown. Sessions that have applications with open files automatically prompt the user to save the files. Don't use the Shut Down command on the Start menu to shut down a Terminal server, because none of these niceties will occur.

The Windows 2000 Command List in the Help files contains an alphabetical listing of every available command, along with syntax information.

The
Complete
Reference

Chapter 10

System Maintenance Tools

Windows 2000 provides housekeeping tools you can use to make sure your system purrs along. Consistent periodic maintenance is important, and those who fail to perform maintenance tasks usually regret the omission. This chapter covers the basic system maintenance tools for all versions of Windows 2000 Server and Windows 2000 Professional.

Defragmentation

When you open a data file in a software application, make changes to the file, and save it again, the file's original location on the drive may not have room for the new, larger document. The operating system splits the document, using one part of the drive for some of the file and another part for the rest. As you continue to expand the size of the file, it may be saved to multiple locations on the drive. The file is said to be fragmented (or *fragged*). Every time you open a file that's fragmented, the system must search the drive to find all its parts. This searching procedure slows down your work because it takes multiple disk reads to load the file.

When you delete files and folders, especially if you delete groups of files and folders, you create small locations of available space, and as you continue to work, creating and saving files, it's less likely that the files will nestle neatly into one contiguous space. Eventually, every time you create a file or a folder, it requires more time to complete the write to the drive, because the system must make multiple writes to multiple locations to hold the new object. Your drive is fragmented.

Disk Defragmenter, which is part of your Windows 2000 system, can optimize your drive by defragmenting the files (commonly called *defragging*). It works by gathering all the pieces of a file and writing them back to the drive in one contiguous location. The program makes room for each file by moving other files (which may also be fragmented) out of the way, placing them in a temporary location until it's their turn to be defragmented.

To launch Disk Defragmenter, open the Accessories submenu, point to the System Tools submenu, and choose Disk Defragmenter. You must have administrator permissions to use this software.

You can create a desktop or taskbar shortcut to the Disk Defragmenter. Right-drag the program file (%SystemRoot%\System32\dfrg.msc) to the desktop, and choose Create Shortcut(s) Here from the menu that appears when you release the mouse. You can place the shortcut on a taskbar toolbar if you wish (see Chapter 6 for more information).

Analyzing the Drive

The Disk Defragmenter window, seen in Figure 10-1, lists the local drives, along with information about the installed file system, capacity, and usage. It's a good idea to have Disk Defragmenter analyze the disk before running a defragmentation procedure. In fact, it's foolish not to analyze first, because defragging is an intensive, lengthy procedure, and an analysis could show there's no need to defrag the drive.

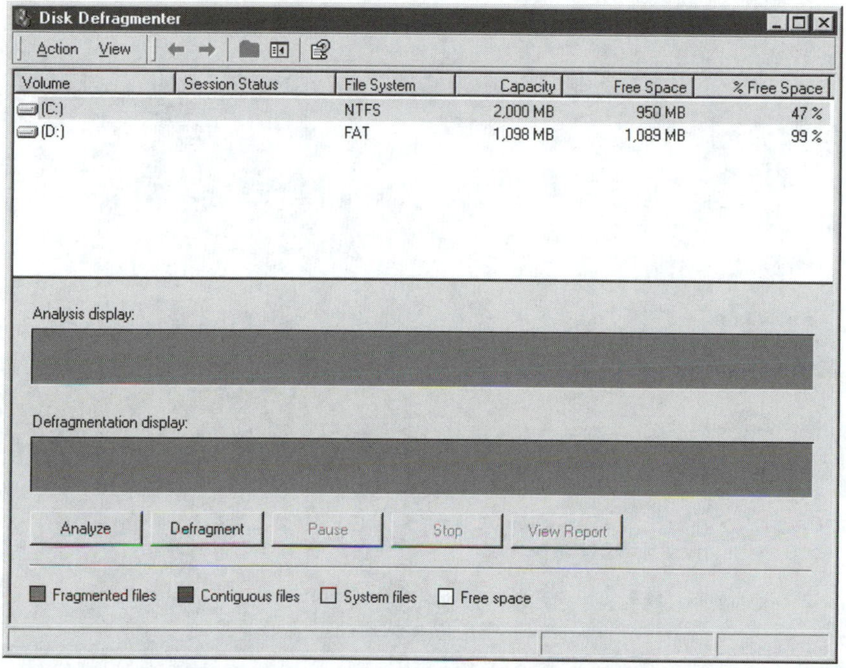

Figure 10-1. *All local drives are displayed in the Disk Defragmenter window*

Starting an analysis is easy—there is no shortage of methods for launching the Analyze process:

- Right-click a drive and choose Analyze from the shortcut menu.
- Select a drive and click the Analyze button.
- Select a drive and choose Analyze from the Action menu.

Tip *Open files cannot be analyzed (or defragged), so close all applications and utilities before beginning this process.*

The Analyze function inspects the drive, and you can watch the progress in the Analysis Display bar. The display is color-coded to signify whether the files being inspected are fragmented or contiguous (see Figure 10-2). There is also a color code to differentiate system files from application/data files.

You can click the Pause button to halt the process if you need to retrieve a file or perform some other task on the computer. The button changes to Resume so you can start the analysis again. Use the Stop button to halt the entire process. The analysis

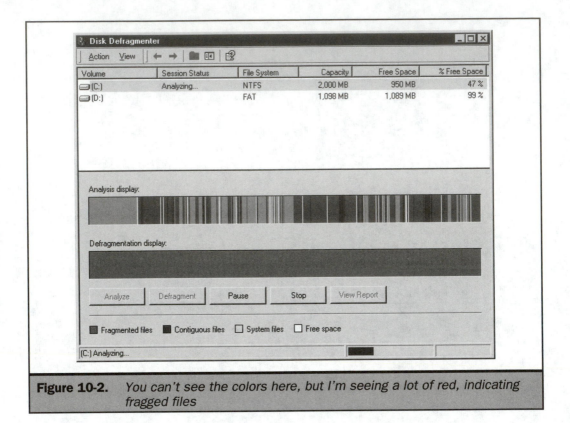

Figure 10-2. *You can't see the colors here, but I'm seeing a lot of red, indicating fragged files*

doesn't take long, and when it's complete, a message box displays to tell you whether your drive needs to be defragmented.

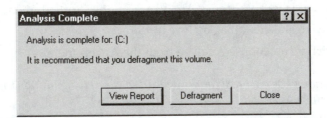

For detailed information, click View Report to see which files and folders are badly fragmented and the number of fragmented segments that exist for each (see Figure 10-3). Disk Defragmenter analyzes and defrags both folders and files.

 You can use the buttons on the Analysis Report window to print the report, or save it as a text file (if you have some reason to require a permanent record).

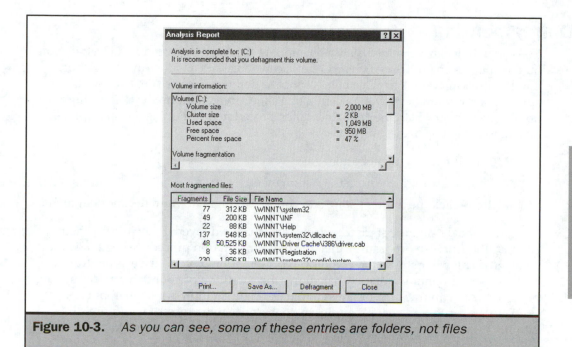

Figure 10-3.   *As you can see, some of these entries are folders, not files*

Scroll through the list of folders and files on the report, and if you see the names of files you use frequently, that's probably why your system has seemed sluggish. The more fragmented files you open, and the greater the number of fragments, the slower your system performs. If the defragmentation level of the drive is acceptable, the Analysis Complete message box tells you so.

You can view the report and if you decide you want to defrag the drive even though Disk Defragmenter doesn't find it necessary, you can. You should run the Analyze procedure regularly; the frequency depends on the activity level of the computer. File servers that are accessed by a large number of users should be analyzed every few days.

Tip   *When you do housekeeping chores, and delete a large number of files or folders at one time, run an analysis after you've completed the task.*

Defragmenting

You can defrag a drive immediately after running the Analyze procedure (a Defragment button appears on both the Analysis Complete message box and the Analysis Report window), or wait until later. Open files cannot be defragged, so be sure to close all applications and utilities. If you're defragging a file server, perform the task during non-business hours. Start the defragmentation procedure by selecting the appropriate drive and using one of these methods:

- Click the Defragment button.
- Choose Defragment from the Action menu.
- Right-click the drive's listing and choose Defragment from the shortcut menu.

Before the defragging starts, the drive is re-analyzed (even if you just finished running the Analyze procedure); then the defragmentation procedure begins. The Analyze display bar shows the graphical representation of your drive as analyzed, and the Defragmentation display bar shows the condition of your drive as defragging proceeds. You can track the progress in the Defragmentation display bar, but it's probably better to find something else to do, because this process takes quite a bit of time. When defragmentation is complete, a message announces that fact.

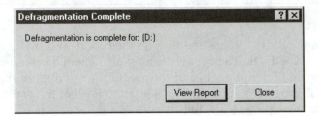

Use the View Report button on the message box to see a detailed report on the drive's new fragmentation state.

Troubleshooting Defragmentation

Don't be surprised if, after the defragging process is complete, your drive is still somewhat fragmented. There are a number of scenarios that can cause this, and some of them can be corrected.

Defragmenting the System Paging File

The *system paging file* (sometimes called the *swap file*) is always held open for exclusive use by the operating system, and therefore cannot be defragmented. If the paging file becomes fragmented, performance suffers quite noticeably. You can remedy the problem if you have a second drive or partition on your computer. Here's how:

1. Open the System applet in Control Panel, or right-click My Computer and choose Properties from the shortcut menu.

2. In the System Properties dialog box, move to the Advanced tab and click Performance options.

3. Click Change to display the Virtual Memory dialog box seen in Figure 10-4.

4. Select another drive and configure a paging file with the same size specifications as the original paging file.

5. Change the minimum and maximum size of the original paging file to 0MB.

6. Reboot to force the system to use the new paging file.

Run Disk Defragmenter on the drive that originally held the paging file. You're not defragging the paging file, of course, you're defragging the drive, which should create enough contiguous space to hold the paging file. Move the paging file back to its original drive, using the steps described here. After you reboot, the paging file is created anew, as a contiguous file, on the original drive.

Insufficient Free Space Impairs Defragmentation

If you defrag a drive and the report that displays afterwards shows that many files are still fragmented, you may not have had enough free space on the disk to permit the

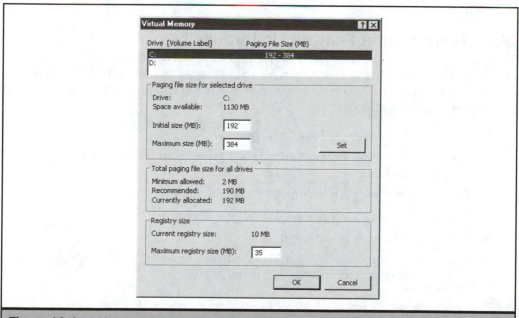

Figure 10-4. *You must move the paging file to another drive to defragment it*

software to temporarily "park" file fragments. Run the Analyze procedure again to see if the software recommends defragmenting the drive (this frequently occurs). In fact, even if the analysis reports back that the drive doesn't need to be defragged, you still may want to run the defragmentation process to optimize the drive a bit more.

As drives get crowded and free space shrinks, it's not uncommon to have to run the defragmentation utility several times in a row in order to get a drive defragged enough to improve productivity. Each time the process runs, Disk Defragmenter does as much as possible, given the constraints of inadequate disk space to use for "parking" files to make room for unfragged files.

The solution is to move a substantial number of files off the drive, copying the files to another drive or another computer on the network. That solution works best after you've defragged the drive once or twice in a single session. Look at the report and note the names of the files that have been successfully defragged (find the largest contiguous files in the list). Copy those files to another drive or computer to give Disk Defragmenter chunks of contiguous space to work with. During the defragging process, the software also tries to put all the free space in contiguous blocks, which enhances the probability that the files you removed can be put back into contiguous locations.

Limitations of Disk Defragmenter

There are a couple of limitations you should know about. One is major (the program is deliberately limited in its feature list), the other minor (a system procedure involving NTFS volumes).

Disk Defragmenter Feature Limitations

There are some serious limitations on the defragmentation program that's installed with Windows 2000. Microsoft programmers didn't write this software; it's obtained from Executive Software, who provided a very limited version of the full retail product. Here are the limitations:

- You cannot schedule the Disk Defragmenter.
- You can only defrag local volumes, this version has no capacity for remote procedures.
- You can defrag only one volume at a time.
- You cannot defrag a volume while you're scanning another volume.
- The program cannot be scripted.
- You can only run one Microsoft Management Console (MMC) snap-in at one time (see Chapter 8 for information about MMC).

 You can purchase a full retail copy of the program from Executive Software (http://www.execsoft.com).

Because file servers are the most common victims of fragmentation, and at the same time cannot be defragmented during normal business hours, the lack of scheduling is bothersome (unless you like coming to the office at 2 A.M.). For that reason alone, it's worth investigating the cost of purchasing the full product.

Disk Space Reserved in NTFS

If you're running NTFS, there's a Master File Table (MFT) that must be located at the beginning of the volume. The MFT holds information about the location of files (or multiple locations of files for those files that are fragmented). Windows reserves space at the beginning of the volume for the MFT, so that space isn't available to the defragmentation application.

Scheduled Tasks

Scheduled Tasks is a task scheduler that's installed automatically with Windows 2000, and you can use it to run scripts and programs on a schedule you devise. The tasks you create are files (with the extension .job) that can be exchanged via e-mail, or copied to remote computers, permitting you to create and run scheduled tasks on other computers. The task files are located in %SystemRoot%\Tasks.

You can launch this utility from the Control Panel, or from the Start menu (in the System Tools submenu under Accessories). The Scheduled Tasks window opens to display an icon named Add Scheduled Task, along with icons for any existing tasks.

 Be sure the date and time of the computer are correct when you're running scheduled tasks.

AT Command and the Task Scheduler

If you used the AT command in previous versions of Windows, you're familiar with the concept of scheduling programs. The AT command is still available in Windows 2000, and you can use it to schedule tasks.

Task Scheduler and the AT command work together. When you schedule a task via the AT command, that task appears in the Scheduled Tasks window. You can reconfigure the task using the switches available in the AT command, or use the features in Scheduled Tasks to modify the configuration of a task you scheduled with the AT command. However, once you use Scheduled Tasks to change the configuration, the AT modifiers no longer work on that task—you've committed your modification efforts to Scheduled Tasks.

You can choose among three methods for creating a new task:

- Launch the Scheduled Tasks Wizard.
- Configure a task in a dialog box.
- Drag a program, script, or document to the Scheduled Tasks window.

LEARNING THE BASICS

Scheduled Tasks Execution File

If you're fascinated by the behind-the-scenes stuff, you may be interested to know that Scheduled Tasks isn't an application, or at least it has no executable. The utility runs as a DLL launched by Explorer.exe, with the path statement:

```
%SystemRoot%\explorer.exe :
:{20D04FE0-3AEA-1069-A2D8-08002B30309D}\:
:{21EC2020-3AEA-1069-A2DD-08002B30309D}\::{D6277990-4C6A-11CF-8D87-00AA0060F5BF}
```

where:

{20D04FE0-3AEA-1069-A2D8-08002B30309D} is a CLSID for My Computer objects.

{21EC2020-3AEA-1069-A2DD-08002B30309D} is a CLSID for Control Panel objects.

{D6277990-4C6A-11CF-8D87-00AA0060F5BF} is a CLSID for a variety of icons and objects referencing Mstask.dll.

Using the Scheduled Tasks Wizard

Open the Add Scheduled Task icon to launch the wizard, and click Next to move past the welcome window. The wizard presents a list of the application files on your computer:

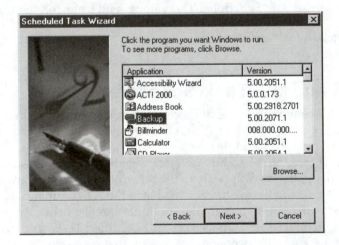

The list of applications displayed in the wizard window includes the apps you installed with the operating system, and any third-party software you installed that appears in the list of applications in the Add/Remove Programs window. If the application you want to schedule isn't in the list, click Browse to open the Select Program To Schedule window.

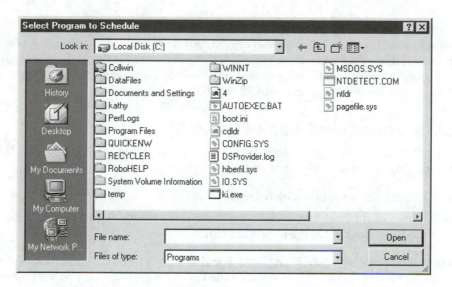

This window is similar to any Open window, and you can select a local application, script, or document. Or you can troll the network to select an object on a remote computer.

Don't configure Windows Backup from the Scheduled Tasks window; it works in the other direction. The backup program has its own scheduling function, and using it transfers the scheduled backup job to the Scheduled Tasks list.

You begin configuring the task in the next wizard window (shown in the following illustration). Note that the option When I Log On is connected to a username, which you enter in a subsequent window.

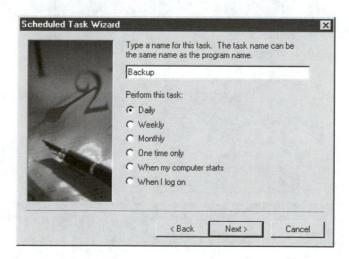

Continue to go through the wizard window to configure this task. The last wizard window offers the usual Finish button, but there's also an option to let the Finish button open the Properties dialog box that is created for the task. The task's dialog box offers additional configuration options (see the next section on creating a task manually for information about all the dialog box options).

Creating a Scheduled Task Manually

If you want to leap right to the Properties dialog box to configure your task, instead of stepping through the wizard, use one of these methods to create a new task:

- Choose File, New, Scheduled Task.
- Right-click a blank spot in the Scheduled Tasks window and choose New, Scheduled Task from the shortcut menu.

A new icon appears, titled New Task. The title is in Edit mode so you can enter a name for the new task. Then right-click on the task icon and choose Properties from the shortcut menu to open the task's Properties dialog box (see Figure 10-5).

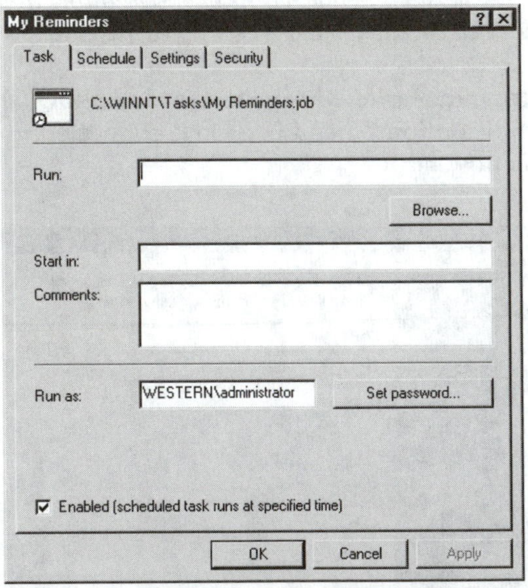

Figure 10-5. *Configure a new task manually using its Properties dialog box*

Scheduled Tasks Properties—Task Tab

The options on the Task tab are pretty much self-explanatory, but there are a couple of guidelines I should point out:

- If the path to the target file contains spaces, enclose the entire path in quotation marks.

- You can add parameters to the executable file.

Scheduled Tasks Properties—Schedule Tab

The Schedule tab is the place to specify the frequency for the schedule, but there's a difference between the options presented in the wizard and those presented in the Properties dialog box. The difference is a missing ingredient. The wizard offers a Weekdays option under the Daily category; the Properties dialog box doesn't. If you want to run this task only on weekdays, you must select Weekly and then click the individual days of the week to create your workweek. You can narrow or broaden the schedule configuration by clicking Advanced, and the options that are offered differ depending on the schedule category you chose.

 There are no advanced options for System Startup, Logon, or When Idle.

Scheduled Tasks Properties—Settings Tab

The Settings tab offers options that let you control the way the task operates under certain system conditions (see Figure 10-6).

In the Scheduled Task Completed section of the Settings tab, you have two options:

- *You can delete the task if it's not scheduled to run again.* This applies to tasks that have an end date (including tasks that were run once, of course). The job, and its file, is removed after the last automatic occurrence. Don't select this option if this task might be reincarnated periodically.

- *You can stop the task if it runs for more than a specified time.* Enter the duration of time you'll permit for this task to complete its job (the default is 72 hours, which is ridiculous). This option is useful for time-consuming tasks that you configure for middle-of-the-night operations and you want to make sure they're not running when the business day begins.

 Don't specify a duration limit for backing up (or for any other critical task), because you want that task to run to completion regardless of the amount of time it requires. Instead, move the start time to an earlier setting to insure the task is finished before the workday begins.

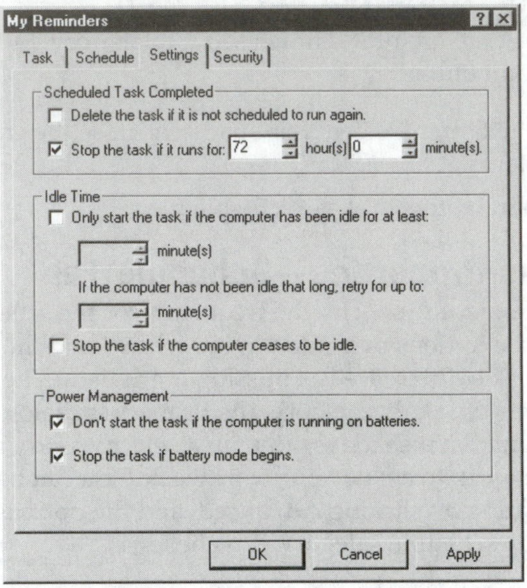

Figure 10-6.   *Configure the behavior of the task in the Settings tab*

In the Idle Time section of the Settings tab, specify the options for a task that you configured for execution during idle time.

The definition of *idle time* is "no mouse or keyboard activity." That, of course, doesn't mean a computer is idle, because all sorts of stuff could be going on, including downloads, database searches, or other automated tasks. The idle time options don't help you make scheduled tasks run more efficiently, and you shouldn't schedule two processor-intensive or I/O intensive tasks at the same time unless you're prepared to let them run for longer than they would if they were running alone.

In the Power Management section of the Settings tab, specify the behavior you desire if battery power issues arise when the task is scheduled (or already running). This option applies to laptops, it has nothing to do with computers that are switched over to UPS power devices when electrical power is lost. (In fact, if you're running UPS software such as PowerChute, all programs, including automated tasks, are usually configured for shutdown.) An option to wake the computer to run this task appears for computers that support that feature.

Scheduled Tasks Properties—Security Tab

Task security is based on the standard Windows 2000 security permissions, using the NTFS file system security definitions. In the Security tab (see Figure 10-7), you can specify the users who can view, delete, modify, or use a task.

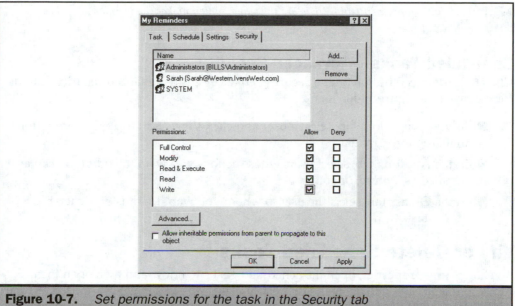

Figure 10-7. *Set permissions for the task in the Security tab*

Tip *The program, script, or document that is connected to the task may also have security restrictions applied if the target computer is running NTFS. Be careful not to create a conflict between these security levels.*

Add or remove a user and set permissions for that user's responsibility for the task. Table 10-1 describes the available permissions.

Permission Level	Rights
Full Control	View, run, change, delete, change owner
Modify	View, run, change, delete
Read & Execute	View, run
Read	View
Write	View, run, change, delete

Table 10-1. *Permissions for Managing Scheduled Tasks*

The rights for Modify and Write are the same, which makes me wonder why they both exist.

Scheduled Tasks—Advanced Security

Click the Advanced button on the Security tab to configure advanced security options for the task (see Figure 10-8).

■ In the Permissions tab, select a user and click View/Edit to apply permissions that are more granular.

■ In the Auditing tab, select users whose actions you want to audit (you can audit for success, failure, or both).

■ In the Owner tab, select the user to whom you want to transfer ownership of this task.

Modify or Delete Scheduled Tasks

To change any properties, open the Scheduled Tasks window and then open the task. Move to the appropriate tab of the Properties dialog box and make the needed changes. To delete a scheduled task, select it and choose your favorite method for deleting:

■ Press the DEL key.

■ Click the delete icon on the toolbar.

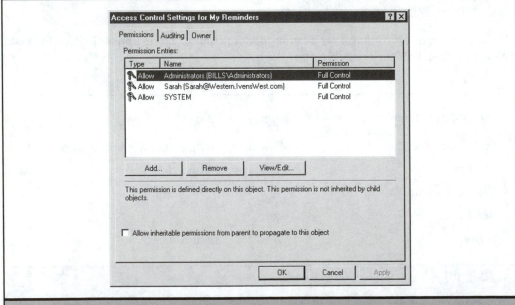

Figure 10-8.   *Advanced security options are available for a scheduled task*

- Right-click the task and choose Delete from the shortcut menu.
- Choose Delete from the File menu.

Deleted tasks are sent to the Recycle Bin. If you don't want a task to run, but you think you might need it in the future, instead of deleting it, disable it. Just clear the Enabled check box on the Task tab of the task's Properties dialog box.

Run and Stop Scheduled Tasks

You can run any task at any time if you don't want to wait for the next scheduled occurrence. In the Scheduled Tasks window, select the task and choose File, Run (or right-click the task and choose Run from the shortcut menu). If a task is running and you want to stop it, open the Scheduled Tasks window, right-click on the task's object, and choose End Task from the shortcut menu. It may take a moment or two for the message to reach the task.

Check the Status of Scheduled Tasks

You can gain information about the status of a task by changing the view of the Scheduled Tasks window to the Details view. The columns provide information about each task (see Figure 10-9).

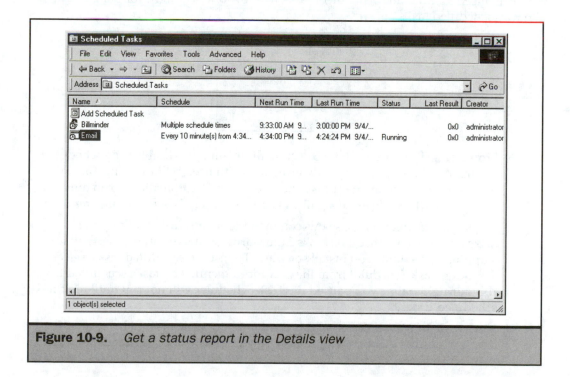

Figure 10-9. *Get a status report in the Details view*

The Status column can have any of the following notations:

Notation	Meaning
Empty	The task is not currently running. The task has run successfully.
Running	The task is currently running.
Missed	One or more attempts to run this task were missed.
Could not start	The most recent attempt to start the task failed.

Check the log file to see detailed information about the performance of tasks. You can access the log file by choosing Advanced, View Log on the Scheduled Tasks folder menu bar, or by opening the log into Notepad. The log file is %SystemRoot%\SchedLgU.Txt.

 Click on a column to sort the list by that column—click the same column again to reverse the sort order.

Setting Global Options for Scheduled Tasks

The Advanced menu in the Scheduled Tasks window offers options for manipulating the way scheduled tasks operate.

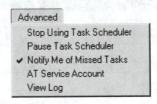

- **Stop Using Task Scheduler**   Selecting this command disables any scheduled tasks until you return to the Advanced menu and select Start Using Task Scheduler. In addition, the Task Scheduler will not automatically run the next time you start Windows 2000 unless you've restarted it before rebooting.

- **Pause Task Scheduler**   Use this command to temporarily halt running tasks and prevent scheduled tasks from starting. This command is useful for stopping tasks while you install software. To resume scheduled tasks, select Continue Task Scheduler from the Advanced menu. Any tasks scheduled to run during the time you paused the Task Scheduler will not run until their next scheduled times.

- **Notify Me of Missed Tasks**   This command does not mean what it says. It does not notify you of missed tasks; it only notifies you about a failure of the

Schedule Task service itself. Tasks that fail to run due to corrupt or missing executables don't kick off a notification.

■ **AT Service Account** Use this command to change the user account that runs tasks that are scheduled with the AT command (the default account is System). Selecting the command opens the AT Service Account Configuration dialog box seen here. Select This Account and enter a user account. You must also enter and confirm the password for that account.

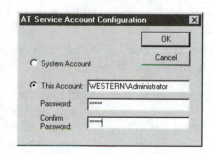

■ **View Log** Select this command to open the task log in Notepad, where you can track the success or failure of your scheduled tasks. A portion of my task log is seen in the following illustration.

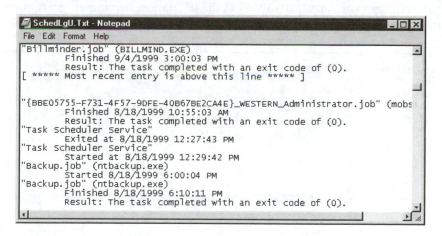

Note *The log file is %SystemRoot%\SchedLgU.Txt.*

Working with Tasks on Remote Computers

You can view, add, or modify the scheduled tasks on a remote computer, depending on the permissions you have for manipulating that computer. Even without the ability to access the tasks on another computer, you can send tasks to other users.

Scheduled Tasks Folder vs. Tasks Folder

When you are working with tasks on remote computers, it's important to understand the difference between the Scheduled Tasks Folder and the Tasks folder under the SystemRoot (usually WINNT).

If you open the %SystemRoot%\Tasks folder on a remote computer, it's going to look extremely familiar, because you're looking at the contents of your own %SystemRoot%\Tasks folder (it's a mirror image—the Recycle Bin works the same way).

- If you delete a job from what seems to be the remote Tasks folder, you're deleting it from your own folder.

- The system will not permit you to drag a job between Tasks folders, because you're really trying to drag a job to itself.

As an example, I'll demonstrate the views from two computers named West and Bills on my network.

Working on Bills, I open the local %SystemRoot%\Tasks folder, and then expand My Network Places to open the %SystemRoot%\Tasks folder on West. You can see the results in Figure 10-10.

Working on West, I open the local Scheduled Tasks folder (by expanding the Control Panel object in the left pane of My Computer, which is configured to show folders). Then I expand My Network Places to open the Scheduled Tasks folder on Bills (the folder is automatically listed in the left pane when viewing a remote computer; there is no Control Panel listing). You can see the results in Figure 10-11.

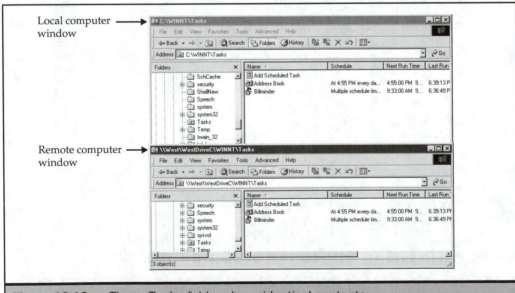

Figure 10-10.   *These Tasks folders have identical contents*

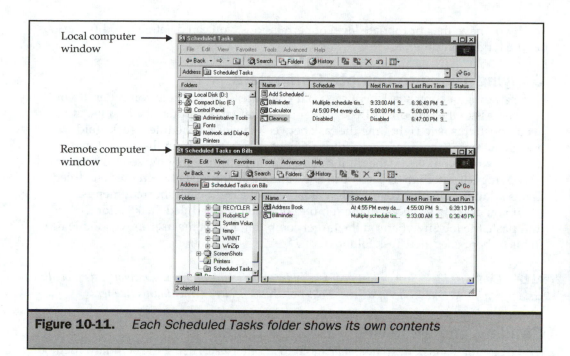

Local computer window

Remote computer window

Figure 10-11. *Each Scheduled Tasks folder shows its own contents*

View Tasks on a Remote Computer

To view the Scheduled Tasks folder on another computer, open My Network Places and expand the remote computer listing to locate the Scheduled Tasks folder. Use the Details view to gain the most information.

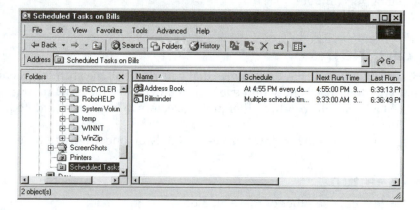

- The drive containing the Scheduled Tasks folder must be shared to provide access to the folder.

- You cannot map a drive to the Scheduled Tasks folder.

If you have the appropriate level of permissions, you can delete or modify the jobs on the target computer.

Copying Tasks to Remote Computers

You can drag or copy a task between your computer and a remote computer. If you have access to the Scheduled Tasks folder on the target computer, the best way to accomplish this is to right-drag the task between the local Scheduled Tasks folder and the remote Scheduled Tasks folder. Choose Copy Here from the menu that appears when you release the right mouse button (left-dragging moves the job instead of copying it). Alternatively, you can copy and paste the job between the Scheduled Tasks folders, using the commands available on the right-click shortcut menus.

If you don't have access to the remote computer's Scheduled Tasks folder, copy and paste the job anywhere on the target computer and let the user move the file in to his or her Scheduled Task folder.

 Don't use the %SystemRoot%\Tasks folder as the source or target of a copy/paste procedure. See the section "Scheduled Tasks Folder vs. Tasks Folder" earlier in this chapter.

Sending and Receiving Tasks via E-mail

You can e-mail a task file (*<taskname>*.job) to another user, using the standard method for attaching a file to a message. The recipient merely needs to drag or copy/cut/paste the file to the Scheduled Tasks folder.

- The file on which the job depends (an executable or document file) must exist on the target computer.

- The properties of the job may need to be adjusted to reflect the path to the file on the target computer.

Disk Cleanup

Disk Cleanup is like a trash hauling service that gets rid of all the stuff that's hanging around that you don't need and won't ever use again. Unlike the junk in your house, you can't hold a lawn sale to entice other junk-collectors to buy your outdated, unwanted computer files.

Disk Cleanup works only on local drives, and only on one drive at a time.

Run Disk Cleanup

To run Disk Cleanup, use either of these methods:

- Choose Start | Run and enter **cleanmgr**, and then click OK.
- Choose Disk Cleanup from the System Tools submenu of the Accessories menu.

The program opens by asking you to select the drive to clean up.

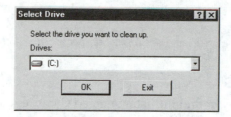

The program scans your drive to see how many, and which, files can be removed.

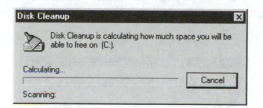

Decide What to Delete

After the analysis is complete, the Disk Cleanup dialog box seen in Figure 10-12 displays.

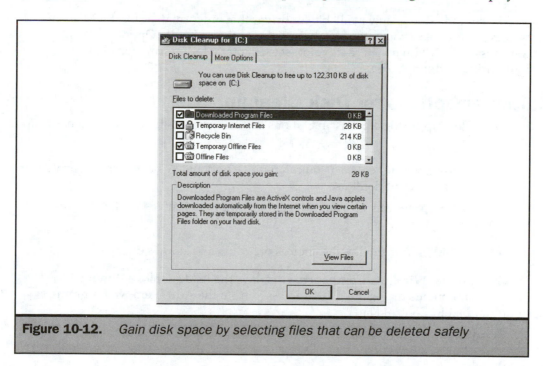

Figure 10-12. *Gain disk space by selecting files that can be deleted safely*

LEARNING THE BASICS

You can select additional file categories, and deselect the categories that were preselected for you. As you change the settings, the total amount of disk space you'll regain is displayed. Select and deselect categories; then click OK to clean up your drive.

 Click a listing and select View Files to see the specific files included by Disk Cleanup.

Compress Old Files

Scroll through the display to find the listing named Compress old files. This is not a file type that Disk Cleanup is offering to remove; it's an offer to keep older files in a compressed format. Compressing the files uses less disk space.

Select the Compress old files listing and click Options to specify how many days must have elapsed since the last time you accessed a file in order to qualify the file for compression.

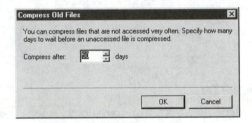

File compression is only available for drives that are formatted for the NTFS file system. If you opt to compress files, be sure to configure Folder Options to display compressed files with an alternate color (see Chapter 6 for information about configuring folder options).

Additional Options for Disk Cleanup

The Disk Cleanup dialog box has an Options tab that presents two additional clean-up alternatives:

- **Windows components,** so you can remove optional Windows components that you installed but don't use.

- **Installed programs,** so you can remove programs you've installed but aren't planning to use.

Selecting either of the following choices produces a Windows dialog box:

- **Optional Windows Components** displays the Add/Remove Windows Components dialog box that is accessed from the Add/Remove Programs applet in Control Panel.

- **Installed Programs** displays the Add/Remove Programs dialog box that lists installed software.

Backup

Drives die, motherboards go to computer heaven, users destroy files, and all sorts of other disasters occur with frightening regularity. You can replace drives, motherboards, and even users, but you can't replace data unless you have an efficient backup strategy.

Backing up isn't just a hedge against disasters; it's also protection for recovering from mistakes. Backups are used to restore files that were accidentally deleted more often than they're used to recover from disk disasters. Windows Backup contains the Emergency Repair Disk Wizard, which you can use to create a floppy disk that will help you repair your system if it won't start, or if system files are damaged or missing. See Chapter 5 for information about creating and using the ERD.

Backup Features New to Windows 2000

If you're migrating to Windows 2000 from Windows NT, here are some of the functions that have been added to the backup feature.

Multiple Target Media Types

Rejoice! Finally, you can back up files to storage devices in addition to tape drives. This long overdue feature means you can use any of the following target media types:

- Tape
- Removable disk (Jaz, Zip, SparQ, etc.)
- Hard drive (logical drive, another physical hard drive, etc.)
- Recordable CD-ROM

Technically, you can use floppy disks, but you'd have to bring in a cot and food supplies to last through all those insertions of the next disk.

Support for QIC and other floppy-based tape drives has been dropped.

Backup/Restore for System State

Backup includes the ability to back up and restore the Windows 2000 System State. The System State data differs by computer type, as follows:

- For all Windows 2000 computers, System State data includes system files, the registry, the COM+ Class Registration database, and the system boot files.

■ For Windows 2000 servers that are domain controllers, System State data includes the Active Directory directory services database and the Sysvol directory.

■ For Windows 2000 servers that are certificate servers, System State data includes the Certificate Services database.

Integration with Remote Storage Services

Remote Storage is a Windows 2000 feature that lets you store data on tape in a library and provide user access to that data. This means you can free up disk space for data that is old and infrequently used, and make that data available via a library of archived files. See Chapter 27 for information about managing Remote Storage Services.

Integration with Task Scheduler

When you configure the backup application for automated processing, the schedule can be accessed through the Task Scheduler.

Backup Storage Media Managed Separately

The target media is handled by the Removable Storage Manager (RSM), which is part of Windows 2000. The service creates libraries of removable media and organizes everything for easy access. See Chapter 27 for more information about Removable Storage.

Backup Types

Windows Backup offers five specific backup types to choose from:

■ **Normal**   Backs up all the selected files, and clears the Archive attribute (marks the files on the disk to indicate they have been backed up).

■ **Copy**   Backs up all the selected files but does not clear the Archive attribute.

■ **Incremental**   Looks at the selected files and only backs up those that have changed since the last backup. For the files are backed up, the Archive attribute is cleared.

■ **Differential**   Only backs up files that have changed since the last backup, but does not clear the Archive attribute.

■ **Daily**   Backs up those files that have been modified or added today. The Archive attribute is not cleared.

| Note | *The only use I can think of for a Daily backup type is to back up the files you were working on today, so you can take them home to continue your work.* |

Quick Restores Are Better than Quick Backups

The way to decide which type of backup to perform is to ask yourself why you're backing up. The answer is usually "So when disaster strikes, I can get back to work quickly."

This means the reason for backup is to restore everything as quickly as possible, so you don't have to reinvent all the work you've done. If you follow that logic to its natural conclusion, you realize that you should have a backup philosophy that makes restoring convenient, not one that makes backing up convenient.

Any backup type except full backup makes restoring your system more time-consuming.

Backing Up

To launch the backup application, open the System Tools submenu on the Accessories menu and select Backup. The Backup program window that opens is shown in Figure 10-13.

You can use a wizard to accomplish your task, or move to the appropriate tab to perform your task manually. For backing up, the tasks you need to accomplish include:

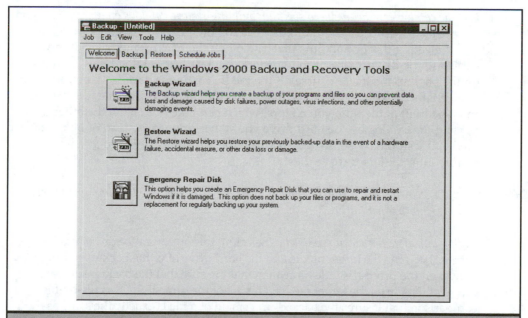

Figure 10-13.   *The Backup program window offers one-click access to all the features in the application*

- Configuring options for the behavior of the Backup program
- Choosing a backup type
- Choosing the folders and files to back up
- Choosing the target media

Configuring the Backup Software

Choose Tools | Options to open the Options dialog box in which you configure default options and the behavior of the software.

General Settings

On the General tab, select or deselect the following features:

- *Compute selection information before backup and restore operations.* The system will calculate the number of folders and files in your backup selection, and the disk space they need, before beginning the operation. For backing up, this is only necessary if the drive(s) you're backing up are much larger than the capacity of your target media and you want to know how many tapes or disks you'll need. For restoring, this is only necessary if you're restoring to a drive that already contains data.

- *Use the catalogs on the media to speed up building restore catalogs on disk.* When you restore a backup, the system builds a catalog on the target disk before restoring files. Selecting this option puts that catalog on the backup media, so it can be copied to the drive if you need to restore the data (the catalog takes up space on the backup media, of course). If the media catalog is damaged, or you have a multitape backup and the tape that holds the catalog is missing, the catalog must be built at the time you restore, which can take hours. On the other hand, placing the catalog on the hard drive you're backing up, instead of on the target media, doesn't make sense because the odds are you're going to attempt a restore after that hard drive dies.

> **Tip** *For the best insurance, write the catalog to the hard drive you're backing up and then copy it to another hard drive.*

- *Verify data after the backup completes.* Selecting this option causes a verification process between the target media and the hard drive after the backup is completed. However, the process is little more than making sure that the backup software can read the file on the target media. This is not the same thing as a file-by-file comparison that insures the backed-up version of a file is exactly the same as the original file. However, if the backup software can't read the file, it's frequently an indication that there's a problem with the media or even the type of media. While this makes an interesting test, a more definitive test is to create a small backup and restore it, and then make sure everything on the drive is the same as it was before the restoral.

■ *Back up the contents of mounted drives.* If you're using mounted drives, this insures that the data on the mounted drive is backed up. Deselecting this option means that only the path information about the mounted drive is backed up.

■ *Show alert message when I start Backup and Removable Storage is not running.* Select this option to receive a warning if the Removable Storage service isn't running. This is only necessary if your target media is handled by the Removable Storage service, which means tape or optical disk.

■ *Show alert message when I start Backup and there is compatible import media available.* Select this option if you use media that is handled by the Removable Storage service and you want to know if and when there is new media available in the media pool.

■ *Show alert message when new media is inserted into Removable Storage.* Select this option if you use media that is handled by the Removable Storage service and you want to know that new media has been inserted in the target device.

■ *Always move new import media to the Backup media pool.* Select this option if you use media that is handled by the Removable Storage service and you want to move new media that's been detected by the service to the media used by Backup.

Restore Settings

The configuration items on the Restore tab apply to partial restores, not recovery from a disk disaster in which you're rebuilding your system. Select the default behavior for restoring files that already exist on the disk, choosing from the following:

■ Don't replace existing files.

■ Replace existing files when the files on the disk are older than the files on the restore media.

■ Always replace existing files.

The first option is the safest, of course. However, remember you are only setting the default configuration, and when you actually restore, you're offered a chance to change the defaults.

Backup Type Settings

Use the drop-down list in this tab to select the default backup type (all five types are described in the "Backup Types" section earlier in this chapter). This setting only sets the default for your backup session, and you can change the type when you perform a backup.

Backup Log Settings

Choose the option for logging the backup operation:

■ **Detailed,** which logs the names of every backed-up file and folder.

■ **Summary,** which logs the major processes, including the time the backup began and a list of any files that couldn't be backed up.

■ **None,** which means no log is kept.

Backup logs are named backupXX.log (where XX starts with 01) and are kept in the directory \Documents and Settings\<LoggedOnUserName>\Local Settings\Application Data\Microsoft\Windows\NTBackup\data. Unlike previous versions of Windows Backup, you cannot change the location.

Excluded File Settings

You can exclude files from the backup, and a number of files are preselected for exclusion regardless of the user who generates the backup. You can add files to that list.

In addition, you can specify additional files to be excluded when you are the user who initiates the backup. If you want to create sets of excluded files for other users, they must log on to create that excluded file set.

The excluded files list is kept in the registry at HKEY_LOCAL_MACHINE\System\CurrentControlSet\Control\BackupRestore\FilesNotToBackup, and these files are excluded regardless of whether you're using Windows Backup or a third-party application.

Creating a Backup

Begin your backup by launching the Backup Wizard or by moving to the Backup tab to manually establish the settings for your backup.

 If you use the wizard, first use the Backup tab to check (or change) the target in the Backup Media or Filename field.

The wizard offers three choices:

■ A full backup (everything on the computer)

■ Selected files (you select the drives, folders and files to backup from a tree of the system hierarchy)

■ System State only

If you don't use the wizard, preferring to configure the backup manually, go to the Backup tab and select the folders and files that you want to include in the backup. The Backup tab displays a tree of the system hierarchy, and you can expand it to include the objects you want to back up (see Figure 10-14). Your pointer turns into a check mark and deposits a check mark with every click. Clicking again toggles the check mark off.

■ Click the check box next to an object to select it.

■ Click the drive or folder object to display its contents in the right pane.

 Tip   *Remember to select the System State for the local computer (you cannot back up the System State on a remote computer).*

There are two options available for selecting storage media (the Backup media or filename field at the bottom of the Backup tab window):

■ *You can back up to a file on a drive.* A drive can be a hard disk or any other type of removable or nonremovable media. If you're using a drive, enter the path and filename (you can use a UNC), or click Browse to select the target drive.

■ *You can back up the data to a tape device.* The tape device option is available only if the system detects a tape device on the computer. If you choose to use the tape device, the media is managed by the Removable Storage system.

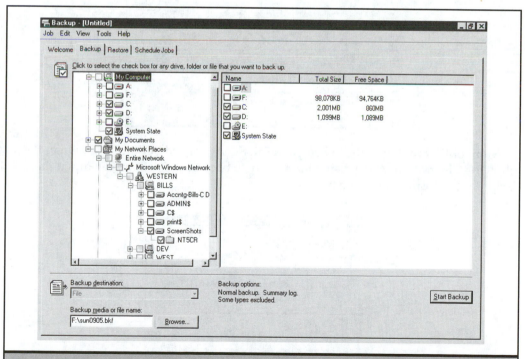

Figure 10-14.   *Select the elements you want to include in the backup*

The file option is always available, even if there is a tape device on the computer.

Choose Save Selections from the Job menu to retain the selections and options you've created as a backup selection file. You can load this job anytime you want to use it, and you can create additional backup jobs with different file and folder selections. The backup selection job is saved as *filename*.bks.

   The backup selection file can be used to specify the files and folders to back up if you want to run backups from the command line. See the section "Using Backup Batch Files" later in this chapter.

Click Start Backup when you've finished making your selections. The Backup Job Information dialog box appears, prompting for additional information about this backup job.

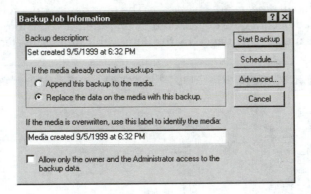

More options are available when you click the Advanced button, as shown in the following illustration. And when you're ready to back up, click Start Backup in the Backup Job Information dialog box.

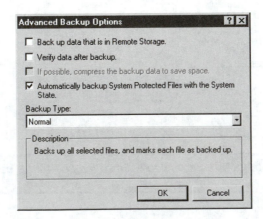

Scheduling a Backup

If you'd prefer to schedule the backup to run at a later time (it's automatically added to your Scheduled Tasks), click Schedule. If you haven't saved the selection file, a message displays to tell you that you have to save your selections before you can schedule a backup. Click Yes to perform the task, and enter a name for this set of options in the Save Selections dialog box.

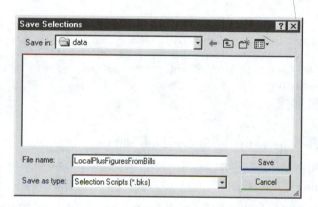

The system prompts for a password for this backup selection file. If you're not worried about the security of this computer or the selection file, you can opt to skip the password. In the Schedule Job dialog box, enter a job name for the backup—this is the name that appears in the Scheduled Tasks window—and click OK. Then click Properties and enter the schedule.

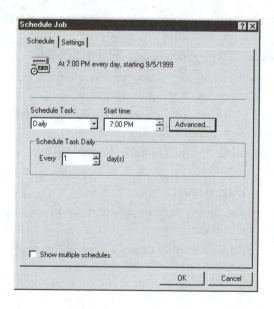

Using Backup Batch Files

If you're comfortable with the command line, you can run your backup procedures via a batch file, with the Ntbackup command. The Ntbackup command does not support filenames as targets, not even in the form of wildcards. However, as a workaround, you can specify an input file that contains a list of filenames.

The syntax for Ntbackup is

```
ntbackup backup [systemstate] "bks file name" /J <"job name"> [/P <"pool name">}]
[/G <{"guid name">] [/T < "tape name">] [/N <"media name">] [/F <"file name">]
[/D <"set description">] [/DS <"server name">] [/IS <"server name">]
[/A] [/V:{yes|no}] [/R:{yes|no}] [/L:{f|s|n}] [/M <backup type>]
[/RS:{yes|no}] [/HC:{on|off}]
```

where:

- **systemstate** Backs up the System State data.
- *bks file name* Is the name of a backup selection file (.bks file) you want to use.
- /J *<job name>* Is the job name you want to use in the log file.
- /P *<pool name>* Is the media pool from which you want to use media (usually the Backup media pool—see Chapter 27 for information about Removable Storage and media pools). You cannot use the /A /G /F /T switches if you use this parameter.
- /A Forces an append to an existing backup on the target drive. Either /G or /T is required with this switch.
- /G *<"guid name">* Overwrites or appends to the tape drive identified by this guid (Globally Unique Identifier).
- /T *<"tape name">* Overwrites or appends to this tape.
- /N *<"media name">* Specifies a new tape name (don't use /A with this switch because a new tape has no existing backup).
- /F *<"file name">* Is the filename for the backup job (including the path). Do not use the /P /G /T switches with this parameter.
- /D *<"set description">* Is the label for the backup set.
- /DS *<"server name">* Is for Exchange Server, and backs up the directory service file on the named server.
- /IS *<"server name">* Is for Exchange Server, and backs up the Information Stores on the named server.
- /V:*<yes|no>* Specifies whether or not to verify the data after the backup is complete.

- **/R:<yes|no>** Specifies that access to the tape is restricted to the owner or members of the Administrators group.

- **/L:<f|s|n>** Specifies the log file setting (**f**=full, **s**=summary, **n**=none).

- **/M** *<backup type>* The backup type (see the section on backup types earlier in this chapter).

- **/RS:<yes|no>** Specifies whether or not to back up the Removable Storage database.

- **/HC:<on|off>** Turns hardware compression on or off on a tape drive (if the drive supports that feature).

Before you use the command line, open the GUI backup application and create the list of files and folders you want to back up, and save those settings in a .bks file. In addition, use the Options dialog box to set global configuration options. The following switches default to the settings you configured in the GUI application (unless you specifically change them in the command line): **/V /R /L /M /RS /HC**.

If you create multiple GUI configurations, you can create multiple backup batch files. Use the AT command or the Task Scheduler to automate the launching of your backup batch files.

Troubleshooting Tape Devices

Using the term "troubleshooting" implies solutions, but there are some complications inherent in the Windows 2000 backup utility that lack solutions, or have solutions you may not find acceptable. The problems impact users who back up to tape devices. The need to manage tape media with the Removable Storage Manager (RSM) and the media pool has made backing up to tape more complex. If you're migrating from Windows NT 4, especially if you used batch files to back up, you're probably going to have mixed emotions about the new features in the Windows 2000 backup utility.

For many organizations, tapes used to be merely another media form, and backups wrote to whatever tape was in the tape drive. Any employee could mount a tape, change a tape, and remove a tape from the drive. For example, if every Wednesday someone inserted the tape labeled "Wednesday" before leaving for the day, the IT department was assured a middle-of-the-night automated backup would be written to the right tape. There were only two requirements for success:

- The employee who inserted the tape in the drive had to be able to read (at least the days of the week).

- The automated backup commands included the appropriate instructions regarding overwriting or appending.

This is no longer the case. In fact, your Windows NT 4 backup batch files won't work in Windows 2000 because they don't contain the switches that control the target media.

RSM provides robust features for organizations that need a method of tracking and controlling removable media. However, using RSM means that tapes can no longer be casually placed in a tape drive. Tapes must be prepared by RSM, named, assigned to media pools, and otherwise manipulated via software.

Given all of this, here are some guidelines for preventing problems when backing up to tape:

■ Be sure to prepare a sufficient number of tapes for your backup before starting the backup (you can't just grab another tape if you need it). Use the Computer Management functions to move them into the Backup pool or the Import pool (if Backup sees a tape in the Import pool, it will ask if you want to import it).

■ Use physical labels on tapes to duplicate the tape's RSM information.

■ Keep a manual log book of tapes indicating when they were last used, in order to make sure you can successfully restore if you have a disk disaster. Alternatively (or additionally), you can configure Backup to write a detailed log, and then print the logs and store them.

Restoring from a Backup

You must use the GUI backup application to restore files you backed up from the Backup application or from the command line (there is no restore operation available via the command line).

The backup type affects the restore method, so when you are faced with a restore operation, the first step is to identify the backup files you need:

■ If you always perform a Normal backup type, you need only the last backup.

■ If you perform Differential backups, you need the last Normal backup and the last Differential backup.

■ If you perform Incremental backups, you need the last Normal backup and every Incremental backup since the last Normal backup. The Incremental backups must be restored in the same order in which they were created.

Restoring Files and Folders

To restore files and folders, open Backup and choose the Restore tab (you could also use the wizard). The left pane displays a tree view of your backup sets, and you can expand a set to select individual folders and files, or select a set to restore the entire contents (see Figure 10-15).

Caution *Do not restore a backup of an NTFS volume to a FAT volume.*

Disaster Recovery

If you have a disk failure (or a computer failure) and have to rebuild a computer, the recovery process has only two steps:

1. Install the operating system with the same volume, hardware, and configuration options used on the failed system.

2. Restore the backup from the failed drive.

As long you backed up the System State, the registry can handle the software and hardware that's restored. If you didn't back up the registry, you must reinstall the software using the same directory structure as the original configuration before restoring the backup.

If the computer you're restoring is running Windows 2000 Professional, or is a member server, that's all you have to do. However, if the computer you're restoring is a domain controller, you have to take special steps, which are covered in this section.

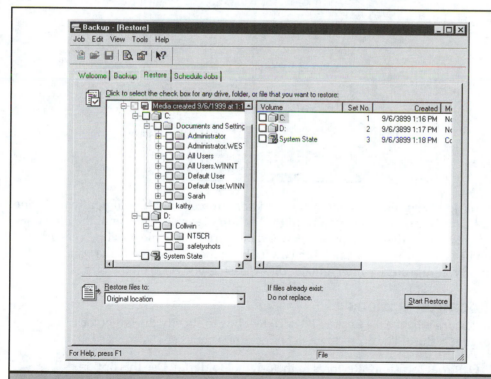

Figure 10-15.   *To restore specific folders and files, expand the backup set*

This section covers regular files and folders, not the System State files, which are restored with special procedures.

Set Restore Options

When you're restoring folders and files, you have some options about the way you want to accomplish the task.

File Replacement Options

Select Options from the Tools menu and go to the Restore tab to specify the conditions for restoring files.

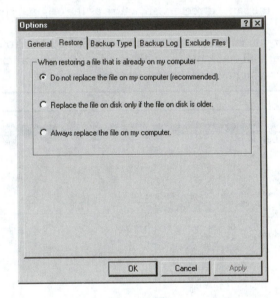

The options you select depend on your reason for restoring files. If you're replacing files that have been corrupted, you want the backup files restored even if the filenames already exist on the drive and have a newer date. Perhaps the file was fine yesterday and you backed it up. Today something awful happened to the file while you were using it. If you're restoring after a major disk disaster, you need all the files.

File Location Options

On the Restore tab, use the Restore Files To text box to specify the target location for the files you restore. The drop-down list offers three choices:

- **Original location**   Restores to the original folder(s). Use this option when you're restoring folders or files that have been corrupted or inadvertently deleted.

- **Alternate location**   Restores to a folder that you designate. Use this option to restore older files that you may need, but take care that you do not overwrite any existing files. The original folder structure is retained in the alternate folder.

- **Single folder**   The only time to use this option is when you know you've lost a file on the drive and you can't find it in the backup folder you thought it was in (or you don't have time to search for it). This option doesn't transfer folders, so the original folder structure is lost. All the files are dumped into the target folder.

Advanced Options

After you've made your file replacement and location selections, click Start Restore. A Confirm Restore message box opens to offer the opportunity to set advanced options before beginning the file transfer. Click Advanced to see the available options.

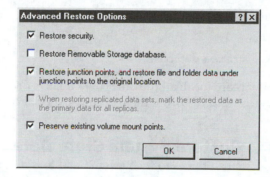

- **Restore Security** applies only to NTFS file systems.

- **Restore Removable Storage Database** applies if you use Removable Storage on the drive you backed up. If you select this option, the database on the backup media will replace the current database on the drive, regardless of your settings for overwriting files.

- **Restore Junction Points And Their Data** applies if you've created junction points. If you omit this option, junction points are restored but the data isn't (which may make the data inaccessible).

- **Preserve Existing Volume Mount Points** keeps the current mount points on the target drive. If you're restoring to a new disk (perhaps as a result of a disk disaster), the new mount points may not match those on the backup.

When you have selected the advanced options you need, click OK and then OK again to begin restoring files.

Excluded Files

Certain files that may be on the backup set are not restored, and you can add to the list in the Exclude Files tab of the Options dialog box. The default excluded files are written to

the registry in HKEY_LOCAL_MACHINE\SYSTEM\CurrentControlSet\Control\
BackupRestore\KeysNotToRestore and those files won't be restored whether you use
Windows Backup or a third-party application.

Restoring Domain Controllers

When you back up the System State on a domain controller, the data contains the
following elements (depending on the system services you've installed):

- Registry
- System boot files
- Active Directory
- SYSVOL directory
- Directory services
- Certificate Services
- COM+ Class Registration database

Only the first two items are local; all the other data objects provide domain-wide or
organization-wide services, and restoring them requires special considerations and
special steps.

Use Safe Mode to Restore System State Data

In order to restore the system services to the System State folder of a domain controller,
you must reboot into Directory Services Restore Mode (which is a form of Safe Mode).
To accomplish this, restart the computer and press F8 when the operating system menu
choices display on your monitor. From the list of boot options, select Directory Services
Restore Mode (Windows 2000 domain controllers only). Here's what to expect:

- A message appears: "The system is booting in safemode – Directory
  Services Repair".
- Select Windows 2000 as the operating system to start.
- The words "safe mode" appear in the four corners of your screen.
- Message boxes appear (Preparing Network Connections, Applying Security).
- The standard Welcome to Windows dialog box that tells you to "Press
  CTRL-ALT-DELETE to begin" appears.
- You press CTRL-ALT-DEL and log on as the local Administrator.
- A message box appears to explain that Windows is running in safe mode,
  giving details about the variety of things you may want to try to get your
  computer to boot normally. Click OK.

■ The desktop appears with the four safe mode text announcements in the corners. Use the Start menu to open Backup and move to the Restore tab (or run the Restore Wizard).

Authoritative Restores

If you have other domain controllers in addition to the DC you're restoring, you may need to run an *authoritative restore* instead of the usual restore procedure (which is nonauthoritative). When you restore normally, the AD is restored with its original update sequence number. Because the sequence number is outdated, the AD database will be overwritten during the next replication event. However, suppose your AD database had become corrupt, and was replicated to the other DCs? After you restore the System State, with its pristine precorruption data, the next replication will destroy it.

An authoritative restore is one in which the restored AD data is replicated to other domain controllers. If the reason you're restoring the System State data is that the AD on the DC had become corrupted and that corrupted data was replicated to other DCs, you need an authoritative restore.

   The definition of corrupted includes (and is most commonly caused by) a mistaken deletion of one or more important objects in the AD.

A nonauthoritative restore is one in which the restored data is later replaced by replicated AD data from another domain controller. If the reason you're restoring the System State data is that you're replacing a DC after a crash or a hardware upgrade, you should run a nonauthoritative restore so the computer can catch up.

To create an authoritative restore, you must run the Ntdsutil utility before you restart the server after restoring the System State data. Ntdsutil is on the Windows 2000 CD-ROM in the \Support\Reskit\Netmgmt directory.

Ntdsutil lets you mark Active Directory objects for an authoritative restore. This really means that an object's update sequence number is changed to make it higher than any other update sequence number in the Active Directory replication system. The data with the highest sequence number is the data that's replicated throughout the organization.

   Ntdsutil adds 100,000 to the sequence number it finds in the restored data.

Here's how to use the Ntdsutil utility:

1. While you're still in Directory Services Restore Safe Mode, copy Ntdsutil.exe and Ntdsutil.doc to the local drive.

2. From the Start menu, point to Programs and click Command Prompt.

3. Open a command prompt from the Start menu (Programs, Accessories, Command Prompt).

4. Enter **Ntdsutil**.

At this point, the commands you enter depend on the distributed services that are in the System State folder, and the documentation for Ntdsutil explains the choices.

After you've completed your work at the command prompt, restart the computer and boot normally. The restored System State data will become the source for the next replication procedure.

Restore System State to a Different Location

Depending on the reason you're restoring data, you may want to restore the System State to a different location during the restore process. When you restore the System State data to the System State folder, the System State data that is currently on your computer is totally replaced with the System State data you are restoring.

When you restore the System State data to an alternate location, only the registry files, SYSVOL directory files, and system boot files are restored to the alternate location. The Active Directory, directory services database, Certificate Services database, and COM+ Class Registration database are not restored to the alternate location.

Therefore, if the problem that caused you to restore is only with the local computer, use an alternate location during the restore process and then copy the files to the System State folder. The system services (Active Directory, etc.) in the System State folder won't be replaced with the earlier data on the backup.

Note   *Even if you opt to restore the System State to an alternate location, you must follow the steps described above for restoring in Safe Mode.*

It's urgent that you test your backup plan by creating a backup and restoring it before you have a disaster.

The
Complete Reference

Chapter 11

Internet Explorer 5

W indows 2000 includes several user-oriented, Internet-related applications. This chapter covers the two most common: Internet Explorer and Outlook Express. Internet Explorer enables you to browse Web, FTP, and gopher sites on the Internet. Outlook Express is a combined application for e-mail, newsgroups, contact management, and directory services (not to be confused with the Active Directory).

Internet Explorer 5

Internet Explorer is a Web browser included with Windows 2000 that enables you to access sites on the Internet, including Web, FTP, and gopher sites. You also can use it to browse local folders and network shares. This section of the chapter focuses on configuring and using Internet Explorer to access Web and FTP sites.

This chapter doesn't cover gopher since gopher's use is declining on the Internet. Gopher sites look and function much like FTP sites in Internet Explorer, but with an expanded structure. To access a gopher site, enter **gopher://address** *in the Internet Explorer address bar, where* address *is the URL for the gopher site.*

When you install Windows 2000, Setup installs Internet Explorer and Outlook Express automatically, so your first step is to configure Internet Explorer's settings.

Configuring Internet Explorer

Configuring Internet Explorer is relatively easy, but there are several different configuration categories with several options each. If your desktop contains an Internet Explorer icon, right-click the icon and choose Properties to display the Internet Properties sheet. If there is no Internet Explorer icon on the desktop, choose Start | Programs | Internet Explorer to start the program, and then choose Tools | Internet Options to display the Internet Options Properties dialog box. The following sections explain configuration options for each property page.

If you haven't set up an Internet connection yet, or don't want to go online while you configure Internet Explorer, choose Stay Offline when prompted.

Configuring General Properties

The General page of the Internet Properties dialog box lets you configure the default home page, how Internet Explorer handles temporary files, the site history, and various aspects of the Internet Explorer interface such as colors and fonts. Figure 11-1 shows the General tab.

DEFINING THE DEFAULT HOME PAGE   Use the Home page group of controls to specify the default home page, which Internet Explorer loads at startup (and also when

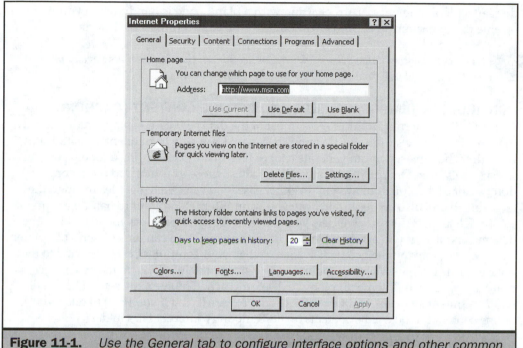

Figure 11-1.   *Use the General tab to configure interface options and other common properties*

you click the Home button on the toolbar). Microsoft sets the home page by default to www.msn.com to drive traffic to its site (a little captive marketing), but you can set the page to whatever site you wish, whether to a local folder, network share, intranet site, Internet URL (Uniform Resource Locater), or no site at all (blank).

To specify a site, click in the Address field and type the UNC (Uniform Naming Convention) pathname or URL to the desired resource. A UNC pathname takes the form *computer**share*, where *computer* is the name of the computer on the LAN hosting the resource and *share* is the name of the share. For example, a share named Documents on a server named Fred would have the UNC pathname \\\\Fred\\Documents. In Windows 2000 you also can specify a folder within the share, such as \\\\Fred\\Documents\\MyStuff. To specify a local folder, type the path to the folder in the Address field. For Web addresses, use the URL for the address in the form http://*location* or ftp://*location*, where *location* is the IP address or DNS name of the site, such as http://www.cnn.com.

If you're already viewing the page or resource you want to define as the home page in Internet Explorer, just click Use Current. Internet Explorer automatically stores the address of the current page to the Address field.

The Use Default button sets the default home page back to http://www.msn.com. Use Blank sets the default home page to *about:blank*, which causes Internet Explorer to display a blank page at startup. Starting with a blank page is handy when you want to be able to open Internet Explorer without actually connecting to the Internet.

You can use the option Never Dial A Connection on the Connections page to prevent Internet Explorer from attempting to connect at startup.

CONFIGURING TEMPORARY FILES AND OFFLINE CONTENT (CACHING)   As you visit sites, Internet Explorer *caches* most of the data so it can display it more quickly the next time you visit the site. Caching speeds up browsing to frequently visited sites. Over time, however, you can generate a lot of files in the cache, using a lot of space on the system's disk. Or, you might have visited sites whose graphics and other content you don't want cached on your system. In either case, you can delete the files through the General tab and also configure the way you want Internet Explorer to handle caching.

To delete cache files, click Delete Files. Internet Explorer prompts you to confirm the deletion and asks if you also want to delete *offline content*. You can direct Internet Explorer to cache sites, making their content available when your computer isn't connected to the Internet. This is a handy feature for browsing a site's content offline, reducing connect charges. If you want Internet Explorer to delete all cached offline sites, select Delete All Offline Content and click OK. Leave the check box deselected if you want to retain the offline content but delete the contents of the Temporary Internet Files folder.

Working with offline content is explained in the section " Configuring Temporary Files and Offline Content" later in this chapter.

To control the way Internet Explorer handles caching and to view the objects in the cache, click Settings on the General tab to access the Settings dialog box (see Figure 11-2).

The first four options on the Settings page specify when Internet Explorer checks for new versions of pages stored in the cache (when it updates the cache). These options, and their methods, include:

- **Every Visit To The Page**   Each time you visit a page, Internet Explorer checks to see if the page has been updated since you last viewed it. If an update has occurred, Internet Explorer downloads the page and stores it in the cache. If there hasn't been an update, Internet Explorer pulls the existing data from the cache to display the page.

- **Every Time You Start Internet Explorer**   Internet Explorer does not check for updates to pages within the same Internet Explorer session. It only checks for updates if you haven't visited the page in the current session (since you started Internet Explorer).

- **Automatically**   Internet Explorer checks for updates of a page only after restarting Internet Explorer or on a different day. Internet Explorer will download updates less frequently if it determines that data changes infrequently on the page.

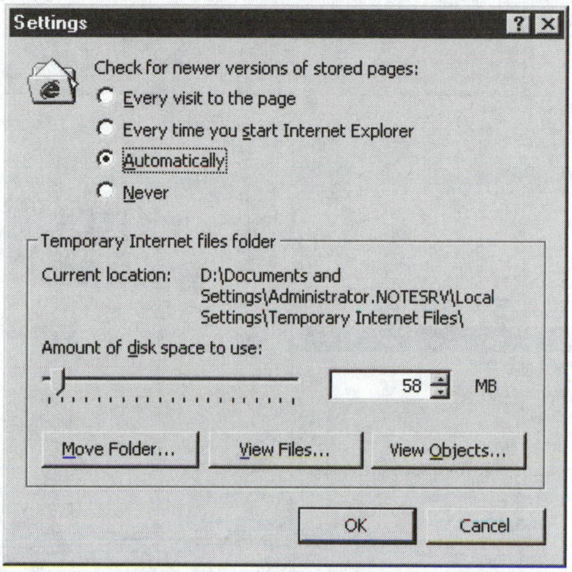

Figure 11-2.   *Configure caching settings in the Settings dialog box*

■ **Never**   Internet Explorer always pulls previously viewed pages from the cache and doesn't check for updates.

Click the Refresh button on the toolbar to reload a page. Hold down the CTRL *key while you click Refresh to force an update.*

The Settings dialog box also lets you configure general cache settings. Use the slider to specify the amount of disk space to allocate to the cache folder. Click Move Folder to relocate the Internet Explorer cache to a different folder. By default, Windows 2000 stores the cache in \Documents and Settings\<*UserName*>\Local Settings\Temporary Internet Files. You might want to move the folder if you're running out of space on the target drive.

The View Files button opens the Temporary Internet Files folder so you can view its contents (cached Web pages, graphics, cookies, etc.). Click View Objects to explore the Downloaded Programs folder, which contains downloaded ActiveX and Java controls.

CONFIGURING AND CLEARING THE HISTORY   Internet Explorer maintains a History folder with shortcuts to the pages you've visited recently. Clicking History on the toolbar opens the History pane, which organizes visited pages by date.

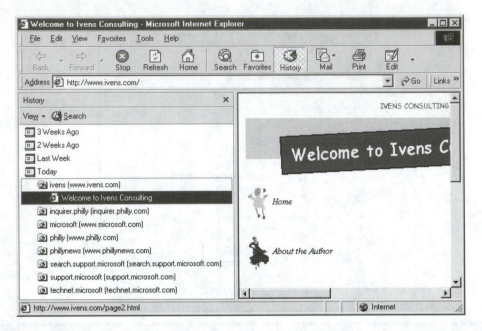

The History pane gives you a quick way to revisit sites you've been to in the recent past. You simply open the week or date you want to use and click the desired Web page to view it. By default, Internet Explorer keeps track of pages for 20 days. When the time expires, Internet Explorer removes the pages from your History folder.

Use the History group on the General page of the Internet Options tab to specify the number of days you want Internet Explorer to retain pages in the History folder. There's also an option to clear the History folder, which removes all references to visited sites.

Configuring Security

Use the Security page of Internet Explorer properties to configure security zones and content. A *security zone* is a group of sites that share a common set of security settings. Windows 2000 predefines four zones:

- **Internet**   This zone comprises all sites on the Internet. You can specify security settings for the Internet zone but not define which sites it contains (which is logical, since the Internet is so vast). Instead, the Internet zone comprises all zones not listed in the other three zones. Although Windows 2000 uses the Medium security level for the Internet zone, you should consider using High to protect against unknown malicious sites and controls.

- **Local Intranet**   The local intranet zone includes any sites hosted within your intranet. An intranet typically consists of systems within a given local area network (LAN), but could also include sites in a wide area network (WAN).

- **Trusted Sites**   Place in this zone those sites that you trust and for which you want to apply less restrictive security.

■ **Restricted Sites**   Place in this zone those sites you *don't* trust, which typically are those that you know or suspect can cause damage to your system, intrude on your privacy, and so on.

You set security options on a per-zone basis. You can choose among High, Medium, Medium-low, or Low, depending on the zone and the security settings you want to apply to each. High applies the most security and Low applies the least. These security levels control such events and tasks as downloading signed ActiveX controls, running ActiveX controls and plug-ins, and handling cookies and downloads. You can select one of the four primary security levels for each zone or define a security set based on one of the four zones. To use one of the predefined levels, select it using the slider control. Click Custom Level to access the Security Settings dialog (see Figure 11-3) to set individual settings. Click Default Level if you want to use one of the predefined security levels for the zone.

Although you can't define the sites in the Internet zone, you can define which sites reside in the Local Intranet, Trusted Sites, and Restricted Sites zones. All zones not defined in these three are implicitly included in the Internet zone.

CONFIGURING THE LOCAL INTRANET ZONE   Click the Local Intranet icon and click Sites to specify the sites that comprise your local intranet. Windows 2000 presents the Local Intranet dialog box with the following three options:

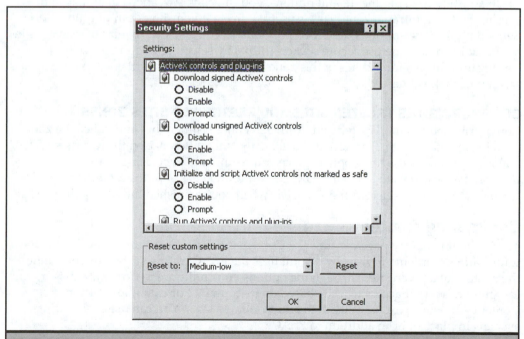

Figure 11-3.   *Use the Security Settings dialog to configure individual security settings for the selected zone*

■ **Include All Local (Intranet) Sites Not Listed In Other Zones**   Select this option to include all sites defined by the system administrator as being local sites.

If you're an administrator, you can use the Microsoft Internet Explorer Administrator Kit (IEAK) to create systemwide settings for your intranet sites, security zones, and other systemwide configuration options. Download the IEAK from Microsoft's Internet Explorer Web page.

■ **Include All Sites That Bypass The Proxy Server**   Select this option to include all sites that bypass your network's proxy server in the Local Intranet zone.

Tip

To define sites that bypass the proxy server, open the Connections tab of the Internet Options properties, click LAN Settings, click Advanced, and enter the URLs in the Exceptions list.

■ **Include All Network Paths (UNCs)**   Select this option to include in the Local intranet zone all UNC paths you specify during browsing. A UNC takes the form *server**share*, where *server* is the name of the computer hosting the resource and *share* is the resource's share name. In Windows 2000 the UNC can include a folder name as well, such as \\BigServer\Documents\MyStuff.

In addition to using the default options, you can click Advanced to add specific sites to the Local intranet zone. This is useful when a given site doesn't fit the criteria defined by the three options described previously. You also can require that all sites in the Local Intranet zone use secure sockets (https) by selecting Require Server Verification (https:) for all sites in this zone on the Local Intranet dialog, which appears when you click Advanced.

CONFIGURING THE TRUSTED SITES AND RESTRICTED SITES ZONES

Configuring sites in the Trusted and Restricted zones is much the same. Click the zone in question and click Sites. For the Trusted zone, the only difference on the Restricted Sites dialog is the lack of the https option (since you're unlikely to be using https on an untrusted, restricted site). Type the URL for a site, and click Add to add it to the list. Use Remove to remove a selected site. Click OK when you're finished modifying the site list.

Configuring Content

The Content property page controls the Content Advisor, Certificates, and Personal Information. Content Advisor by default uses the RSACi rating system to determine the content of a given site. Through the options you configure in Content Advisor, you can grant or restrict access to a site based on its content. For example, you can use Content Advisor to exclude access to adult-oriented sites. You can use other rating systems in place of or in addition to RSACi.

Certificates digitally identify you, a certification authority (which grants certificates), and publishers (such as software developers). You can use a certificate to sign an e-mail message, for example, to prove that the message came from you. Certificates can be used for other purposes as well, such as authentication (depending on the function of the certificate).

The Personal Information section of the Content page lets you define a profile with your personal information (name, address, etc.), which you can provide to a Web site that requests it. You also can configure the way you want Internet Explorer to handle automatic completion of addresses, usernames, passwords, and other information.

CONTENT ADVISOR   Content Advisor uses various rating systems to identify the content of a site so you can potentially block sites that contain certain topics such as nudity, violence, and so on. Site rating is entirely voluntary, however, so using a rating system is no guarantee that offensive or unwanted sites won't come through anyway. Many sites do employ some rating service, however, so you can at least filter a majority of the sites. In addition, you can configure Internet Explorer (IE) to exclude sites that are not rated. Content Advisor is turned off by default. Click Enable on the Content page to open the Content Advisor dialog box shown in Figure 11-4.

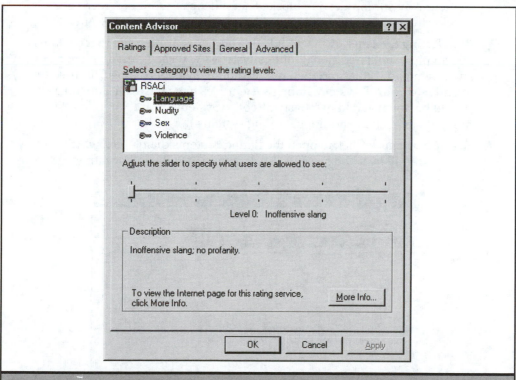

Figure 11-4.   *Use Content Advisor to prevent sites with specific types of content from being displayed*

The Ratings tab lets you specify the level of censorship applied to the selected category. Click a category and use the slider to specify what the user is allowed to view from sites rated by the selected rating system. Click More Info to view the home page for the selected rating system.

The Approved Sites tab lets you create a list of Web sites that can always be viewed regardless of rating level (useful for viewing certain sites that are unrated when you have otherwise excluded unrated sites). Simply type the URL for the site in the Allow This Web Site field and click Always to allow the site; click Never to exclude it. To remove a site from the list of approved sites, select the site and click Remove.

The General page of the Content Advisor controls miscellaneous options:

- **Users Can See Sites That Have No Rating** Select this option to allow users to view unrated sites. Deselect to exclude unrated sites.

- **Supervisor Can Type A Password To Allow Users To View Restricted Content** Select this option if you want Internet Explorer to display a dialog in which you enter the supervisor password to access a site that would otherwise be blocked by Content Advisor.

- **Change Password** Click to specify a Supervisor password required to bypass Content Advisor for viewing blocked sites. If a password has been set previously, you must provide the old password to assign a new one.

- **Find Rating Systems** Click to travel to a Microsoft Web site that contains information about additional ratings systems. You can select a link to a system and download its file, and then use the Rating Systems dialog (discussed next) to add it to your IE system. Rating system files have the extension .rat and should be downloaded to %SystemRoot%\System. (You'll often find links on rating system sites to additional rating systems.)

- **Rating Systems** Click to open the Rating Systems dialog box, which displays your currently installed systems. Click Add to install another rating system.

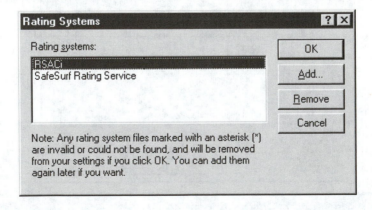

The Content Advisor's Advanced tab lets you specify a ratings bureau to use in conjunction with certain rating systems. URLs are checked by the ratings bureau before a page is opened. A ratings bureau provides a more dynamic rating system, updating its rating data on a continual basis (usually making determinations by reading metatags on Web pages). Using a ratings bureau can slow down access, however, since the ratings bureau is contacted for each page. You also can specify rules on the Advanced page that define how content is handled by Content Advisor.

USING CERTIFICATES   Certificates provide a means of authentication and validation. Some sites use certificates to allow access. You can use certificates to identify e-mail you send as having come from you, rather than being forged by someone else. You can use certificates to encrypt data for transmission across nonsecured networks such as the Internet. And certificates serve several other purposes for authentication and positive identification. Through the Certificates group on the Content property page, you can install, import, and export certificates, define the purpose of a certificate, and perform other tasks related to configuring and using certificates.

When you click Certificates, Internet Explorer displays the Certificates dialog box shown in Figure 11-5. You can view your own certificates, certificates issued to others, intermediate certificate authorities (CAs), and trusted root CAs. To view or manage certificates for a given category, click the category's tab.

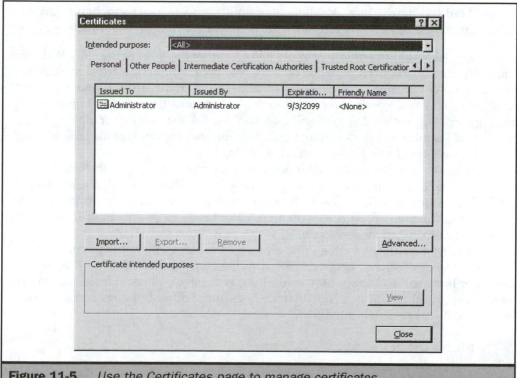

Figure 11-5.   *Use the Certificates page to manage certificates*

LEARNING THE BASICS

Before you can use a certificate you have to acquire one. You can't create certificates yourself, but instead must obtain one from a Certificate Authority, or CA. Some CAs provide certificates for free, while others charge an annual fee. Some CAs charge for certain types of certificates but not for others. Windows 2000 servers can act as CAs for a LAN or enterprise. Public CAs distribute certificates via the Internet, typically from their respective Web sites. The following list identifies several public CAs and their sites:

■ **VeriSign, Inc.** provides digital certificates for individuals and organizations, ISVs, and secure servers. http://www.verisign.com

■ **Thawte, Inc.** offers personal and server certification services for Netscape, MSIE, PGP and other generic X.509 software users. http://www.thawte.com

■ **BelSign** provides digital certification in Europe for individuals and servers. http://www.belsign.be

■ **Certco** offers digital certificates to financial institutions but not to individuals. http://www.certco.com

■ **GNS CA** offers digital certificates to organizations of all sizes based on Entrust technology. http://champlain.gns.ca

■ **Keywitness Canada** provides certificates for individuals and corporations. http://www.keywitness.ca

■ **Trade Authority** provides digital key and certificate management primarily for customers requiring multiple digital certificates. http://www.tradewave.com

To request a public certificate, simply point Internet Explorer to the CA's Web site and follow the instructions provided by the CA to obtain the certificate. Generally the process involves the need to provide personal data and credit card information (if the certificate isn't free). You then receive the certificate as an attachment to an e-mail message, or by downloading the certificate from the CA's secure server. Some certificates install themselves automatically into Internet Explorer, while others require manual installation through the Certificates dialog box.

To request a certificate from a Windows 2000 enterprise CA, open the Certificates console in the MMC. Right-click where you want the certificate installed, and choose All Tasks, Request New Certificate. The wizard will prompt you for information about the type and function of certificate you need. Click Install Certificate at the completion of the wizard to install the certificate.

To request a certificate from a stand-alone server, point Internet Explorer to http://*servername*/certsrv, where *servername* is the name of the Windows 2000 Server computer hosting the CA service. The resulting Web page will provide the mechanism for you to request certificates. Note that the page might differ from one server to the next, since the pages can be modified.

Tip   *You can use the Certificates MMC snap-in to manage certificates on your system.*

If the mechanism you use to obtain a certificate doesn't install the certificate automatically in Internet Explorer, you can use the Certificates page to install it. To do so, click Import. Internet Explorer starts a wizard to help you install the certificate. You'll need to specify the file containing the certificate, the password for the key, and other options. Follow the prompts to complete the installation.

You also can export a certificate to move it to a different computer or send the certificate to someone else. In the Certificates dialog box, click the certificate you want to export and then click Export. Internet Explorer provides a wizard to help you export the certificate to a file. You then can copy the file to another system or send it to another user.

When you click Advanced on the Certificates dialog, Internet Explorer displays the Advanced Options dialog box shown in Figure 11-6. Use this dialog box to configure certificate purposes and set the default certificate export file format.

In addition to offering a means of managing certificates, Internet Explorer's Content property page lets you view and manage the list of software and certificate publishers that you trust. Internet Explorer will install applications (such as plug-ins) from trusted publishers, or publishers certified by a listed CA, without prompting you for verification. To view the list of trusted publishers, click Publishers on the Content page. You can remove a publisher by selecting it in the list and clicking Remove. Note that this dialog box only supports removing a publisher from the list through the dialog. To add a publisher to the list, download a plug-in or other application from the publisher

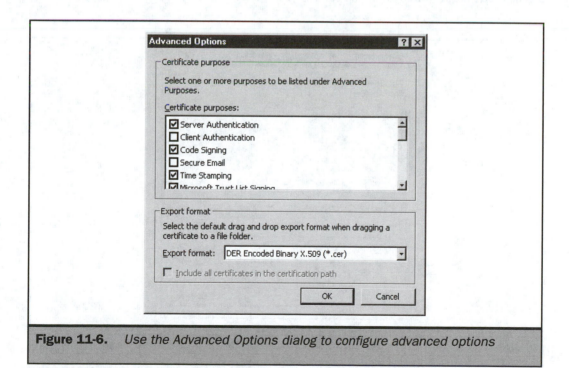

Figure 11-6.   *Use the Advanced Options dialog to configure advanced options*

LEARNING THE BASICS

and when prompted by Internet Explorer, specify that you always want to trust software from that particular publisher.

CONFIGURING PERSONAL INFORMATION   The Personal Information group on the Content page lets you manage personal profile data and personal settings that control AutoComplete features (Internet Explorer automatically completes data as you type it). Click AutoComplete to access the AutoComplete Settings dialog shown in Figure 11-7. The following list explains the options:

- **Use AutoComplete For**   Select the items that you want Internet Explorer to automatically complete for you, including Web addresses, forms, usernames, and passwords. You also can have Internet Explorer prompt you to save passwords in your password cache. The Forms option can fill in nearly any field in a Web page, including names, account numbers, etc. It's useful for automatically completing entries that are not normally cached.

- **Clear Forms**   Click to clear the AutoComplete history for form entries.

- **Clear Passwords**   Click to clear the AutoComplete history for passwords.

In addition to controlling AutoComplete properties, the Personal Information group on the Content page provides a means to create a personal profile in the Address book. This profile holds information about you such as your name, address, phone number, e-mail

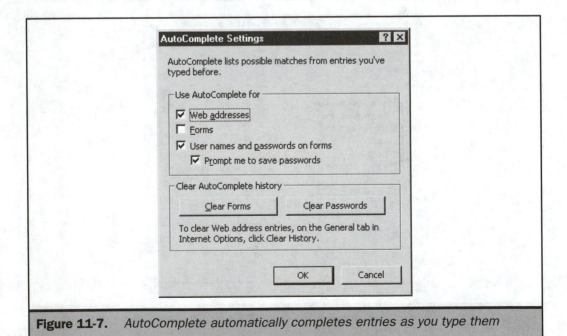

Figure 11-7.   *AutoComplete automatically completes entries as you type them*

and address. If you often visit sites that require this information, the site can pull the data from your profile rather than requiring you to type it all in. To create a profile, click My Profile. Select Create to create a new entry or Select to choose an existing entry for modification. The Main Identity Properties dialog box (see Figure 11-8) provides pages for entering a variety of personal information, which are generally self-explanatory.

Configuring Connections

Internet Explorer can't do anything without a connection to the Internet, so you naturally need a way to create a connection and specify connection properties. The Connections page of the Internet Options dialog box provides a centralized location for creating and configuring dial-up connections and specifying LAN and proxy settings for Internet Explorer.

If you aren't very familiar with Internet connection properties, you can use the Internet Connection Wizard to step you through the process of creating a dial-up account. You can use the wizard to sign up for a new Internet account if you currently don't have one (have your credit card handy), transfer an existing account to this computer, or configure the account manually. Rather than cover the wizard, this chapter assumes you're creating an account manually. (If you decide to use the Internet Connection Wizard, the same information and settings apply.)

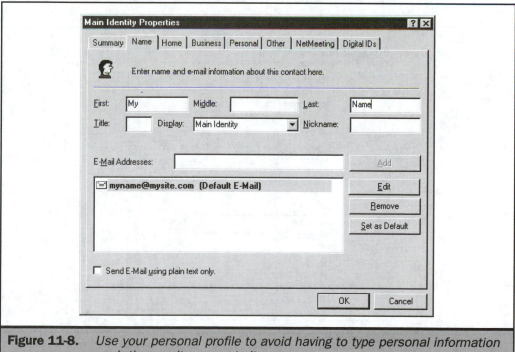

Figure 11-8.   *Use your personal profile to avoid having to type personal information each time a site requests it*

ADDING A DIAL-UP ACCOUNT   Open the Connections property page, and click
Add to add a new dial-up connection. Internet Explorer starts the Network Connection
Wizard. You can choose to create a dial-up connection to a private network, the
Internet, or a direct cable connection to another local computer. Choose the option
Dial-Up To Private Network to create a connection to an Internet Service Provider.
Windows 2000 prompts you to specify the connection device (usually a modem), the
phone number to dial, the users who can access the connection (everyone or just
yourself), and a name for the connection. At the completion of the wizard, Windows
2000 displays the Dial-Up Connection Settings dialog box shown in Figure 11-9.

Specify the following properties in the Connection Settings dialog box:

- **Automatically Detect Settings**   Select this option to have the connection
  automatically derive settings from a file provided by a system administrator.

- **User Automatic Configuration Script**   Select this option and specify the URL
  or filename for a script to be used to automatically configure all of Internet
  Explorer's settings. (Scripts are created and distributed by the administrator,
  using the Internet Explorer Administration Kit.)

- **Use a Proxy Server**   Select this option if you connect to the Internet through a
  proxy server. A proxy server acts as a middleman between the local network

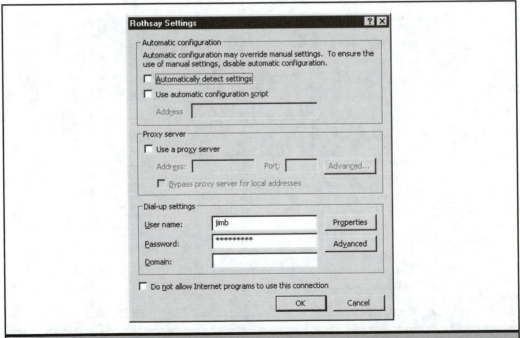

Figure 11-9.   *Use this dialog to configure a new or existing dial-up connection*

and the Internet, essentially hiding the local network from computers on the Internet. Using a proxy server increases security for local systems, but is not a substitute for a good firewall.

- **Address** Specify the IP address or FQDN (Fully Qualified Domain Name) of the proxy server.

- **Port** Specify a port if you only need proxy access through a single port (see Advanced).

- **Advanced** Click to open the Proxy Settings dialog box, in which you can enter individual proxy settings for http, secure sockets, and other protocols, as well as their respective port numbers. You also can specify that the same settings be used to proxy all protocols and specify a list of addresses for which Internet Explorer will bypass the proxy server.

- **Bypass Proxy Server For Local Addresses** Select this option to bypass the proxy server and connect directly for local addresses (those in your own intranet/subnet).

- **User Name** Specify the user account name used to log onto the remote service.

- **Password** Specify the password for the logon account.

- **Domain** If you are logging on with a domain account, specify the domain name.

- **Properties** Click to set other connection properties (see the explanation that immediately follows this list).

- **Advanced** Click to specify the number of dial attempts, pause between attempts, and automatic disconnect settings (disconnect on idle, or connection no longer needed).

- **Do Not Allow Internet Programs To Use This Connection** Select to prevent programs other than Internet Explorer from using this connection to connect to the Internet.

You'll probably need to specify other settings in addition to those in the previous list. Click Properties to access an additional Properties dialog box for this connection. Use the General tab to configure modem settings and the Options tab for dialing properties. The Security tab provides a place to configure the way this connection treats your password (encrypted or clear text), and to configure advanced settings such as the authentication protocol used to establish the connection (CHAP, PAP, etc.).

Use the Networking tab to specify the type of dial-up server to which you're connecting. In most cases PPP is the correct option, because nearly all ISPs, as well as Windows 9x, Windows NT, and Windows 2000 servers, use PPP as the protocol. If your ISP or network administrator instructs you to, select the SLIP (Serial Line Interface Protocol) option.

The Networking tab also provides a place for you to specify which protocols, clients, and services are used for this connection. Simply select the ones that are required and deselect those that are not. If you need to install a protocol, client, or service not listed, click Install and follow the prompts to add the item; then click Properties to configure its settings. For example, click TCP/IP to configure address, DNS, gateway, and other properties for that protocol.

> **Note** *See Chapter 13 for a detailed explanation of TCP/IP settings.*

The Sharing tab gives you access to a feature new in Windows 2000—Internet Connection Sharing. You can configure the dial-up connection so it is shared by other users on the network, enabling multiple users to connect to the Internet through this single modem and dial-up account. In effect, the sharing system becomes a DHCP allocator and router, allocating IP addresses to other computers that need to access the Internet, using a range of addresses preconfigured at 169.x.x.x. It also manages traffic between those computers and the Internet. The Internet Connection Sharing system also installs a DNS allocator, although both the DHCP and DNS allocators stop working in the presence of an authorized DHCP service.

To share a connection, select Enable Internet Connection Sharing for this connection. From the drop-down list, select the local network connection where the other client computers are located (there is only one listed if you have only one network adapter). If you want the computer to dial the connection automatically whenever anyone tries to connect to the Internet, select Enable On-Demand Dialing.

To configure the clients to use the shared connection, configure the TCP/IP properties for their LAN connection to retrieve an IP address automatically through DHCP. Configure their Internet applications to connect to the Internet through the LAN. After the configuration options are in place, the connection is automatic for the clients who share this connection. (Depending on the operating system of the clients, you might have to restart the computer in order to have the IP address change become effective.)

CONFIGURING DIALING OPTIONS The Connections property page includes three options that control the way Windows 2000 connects to the Internet:

- **Never Dial A Connection** Internet Explorer will not attempt to connect automatically to the Internet through a dial-up connection. Choose this option if you want to control when Internet Explorer dials your account.

- **Dial Whenever A Network Connection Is Not Present** Internet Explorer will dial the Internet connection automatically if a network connection to the Internet is not currently established.

- **Always Dial My Default Connection** Internet Explorer will always dial the default connection at startup regardless of the presence of a current network connection. To set the default connection, select the appropriate connection and click Set Default.

CONFIGURING LAN SETTINGS If you connect to the Internet through a LAN (including through a shared dial-up connection on the LAN), click LAN Settings to access the Local Area Network (LAN) Settings dialog shown in Figure 11-10. See the

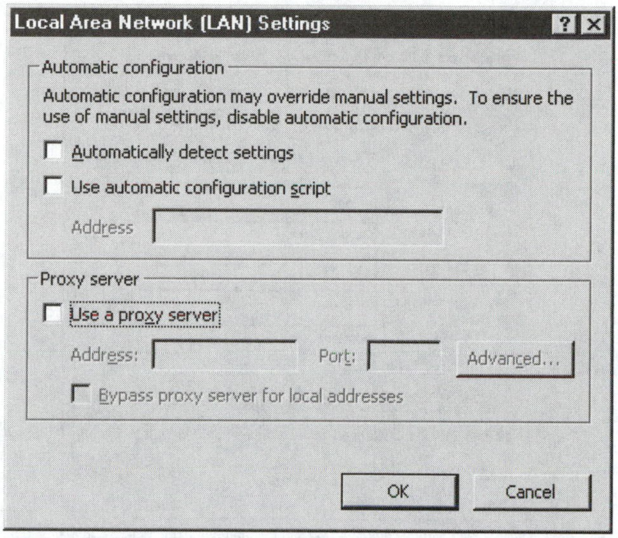

Figure 11-10.   *The settings for a LAN connection are the same as for a dial-up but without the user account, password, and domain properties*

section "Adding a Dial-Up Account" earlier in this chapter for an explanation of the options in this dialog box.

Configuring Programs

You can use Internet Explorer to send and receive e-mail and to access newsgroups. The Programs tab (see Figure 11-11) gives you a place to specify the applications for a specific set of tasks. When you click the Mail icon on the toolbar and select Read Mail, for example, Internet Explorer automatically opens Outlook Express, because Outlook Express is defined in the Programs tab as the application for e-mail.

To use a program other than the default for a given task, first install the program. If you prefer to use Outlook for e-mail, for example, install Outlook. Then select from each drop-down list the application you want to use for the given task. To restore the default settings, click Reset Web Settings. Internet Explorer will reset all the settings to the original defaults, and also give you the option of resetting the home page to the default (www.msn.com).

Use the option at the bottom of the Programs tab to ask Internet Explorer to check whether it is the default browser at each startup. This option is useful if you have (or plan to install) another browser but want IE to be the default browser. If you want to use a different browser as the default, deselect this option to prevent Internet Explorer from performing the check.

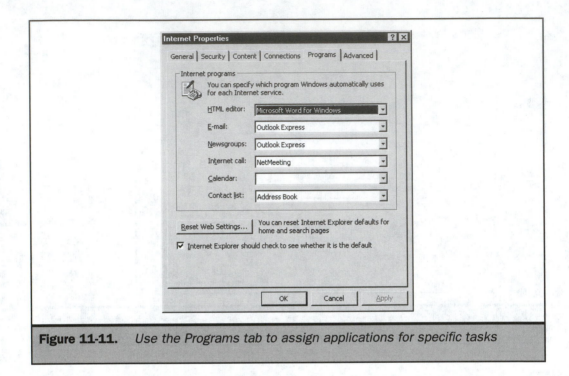

Figure 11-11. *Use the Programs tab to assign applications for specific tasks*

Configuring Advanced Properties

The Advanced tab of the Internet Options Properties dialog box (see Figure 11-12) offers numerous advanced options that control the way Internet Explorer handles specific objects, tasks, and events. The settings are organized by category. Scan through the list and select/deselect options as needed. Click the Question Mark button, and then click on the setting if you need to see a tooltip with more information about the setting's purpose.

Internet Explorer Commands and Features

Internet Explorer is relatively easy to use, and you should have no trouble becoming comfortable with it. If you're moving over from a different browser, this section will bring you up to speed.

Browsing with Internet Explorer

By default, Internet Explorer includes a toolbar, address bar, and links bar. The toolbar offers often-used functions to control browsing, search for information, and access frequently or recently used pages. The address bar provides a place for you to type the URL of the page or site you want to view. You can specify the

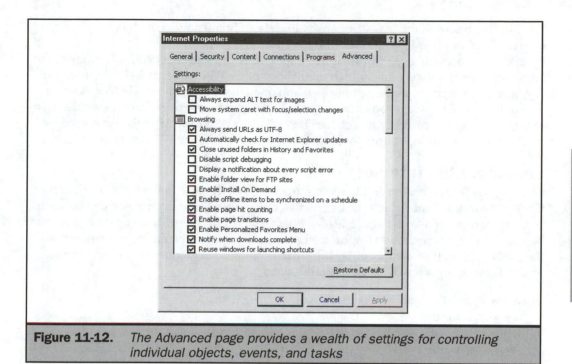

Figure 11-12. *The Advanced page provides a wealth of settings for controlling individual objects, events, and tasks*

friendly name of the site, such as www.microsoft.com, or specify the full URL, such as http://www.microsoft.com. You can also specify a specific page at the target site, such as http://www.microsoft.com/windows/.

To connect to an FTP site, preface the address with ftp://, as in ftp://ftp.microsoft.com (see "Downloading and Uploading with FTP" later in this chapter). To browse a local folder or shared resource on the LAN, specify the local or network path, such as C:\My Documents or \\Server1\Documents\jboyce.

Select the Show Friendly URLs option on Internet Explorer's Advanced property page if you want Internet Explorer's status bar to show the short site name rather than the full URL.

As you're viewing pages, click the Back button on the toolbar or press the BACKSPACE key on the keyboard to see viewed pages in reverse order (view the last page displayed prior to the current page). Click the Forward button to move forward through the page sequence. Click the Stop button to stop the current page from loading or stop Internet Explorer from attempting to load the page referenced by a link you've just clicked or an address you've typed in the address bar.

The Refresh button on the toolbar refreshes (reloads) the current page to make sure you have the most current version of the page. This is the same as Reload in Netscape.

The Home button on the toolbar opens your default home page, which is the page Internet Explorer displays automatically at startup.

As you're browsing, you'll find links in the pages you view. Clicking a link opens the object associated with the link, which might be another Web page, an FTP site, a file, etc. If you want to keep the current page open and open the link in a new window, hold down the SHIFT key when you click on the link. To open a new page from the address bar without closing the current page, choose File | New | Window. After the new window opens, click Stop to stop it from loading, and then enter the new URL in the address bar.

Searching the Internet

Clicking the Search button on the toolbar opens a Search pane to the left of the Internet Explorer window. The Search pane contents, by default, come from ie.search.msn.com. You can search for a Web page, address, business, etc., by typing search text in the text box and clicking Search. You might prefer to use a different search engine rather than the MSN engine. If so, simply enter the URL for the search engine site in the address bar. Following are a few additional search sites:

> www.altavista.com
> www.yahoo.com
> www.lycos.com
> search.cnet.com

You can change the default search page in Internet Explorer by editing the registry. Use a registry editor to go to HKEY_LOCAL_MACHINE\SOFTWARE\Microsoft\ Internet Explorer\Search. Change the value of SearchAssistant to point to the URL of the desired search engine. If that search engine provides a page for customizing its appearance, you can also change the value of CustomizeSearch to point to the URL for the customization page. When you close the registry editor, the change goes into effect immediately.

Finding, Using, and Printing Data on a Page

Sometimes, when you're viewing a page with a lot of data, you need a way to search the page for specific text. To find data on a page, let the page load in its entirety and choose Edit | Find, or press CTRL-F. Internet Explorer opens a dialog box in which you specify the text to find (and use other search options as needed). Click Find Next to perform the search.

After you've found some useful data on a page, you might want to copy that data for use in another document. Internet Explorer fully supports the Windows clipboard, so you can easily copy data from a page to the clipboard. Just highlight the data and use the usual clipboard methods (CTRL-C, or Edit | Copy, followed by CTRL-V, or Edit | Paste).

You also can print the current page or a portion of the page. To print the entire page, click the Print icon on the toolbar or choose File | Print to use the Print dialog box (in case you want to specify printing options). If you want to print a selection from the page, highlight the selection and choose File | Print | Selection.

If you find a page that really impresses you and you'd like to know how it is coded, choose View | Source. Internet Explorer opens Notepad and displays the page's source code.

Controlling the Internet Explorer Interface

Internet Explorer provides a handful of options for controlling the user interface. You can specify which of the toolbars to display, and customize the Standard Buttons toolbar. You also can turn the Explorer bar on or off, and specify its contents.

CONFIGURING TOOLBARS   Choose View | Toolbars to specify which of the four toolbars are displayed at the top of the Internet Explorer window. To customize the Standard Buttons toolbar, click View | Toolbars | Customize to open the Customize Toolbar dialog box.

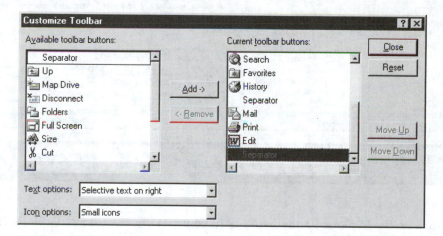

You can add and remove commands, define the way Internet Explorer shows text on the toolbar, choose between small and large icons, and change the order of buttons on the toolbar.

    Click Reset on the Customize Toolbar dialog box to return the toolbar to its default configuration.

USING THE EXPLORER BAR   The Explorer Bar is a special pane that appears to the left of the Internet Explorer window. You can configure the Explorer Bar to show your default search page, the Favorites folder, the History folder, or your system folders. Figure 11-13 shows the Explorer Bar with the system folders displayed.

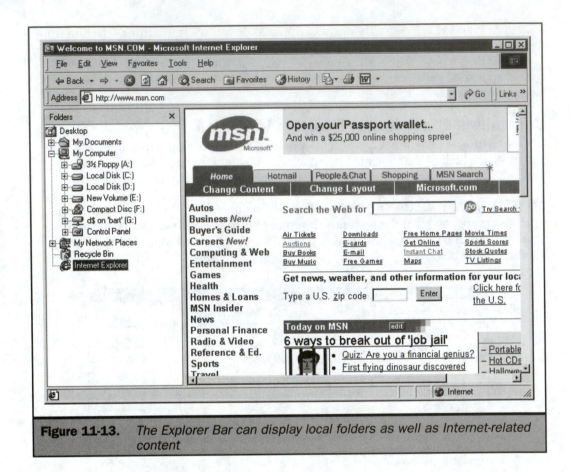

Figure 11-13.   *The Explorer Bar can display local folders as well as Internet-related content*

To turn on the Explorer Bar and specify its contents, choose View | Explorer Bar; then select the object you want to display.

Working with Favorites and History

The Favorites folder serves as a repository of pages and other URLs you use most often, or want to save for future use. To view a resource stored in your Favorites, click Favorites, and then locate and click the target object in the menu. If you have the Favorites folder displayed in the Explorer Bar, simply click the shortcut located there to open the target URL.

The Favorites folder is located on your hard drive in the \Documents and Settings\<*UserName*>\Favorites folder. You can copy or create URL shortcuts directly into the Favorites folder, or use Internet Explorer to save the current URL to the folder. To save the current URL, choose Favorites | Add to Favorites. Specify a name for the object and (optionally) a location for the shortcut. If you don't specify a location, Windows 2000 places the shortcut in the main Favorites folder.

   Although you can use a standard Explorer folder window to manage your Favorites folder, you might prefer to use a more localized approach. Choose Favorites | Organize Favorites to open the Organize Favorites dialog box. Use the controls in this dialog box to create folders under the main Favorites folder, or rename, move, or delete folders and shortcuts.

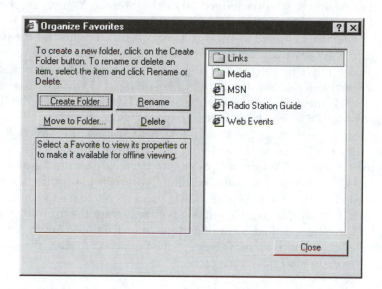

   The History folder contains shortcuts for the URLs you've viewed recently. You can click on a link in the History folder to open the associated URL. The History folder is particularly useful if you want to revisit a site you've been to recently. To display the History folder, choose View | Explorer Bar | History. (Use the General tab of the Internet Options Properties dialog box to configure how long URLs are kept in the History folder and to clear the folder.)

Working with E-Mail

You can use the Tools | Mail and News submenu to open your e-mail or newsgroup program to read and compose messages, send a link or page to someone else as an attachment, and work with newsgroups. See the section "Outlook Express" later in this chapter for detailed information on setting up Outlook Express for e-mail and newsgroup access.

Downloading and Uploading with FTP

FTP stands for File Transfer Protocol, which is a file transfer mechanism that originated in the UNIX world. You can use FTP to upload and download files to and from an FTP site hosted by an FTP server. Although the command-line version of FTP offers several additional commands and features for advanced users, Internet Explorer serves as a good FTP platform for most situations.

Nonsecured FTP sites allow you to log on anonymously. When logging on anonymously, you use the username **anonymous** and (usually) your e-mail address as the password. In most cases, you can enter anything for the password and gain access to the site. Some sites don't allow anonymous access but instead require that you provide a username and password defined on the FTP server. You obtain the username and password from the FTP site manager or organization.

Subject to the security applied to various directories on the site and the username you use to log in, you can download files from the site to your computer or upload files to the host. You can move within the directory structure of the site (again subject to security restrictions) to locate the directory or file you need to work with.

To access an FTP site, type **ftp://***site* in the address bar, where *site* is the IP address or DNS name of the FTP server, such as ftp://ftp.microsoft.com or ftp://support.somedomain.com. By default, Internet Explorer attempts to log onto an FTP site using the anonymous account. To log on as a different user, specify the username in the address in the format ftp://*user@site*, where *user* is the account name, such as ftp://me@ftp.somedomain.com. Internet Explorer will prompt you for a password if needed. Or type the FTP site's URL, press ENTER to try to connect, choose File | Login As to display the Login As dialog box, and enter the username. Click Login to log on with the specified account and password. Choose Login Anonymously to log on with the anonymous account. Select Save Password to store the password for the specified account in your password cache.

Tip	*You can right-click in the Internet Explorer window and choose Login As to change the login account.*

After you've logged into the site, you can download files simply by double-clicking their icons. If you've logged into a site that grants you write permission (upload), you can upload files to the site. To do so, connect to the site and open the target directory. Drag and drop the file from the desktop or an Explorer window to the Internet Explorer window, or use the clipboard to copy and paste the file to the site.

Outlook Express

Windows 2000 includes Outlook Express 5, an updated version of Microsoft's popular communications program. With Outlook Express, you can send and receive e-mail through multiple mail accounts, work with newsgroups, and search directory services for addresses, names, etc. Rather than concentrate on how to use Outlook Express to perform common tasks such as sending and receiving e-mail, this chapter focuses on configuring Outlook Express and creating accounts. When you install Windows 2000,

Setup automatically installs Outlook Express along with Internet Explorer, so all you have to do is start configuring it.

Creating Mail Accounts

Before you can send and receive e-mail through Outlook Express, you need to create at least one account. You can create and use several e-mail accounts in Outlook Express to manage e-mail from several different mail servers and/or e-mail accounts. For example, if you have a CompuServe account, work account, and other private account, you can use Outlook Express to work with all three in a single Inbox.

The first time you run Outlook Express, it starts the Internet Connection Wizard to create a mail account. To create accounts manually, open Outlook Express and choose Tools | Accounts. Click Add | Mail to start the Internet Connection Wizard. The wizard prompts you for the following data:

- **Display Name**   The name that appears in the From field of outgoing messages. Usually this is your full name—e.g., Joe Blow.

- **E-mail Address**   Specify the full e-mail address for an existing account in the form *account@domain*, such as asleep@mydesk.net. The wizard also gives you the option of signing up for a new e-mail account with Hotmail (coincidentally owned by Microsoft).

- **Incoming Mail Server Type**   Choose POP3 if you're using a regular POP3 account such as those provided by an ISP or your office mail server. Choose HTTP if you're setting up an account for an HTTP-based mail service such as Hotmail. Choose IMAP if your server is an IMAP server.

- **Incoming Mail (POP3, IMAP, Or HTTP) Server**   Specify the IP address or DNS name of the mail server hosting your account.

- **Outgoing Mail (SMTP) Server**   Specify the IP address or DNS name of the mail server that processes your outgoing mail. In most cases it will be the same as your incoming mail server, but it could be different. The SMTP server is always connected to the host (ISP), and you can get the exact name of the server from the host administrator. This option is disabled for HTTP servers since you use a Web browser to send mail.

- **My HTTP Mail Service Provider Is**   Select Hotmail or Other, depending on your mail provider. This option only applies if you select HTTP as the server type.

- **Log On Using Secure Password Authentication (SPA)**   Select this option if the mail server requires you to use SPA to authenticate against your e-mail account.

After you create the account, you can configure the properties that define the way the account functions. In Outlook Express, choose Tools | Accounts to open the Internet Accounts Properties dialog box. Move to the Mail tab and click the account you want to modify; then click Properties to change the account properties. In the

General tab shown in Figure 11-14, specify the name for the account and general user information. The following list explains the options:

- **Mail Account** This is the name by which the mail account appears in the Internet Accounts list. It has no relationship to your mailbox account name or the server name; it's simply a reference for you to use to identify the account. Specify a descriptive name that identifies the account (Work, Personal, etc.).

- **Name** This display name appears in the From field of messages that you send.

- **Organization** Optionally specifies your business, department, organization, etc.

- **E-Mail Address** This e-mail address is used when composing new messages. A recipient will see this address by double-clicking your name in the From field of a received message.

- **Reply Address** This e-mail address is used when replying to a message. The reply address can be different from the E-mail address setting. If you don't specify an address here, the address defined by E-mail address is used for replies.

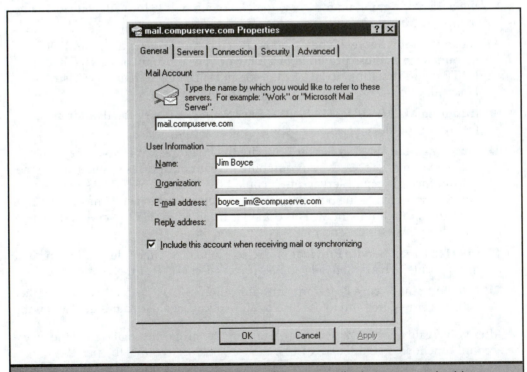

Figure 11-14. *Use the General tab to configure your display name and address*

■ **Include This Account When Receiving Mail Or Synchronizing**   Select this option if you want Outlook Express to automatically send and receive mail through this account when you click Send/Recv on the toolbar or choose Tools | Send and Receive All (or Receive All or Send All). Deselect this option if you don't want the account to check automatically, but prefer to initiate mail transfers manually.

The Servers tab of the account's Properties dialog box defines the settings for the incoming and outgoing mail servers, mailbox account and password, and authentication options (see Figure 11-15). In most cases, the incoming and outgoing servers are the same. In some cases, however, organizations separate the two for administrative or security reasons. Another situation in which they might be different is if you are connecting to a mail server that doesn't support sending from your current location. For example, your ISP's mail server might restrict outgoing mail to only those subnets it hosts, preventing nonsubscribers from using their mail server for forwarding mail. So if you dial into a different ISP or connect at work (and connecting from a subnet not managed by the ISP holding the mail account), you won't be able to send outgoing mail through that server. You'll have to specify a different outgoing mail server that accepts mail from your location.

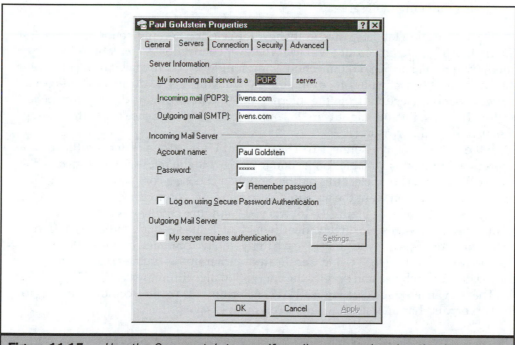

Figure 11-15.   *Use the Servers tab to specify mail server and authentication properties*

The following list summarizes the options on the Servers page:

- **My Incoming Mail Server Is A *<servertype>* Server**   This read-only property specifies the incoming mail server type.

- **Incoming Mail (POP3)**   Specify the IP address or DNS name of the mail server on which your mailbox resides (where you receive mail).

- **Outgoing Mail (SMTP)**   Specify the IP address or DNS name of the mail server the account uses to send mail.

- **Account Name**   Specify the account name on the incoming mail server.

- **Password**   Specify the password for the mail account.

- **Remember Password**   Select this option to store the password in your local password cache.

- **Log On Using Secure Password Authentication**   Select this option if your mail server uses SPA to authenticate your login to the mail server.

- **My Server Requires Authentication**   Select this option if the outgoing mail server requires that you log on to send mail. Some ISPs configure their servers in this way to prevent mail forwarding through the server by nonmembers.

- **Settings**   Click to specify account, password, and authentication options for the outgoing mail server.

The Connection tab lets you specify how the selected account connects to the Internet. By default, an account will use whatever connection is available without attempting to dial a specific connection. For example, if you're dialed into your home ISP and want to check your office e-mail, you'll only be able to do so if the office mail server allows connections from the Internet rather than through a dial-up connection within the LAN. So you might want to configure an account to use a specific dial-up connection for that reason.

If the option Always Connect To This Account Using is deselected, Outlook Express will use any available connection to connect to the mail server(s) specified in the account properties. Select this option, and then choose a connection from the drop-down list if you want the account to use a specific connection.

The Security tab (see Figure 11-16) lets you configure certificates for digitally signing your messages (positively identifying you as the sender), and also configure encryption for securing your messages. After you have obtained and installed the necessary certificates (see "Using Certificates" earlier in this chapter), select the certificates for each use and specify the encryption algorithm to use.

The Advanced page (see Figure 11-17) determines how the account connects to the server, and handles sending and receiving messages.

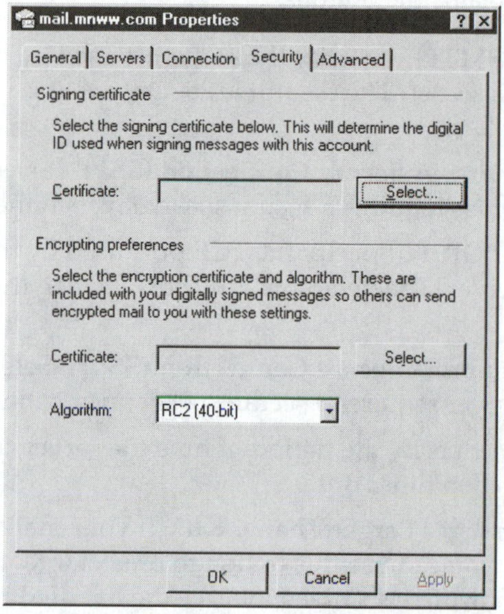

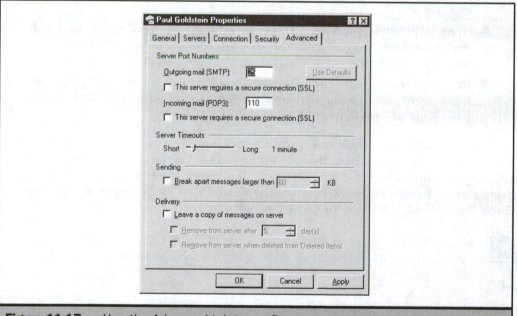

Figure 11-16. *Use the Security tab to assign certificates for digital signing and encryption of messages*

Figure 11-17. *Use the Advanced tab to configure server connection and mail handling options*

The following list explains the options:

- **Outgoing Mail (SMTP)**   Specify the TCP port used by the SMTP service on the outgoing mail server. The default is 25. Only change this if the server uses a different port.

- **This Server Requires A Secure Connection (SSL)**   Select this option if the outgoing mail server requires a secure socket layer connection.

- **Incoming Mail (POP3)**   Specify the TCP port used by the POP3 service on the incoming mail server. The default is 110. Only change this if the server uses a different port.

- **This Server Requires A Secure Connection (SSL)**   Select this option if the incoming mail server requires a secure socket layer connection.

- **Server timeouts**   Specify the period of time the server can be unresponsive before the connection times out.

- **Break Apart Messages Larger Than *n* KB**   If your mail server imposes a limit on message size, you can use this option to break large messages into multiple messages, each of which is small enough to be handled by the server.

- **Leave A Copy Of Messages On The Server**   Select this option to leave a copy of your messages on the server. Deselect this option if you want the messages downloaded to your computer and then deleted from the server. You'll probably need to deselect this option if your mail server imposes a limit on mailbox size.

- **Remove From Server After *n* Days**   Select this option and specify a time limit if you want server-saved messages deleted from the server after that time period has elapsed.

- **Remove From Server When Deleted From 'Deleted Items'**   Select this option if you want saved messages deleted from the server when you delete them from your Deleted Items folder.

Create an account in Outlook Express for each e-mail account you want to access through Outlook Express. Note that one of the accounts serves as the default account, and new messages are sent through the default account. To send or reply to a message using a provider other than the default, select it using the From drop-down list (just above the To field) when you compose the message.

Identities enable you to create multiple "personalities" in Outlook Express and use those identifies to, for example, keep your work and personal e-mail separate.

Creating Newsgroup Accounts

A news service (in the context of newsgroups) is essentially an electronic bulletin board where you can post messages (with attachments if desired) and read other peoples' messages. An area of specific interest on a news server is called a *newsgroup*. At last count there were over 40,000 public newsgroups on the Internet, and the number grows daily. Private news servers enable authorized users to communicate about topics hosted by the private server (such as beta software newsgroups or news servers internal to a company). You can use Outlook Express to work with both private and public newsgroups.

To create a news account, choose Tools | Accounts to open the Internet Accounts Properties dialog box. Click Add | News to start the Internet Connection Wizard. The wizard prompts you for the following information:

- **Display Name**   This is the name that appears in the From field of messages you post in newsgroups.

- **E-Mail Address**   This e-mail address appears with your name in the headers of messages you post in newsgroups.

- **News (NNTP) Server**   Specify the IP address or DNS name of the news server. In the case of most ISPs, the news server name is news.*domain*, where *domain* is the ISP's domain (for example: news.compuserve.com).

- **My News Server Requires Me To Log On**   Select this option if the news server requires that you specify a user account and password to connect to the news server. Some ISPs restrict news server access to only those subnets they host, which restricts access to members. Others use authentication to achieve the same purpose.

After you create a news account you can modify additional properties of the account. As with a mail account, choose Tools | Accounts to open the Internet Accounts Properties dialog box. Move to the News tab, select the news account you want to modify and click Properties.

The General, Server, and Connection tabs of a news account's properties controls the same options as their e-mail account counterparts. The Advanced tab (see Figure 11-18) controls connection, authentication, and posting options as explained in the following list:

- **News (NNTP)**   Specify the TCP port used by the news server. The default is 119. Only change this setting if you know the server uses a different port.

- **This Server Requires A Secure Connection (SSL)**   Select this option if the news server requires a secure socket layer connection to authenticate.

LEARNING THE BASICS

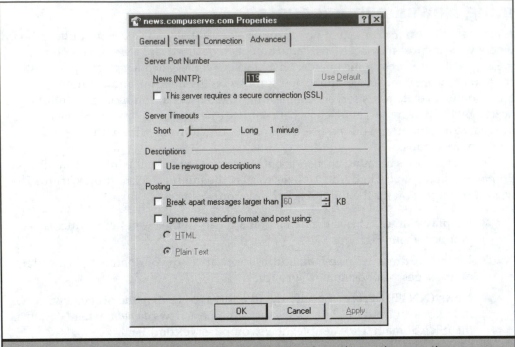

Figure 11-18. *Set connection, authentication, and posting options on the Advanced tab*

■ **Server Timeouts** Specify the amount of time the server can be unresponsive before the connection times out.

■ **Use Newsgroup Descriptions** Some newsgroups have descriptions that explain their content. Select this option if you want newsgroup descriptions downloaded when you download the list of newsgroups from the server. Deselect the option to download only newsgroup names (which reduces the time required to download a large number of newsgroups).

■ **Break Apart Messages Larger Than *n* KB** If the server won't accept messages larger than a given size, use this option to break large messages into multiple messages of a size accepted by the server.

■ **Ignore News Sending Format And Post Using** Select this option to ignore the default setting in Outlook Express for sending messages and select a corresponding option (HTML or plain text).

Creating Directory Service Accounts

A *directory service* in the context of Outlook Express is a server that hosts information in a directory. For example, a server might host information about people and their personal information (such as e-mail address, phone number, address, etc.). You can use Outlook Express to connect to a directory service to retrieve information from the service. Outlook Express uses Lightweight Directory Access Protocol (LDAP) to retrieve the information from the service.

Outlook Express includes several predefined directory service accounts for the most popular directory services on the Internet. You can create new accounts as well, by opening the Internet Accounts Properties dialog box in Outlook Express and clicking Add | Directory Service. Outlook Express runs a wizard to prompt you for information about the directory service. The following list summarizes a directory service account's properties:

- **Directory Service Account**   This is the account name in Outlook Express for the directory service account.

- **Server Name**   Specify the IP address or DNS name of the directory server.

- **This Server Requires Me To Log On**   Select this option if the directory service requires a password to log on.

- **Account Name / Password**   Specify the account and password (if any) required to log onto the directory service.

- **Log On Using Secure Password Authentication**   Select this option if the server uses SPA for secure authentication.

- **Check Names Against This Server When Sending Mail**   Select this option if you want Outlook Express to automatically connect to the directory service to verify the address of e-mail recipients.

- **Directory Service (LDAP)**   Specify the TCP port used by the LDAP server.

- **This Server Requires A Secure Connection (SSL)**   Select this option if the server requires a secure socket layer connection.

- **Search Timeout**   Specify the amount of time the server can be unresponsive before the connection times out.

- **Maximum Number Of Matches To Return**   Specify the maximum number of search results you want the server to return for a given query.

- **Search Base**   Some directory services structure data in categories such as countries, departments, etc. Use this option to specify the point in the directory at which you want to begin a search.

■ **Use Simple Search Filter**   Select this option to use simple search query options for a search. If this option is selected, the Find People dialog box (explained next) omits the Advanced search tab that provides additional user-definable search criteria.

You don't have to use Outlook Express specifically to browse a directory service. You can use the features in Windows 2000 instead. Click Start | Search | For People to open the Find People dialog box. (You can open the same dialog in Outlook Express by choosing Edit | Find | People.) Select the service you want to use from the drop-down list, specify the search criteria, and click Find Now.

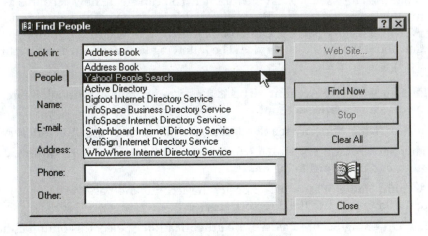

Setting Outlook Express Options

In addition to the properties you can configure for the various types of accounts, Outlook Express also provides several options that control the way the Outlook Express interface appears, how messages are sent and received, and other global options. To view or configure these options, choose Tools | Options. The following sections provide an overview of the various options for Outlook Express.

General Tab

The General tab (see Figure 11-19) controls a handful of general Outlook Express settings that control the actions Outlook Express takes at startup and what action it takes when a message is received. Most of the options are self-explanatory. The option Check For New Message Every n Minutes determines whether or not Outlook Express will automatically attempt to send and receive e-mail. If you want to control when Outlook Express processes your mail (not dialing a connection in the middle of the night, for example), deselect this option. Select this option if you do want Outlook Express to automatically check for mail, and select an option from the associated drop-down list to specify how Outlook Express should react if there is no current connection when the specified time arrives.

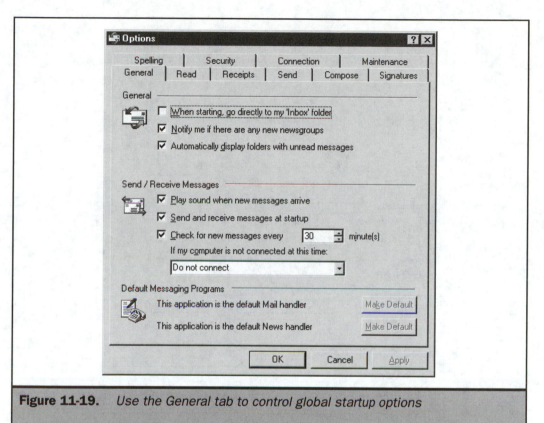

Figure 11-19.   *Use the General tab to control global startup options*

Read Tab

The Read tab (see Figure 11-20) applies primarily to news accounts but also affects mail accounts. You can have Outlook Express automatically expand message threads when you open a newsgroup, automatically download a message previewed in the Preview pane, and control other news message options.

Receipts Tab

The Receipts tab controls options for requesting receipts for sent messages and responding to receipt requests for received messages. The following list summarizes the options:

■ **Request A Read Receipt For All Sent Messages**   Select this option if you want Outlook Express to request a read receipt from recipients of all messages that you send.

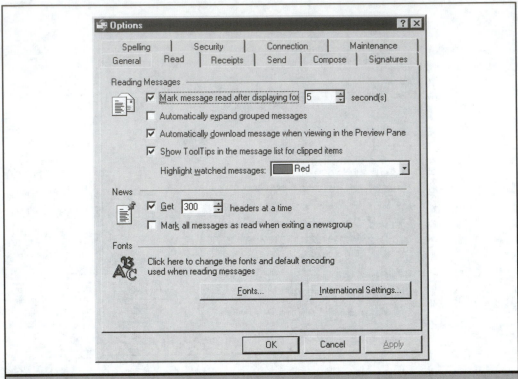

Figure 11-20.   *Use the Read tab to control how Outlook Express processes messages and news headers*

■ **Never Send A Read Receipt**   Select this option to prevent Outlook Express from sending receipts to senders for messages you've received and read.

■ **Notify Me For Each Read Receipt Request**   Use this option to have Outlook Express prompt you when a sender requests a read receipt for a message you have read.

■ **Always Send A Read Receipt**   Automatically send a receipt for all messages you've read, if requested by the sender.

■ **Unless It Is Sent To A Mailing List**   Use this option to prevent Outlook Express from sending a read receipt if the message was sent to a distribution group, and your name is not in the To or CC fields.

■ **Secure Receipts**   Click to set options for secure receipts, which enable you to request a digitally signed receipt to verify that the receipt is valid and came from the recipient.

Send Tab

The Send tab (see Figure 11-21) provides several options to control how Outlook Express processes outgoing messages. For example, you can save a copy of each sent message in the Sent Items folder, automatically place recipients in the address book, and specify the format for outgoing messages (HTML or plain text). The options on the Send page are generally self-explanatory.

Compose Tab

The Compose tab lets you configure various options that affect the way Outlook Express handles composition of new messages. You can specify the font used for both mail and news postings, use stationary for the background of HTML-based messages, and attach electronic business cards to messages. Use the Stationary group of controls to select and edit the stationary to apply to mail and news messages. Use the Business Cards group to create and edit electronic business cards and assign them to mail and news messages. You should find the options on the Compose tab self-explanatory.

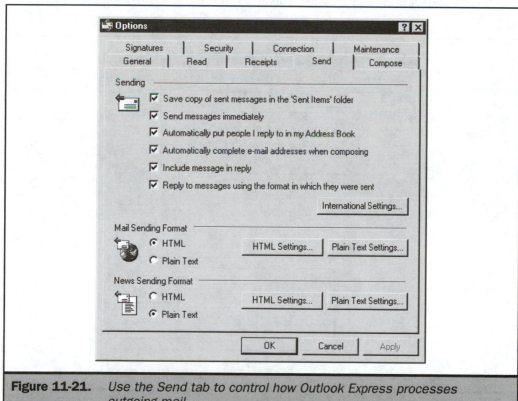

Figure 11-21. *Use the Send tab to control how Outlook Express processes outgoing mail*

Signatures Tab

A *signature* is a string of predefined text (or a file) that you can automatically attach to outgoing messages including (optionally) replies and forwards. For example, some people like to include a favorite quote at the bottom of each message, or include their address, phone, or other information on each message. Use the Signatures tab (see Figure 11-22) to define and assign message signatures.

To create a new signature, click New. Use the Edit Signature group to either type the text or select the file to be used as the signature. You can rename the signature using the Rename button. Click Advanced if you want to specify the accounts for which a selected signature is used.

Security Tab

The Security tab of the Options Properties dialog box lets you specify which security zone Outlook Express uses to process messages. The selection you make can have an impact on how Outlook Express handles such things as incoming attachments. Select the Internet zone for the least restrictive but most functional option, or select the Restricted zone for optimum security. You also can use the Security page to obtain and

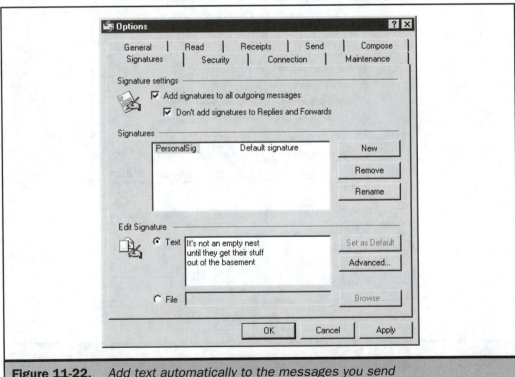

Figure 11-22. *Add text automatically to the messages you send*

configure digital IDs (certificates) for use in securing your messages, both through positive identification to prevent forging and encryption. See the section "Configuring Security" earlier in this chapter for more information on zones and security settings.

Connection Tab

The Connection tab specifies the connection Outlook Express uses to connect to the Internet, and determines how Outlook Express handles dialing. The page includes the following options:

- **Ask Before Switching Dial-Up Connections**   If Outlook Express needs to process messages through an account that uses a connection other than the current one, selecting this option will cause Outlook Express to prompt you to allow the connection change. Otherwise, Outlook Express will automatically disconnect the current connection and dial the required one.

- **Hang Up After Sending And Receiving**   Select this option to have Outlook Express automatically hang up the connection when it finishes processing messages.

- **Change**   By default, Outlook Express uses the same Internet connection as Internet Explorer. Click this if you want to specify a different connection for Outlook Express to use (such as using a LAN connection to connect to a local mail or news server).

Maintenance Tab

The Maintenance tab (see Figure 11-23) offers several options that control general maintenance functions such as cleaning out old deleted messages, compacting the message folders to conserve space, etc. You also can configure Outlook Express to log communication sessions for troubleshooting a connection. The options on the Maintenance page are generally self-explanatory.

Advanced E-Mail Features

Sending and receiving messages through a mail server or news server is no real challenge for the average user, so those topics aren't covered in this chapter. Two features that add flexibility and power to Outlook Express are covered, however, since they are not as intuitive as the Outlook Express basic features.

Using Message Rules

A *message filter* or *message rule* lets Outlook Express process messages and take certain actions on a message depending on its source, content, account, etc. For example, you might want to keep your work mail separate from your personal mail. You could create a separate folder for each, and then create message rules that move the messages into

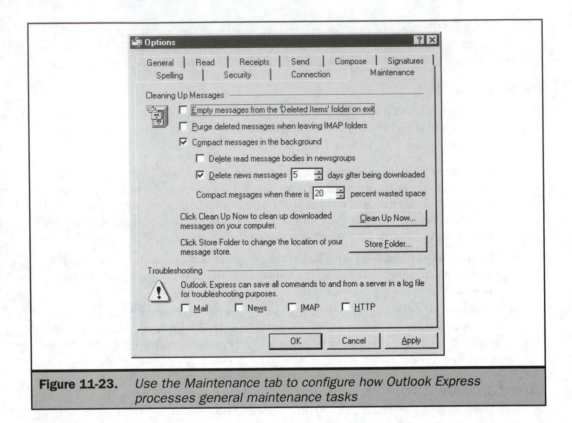

Figure 11-23.   *Use the Maintenance tab to configure how Outlook Express processes general maintenance tasks*

their respective folders based on the account they came from (work or personal). Message rules are also useful for filtering out unwanted messages. Rather than download the messages, you might simply delete them or automatically reply with a message asking to be removed from the distribution list. If you frequently receive unwanted e-mail from a certain domain, you can use message rules to exclude any e-mail from that domain.

Choose Tools | Message Rules | Mail to access the Message Rules dialog box to view or configure message rules for mail. If no rules are defined, Outlook Express automatically opens the New Mail Rule dialog (see Figure 11-24) so you can create a rule.

You create a mail rule by selecting the conditions for the rule, the action to take if the conditions are met, and a name for the rule. Using the previous example of separating work mail from personal mail, you'd create a rule using the criteria Where The Message Is From The Specified Account. Next, select Move It To The Specified Folder, and then select the account in question and a folder using the options provided in the Rule Description box. Click OK to create the rule.

You can use combinations of conditions to fine-tune how a given rule will work. Each condition is generally self-explanatory. The process of creating message rules for newsgroups is much the same, although the conditions and actions are somewhat different due to the differences between mail and news messages.

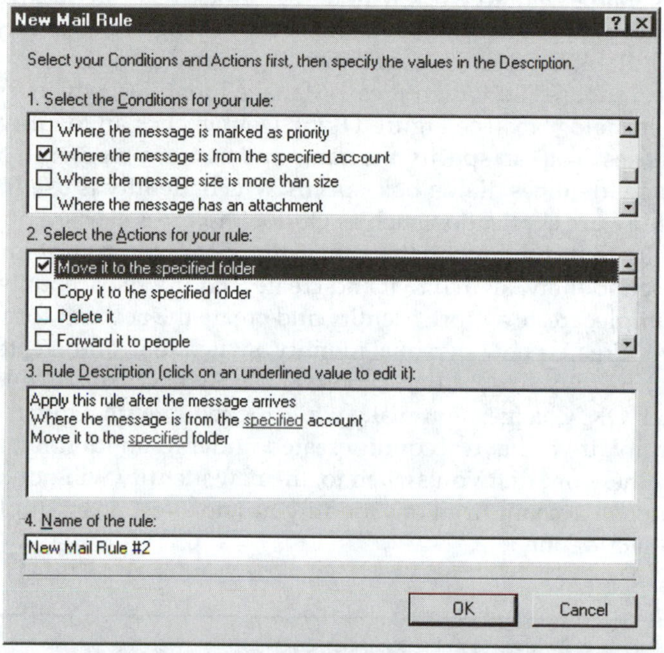

Figure 11-24. *Create a new rule using the New Mail Rule dialog box*

One particularly nice feature in Outlook Express is the ability to block messages coming from certain domains. For example, assume you receive spam (unsolicited mail) from a certain address, or from a set of addresses in a specific domain. You can block these messages from reaching you by adding the address or domain to the list of blocked addresses. To do so, choose Tools | Message Rules | Blocked Senders List. Click Add to access the Add Sender dialog box, and enter the e-mail address or domain you want to block, choose the types of messages to block, and click OK. Add any other addresses or domains as needed and close the Message Rules dialog box. To receive messages from a blocked address or domain, simply remove it from the list.

Using Identities

Identities are another new useful feature in Outlook Express 5. Identities provide a framework in which you create accounts. Since each identity can include its own accounts, identities make it easy to support multiple users on a single computer. For example, you might have a small group of people who share a single workstation and logon account, but who need to keep their e-mail separate. Or you might want to create identities to separate accounts for different family members on a home computer. When a particular person needs access to his accounts, he switches to his identity and

Outlook Express enables him to work with his accounts. You can password-protect each identity to keep other people from using or modifying your identity.

By default, Outlook Express creates an identity named Main Identity. To create or manage identities, choose File | Identities | Manage Identities, which displays the Manage Identities dialog box (see Figure 11-25). Double-click an identity in the list to change its properties. You can specify the name and assign a password to the identity.

On the Manage Identities dialog box, specify which identity is used by default when an identity-aware application such as Outlook Express starts. You also can specify the identity to be used when the application does not prompt for an identity. After you create an identity, switch to it and create/modify the accounts for the identity. For example, create a work identity and create the account for your work e-mail account(s). Create a new personal identity, switch to it, and create your personal e-mail account(s). To switch identities, choose File | Switch Identity, select the desired identity, and click OK. Changes you make while logged in with a given identity apply only to that identity. If you have accounts created under Main Identity, for example, and then create a new one that you switch to, the new identity will not contain those accounts. Deleting an account from one identity has no effect on a "duplicate" account specified in another identity.

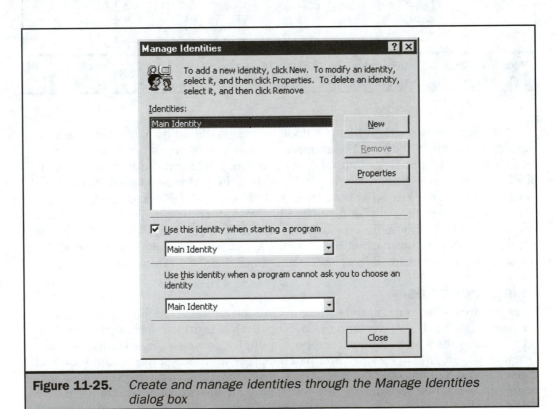

Figure 11-25. *Create and manage identities through the Manage Identities dialog box*

The
Complete
Reference

Chapter 12

Printing

The installation and configuration of printers and printing services in Windows 2000 seems amazingly simple if you've installed and configured other NOS print services and print servers. After printers are installed and configured, users can access the printers across the network quite easily. Achieving all this simplicity takes a great deal of complicated process by the operating system, all performed in the background.

In this chapter, I'll cover printing for Windows 2000 and then the legacy client issues connected to printing.

Printing Basics

Windows 2000 is a protected-mode operating system with no direct access to hardware. Therefore, virtual printers (sometimes called *logical* printers) are used to control the printing features and to interact with the physical printing devices. Sending a print job to the printer means sending the job to the logical device. The important things to keep in mind are the following:

- The icons that are displayed in printer listings represent virtual printers.

- Users send a print job to a virtual printer, not a physical printer.

- Installed printer drivers are loaded at print time and sent to the virtual printer.

- Configuration changes to a printer's properties are made to the virtual printer, but the options must match the capabilities of the physical printer.

New Windows 2000 Printing Features

If you're migrating to Windows 2000 from Windows NT, you're probably anxious to know what's new and different in printing. There are quite a few enhancements and improvements to printing in Windows 2000, and they're covered in detail throughout this chapter. However, for the impatiently curious, here's a brief overview of some of the important changes.

- **Remote Port Administration** Remote administration of printers has been extended to include the ability to perform remote printer port administration.

- **Standard Port for TCP/IP** A new port, called the *standard* port, is available for easy installation of most TCP/IP printers on your network. If you ever set up TCP/IP printing in Windows NT 4, you'll appreciate the fact that you don't have to go through all those steps in all those dialog boxes.

- **Internet printing** Printing is integrated with the Internet, and users can access print servers on an intranet or on the Internet via a URL.

 **Printing Processes**

Before a print job is actually sent to the printer, the operating system performs a number of processes. What follows is a brief overview of those processes, starting at the point a user sends a document to a printer. (I'm assuming the software is a Windows application.)

Load the Printer Driver

The printer driver is loaded into memory, which makes all of the printer-specific codes and instruction sets available to the processes that follow.

Usually, the driver is called by the Windows 2000 Graphics Device Interface (GDI), which is active in the software session because it manages the WYSIWYG interface presented to the user. However, some Windows applications actually load the printer driver into memory when they're launched and use it to provide the WYSIWYG interface.

Create the Output File

The sending application generates an output file. This file contains instructions, called *Device Driver Interface (DDI) calls,* which are sent to the printer driver. The output file is called a *DDI Journal file.*

The application uses the GDI to generate this file. The graphics engine (%SystemRoot%\System32\gdi32.dll) translates the GDI commands into the DDI commands that can be read by the operating system's print processors and by the printer driver.

Process the Output File

The output file is passed to the local spooler, which examines the data type and then passes the print job to the print processor. It also sends information about the data type. The print processor creates the print data format that the physical printer expects. See the sections on print processors later in this chapter for information about data types and data formats.

 It doesn't matter whether the file is being sent to a local or network physical printer; the output file is always passed to the local spooler.

Route the Print Job

The client computer uses a Remote Procedure Call (RPC) to send the print job to the Windows 2000 router. The router accepts the job from the client computer and checks the location of the physical printer. Then the router sends the processed job to the spooler located on the computer to which the physical printer is attached (the print server). If the printer is local, that just means the processed job is sent back to the client spooler and the local computer is considered to be the print server.

Send the Print Job

The spooler on the print server hands the print job off to the operating system's print monitor. The print monitor checks the destination port, and if it is free, it sends the print job. If the port is not free, the print monitor holds the print job in the queue in the spooler until the port is free.

Printing Components

All the steps the operating system performs to move a print job from an application to a physical printer require the use of a number of components and processes provided by the operating system.

Spooler

The *spooler* is software—a group of DLLs that take care of the chores that must be accomplished when a document is sent to the printer. Those chores include

- Tracking the printer ports associated with each printer.
- Tracking the configuration of the physical printer, such as memory, trays, and so on.
- Assigning priorities to the print jobs in the queue.
- Sending the print job through a series of software processes that depend on the type of job, the type of data, and the location of the physical printer.
- Sending the job to the physical printer.

The spooler receives the print job, stores the job on disk, and then passes the job through the print processes and on to the physical printer. As soon as the print job is stored on disk, the user can go back to work in the sending application. All of the print process is done in the background.

By default, the directory used for spooling is %SystemRoot%\system32\ spool\printers. You can change the location of the spooler, and it's frequently a good idea to do so if you have another drive (with more free space) on the computer. The spool files on a print server can take up quite a bit of disk space.

If the print server has a second drive that's attached to a separate controller, you can also improve I/O performance on the default spooler drive by moving the spooler to the other, separate drive.

To move the spooler, open the Printers folder and choose Server Properties from the File menu ("Server" means print server, so this menu item is present on workstations that provide shared printers). In the Print Server Properties dialog box, move to the Advanced tab, which displays the location of the spool folder. Enter a new location, with these guidelines in mind:

- Don't put the spool folder on the root (I used D:\printing\spool\printers).

- Don't perform this action while print jobs are active; they'll never print.

- If the directory doesn't exist, it's created for you, but if the directory is a subdirectory, the parent directory must already exist. In other words, the system is willing to create only the bottom level of the path automatically, so it's best to create the directory manually before moving the spooler.

- If the spooler is on an NTFS partition, be sure that Everyone has write permissions for the spool directory.

The new location is written back to the registry immediately and is effective immediately. The registry key is HKEY_LOCAL_MACHINE\Software\Microsoft\Windows NT\CurrentVersion\Print\Printers. The data item is DefaultSpoolDirectory (a REG_SZ data type).

If the new location doesn't take effect, stop and restart the Print Spooler service. Open the Services applet in Control Panel (in Windows 2000 you have to drill down from the Administrative Tools applet in Control Panel). The Print Spooler service has a startup configuration of automatic (the service is started during the operating system startup), but you can stop and restart it in the dialog box by right-clicking on the listing and choosing Stop. Then right-click and choose Start.

You can also stop and start the Print Spooler service from the command line with the commands **net stop spooler** and **net start spooler**.

Spool Files

The spooler directory holds the spool files (the list of spool files is called the *queue*). For each spooled print job, there are two files written to the spooler directory:

- **The spool file**   This file is actually the print job. It has an .spl extension.
- **The shadow file**   This file contains the administrative information needed to print the job (the target printer, the job's priority, the name of the sending user, and so on). The file has an extension of .shd.

If the print server is shut down before all the spooled jobs are printed, when the print server is restarted, printing restarts, because the presence of spool and shadow files starts the printing process.

Print Queue

The lineup of print job files in the spool directory waiting to be sent to the physical printer is called the queue.

If you have Novell NetWare or OS/2 in your professional history, you have to redefine the definition of the word "queue." The queue used by those other network operating systems is the primary software interface between the applications and the physical printer. The queue's relationship to the printer is a one-to-one concept.

In OS/2, for example, when a user sends a print job to a printer, the job is intercepted by the OS/2 spooler, which holds the job in a queue that is really a virtual alias to a specific physical printer. The print job is submitted to the queue for handling; the queue is not a collection of print files that have already been "handled" by the operating system. The spooler and the queue are a merged concept. The printer driver, the spooler, and the queue do not individually manipulate the print job; the job is grabbed, held, and shipped to the physical printer by one entity, the queue.

NetWare 3.x (and NetWare 4.x if you opt to use a queue instead of a virtual printer) operates in much the same manner as OS/2, except setting up the queue and the printer server requires much more work.

Printer Drivers

Printer drivers translate the data and codes in the print job document into the form needed by the printer. The operating system uses the printer driver for three specific tasks, and breaks down the functions of the printer driver into those distinct parts. The three individual parts, each of which is a set of files, are the following:

- Graphics drivers
- Printer interface drivers
- Characterization data files

Each of these components plays a specific role in print processing.

Graphics Drivers

The imaging functions (rendering of graphic images) are implemented by Windows 2000 as a DLL. The Print Graphics Driver DLL provides the API calls that are used as a graphics device interface during the building of the DDI Journal file. The graphics driver also converts the DDI commands into commands that printers can accept.

These files are stored in subdirectories under %SystemRoot%\System32\spool\drivers\w32x86.

Printer Interface Drivers

The printer interface files (which are .dll files) provide the options a user can choose when configuring a printer. Specifically, they display the Properties and Preferences dialog boxes.

Characterization Data Files

These files contain the information provided by printer manufacturers about the capabilities and configuration options, such as whether it prints on both sides of the paper, the maximum paper size it accepts, and so on.

For raster printers, these files are called minidrivers and are usually implemented as DLLs (although you may see other extensions such as .gpd or .pcd). They are source-code compatible across platforms and processors.

For PostScript printers, these are *PostScript Printer Description (PPD) files*, which are text files provided by the manufacturer. They are binary compatible across platforms and processors.

Windows 2000 Print Processor

The print processor does the rendering of the print job after it receives the file from the spooler. *Rendering* means translating all the data in the print job into data that is understood and accepted by the printer.

Before passing the job, the spooler checks for the data type; if rendering is necessary, it passes along rendering information to the print processor in addition to the print job. The question of whether or not the job needs processing is dependent upon the data type sent by the client application.

During the configuration of a printer, the default data type option is RAW and it would be unusual to change that. The default data type, however, is only used if the application fails to specify a data type for the print job. Most applications that are written for Windows 2000 (and Windows NT 4) send print jobs with NT EMF as the data type, and the print processor can pass the job to the printer with full confidence that the printer can understand and handle the print job.

You can find the print processor and configuration for data type in the printer's Properties dialog box by clicking the Print Processor button on the Advanced tab.

The various data types are as follows:

- **RAW**   This data type indicates that the job has been rendered and is ready for the printer. The print processor takes no action. RAW is used by non-Windows NT 4/Windows 2000 clients and is the default data type for PostScript printers.

- **RAW [FF appended]**   This data type indicates that the client has sent a document with no form feed at the end of the job (needed to make the last page eject). The print processor adds a form feed and takes no other action.

- **RAW [FF auto]**   This data type indicates the same as RAW [FF appended], but the print process checks for the presence of a form feed at the end of the job, and adds one if it's missing.

- **TEXT**   This data type indicates that the job is simple text, and is usually applied to print jobs that are being sent to PostScript printers or plotters (which don't accept text as a valid data type). The print processor uses the printer driver to render the job into printer commands that are acceptable to the target printer.

■ **NT EMF**   The Enhanced Metafiles (EMF) data type is the default, used by most application that are written for Windows 2000 or Windows NT 4. EMF information is generated by the GDI before spooling; then the spooler delivers the print job to the queue in the background. EMF files are typically smaller than RAW data type files. More important, they are portable and can be translated to meet the expectations of any printer.

Other Print Processors

In addition to the print processor that is built into Windows 2000, you can add third-party print processors to your system. These processors are made available by software companies that ship applications that produce data requiring special handling in order to be understood by the printer.

A Macintosh print processor, Sfmsprt.dll, is available with Windows 2000. It's invoked if you've installed Macintosh services in your system. When a Macintosh computer sends a print job to the server (Windows 2000 print servers handle the Macintosh printing needs), the Macintosh print processor examines the target printer and applies the appropriate services. Along the way, the Macintosh client spools the document to the Windows 2000 print server, freeing up the client workstation for other tasks.

If the printer is PostScript, the print processor assigns RAW as the data type. If the printer is not PostScript, it assigns PSCRIPT1 as the data type and turns the code into pages made up of bitmap images that imitate the way the job would look if it were printed by a PostScript printer. A Raster Image Processor (RIP) that's built into the Macintosh print processor performs this task. Those images are sent to the Windows 2000 graphics engine, which produces the bitmapped product for the printer.

There's a limitation in the non-PostScript scenario that usually annoys the heck out of Macintosh users (who tend to be extremely fussy about graphics). The impediment is a 300dpi limit on resolution, regardless of the capabilities of the physical printer. In addition (and once again causing annoyance to Macintosh users), RIP output is limited to monochrome, even if the target printer supports color. The best way to handle Macintosh print clients is to have PostScript printers (color would be appreciated).

Print Router

The *print router* accepts requests to print from clients and determines the spooler component that should be used to fulfill the request. It works between the client and the print server (which may be the same computer, of course). The print router is implemented with Winspool.drv in %SystemRoot%\System32, and the communication between the client and the print router is accomplished with RPCs.

The first task of the print router is to find the physical printer to which the print job is to be delivered. When the printer is found, the router looks at the printer driver attached to it and compares that to the printer driver on the client computer (if there is one). If there is no printer driver on the client, or if the date of the client's printer driver is earlier than the date of the driver on the print server, the driver on the print server is loaded for the client.

If the client receives no error message (an error message being "printer not found") from the print router, the job is processed by the client (now assured of having the correct driver), which means the job is placed in the local spooler. If the print server is not the client computer, the print router copies the job from the client spooler to the print server spooler.

Print Monitors

The *print monitor* is the component that controls the port as well as the communication between the port and the spooler. It sends the print jobs to the port by performing the following tasks:

- Accesses the port (sends the print job)
- Releases access to the port at the end of a print job
- Sends notification to the spooler when a print job has finished printing (the spooler then deletes the job from the queue)
- Monitors the printer for error messages

A print monitor that performs the tasks described here is sometimes called a *port monitor*. If the printer supports bidirectional printing, a print monitor also acts as a *language monitor*, facilitating the two-way communication between the printer and the print server's spooler. This gives the spooler the configuration and status information about the printer.

However, the most important job of a print monitor is to control port I/O, and there are print monitors for any type of port you use or install in your Windows 2000 system.

Local Print Monitor

The local print monitor (%SystemRoot%\System32\Localmon.dll) controls the local ports. The following port assignments for printers are considered local (any printer can be configured to print to any port in this list):

- Parallel
- Serial
- File (the print monitor prompts for a filename when you use this port)
- Explicit filenames (each job sent to a specific filename overwrites the last job sent to that filename)
- UNC designations for a shared remote printer
- NUL
- IR (infrared, which is available only if the computer supports it)

LEARNING THE BASICS

Use the NUL Port for Testing

The NUL port is generally used for testing network printing. Set a printer to use the NUL port and pause it (so you can see jobs waiting; otherwise the jobs pass through the port too fast to watch them). Then send a job to that printer from a connected client. You should be able to see the job when you open the printer object. If you don't see the job, check the setup to make sure the printer is configured for the NUL port. If you do see the job, your test is successful. Resume printing, which really does nothing because jobs sent to a NUL port just disappear. Instead of paper, documents print to thin air as they travel to lost document la-la land.

HP Print Monitor

The Hewlett Packard monitor (Hpmon.dll) controls HP devices such as printer-installed network adapters and JetDirect adapters. Today's JetDirect devices are able to use TCP/IP, but legacy devices that can't use TCP/IP will need the HP print monitor.

The HP print monitor requires the DLC (Data Link Control) protocol. DLC only needs to be running on the print server (see "Installing DLC" later in this section).

After you install the DLC protocol, you can add an HP port to the computer that holds the printer requiring the HP print monitor. To add the HP port (which installs the printer at the same time), follow these steps:

1. Open the Printers folder.

2. Open the Add Printer object to start the Add Printer Wizard and click Next.

3. Select Local Printer, and make sure the automatic detection check box is deselected; then click Next.

4. Select the Create A New Port option to activate the Type text box.

5. Click the arrow to the right of the Type text box and select Hewlett-Packard Network Port from the drop-down list (if it's not listed, the DLC protocol is not installed).

6. Click Refresh; then select the printer card address from the Card Address list.

7. Enter a name for this printer and click OK.

8. Follow the onscreen instructions to complete the installation for this printer.

Installing DLC

DLC is a protocol and must be installed along with the other protocols attached to your network connection:

1. Open the Network And Dial-Up Connections applet in Control Panel, and right-click the Local Area Connection.

2. Choose Properties from the shortcut menu to open the Properties dialog box.

3. Click Install; then select Protocol and click Add.

4. Select DLC and click OK.

Digital Print Monitor

The Digital print monitor controls any Digital Network ports you install in order to use Digital Equipment Corporation (DEC) PrintServer devices. In addition, some individual DEC printers require this port and attendant port monitor. This monitor must be obtained from the manufacturer (http://www.compaq.com). Use the Have Disk option to install the printer and port.

Lexmark Print Monitors

If you have Lexmark printing devices, you should have received the Lexmark print monitor software with the device. If not, try http://www.lexmark.com. The Lexmark print monitors control the advanced features available in the printers, all of which require communication with the port (which is, of course, the job of the print monitor).

Lexmark offers two print monitors:

- Lexmark TCP/IP print monitor, which controls any Lexmark TCP/IP network port.

- Lexmark DLC print monitor, which controls any Lexmark DLC network ports.

Use the Have Disk option to install the printer on the appropriate port.

Macintosh Print Monitor

The Macintosh print monitor (Sfmmon.dll) controls printing over AppleTalk protocols. Only a print server that's a Windows 2000 Server can receive Macintosh AppleTalk print jobs; Windows 2000 Professional cannot print jobs from Macintosh clients.

To support Macintosh printing, you must have a transport to communicate between the client and the print server (AppleTalk protocol), the printing services to produce the print job (Print Services for Macintosh, which supplies the Macintosh print monitor), and an AppleTalk port (installed when you install the printer).

To install the AppleTalk protocol, follow these steps:

1. Open the Network And Dial-Up Connection applet in Control Panel.

2. Open the Local Area Connection object.

3. In the Local Area Connection Status dialog box, click the Properties button.

4. In the Local Area Connection Properties dialog box, click Install.

5. Select Protocol and click Add.

6. Select AppleTalk Protocol and click OK.

The files are transferred from the Windows 2000 CD-ROM. To your Macintosh clients, the Windows 2000 print server looks like an AppleTalk device

LEARNING THE BASICS

To add Print Services for Macintosh to the appropriate print server, use these steps:

1. Open the Add/Remove Programs applet in the Control Panel.

2. Click the Add/Remove Windows Components icon to open the Windows Components Wizard, and click Next to get past the introductory window (unless the wizard moves on automatically, which this wizard seems to do).

3. In the next wizard window, scroll through the Components list to locate Other Network File And Print Services. Select that listing, but don't click the check box to select the installation option.

4. Click Details to display the available services, which are File Services For Macintosh, Print Services For Macintosh, and Print Services For UNIX.

5. Select Print Services For Macintosh and click OK.

6. Follow any additional prompts to install the services from the Windows 2000 CD-ROM.

Note   *If you perform this exercise on Windows 2000 Professional, you should see only Print Services For UNIX because Windows 2000 Professional does not support Macintosh File And Print services.*

To install an AppleTalk port and the attendant printer, follow these steps:

1. Open the Printers folder.

2. Open the Add Printer object to start the Add Printer Wizard and click Next.

3. Select Local Printer, and make sure the automatic detection check box is deselected; then click Next.

4. Select the Create A New Port option to activate the Type text box.

5. Click the arrow to the right of the Type text box and select AppleTalk Printing devices; then click Next.

6. From the AppleTalk Printing Devices list, click the AppleTalk printer you want to add, and then click OK.

7. Click Yes to capture this AppleTalk device.

8. Follow the onscreen instructions to complete the installation for this printer.

If you're wondering what you need to install, here are the guidelines:

■ To print from Windows 2000 to an AppleTalk printer, you only need to install the AppleTalk protocol, which lets you add an AppleTalk port (available for both Windows 2000 servers and workstations).

■ If you want to have Macintoshes print to Windows 2000 shared printers, you must have both the AppleTalk protocol and the Services For Macintosh installed (available only on Windows 2000 servers).

LPR Print Monitors

In the UNIX environment, an application can use a *line printer remote (LPR)* service to send a document to a print spooler service on another computer. LPR is a part of the protocols developed with and for TCP/IP to provide printing services for UNIX (actually, it started with Berkeley UNIX, which only some of us who are quite old can remember). Today, LRP still works for many UNIX clients.

In Windows NT 4, LPR was needed for printing across TCP/IP (even if there were no UNIX computers in sight), but that's all changed with Windows 2000, which treats TCP/IP as a standard port. That doesn't mean you won't need LPR; it just means you won't need it for printing over TCP/IP within the Windows 2000 environment. However, you will need LRP to providing printing services in an environment that includes UNIX.

LPR protocols permit client applications to send print jobs directly to a print spooler on a print server. The client side of this is called LPR, and the host side is called *line printer daemon (LPD)*. Microsoft Print Services For UNIX provides both the LPR and LPD services.

On the client side, Windows 2000 supports LPR with an executable file named Lpr.exe (in %SystemRoot%\System32). This executable, when launched, supplies the print monitor (Lprmon.dll) that communicates with the LPD services (which are native to the UNIX host).

On the server side, Windows 2000 provides LPD services through Lpdsvc.dll. This service can support any print format, but it has no processing power. The client application must send the format expected by the printer.

To print from a UNIX client to a Windows 2000 printer, the client must have a supported version of LPR (not all flavors of UNIX support the LPR standards that are supported by Windows 2000). Lpdsvc on the print server receives the documents from the LPR utilities running on the client UNIX machine (the LPR utilities are native to the client, so you don't need to install them). In addition, the Windows 2000 print server must be running Print Services For UNIX.

To print from a Windows 2000 computer to a printer hosted by a UNIX print server, Lpr.exe supplies Lprmon.dll, which communicates with the native LPD UNIX service on the host. This also requires the installation of Print Services For UNIX.

To install Print Services For UNIX, follow these steps on either Windows 2000 Server or Professional:

1. Open the Add/Remove Programs applet in the Control Panel.

2. Click the Add/Remove Windows Components icon to open the Windows Components Wizard.

3. In the next wizard window, scroll through the Components list to locate Other Network File And Print Services. Select that listing, but don't click the check box to select the installation option.

4. Click Details to display the available services, which are File Services For Macintosh, Print Services For Macintosh, and Print Services For UNIX. (Windows 2000 Professional only offers Print Services For UNIX.)

5. Select Print Services For UNIX and click OK.

6. Follow the additional prompts to install the services from the Windows 2000 CD-ROM.

If the Windows 2000 computer is the print server, the LPD services must be started (client services are started by the Lpr executable), and an LPR port must be created for the printer.

Usually, LPD services (TCP/IP Print Server services) are started automatically when they're installed during the installation of Print Services For UNIX. To make sure, follow these steps:

1. Open the Administrative Tools applet in Control Panel.

2. Open the Services applet.

3. Scroll to the listing for TCP/IP Print Server.

4. Be sure the service is started.

5. Be sure the service is configured to start automatically.

To add a port to the Windows 2000 print server that's providing print services for UNIX clients, follow these steps:

1. Open the Printers folder and open the Add Printer object.

2. The Add Printer Wizard appears.

3. Select Local Printer and be sure the option to autodetect the printer is not selected. Click Next.

4. In the next window, select the option Create A New Port to enable the Type text box.

5. Click the Down arrow next to the Type box and choose LPR port, which is listed as a result of installing Print Services For UNIX. Click Next.

6. In the Name Or Address field, enter the DNS name or the IP address of the host for this printer.

7. In the Name Of Printer Or Print Queue On That Server field, enter the name of the installed printer (the identification used by the host computer).

Summary of Printer Ports for Windows 2000

Having gone over the details of print monitors and their attendant ports, Table 12-1 presents a summary for quick reference.

Print Providers

The last component in Windows 2000 printing is the *print provider*. The print provider sends the job to the physical device, using the configuration options for that device. In effect, it implements the choices you make in the Properties dialog box for the printer.

For example, if you've opted to print spooled jobs as soon as spooling begins, it sends the job to the printer immediately instead of waiting for the entire job to be received. The options available for configuring printers are discussed later in this chapter.

Windows 2000 includes two print providers: local and remote.

LEARNING
THE BASICS

Port	Target Printer(s)	Availability
Local port (parallel, serial, USB, UNC)	Printers connected to the port	Built in
Standard TCP/IP port	TCP/IP printers on the network	Built in
AppleTalk printing devices	AppleTalk printers	After installing the AppleTalk protocol
HP network port	Printers that use older HP JetDirect adapters (use the TCP/IP port for newer JetDirect cards)	After installing DLC network protocol
LPR port	TCP/IP printers connected to a UNIX (or VAX) server	After installing Print Services For UNIX
Port for NetWare	NetWare printing resources	After installing NWLink protocol and Client Services For NetWare

Table 12-1. *Printer Ports Available in Windows 2000*

Local Print Provider

The local print provider is Localspl.dll, which is in the %SystemRoote%\System32 directory. It sends print jobs to the locally attached printer. To accomplish this, it performs the following tasks (using RPC calls):

- When the print job is received (from a local application or a remote user), it writes the job to disk as a spool file. It also writes the shadow file.

- If there is a configuration option for separator pages, it processes them.

- It checks to see which print processor is needed for the print job's data type and passes the job to that print processor. When the print processor finishes making modifications (if any are necessary), it passes the job back to the local print provider.

- It checks the port for the target printer, and then passes the job to the print monitor attached to that port.

Remote Print Providers

Both of the remote print providers are .dll files in the %SystemRoot%\System32 directory. Remote print providers are employed when a Windows 2000 computer sends print jobs to a remote print server:

- Win32spl.dll moves print jobs to Windows print servers.

- NWProvau.dll moves print jobs to Novell NetWare print servers.

If the target printer is on a print server running a legacy Windows operating system, the Windows 2000 remote print provider contacts the Windows network redirector, which sends the job across the network to the appropriate print server. That server takes over the responsibility of printing the job.

 The Windows redirector is a component of the Windows Network APIs. It lets client computers have access to resources on other computers as if those accessed resources were local. Communication is accomplished via the protocol stack to which it is bound.

The NetWare remote print provider takes control of a print job when the server name is recognized as a NetWare print server. The NetWare print provider turns the job over to the NetWare redirector, which passes the job to the print server. For information about installing IPX/SPX and the NetWare network services, see Chapter 17.

Installing Local Printers

The installation of printers (which is really the installation of printer drivers) in Windows 2000 is a snap. In fact, the addition of Plug and Play to Windows 2000 can make installing a local printer easier (especially if your printer is a Plug and Play candidate). You can install a local printer as long as you have administrative rights on the computer.

Plug and Play Printer Installation

After you physically connect the printer and start the computer, if your printer is detected by Plug and Play it's automatically installed. The Found New Hardware Wizard runs automatically and installs the printer.

If Plug and Play doesn't detect the printer at startup, and you know that's because your printer is not Plug and Play, follow the instructions in the next section, "Manual Installation of Printers."

If you believe the printer should work with Plug and Play, you can try an automatic Plug and Play installation from the Printers folder (on the Settings submenu, or in Control Panel). Open the Add Printer object to launch the Add Printer Wizard. Click Next on the first wizard window, which is an introductory window and performs no action. In the next wizard window, select Local Printer and check the option to Automatically Detect And Install My Plug And Play Printer. Then click Next.

When (or if) the Add Printer Wizard finds the printer, it displays a message telling you so, and asks if you want to print a test page (you should select Yes). Just follow the prompts for any additional configuration requests. When the installation is complete and the printer driver files are copied to your local drive, the test page prints.

If the Add Printer Wizard does not find the printer, a message displays telling you Windows was unable to detect and Plug and Play printers. Click Next to perform a manual installation of the printer (covered next). If you have drivers from the manufacturer, be sure they're handy (if they're on a floppy disk or CD-ROM) or that you know their location on your hard drive (if you downloaded them).

Manual Installation of Printers

If your printer is not Plug and Play, you must perform a manual installation with the following steps:

1. Open the Add Printer object in the Printers folder to launch the Add Printer Wizard.

2. Click Next on the first wizard window, which is an introductory window and performs no actions.

3. In the next wizard window, select Local Printer and make sure the option to Automatically Detect And Install My Plug And Play Printer is cleared. Then click Next.

4. Select the port on which the printer is connected and click Next.

5. In the next window, select the manufacturer and model of your printer and click Next.

6. Enter a name for the printer and specify whether this printer is to be the default printer for Windows software applications.

7. The next window asks if you want to share the printer with other network users. If you do, select Share As and enter a share name for the printer (or accept the name suggested by Windows, which is usually the name of the printer model). You can add an optional description for the benefit of network users.

> **Tip** *Windows 2000 Server defaults to sharing the printer—Windows 2000 Professional does not.*

8. Specify whether you want to print a test page (it's always a good idea to say Yes).

9. Click Next to see the last wizard window, and click Finish.

The driver files are copied to your hard drive, and the printer's icon appears in the Printers folder.

Printer Model Isn't Listed

If your printer model isn't listed, and you don't have drivers from the manufacturer, click Cancel and return to the wizard after you've contacted the manufacturer to get the drivers. If the printer is a new model, you can also try clicking Windows Update to see if the Microsoft Web site has the driver.

The following options are also available on this wizard window:

- **Have Disk**   Click this button if you want to use printer drivers from the manufacturer. See the following section, "Using Manufacturer Drivers."

- **Windows Update**   Click this button if you want to get a driver from Microsoft's Web site. If you are currently connected to the Internet, your browser automatically heads for the site. If you are not currently connected, a message window opens with a Connect option that you can click to open your Internet connection and launch your browser.

Using Manufacturer Drivers

If you have printer drivers from the manufacturer, click Have Disk as described previously in the "Printer Model Isn't Listed" section. Specify the location of the drivers, and follow the rest of the prompts to finish installing the printer.

Installing USB Printers and IEEE Printers

If your printer connects to a Universal Serial Bus (USB) or IEEE 1394 port, Plug and Play detects it immediately. In fact, Plug and Play opens as soon as you plug the jack into the port; you don't even have to start the Add Printer Wizard. As soon as a USB or IEEE port is detected, that port is added to the list of ports available to the printer, and the automatic installation process selects the port without user intervention.

Installing Infrared Printers

Infrared printers are automatically detected and installed, as long as the printer and computer are both turned on and can see each other. Be sure to position the two devices within about 3 feet of each other. It takes a few seconds for the computer to find the printer, but then everything goes on autopilot and you don't have to do anything else.

If your computer is not infrared capable but your printer is, you can add an infrared transceiver to your serial port with these steps:

1. Open the Add/Remove Hardware applet in Control Panel, and click Next to move past the opening window.

2. In the next window, select Add/Troubleshoot a device and click Next. Wait a few seconds until Windows searches in vain for Plug and Play devices.

3. When the next window appears, select A New Device (the first listing) and click Next.

4. In the next window, select No, I Want To Select The Hardware From A List; then click Next.

5. In the next window, select Infrared devices and click Next.

6. In the next window, select a manufacturer and a device (or select Have Disk if you have manufacturer drivers).

7. Follow the remaining prompts to install the infrared device.

Now you can automatically install the infrared printer.

Infrared Installation Is Truly Automatic

If you haven't yet tried an infrared printer connection, or you don't have infrared capabilities in the desktop computers on your network, examine your laptop. Most of today's laptops have infrared capabilities (look for the little glass window at the back of the unit). So do most of today's laser printers, even the less expensive "personal" models (look for the little glass window on the front of the printer).

I was visiting a colleague and he had a laptop on his lap while he worked on a desktop computer. He swung his chair around to ask me a question, and the laptop's infrared sensor made a "passing contact" with his printer's infrared sensor. We heard the soft noise of hard drive action on the laptop and looked at the screen. The printer was installed on the laptop! Talk about effortless installation!

Installing a Printer Directly to the Network

Printers that have their own network interface connections work faster than printers that are attached to computers via a parallel port. Most of today's Internet connection devices for printers are capable of using TCP/IP to communicate, and Windows 2000 is set up to take advantage of this. You can choose between two methods when you want to add a network-ready printer to the network:

- Add the printer to each user's computer, and eliminate printer-sharing management.

- Add the printer to a computer that acts as a print server, and set up printer sharing.

For administrators of small networks or small branch offices, it's tempting to believe it's less of an administrative headache to let each user install the printer and manage it directly. This passes the headaches to the users. The headaches include:

- No user knows the current state of the printer, because displaying the print queue shows only the user's print jobs.

- Setting print priorities is a useless exercise, because only the querying user's print jobs are involved in the settings.

- Printer errors (out of paper, jams, and so on) are only revealed to the user who sent the current print job. Everyone else just keeps sending jobs.

Administrators who think users will put up with these headaches either have a problem with reality or have done a heck of a job training users to solve their own problems.

Printers that are accessed by multiple users always benefit from the management advantages of printer sharing. Install the direct-connection printer to a print server. If the number of simultaneous accesses doesn't exceed 10, you can use a Windows 2000 Professional workstation (unless you have to support Macintosh or NetWare services). Printing doesn't impose an enormous strain on a computer's processing or I/O levels, so you can use a computer that performs other chores.

Now that I've convinced you to attach the printer with a NIC to a print server (be sure the computer that's acting as a print server is running TCP/IP), here are the instructions for installing the printer:

1. Open the Printers folder and then open the Add Printer object (click Next right away to move past the Add Printer Wizard welcome window).

2. Select Local Printer and clear the check box for automatic detection; then click Next.

3. In the Select the Printer Port window, select Create A New Port. Choose Standard TCP/IP Port from the drop-down list; then click Next to open a new wizard (this wizard adds and configures TCP/IP printer ports).

4. Enter a printer name or an IP address for the printer, name the port (the port and the printer can use the same name), and click Next.

5. Select the device type from the drop-down list or select Custom and configure the device manually.

 The protocol, port number, and data type for the printer are built into the device type, so if you need to perform a manual device installation, make sure you have this information at hand.

Sharing Printers

When you install a printer in Windows 2000 Server, the default configuration is to share the printer. Windows 2000 Professional does not share printers by default during installation, and you must specifically elect to share the printer.

It's common to share all the printers on a network—the exceptions are printers that hold checks, or other specialized and/or sensitive paper types. In Windows 2000, sharing printers offers more features to users and administrators than previous versions of Windows NT.

Creating a Printer Share

If you elected not to share the printer during installation, you can share it at any time thereafter. Open the Printers folder, right-click on the printer's icon, and choose Sharing from the shortcut menu. The printer's Properties dialog box opens to the Sharing tab. Select Shared As, and enter a name for the printer (or accept the default name, which is usually the printer model). The Sharing tab has additional options available (see Figure 12-1):

- Select List in the Directory to publish the printer in the Active Directory.
- Additional drivers cover the needs of remote users who have different versions of Windows. See "Add Drivers for Other Versions of Windows," later in this chapter.

On the General tab of the printer's Properties dialog box, you can add optional descriptive comments:

- Use the Location text box to describe the printer's physical whereabouts. This information is available to users who are searching for printers.
- Use the Comment text box to add information about this printer. The contents of this text box appear when a remote user hovers the mouse pointer over the printer's icon in My Network Places.

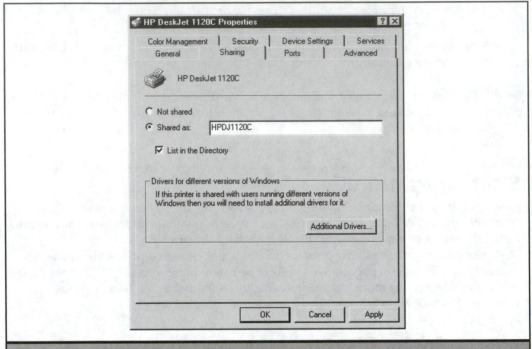

Figure 12-1. *Configure the printer for access by remote users*

Setting Printer Permissions

Printer permissions are set on the Security tab of the printer's Properties dialog box (see Figure 12-2).

The default standard permissions are set forth in Table 12-2.

User or Group	Print	Manage Printer	Manage Documents
Everyone	Y		
Administrators	Y	Y	Y
Creator/Owner			Y
Print Operators	Y	Y	Y
Server Operators	Y	Y	Y

Table 12-2. *Default Printer Permissions*

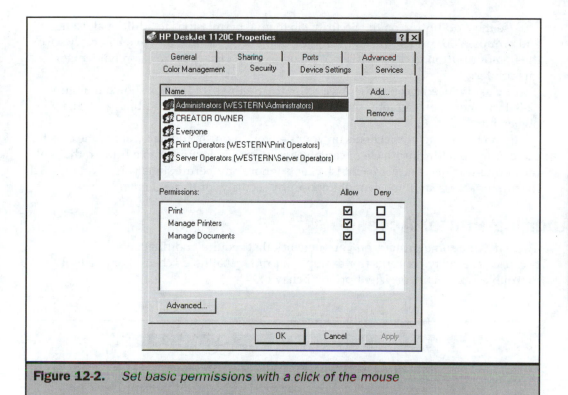

Figure 12-2. *Set basic permissions with a click of the mouse*

Each of the permission levels has a set of rights, as follows:

- Print:
  - Print documents
  - Pause, resume, restart, and cancel the user's own documents
  - Connect to the printer
- Manage Documents:
  - All permissions contained in the Print level
  - Control job setting for all documents
  - Pause, restart, and delete all documents
- Manage Printer:
  - All permissions contained in the Manage Documents level
  - Share a printer
  - Change printer properties
  - Delete printers
  - Change printer permissions

Use the Add button on the Security tab to give permissions to additional users and groups. You can use the listing for the domain or the entire Active Directory. Use the Remove button to delete a user or group from the list of permission holders for this printer.

Click Advanced to open the Access Control Settings dialog box shown in Figure 12-3. From here you can set more granular permissions, enable auditing, and change ownership.

If you have Macintosh clients on your network, you should be aware of the effect on security. If a Macintosh client can physically send a document to a printer, that's all the permission necessary. Macintosh clients ignore any permissions you've established for printer access, and you cannot impose any security for those clients.

Auditing Printer Access

There may be some printers on your network that require auditing, either because of security concerns (for example, a printer that holds checks) or as a tool in troubleshooting inconsistent printer behavior.

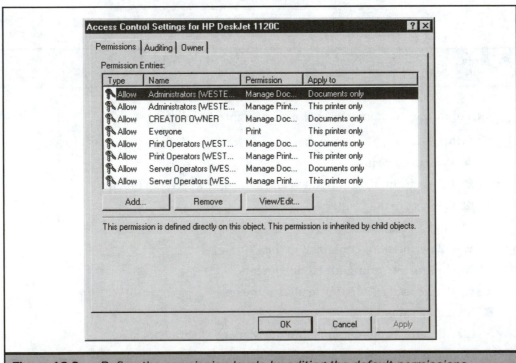

Figure 12-3.   *Refine the permission levels by editing the default permissions*

Setting up printer auditing requires two procedures:

- Enable auditing for the computer (assuming domain policies are configured to allow this).
- Configure auditing on the printer(s).

Enable Auditing for the Computer

Use the MMC to turn on auditing. If the Group Policy snap-in isn't loaded, add it. In the Group Policy Object, select Local Computer; then click Finish and Close. Expand Local Computer Policy to get to Audit Policy (see Figure 12-4).

Right-click Audit Object Access (in the right pane), and select Security from the shortcut menu. Then select the attempts you want to audit: Success, Failure, or both.

Configure the Printer for Auditing

To set up auditing for a printer, click the Advanced button on the Security tab of the printer's Properties dialog box, and move to the Auditing tab. You can audit the action

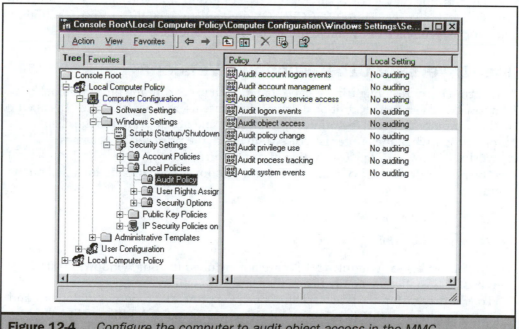

Figure 12-4. *Configure the computer to audit object access in the MMC*

of groups or individuals, or a combination of both. Click Add to open a window in which you can select the target users.

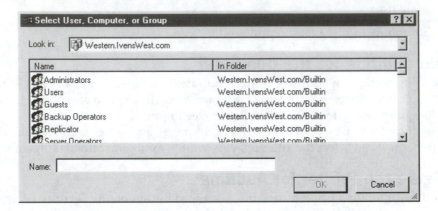

Use the Look In text box at the top of the window to select a domain, or select the entire directory. Then choose the first user or group you want to audit, and click OK (you have to perform this procedure one user at a time).

The Auditing dialog box opens for this user or group, and you can select the events you want to track (see Figure 12-5). Click OK and either repeat the process for another group or user, or click OK again to finish configuring audits.

Adding Drivers for Other Windows Versions

If the printer you're configuring will be shared with users running other versions of Windows, you can install additional drivers for those users. The drivers are installed on the computer to which the printer is connected, and are delivered to the clients automatically when the printer is accessed. In effect, the print server becomes a network sharepoint for the distribution of printer drivers.

The printer drivers for Windows NT 4 and Windows 9x clients are included on the Windows 2000 CD:

- \Printers\NT4\i386
- \Printers\Win9X

Printer drivers for Windows NT 3.x are not included in your Windows 2000 CD and must be installed manually (using the Have Disk option).

To add drivers for down-level clients, open the printer's Properties dialog box and move to the Sharing tab. Click Additional Drivers to open the Additional Drivers dialog box seen in Figure 12-6. Select the drivers you want to install, click OK, and follow the prompts.

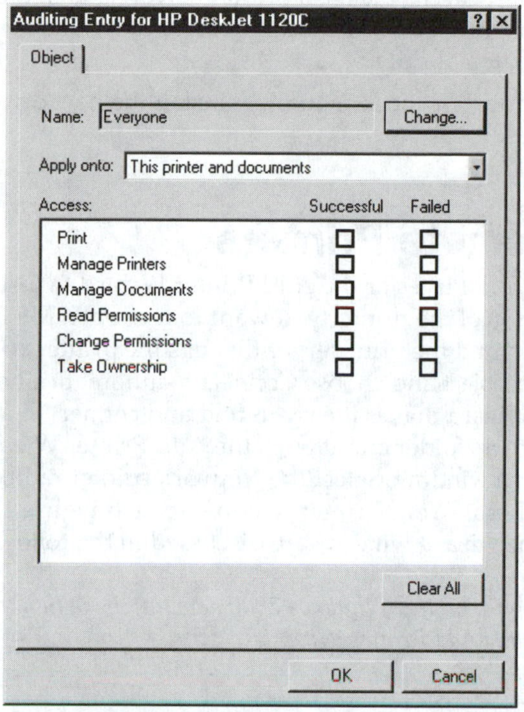

Figure 12-5. *Choose the events you want to audit for this user or group*

If you have manufacturers' drivers, use the Have Disk option. Be aware that you may have to use the Have Disk option for printers that Windows 9*x* and even NT 4 may have supported. For example, in my office, one of the printers (an HP DeskJet 1120C) was not in the Win9X printer directory of the Windows 2000 CD. I used the Windows 98 CD (which supports this printer) as the disk in the Have Disk option to install the drivers on my Windows 2000 print server.

If you update the drivers later, you should be aware that not all your down-level clients will handle the update in the same manner:

- **Windows 2000** checks the local printer driver against the print server when connecting to the network. If the local driver is older, the new driver is downloaded automatically.

- **Windows NT 4** checks the local printer driver against the print server when connecting to the network. If the local driver is older, the new driver is downloaded automatically.

- **Windows NT 3.***x* checks the local printer driver against the print server when the spooler service starts. If the local driver is older, the new driver is downloaded automatically.

- **Windows 9***x* does not check. You must install the new drivers manually on the client machines.

Installing Remote Printers

You can use My Network Places or the Add Printer Wizard to install a remote printer. If you know the location of the printer you want to use, open My Network Places and expand the network to find the print server that has the printer you want to use. Right-click the printer object and choose Connect to automatically install the printer.

The Add Printer Wizard makes it easy to find and connect to a shared remote printer. Open the Printers folder and launch the Add Printer Wizard, clicking Next to move past the welcome window. Select the Network printer radio button and click Next to bring up the Locate Your Printer window seen in Figure 12-7. The choice of methods offered in the wizard window are discussed in the following sections.

> **Note** *If you are not logged on to a Windows 2000 domain, the option to search the directory is not available on the Add Printer Wizard.*

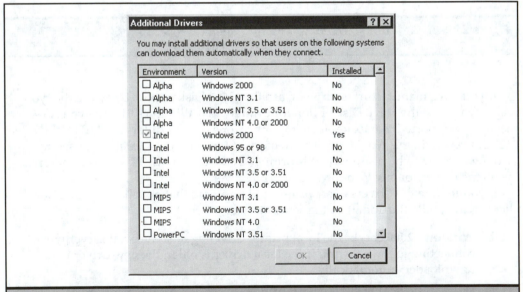

Figure 12-6. *The Windows 2000 driver is selected by default; the rest is up to you*

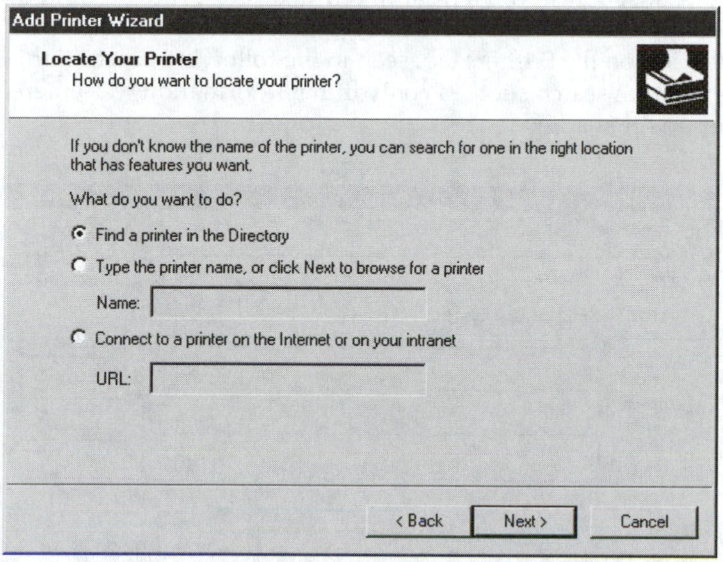

Figure 12-7. *Pick a method for locating a printer on the network*

Searching the Directory

Using the directory is a nifty way to find a printer that has the options you need. (It's assumed that all shared printers are published to the Active Directory). This feature uses the Find Printers dialog box that is part of the Windows 2000 Search function, which can be accessed using any of the following methods:

- Add Printer Wizard
- Search command on the Start menu
- Find Printer command on the Print dialog box

In the Add Printer Wizard, select Find A Printer in the directory, and then click Next, to locate a printer. The Find Printers dialog box opens, and you can use the tabs on this dialog box to specify the features you need.

Enter the Search Criteria

At the top of the dialog box, select Entire Directory to search the Active Directory for your organization, or select your domain. Usually, it's a good idea to select your domain because if you choose Enter Directory you cannot use the Advanced tab of the dialog box. Also, because you'll need to retrieve your print job from the printer, it's normal to select a printer that's located nearby.

The information on the Printers tab, seen in the following illustration, is rather basic, and the location search succeeds only if that information was entered when the printer was set up for sharing.

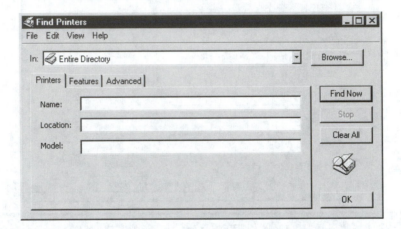

More specific criteria is available in the Features tab, shown in the following illustration. The information you enter is matched against the properties of all the network printers. For example, you might need a printer that is capable of color printing, or prints at a specific resolution.

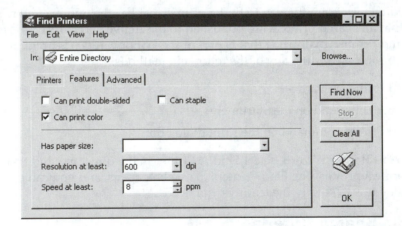

If you really need to narrow down the choices, you can move to the Advanced tab. Click Field to open a drop-down list of characteristics, as seen in Figure 12-8. (The list includes those criteria available on the other two tabs.)

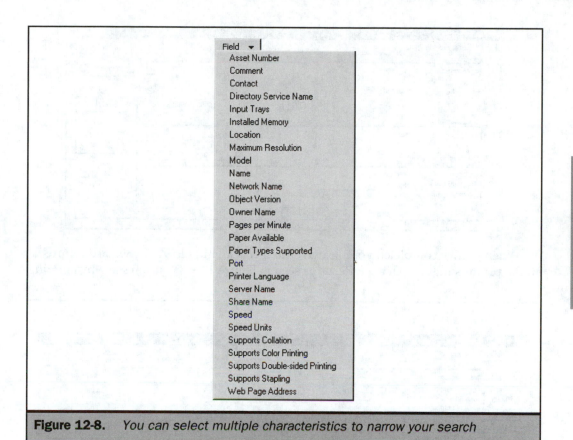

Figure 12-8. *You can select multiple characteristics to narrow your search*

After you select a field, select the condition for the search. For some fields, the condition is True or False (such as support for color printing). For other fields, the choices are broad enough to cover any eventuality, including "guesses."

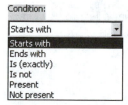

As you choose fields and set the conditions, click Add to build your list of criteria, an example of which is seen in the following illustration.

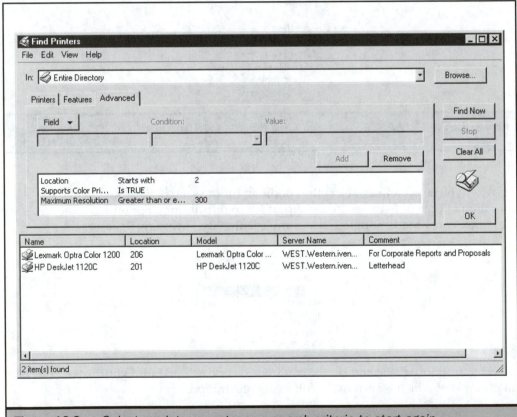

When you've completed your search criteria, click Find Now. The wizard returns all the printers that match the criteria, as seen in Figure 12-9. (You can see why entering

Figure 12-9.   *Select a printer or enter new search criteria to start again*

as much information as possible about a printer makes it easier for other users to locate printers). If no printers appear in the list, you can either enter different criteria, or return to the Add Printer Wizard to change the way you're searching (the other search methods are discussed in the next sections).

Right-click the printer you want to use, and choose Connect from the shortcut menu. The printer is automatically installed and you can begin using it.

 You can click Find Now without entering any information to see a list of all the printers in the directory.

Sort and Filter the Search Results

If the search for printers results in multiple choices, you can sort and filter the results. Select the Details view of the Results box if it isn't already displayed.

SORTING   To sort the display, click on the column heading that has the criteria by which you want to sort. Click again to reverse the order of the sort scheme. For example, if you want to choose among the printers that are connected to a specific computer, click the Server Name column heading. Or, if you like a particular model, sort by the Model heading and then choose the server or location that you want.

FILTERING   Filtering makes it easier to choose a printer when the list of available printers is copious. To filter the display, choose View | Filter from the menu bar of the Find Printers dialog box. This places a new row in the columns of the results display, as seen in Figure 12-10.

The way filtering works is the text you enter for each column is matched against the specifications you set for the filter. After you enter text, click the arrow next to the text box to choose the criteria to apply to your text.

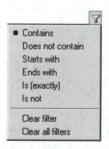

The default criteria (usually "contains") is applied as soon as you enter the text, so if that's your criteria, the column is already displaying your match. If you choose a different criteria, the column redisplays to match the information you want. You can filter as many columns as you need to. To turn off filtering, choose View | Filters again to deselect the option.

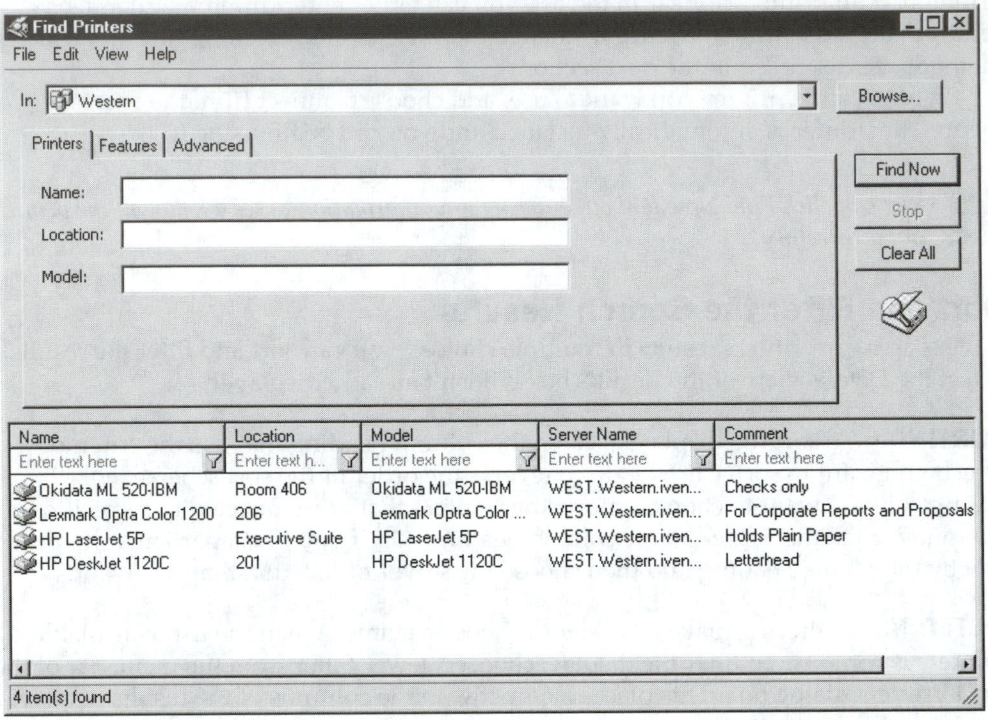

Figure 12-10. *Each column has a new text box for entering the filter criteria*

Save the Search

You can save the search information so the next time you need to locate a printer with the characteristics you've described, you don't have to reinvent the wheel. If you have administrative permissions, you can distribute the search file to other users. To save the search, choose File | Save Search to open the Save Directory Search dialog box. Give the file a descriptive name (for example, Color-2ndFloor or LetterheadInTray). The extension .qds is automatically added to the filename.

You can distribute the search results file to other users. If you selected printers from a domain instead of the whole directory, be sure the target computers and users are in the same domain. If you plan ahead, you can save users a lot of work by creating saved searches by location, paper type, color capabilities, and so on.

Browse the Network

You can browse the Network by selecting that option in the Locate Your Printer Wizard window. If you know the name of the printer, enter it in the Name text box and click Next. If you don't know the name of the printer, just click Next to open a window that displays the network objects. Open the computer that acts as the printer server. If there are multiple print servers on your network, you'll have to open each one individually (which is why knowing the name of the printer is helpful). Then select the printer and click Next to finish the installation process.

You can accomplish the same thing without the Add Printer Wizard by opening My Network Places. Expand the network and open the object for the print server to display the printers. Right-click on the printer you want to use and choose Connect.

Connect an Internet or Intranet Printer

The third option on the Add Printer Wizard's Locate Your Printer window is to connect to a printer on the Internet or on your company's intranet. If your professional printer cooperates by making a printer available through its Web page, you can select the company's printer and send your print job directly to the Web site. If your organization has an intranet, you can send a document from your office in one city to a printer in another city. Enter the URL for the Internet or intranet printer in the wizard window and click Next. Then follow the wizard prompts to complete your task.

If you're not using the Add Printer Wizard, you can open either Internet Explorer or your Printers folder and enter the URL in the address bar. You must be running IIS or Peer Web Services to use this feature. See Chapter 24 for information about IIS.

Using Printer Location Tracking

Windows 2000 has a new feature, called Printer Location Tracking, that automates the process of finding and connecting to a remote printer based on location. Location Tracking is useful for large domains with multiple sites, because it relieves the user of the need to know the location of the target printer. When a user chooses to search the directory for a printer, the system identifies the user's location on the domain and automatically searches the directory for printers in the same location.

Printer Location Tracking Requirements

To use Printer Location Tracking, you need to prepare and configure your domain with this feature in mind, using the following guidelines:

- You have multiple sites in the domain, or multiple subnets in a single site.
- Your network IP addressing scheme is devised to correspond with the physical layout of your network.

■ You have a subnet object for each site (created using Active Directory Sites and Services).

Only clients who participate in the Active Directory can use this feature: Clients running Windows 2000 Professional or Windows 9x with the AD client installed.

You must create a subnet object for each subnet, using Active Directory Sites and Services. After you have created the site and subnet objects, you need to set the location string for each subnet. Then use the Location tab of the subnet Properties dialog box to set the location string (see the next section, "Printer Location Naming Requirements").

Note *The directory service site name does not have to be the same as the location name.*

Printer Location Naming Requirements

Because the process of locating printers is automated, and users count on the accuracy of the information in the AD, you must devise a location naming protocol for all printers in the AD. The protocol for naming locations must follow these rules:

■ The location names take the form *Name/Name/Name/Name/*.

■ The location name can consist of any character except the forward slash, which is used as a separator.

■ The maximum length of each *Name* component is 32 characters.

■ The maximum length of the entire location name string is 260 characters.

For example, in my organization, there are two domains (Eastern and Western) and each domain has two sites:

■ Eastern has the sites Admin and Accounting.

■ Western has the sites HR and Research.

The sites have subnets as follows:

■ Admin has subnets for the 2nd Floor and the 3rd Floor.

■ Accounting has subnets for the 5th Floor and 6th Floor.

■ HR has subnets for West Bldg and West Bldg PH (penthouse).

■ Research has subnets for Lab and the 9th Floor.

The location naming for printers located in the Admin subnet on the 2nd Floor takes the form Eastern/Admin/Floor2. The protocol of using FloorX to designate floors was part of the general planning process for printing. When the protocol was explained to users, it meant that users who wanted to avail themselves of the ability to enter a location Location field in the Find Printers dialog box knew the format of locations. It's important to make sure the Location field is filled in for each printer on the network.

Enabling Printer Location Tracking

Printer Location Tracking is enabled via three processes:

- Configure subnets
- Create a Group Policy to enable the feature
- Enter location information for each printer to match the location system for subnets

Right-click each subnet you're using for location tracking and choose Properties. In the Location tab of the Properties dialog box, enter the location of the subnet in the format *location/location*. For example, using the organization explained in the preceding section, I have a subnet named research/lab.

Open an MMC window and add a Group Policy for the appropriate container (domain or OU). (See Chapter 8 if you need more information about using the MMC.) Expand the console tree as follows: Computer Configuration | Administrative Templates | Printers. In the right pane, double-click Pre-Populate Printer Search Location Text to open its Properties dialog box, and select Enabled on the Policy tab.

Open each printer in the AD and enter location information in the format *location/location* to match the location naming scheme for your subnets. It's a good idea to add one additional location to give users very precise information about the printer, for example, /research/lab/roomA-1 or research/lab/hallway.

Deploying Printers

Printers should be distributed to match user need, although sometimes political and security concerns can upset a perfect, logical plan. I know IT directors who have been told to place a printer in an executive office for the convenience of the person occupying that office (and, of course, the printer is never shared because other users can't freely enter the office to pick up print jobs). If that's the case in your organization, be sure to explain that such printers are additional budget items and you can't afford to use your "printer stock" in such a manner. Good luck!

Physical Security for Printers

Printer security is a concern when printers hold checks, purchase orders, or other paper types that can be dangerous in the wrong hands. In addition, users who print sensitive documents (especially the accounting and human resources departments) should have printers that are located in a secure manner. Secure printers should not be placed in hallways or rooms in which no supervisory users are working. It's best to attach them to the computer that is used by the person who sends sensitive print jobs. If other users must share the printer, you can use the printer permissions to restrict access.

Don't forget to secure the warehouse printers with strict permissions. Pick slips generate shipping, and I've had clients who suffered "shrinkage" (the polite term for employee theft) through the efforts of users who sent pick slips. The orders were picked and packed and shipped to the user's choice of cohorts. If pick slips require the existence of a sales order (a good security measure), be sure to secure your accounting software to prevent unauthorized users from getting to the Sales Order module. However, a clever user who knows how to format a word processing document can send a fake pick slip to the printer (it prints exactly as if it had come from the accounting software) and end-run the need to have a sales order.

One-to-One Printer Drivers

The standard relationship between a virtual printer (the printer icon displayed to users) and the physical printer is one-to-one. All users send print jobs to the virtual printer, which passes the jobs to the physical printer. Users can set print options in their software applications, and the virtual printer handles all the processing so the job prints correctly.

One-to-Many Printer Drivers (Printer Pools)

A *printer pool* is a one-to-many relationship in which a single virtual printer can pass print jobs to multiple physical printers (see Figure 12-11). You can use printer pooling to ensure printing services in mission-critical operations. Pooling is commonly used to spread the printing load in situations where there is so much printing activity that users have to wait too long for documents to emerge from the printer.

To use printer pooling, all the physical printers have to be the same (or at least have an emulation mode that means the single printer driver works). The printers should be located together because users will not know which physical printer received the job and it's not cricket to force users to wander the halls looking for a print job.

To configure printer pooling, right-click the printer you want to use for pooling and choose Properties from the shortcut menu. Move to the Ports tab and select the Enable Printer Pooling check box. Then select the additional ports to which the printers in the

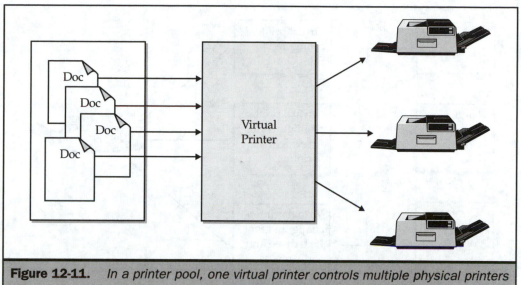

Figure 12-11.   *In a printer pool, one virtual printer controls multiple physical printers*

pool are connected. You can add more parallel ports to this server, and/or select a port that represents another computer (using the UNC) that has a connected printer that is part of this pool.

Many-to-One Printer Drivers

You can configure a many-to-one virtual-to-physical printer setup to take advantage of configuration options on a physical printer (see Figure 12-12). For example, a printer that has two trays may hold letterhead and plain paper (or purchase orders and sales orders). Creating a virtual printer that is configured for a specific form makes it easier for users who want to print to that form. Other reasons to create this scenario include

- Printers accessed by groups who need banners and groups who don't
- Printers used for very large documents that should print at night (deferred printing)

To create multiple virtual printers, use the Add Printer Wizard in the Printers folder to create as many copies of the printer as you need (these are local printers, of course). When prompted about using the current driver, select the option to keep the current driver. The wizard's Name The Printer window displays the same name as the first printer, with the notation "(Copy 2)". You can rename the printer either at this point or later. The printer's name should reflect its configuration. The wizard also asks for a share name and offers a comment field, and you have the same options—enter the information now or do it later.

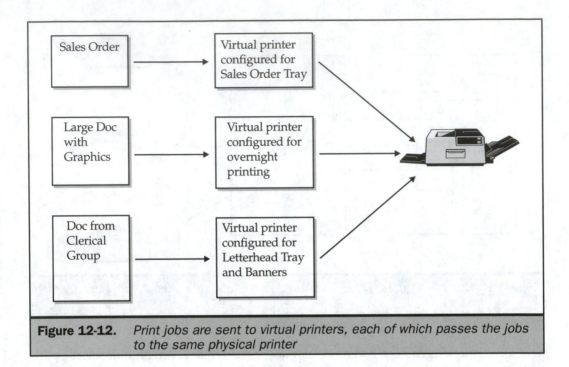

Figure 12-12. *Print jobs are sent to virtual printers, each of which passes the jobs to the same physical printer*

For example, for my Lexmark printer I have the following virtual printer objects:

- Lex-banners
- Lex-nights
- Lex-SO
- Lex-LH

The SO indicates Sales Orders and the LH indicates Letterhead. The Lex-LH printer is the original printer I installed, which I renamed to indicate its configuration.

Now you can configure each printer for its specific use. For example, using my Lexmark, the virtual printer for printing sales orders (which are in Tray #2), has Tray #2 configured for letter-sized paper and the other trays marked unavailable (Figure 12-13).

Printer configuration options are discussed later in this chapter, in the section "Configuring Printers."

Configuring the Print Server

You can set properties for the printer server by opening the Printers folder and choosing File | Server Properties. The properties you set for the server are those that are not printer dependent, and are the defaults for all printers on this server.

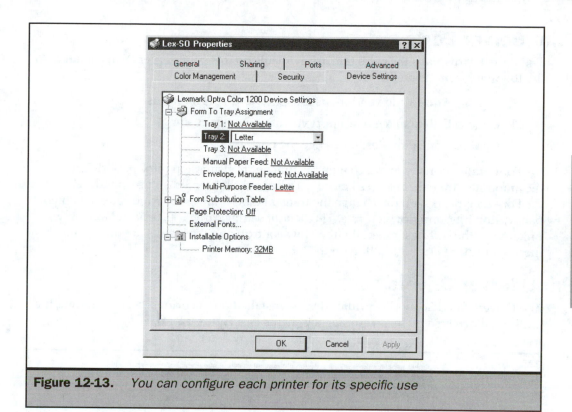

Figure 12-13. *You can configure each printer for its specific use*

Print Server Forms

Windows 2000, like Windows NT 4, deals with paper sizes and formats as forms rather than printer tray options. A form is, by definition, a paper of a particular size. Forms give administrators a way to let users choose a form without having to worry about which tray is to hold which size form. Because most companies operate with network print servers, the printer is frequently not in sight, which means users can't lean over and see that the top tray contains letter-sized paper and the bottom tray contains legal-sized paper. In fact, the user can't see how many trays are in the printer.

With configured forms, when a user chooses to print to legal paper, he or she merely picks the form. The system matches the form to the tray that holds it. Windows applications are capable of presenting different forms to the user, and when a selection is made that is other than a default, the spooler checks the printer's configuration options and includes the codes for the appropriate tray when the document is sent to the printer.

You can use the Forms tab to create new forms. Select Create A New Form and then specify the measurements to match your creation. Give the form a name to make it available to all the printers on this print server (as long as they can physically handle the form).

Print Server Ports

The Ports tab displays the ports that are available on this print server. You can take the following actions on this tab:

- Choose **Add** to add vendor-specific ports and port monitors.
- Choose **Delete** to remove a port you are no longer using.
- Choose **Configure Port** to change the port settings.

For parallel ports, you can change the timeout transmission retry period. This is the amount of time that elapses before it's assumed the printer isn't responding.

For serial ports, you can change the transmission settings for baud rate, data bits, parity, stop bits, and flow controls. The default settings are 9600, 8, N, 1, None. If you tinker with the settings (especially the Flow control) and the results are disastrous, there's a Restore Defaults button on the tab.

Print Server Drivers

The Drivers tab displays the printer drivers installed on the print server, including the additional drivers you loaded for legacy clients (see Figure 12-14).

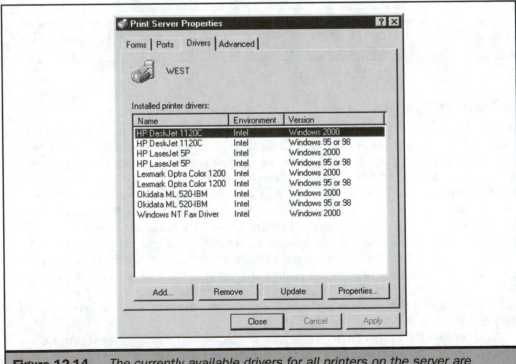

Figure 12-14.   *The currently available drivers for all printers on the server are displayed*

You can add, remove, and update drivers for the printers installed on the server. (Adding and removing drivers launches a wizard.) Click the Properties button to see the driver files (including the help files), and to set permissions for accessing those files. Note that help files attached to printer drivers are not standard help files but the files that provide the text for the What's This? feature.

Server Spooler Options

Move to the Advanced tab to set options for the spooler on the print server (see Figure 12-15). You can change the location of the spool folder; see "Spooler" earlier in this chapter for instructions.

The configurable items that are turned on and off with check boxes on this dialog box are self-explanatory. However, I'd like to point out that leaving the option to Log Spooler Warning Events may send more entries to the System Log in the Event Viewer than you're prepared for. A warning event is logged every time anyone with the appropriate permissions makes any changes to configuration options for a printer or the print server. You may want to stick to error warnings only. And unless you have a very good reason (such as a serious troubleshooting effort), don't elect to Log Spooler Information Events because every printing event will be recorded in the Event Viewer.

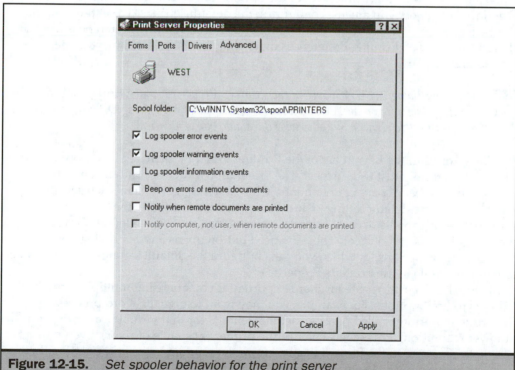

Figure 12-15.   *Set spooler behavior for the print server*

The option to notify users when remote documents are printed is a quick way to alienate users, and the fact that you can notify the sending computer instead of the user doesn't make this option more tolerable. It's not just that the system sends an annoying message to say the document has printed; users also have to click OK to clear the message. Users do not enjoy doing that.

Configuring Printers

You can set printing defaults with a printer's Properties dialog box. The defaults you set can be changed by any users to whom you give permission to manage printers (see "Setting Printer Permissions" earlier in this chapter). The configuration options vary from printer to printer, of course. Color printers have more options than monochrome, PostScript printers have unique options, duplex printers have special options, and so on. However, there are some settings that are global in nature, and those are covered in this section.

Printing Preferences

The Printing Preferences options are the defaults that appear in the Print dialog box when a user chooses this printer. All of the options can be changed by the user for each individual print job; you are just configuring the default settings. To set the defaults, right-click the printer you want to configure and choose Printing Preferences from the shortcut menu. The Printing Preferences dialog box for the selected printer opens, as seen in Figure 12-16.

 The same dialog box is available on the Printer's Properties dialog box by clicking Printing Defaults on the Advanced tab. The title bar says Printing Defaults instead of Printing Preferences, but otherwise the dialog box is identical.

The settings in the Layout tab of the Printing Preferences dialog box should be set to default to those most users expect. The orientation, order of printing, and number of pages on a sheet of paper are standard settings. The Paper/Quality tab sets the paper source (the default setting of automatic selection is usually the best option). If the printer is capable of color printing, you can choose to use a default for gray scale printing instead of color. The Advanced button opens another dialog box with printer-specific options for which you can configure the default settings. These options are also available in the printer's Properties.

These default settings are far more important if you are using multiple virtual printers to limit options. For example, you may want to give the word processing department a printer called "drafts," set the defaults for that virtual printer to print at lower resolution, and eschew color (if the printer is capable of color). Even if users can make changes on the Print dialog box from the sending application, setting these defaults makes it more likely that the options you set will be used.

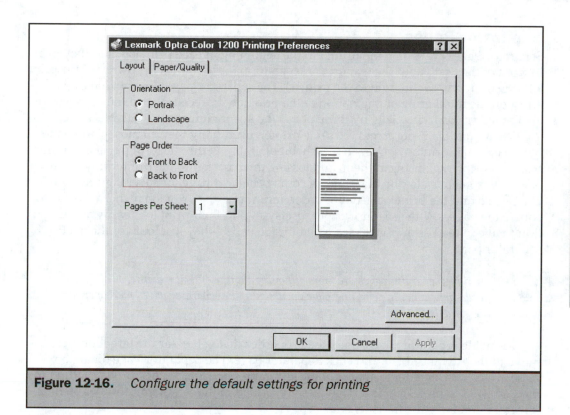

Figure 12-16. *Configure the default settings for printing*

Printer Properties

The configuration of properties for a specific printer is accomplished through the printer's Properties dialog box, which is accessed by right-clicking the printer object and choosing Properties from the shortcut menu. The number of tabs, and the contents of the tabs, vary from printer to printer. However, there are some global options you should examine and set.

General Printer Information

The General tab for all printers includes the printer name, location, and comments. You should use the Location and Comments text boxes to help users identify (and find) printers. Develop a companywide convention for these entries; it's confusing if some printer locations are entered as "Room 304" and others as "305." In fact, to make it easier for users to search for printers, avoid unnecessary words (like "Room"). Click the Printing Preferences button to display the same dialog box discussed in the preceding section.

Separator Pages

Separator pages are sent to the printer at the beginning of each print job, and they print in front of the first page. The text on the separator page identifies the owner of the print job (the user who sent the job to the printer). The separator page does not have any effect on the numbering or pagination of the print job it precedes. (Separator pages are also called *banners*, especially by those of us who spent many years with NetWare.)

When multiple users access the same printer, eventually they all mosey down the hall to get their printouts. Users have a habit of grabbing the sheets of paper emerging from the printer, glancing at them, and tossing them back into the printer tray if they belong to someone else. By that time, of course, the next page (or several more pages) has ejected and the print job is out of order, infuriating the print job owner who has to collate the pages. With separator pages, users can find their print jobs easily and they don't have to read each page to see when the job ends—they just look for the next separator page.

Sometimes separator pages are more annoying than useful. If a printer is accessed by users who usually print one-page documents, the separator pages merely create more recycling.

To enable separator pages, open the Properties dialog box for the target printer, move to the Advanced tab, and click Separator Page. The Separator Page dialog box appears so you can enter the name of the separator page file, or click Browse to find the file you want to use. Separator Page files are located in the %SystemRoot%\System32 directory and have the file extension .sep.

By default, Windows 2000 installs three separator page files, only two of which actually print separator pages:

- **Pcl.sep** for printers that use PCL (printer control language). The separator file also switches dual-language printers to PCL printing before printing the separator page.

- **Sysprint.sep** for printers that use PostScript. The separator file also switches dual-language printers to PostScript before printing the separator page.

- **Pscript.sep** does not print a separator page, and is used for switching dual-language printers to PostScript.

Schedule Printer Availability

A shared printer can be scheduled for use on the Advanced tab of the printer's Properties dialog box. By default, printers are always available. If you want to change the printer's hours of operation, select the Available From radio button and specify a beginning and end time for this printer's availability.

This task is commonly performed when you're using multiple virtual printers for one physical printer. If the printer supports color and has other features that are needed for large, complex documents, you should set time limits for a virtual copy of the printer and have users send documents to the printer before they leave for the evening. This means that slow, complex documents will print during the night, and other users who need the printer won't be inconvenienced. Make sure there is plenty of paper in the printer before everyone leaves (in fact, don't use a printer for overnight printing unless its paper tray is capable of holding four or five hundred sheets of paper).

Another good use of a virtual printer copy available at specific times is for printers that are used for checks or other specialized paper. Set a company policy that checks are in the printer tray for a specific time period, and then match that time to the printer's availability.

Set Default Document Priorities

The Advanced tab also has a Priority text box, which represents the default priority level for each document sent to the printer. By default, the priority is 1, which is the lowest priority. You can change the default priority to any number between 1 and 99.

Setting a priority level for the documents that arrive at a printer is meaningless. The only way to make priority levels work is to establish multiple virtual printers and set a different priority for each. Print jobs that are sent to the virtual printer with high priority will print ahead of the jobs sent to the standard virtual printer. Then use one of these techniques to ensure that users employ printing priorities properly:

- Explain that only higher-priority documents should be sent to the virtual printer marked for high priority (yeah, sure, that works).

- Set permissions for the higher-priority printers so that access is limited to the groups and users that usually have realistic high-priority needs.

Set Spooling Options

There are a variety of spooling options available on the Advanced tab of the printer's Properties dialog box (see Figure 12-17).

SET THE EVENT THAT BEGINS THE PRINTING PROCESS You can choose to start printing after the last page is spooled, or you can print immediately after the document has begun to feed data to the spooler directory. Opting for the former means the spooler does not begin processing the file until it has received the entire file (the application sends an end-of-file marker to indicate the entire file has been sent). The latter choice means the spooler sends pages through the printing process as they are received.

Waiting for the last page to spool before starting print processing means that there is a delay before the document emerges from the printer. However, it ensures that the whole document prints, and that the document is error-free, so a document with corrupt data isn't sent to the printer. This is actually a choice between speed and safety, and you should pick the option that matches your own philosophy.

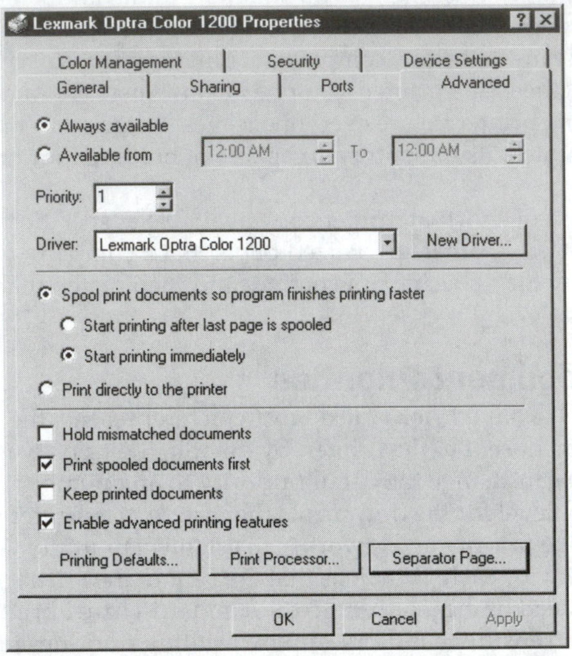

Figure 12-17.   *Select the spooling options for this printer*

USING OR BYPASSING THE SPOOLER   There's an option on the Advanced tab to print directly to the printer. This means you bypass the spooler and move files directly from the application software to the printer. While this may sound terribly efficient, it's not a good idea because the spooler keeps documents intact, separating multiple documents from each other.

   If there's a problem with printing, however, use this option to determine whether the problem originates in the spooler. If a print job that didn't print (or didn't print correctly) prints properly when you bypass the spooler, then you should reinstall the spooler files (see the section "Spooler" earlier in this chapter).

MANAGING MISMATCHED DOCUMENTS   The Advanced tab has an option to hold mismatched documents. A mismatched document is one in which the codes going to the printer don't match the printer's current configuration. For example, a document may be an envelope and the target printer may not have an envelope tray, instead requiring manual insertion of envelopes.

   Selecting the option to hold mismatched documents tells the spooler to move other documents (that are not mismatched) ahead of the document that requires special handling. Eventually, when the spooler is empty except for the mismatched document file, the document is sent to the printer. Most printers will blink some lights at that point to indicate there's a manual feed required to print the job.

By default, the option to hold mismatched documents is not selected, because most printers rarely have empty spoolers and the user waiting for the mismatched document could be ready for retirement before the document is sent to the printer. However, it's imperative for users to understand that anytime a paper form needs to be inserted, they must go to the printer and perform that task. Otherwise, all the jobs behind the mismatched job are held up.

PRINT SPOOLED DOCUMENTS FIRST

PRINT SPOOLED DOCUMENTS FIRST The Advanced tab has an option to print spooled documents first, and that option is selected by default. This means the spooler treats documents that have completed the spooling process with a higher priority than documents that are still in the process of spooling. This means that a large document that was sent to the spooler from an application before another, smaller document was sent will print after the document that was sent later. This is usually just as efficient as it seems. In fact, sometimes a number of small documents arrive at the spooler after the large document is sent, and the small documents are placed in the queue as they finish spooling. When the large document has finished spooling there may be four or five (or more) documents ahead of it in the queue. With this option enabled, the spooler prints the largest document first, then the next largest, and so on. This ensures that large documents don't receive a de facto low priority.

If you clear the option, the spooler looks at document priority before sending print jobs to the printer. If all documents have the same priority, the queue is printed in the order in which the documents finished spooling.

KEEP PRINTED DOCUMENTS

KEEP PRINTED DOCUMENTS This option on the Advanced tab does exactly what it says it does—it tells the spooler to retain the spooler file for every document that is sent to the printer. The only way a spooler file is removed is manually: open My Computer or Windows Explorer and delete the file. You'll have to do this after every print job unless you have more disk space than you know what to do with.

The purpose of this option is to be able to reprint a file from the spooler instead of opening the application again. I'm willing to bet that the number of times administrators have needed this function is so small that it's safe to guess "never."

ENABLE ADVANCED PRINTING FEATURES

ENABLE ADVANCED PRINTING FEATURES This option on the Advanced tab is selected by default, and it makes any advanced features for this printer available to users. Some of those advanced features, such as booklet printing and multiple pages per sheet, require metafile spooling. If there are problems using advanced features (typically, problems only occur if you're using a printer driver that's an emulation instead of the real driver for the printer), you can deselect the option.

> **Note** *Metafiles are files that describe or specify other files. Microsoft uses metafiles for the Windows Metafile (WMF) format. A WMF file contains a sequence of graphical device interface (GDI) commands that are commonly used for printing graphic images.*

Color Management

For printers capable of color printing, you can take advantage of the Windows 2000 Image Color Management (ICM) feature. ICM provides a way to produce consistent color, regardless of the capabilities of a specific device. ICM maps colors and translates color types (RGB to CMYK, for example) to provide accurate and consistent colors. This means the screen color matches the print color, the scanner color matches the screen color, and so forth.

The Color Management tab of a color printer's Properties dialog box provides the opportunity to supply profiles for users who access the printer. When you move to the Color Management tab (available only for color printers that support the color management features), you should see either of the following color profile configurations:

- No profiles are loaded for the printer.
- The sRGB Color Space Profile is loaded.

 The sRGB profile is the default color profile for Windows 2000 and works with all devices that are capable of color management.

You can add a color profile to the printer by clicking Add and selecting a profile from the Add Profile Association dialog box. Color profile files have an extension of .icm and are stored in %SystemRoot%\System32\Spool\Drivers\Color. You can add as many profiles as you wish, and then configure to the printer to automatically select the best profile or let users select a profile.

If you have users who need the color-matching features to prepare high-end graphics or desktop publishing, read the next section, "An Overview of Color Management."

An Overview of Color Management

While it's beyond the scope of this book to enter into a deep and detailed discussion of the color management utilities included in ICM, it seems worthwhile to present an overview so you can decide for yourself whether you need to investigate this feature more fully.

ICM uses APIs to configure colors for input and output devices (monitor, scanner, and printer). You can assign color profiles to printers so that users can access those profiles. The color profile has the data needed to send codes about color to the target devices. You can also add a color profile to a monitor, using the Advanced button in the Settings tab of the Display properties dialog box. In fact, if you add a color profile to a printer, you should add the profile to the monitor (and vice versa). This means that WYSIWYG displays match print jobs, which is important to the preparation of high-end graphics.

Profiles can also be installed in the other direction, by opening the profile and associating it with the monitor and printer. Right-click the profile's object and choose

Associate from the shortcut menu. Then add the monitor and printer(s) to the associated devices list.

Without a color profile, color features can vary from job to job because of the differences in the way hardware uses color. Users who have specialized needs (graphics, desktop publishing) can specify color profiles to match the job they're working on, ensuring consistency across devices and computers. Because profiles add overhead and can slow the printing process, day-to-day color printing shouldn't involve the use of profiles.

Windows 2000 includes version 2.0 of ICM, an upgrade from the original ICM 1.0, which was introduced in Windows 95. It works with any scanners, monitors, and printers that support color management.

Only applications that are written to support the ICM APIs work with color management. (In Windows 2000, the Imaging program on the Accessories menu works with ICM.) When you want to invoke the color management features, choose File | Color Management from the application menu bar.

 Windows applications can support either of two levels of API: there is one set of APIs for RGB and another set for multiple color spaces. The APIs maintain device color profiles and provide color conversion procedures.

Scanners that support color management either create sRGB output or embed a color profile into the image file. The former is preferable because the operating system can work with sRGB output. An embedded color profile is not necessarily available to the other devices. A scanner can create sRGB output in one of two ways:

- It can make a call to ICM, pass ICM the appropriate scanner profile, and point it to the sRGB profile. The Windows 2000 ICM then generates sRGB output that the device can pass onto the application.

- It can use a proprietary system that corrects from the scanner color space to sRGB standards. This isn't very flexible and usually requires software from the manufacturer to complete the process of passing the color data to the application. Unfortunately, some proprietary software isn't compatible with Windows ICM.

The importance of ICM and color profiles is that all components that use an associated color profile can let ICM manage color continuity throughout the entire editing process.

Managing Printing

With the proper permissions, you can manage printers on any print server. In fact, you can manage the print server properties for a remote computer. Windows 2000 is built for remote management of printing, which is why you must pay careful attention to permissions.

Managing Remote Printers

You can access a remote printer for management in several ways: use My Network Places, use the Search command on the Start menu to locate a printer, or use your browser to travel to a remote print server. You have the same powers for manipulating the properties of the Printers folder and the printers contained within it as you have for a local Printers folder.

If you manage a remote printer or a remote print server on a regular basis, you can bring the printers to your own workstation. This is a nifty way to make your job easier. Create a folder for managing printers, or open the Printers folder on your local computer. Then open My Network Places and expand the computer that is the print server you manage remotely. With the windows side-by-side, drag the Printers folder from the remote print server into your local folder, as seen in Figure 12-18.

You can also open the Printers folder on the remote print server and drag individual printer objects to your own computer.

Redirecting Print Jobs

If a printer breaks down, you can move the print jobs that are waiting to print to another printer, as long as the other printer uses the same printer driver. The new

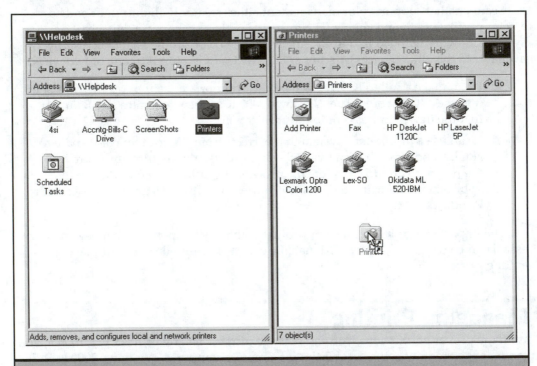

Figure 12-18.   *Bring your work to your own computer*

printer can be on the same print server, or on another print server. The ability to redirect the documents means you don't have to kill the queue and tell users to reprint.

To accomplish this task, open the Printers folder and open the printer that isn't working. The list of print jobs waiting to go to the printer displays in the Printer window. Choose Printer | Properties to open the Properties dialog box, and move to the Ports tab. Then use the appropriate method to move the queue to another printer:

- To move the print jobs to another printer on the same print server, select the port to which the target printer is connected. Click OK.

- To move the print jobs to a printer on another print server, choose Add Port | Local Port | New Port. Then enter the UNC for the remote printer, using the format \\PrintServer\PrinterShareName.

The document that is showing an error message (the document that is currently printing) cannot be transferred and you must delete it. The user who owns the document must resend the print job.

Manipulating Print Jobs in the Queue

When you open a printer by double-clicking its icon in the Printers folder, the window shows all the jobs in the queue, along with information about each job (document name, size, owner, and so on). With the appropriate permission level, you can perform the following actions on documents in the queue:

- Cancel the print job by right-clicking on its listing and choosing Cancel.
- Pause the print job by right-clicking on its listing and choosing Pause.
- Resume a paused print job by right-clicking on its listing and choosing Resume.
- Restart a document that stopped (usually due to a printer jam or out-of-paper error) by right-clicking on its listing and choosing Restart.
- Change the priority of a print job by right-clicking on the job listing and choosing Properties. On the General tab of the Properties dialog box, raise or lower the document's priority.

| Note | *When you resume or restart a print job, it has to wait behind any documents with higher priority that may have arrived in the queue.* |

To perform an action on all the documents in the queue, right-click the printer object in the Printers folder and choose the appropriate command from the shortcut menu:

- Pause printing
- Cancel all documents
- Resume Printing

Note *Users can manipulate only their own jobs, which they access by opening the printer icon that appears in the taskbar during printing.*

Printing to a File

The Windows Print dialog box that appears when you choose File | Print in an application offers an option to print to a disk file. In addition, you can establish a printer that automatically prints to a disk file instead of a physical printer. There are several reasons you might want to do this:

- You want to print the document from another location.
- The printer is temporarily down.
- You want to give the file to another user.

It's a good idea to create a virtual printer that's preconfigured for disk files (see the section "Many-to-One Printer Drivers" earlier in this chapter). To do so, when you add the printer, use File as the port selection. When a user accesses this printer, he or she is prompted for a filename. The file is stored on the user's computer.

To print a disk file, enter the following command at the command line

```
print [/d:device] [[drive:] [path] [filename]]
```

where:

- **d:device** is the output device, which can be a port (e.g., lpt1) or a remote printer (\\PrintServerName\PrinterShareName).
- **drive:path filename** is the path to the file you want to print.

The disk file only prints to the printer that created it. In other words, you cannot configure your HP laser printer to print to a file, and then print the file to a Lexmark laser printer. The codes that the target printer expects are embedded in the disk file.

Printing from DOS

If your printer is connected to your own computer, you won't have a problem when you print from DOS software or from the command line. However, if you are using a remote printer, printing from DOS is not simply a matter of selecting a printer in the software. To print from DOS, you must manually redirect printing, using the following command:

```
net use lptx \\PrintServerName\PrinterShareName
```

where:

- *x* is the port you want to redirect (usually lpt1).

You can make this a permanent command by adding the parameter **/persistent:yes**. For example, to use a printer named HPLJ6 that's connected to a computer named PrtSrv3, enter **net use lpt1 \\PrtSrv3\HPLJ6 /persistent: yes**.

After you've redirected the port, you can send files to the printer via the command line in addition to printing from DOS applications. The persistent parameter survives shutdown, so the remote printer is always available. However, the state of lpt port redirection is a user profile issue, so if multiple users access the computer, each user must invoke the redirection command.

If you have multiple remote printers to choose from, you can redirect lpt2 to one of them, lpt3 to another, and so on. Then, in your DOS software, be sure to establish the ability to print to those ports. For command-line printing, you need only name the port as the target of the command to send the DOS file to the right printer.

The
Complete
Reference

Part III

Connecting with Windows 2000

Chapter 13

Networking with TCP/IP

As a stand-alone operating system, Windows 2000 is like an orphaned child. Much of its functionality is devoted to communications with other systems, and the TCP/IP protocols are the means by which this communication is possible on most Windows 2000 networks. Many of the functions covered in this chapter are invisible to the user after TCP/IP has been properly configured, but you cannot fully understand Windows 2000 until you examine the networking processes that run beneath the surface.

This chapter examines many of these processes, including:

- The use of TCP/IP within the Windows 2000 networking model
- The various TCP/IP protocols and their layered functionality
- The elements of a client TCP/IP configuration
- The automatic configuration of TCP/IP clients using DHCP
- The name registration and resolution processes
- The use of the Windows 2000 TCP/IP utilities

After you have achieved an understanding of these subjects, your conception of Windows 2000 networking—and of the Internet—will become clearer, and you will be more capable of dealing with problems when they arise.

The Ins and Outs of TCP/IP

The growth of Windows 2000 into an enterprise-class network operating system and the meteoric popularity of the Internet are two of the factors that have made the TCP/IP protocol suite into the de facto networking standard that it is today. Enterprise networks have become more heterogeneous in recent years, either through the addition of new technologies or the consolidation of existing ones, and one of the problems resulting from this phenomenon has been the general increase in network traffic congestion due to the different protocol types used by different platforms.

To relieve this congestion, many network administrators have sought to standardize on a single set of network protocols, in the hope of making their network traffic easier to manage. For a number of reasons, the obvious protocol suite of choice is TCP/IP. Among these reasons are:

- **Compatibility** Most major network operating systems in use today are capable of using TCP/IP as a native protocol. Those that do not are now seen as being noticeably lacking in their support for industry standards.
- **Scalability** TCP/IP was designed for use on what is now the world's largest internetwork, the Internet. It provides protocols to suit almost any communications task, with varying degrees of speed, overhead, and reliability.
- **Heterogeneity** TCP/IP is capable of supporting virtually any hardware or operating system platform in use today. Its modular architecture allows

support for new platforms to be added without reengineering the core protocols.

- **Addressability** Every machine on a TCP/IP network is assigned a unique identifier, making it directly addressable by any other machine on the network.

- **Availability** The TCP/IP protocols are designed to be open standards, freely usable by all, and are developed through an "open forum" approach in which contributions from all interested parties are welcome.

TCP/IP is partially responsible for the growing popularity that Windows 2000 enjoys today. It's predecessor' Windows NT's original native protocol, NetBEUI, is suitable for use only on small networks because it has no network layer and is therefore not routable between network segments. The TCP/IP protocols contained most of the functionality required for use with Windows NT and Windows 2000, and what it lacked, Microsoft helped to develop by working with other industry leaders to create new open standards.

Microsoft's TCP/IP Rollout

Development of the TCP/IP protocols for use on the fledgling ARPANET (later called the Internet) began in the 1970s, but some of the innovations that have made it a practical choice for use on private enterprise networks were not conceived until much later. Microsoft's own adoption of TCP/IP for its global corporate internetwork was a telling case in point.

In the early 1990s, as Microsoft's Information Technology Group examined the various candidates that might replace the archaic XNS protocols they were then using, TCP/IP was a front-runner from the very beginning, but it presented certain major obstacles to a worldwide rollout of this size. Primary among these obstacles were the administration and configuration of IP addresses, network name resolution, and the use of broadcasts to locate other computers.

On a small or medium-sized network, the task of assigning IP addresses to workstations is an onerous one; but on a large internetwork spreading over 50 countries, it is a major administrative expense. Not only must the network address assignments be carefully planned and meticulous records be kept at a central location, but the task of actually configuring those thousands of nodes must be dealt with. Do you send trained personnel to every remote sale office? Do you train people who are already there? Do you develop documentation that will (hopefully) enable end users to configure their own workstations?

Name resolution on this scale is another difficult problem. To use TCP/IP with Microsoft operating systems prior to Windows 2000, you had to have a means of equating NetBIOS names with IP addresses. On a local network segment, this was done using broadcasts (which could cause network traffic problems themselves). Connections to machines on other networks required entries in an LMHOSTS file on each workstation, which listed NetBIOS names and their equivalent IP addresses. The task of maintaining these files on so many computers dwarfed even that of assigning IP addresses.

CONNECTING WITH WINDOWS 2000

Fortunately, Microsoft was in a unique position to help resolve these problems. It was clear to Microsoft that the difficulties it was facing would afflict any large corporate adoption of TCP/IP, to some extent. The results of Microsoft's efforts, in collaboration with other network engineers and product manufacturers, were the DHCP and WINS modules that provided IP address configuration and name resolution services, respectively, to network users. By using these services, you could greatly reduce the administrative overhead required by a large TCP/IP network and insulate your users from the need to know anything about protocols and IP addresses.

TCP/IP has yet again undergone a transformation for Microsoft with Windows 2000. It includes many new features and enhancements from the Windows NT 4 implementation (refer to the following section for a list of new features and enhancements). In the purest sense, Windows 2000's TCP/IP implementation has standardized with the rest of the industry. It no longer has to rely on NetBIOS for name resolution. Instead, it uses the Domain Name System (DNS) as it's primary name resolution mechanism. However, NetBIOS and related services are supported for compatibility with older Windows-based systems and applications.

The term TCP/IP is, of course, a misnomer. As it is generally used, the name actually refers to a collection of more than a dozen protocols and is taken from the two that are used most often. The standards on which the protocols are based are published by the Internet Engineering Task Force (IETF) and are known as Requests for Comments (RFCs). These documents are much more accessible than many networking standards, both in their availability and their readability. They can be freely downloaded from many different FTP servers, such as:

- nis.nsf.net
- nisc.jvnc.net
- ftp.isi.edu
- wuarchive.wustl.edu
- src.doc.ic.ac.uk
- ftp.ncren.net
- ftp.sesqui.net

Most of the sites store the documents in a top-level directory called RFC. They are predominantly ASCII text files, with some that contain illustrations available in PostScript format.

Windows 2000's TCP/IP Enhancements

Like almost everything else in the computer world, TCP/IP is continually undergoing changes and enhancements to meet ever-changing business needs. Microsoft is striving to ensure that it's TCP/IP implementation meets and exceeds the expectations brought about by the industry. The new technologies that are adopted within Windows 2000's TCP/IP implementation are listed in Table 13-1.

Feature	Description
Internet Printing Protocol (IPP)	Enables you to print directly to a URL and manage print devices over an intranet or the Internet. More information can be found on IPP in Chapter 12.
Quality of Service (QoS)	Supports QoS-related standards, such as Resource Reservation Protocol (RSVP), Differentiated Quality of Service, and 802.1p in order to obtain higher levels of service quality. Think of QoS as an agreement between two or more machines that guarantees a certain expected level of throughput, traffic control, and more. However, using this feature takes resources (you may be robbing Peter to pay Paul).
Telephony Application Programming Interface (TAPI) 3	Increased support for telephony for Windows 2000.
IP Security (IPSec)	Encryption technology for IP. Often used in Virtual Private Networks (VPNs). Refer to Chapter 21 for more information on security-related topics.
Layer Two Tunneling Protocol (L2TP)	Provides enhancements for secure virtual private networking capabilities.
NDIS 5	New network architecture that supports a multitude of enhancements such as multicasts, bandwidth reservation, power management, and more.
Automatic Client Configuration	The ability for a DHCP client to configure itself to communicate on the network when no DHCP server can be contacted. More information on this feature can be found in "Understanding DHCP" later in this chapter.

Table 13-1.   *New TCP/IP Enhancements for Windows 2000*

CONNECTING WITH
WINDOWS 2000

Feature	Description
High-speed network support	Windows 2000 broadens its support for high-speed networks (defined in RFC 1323) for increased performance and scalability. This includes support for Selective Acknowledgements (SACK), IEEE 1394, wireless networks, IP over ATM (RFC 1577), and much more.
Internet Group Management Protocol version 2 (IGMP v2)	Allows computers to use multicasting-based technologies such as streaming media services.
Protocol Stack Tuning	Windows 2000 automatically adjusts protocol settings, such as increasing the default TCP window size, to increase network performance.
Plug and Play Networking	Windows 2000 now has the ability to automatically recognize networking hardware, such as network interface cards (NICs) and PCMCIA adapters, without manual intervention.
DHCP Enhancements	New features for DHCP include integration with DNS, enhanced monitoring and reporting of usage, rogue DHCP server detection, and much more.

Table 13-1. *New TCP/IP Enhancements for Windows 2000* (continued)

Fitting TCP/IP into the Windows 2000 Networking Model

Windows 2000's networking architecture is particularly well suited for use by different sets of protocols. With the Transport Device Interface (TDI) at the top of the OSI model's Transport layer, and the Network Device Interface Specification (NDIS) interface beneath the Network layer, the core transport protocols are largely isolated from the rest of the networking stack, as shown in the following illustration. As long as they can address these two interfaces, any competent protocols can be used to send data over the network. Indeed, different transport protocols can function simultaneously in Windows 2000, resulting in the double-edged sword of platform interoperability and network traffic congestion.

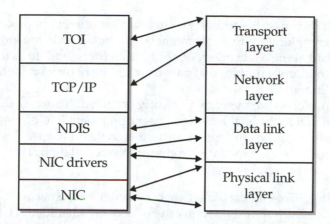

Above the TDI are the *user-mode interfaces* (also known as *application programming interfaces,* or *APIs*). These interfaces are addressed by applications when they require network services. Chief among these interfaces are the NetBIOS interface, which Windows 2000 still supports for file services, and Windows Sockets (Winsock), which is the standard interface for many TCP/IP and Internet utilities for backward-compatibility issues with down-level clients. Other supported APIs are

■ Remote Procedure Calls (RPCs)
■ Server Message Blocks (SMBs)
■ Named Pipes
■ Mail Slots

These APIs are not necessarily associated with a particular set of protocols. The original Windows NT release, for example, could only pass data from its APIs to the NetBEUI protocol and then to an NDIS driver. This simplified system lacked the functionality of TCP/IP but provided basic network services on a small scale.

The TDI provides a distributed interface that enables network requests from the different APIs to be directed to whichever protocol is needed to access the required resource. NetBIOS file requests, for example, can be directed to the TCP/IP protocols when accessing a Windows 2000 drive on the network, or to the NWLink protocol when the application needs a file from a NetWare server. Multiple applications running in Windows 2000 might be processing several network requests simultaneously, meaning that various function calls can be passing through the TDI to the TCP/IP protocol stack, or the NWLink stack, or both, at the same time.

All the protocol stacks operating on a Windows 2000 machine deliver their network service requests to the same place—the NDIS interface. NDIS is the standard used to create the device driver that provides access to the networking hardware. Thus the network architecture of Windows 2000 can be seen as a series of funneling procedures. Applications at the top of the model generate requests that can utilize any of a handful of APIs. The APIs then pass the requests on to a smaller number of protocols (usually one or two). Different kinds of requests might be intermingled in the individual protocol stacks; and at the NDIS interface, they are all funneled into a single stream and packaged into discrete packets that pass through the network adapter and out onto the network medium itself.

The TCP/IP protocols are therefore primarily occupied in moving the application requests from the TDI to the NDIS interface, packaging them into discrete units called *datagrams* so that they can be efficiently transmitted to their ultimate destination. The process is, of course, reversed for data arriving at the workstation. This packaging can be said to consist of three basic functions:

- **Addressing**   To send data to another computer on the network, there must be a means by which the destination can be uniquely identified. TCP/IP provides its own identification system, in the form of an IP address for each machine on the network.

- **Routing**   A Data Link-level protocol such as Ethernet or token ring is not concerned with the ultimate delivery of network packets, only with transmitting them to the next machine on the network. TCP/IP provides the means by which network traffic is efficiently and reliably routed through multiple network segments to its destination.

- **Multiplexing**   Because an operating system like Windows 2000 can be running several programs at once, network requests are multiplexed over the cable (that is, packets with different origins and purposes are intermingled in the network data stream). Individual packets must therefore be identifiable in order for the requests to reach the appropriate application process in the destination computer. TCP/IP accomplishes this by assigning a port number to each process, which in combination with an IP address uniquely identifies the actual process on the network to which the packet must be delivered. The combination of an IP address and a port number is called a *socket*.

Exploring the TCP/IP Protocol Stack

The TCP/IP protocols, as realized on Windows 2000, can be broken down into four functional layers that roughly correspond to those of the OSI reference model, as shown in Figure 13-1.

- Application
- Transport
- Network (also known as the Internet layer)
- Network Access

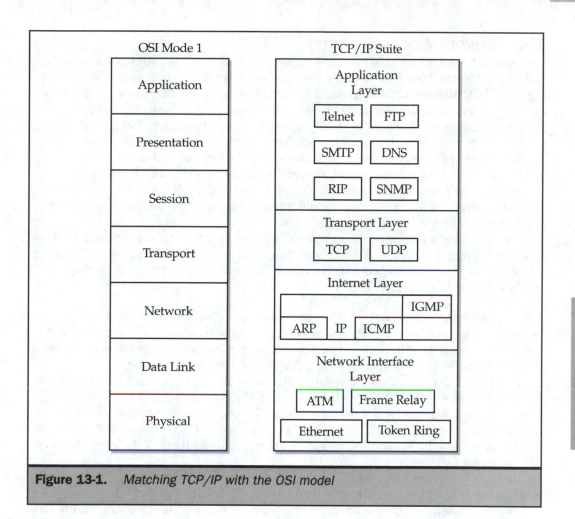

Figure 13-1.   *Matching TCP/IP with the OSI model*

As with the OSI reference model, the functionality of the various TCP/IP protocols is divided into layers that make the process of data encapsulation more comprehensible. As a message is passed down from the user interface at the top of the networking stack to the actual network medium (usually a cable) at the bottom, data processed by an upper-layer protocol is repeatedly encapsulated by protocols operating at each successive lower layer. This results in a compound packet that is transmitted to the destination system, where the whole process is repeated in reverse, as the message travels up through the layers.

With TCP/IP, examining the layers at which the suite of protocols function is a means of understanding how they have been adapted for use on Windows 2000 networks.

The Network Access Layer

The Network Access protocols operate at the bottom of the TCP/IP protocol stack, working just above the Data Link layer to facilitate the transmission of datagrams over the network medium. TCP/IP has its own addressing system, by which it identifies the other computers on the network. Once the IP datagrams reach the NDIS interface, however, they are repackaged again into frames that are appropriate for the network type being used.

Every network type, whether Ethernet, Token Ring, or something else, has its own way of identifying the computers on the network. Most of the network types in use today accomplish this identification through the use of a hardware address that is coded into every network adapter by its manufacturer. This Media Access Control (MAC) address is used in the outermost frame of every network packet to identify the computer to which it should be sent.

Therefore, for an IP datagram to be sent out over the network, there must be a way of determining what hardware address corresponds to the given IP address. This is the job of the Network Access protocols, of which the most commonly known is the Address Resolution Protocol (ARP).

ARP   ARP functions between the Network and Data Link layers on Ethernet networks. It cannot operate until it is provided with the IP address of the computer to which a datagram is to be sent. No datagram can be transmitted over the network until ARP supplies the Data Link layer with a destination hardware address.

When ARP receives a datagram from the Network layer, it reads the IP address of the intended destination from the IP header and then generates an *address resolution request packet,* which is broadcast to the entire local network. The address resolution request contains the IP address of the destination computer (if the destination is on the same network segment) or the IP address of the workstation's default gateway (if it is not).

Each computer on the network segment processes the ARP packet and notes the IP address carried within. If a computer on the network detects its own IP address in an ARP packet, it responds to the sender with a reply containing the hardware address of its network adapter. The ARP passes this address along to the Data Link layer protocol, which uses it to frame the packet and eventually transmit it over the network.

ARP also maintains a cache of IP addresses and their corresponding hardware addresses, to reduce the number of redundant broadcasts transmitted over the network. The cache is erased whenever the computer is shut down or rebooted, to prevent incorrect transmissions due to changes in network hardware.

> **Note**   *ARP broadcasts are limited to the local network segment. A computer's Data Link protocol is concerned only with the transmission of the frame to the next computer down the line. In most cases, this will be a gateway to another network segment and not the computer whose IP address is specified as the final destination of the message.*

ARP is only one of many Network Access protocols designed to support the extremely wide and varied array of platforms that can utilize TCP/IP.

The Network Layer

The Internet Protocol (IP), which operates at the Network layer of the TCP/IP stack, is the central protocol of the entire suite and the core of TCP/IP's functionality. All the upper-layer protocols in the suite are packaged within IP datagrams before being passed to the NDIS interface. IP performs many of the key functions that enable the TCP/IP suite to operate, including the following:

- The packaging of upper layer traffic into datagrams, the fundamental TCP/IP transmission unit
- The implementation of the TCP/IP addressing system
- The routing of datagrams between networks
- The fragmentation and defragmentation of datagrams to accommodate the limitations of the network types between the source and the destination
- The passing of data between the Transport and Network Access layers (in both directions)

IP is a connectionless, unreliable protocol. *Connectionless* means that it transmits packets without first establishing that the destination computer is operating and ready to receive data; *unreliable* means that it has no inherent mechanisms that provide error detection and correction. These apparent deficiencies are not really a problem because IP can always be used in conjunction with other protocols that provide these services if needed. As a basic carrier medium for network communications, the intention behind IP's design is to provide only the common services needed by all transmissions, so that an appropriate transport protocol can be selected to suit the specific needs of the data being transmitted.

The rest of this section describes the means by which IP datagrams are carried from system to system to their ultimate destination, as well as examining the header of the IP datagram, which contains the information needed to complete the transmission. In addition, the Internet Control Message Protocol is introduced, which performs many different functions that assist the efforts of the Internet Protocol.

IP ROUTING IP is also responsible for the routing of datagrams to adjacent network segments. Every computer running TCP/IP on an internetwork has access to one or more gateways that it uses to transmit data to systems on other networks. A *gateway*, in TCP/IP parlance, is a device that passes packets between two or more networks. The term does not necessarily imply the existence of a protocol translation, as it does in the general networking vocabulary. A TCP/IP system that functions as a gateway between the source of a transmission and its destination is also known as an *intermediate system*. The source and destination themselves are called *end systems*.

TCP/IP traffic on an intermediate system travels up to Network layer, and no higher. IP is aware only of the computers on its local network segment and the adjacent segments that can be accessed through local gateways. When it receives a packet destined for a computer on another segment, IP sends it to one of the local gateways to continue it on its way. That particular gateway is selected for one of the following reasons:

- It provides direct access to the network on which the destination computer resides.

- It is registered in the computer's routing table as the best possible route to the destination network.

- It is the computer's default gateway.

THE IP HEADER   As with any network protocol, IP places its own header onto each packet it receives from the upper layers, encapsulating it for transmission and inserting the information needed to perform all the protocol's functions. The IP header, illustrated in Figure 13-2, is either 20 or 24 bytes long, depending on the inclusion of certain options. Bytes, in TCP/IP-speak, are referred to as *octets*, and the header is broken into 32-bit *words*, of which there are five or six. After the header is applied, the packet is referred to as a *datagram*, and it is passed down to the Network Access layer. The datagram will be encapsulated again by the Data Link layer, before it is actually transmitted over the network.

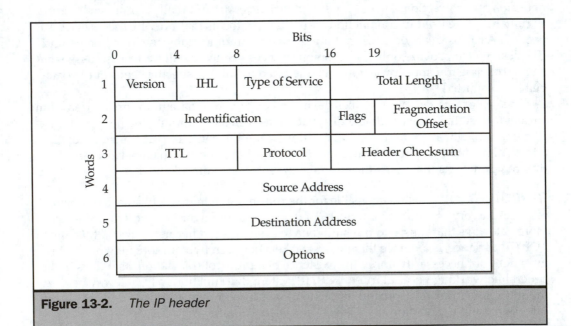

Figure 13-2.   *The IP header*

The IP header consists of the following fields:

- **First Word**

  - **Version (4 bits)**   Indicates the IP header version.

  - **Internet Header Length (4 bits)**   Specifies the overall length of the IP header (in 32-bit words), thus indicating whether the optional sixth word is present.

  - **Type of Service (8 bits)**   Indicates the desired network service priority for this datagram.

  - **Total Length (16 bits)**   Specifies the total length of the datagram in octets (bytes); can be used to determine whether fragmentation of datagrams is needed to complete the transmission.

- **Second Word**

  - **Identification (16 bits)**   When datagrams are fragmented or defragmented, this field specifies the datagram to which a particular fragment belongs.

  - **Flags (3 bits)**   Specifies whether the datagram can be fragmented and whether all the fragments composing the original datagram have been received.

  - **Fragmentation Offset (13 bits)**   Used to reassemble fragments in the proper order, this field provides the starting point (measured in 64-bit units) of this fragment in the datagram.

- **Third Word**

  - **Time to Live (8 bits)**   Specifies how long (in seconds) the datagram can remain active on the internetwork. This allows undeliverable datagrams to be removed from the network after a set time period. Every system that processes the datagram decrements this value by at least one second.

  - **Protocol (8 bits)**   Indicates the protocol at the Transport layer of the destination computer for which this datagram is destined.

  - **Header Checksum (16 bits)**   Verifies that the IP header (but not the data) has been transmitted correctly. The checksum is verified by each intermediate system and recomputed before being sent to the next node.

- **Fourth Word**

  - **Source Address (32 bits)**   The IP address of the transmitting computer.

- **Fifth Word**

  - **Destination Address (32 bits)**   The IP address of the end system to which the datagram is being sent.

- **Sixth Word (optional)**

CONNECTING WITH
WINDOWS 2000

■ **Options (variable)** Provides routing, security, or time-stamp services for IP transmissions. The options field is itself optional, but must be supported by all implementations of IP.

■ **Padding (variable)** Zeros added to fill out the sixth word to a full 32 bits.

Although it is the most heavily used of the TCP/IP protocols, IP by itself is not capable of coping with some of the situations that might be encountered during the transmission of datagrams. In these cases, a "helper" protocol is needed to perform additional transmission control functions.

THE INTERNET CONTROL MESSAGE PROTOCOL The Internet Control Message Protocol (ICMP) operates at the Network layer. It is used to perform a number of diagnostic and administrative functions that aid in the transmission of IP packets. The ping utility, for example, uses ICMP packets to verify the existence of particular IP addresses on the network.

Similar ICMP packets are also used to provide a sending computer with reports on the status of its transmissions, such as:

■ Messages stating that a datagram's destination address is unreachable, specifying further whether it is the destination's network, host, protocol, or port that is unavailable.

■ ICMP Source Quench messages indicating that an intermediate or end system is being overwhelmed by incoming packets. This enables the sending node to initiate flow control procedures by slowing down its transmissions until the complaint messages cease.

■ Reports that packets have been discarded by an intermediate or end system due to packet header corruption.

■ Warnings that datagrams will have to be fragmented before they can be successfully transmitted to the destination.

Routing advice, in the form of ICMP Redirect packets, inform a sending node of conditions beyond the adjacent network segments. When the transmitting computer is on a segment with more than one usable gateway, these packets enable the sender to select the gateway that provides the most efficient route to the destination.

These functions should not be confused with those providing true connection-oriented service and error detection. ICMP aids in the delivery of IP datagrams to the destination but does not guarantee reliable service.

The Transport Layer

As in the OSI reference model, the TCP/IP Transport layer sits atop the Network layer. Transport protocols are encapsulated within IP datagrams for transmission over the network and provide different levels of service, depending on the needs of the application. The two main protocols that operate at the Transport layer are the Transport Control Protocol (TCP) and the User Datagram Protocol (UDP), both of which are profiled in the following two sections. TCP is used when more reliable service is required, and UDP when guaranteed delivery is less critical. As you saw in the diagram earlier, the Protocol field of the IP header identifies which transport protocol is being carried within the datagram, so that the receiving workstation knows how to process the packet.

THE TRANSPORT CONTROL PROTOCOL (TCP)   TCP is the primary connection-oriented, reliable protocol used in TCP/IP communications. Applications use it in situations that require data transmissions that are verifiable as being absolutely accurate, such as ftp file transfers. Unlike IP, TCP data transmissions never begin until a three-way handshake with the destination system has been completed. This creates a virtual connection between the two systems, a prearranged agreement between the two machines for the exchange of packets. After the connection is established, all the datagrams transmitted during that session are considered to be *segments* of that transmission. The entire series of datagrams transmitted during the session is called a *sequence*.

The reliability of TCP communications is provided by an error detection and correction system called *positive acknowledgment with retransmission*. This means that the receiving computer examines the checksum included with each packet and sends periodic acknowledgments back to the sender indicating that the incoming packets up to a certain point have been received intact. The transmitting system automatically resends any packets not positively acknowledged by the receiver.

TCP also provides flow control and packet reordering services for every transmission. Even though a virtual connection exists between the two end systems, individual IP packets can travel different routes to the same destination, possibly even arriving in a different order from that in which they were sent.

The header of a TCP packet, shown in Figure 13-3, is admittedly complex, even though it is the same size as the IP header, because it has a great deal to do. The TCP header is carried within the IP header and is read only by the end system receiving the packet. Because the destination system must acknowledge receipt of the transmitted data, TCP is necessarily a bidirectional protocol. The same header is used to send data packets in one direction and acknowledgments in the other.

The TCP header is formatted as follows:

- **First Word**
  - **Source Port (16 bits)**   Specifies the port number of the application process at the source computer sending the transmission.
  - **Destination Port (16 bits)**   Specifies the port number of the application process at the destination computer that will receive the transmission.

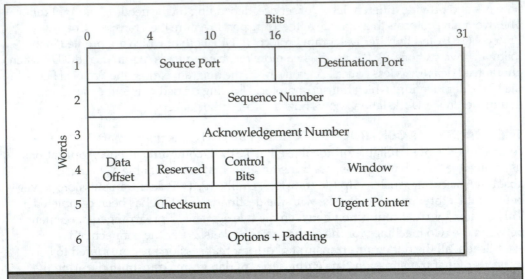

Figure 13-3. *The TCP header*

- **Second Word**
  - **Sequence Number (32 bits)**   Ensures that segments are processed in the correct order at the destination by specifying the number of the first data octet in the segment out of the entire sequence.

- **Third Word**
  - **Acknowledgment Number (32 bits)**   Specifies the sequence number of the segment that will next be received by the destination; indicates that all prior segments have been received correctly and acknowledged.

- **Fourth Word**
  - **Data Offset (4 bits)**   Specifies the length of the TCP header in 32-bit words, thus indicating the beginning of the data field and whether the optional sixth word is present in the header.

  - **Reserved (6 bits)**   Currently unused; the value must be zero.

  - **Control Bits (6 bits)**   Binary flags that can be turned on to indicate the segment's function or purpose:

    URG: Urgent Pointer field significant
    ACK: Acknowledgment field significant
    PSH: Push Function
    RST: Reset the connection

SYN: Synchronize sequence numbers

FIN: No more data from sender

- **Window (16 bits)** Provides flow control by specifying the number of octets (beginning at the sequence number in the Acknowledgment Number field) that the destination computer can accept from the source.

- **Fifth Word**

  - **Checksum (16 bits)** Provides error correction by checking both the TCP header and data fields, as well as a pseudo-header containing the source address, destination address and protocol values from the IP header and the overall length of the TCP packet. The pseudo-header enables the Transport layer to reverify that the datagrams have been sent to the correct destination.

  - **Urgent Pointer (16 bits)** When the URG control bit is turned on, this field specifies the location of urgent data (in relation to the Sequence Number of this segment).

- **Sixth Word (optional)**

  - **Options (variable)** Optional field used only to specify the maximum segment size allowed by the sending computer during the TCP handshake (when the SYN control bit is set).

  - **Padding (variable)** Zeros added to fill out the sixth word to a full 32 bits.

ANATOMY OF A TCP SESSION To begin a TCP session, one end system transmits a packet that has the SYN control bit turned on and contains a randomly selected sequence number. The destination system replies to the sender with a packet that has the ACK control bit turned on and specifies its own beginning sequence number, and then returns a SYN. Each system maintains its own numbering of the bytes in the sequence, while remaining aware of the other machine's numbers as well.

The sequence numbering begun in the first packet is continually incremented by both systems during the entire duration of the TCP connection. When it actually begins to transmit data, the transmitting computer specifies in each packet the number of the first byte contained in that packet's data field. If packets should arrive at the destination in the wrong sequence, the receiving system uses the sequence numbers to reassemble them in the correct order.

During the data transmission, the transmitting system computes a checksum for each packet and includes the result in the TCP header. The destination computer recomputes the checksum for each packet received and compares the result to the value provided in the checksum field. If the values match, the packet is verified as having been transmitted without error.

The receiver sends periodic acknowledgment packets back to the sender, each containing the number of the highest verified packet received thus far, in the Acknowledgment Number field. The sender can safely assume that all packets with lower numbers have been received and verified (preventing the receiver from having to acknowledge every packet). If the sender fails to receive an acknowledgment in a given period of time, it begins to resend packets beginning at the last acknowledgment number it has received.

Acknowledgment packets also contain a Windows value that indicates to the sender how many packets the destination system is capable of receiving at that moment. If this number increases in successive acknowledgment packets, the transmission rate can be increased. If the Windows value drops, the transmission rate is slowed, giving the receiver time to catch up (creating what is called a *sliding window*).

When it has finished sending data, the transmitting node sends a packet with the FIN control bit turned on to the destination, breaking down the connection and ending the sequence.

> **Note** *During the FIN-ACK-FIN transmissions, the last FIN can be delayed for up to two minutes (per the RFC). This is because designers assumed the last FIN packet could get lost somewhere on the net. Rather than holding a connection in a half-open state, the FIN is reset after the two-minute interval.*

TCP provides highly reliable data transfers, but at a significant price. Not only does the TCP header in each packet add to the overall transmission volume, but also the need for acknowledgments significantly increases the overall number of packets transmitted. It is easy to see why this kind of guaranteed service is implemented at the Transport layer as an option and not at the Network layer. If IP provided all these services, TCP/IP networks would slow down to a crawl.

THE USER DATAGRAM PROTOCOL   UDP provides a low-overhead alternative to TCP for use when the reliable transfer of data is not critical. It is connectionless, with each packet sent and processed independently of the others, and requires only a two-word header. There is no explicit acknowledgment of received packets during a UDP transmission (for example, a NetBIOS broadcast). Replies to UDP requests can be returned to the sender, but they are processed at the application level.

UDP is not typically used for the transfer of large binary data files, in which a single incorrect bit can cause the file to be ruined. UDP is more likely to be used for the transmission of a short query to another computer. If the sender receives no response, the entire request can usually be retransmitted using less overall traffic volume than the establishment of a TCP connection.

> **Note** *Some applications have begun to use UDP to stream audio and video over the Internet because the control overhead is so much lower, and also because an audio or video stream can recover from an occasional lost packet more easily than most binary files.*

Compared to the TCP header, UDP is simple and minimal. It is shown in the following illustration.

Bits

0   16   31

	Source Port	Destination Port
Words 1	Source Port	Destination Port
2	Length	Checksum

The UDP header layout is as follows:

■ **First Word**

　　■ **Source Port (16 bits)**   Specifies the port number of the application process generating the UDP transmission (optional, padded with zeros if omitted).

　　■ **Destination Port (16 bits)**   Specifies the port number of the application process in the destination system to which the UDP transmission is directed.

■ **Second Word**

　　■ **Length (16 bits)**   Specifies the overall length of the UDP packet in octets, including the data but excluding the IP header and any Data Link frames.

　　■ **Checksum (16 bits)**   Specifies the result of a checksum computation on the UDP header and data, plus a pseudo-header that consists of the IP header's Source Address, Destination Address, and Protocol fields.

The Application Layer

The TCP/IP suite includes many different protocols that operate above the Transport Device Interface. Some, like ftp and Telnet, are applications themselves, as well as protocols, and are included with most implementations of the TCP/IP suite to provide basic file transfer and terminal emulation services to users on any platform, with a standardized interface.

THE COMMON...   Other Application layer protocols are used to provide specific TCP/IP services to programs. Simple Mail Transfer Protocol (SMTP), for example, is used by many programs to send e-mail over TCP/IP networks. Other protocols, such as the Domain Name System (DNS), provide more generalized services. DNS is used by many applications to resolve Internet host names into IP addresses.

THE OBSCURE...   Although the examples cited thus far are rather well known, some application protocols operate almost invisibly to the user. The Router Information Protocol (RIP), for example, disseminates data to other computers on the network that helps them make more intelligent routing decisions.

HOW IT WORKS   Application protocols are, logically, closest to the user interface and are often directly involved with the process that generates the request for network resources. When such a request is processed, it is passed down the layers of the networking stack and encapsulated using the various protocols discussed in the preceding sections.

Thus, when you connect to an ftp server on the Internet and download a file, the ftp server at the remote site accesses the file and creates a packet by applying the header for the FTP application protocol. The entire packet is then passed down to the Transport layer, where it becomes the data field in a TCP packet. At the Network layer, the packet is divided up into units of the proper size to transmit over the network. An IP header is applied to each, and the packets can now properly be called a series of datagrams.

Except for minor changes to the IP headers while in transit, these datagrams will remain unopened until they arrive at their destination. While they are on the network, the outermost layer of the data packets, the Data Link frame, can change several times during the packets' journey from the ftp server to your workstation. The datagrams might arrive at your computer encased within Ethernet packets, and they might even start out that way when they leave the ftp server; but there could be 20 gateways or more between the source and the destination systems, running an untold number of different Data Link protocols.

After the packets arrive at your computer, the process begins in reverse. IP passes the datagrams up to the TCP protocol (which was specified in the IP header), where they are assembled into the correct order and fed to the FTP protocol (identified by its port number in the TCP header), which writes the received file to your hard disk drive.

All the TCP/IP protocols discussed in the preceding sections work together to transmit data over the network. By default, Windows 2000 installs them as part of the network communications stack. In Windows 2000, TCP/IP is often referred to as though it is a single protocol, when actually the entire family of protocols is implied.

Installing and Configuring TCP/IP

TCP/IP has been the default protocol since Windows NT 4.0 and will be installed during the operating system's setup routine. However, this time TCP/IP is prerequisite for you to log on, use Active Directory (AD), Domain Name System (DNS), and much more. The TCP/IP stack in Windows 2000 includes support for all the protocols discussed in the preceding sections, as well as a large collection of services and utilities that enable you to utilize, manage, and troubleshoot TCP/IP. The Windows 2000 Server product ships with many more TCP/IP-based services that facilitate the administration of large numbers of TCP/IP users on a network.

TCP/IP can also, optionally, be installed after the operating system is already in place, by clicking the Add button on the Local Area Connections Property page. If you have been relying on other protocols, such as NetBEUI, to communicate with other Windows computers on your local network, I highly recommend removing it after all your machines have been configured to use TCP/IP. It's always a good rule of thumb to keep the number of protocols that you're using down to a bare minimum.

After TCP/IP is installed, whether through the installation program or the Local Area Connections Properties page, you must provide the settings needed to identify your machine and ready it for interaction with the rest of the TCP/IP network. Windows 2000 continues to include a feature called the Dynamic Host Configuration Protocol (DHCP) that can enable a Windows 2000 server to automatically provide your systems with all the TCP/IP configuration settings that it requires. DHCP, discussed in the "Understanding DHCP" section later in this chapter, enables you to skip all the settings covered in the coming sections. For now, you'll learn about each of the settings required for effective TCP/IP communications and how a computer uses them to communicate with the network.

All the settings required to use TCP/IP on Windows 2000 are configured in the Internet Protocol (TCP/IP) Properties page, as shown in Figure 13-4.

To get to the Internet Protocol (TCP/IP) Properties page:

1. Select Network And Dial-Up Connections from the Start | Settings menu.

2. Right-click on the Local Area Connection icon and select Properties.

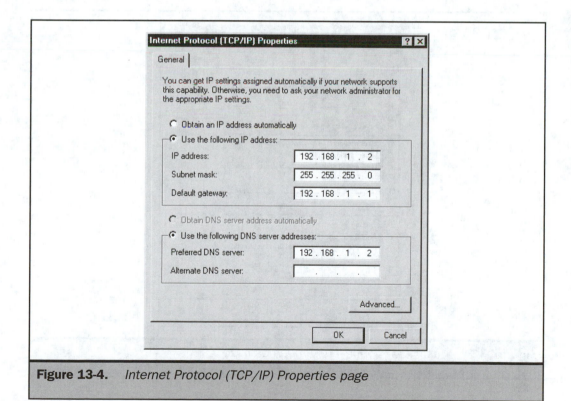

Figure 13-4. *Internet Protocol (TCP/IP) Properties page*

3. On the Local Area Connection Properties page shown in Figure 13-5, select the Internet Protocol (TCP/IP) and then click the Properties button.

You are then presented with the Internet Protocol (TCP/IP) Properties page, which contains the four most crucial settings for a TCP/IP stack, on any platform:

- IP address
- Subnet mask
- Default gateway
- Preferred and alternate DNS servers

IP Addressing

The IP address is the means by which computers are identified on a TCP/IP network. It identifies both the host itself and the network on which it resides. Each computer must be assigned an address that is different from those of all other computers on the network. Otherwise, datagrams might be delivered to the wrong system, causing all sorts of problems for both of the conflicting workstations.

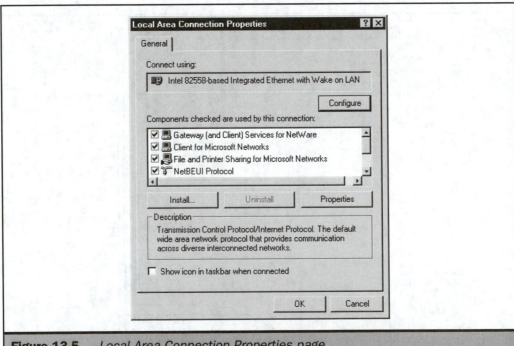

Figure 13-5. *Local Area Connection Properties page*

On a TCP/IP network, the term "host" is not necessarily synonymous with a computer. A host is a network interface, of which there can be more than one in a single system. In such a case, each host must have its own IP address.

IP addresses traditionally are 32 bits long and are expressed as four-decimal values from 0 to 255, representing 8 bits each, separated by periods. For example, the IP address 192.168.1.146 is equivalent to

```
11000000.10101000.00000001.10010010
```

in binary. With the onslaught of Internet domain name registrations, the number of available IP addresses is quickly dwindling. As a result, the IP addressing convention has had to undergo some changes. These changes are reflected in the new version, IP version 6 (IPv6). Whether you use the traditional IP addressing scheme (32-bits) or IPv6, the point is that every computer on your network must be assigned a unique IP address.

If your network is not connected to the Internet, the addresses are assigned to individual hosts by your network administrators. The actual addresses themselves can be any legal combination of numbers, as long as each assigned address is unique. In Chapter 2, Table 2-1 lists private IP addresses that can be used internally by anyone. This is known as an *unregistered* network because it is a wholly private arrangement within the confines of your organization.

If your network is connected to the Internet, however, you will have one or more machines with *registered* IP addresses. To prevent address duplication, you must register the IP addresses of Internet hosts with an Internet authority, such as Network Solutions (http://www.networksolutions.com/). A private network can elect to use registered IP addresses for all its hosts, or it can maintain an unregistered network for internal users and register only the machines directly accessible from the Internet, such as World Wide Web and ftp servers. In the case of the latter, users with unregistered IP addresses typically access the Internet through a firewall or proxy server that prevents unauthorized access to the local network from outside machines.

When you are configuring a computer to use TCP/IP, you should either receive an IP address from your network administrator (who must keep some record of the address assignments for the network), or use Windows 2000's DHCP server, which assigns addresses automatically from a pool configured by the administrator.

  The one thing that you should not do is select a random IP address just to see if it works. IP address conflicts are one of the most common problems on TCP/IP networks, and one of the most difficult to troubleshoot. Remember, the IP address that you just "borrowed" might belong to your boss. Also, IP stacks will shut down in the event of a duplicate.

Subnet Mask

The *subnet mask* is probably the most misunderstood of the TCP/IP configuration settings. People see the values assigned to this setting like 255.255.255.0 and mistake them for actual IP addresses, or they might know what value should be assigned but fail to understand why.

The subnet mask is actually based on a very simple concept. If you recall, in the last section you learned that the IP address identifies both the network and the actual host on that network. The only purpose of the subnet mask is to designate what part of the IP address identifies the network on which the host resides and what part identifies the host itself.

This is more easily understood if you think of the subnet mask in binary terms. All IP addresses are 32-bit binary values. They are notated in decimal form only for the sake of convenience. A subnet mask value of 255.255.255.0, when expressed in binary form, appears like this:

```
11111111.11111111.11111111.00000000
```

This value means that, for the IP address associated with this mask, all the digits with the value 1 identify the network, and all the zeros identify the host on that network (the 1's *mask* the network ID). Thus, if the machine's IP address is 123.45.67.89, then 123.45.67 identifies the network, and 89 identifies the host.

IP Address Types

When you understand what the subnet mask is used for, the next logical question is to ask why different networks require different numbers of digits to identify them. The answer to this, as with most TCP/IP questions, is found on the Internet. The TCP/IP protocols were designed for use on what is now known as the Internet. Although no one could have predicted its phenomenal growth, the Internet was designed to be a highly scalable network requiring a minimum of centralized administration.

TCP/IP's developers understood even in the early days that the idea of registering a unique address for every host on the network with some sort of administrative body was impractical. The cost would have been too high even then. They decided, therefore, that only networks would be registered and that the administrators of the networks would be responsible for maintaining the IP address assignments for the individual hosts.

It was then decided that three different network classes would be created, which would be registered to individual networks based on the number of hosts that they had to connect to the Internet. Table 13-2 lists the classes, the subnet mask for each, the maximum number of possible networks of that class using the current system, and the number of unique host addresses available to a single network of each class.

Address Class	Default Subnet Mask	Number of Networks	Number of Hosts
A	255.0.0.0	126	16,777,214
B	255.255.0.0	16,384	65,534
C	255.255.255.0	2,097,152	254

Table 13-2.   *Address Class Characteristics*

Note   *Two additional address classes are D and E. Class D addresses are typically used for multicasting, and Class E addresses are reserved for experimental use.*

On a practical level, this means that if you wanted to register your network in order to connect it to the Internet, you could obtain a class C address from an Internet authority. They would assign you a network address that you would use for the first three octets of all your IP addresses, such as 199.45.67. You would then be free to assign the 254 possible values for the fourth octet however you want, as long as there was no duplication. The subnet mask on all your machines would be 255.255.255.0, indicating that only the last octet is being used to identify the host.

If you had more than 254 nodes on your network, you would have to get another class C address. If you had a sufficiently large network to register, then you could possibly get a class B address, which would support up to 65,534 hosts. You would then assign the last two octets yourself and use a subnet mask of 255.255.0.0.

Save the Internet

When the Internet was conceived, no one had even the remote idea that it would become as popular a communications medium as it is today. The concepts and protocols used on the Internet were developed with scalability in mind, though, and it is a worthy testament to their creators that the system has far exceeded its intended design limits.

The time is rapidly approaching, however, when we must begin to think about conserving our Internet resources, just as we must be concerned about fossil fuels, clean water, and the rain forests. The time is past when we can blithely assign class B and C addresses to organizations that do not intend to fully make use of them.

There might soon come a time when you have to register a new network, and you turn on the Internet authority faucet to find that there are no more addresses to be had.

The time to begin conserving is now! Don't use registered addresses for every node on your network unless you have a genuine need to do so. Use one of the many firewall or proxy server products on the market to provide Internet services to users on your internal network. The users will have the same access they always had, you'll ensure the security of your network, and most of all, you'll be able to sleep at night, knowing that you are doing your part to preserve our dwindling Internet resources.

IP VERSION 6   One of the primary reasons for IPv6 is to accommodate the explosive growth of registered IP addresses. IPv6 is not exactly mainstream yet, but don't be surprised when you have to use the new IP addressing scheme because it's just around the corner.

IPv6, also known as IP Next Generation (IPng), is defined in RFC 1883. The principles behind IPv6 are similar to current IP addressing scheme (IPv4), but instead of using 32-bit addressing, it uses 128-bit addressing. As you can imagine, this significantly expands the number of available IP address. To accommodate the 128-bit addressing, IPv6 uses eight sets of four hexadecimal digits that are separated by a colon (:). So, an IPv6 IP address would look like this:

4321:0:1:2:3:4:567:89ab

This, and other changes defined in RFC 1886, affect DNS. RFC 1886:

- Defines the new resource record type, AAAA, that is equipped to handle the new 128-bit addressing format.

- Establishes ip6.int, which is the new reverse lookup (IP address to name mappings) namespace.

For more information on DNS, refer to Chapter 14.

What Is a Subnet?

Subnet masking is not always as simple as you have seen in the examples given thus far. Sometimes the dividing line between the network and the host portions of an IP address does not fall neatly between the octets.

A *subnet* is simply a logical subdivision imposed on a network address for organizational purposes. For example, a large corporation that has a registered class B network address is not likely to assign addresses to its nodes by numbering them consecutively from 0.0 to 255.555.

The more practical scenario would be to divide the network into a series of subnets, which are usually based on the wiring scheme of the facilities. By creating subnets corresponding to the Ethernet or token ring networks that make up the enterprise, the task of assigning and maintaining the IP addresses can be divided among the administrators responsible for each network.

Therefore, in this scenario, the class B network address would dictate the values of the first two octets of an IP address, and the subnet would dictate the value of the third octet, leaving the fourth to identify the host. The subnet mask in such a situation would be 255.255.255.0 because the first three octets are defining the network address, regardless of whether it is registered.

Suppose, however, that you have a class C address and you find yourself in the same situation. The first three octets of your IP addresses are dictated by the registered network address, but you still want to create subnets because your workstations are on several different network segments. You can still do this, if you again think of the subnet mask in binary terms. Instead of using the class C subnet mask as it stands, you can assign some of the bits in the fourth octet to the network address as well, like this:

```
1111111.11111111.11111111.11110000
```

Converting this address back to decimal form yields a subnet mask of 255.255.255.240. This arrangement enables you to define up to 14 network addresses (not 16, because values of all zeros or all ones are not allowed) composed of up to 14 hosts on each. You can alter the bit arrangement in favor of more networks or more hosts as needed. To assign network and host addresses using this method, it is a good idea to work out the proper values in binary form and then convert them to decimals to avoid errors. Because most humans do not think in binary terms, a good calculator is helpful in this task.

In most cases, the value for your workstation's subnet mask will be supplied to you along with your IP address, either by hand or through a DHCP server, especially if a complicated subnetting arrangement like this is being used. Remember, though, that subnetting is a local phenomenon. TCP/IP applications treat all IP addresses alike, regardless of which bits are used to identify the network.

Default Gateway

The default gateway setting on the Internet Protocol (TCP/IP) Properties page is the address of a gateway system on your local network segment that provides access to the rest of the internetwork. This can be a computer, a switch, or a router that joins two or more of the segments on your network. You can have more than one gateway on your local segment, but this is the one that your computer will use by default when trying to connect to a computer on another network.

If you can connect to other systems on the local network but not to those on other networks, then it is likely either that you have specified an incorrect value for the default gateway, or that the gateway itself is malfunctioning.

The use of the default gateway to access certain destinations can be automatically overridden in your workstation by the receipt of an ICMP redirect message, which would contain the address of another gateway that provides a more efficient route to the destination.

Advanced IP Addressing

As mentioned earlier, a computer can have more than one network interface, each of which must have its own TCP/IP configuration settings. The Internet Protocol (TCP/IP) Properties page of the Local Area Connection Properties window contains a selector that enables you to choose from the network adapters installed in your machine, so that you can provide the different settings needed for each.

It is also possible, however, to assign more than one IP address to a single network host adapter. When you click the Advanced button on the Internet Protocol (TCP/IP) Properties page, you are presented with the Advanced TCP/IP Settings dialog box (see Figure 13-6) under the IP Settings tab where you can enter additional addresses for each installed network adapter.

The most common scenario in which a user would want to assign multiple addresses to a single adapter is in the case of a machine used as a server on the Internet. You can, for example, run a World Wide Web (WWW) server, such as Internet Information Server 5 (see Chapter 23), on a Windows 2000 machine directly connected to the Internet and host Web sites for different customers, providing each site with its own IP address. Internet users could then access the different sites associated with each of the IP addresses, never knowing that they were all running on the same machine.

The IP Settings tab in the Advanced TCP/IP Settings dialog box also enables you to specify the addresses of additional gateways for each adapter. Unlike the additional IP

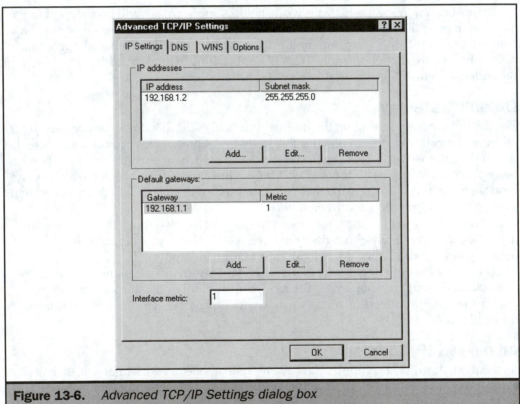

Figure 13-6.   *Advanced TCP/IP Settings dialog box*

addresses, however, which all remain active simultaneously, additional gateways are only used (in the order listed) when the primary default gateway is unreachable.

Preferred and Alternate DNS Servers

Many of you using Windows-based operating systems, especially those using Windows-only network environments, are accustomed to using DNS mainly for external resolution. Moreover, you may have never been responsible for DNS because it was always taken care of by your ISP rather than being managed internally. For instance, when you visit a Web site, you're using DNS to resolve a name (www.microsoft.com, for example) to its corresponding IP address. However, internal name resolution typically relies on NetBIOS and WINS, not DNS, to communicate with other computers on the network.

DNS has taken over the name resolution responsibility within Windows 2000 (see Chapter 14 for more information on DNS). Anytime you request to contact another computer on your network or on the Internet, DNS is the service providing the necessary name to IP address translation. Although NetBIOS is still supported by Windows 2000, it is still a part of the operating system primarily because of legacy applications and systems that rely on NetBIOS.

As a result of Windows 2000's dependence on DNS, you must configure all computers on your network to at least use a preferred DNS server. The alternate is recommended but optional. The preferred and secondary DNS servers' IP addresses can either be manually entered or you can allow DHCP to pass the information to clients.

 If you're using DHCP to configure clients (including assigning DNS IP addresses), make sure that you check the radio button beside Obtain DNS Server Address Automatically to ensure that client is getting the right information for using DNS.

Understanding DHCP

As mentioned earlier, TCP/IP users and administrators can avoid all the machine configuration chores discussed thus far in this chapter by using a Dynamic Host Configuration Protocol (DHCP) server to assign the configuration settings automatically.

To resolve the problem of IP address assignment and administration on a large scale, Microsoft worked with other networking professionals to create the Dynamic Host Configuration Protocol. DHCP is an open standard defined in the IETF's Requests for Comments. Other manufacturers market DHCP servers, but Microsoft includes theirs in the Windows 2000 Server package.

DHCP resolves some of the biggest problems inherent in TCP/IP, as it was originally conceived. It eliminates the chore of configuring every workstation individually, and it makes the assignment of duplicate IP addresses virtually impossible. The use of DHCP is recommended on all Windows 2000 networks, but only when it is used on all of the network's systems. Problems can arise when a mixed environment is created, in which some computers use DHCP while others do not. Even when you have systems that must be assigned a specific IP address, assign it using DHCP, if only for reasons of efficient record keeping.

Origins of DHCP

DHCP has its origins in BOOTP, and earlier protocol designed for use with diskless workstations. A BOOTP server stored IP addresses and other configuration settings for workstations, keyed according to the MAC address hard-coded into each workstation's network interface adapter. As a computer on the network was booted, its TCP/IP settings would be delivered to it by the server. After the TCP/IP stack was operational, BOOTP would transfer an executable operating system boot file to the workstation using TFTP (the Trivial File Transfer Protocol, a UDP version of FTP), and the workstation would then be ready for use.

BOOTP resolved one of TCP/IP's basic problems by eliminating the need for each workstation to be manually configured by an administrator or an end user. It did not really alleviate the administrative problem of IP address assignment, however, because it only provided a central location for the storage of the configuration settings. The IP settings for each individual workstation still had to be specified by the administrator and manually stored on the server. If duplicate IP addresses were accidentally entered into the configurations of two different machines, BOOTP could do nothing to detect, prevent, or remedy the situation.

IP Address Allocation

DHCP was designed to be an improvement over BOOTP. It retains the best aspects of its predecessor, which is the storage and automatic delivery of TCP/IP configuration data, and builds on it to create an even better solution.

DHCP is capable of assigning IP addresses to its clients in three different ways:

- **Manual allocation**   Essentially the equivalent of the BOOTP service, IP addresses and other configuration settings are individually entered by the administrator, stored on the server, and delivered to predetermined clients.

- **Automatic allocation**   This is what we call using a *static pool*. As a DHCP client workstation boots on the network for the first time, the DHCP server assigns it an IP address and other configuration settings from a pool of available addresses that the administrator has configured the server to use. These become the permanent settings for the machine.

- **Dynamic allocation**   This is the same as automatic allocation, except that the TCP/IP settings are not permanently assigned, but only leased for a specified amount of time. The lease must be periodically renewed through (automatic) negotiations between the DHCP client and the server.

These three methods can be used simultaneously, providing all the options that network administrators should require. Manual allocation is a necessary holdover from

BOOTP because often certain computers on the network must have a particular IP address permanently assigned, such as World Wide Web and ftp servers. The advantage to using DHCP for such computers (rather than simply configuring then manually) is that all IP address information for the entire network can be stored in one place, and that DHCP will prevent any other DHCP client from using the addresses that have been manually allocated.

A network that rarely changes can use DHCP to automatically allocate IP addresses, creating a permanent network configuration. If a computer is moved from one subnet to another, it will automatically be assigned a new IP address for that subnet. The address on the old subnet, however, will remain allocated until the administrator manually deletes the assignments from the DHCP table.

When a computer is dynamically allocated an IP address, its lease must be renewed periodically or it will expire, causing the address to be returned to the pool of available addresses. The lease renewal process is automatic and invisible to the user, unless it fails. If the computer is moved to a different subnet, it is assigned an appropriate IP address for its new location. The old address assignment is returned to the pool when its lease expires.

Thus, dynamic allocation resolved the problem of the "roving user," the portable computers that can be logged onto the network from different offices, different buildings, or even different cities.

Other DHCP Capabilities

The controlled allocation of IP addresses is clearly DHCP's primary strength, but an IP address alone is not sufficient to fully configure a client's TCP/IP stack. DHCP can also supply a client with settings for more than 50 other TCP/IP-related parameters, many of which are intended only for use with non-Microsoft clients.

A Windows 2000 or down-level DHCP client can be furnished with any or all of the following configuration parameters (these are the most common parameters passed to clients):

- **IP address** A 32-bit dotted decimal address used to identify a particular host on an IP network.

- **Subnet mask** A 32-bit dotted decimal value used to differentiate the network address bits of an IP address from the host address bits.

- **Router** The IP addresses of the default gateway systems that a client will use to access remote networks (accessed in the order they are listed).

- **DNS servers** The IP addresses of the DNS servers that will be used by a client to resolve Internet host names into IP addresses (accessed in the order they are listed).

- **Domain name** The name of the client's domain.

CONNECTING WITH
WINDOWS 2000

- **WINS/NBNS (Windows Internet Naming System/ NetBIOS Name Server) addresses** The IP addresses of the WINS servers that the client will use for NetBIOS name registration and resolution services.

- **WINS/NBT (Windows Internet Naming System/NetBIOS over TCP/IP) node type** A code used to specify which name resolution techniques will be used by the client, and in what order.

- **NetBIOS scope ID** A character string used to identify a group of NetBIOS machines that can communicate only with each other. (This is one to avoid; it almost always causes more problems than it's worth.)

There are several other parameters that are less commonly used than those listed above but which nonetheless may be useful to clients, depending on your environment. To name a few:

- Cookie servers
- LPR servers
- Impress servers
- Resource location servers
- Host name

New Features for DHCP in Windows 2000

Windows 2000 continues to improve upon the many TCP/IP-related services that it has inherited from previous versions. DHCP is no exception, and the following is a list of new features for DHCP:

- Integration of DHCP with DNS
- Enhanced monitoring and reporting
- Support for vendor-specific and user class options
- Multicast address allocation
- Detecting and preventing unauthorized DHCP servers
- AD integration
- Support for Windows 2000 Clustering Service
- Automatic client configuration

Automatic Client Configuration

Another noteworthy enhancement to Windows 2000's DHCP involves the DHCP client. Windows 2000 and Windows 98 clients configured to use DHCP can automatically configure themselves with an IP address and subnet mask in the event that a DHCP server can't be contacted. The procedure that the DHCP client service goes through before actually assigning itself this information depends on whether or not a DHCP server has previously been contacted.

After a fresh installation attempt, the DHCP client service attempts to find a DHCP server to get all the TCP/IP information necessary to function on the network. If the search fails, the client automatically configures itself with a Class B IP address and subnet mask. More specifically, it assigns itself with an IP address within the 169.254.0.0 to 169.254.255.255 address range with a subnet mask of 255.255.0.0. It then announces this address to the world to see if another computer already has taken this address. The client periodically (default is every five minutes) tries to contact a DHCP server until it's successful. Figure 13-7 illustrates this process.

The last procedure involves a client that has previously contacted and received TCP/IP information from a DHCP server. In this case, the client is contacting the DHCP server in order to renew a lease. If the client fails to contact the DHCP server, it pings its assigned default gateway. When the ping is successful, the client treats the failed communication with the DHCP server as a temporary setback and continues to use the lease that it has. For instance, the DHCP server could be down for maintenance or may have connectivity problems of its own. The client also continues to try to contact the DHCP server for a lease renewal. Only when the ping fails does the client automatically configure itself with the Class B IP address mentioned above.

DISABLING AUTOMATIC CLIENT CONFIGURATION   Automatic client configuration is definitely an improvement to the DHCP service. However, it does have its drawbacks. For example, would a client be able to contact other machines with the Class B IP address? In most cases, the answer would be no because of the subnet differences. The client would only be able to contact those computers on the same

CONNECTING WITH WINDOWS 2000

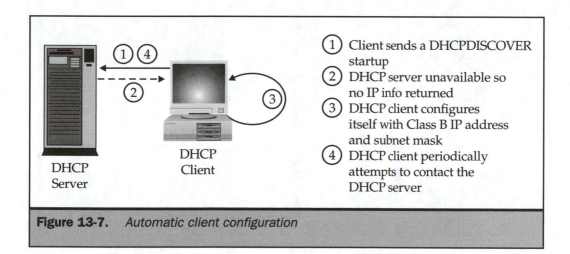

① Client sends a DHCPDISCOVER startup

② DHCP server unavailable so no IP info returned

③ DHCP client configures itself with Class B IP address and subnet mask

④ DHCP client periodically attempts to contact the DHCP server

DHCP Server

DHCP Client

Figure 13-7.   *Automatic client configuration*

subnet. Also, the client is unable to automatically configure itself with a default gateway or DNS server IP address that would help it communicate. Therefore, this feature is generally only useful in very small environments.

If you feel that this feature does not bring added benefit to your environment, you have the option to disable it. To disable automatic client configuration on a Windows 2000 computer, do the following:

■ From the Start | Run menu, type **REGEDT32** to start the Registry editor as shown in Figure 13-8.

```
Open
HKEY_LOCAL_MACHINE\SYSTEM\CurrentControlSet\Services\Tcpip\Paramete
rs\Interfaces\<Network Adapter>
```

Add the value IPAutoconfigurationEnabled and set it to 0.

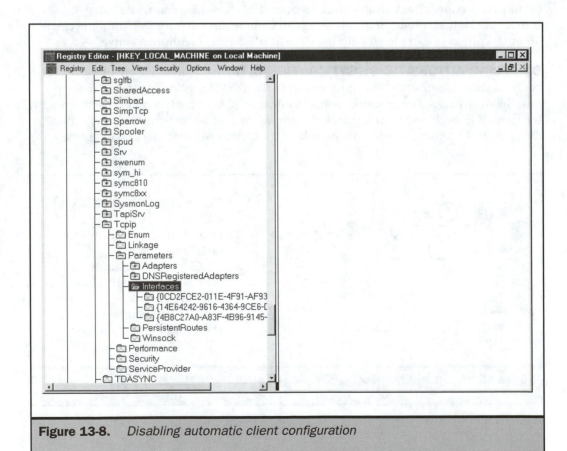

Figure 13-8.   *Disabling automatic client configuration*

Detecting and Preventing Unauthorized DHCP Servers

The DHCP service is a tremendous improvement over manually configuring IP addresses and other TCP/IP-related settings for every computer on the network. However, network administration can get pretty hairy when you have unauthorized DHCP servers contending with authorized DHCP servers for rights on who gets to pass information to clients. For instance, a user decides to install the DHCP Server service on his/her computer to pass information to a select few computers in a lab. As it turns out, what was intended to be a local DHCP server actually services other clients on the network. The change may render the clients useless.

Most of the time these situations are accidental, but they affect the network nonetheless. Previous versions of DHCP weren't able to adequately cope with such problems. Administrators had to keep on their toes to ensure that only the DHCP servers that they created and/or managed were allowed on the network.

One of the many enhancements to DHCP is the ability to detect and prevent unauthorized DHCP servers on the network. Each DHCP server installation must go through an authorization step either by checking with AD or by being led by someone with administrative privileges. Otherwise, the DHCP Server service is not allowed to service clients, and a message like the one in Figure 13-9 is displayed in the DHCP snap-in.

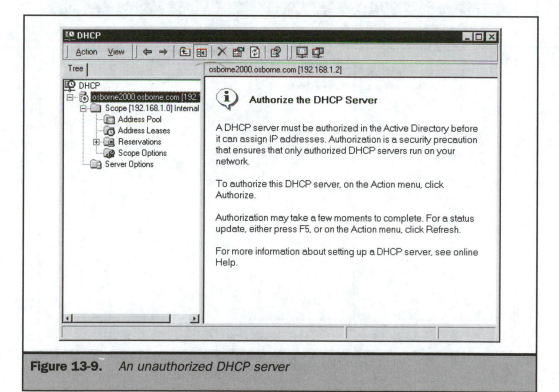

Figure 13-9. *An unauthorized DHCP server*

AD can store a list of authorized DHCP servers so that when a new DHCP server starts up, it tries to find out whether or not it's authorized. If it is authorized, it sends out DHCPINFORM messages to find out if it is authorized in other directory services as well. If the DHCP server isn't authorized but needs to be, you must do the following:

1. Within the DHCP snap-in, select the unauthorized DHCP server in the left pane.

2. Select Authorize from the Action menu.

3. You may have to wait several minutes before the authorization process finishes. If you're impatient like I am, you may want to hit F5 to refresh the DHCP snap-in window until you've been authorized (see Figure 13-10).

DHCP Communications

When a Windows 2000 or down-level client is configured to use DHCP to obtain its TCP/IP configuration settings, it undergoes a negotiation process with a DHCP server that results in a lease arrangement. The communications with the server are carried out

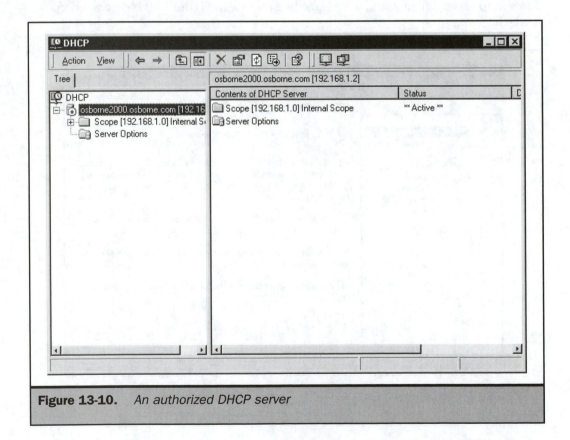

Figure 13-10.   *An authorized DHCP server*

using the protocol defined in the DHCP Request for Comment, published by the Internet Engineering Task Force (IETF).

The actual Dynamic Host Configuration Protocol consists of a single packet type that is used for all DHCP client/server communications. Carried by the User Datagram Protocol (UDP), the packet header contains a DHCP Message Type field that identifies the function of that packet, from among the choices shown in Table 13-3.

The various message types are used in the communications between DHCP servers and clients to allot IP addresses and periodically renew them, as detailed in the following sections.

Lease Negotiations

Before a lease has been negotiated, a potential DHCP client is operating a TCP/IP stack without an IP address, so its communication capabilities are obviously limited. It is able, however, to broadcast a DHCPDISCOVER message, in the hope of locating a DHCP server. Broadcasts are normally limited to the local network segment, but DHCP, being an open standard, is supported by many of the routers on the market, enabling them to propagate DHCP broadcasts across network boundaries. In this way, a single DHCP server can maintain clients on multiple network segments.

The DHCPDISCOVER packet contains the MAC address of the workstation, enabling DHCP servers to reply using unicasts rather than broadcasts. All DHCP servers receiving the broadcast are obliged to reply to the client with a DHCPOFFER packet containing an IP address and other configuration settings for the client's

Value	Message Type	Purpose
1	DHCPDISCOVER	Used by clients to locate DHCP servers
2	DHCPOFFER	Used by servers to offer IP addresses to clients
3	DHCPREQUEST	Used by clients to request a specific IP address
4	DHCPDECLINE	Used by clients to reject an offered IP address
5	DHCPACK	Used by servers to acknowledge a client's acceptance of an IP address
6	DHCPNAK	Used by servers to reject a client's acceptance of an IP address
7	DHCPRELEASE	Used by clients to terminate the lease of an IP address

Table 13-3. *Communication Characteristics Between the DHCP Server and Client*

consideration. If the client receives multiple DHCPOFFER packets, it selects one and broadcasts a DHCPREQUEST containing the IP address and settings that it intends to accept. This message is broadcast both to inform the selected server of its acceptance and to notify the other servers that their offers are being rejected.

During this period, the IP address offered by the server is not yet fully committed to that client. Under certain circumstances, those same settings might be offered to another potential client in the interim. Upon receiving a DHCPREQUEST, however, the server commits the offered settings to the client, writing them to its database and creating a *bound client.* It then sends a DHCPACK packet to the client, informing it of its acknowledgment. The exchanges involved in a successful lease negotiation are shown in the following illustration. If, for any reason, the lease cannot be finalized, the server sends a DHCPNACK packet, and the client begins the entire process again with a new DHCPDISCOVER packet.

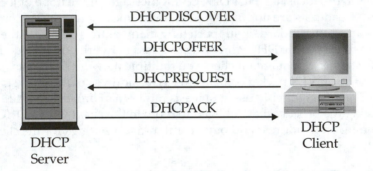

On receipt of the DHCPACK, the client performs a final check of the offered IP address using the Address Resolution Protocol to look for a duplicate address on the network. If one is found, the client sends a DHCPDECLINE packet to the server, nullifying the entire transaction. Otherwise, the settings are used to configure the TCP/IP stack and a network logon can commence.

Lease Renewal

After a lease has been negotiated, the DHCP client has the right to utilize the settings allocated to it for a period of time that is configured at the server. The default lease period is eight days, as shown in Figure 13-11. Each time the workstation logs onto the network, it renews the lease by broadcasting a DHCPREQUEST message containing the *lease identification cookie,* the combination of the workstation's MAC address and IP address that uniquely identifies the lease to the server.

Under normal conditions, the server replies with a DHCPACK message as before. If the server detects that the client is on a different subnet from the one where the lease was negotiated, it will issue a DHCPNACK message, terminating the lease and forcing a renegotiation. If the client receives no response to the request after ten attempts, it will broadcast a DHCPDISCOVER in the hope of negotiating a new lease.

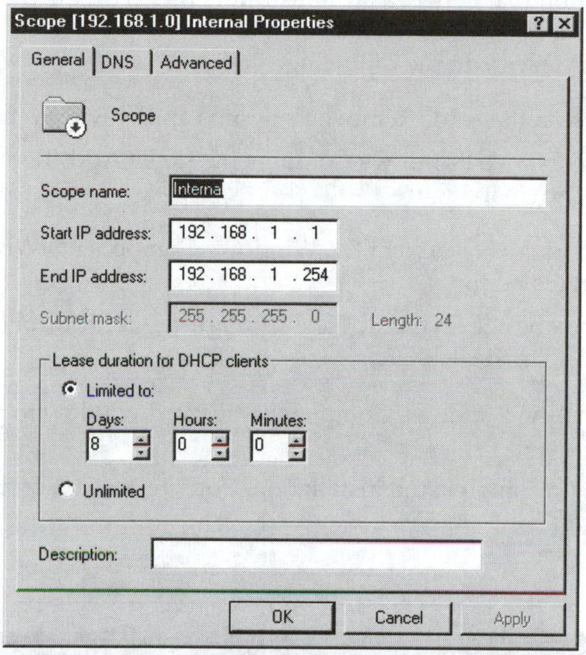

Figure 13-11.   *DHCP's default lease period*

CONNECTING WITH
WINDOWS 2000

If the client reaches the time at which 50 percent of its current lease period has expired, it moves from the *bound* state to the *renewing* state. DHCPREQUEST messages are then sent as unicasts to the server holding the lease rather than broadcasts. At 87.5 percent of the lease period, the client moves into the *rebinding* state, in which it begins broadcasting DHCPREQUEST messages again, soliciting a response from any DHCP server. If the entire lease period expires without a response from a DHCP server, the client enters the *unbound* state, and it goes through the process of automatically configuring itself with a Class B IP address and subnet mask.

Running the Microsoft DHCP Server

Microsoft's DHCP server consists of an application for managing, tracking, and allocating TCP/IP configuration settings and a protocol for delivering those settings to DHCP clients. The DHCP server that ships with Windows 2000 Server runs as a service after being installed through the Local Area Connections Properties page or through the Add/Remove Programs applet in the Control Panel. Also included is the DHCP snap-in, an application that network administrators use to define the configuration settings to be furnished to DHCP clients.

To install DHCP server, do the following:

1. Double-click on the Add/Remove Programs applet within the Control Panel.

2. Select Add/Remove Windows Components in the Add/Remove Programs window as shown in Figure 13-12.

3. Select Networking Services in the Windows Components Wizard window and click the Details button.

4. Check the box beside Dynamic Host Configuration Protocol (DHCP), as shown in Figure 13-13, and click OK.

5. Click Next in the Windows Components Wizard window to proceed to install the service.

6. Click Finish to complete the installation. You are now ready to configure the DHCP server.

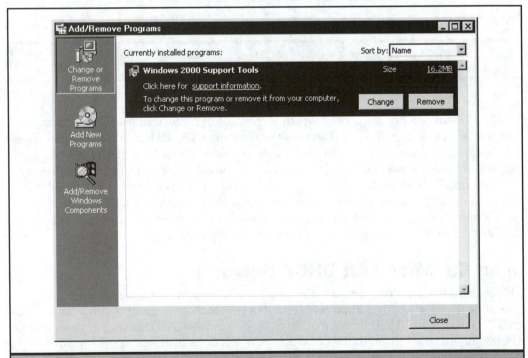

Figure 13-12.   *Add/Remove Programs window*

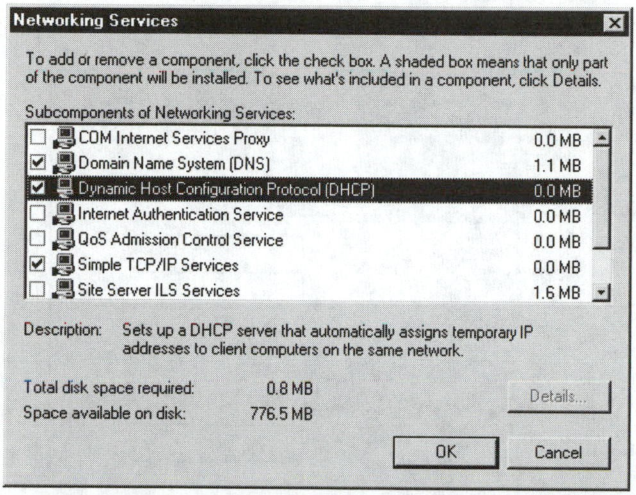

Figure 13-13.   *Installing DHCP*

Configuring Client to Use DHCP

When you elect to make a Windows 2000 machine into a DHCP client, you need to click the radio button on the Internet Protocol (TCP/IP) Properties page to have all the required TCP/IP configuration settings automatically assigned to your machine (as shown in Figure 13-14). In addition, the settings are all stored in a central location, the DHCP server, which prevents the need to manually maintain a record of IP address assignments.

Settings for many of a DHCP client's parameters (except the IP address and subnet mask) can also be applied at the client computer. A client-specified setting will always override one supplied by DHCP. For this reason, if you are converting computers from local configurations to DHCP, be sure to remove the existing, hard-coded TCP/IP settings on the client.

Configuring the DHCP Server

You configure TCP/IP settings in the DHCP Manager by creating scopes and then assigning properties to them. A *scope* is a collection of IP addresses that can be dynamically or automatically allocated to DHCP clients as needed. You create a scope by defining a range of consecutive IP addresses in the New Scope dialog box (see Figure 13-15) and specifying the subnet mask that should be supplied with them. If necessary, you can exclude some of the addresses in the range from allocation. You can also modify the duration of the leases that will be negotiated between clients and the server.

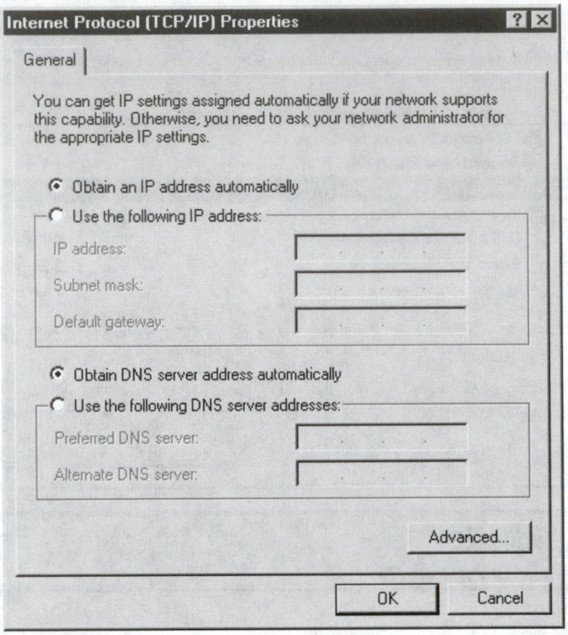

Internet Protocol (TCP/IP) Properties   [?] [X]

General

You can get IP settings assigned automatically if your network supports this capability. Otherwise, you need to ask your network administrator for the appropriate IP settings.

(•) Obtain an IP address automatically

( ) Use the following IP address:

IP address:

Subnet mask:

Default gateway:

(•) Obtain DNS server address automatically

( ) Use the following DNS server addresses:

Preferred DNS server:

Alternate DNS server:

Advanced...

OK   Cancel

Figure 13-14. *Configuring a client to use DHCP*

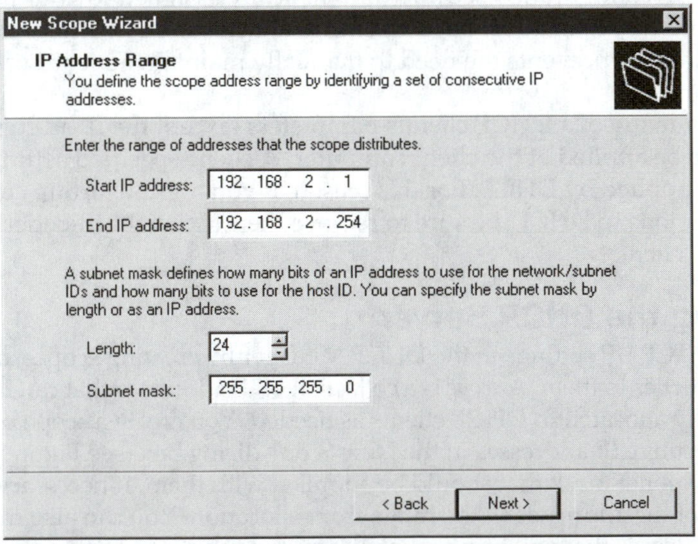

New Scope Wizard   [X]

IP Address Range
You define the scope address range by identifying a set of consecutive IP addresses.

Enter the range of addresses that the scope distributes.

Start IP address: 192 . 168 . 2 . 1

End IP address: 192 . 168 . 2 . 254

A subnet mask defines how many bits of an IP address to use for the network/subnet IDs and how many bits to use for the host ID. You can specify the subnet mask by length or as an IP address.

Length: 24

Subnet mask: 255 . 255 . 255 . 0

< Back   Next >   Cancel

Figure 13-15. *Defining a scope's IP address range*

Note *You can configure the DHCP server, but it won't start servicing clients until you authorize it.*

After you have created a scope, you define the additional settings (from the list shown in the earlier section "Other DHCP Capabilities") that you want to deliver along with scopes, or specify only the options to be delivered with the addresses of a particular scope. The reason for these options is that separate scopes would typically have to be defined for each subnet on your network because certain settings (such as default gateways) would necessarily differ.

A typical medium-sized network, for example, might consist of several subnets and for each you would create a scope. Settings like those for the domain name, the DNS servers, and the WINS/NBT node are probably going to be the same for all the clients in the enterprise, so they are best defined as global options. Routers and WINS/NBNS servers will more likely have to be defined as scope options, as there might be different values for different scopes. Figure 13-16 shows an example of the options that can be defined within a scope.

It is up to the administrator to supply correct settings for all the required TCP/IP configuration parameters. The objective is usually to provide clients with a complete TCP/IP configuration solution, but any settings that are omitted or incorrectly configured will cause TCP/IP communications at the client to malfunction without warning.

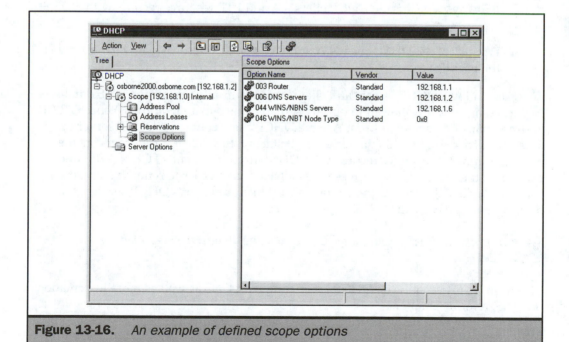

Figure 13-16. *An example of defined scope options*

CONNECTING WITH
WINDOWS 2000

A DHCP server cannot itself use DHCP to obtain its own TCP/IP configuration (even from another DHCP server). Its settings must be manually configured in the Internet Protocol (TCP/IP) Properties dialog box.

DHCP and Name Resolution

As you will learn in the following sections, another major concern when using TCP/IP on the enterprise internetwork is name resolution. Just as DHCP maintains a listing of its clients' MAC addresses and their equivalent IP addresses, so there must be a means to equate IP addresses with host names assigned to all computers in a Windows 2000 network environment. Equally important is equating IP addresses with any NetBIOS names from down-level clients.

DHCP and DNS

DHCP has a rather interesting relationship with DNS because it isn't necessarily just responsible for passing a DNS IP address to the client. Instead, DHCP can be made responsible for registering clients when Dynamic DNS (DDNS) and the DHCP option code 81 are enabled. Option code 81 allows for DHCP clients to return their fully qualified domain name (FQDN) to the DHCP server. In turn, the DHCP server can register clients with DDNS or the clients themselves can register with the name resolution service. This option code gives the DHCP server three options for processing DDNS information for a DHCP client:

- It always registers the DHCP client's A and PTR resource records with DDNS.
- It never registers DHCP client's A resource record.
- It registers the DHCP client's A and PTR resource records with DDNS only at the client's request.

DDNS allows DHCP servers and clients to dynamically update the DNS database. In particular, they are allowed to update A (name maps to an IP address) and PTR (IP address maps to a name) records. When a DHCP client contacts a DHCP server to obtain network configuration parameters at startup, the DHCP server registers the client's A and PTR resource records with DDNS from the client's FQDN. With one exception, the same process applies when a DHCP client tries to renew a lease. It contacts the DHCP server to get a renewal, but then the client's DHCP service can perform the update with DDNS.

 It is imperative that you test the DHCP and DDNS interactions with down-level clients.

For more information on DHCP interacting with DNS as well as more information on DNS, refer to Chapter 14.

DHCP and WINS

DHCP, in resolving the problem of IP address administration, exacerbates the problem of NetBIOS name resolution. When IP addresses are automatically or dynamically allocated to network clients, it becomes all but impossible for the network administrator to keep up with the ever-changing assignments. For that reason, WINS, the Window Internet Naming System, works together with DHCP to provide an automatic NetBIOS name server that is updated whenever DHCP assigns a new IP address. On a Windows 2000 network running DHCP, WINS is a necessity only when NetBIOS is still present (the presence of down-level clients).

For more information, see the sections on "WINS Name Registration" and "WINS Name Resolution" later in this chapter.

Understanding Name Registration and Resolution

When it comes to network communications, the TCP/IP protocols are entirely reliant on IP addresses for the identification of other systems. In addition, host names and NetBIOS names are used to identify networked computers so that it's easier to contact other computers. It would be extremely difficult, if not impossible, to remember the IP address for every computer or every Web site that you want to contact. And this is assuming that the IP addresses will never change!

Microsoft operating systems prior to Windows 2000, such as Windows NT, have always based their network communications on NetBIOS names. Windows 2000 still permits NetBIOS for compatibility, but it is designed to work with host names instead of NetBIOS names. Either way, there must be mechanisms by which these various names can be equated with IP addresses.

Several mechanisms, with varying levels of sophistication, can be used by Windows 2000 to accomplish these tasks; but they all can be reduced to what is ultimately a database containing the names and their equivalent addresses. The differences in the mechanisms center on the methods used to get the information into the database and the ways in which it is retrieved. These two tasks are known as *name registration* and *name resolution*, respectively.

If you are running a Windows 2000 network with down-level clients, you will need to have at least two separate name resolution mechanisms. Host names and NetBIOS names are always treated separately in this respect, even if a computer uses the same name for both. If your network doesn't use down-level clients or NetBIOS-based applications, you can dispense with the NetBIOS names.

The following sections examine the various mechanisms that can be used by Windows 2000 for the registration and resolution of both host names and NetBIOS names. For host names, these mechanisms are listed here:

- The HOSTS file
- The Domain Name Service

For NetBIOS names, the mechanisms are

- Network Broadcasts
- The Windows Internet Naming Service (WINS)
- The LMHOSTS file

All Windows-based computers use at least one of these mechanisms during every TCP/IP exchange over the network that uses a name instead of an IP address. Understanding how they work can help you maximize the efficiency of your network and keep network traffic levels to a minimum.

For a complete understanding of host names, domain hierarchy, DNS, and more, refer to Chapter 14.

Host Names

The TCP/IP protocols were initially developed for use on the Internet, and one of the requirements for their design was that they be completely self-sufficient in their addressing. Because they were going to be used on a wide variety of computing platforms, the existence of a MAC address, such as is found on all Ethernet and token ring adapters, could not be taken as a given. An IP address is therefore assigned to every host on a TCP/IP network, providing an ideal means of identification for the computers doing the communicating.

IP addresses have, unfortunately, proven to be a less than ideal means of computer identification for humans. Think of how many World Wide Web and ftp servers you know by their host names, such as www.intel.com and ftp.microsoft.com, and imagine having to remember up to 12 digits for each one instead. Internet host names were devised solely as a means to provide friendly names for the user interface.

As you saw earlier in this chapter, the IP header does not carry the host names of the source and destination computers, only the IP addresses. Whenever an application, such as a Web browser or an ftp client, attempts to connect to another computer whose host name has been specified by the user, the first step in the process is to resolve the name into an IP address.

Because they are not directly associated with the TCP/IP communications processes, host names can be considered independently of IP addresses. For example, a computer with a single network adapter and one IP address can have many host names. You can run a Web server, an ftp server, and a DNS on the same machine and use a different host name for each, with all of them pointing to the same IP address.

Domain Names

A host name consists of several words separated by periods. There are two or more domain names that identify the organization running the network, plus a name that identifies the specific computer. The names are organized hierarchically, with the most specific name (that is, the computer's name) first, followed by the domain names. The last word always specifies the top-level domain name.

The purpose of this arrangement is to distribute the task of administering the host names among each of the organizations running Internet computers. This way, no one body or organization is saddled with the task of administering the entire Internet, which would today be a Herculean labor.

> **Note**   *As with IP addresses, every computer's host name must be unique.*

Using a HOSTS File

The simplest way to resolve host names is to maintain a table of those names and their equivalent IP addresses. That is all that a HOSTS file is—an ASCII file, stored on the local hard drive, that lists IP addresses on the left and host names on the right. When a user supplies an application with a host name, it looks it up in the HOSTS file. If the name is found, its equivalent IP address is used to create the network connection. If it is not found, the operation fails.

At one time, name resolution services for the entire Internet were provided through a single HOSTS table containing thousands of entries that had to be regularly downloaded by Internet users to upgrade their systems.

The problems with this method are obvious. The name registration method—that is, the means by which the names and addresses are inserted into the file—is wholly manual. Users or administrators must individually modify or upgrade the HOSTS file on every network computer to include the name and address of every host to be contacted by name. Also, as the number of entries increases, the file can quickly become unwieldy and name resolution performance begins to suffer. Can you imagine trying to manage your company's HOSTS file with hundreds, if not thousands, of name-to-IP-address mappings? Each change to the file would require all computers on the network to get an update, meaning that the entire HOSTS file would need to be transferred to each of them.

Using the Domain Name System

The Domain Name System, or DNS, is the more commonly used method of Internet host name resolution because it enables users to connect to any site anywhere on the Internet, by name. This might seem like an incredible feat, particularly in light of the Internet's growth in the past few years, but the DNS takes advantage of, and is indeed the primary reason for, the domain-based structure of Internet host names.

The Domain Name System consists of thousands of DNS servers located all over the Internet. When you register a domain name, you are required to specify a primary and a backup DNS server. These are known as the *authoritative servers* for your domain. A DNS server is a UNIX daemon or a Windows 2000 service that is responsible for maintaining and publishing a database of the host names and addresses in its own domain.

A domain's DNS servers do not necessarily have to be located on its local network. Many Internet Service Providers (ISPs) will provide the use of their DNS servers for a fee. What's important is that an Internet authority, or whatever other body has registered the domain name, has a record of the DNS servers responsible for that domain's hosts.

Because individual network administrators are responsible for assigning the host names within their domains, they must also be responsible for maintaining the DNS records of those names. Surprisingly, the registration of a domain's host names in its DNS servers is no less of a manual operation than in a HOSTS file. If you add a new ftp server to your network, for example, you must manually add or edit a DNS resource record, specifying the name and address of the new machine.

Windows 2000's DNS, however, has adopted the new technology of dynamically registering computers instead of tediously, manually updating resource records. Clients are able to have their host (A) and pointer (PTR) resource records registered automatically with the DNS server. Also, Windows 2000's DNS can be integrated with AD, which enhances security, replication of the DNS database, administration, and much more. Chapter 14 covers DNS and related topics in great detail.

How DNS Resolves Host names

When a client supplies the host name of a remote system in a TCP/IP application, the first step taken by the application is to resolve the name. It does this by using built-in code libraries called the *resolver* to obtain the IP address of the DNS server that it should use from the computer's TCP/IP configuration settings. The client then sends a name resolution request to the first DNS server specified.

If the name to be resolved is located on the local domain, then the DNS functions like a networked HOSTS file. It looks up the name in its own tables and returns the IP address to the client. If the name is not in the local domain, however, the DNS will fail to find a listing for it (unless it is cached in the DNS from a previous query). The DNS then forwards the request to the core servers at the host name's top-level domain. The IP addresses of the core servers for the standard U.S. top-level domains (.com, .edu, .mil, .org, .net, and .gov) are preconfigured into the DNS server.

When a host name query is forwarded to one of the core servers by a DNS, its reply contains only the IP address of the authoritative server for the domain on which the host is located. The client's DNS then sends another query to that authoritative server, which returns the IP address of the actual machine using the host name.

To prevent repeated queries on the same names, a DNS server also caches the information for the host names that it has resolved. This is one reason why you might notice a delay when connecting to a new machine over the Internet, although commonly used sites are accessed more quickly.

The DNS might seem like a fairly complex mechanism for what is essentially a simple task, but remember that it was designed to be a scalable solution at a time when the Internet was less than a tenth of its current size. That it has continued to be an effective means of registering and resolving host names after all the growth it has undergone demonstrates the excellence of its design.

NetBIOS Names

Although NetBIOS is no longer required on a Windows 2000 network, it is essential for backward compatibility with older Windows-based systems, such as Windows 9x and Windows NT, that use NetBIOS to communicate. Therefore, Windows 2000 still is able to support those systems and applications that require NetBIOS.

NetBIOS is a software interface that has been used for many years to provide network communication capabilities to applications. Some of the original Windows NT networking architecture that has been incorporated into Windows 2000 relied solely on NetBIOS's own naming system to identify other computers on the network.

A NetBIOS name consists of 16 characters, the last of which Windows 2000 reserves to identify the special functions of certain computers, such as domain controllers or browsers. When NetBIOS is enabled, every computer is assigned a NetBIOS name by the operating system. The name might or might not correspond to the user's logon name or the computer's host name. You use NetBIOS names whenever you type a UNC pathname that refers to a Windows network system such as the one shown in Figure 13-17.

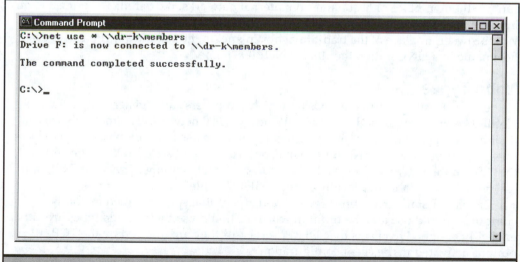

Figure 13-17.   *Connecting to a machine using its UNC pathname*

CONNECTING WITH
WINDOWS 2000

NetBIOS is no longer a necessity unless you have down-level clients or NetBIOS-dependent applications, but it is still an integral part of Windows 2000 networking. The Workstation and Server services that run on all Windows 2000 computers use NetBIOS as well as *direct hosting* to provide the core file-sharing services needed from any network operating system. Direct hosting is a protocol that uses DNS for name resolution rather than NetBIOS. The default configuration is that both NetBIOS and direct hosting are enabled and are used simultaneously to resolve names for new connections with other machines.

Because it runs above the Transport Device Interface, NetBIOS can theoretically use any compatible protocols for its lower-level communications needs. Originally, operating systems prior to Windows 2000 used NetBEUI (the NetBIOS Extended User Interface) to carry its NetBIOS traffic. NetBEUI is not routable, however, so when TCP/IP was proposed as an alternative, networking authorities began work on an open standard (later published as an RFC) to define the way in which NetBIOS services could be provided using the TCP/IP protocols. This standard became known as NetBIOS over TCP/IP, or NetBT.

The NetBT standard defines two kinds of NetBIOS services: session and datagram. Session services use TCP to provide fully reliable, connection-oriented message transmissions, whereas datagram services use UDP and are subject to the low overhead and relative unreliability of the protocol.

The network service requests generated by the NetBIOS interface use the NetBIOS computer names to refer to other systems. For TCP/IP to carry requests over the network, the NetBIOS names, like host names, must first be resolved into IP addresses.

Because NetBIOS names are resolved into IP addresses before transmission, you can use them in place of host names on internal networks, if desired. To connect to an intranet Web server, for example, a user can specify the server's NetBIOS name in a Web browser, in place of the traditional host name. In the same way, you can use a host name in a UNC path rather than a NetBIOS name.

Node Types

There are several different methods by which computers can register and resolve NetBIOS names into IP addresses on a Windows 2000 network. The methods vary in their capabilities and their efficiency. A computer can use network broadcasts to locate the system with a specific NetBIOS name; or it can consult a NetBIOS Name Server (NBNS) on the network, such as the Windows Internet Naming Service (WINS); or it can use a lookup table in a locally stored LMHOSTS file.

The NetBT standard defines several node types that specify which methods a computer should use and the order in which it should use them. Node types are either explicitly assigned to clients by a DHCP server, or they are inferred by the TCP/IP options activated in the client configuration.

The node defined in the NetBT standard document is as follows:

- **B-node**   The client uses network broadcasts for both name registration and resolution.

- **P-node**   The client directs unicast communications to a NetBIOS Name Server for name registration and resolution.

- **M-node**   The client uses broadcasts for name registration; for name resolution, the client uses broadcasts first and if unsuccessful, directs unicast communications to a NetBIOS Name Server.

- **H-node**   The client directs unicast communications to a NetBIOS name server for both name registration and resolution; if the NBNS is unavailable, the client uses broadcasts until an NBNS is contacted.

Originally, operating systems prior to Windows 2000 provided enhanced B-node service for NetBIOS name registration and resolution. The service was enhanced because if the broadcast method failed to resolve a name, the computer's LMHOSTS file was consulted as an alternative. This enabled users to contact systems on other network segments, as long as they had been manually entered into LMHOSTS.

Windows 2000 still includes WINS (see Figure 13-18), a NetBIOS name server that can store the NetBIOS names and IP addresses for an entire internetwork in its database, making them available to users all over the enterprise. When they use WINS,

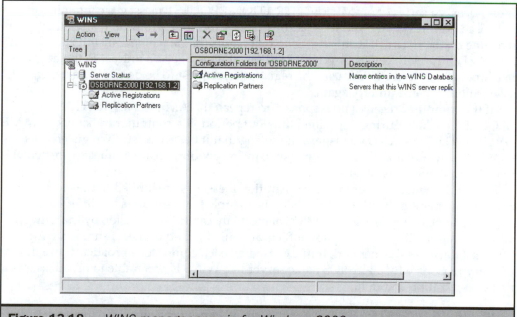

Figure 13-18.   *WINS manager snap-in for Windows 2000*

down-level computers are said to be enhanced H-nodes. They first attempt to resolve NetBIOS names using WINS, revert to broadcasts if WINS is unsuccessful or unavailable, and then consult the LMHOSTS file if broadcasts fail to resolve the name.

NetBIOS Name Registration

Whenever a down-level machine logs onto the network, it is required by the NetBT standard to register its NetBIOS name, to ensure that no other system is using a duplicate name and that the IP address is correct. If you move a workstation to another subnet and manually change its IP address, the registration process ensures that other systems and WINS servers are all aware of the change.

The name registration method used by the workstation depends on its node type. B-nodes and M-nodes use broadcast transmissions to register their names, whereas H-nodes and P-nodes send unicast messages directly to the WINS server. These two methods are discussed in the following sections. One of the two is used by every down-level system that is connected to the network.

BROADCAST NAME REGISTRATION   A system that uses broadcasts to register its NetBIOS name (B-nodes and M-nodes) does not perform a registration in the same sense as the other node types. The name is not entered into a table or stored on other network systems. Instead, the system uses broadcasts to "claim" its NetBIOS name and check to see if any other system is already using it.

The registration process begins as soon as the computer logs onto the network. It broadcasts a series of NAME REGISTRATION REQUEST messages containing its proposed NetBIOS name and its IP address, using the UDP protocol. If any other machine on the network is already using that name, that machine transmits a NEGATIVE NAME REGISTRATION RESPONSE message as a unicast to the new machine's IP address. This causes the registration request to be denied. The user must select another name and try again.

If the computer receives no responses to repeated NAME REGISTRATION REQUEST packets during a specified time-out period, the computer transmits a NAME OVERWRITE DEMAND message, announcing that it has successfully registered its name. That workstation is now responsible for responding to any requests directed at that NetBIOS name by other systems.

Like all broadcasts, these name registration messages are limited to the local network segment only. This means that it is possible for computers on different networks to be using the same NetBIOS name. Only careful supervision by the networks' administrators will prevent name conflicts and misdirected packets from occurring. This and the excessive network traffic caused by each computer's broadcasts are the primary reasons why a NetBIOS name server like WINS is preferable to broadcasts as a name registration solution.

WINS NAME REGISTRATION   A WINS client computer begins its name registration procedure by generating the same NAME REGISTRATION REQUEST packet used in the broadcast method. This time, however, the packet is sent as a unicast directly to the WINS server specified in the WINS Configuration tab of the Microsoft TCP/IP Properties dialog box (see Figure 13-19). If no other system is using the name, the WINS server returns a POSITIVE NAME REGISTRATION RESPONSE to the sender and writes the NetBIOS name and IP address to its database.

If the WINS server finds that another system has already registered that NetBIOS name, the WINS server challenges that system to defend its registered name by sending it a NAME QUERY REQUEST message. If the system does not respond or sends a NEGATIVE NAME QUERY RESPONSE, then the WINS server registers the name to the new system and sends it a POSITIVE NAME REGISTRATION RESPONSE. If the challenged system returns a POSITIVE NAME QUERY RESPONSE, then it has successfully defended its name against the challenge. WINS then sends a NEGATIVE NAME REGISTRATION RESPONSE message to the original system, informing it that its registration attempt has failed.

When WINS successfully registers a NetBIOS name, it assigns an expiration date to the registration in the form of a time-to-live (TTL) value. Each time the system logs onto the network, the value is renewed. Until that time period expires, any attempt to register that NetBIOS name will be challenged. If no logons occur in the specified time period, however, the NetBIOS name is released and will be reassigned by the WINS

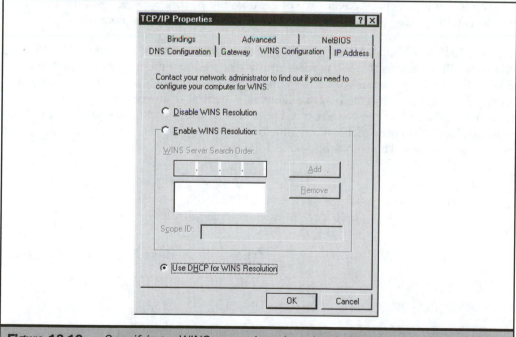

Figure 13-19.   *Specifying a WINS server in a down-level client*

server on demand, with no challenge. If the name remains unused for a specified time period, it is declared extinct and purged from the WINS database.

Notice that this entire transaction is conducted using unicast messages between the three computers involved. There are no broadcasts flooding the network at all. This is one of the primary advantages of WINS.

NetBIOS Name Resolution

All Windows 2000 and down-level systems maintain a cache of NetBIOS names that they have previously resolved if NetBIOS is enabled. When a computer has to resolve a NetBIOS name, the cache is always consulted first. If the name is not found in the cache, the next resolution method used is determined by the system's node type. A non-WINS client will proceed to use broadcasts to resolve the name and then consult its local LMHOSTS file.

A WINS client can use all of the available methods to resolve NetBIOS names. It begins by consulting the NetBIOS name cache, and then proceeds to the WINS server. Broadcasts are used next if the WINS server fails, and then the LMHOSTS file.

 Remember that NetBIOS and DNS name resolution is done simultaneously. If first attempts fail to resolve the name, broadcasts are used.

The following sections cover each of the possible NetBIOS name resolution methods in the order that they would be used by a WINS-enabled computer.

THE NETBIOS NAME CACHE   During each network session, a client system stores all the NetBIOS names that it has successfully resolved in a memory cache so that they can be reused. Because it is stored in memory, the cache is by far the fastest and most efficient name resolution method available. It is the first resource accessed by all node types when they must resolve a name. You can view the current contents of your system's NetBIOS name cache at any time by using the nbtstat -c command in a Command Prompt. The results appear as follows:

```
c:\>nbtstat -c
Node IpAddress: [194.10.34.8] Scope Id: []
                NetBIOS Remote Cache Name Table
```

Name		Type	Host Address	Life[sec]
FTP.MICROSOFT.COM	<03>	UNIQUE	198.105.232.1	-1
FTP.MICROSOFT.COM	<00>	UNIQUE	198.105.232.1	-1
FTP.MICROSOFT.COM	<20>	UNIQUE	198.105.232.1	-1
SMITHJ	<03>	UNIQUE	167.171.2.56	-1

Name		Type	Host Address	Life[sec]
SMITHJ	<00>	UNIQUE	167.171.2.56	-1
SMITHJ	<20>	UNIQUE	167.171.2.56	-1
ACCTGSERVER	<03>	UNIQUE	167.171.4.37	-1
ACCTGSERVER	<00>	UNIQUE	167.171.4.37	-1
ACCTGSERVER	<20>	UNIQUE	167.171.4.37	-1
SALES3	<03>	UNIQUE	167.171.2.120	-1
SALES3	<00>	UNIQUE	167.171.2.120	-1
SALES3	<20>	UNIQUE	167.171.2.120	-1

The NetBIOS name cache is erased whenever the computer is shut down or logged off the network. This ensures that the data in the cache is always up to date. You can use an LMHOSTS file to preload often-used NetBIOS names and their IP addresses into the cache, making them immediately available for use at all times (see "Using an LMHOSTS File," later in this chapter).

WINS NAME RESOLUTION   WINS is designed to be an enterprise network solution for the registration and resolution of NetBIOS names. It is the only mechanism available to a Windows 2000 network that automatically maintains a database of a network's NetBIOS names and their IP addresses. Unlike the broadcast method, WINS uses only unicast network transmissions, enabling it to function irrespective of the boundaries between network segments and greatly reducing the overall network traffic generated by NetBIOS name resolution activities.

WINS is supplied with the Windows 2000 Server product, where it runs as a service. A WINS snap-in manager application is included, as shown in Figure 13-18, enabling you to manage all the WINS servers on an enterprise network from a central location. For speed and fault tolerance, you can run several WINS servers on an enterprise network. The WINS databases can be automatically replicated among the servers at preset intervals or at specified times of day. You can, therefore, schedule WINS replication to occur over WAN links during low-traffic periods, providing a unified enterprise database for a worldwide network.

WINS also provides its clients with the capability to browse machines on other network segments, without requiring the services of master browsers on those networks. This enables users to easily communicate with other machines at remote sites without wasting WAN bandwidth on browser traffic.

When a WINS client needs a NetBIOS name resolved, it sends a unicast NAME QUERY REQUEST to the first WINS server specified in the WINS Address page of its Microsoft TCP/IP Properties dialog box. The WINS server then replies with a POSITIVE NAME QUERY RESPONSE containing the requested name and its IP address, or a NEGATIVE NAME QUERY RESPONSE, signifying that there is no record of the name in the database.

If there is any delay in responding, the WINS server will send WACK (or WAIT FOR ACKNOWLEDGMENT RESPONSE) packets to the client so that it will not proceed to the next resolution method.

If the WINS server fails to resolve the name, whether by sending a negative response or no response at all, the client contacts its secondary WINS server and repeats the process. If the secondary server fails, an H-node system proceeds to use broadcasts to resolve the name. If the WINS servers have failed to respond at all to resolution requests, however, the client will continue attempting to contact them and revert back to WINS name resolution at the earliest possible opportunity.

BROADCAST NAME RESOLUTION   When NetBIOS names are resolved using broadcasts, it is the responsibility of all registered systems to respond to requests specifying their names. A computer using broadcast name resolution generates the same NAME QUERY REQUEST packet as a WINS client, except that it is broadcast to all the systems on the local subnet. Each system receiving the packet must examine the name carried within, for which the IP address is requested.

If the packet contains an unrecognized name, it is silently discarded. A computer recognizing its own name in a query request, however, must respond to the sender with a POSITIVE NAME QUERY RESPONSE packet containing its IP address, sent as a unicast.

The broadcast method of name resolution is attempted by all down-level systems that are not WINS clients, after the name cache is consulted. If the name to be resolved belongs to a system on another network segment, the broadcasts cannot reach it, and the method will fail after the broadcast timeout period is reached.

USING AN LMHOSTS FILE   When an attempt to resolve a NetBIOS name using broadcasts fails, the next alternative is to consult the LMHOSTS file on the local hard drive. Non-WINS clients do this automatically. For a WINS client to use LMHOSTS after both the WINS and broadcasts methods fail, you must check the Enable LMHOSTS Lookup check box in the WINS Address page of the Microsoft TCP/IP Properties dialog box as shown in Figure 13-20.

Use of the LMHOSTS file is not included in the NetBT standard as part of the node type definitions. Clients are therefore referred to as enhanced B-node and H-node systems when they use LMHOSTS.

An LMHOSTS file is similar to the HOSTS file used for host name resolution except that it lists NetBIOS names instead. It is located in the same directory as HOSTS, \%systemroot%\system32\drivers\etc, and Windows 2000 as well as down-level provides a sample file called LMHOSTS.SAM for you to use as a model for your own file.

For a system that is not a WINS client, LMHOSTS is the only name resolution method available for computers on other network segments. You register the NetBIOS names in LMHOSTS by manually editing the file and adding an entry for each system you will be contacting. Each entry should contain the system's IP address at the left

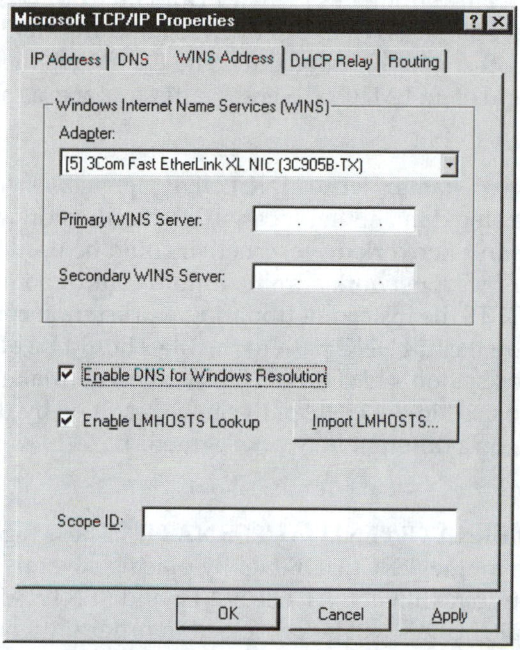

Figure 13-20. *Enabling LMHOSTS name resolution*

margin followed by the associated NetBIOS name on the same line, separated by at least one space.

Unlike HOSTS, LMHOSTS files can contain additional options that aid in the name resolution process. These options are as follows:

■ **#PRE** The #PRE tag, when added to an entry in the LMHOSTS file, causes that entry to be preloaded into the NetBIOS name cache whenever the system boots. Adding your most commonly accessed systems to the LMHOSTS file in this way will speed up name resolution, even for WINS clients. The #PRE tag should be appended to the end of an LMHOSTS entry, with one or more spaces separating it from the NetBIOS name, as shown:

```
139.41.129.8  smithj  #pre
```

■ **#DOM:<domain name>** The #DOM tag used is used to associate an LMHOSTS entry with the Windows NT domain specified in the *<domain name>* variable. This causes the computer in this entry to receive the domain browse list from the specified domain's Primary Domain Controller (PDC). That way, computers that don't use WINS can browse the computers in the domain that are located on other network segments. The #DOM tag, with its variable, is placed at the end of an LMHOSTS entry, after a space, as shown:

```
139.41.129.8  smithj  #DOM
```

■ **#INCLUDE <path name>**   The #INCLUDE tag enables you to access an LMHOSTS file stored in another location. Typically, you would use this feature to access a file on a network drive, where it could be used by other clients at the same time. That way, network administrators could update a single, centrally located LMHOSTS file instead of updating workstation copies individually. The tag, followed by the full UNC path to the file, should be placed on a line of its own in the workstation's LMHOSTS file, as shown. (Make sure that the NetBIOS name used in the UNC path can be resolved by using the #PRE tag if the machine is on a different network segment.)

```
#INCLUDE \\server1\share\etc\lmhosts
```

■ **#BEGIN_ALTERNATE/#END_ALTERNATE**   These tags are used to provide fault tolerance for the #INCLUDE tag. By placing several #INCLUDE statements between #BEGIN_ALTERNATE and #END_ALTERNATE tags, as shown, the #INCLUDEs will be processed in order until one is successfully accessed. After one #INCLUDE is successfully read, those following are ignored, and processing continues at the next line after the #END_ALTERNATE statement.

```
#BEGIN_ALTERNATE
#INCLUDE\\server1\share\etc\lmhosts
#INCLUDE\\server2\share\etc\lmhosts
#END_ALTERNATE
```

■ **\Oxhh**   This tag is used to specify special characters in NetBIOS names by their hexadecimal values. If an application requires a certain character in the NetBIOS name's 16th position, you can supply it by enclosing the name in quotation marks and using \Oxhh (replacing hh with the hexadecimal value of the character needed) in the appropriate position. The \Oxhh replaces only a single character of the NetBIOS name. Be sure to include the proper number of spaces between the quotation marks to account for the 16 positions of the name, as shown:

```
139.41.129.18  "application   \ox14"
```

Installing WINS

As you can see, if you're going to support NetBIOS names in Windows 2000 either because of down-level machines or NetBIOS-based applications, it is important to use WINS. This significantly reduces NetBIOS name resolutions and, more importantly, reduces network traffic.

To install WINS on Windows 2000, do the following:

1. Double-click Add/Remove Programs from the Control Panel.

2. In the Add/Remove Programs window, select Add/Remove Windows Components to bring up the Windows Components Wizard.

3. In the Windows Components Wizard page, select Networking Services and then click the Details button.

4. Check the box next to Windows Internet Naming Service (WINS) and click OK. This will return you to the Windows Components Wizard page.

5. Click Next to begin installing the WINS service.

6. Click Finish to complete the installation.

When to Stop Relying on NetBIOS

Microsoft is striving for a purer TCP/IP implementation in Windows 2000 network environments. It no longer requires NetBIOS to be overlaid on TCP/IP for name resolution; DNS has won that title. Also, it is only supported because of legacy systems and applications.

DNS is simply a more scalable and reliable solution for name resolution. It's stood the test of time, and the Internet is the best example of its success. To familiarize yourself more with DNS and how it affects your Windows 2000 environment, refer to Chapter 14.

As you can probably already imagine, the sooner you stop using NetBIOS, the better off your Windows 2000 environment will be. The first step is to upgrade all your down-level clients to Windows 2000. Unfortunately, your job is not done at this point. The next step is for you to verify which applications are dependent upon NetBIOS. If you do have NetBIOS-based applications (and you still need to use them), check with the vendor to see if they have an upgraded version that doesn't rely on NetBIOS. Once you disable NetBIOS, any applications that rely on it will either stop working properly, or not work at all. The final step is to actually disable NetBIOS on all Windows 2000 machines. To do so, follow these steps:

1. From the Start | Settings menu, select Network And Dial-Up Connections.

2. Right-click on the Local Area Connection icon and select Properties.

3. On the Local Area Connection icon Properties page, scroll down until you find Internet Protocol (TCP/IP). Click on it so that it is highlighted.

4. Click the Properties button to display the Internet Protocol (TCP/IP) Properties page as shown in Figure 13-4.

5. Click the Advanced button located in the bottom right-hand corner to display the Advanced TCP/IP Settings dialog box.

6. Select the WINS tab, as shown in Figure 13-21, and select the radio button beside Disable NetBIOS Over TCP/IP.

7. Click the OK button three times to close the previously opened windows.

Using TCP/IP Tools

Windows 2000's implementation of the TCP/IP protocols includes a collection of tools and utilities that enables users and administrators to monitor and troubleshoot TCP/IP activities. Many of these utilities are Windows 2000 versions of programs developed for other TCP/IP environments that have become standard tools for network administrators.

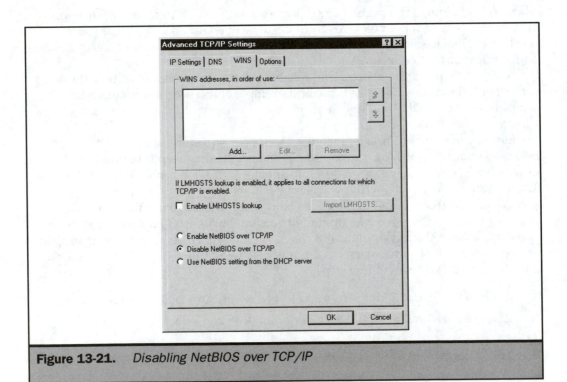

Figure 13-21. *Disabling NetBIOS over TCP/IP*

Ping

Ping is the most basic and most commonly known TCP/IP utility. It is the basic tool that you use to determine whether the TCP/IP stack on your computer is functioning, whether another computer on the network can be contacted, or whether a DNS server can resolve a host name into an IP address. In Figure 13-22, ping is used to check whether the DC called OSBORNE2000 can contact a machine called WIN98CLIENT.

Ping operates by sending ECHO REQUEST packets to the destination specified on the command line using the Internet Control Message Protocol. The destination system returns an ECHO RESPONSE packet for each request it receives, and ping displays the size of each packet sent (in bytes), the round-trip time (in milliseconds), and the packet's time-to-live value.

Tracert

The *tracert* program, known as *traceroute* on UNIX systems, identifies the route taken by IP datagrams to reach a specified destination. Apart from being entertaining (especially when used to trace Internet connections), it is useful in troubleshooting routing problems. When you have a multihomed Windows 2000 system, tracert is a sure way of determining which network the system is using to reach a particular destination.

Using the same ICMP packets as ping, tracert sends successive ECHO REQUEST messages to the destination address with incrementing time-to-live (TTL) values.

CONNECTING WITH WINDOWS 2000

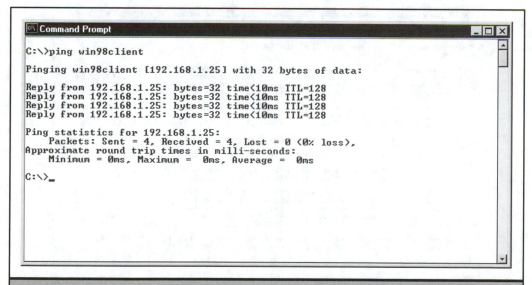

```
C:\>ping win98client

Pinging win98client [192.168.1.25] with 32 bytes of data:

Reply from 192.168.1.25: bytes=32 time<10ms TTL=128
Reply from 192.168.1.25: bytes=32 time<10ms TTL=128
Reply from 192.168.1.25: bytes=32 time<10ms TTL=128
Reply from 192.168.1.25: bytes=32 time<10ms TTL=128

Ping statistics for 192.168.1.25:
    Packets: Sent = 4, Received = 4, Lost = 0 (0% loss),
Approximate round trip times in milli-seconds:
    Minimum = 0ms, Maximum =  0ms, Average =  0ms

C:\>_
```

Figure 13-22.   *Using the ping utility*

Because each intermediate system that a packet travels through reduces the TTL value by one, each request times out one hop farther along the route to the destination.

As each successive packet times out, it returns a message to the source containing the address of the gateway where the TTL value reached zero. These addresses are resolved and displayed on the host computer, along with the time interval for each hop.

When used with Internet addresses, as shown in Figure 13-23, tracert provides a fascinating insight into the international telecommunications network. Because Windows 2000 resolves the IP addresses of each gateway, you can often identify the sites through which your packets are passing on the way to their destination. Trace the route to a Web server in Europe, and you can see from the elapsed times the point at which your signal crosses the ocean.

Ipconfig

Ipconfig is a command-line utility that displays the current IP configuration settings for your computer. When you use ipconfig with the /all switch, it displays the current IP configuration settings for each of the network adapters installed in your computer. This is particularly useful on DHCP client systems, where there is no other way to determine this information without access to the DHCP Manager program on the server. Ipconfig's display appears as follows:

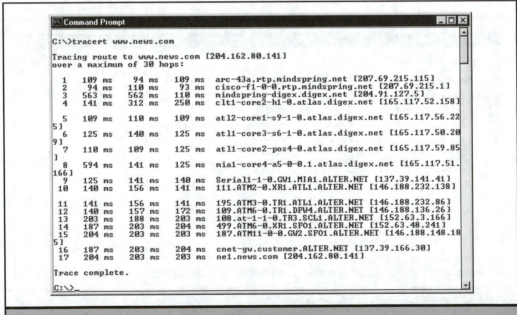

Figure 13-23. *Tracing a route to a Web site*

```
C:\>ipconfig
Windows 2000 IP Configuration
Ethernet adapter Local Area Connection:
        Connection-specific DNS Suffix  . :
        IP Address. . . . . . . . . . . . : 192.168.1.2
        Subnet Mask . . . . . . . . . . . : 255.255.255.0
        Default Gateway . . . . . . . . . : 192.168.1.1


C:\>ipconfig/all
Windows 2000 IP Configuration
        Host Name . . . . . . . . . . . . : OSBORNE2000
        Primary DNS Suffix  . . . . . . . : osborne.com
        Node Type . . . . . . . . . . . . : Broadcast
        IP Routing Enabled. . . . . . . . : No
        WINS Proxy Enabled. . . . . . . . : No
        DNS Suffix Search List. . . . . . : osborne.com
Ethernet adapter Local Area Connection:
        Connection-specific DNS Suffix  . :
        Description . . . . . . . . . . . : Intel 82558-based
        Integrated Ethernet with Wake on LAN*
        Physical Address. . . . . . . . . : 00-A0-C9-EC-1D-09
        DHCP Enabled. . . . . . . . . . . : No
        IP Address. . . . . . . . . . . . : 192.168.1.2
        Subnet Mask . . . . . . . . . . . : 255.255.255.0
        Default Gateway . . . . . . . . . : 192.168.1.1
        DNS Servers . . . . . . . . . . . : 192.168.1.2
```

Netstat

Netstat is a command that lists the TCP/IP connections currently in use by the workstation, as well as communications statistics for the network interface and for the IP, TCP, and UDP protocols, as follows:

ACTIVE CONNECTIONS:

Proto	Local Address	Foreign Address	State
TCP	smithj:1372	ftp.mycorp.com:ftp	TIME_WAIT
TCP	smithj:1390	www.mycorp.com:80	ESTABLISHED
UDP	smithj:nbname	*:*	
UDP	smithj:nbdatagram	*:*	
UDP	smithj:nbname	*:*	
UDP	smithj:nbdatagram	*:*	

Interface Statistics	Received	Sent
Bytes	4441152	86989
Unicast packets	1230	902
Non-Unicast packets	4087	80
Discards	0	0
Errors	0	0
Unknown protocols	9456	

IP Statistics

Packets Received	=	3705
Received Header Errors	=	0
Received Address Errors	=	14
Datagrams Forwarded	=	0
Unknown Protocols Received	=	0
Received Packets Discarded	=	0
Received Packets Delivered	=	3691
Output Requests	=	961
Routing Discards	=	0
Discarded Output Packets	=	0
Output Packet No Route	=	0
Reassembly Required	=	0
Reassembly Successful	=	0
Reassembly Failures	=	0
Datagrams Successfully Fragmented	=	0
Datagrams Failing Fragmentation	=	0
Fragments Created	=	0

TCP Statistics

Active Opens	=	28
Passive Opens	=	11
Failed Connection Attempts	=	0
Reset Connections	=	17
Current Connections	=	0
Segments Received	=	1160
Segments Sent	=	846
Segments Retransmitted	=	4

UDP Statistics

Datagrams Received	=	232
No Ports	=	2299
Receive Errors	=	0
Datagrams Sent	=	101

With Netstat, you can see what type of connection an application is using and how much data is being transmitted or received. By using the *interval* parameter, the Netstat display can be continually updated to show you the ongoing progress of network communications as they are happening.

ARP

The ARP utility displays the current contents of the system's Address Resolution Protocol cache. This cache contains the MAC addresses and IP addresses of the machines on your local network that have recently been involved in TCP/IP communications.

The cache contains entries for the system that your workstation has contacted, as well as others, because the reply packets generated by Windows 2000 machines in response to ARP requests are transmitted as broadcasts. This enables all the systems on a network to benefit from one machine's request. The ARP cache is purged periodically to ensure that the data remains current. You can, however, use the -s parameter to add entries to the ARP table that will remain there permanently, enabling you to reduce the number of redundant queries sent over the network.

CONNECTING WITH
WINDOWS 2000

Route

As discussed earlier in this chapter, a Windows 2000 system maintains a table that contains a record of the routing information received from other systems, in the form of ICMP Redirect packets. You can use the Route command to display, edit, add, or delete entries in the table. You can, for example, specify that a gateway other than the default be used when transmitting to a specific destination.

The output of the ROUTE PRINT command is as follows:

ACTIVE ROUTES:

Network Address	Netmask	Gateway Address	Interface	Metric
0.0.0.0	0.0.0.0	120.110.10.100	120.110.10.1	1
120.110.10.0	255.255.255.0	120.110.10.1	120.110.10.1	1
120.110.10.1	255.255.255.255	127.0.0.1	127.0.0.1	1
120.255.255.255	255.255.255.255	120.110.10.1	120.110.10.1	1
127.0.0.0	255.0.0.0	127.0.0.1	127.0.0.1	1
224.0.0.0	224.0.0.0	120.110.10.1	120.110.10.1	1
255.255.255.255	255.255.255.255	120.110.10.1	120.110.10.1	1

Nbtstat

The nbtstat command enables you to display various statistics regarding the NetBIOS over TCP/IP (NetBT) activities on your computer. With nbtstat, you can display the contents of the NetBIOS name cache, list the current NetBT sessions in progress, show protocol statistics at regular intervals, and even reload the cache by processing the LMHOSTS file. You can, therefore, make changes to the file to take effect immediately.

The Complete Reference

Chapter 14

Understanding DNS

The Domain Name System (DNS) is a hierarchical name resolution mechanism that has stood the test of time for most, if not all, operating system platforms. In fact, although the entire Internet relies on its service, many of you are not even aware of its existence! DNS has been available for Windows NT-based environments, but it hasn't necessarily been an integral part of the operating system. Windows 2000, however, has incorporated DNS and is extremely reliant on it (that is an understatement).

To help you fully appreciate DNS and Windows 2000's dependence on it, this chapter examines DNS fundamentals, installation and configuration issues, integration with other services, and much more. After reading this chapter, you'll have a thorough understanding of DNS, but more importantly, you'll be able to use it effectively within your own Windows 2000 environment.

DNS Fundamentals

DNS provides name resolution for TCP/IP networked environments. TCP/IP uses IP addresses, not names, to communicate with other machines (refer to Chapter 13 for more information on TCP/IP). This means you are able to get to other machines simply by typing a name rather than an IP address. For instance, to get to Microsoft's Web site, you enter **http://www.microsoft.com/** in a Web browser rather than typing in a cryptic IP address such as **http://207.206.205.204/.** Even if you're one of the lucky ones with a photographic memory, it would be an overwhelming task to remember the IP address of every host you contact. Furthermore, servers move to different locations, frequently requiring a change in the IP address.

The most elementary way of describing DNS is to say that it provides convenience to you by translating easy-to-remember names to IP addresses. Typically, DNS is associated with the Internet or UNIX-based environments. If your Windows-based network environment currently uses DNS, chances are that you are using it primarily for communicating on the Internet or with non-Microsoft operating systems. Only a small percentage of administrators rely on DNS for name resolution on the LAN. However, Windows 2000 network environments depend on DNS to communicate with other machines on the Internet, with non-Microsoft operating systems, as well as with machines on the LAN. DNS is pushing Microsoft operating systems' dependency on NetBIOS out the window.

Hosts Files—DNS's Precursor

Translating names to IP addresses has always been a challenge in TCP/IP networks. One of the first mechanisms designed to overcome this challenge was the use of *hosts* files. Hosts files are flat, ASCII files that contain computer host names and corresponding IP addresses in a two-column list as illustrated in Figure 14-1. Each computer on the network needs to have its own copy of the hosts file so that it can contact other computers by host name. Any changes that are made need to be reflected in all hosts files that exist on the network.

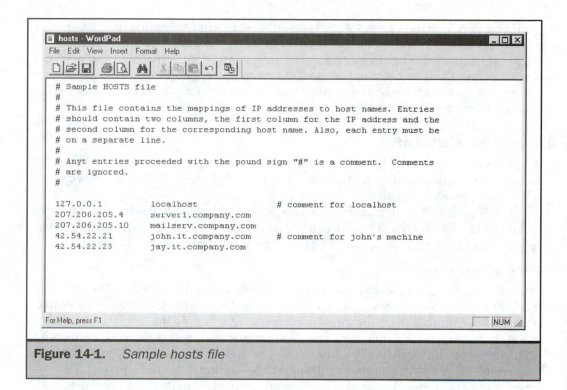

```
# Sample HOSTS file
#
# This file contains the mappings of IP addresses to host names. Entries
# should contain two columns, the first column for the IP address and the
# second column for the corresponding host name. Also, each entry must be
# on a separate line.
#
# Anyt entries proceeded with the pound sign "#" is a comment.  Comments
# are ignored.
#

127.0.0.1          localhost                 # comment for localhost
207.206.205.4      server1.company.com
207.206.205.10     mailserv.company.com
42.54.22.21        john.it.company.com       # comment for john's machine
42.54.22.23        jay.it.company.com
```

Figure 14-1.   *Sample hosts file*

Although hosts files are still in use today, their occurrence is rare and usually only in small TCP/IP environments. There are just too many disadvantages to using hosts files for name resolution, including:

- You risk the possibility that not all hosts files are up-to-date.
- Security can easily be compromised.
- The process can grow large and cumbersome to the point of becoming an administrative nightmare.
- Duplicate host names and IP addresses are more prevalent.
- Extremely difficult to perform queries.
- Entries are static and susceptible to error.
- Multiple copies must be maintained as machines are added and removed.

Note   *Windows 2000 still supports the use of hosts files, but they can't be used as an alternative to DNS. The hosts file in Windows 2000 can be located in the %SystemRoot%\System32\Drivers\Etc directory. It is in the same format as the 4.3 Berkeley Software Distribution (BSD) UNIX /etc/hosts file.*

If you decide to use or keep using hosts files, you must realize that the hosts file is queried before DNS. Once the query finds an entry, the name resolution process begins. If the hosts file has an incorrect or different entry for the machine you're trying to contact, you will not get to the proper site or you will get nothing at all. Therefore, any entries that you have will be used instead of DNS, which could cause more troubles than you would wish to face.

DNS to the Rescue

All of the limitations with hosts files prompted the development of a more reliable, secure, and scalable solution to the name resolution challenge. DNS is the answer to overcoming those limitations.

DNS is essentially a database with its own set of tools used to provide maintenance and querying capabilities. It is also distributed in nature, meaning that each domain is responsible for itself. Your domain's database must be maintained and accurate.

DNS Hierarchy

There are DNS servers that contain information about all other domains. These machines are called *root servers* because they are the final authority for their respective domains. The topmost root domain is unnamed (and is simply the "."). The next level in the chain is a top-level domain. Examples of top-level domains are .edu, .com, .org, .mil, .net, .gov, and two-letter country codes. The .com namespace root server is responsible for keeping records for all namespaces ending in .com. Table 14-1 provides a list of top-level domains and a short description of their intended use.

Top-level Domain	Description
.com	Intended for companies or other commercial-related activity
.edu	Intended for educational organizations only
.gov	Intended for federal governmental organizations
.int	Intended for international organizations
.mil	Intended for United States military agencies and operations
.net	Intended for network providers
.org	Intended for noncommercial organizations but can be used by organizations that don't fall into any of the previous categories

Table 14-1.   *Top-Level Domains and Respective Descriptions*

The top-level domains have secondary or second-level domains branching from them. Figure 14-2 shows DNS's hierarchical structure and some familiar names on the second-level domains. Optionally, under the second-level domains, there may be subdomains, such as it.company.com or compsci.ncsu.edu. The last link in the DNS hierarchy is the actual host name.

One of the easiest ways to remember the hierarchical structure of DNS is to look at it as if it were a family tree. This can include your immediate family (your parents, yourself, and your siblings), or it can include as many generations as you can imagine. The point is that name and other characteristics of a domain (the parent) are appended to any directly related subdomains (children). Of course, in a family tree you have name changes, marriage into other families, and other factors that may alter a family tree structure. But if you can think of better analogies, then great, you get my point.

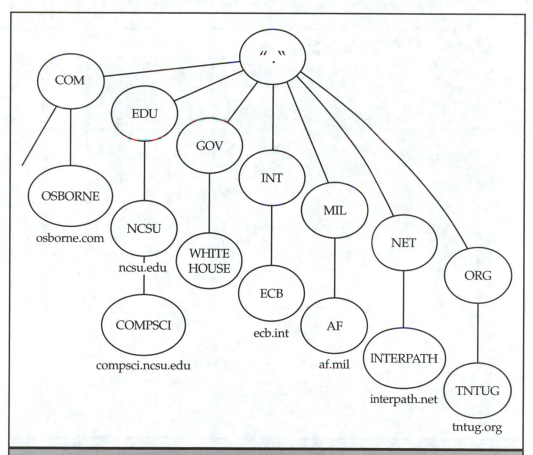

Figure 14-2. *DNS hierarchy with levels of domains*

Note *There is another type of domain called the reverse domain. Reverse domains are unique domains used for IP address-to-name mappings (the opposite of name to IP address resolution), commonly referred to as reverse name lookup. Two are in existence today: in-addr.arpa and IP6.INT. The latter reverse domain is used for IP version 6 reverse lookups. For more information, see "Name Resolution" later in this chapter.*

You must register a domain name with an Internet authority, such as Network Solutions (http://www.networksolutions.com/) shown in Figure 14-3, in order to claim a domain namespace. The Internet craze has sparked a flurry of domain

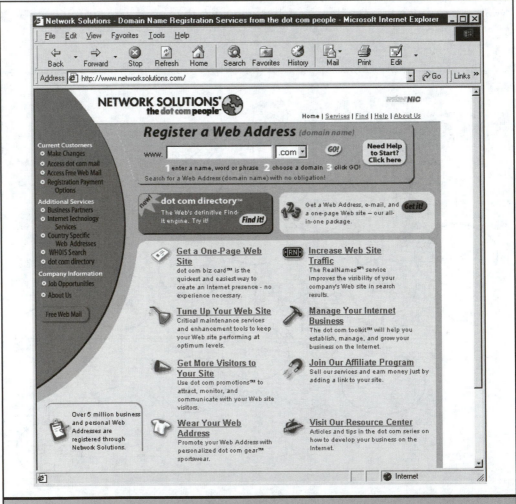

Figure 14-3. *Registering a domain name*

registrations especially in the .com domain, so your choices for the domain name you want are narrowing every day.

Using DNS doesn't necessarily mean that you also have to be connected to the Internet. Windows 2000 requires DNS whether you're connected to the Internet or not. You also aren't obligated to supply your environment's entire DNS infrastructure to the rest of the world. You can create private networks that are not visible on the Internet, using your own domain namespaces.

Now, you may be thinking that your DNS for company.com can provide name resolution for all sites that you contact, including those that reside halfway around the world. In truth, it is only responsible for, and has the authority to provide, name resolution for the company's domain namespace, and therefore it isn't a root domain. The section "Name Resolution," following shortly, looks at what's really happening when you try to reach a site that isn't in your domain namespace.

Host Names

The TCP/IP protocols were initially developed for use on the Internet, and one of the requirements for their design was that they be completely self-sufficient in their addressing. Because they were going to be used on a wide variety of computing platforms, the existence of a MAC address, such as is found on all Ethernet and token ring adapters, could not be taken as a given. An IP address is therefore assigned to every host (computer) on a TCP/IP network, providing an ideal means of identification for the computers doing the communicating.

IP addresses have, unfortunately, proven to be a less than ideal means of computer identification for humans. Think of how many World Wide Web and ftp servers you know by their host names, such as www.intel.com and ftp.microsoft.com, and imagine having to remember 12 digits or more for each one instead. Host names were devised solely as a means to provide friendly names for the user interface.

The IP header does not carry the host names of the source and destination computers, only the IP addresses. Whenever an application, such as a Web browser or an ftp client, attempts to connect to another computer whose host name has been specified by the user, the first step in the process is to resolve the name into an IP address.

Because they are not directly associated with the TCP/IP communications processes, host names can be considered independently of IP addresses. For example, a computer with a single network adapter and one IP address can have many host names. You can run a Web server, an ftp server, and DNS on the same machine and use a different host name for each, with all of them pointing to the same IP address.

Each host name refers to a computer. For example, Karen or Osborne2000 can be host names. A host name is the leftmost portion of a fully qualified domain name (FQDN), which defines its place within the DNS hierarchy. Karen.traveler.company.com is an FQDN and is graphically represented in Figure 14-4. The FQDN is used by DNS for name resolution.

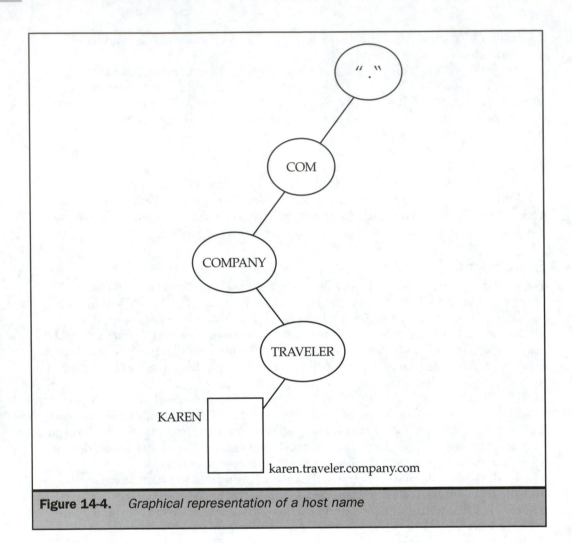

Figure 14-4. *Graphical representation of a host name*

Zones

If you thought that DNS could not be segmented anymore, think again. There are defined areas within DNS called *zones* that correspond to a series of records stored on a DNS server. Each zone can contain a domain, a portion of a domain, or multiple domains. One or more DNS servers are responsible for each zone. A sample zone is illustrated in Figure 14-5.

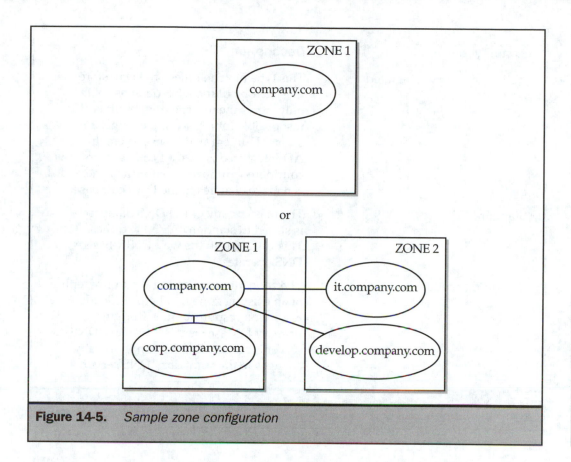

Figure 14-5. *Sample zone configuration*

The easiest way to think of zones is to treat them as partitions in the DNS namespace but they aren't domains. DNS servers in assigned zones answer queries about their zone and are authoritative. Some advantages to using zones include:

1. The ability to delegate responsibilities for specific areas in the DNS namespace to specific DNS servers

2. Increased performance

3. A zone fits topologically or geographically dispersed environments

4. Greater control over the namespace

ZONE TYPES   Windows 2000 supports three types of zones: Active Directory-integrated, standard primary, and standard secondary. These are described in Table 14-2.

Zone Type	Description
Active Directory-integrated	This type of zone relies on AD to store the master copy of the DNS database. AD not only stores the information, but it is also responsible for replicating changes to other AD-integrated DNS servers. In AD-integrated zones, all DNS servers are considered authoritative for the zone and can make changes to the DNS database.
Standard Primary	The master copy of the DNS database is stored in standard ASCII text files. This is similar to the way UNIX-based DNS operates.
Standard Secondary	The zone information is a read-only replica of an existing zone that helps offload name resolution responsibilities from the primary DNS server. The primary DNS server is responsible for supplying any changes to the secondary DNS server.

Table 14-2.   *Zone Types and Descriptions*

REPLICATION   Standard DNS employs a primary and one or more secondary DNS servers for each zone. Changes to the DNS database can only be made to the primary to avoid the risk of corruption. This is similar to a single-master Windows NT 4.0 domain model. As a result, secondary DNS servers use a read-only copy of the DNS database.

The secondary DNS servers keep up-to-date and synchronized with the primary DNS server through a replication mechanism appropriately called *zone transfer*. Zone transfers replicate the entire contents of the primary DNS database to secondary DNS servers. These transfers are initiated by the following actions:

■ When the secondary DNS server starts up.

■ At specified intervals, the secondary DNS server checks to see if the DNS database has been changed.

Name Resolution

Name resolution is the process of translating a name into an IP address that is recognizable by the TCP/IP protocol. This process makes it easier on all of us because we can use friendlier ways (names) instead of IP addresses to contact another machine.

Let's say you want to check out the latest in world news using your Web browser. You type in the address of the site that you wish to contact (for example, http://www.cnn.com/). Your Web browser calls a group of functions or libraries that are collectively called a *resolver* and pass the name that you want translated. Windows 2000 first checks for a local hosts file, and if it's present, the OS searches the hosts file for the name and corresponding IP address. Hopefully, you took my earlier advice and you don't have to worry about how the hosts file is configured, because you're not using one. Otherwise, the query fails with the hosts file and Windows 2000 uses DNS if it's enabled on the client. For more information on configuring client machines, see "Configuring Clients to Use DNS" later in this chapter.

> **Note** *Down-level clients (Windows 3.x, 9x, etc.) try resolving the NetBIOS name before using DNS resolution. The exception to this rule is for Windows NT 4.0 machines when the name contains a period or it's greater than the NetBIOS limitation of 15 characters in length.*

The resolver then asks the primary DNS server if it can translate the name. If there isn't a match in the DNS's cache or zone file, it won't resolve the name. DNS is persistent; instead of stopping there, it asks another DNS server. Typically, another DNS server is installed at or close to where your company's network meets the Internet, and one of its primary purposes is to forward queries to DNS servers on the outside. This type of DNS server is appropriately called a *forwarder*. The internal DNS server queries the forwarder, which first checks to see if it can resolve the name. If not, it passes the query to other DNS servers on the Internet until either a match is made or the query fails. A successful name resolution is then placed in the local DNS server's cache so that when others attempt to go to CNN's Web site, the resolution will be much quicker. Figure 14-6 illustrates the process of resolving a name to an IP address.

I've given an overview of the name resolution process, but I haven't explained enough about the types of queries that are made. The following queries are used in the name resolution process:

- **Iterative** Iterative queries are analogous to a referral system. They start from the topmost level and work themselves down until they reach an authority where the host resides. DNS servers, usually not clients, send an iterative query to a DNS server. The receiving DNS server checks its cache and zone for a match, and if it can't resolve the name, it refers the original DNS server to another DNS server that can more appropriately handle the request.

- **Recursive** A recursive query maps an IP address to a name. Since DNS is indexed by name, a recursive query could take an exceptionally long time to find the answer. To solve this dilemma, it uses the in-addr.arpa domain, which uses the same hierarchy but uses IP addresses instead of names. Typically, troubleshooting tools or security-based applications use recursive queries but a DNS server can also use them. If a security-based application on a client sends a recursive query, it expects to get resolution, but it is unaware of the iterative queries being made, if any, between DNS servers.

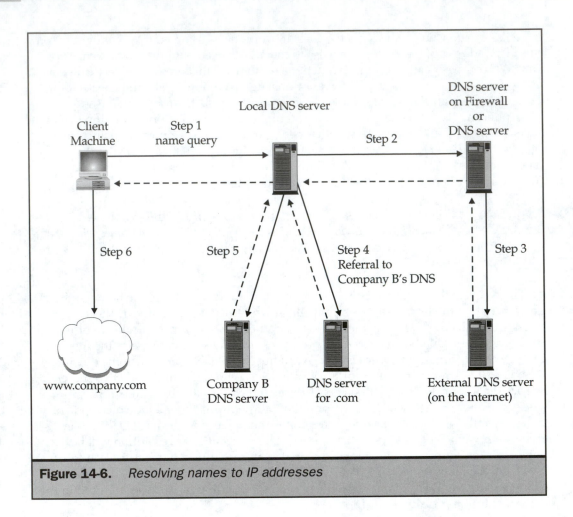

Figure 14-6. *Resolving names to IP addresses*

■ **Inverse** These queries are requests from a machine to find a name after it
supplies the IP address. The difference from a reverse lookup (explained in
"Creating a Reverse Lookup Zone," later in this chapter) is that the DNS server
only checks its zone files for a match. If the answer is not found within the zone
file, the query stops because it failed. This type of query is rarely performed by
an application and is only supported with Windows 2000's DNS for backward
compatibility issues with older DNS versions.

Most people tend to think that name resolution applies mostly to external
resolution with the Internet (granted this is an area that most of us are very familiar
with). On the contrary, the same name resolution process applies to internal resolution.
Windows 2000 no longer has to rely on WINS but instead focuses on DNS for internal
and external name resolution.

DNS CACHING   DNS servers (especially those tied to the Internet) will more than likely talk to many other DNS servers. For instance a DNS server may send one or several queries out to fulfill name resolution. As it finds other DNS servers that have authority for particular namespaces, it caches or stores them for future reference. This greatly increases the chances that other queries will be resolved much faster and more efficiently.

Once the server caches a result, it is stored for a specified period of time. This time is referred to as the Time to Live (TTL). The default TTL for Windows 2000 DNS is one hour. Immediately, the TTL clock starts ticking and will eventually expire if a query for that namespace isn't made during that time. When the TTL expires, the query result is deleted from the DNS server's cache.

DNS Database Files and Resource Records

DNS is composed of many different database files that structure the DNS database and define its functionality within your environment. The files that make up the database are listed in Table 14-3.

CONNECTING WITH WINDOWS 2000

Filename	Description
BIND Boot File	Defines startup parameters such as whether or not the DNS server is primary or secondary. This file is not used by default because startup parameters are stored in the registry, and it is supported mainly for compliance with BIND implementations.
Forward Lookup File	Contain information to resolve names within the domain. They are required to contain SOA and NS records (defined later in this chapter), but they can also contain other resource records as well.
Reverse Lookup File	This file contains information (SOA, NS, and PTR records) that is needed to resolve IP addresses to names. It may also rely on two special, reverse domains (in-addr.arpa and IP6.INT) for resolution. While reverse lookups are out of the ordinary, they are especially useful for troubleshooting connections as well as providing an additional layer of security for applications that connect based on host names.

Table 14-3.   *Files That Make Up DNS*

Filename	Description
Root Hints File	Also known as the cache file or cache hints file, it contains names and IP addresses of root servers outside its authoritative domain. Although this helps resolve names outside of its authoritative domain, the root hints file doesn't actually resolve the names.
Zone File	Zone files store information that is pertinent to a specific zone to which they belong, such as the SOA record. They can be stored in plain text; however, I recommend that you integrate DNS and AD if possible so that the zone files are stored in the AD database. This creates a more robust and fault-tolerant environment.

Table 14-3.   *Files That Make Up DNS* (continued)

The DNS database consists of one or more zone files. Within each of the files (mentioned in Table 14-3) that constitute a zone, is a collection of resource records. There is a plethora of resource records available in DNS, but some are more common than others and some are specific to Windows 2000.

The following is a list of the most common resource records for the DNS database:

- **A**   This resource record specifies a host address. It maps a static host name to an IP address. For example,

```
w2kserverdns.mycompany.com  IN   A    127.0.0.1
```

is an A record for the machine's host name and IP address.

- **AAAA**   The AAAA resource record is not as common right now but soon will be with the influx of people registering domains and IP addresses. AAAA is similar to the A resource record in that it is a host record, but it is specifically designed for IPv6 128-bit IP addresses. An example of an AAAA resource record is the following:

```
ipv6name.osborne.com  IN    AAAA    4321:0:1:2:3:4:567:89ab
```

- **CNAME** Canonical name (CNAME) resource records define aliases for their true host name, hence the name canonical. As you can imagine, creating multiple (CNAME) resource records allows you to map multiple host names to a single IP address. For instance, some Web sites can be contacted by specifying either domain.com or www.domain.com.

- **MX** The Mail Exchange (MX) resource record provides information for message routing for the specified domain. Multiple MX records can be used to specify multiple mail servers, and they can be ranked according to preference. This adds another layer of fault tolerance to your environment by offering messages another route to other mail servers. The following illustration is an example of an MX resource record.

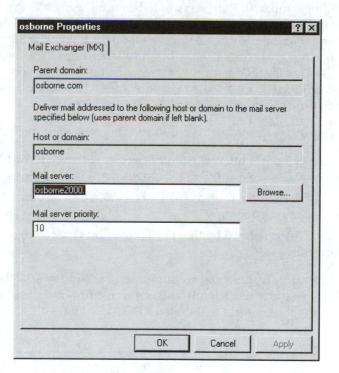

- **NS** Name Server (NS) resource records lists other name servers that contain information for a domain. NS resource records also help define the DNS database by listing secondary servers for the zone and primary servers for zones branching from it.

- **PTR** A pointer (PTR) resource record is essentially the reverse of a host (A) resource record because it provides information for reverse lookups. It adds the special domain, in-addr.arpa, mentioned earlier for the static translation. For instance, for machine me.mydomain.com with IP address 100.99.98.97, the corresponding PTR resource record would look this:

```
97.98.99.100.in-addr.arpa     IN  PTR      me.mydomain.com
```

- **SOA** The Start of Authority (SOA) resource record defines the zone for which the server is authoritative. It also contains many fields such as primary DNS server name, time-to-live (TTL) value, retry and refresh rates (how long secondary DNS servers wait for a response), serial number (used to determine if changes have been made to DNS and if synchronization is required in the zone), and more.

- **SRV** The Service locator (SRV) resource record specifies multiple servers that are providing similar TCP/IP services to be found using a single DNS query. This is very similar to the MX resource record in that you can list multiple servers for a particular service. However, it doesn't have the limitation of listing for only one type of service like the MX resource record. One of the more popular uses for the SRV resource record is listing multiple servers for the World Wide Web (WWW) related services. Also, DCs in Windows 2000 register with DNS using this resource record.

A few other resource records are Microsoft specific, including the following:

- **WINS** The Windows Internet Naming Service resource record allows Windows 2000 DNS to use WINS to help resolve a host name.

- **WINS-R** This resource record is similar to the WINS resource record but is used only for reverse lookups.

- **ATMA** ATMA is defined by the ATF Forum and is used to resolve names to ATM addresses.

Several other resource records that are supported by Windows 2000 DNS are given in Table 14-4. These resource records are neither specific to Windows 2000 nor are they commonly used, but they conform to the cited RFC.

Resource Record Type	RFC
AFSDB	1183
HINFO	1034
ISDN	1183

Table 14-4. *Resource Record Types and Corresponding RFCs*

Resource Record Type	RFC
MB	1035
MG	1035
MINFO	1035
MR	1035
RP	1183
RT	1183
TXT	1035
WKS	1035
X.25	1183

Table 14-4.   *Resource Record Types and Corresponding RFCs* (continued)

CONNECTING WITH
WINDOWS 2000

Installing DNS

You can install DNS in several ways, including these:

- Install DNS during the initial setup of Windows 2000.
- Use DCPROMO to install DNS when you are configuring a DC.
- Install the service manually anytime after you've installed Windows 2000.

Before you begin installing DNS, make sure that you assign a static IP address to the computer. For more information on configuring TCP/IP, refer to Chapter 13. Installing DNS does the following:

- It installs the DNS Manager snap-in for the Microsoft Management Console (MMC) used to configure and manage the DNS service.
- It creates the %Systemroot%\System32\Dns directory that contains the DNS database files described earlier
- It adds the DNS service to the Registry. In particular, it adds HKEY_LOCAL_MACHINE\System\CurrentControlSet\Services\Dns key, as shown in Figure 14-7.

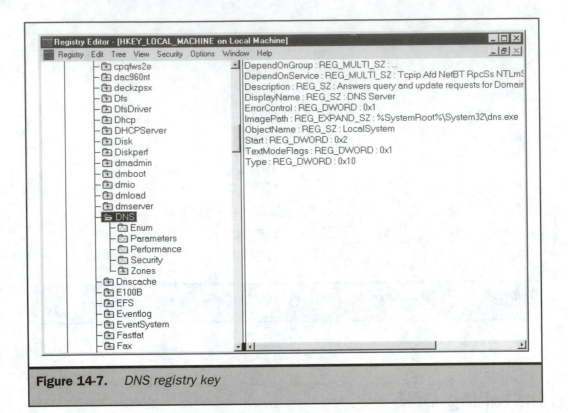

Figure 14-7.   *DNS registry key*

Installing DNS During the Windows 2000 Installation

During the Windows 2000 installation process, the setup program presents a set of network configuration options that you can choose to install. DNS is one of those network services you can choose to install along with your standard network configuration.

Personally, I would refrain from installing DNS during the Windows 2000 setup for a couple of reasons. First, it is always a good idea to make sure that the Windows 2000 installation is successful. This includes, but isn't limited to, testing your TCP/IP connectivity with other machines on the network and verifying that all services have initiated properly. The second reason is that installing the service later doesn't require the machine to be restarted (as was required with previous versions of Windows NT).

Using DCPROMO to Install DNS

DCPROMO, also known as the Active Directory Installation Wizard, is a utility used to promote a stand-alone server to a DC (explained in more detail in Chapter 2). If you use DCPROMO to promote a server to DC status, it gives you the option to install DNS as well. Now, there are two real advantages of using DCPROMO to install DNS. First, Windows 2000 automatically configures some of the initial DNS server settings, such as creating zones, from the information you specified during the upgrade process. Also, the combination allows you to support dynamic updates (see "Enabling Dynamic DNS" later in this chapter).

If the server you are promoting is the first DC for the domain, DCPROMO also specifies the primary DNS server (itself) and creates forward and reverse zones. Refer to "Configuring DNS" for more information on integrating DNS into your environment.

The disadvantage of using DCPROMO to install DNS is that you may not want the machine to be a DC. This may be because you're not sure if the server should be a DC, you don't want to use DDNS, you're coexisting with non-Microsoft DNS servers, or some other reason.

Manually Installing DNS

To manually install Microsoft's DNS Server, perform the following steps:

1. Double-click the Add/Remove Programs applet within the Control Panel.

2. Click on Add/Remove Windows Components to invoke the Windows Components Wizard.

3. Highlight the Networking Services option and click Details.

4. Check the box beside Dynamic Name Service (DNS) as shown in the following illustration, and then click OK.

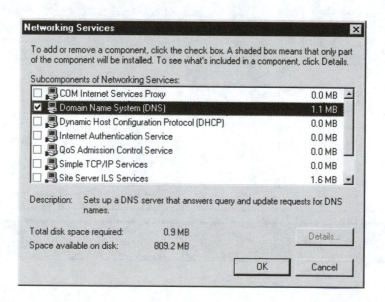

5. Click Next to begin installing DNS. If Windows 2000 can't find the system files needed, you are prompted to insert the CD or specify their location.

6. If you have another DNS server on your network, specify the Primary DNS Server's IP address in the Primary DNS Server box. Otherwise, click OK twice and then select Finish to complete the installation.

7. Close the Add/Remove Programs window and you're done.

Configuring DNS

After installing the DNS service, you use the DNS Manager, shown in Figure 14-8, to configure the service to provide your network environment with DNS name resolution. For those of you who are familiar with previous versions of Microsoft's DNS, you're in luck because the principles behind configuring DNS are similar to earlier versions.

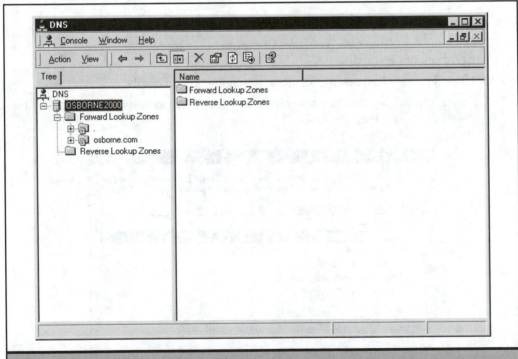

Figure 14-8.   *DNS Manager interface*

There are, of course, more configuration options than before, such as AD integration and interface enhancements, but you'll still feel comfortable configuring the new DNS service.

> **Note**   *You can choose to manually administer and manage the DNS database, but the easiest and recommended way is to use the DNS Manager. Stick to using only one method so you don't run the risk of corrupting the DNS service.*

Unless you're upgrading an existing DNS server (Microsoft or non-Microsoft), the beginning part of the process is the same as before, too. You specify a primary DNS server and then configure both the forward and reverse lookup zones.

The following sections on configuring DNS assume that you're using the DNS Manager to administer and manage DNS. Moreover, the context describes using the DNS version included with Windows 2000.

Configuring a DNS Server

The first step in configuring the DNS server is to specify the primary DNS server. The primary DNS server has authority and answers queries for the zone you're about to set up. Unless you've used DCPROMO to install and initially configure DNS for the Windows 2000 domain, you are prompted to supply a name for the primary DNS server when you start the DNS Manager.

Creating a Forward Lookup Zone

In order for DNS to provide name resolution to a Windows 2000 environment, you must configure at least one forward lookup zone for each zone in the namespace. To create a new forward lookup zone, do the following:

1. Start the DNS Manager (named DNS on the toolbar) from Start | Programs | Administrative Tools.

2. In the left pane, select the domain you wish to create a forward lookup zone in to view the Forward Lookup Zone folder in the right pane as shown in Figure 14-9.

3. Right-click on the Forward Lookup Zone folder and select New Zone. This initiates the New Zone Wizard.

4. Click Next to continue. The next screen asks you to select which type of zone (Active Directory-integrated, Standard Primary, or Standard Secondary) you wish to create. A brief description of each of these zone types is given to help you choose which zone type is more appropriate. This screen is shown in Figure 14-10. For this example, I'm choosing a new Standard Primary zone for the authors.osborne.com domain. Click Next to continue.

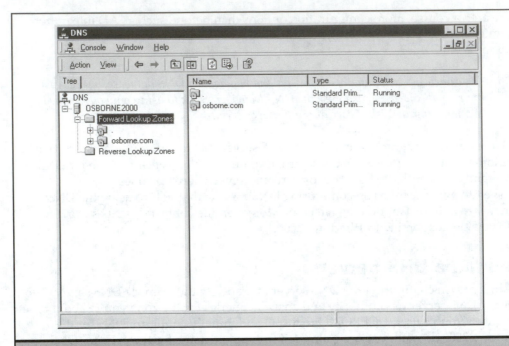

Figure 14-9.   *Viewing zones of a domain*

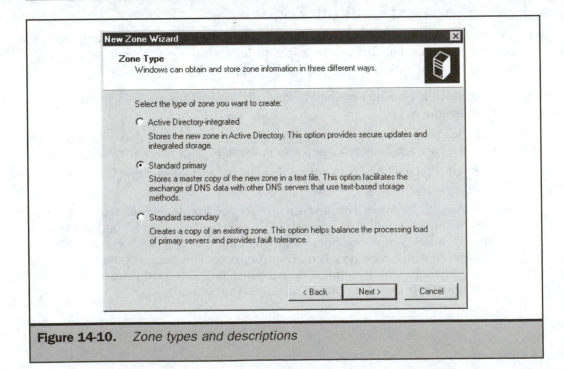

Figure 14-10.   *Zone types and descriptions*

5. Type in the zone name. Since I'm creating a new zone for the authors.osborne.com domain, I typed in the name of the domain. Click Next to continue.

6. The New Zone Wizard then asks you to supply the zone database filename with a .dns extension. I strongly recommend that you keep the name that Windows 2000 suggests. On this screen you can also specify an existing zone file if you're migrating a zone from another server. Before continuing to specify an existing file, be sure to copy it into the %SystemRoot%\System32\Dns directory. Click Next to continue.

7. The next and final screen, as illustrated in Figure 14-11, gives you a summary of the zone information you are about to create. Review the information for accuracy, and then click Finish to create the forward lookup zone.

Creating a Reverse Lookup Zone

Technically, a reverse lookup zone is not required for DNS to properly function within your environment. However, I recommend creating one because it helps you maintain and troubleshoot DNS by giving you the ability to use tools, such as NSLOOKUP (described in the section "NSLOOKUP," later in this chapter). Some applications may even require reverse lookup zones for security reasons.

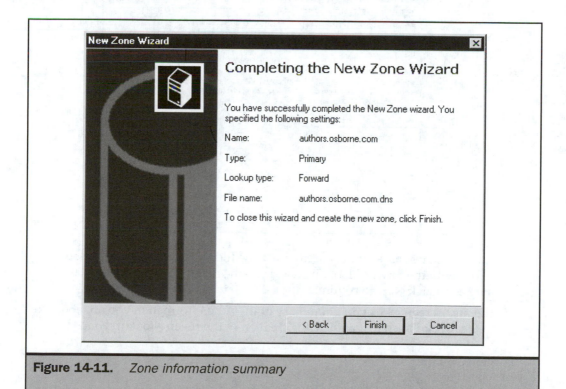

Figure 14-11.   *Zone information summary*

To create a reverse lookup zone, do the following:

1. Start the DNS Manager (named DNS on the toolbar) from Start | Programs | Administrative Tools.

2. In the left pane, select the domain you wish to create a reverse lookup zone in order to view the Reverse Lookup Zone folder in the right pane.

3. Right-click on the Reverse Lookup Zone folder and select New Zone. This initiates the New Zone Wizard. Click Next to continue.

4. Select either Active Directory-integrated, Standard Primary, or Standard Secondary for the zone type. For this example, I'm choosing Standard Primary.

5. Enter the network ID and subnet mask for the server. In this case, the server's IP address is 192.168.1.2 with a subnet mask of 255.255.255.0. So, in the following illustration, the network ID is 192.168.1. The 255s mask the network ID. For more information on TCP/IP, refer to Chapter 13. Click Next to continue.

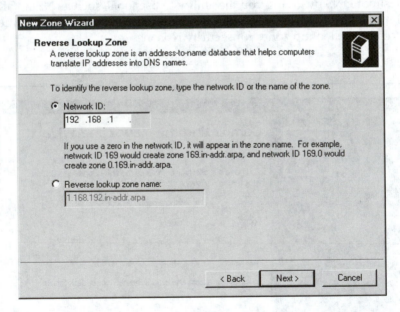

6. The next screen asks you to specify the zone filename. As I recommended before with the forward lookup zone, keep the name that Windows 2000 suggests. Click Next to continue.

7. The next screen gives you a summary of the zone information you are about to create. Click Finish to complete the creation of the reverse lookup zone.

Enabling Dynamic DNS

One of the best features of Windows 2000 DNS is its ability to dynamically update the DNS database. DDNS is based on RFC 2136, and it adds the UPDATE API, which allows servers (DHCP, DC, and DNS servers) and client machines to update resource records in the DNS database. This is in contrast to the older, static DNS servers where you had to manually update a zone's resource records anytime a change occurred. What does DDNS mean to you? It means that you don't have to be burdened with constant manual updates to the DNS database, even when you use DHCP for client machines. Windows 2000 does a lot of the work for you.

In order to take advantage of DDNS, you must integrate DNS and AD. DNS and AD integration issues are examined later in this chapter in "Integrating DNS with Active Directory." For now, I'm going to keep it simple and just say that you must promote the DNS server to a DC to use DDNS.

Promoting a DNS server to a DC to allow dynamic updates is different from a zone being AD-integrated. An AD-integrated zone keeps the DNS database within the AD structure and permits you to join the DNS replication scheme to AD.

After you've promoted the DNS server to AD, you can allow dynamic updates. To configure the zone to use DDNS, do the following:

1. Open the DNS Manager from the Start | Programs | Administrative Tools menu.

2. Right-click on the forward zone that you wish to allow dynamic updates and select Properties. If you've configured a root "." server for your Windows 2000 network, I recommend that you don't allow dynamic updates for the root. Instead, configure DDNS on top-level domains or subdomains.

3. On the General Tab, select Yes for Allow Dynamic Updates? as shown in Figure 14-12.

4. Click OK.

Other DNS Server Configuration Options

A wide variety of options can be configured within DNS. I've already discussed specifying a primary DNS server, creating forward and reverse zones, and enabling DDNS. These options are essential, but others may or may not play as important a role in your environment. It totally depends on you and your network environment. The configuration options discussed in the following sections are important and appropriate for any Windows 2000 network environment.

CONNECTING WITH WINDOWS 2000

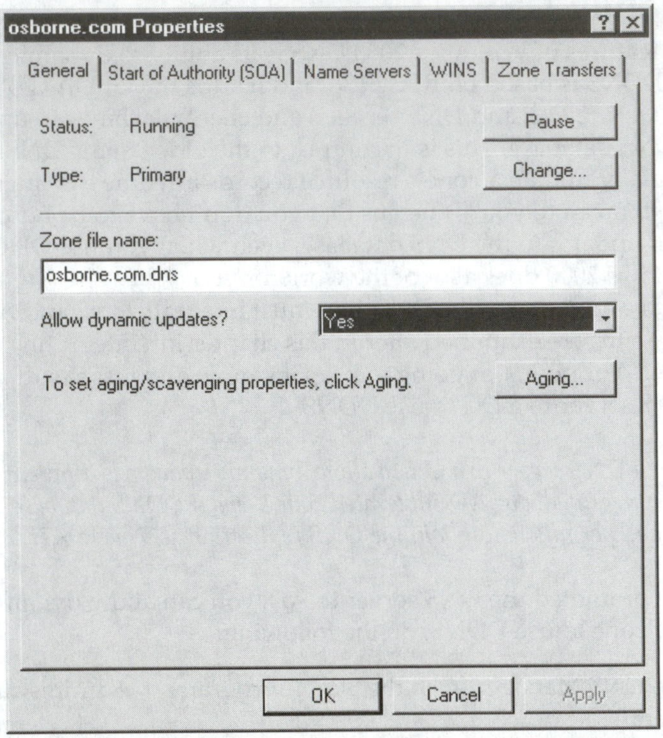

Figure 14-12.   *Allowing dynamic updates*

Adding Resource Records

After zones are created, you can add other resource records to the DNS database. There are many resource records that you can choose to create. See "DNS Database Files and Resource Records" earlier in this chapter for a list of resource records that you can add. The exception, however, is that some resource records can't be added because they have already been created when the zone was created. For example, the SOA record is created automatically when the zone is defined.

Caution   *If you employ DDNS, you'll want to be careful of which resource records you'll be adding. Don't bother creating resource records for machines that can automatically register themselves in the DNS database.*

To add a resource record, simply right-click on the zone in which you'd like to add a resource record and choose New *<resource record>* of your choice. The most common ones are readily available to you. For example, in Figure 14-13, the Mail Exchange (MX) record is highlighted and can be selected if you wish to create the record.

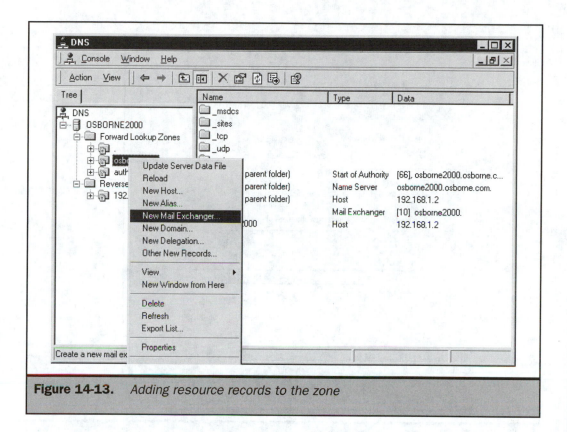

Figure 14-13.   *Adding resource records to the zone*

Testing Your Configurations

It's very important to test configurations before they are put into production
environments. This is especially important after you create forward and reverse lookup
zones or enable DDNS.

Windows 2000's DNS makes it really easy for you to test the functionality of your
zones by providing a facility in the DNS Manager that tests queries for the two zones.
To test the zones, do the following:

1. Open the DNS Manager from the Start | Programs | Administrative Tools menu.

2. In the left pane, right-click on the primary DNS server for the zones you wish to
   test and select Properties.

3. Under the Monitoring tab, check the test type you wish to perform. You have
   two options, a simple or a recursive query, as shown in Figure 14-14.

4. You now have two additional options. You can either perform the test
   immediately or specify a time interval. To test immediately, press the Test
   Now button.

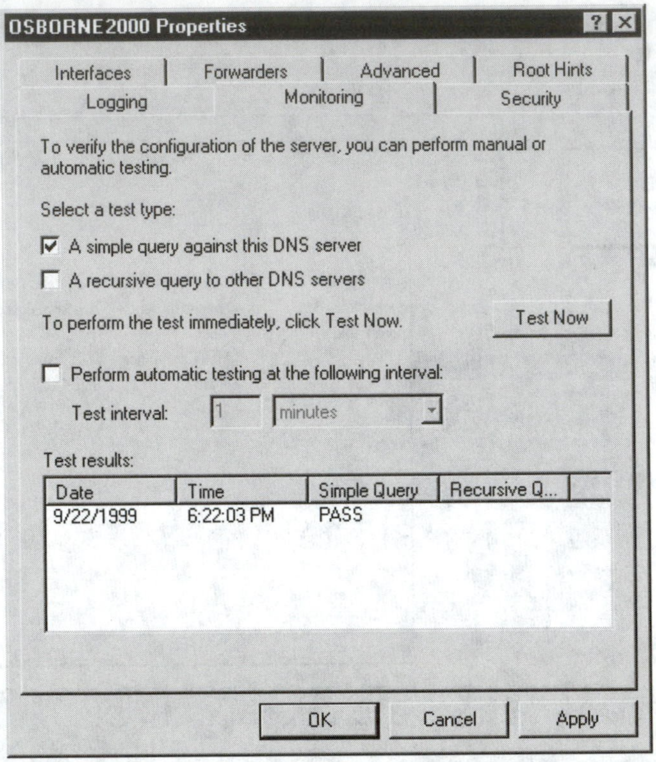

Figure 14-14.   *Testing the DNS configuration*

5. Test results are displayed in the test results box at the bottom of the window.

6. Click OK to exit the DNS server's Properties window.

Another option at your disposal is to use the NSLOOKUP utility to test your DNS server. It can be especially useful for testing reverse lookups. NSLOOKUP is covered in detail later in this chapter.

Logging Options

Logging is a useful way of getting information from the DNS service, and it can be used for troubleshooting purposes as well. Figure 14-15 shows the options within the Logging tab. The following is a list of events that can be logged:

- Query
- Notify
- Update

- Questions
- Answers
- Send
- Receive
- UDP
- TCP
- Full packets
- Write through

The information from these events is logged in the %SystemRoot%\System32\ Dns\dns.log file.

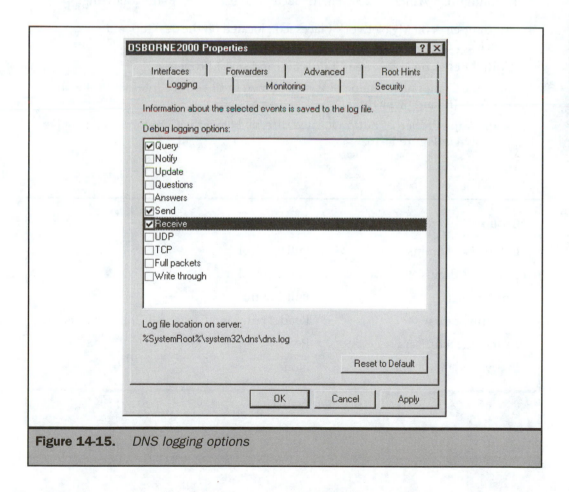

Figure 14-15. *DNS logging options*

Security Options

DNS gives you the ability to delegate permissions to groups and users for administering and managing the service. You can choose to tighten or loosen the security on DNS. Before doing so, carefully plan and prepare the security permissions so that the service isn't compromised in any way. For more information on security, refer to Chapter 21.

Table 14-5 shows some of the default permissions for DNS.

Configuring Clients to Use DNS

Client machines must be aware of or notified to use DNS for name resolution in a Windows 2000 network environment. The vast majority of you are probably already having clients use DNS to get out onto the Internet (unless you're using a proxy). Now, however, DNS is also providing name resolution for Windows machines in the internal network, so it's imperative that you configure them to use DNS either through manual configuration or through DHCP.

To configure a Windows 2000 client machine to use DNS, do the following:

1. Right-click on My Network Places icon located on the desktop and select Properties.

2. Right-click on Local Area Connection and select Properties.

3. In the Components dialog box, scroll down until you see Internet Protocol (TCP/IP) and highlight it.

4. Click the Properties button located directly below the Components dialog box shown in Figure 14-16.

Group	Permissions
Enterprise Admins	Full Control
Domain Admins	Full Control
DnsAdmins	Full Control
Administrators	Read, Write, and Create All Child Objects
Authenticated Users	Read
Everyone	None

Table 14-5.   *Groups and Associated Permissions for DNS*

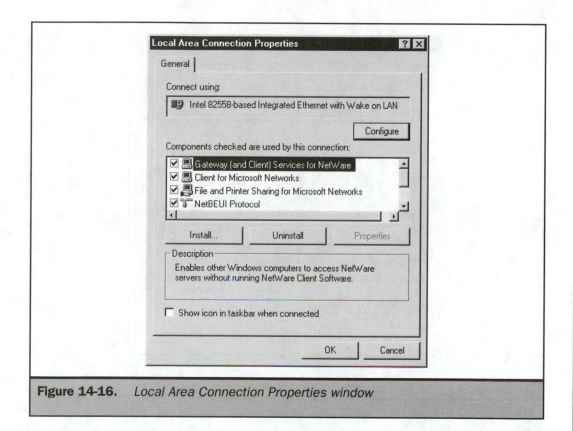

Figure 14-16. *Local Area Connection Properties window*

5. If you're using DHCP, make sure that Obtain DNS Server Address Automatically is selected. Otherwise, specify the IP address for the primary and secondary DNS server as in Figure 14-17.

6. Click OK to close the Internet Protocol (TCP/IP) Properties window.

7. Click OK to close the Local Area Connection Properties window.

Integrating DDNS with DHCP

DDNS and DHCP are two services that complement one another. DDNS allows servers (including DHCP) and client machines to dynamically update the DNS database. In particular, they are allowed to update A (name maps to an IP address) and PTR (IP address maps to a name) records. DHCP, on the other hand, dynamically assigns IP addresses and other TCP/IP-related information to its clients. More information can be found on DHCP in Chapter 13. Integration of the two services enables both of them to communicate and keep track of the constantly changing IP addresses and their corresponding host names.

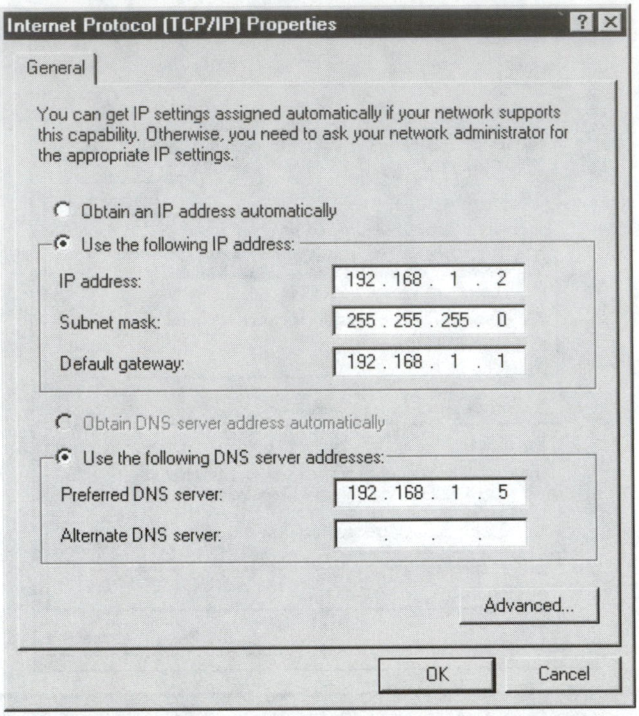

Figure 14-17.   *Internet Protocol (TCP/IP) Properties window*

Microsoft is currently working with the Internet Engineering Task Force (IETF) for the DHCP-DNS interaction specifications, which can be found at the following location: ftp://ftp.ietf.cnri.reston.va.us/internet-drafts/draft-ietf-dhc-dhcp-dns-10.txt

Many important concepts are contained within this document, but the two most notable are how the DHCP server is used to update A and PTR records and the specifications for the new DHCP option code 81 (a.k.a. Client FQDN).

The Registration and Update Process

Windows 2000 client machines can use DHCP to obtain network configuration parameters such as an IP address, subnet mask, default gateway, and much more at startup. The DHCP server optionally can then register the client's A and PTR resource records with DDNS from the client's fully qualified domain name (FQDN) as shown in the following illustration. When an update occurs after a specified period of time, the client's DHCP service or the DHCP server updates the client's A and PTR resource record with DDNS.

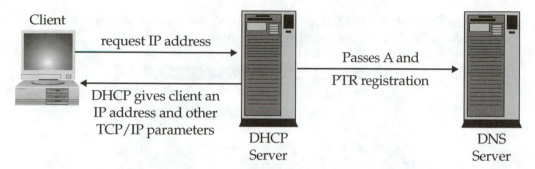

In summary, there are three possible scenarios for Windows 2000 clients interacting and registering with DDNS. They are the following:

■ Windows 2000 clients can register with DDNS without DHCP interaction.

■ A Windows 2000 DHCP server can register on behalf of Windows 2000 clients. The process of who does the registration can be negotiated.

■ A Windows 2000 DHCP server can register on behalf of Windows 2000 clients without negotiating.

DOWN-LEVEL CLIENTS   The registration and update process for down-level clients is a bit trickier. They go through the same process of obtaining information from a DHCP server, and the DHCP server registers the down-level client's A and PTR resource records with DDNS. However, when an update occurs, the registration is different because they don't support DDNS.

By default, the Enable Updates For DNS Clients That Do Not Support Dynamic Updates option is turned on. Don't trust this option because down-level clients cannot and will not update with DDNS directly. Instead, this option means that down-level clients can have their resource records updated with DDNS, but the DHCP server serves as the middleman. Only the DHCP server can register on behalf of a down-level client. Since the down-level client is inherently unaware of AD, it is also oblivious to the nonnegotiated registration process.

DISABLING DYNAMIC UPDATES FOR DOWN-LEVEL CLIENTS   You are given the choice of whether you want to keep the Enable Updates For DNS Clients That Do Not Support Dynamic Updates option enabled within DHCP. And, more importantly, you don't have to go searching through the registry to disable this option, because it's built within the DHCP interface. To disable this option do the following:

1. Open the DHCP console window from the Start | Programs | Administrative Tools menu.

2. Right-click on the scope you wish to configure, and choose Properties.

CONNECTING WITH
WINDOWS 2000

3. In the DNS tab (see the following illustration), deselect the option Enable Updates For DNS Client That Do Not Support Dynamic Updates.

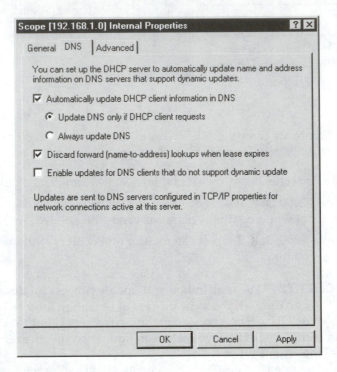

4. Click OK to exit the Scope Properties window.

5. Exit the DHCP console.

DHCP Option 81

The IETF draft mentioned earlier also describes an additional DHCP option code (option code 81). This option code gives the DHCP server three options for processing DNS information for a DHCP client:

- It always registers the DHCP client's A and PTR resource records with DDNS.
- It never registers DHCP client's A resource record.
- It registers the DHCP client's A and PTR resource records with DDNS only at the client's request.

Integrating DNS with Active Directory

By now you are well aware that Windows 2000 (AD in particular) relies on DNS to resolve names to IP addresses and vice versa. DNS is one of the underlying mechanisms for Windows 2000, and you've already seen that the integration of the two is especially important for locating DCs in the AD schema as well as for allowing dynamic updates from servers and clients.

The one important thing yet to be examined is integrating the DNS zone structure within the AD. Combining the two services in this manner gives you the ability to use AD to store and replicate zone information.

> **Note**   *The AD is covered in-depth in Chapter 15.*

Storing the DNS database

Traditional versions of DNS store the DNS database in ASCII text files on the primary DNS servers. Secondary DNS servers use the same information as the primary, but the files are read-only. Therefore, any changes that are to be made to the DNS database must occur on the primary DNS server. Moreover, when changes are made to the DNS database, the information is replicated (via zone transfer) to all secondary DNS servers for that zone.

The limitations for the traditional way of storing the DNS database are rather straightforward. They include, but aren't limited to:

- DNS has a single point of failure. If the primary server goes down, changes to DNS can't be made.

- As the DNS database gets larger, the zone transfer times increase because the entire DNS database is sent.

- The database is in ASCII format (need I say more?).

Don't get me wrong. I'm not saying that this method is bad or error prone. It is an irrefutable fact that DNS has been very successful since its inception, and it will continue to provide exceptional name resolution for the entire world. What I am saying, though, is that integrating DNS zones to the AD schema provides an enhancement to the traditional method.

Once AD is installed on a DNS server, you can continue to use standard methods for storing and replicating DNS zone information, but the benefits come when you use AD. With AD, all the zone information is stored in the AD structure rather than in text files. The zone text files become AD objects and are replicated by AD.

The benefits of using AD-integrated zones are enormous. To name a few, they include:

- It removes the single point of failure if you have multiple DCs and DNS servers. Updates can be made to more than just one DNS server for the zone.

- AD controls the replication intervals, and only the changes made to DNS are replicated instead of transferring the entire zone. This makes DNS replication faster and more efficient than standard zone transfers.

- You only have to deal with one replication technology. This makes DNS administration and management much simpler.

CONNECTING WITH
WINDOWS 2000

■ AD sites can be used to manage the replication traffic on the LAN and WAN.

■ It strengthens security. You can now use an access control list (ACL) to tighten security of the DNS database. You can also control access of zone objects as well as resource records.

■ Zone information is automatically propagated to new DCs within that zone.

Changing Zone Types

Even if you've already been using standard primary Windows 2000 DNS zones, it's not too late to make the switch to using AD-integrated zones and take advantage of the benefits it brings. To change a zone to AD-integrated status, do the following:

1. Open the DNS Manager from the Start | Programs | Administrative Tools menu.

2. Right-click on the primary zone you want to change to AD-integrated and select Properties. You should see a window similar to the one in the following illustration.

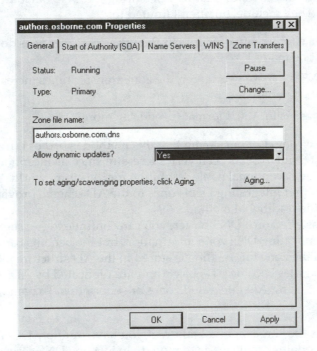

3. Under the General tab, click the Change button.

4. Change the zone type from Standard Primary to Active Directory-integrated as shown in the following illustration.

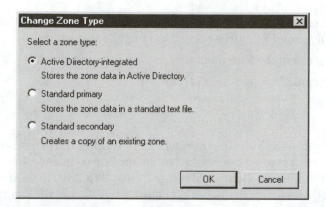

5. Click OK to close the Change Zone Type window.

6. Click OK to close the <Zone> Properties window.

7. Exit the DNS Manager.

Maintaining and Troubleshooting DNS

Unfortunately, DNS isn't one of those services that you just install and forget about (most aren't). You'll need to keep watch over it, not necessarily because you'll have trouble with it, but because taking a proactive stance always ensures less stress and fewer headaches.

The sections to follow show you some useful utilities and procedures that can be used to maintain or troubleshoot DNS.

DNSCMD

Those of you coming from a UNIX or scripting background are going to feel at home with DNSCMD. DNSCMD is a command-line utility found in the Windows 2000 Resource Kit that is used to manage DNS servers.

This tool can be used for a variety of different tasks including:

■ Create script or batch files to automate daily administrative processes in DNS. This is useful when you have standard primary zone using text-based files.

■ Update resource records

■ Set up and configure new DNS servers

Installing the DNSCMD utility is extremely easy. All you need to do is the following:

1. Copy DNSCMD from the \Support\Enterprise\Reskit folder on the Windows 2000 Server CD-ROM to the folder of your choice on the DNS server. For

example, copy the file into the C:\DNS Utilities folder. Note that the Windows 2000 Professional Resource Kit doesn't include this utility.

2. Type **dnscmd** in the Run menu or from a command prompt.

3. Type **dnscmd /?** for parameters and help.

Ping

Ping is a utility within the built-in suite of TCP/IP utilities. It is commonly used on TCP/IP networks but is often overlooked as an applicable troubleshooting tool for DNS. Ping uses the Internet Control Message Protocol (ICMP) to verify the existence of particular IP addresses on the network. Figure 14-18 shows the ping utility used to verify connectivity to www.unknown.com.

Ping helps distinguish where the problem(s) may be because you quickly determine whether or not there are connectivity issues with other machines including the DNS server. For instance, if a client is having difficulty resolving names, this is one of the first utilities that you should use to see any connectivity issues from the client to the DNS server. You can then proceed to see if you can ping other machines on the network. If a ping successfully reaches another machine on the network, you may be able to narrow the scope of the problem to DNS configuration error on the client, a DNS server problem, and so on.

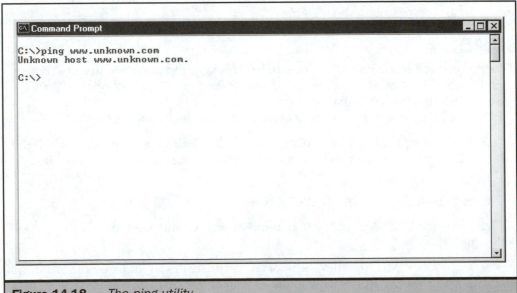

Figure 14-18.   *The ping utility*

IPCONFIG

IPCONFIG is another command-line TCP/IP utility that can be used for DNS. Typing IPCONFIG at a Command prompt, like the one in Figure 14-19, displays a computer's TCP/IP network configuration. For example, you can use this to verify DNS server entries in your TCP/IP network configuration.

   This utility can also be used to manually renew a client's DNS registration, troubleshoot a failed DNS name registration, or troubleshoot a dynamic update to a DNS server. To renew or troubleshoot a client's DNS registration, simply open a Command prompt and type **ipconfig /registerdns**. The command refreshes DHCP leases and reregisters the computer's host name.

  You can only use the ipconfig /registerdns option on systems configured to use DHCP.

NSLOOKUP

NSLOOKUP is a diagnostic utility that displays information from DNS. More specifically, it allows you to have a dialog with DNS and lets you examine resource records. Like the utilities mentioned earlier, NSLOOKUP is run from the command line. It has the following syntax:

```
nslookup [-option ...] [hostname | - [server]]
```

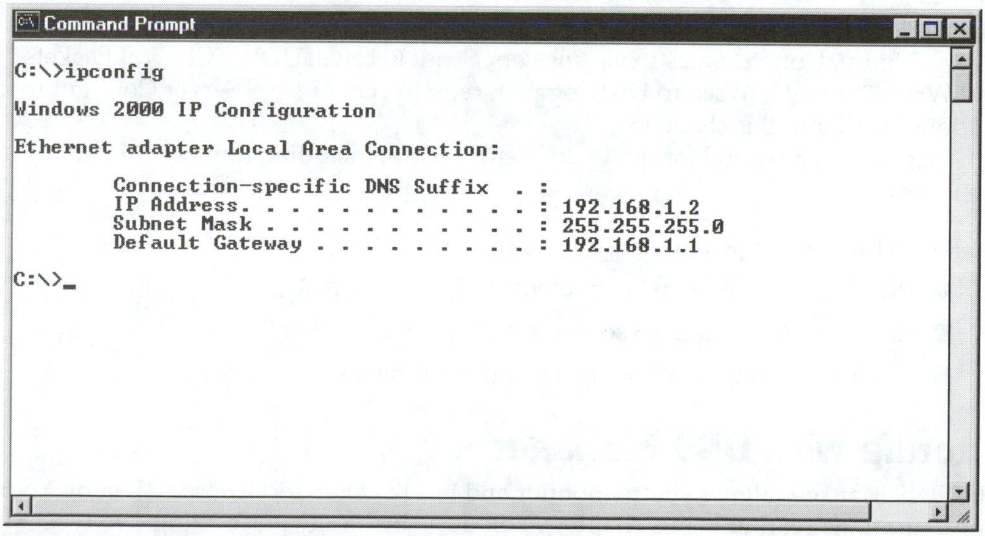

```
Command Prompt                                                  _ □ X

C:\>ipconfig

Windows 2000 IP Configuration

Ethernet adapter Local Area Connection:

        Connection-specific DNS Suffix  . :
        IP Address. . . . . . . . . . . . : 192.168.1.2
        Subnet Mask . . . . . . . . . . . : 255.255.255.0
        Default Gateway . . . . . . . . . : 192.168.1.1

C:\>_
```

Figure 14-19.   *Using the IPCONFIG utility*

where:

- **-option ...**   specifies one of more command-line options. For a list of commands, type NSLOOKUP/? Every option is preceded with a hyphen (-) or an equal sign (=) and ends with a value. You can also specify more than one option.

- **hostname**   uses the host name you specify or defaults to the *server* you specified.

- **server**   uses the DNS server you specify. Otherwise, it defaults to the DNS server specified in your TCP/IP network configuration.

For example, typing **nslookup -querytype=mx company.com** displays the mail exchange record for company.com.

There are many other appropriate uses for the NSLOOKUP utility, including the following:

- Verify resource records within a zone.

- Verify that the DNS server is responding to requests. For example, typing **nslookup 207.206.205.204 127.0.0.1**, where the first IP address is the DNS server "localhost" is returned if the server is responding.

- Verify that DCs are correctly added to the zones with the SRV resource record.

- Test WINS-sourced responsiveness.

Logging

The DNS Manager allows you to configure additional logging options, including Query, Notify, Update, Questions, Answers, Send, Receive, UDP, TCP, Full Packets, and Write Through. To set up DNS logging, refer to "Other DNS Server Configuration Options" earlier in this chapter.

Logging can be useful for many different reasons, including (but not limited to) the following:

- Debugging registrations, queries, and more

- Providing statistical measurements of DNS activities

- Capacity-planning DNS server utilization

- Troubleshooting client name resolution problems

Monitoring with DNS Manager

The DNS Manager allows you to monitor and test the DNS service (see "Testing Your Configurations" earlier in this chapter). You do so by locally performing two types of queries:

- **Simple**   This query tests forward lookup (name mapping to an IP address) capabilities of the DNS server.

- **Recursive**   This query tests reverse lookup (IP address mapping to a name) capabilities of the DNS server. If another server is present in the same zone, it forwards the query to the other DNS server. In order to perform this test, you must have defined a reverse lookup zone.

The results of the tests are recorded in the results section of the window. The DNS Manager will tell you that it either passed or failed.

You can also configure DNS to automatically perform these queries at specified time intervals. This is particularly useful if you have recently installed and configured a DNS and you want to keep a close watch on it until you feel comfortable that everything is working properly.

CONNECTING WITH
WINDOWS 2000

The Complete Reference

Chapter 15

Understanding Active Directory

Active Directory (AD) is one of the most important, core services of Windows 2000. It revolutionizes the organization of Windows 2000 network environments, especially when compared to the organizational models of Windows NT.

AD completely changes our familiarity with Windows-based environments. It is a centralized service for managing otherwise distributed directory services. All services that use a directory to store information in Windows 2000 use AD. The information that it holds is stored as objects (another unfamiliar concept to the Windows world). This chapter sheds light on what AD is and how it encompasses many, if not all, aspects of Windows 2000 network environments.

Directory Services

Let's face it, directories exist everywhere. They are repositories of various types of information. The epitome of a directory that's been in existence for as long as you can remember is the telephone book. It lists names, addresses, and phone numbers for everyone to use. Also, for those of you who'd rather not take the time to look up a person's or company's phone number, the baby bells are also offering the directory assistance extension (a directory extension) to the phone book. Now all you have to do is call 411 and say the person's or company's name and their location to get the information you need.

The directory isn't a new concept within the computer world either, but they have traditionally been disparate and incongruent. Applications, such as e-mail or database systems, all provide their own type of directory for the network. Also, prior versions to Windows 2000, namely Windows NT 3.*x* and 4.0, have many directory-related services. For instance, a user and his or her associated security permissions, descriptions, and profiles are kept within Windows NT's SAM. Any other directory that isn't contained within the SAM must be kept either in the Registry or by the application that uses that information. When you combine the ability to send and receive e-mail, you're creating two different directories, one for the user account and another for the e-mail account. Now, it is important to note that a Windows NT user account can be associated with Microsoft's Exchange Server (versions 5.5 and below) but the two services are only loosely integrated; they still remain separate directories (you still need to create two accounts).

Directory services, on the other hand, reach beyond the standard directory functionality by providing a more unified directory that can incorporate a variety of information from many sources. These sources may be several different applications from a single vendor or may allow other vendors to publish and share information to a single directory.

The Purpose of Directory Services

Computers have taken over almost every business facet from filing to forecasting, and the information keeps piling up. The traditional way of keeping up with the vast amounts of information is to store it on separate distributed systems. This drastically affects the way companies do business because the communication between those systems is often limited in the best-case scenario. In fact, most directories are disparate in nature, which brings a higher learning curve (administrators must learn a variety of different systems), additional workloads, and an increase in costs to support them. Using the example above, if you were to provide only file/print and e-mail services to your users, you would essentially have to double your administrative efforts because you have two accounts to deal with, not one. Also, what happens when a user leaves your company? Are there multiple applications that you must turn to in order to deactivate or remove the account?

Directory services are changing the way companies do business by encompassing the needs of the business rather than just a particular subset of the business such as e-mail. Directory services are the means by which to organize the information that floods us on a daily basis. They serve as a repository where various types of objects containing information (names, addresses, phone numbers, e-mail addresses, birthdays, department location, and much more) can be stored and retrieved by everyone. The stored objects don't necessarily have to be users; they can be items in a grocery store, computers, printing devices, and so on. Directory services aren't mere centralized databases. Instead, a directory service can be considered a specialized database where all services and information with regard to the network can be stored and located.

In addition, directory services allow you to centrally manage (add, delete, and modify) the information contained within them. In other words, you don't need to go to the individual applications to manage users who are allowed to use the database, reconfigure permissions for a user, delete an e-mail account, or manage a printer's settings.

Directory services try to bring unity to otherwise separate, diverse network environments. By combining network services and information into a single entity, you simplify the administrative support model and thus reduce total cost of ownership (TCO). The exact amount of reduction in TCO is difficult to determine. Generally speaking, the reduction in TCO is proportional to the size of your environment. For example, small environments with one or two servers supporting the infrastructure probably won't see as much of a benefit as, say, a large company with hundreds or thousands of servers and services to support. The important thing to remember is that every network environment benefits from a single common directory service.

There are many directory services that exist for network environments today. They include but aren't limited to:

- Directory Access Protocol (DAP)
- Directory System Protocol (DSP)
- Directory Information Shadowing Protocol (DISP)
- Lightweight Directory Access Protocol (LDAP)
- X.500
- Novell Directory Services (NDS)
- Active Directory (AD)

CONNECTING WITH
WINDOWS 2000

Directory services must adhere to standards to provide the greatest amount of accessibility from different application vendors that may be present on any given network. They must also ensure the following:

- **Extensibility**   To change and extend itself as business changes
- **Flexibility**   To store a wide variety of information
- **Scalability**   To accommodate all sizes of network environments
- **Security**   To provide a secure means to store, locate, and manage information

DAP and X.500

X.500 is an open standard that has been adopted by many companies, including Microsoft, for their directory service model. It defines the entire gamut for protocols commonly used for directory services including namespace concerns, functionality, authentication, and much more.

One of several protocols that X.500 defines is the *Directory Access Protocol (DAP)*, which helps clients access and communicate with the directory. Microsoft and others have deemed DAP as a full OSI protocol, meaning it has a large range of functionality compared to other directory service-related protocols. Contrary to what you may believe, this increased functionality and complexity are DAP's major downfall as well. It is just too heavy and cumbersome a protocol to be efficient with personal computers, thin clients, and the Internet.

PCs, thin clients, and the concerns surrounding the growing Internet required a more lightweight protocol that included only the most vital functionality. As a result, a new directory service protocol, the *Lightweight Directory Service Protocol (LDAP)*, emerged to remove the constraints posed by DAP.

LDAP

LDAP is modeled from X.500 and DAP. As the name implies, LDAP is a smaller protocol than its predecessors are, and its design utilizes their best attributes for greater versatility. Moreover, it's designed specifically for managing and querying information in a directory service over a TCP connection (port 389).

LDAP acceptance and adoption is becoming more and more commonplace in the industry as software vendors strive to provide unified directory services. In fact, LDAP has been widely accepted to support the Internet. All the major players, including Microsoft, use LDAP as an underlying structure for their own directory services. For example, Microsoft's AD uses LDAP natively (supports the latest LDAP, version 3) but has also incorporated extensions to accommodate the needs of a Windows 2000 AD environment.

LDAP Architecture Basics

LDAP supports both client- and server-side communications but most vendors primarily use it for clients to manage and query information in their own directory service. It is hierarchic or treelike in structure, which allows for better storing and searching of objects in the directory tree. The *directory information tree* (DIT) contains the information for a network environment, and subtrees can branch off the trunk. This is similar to the hierarchical nature of DNS, which you read about in Chapter 14. Each object in the DIT, such as a user or printer, is referred to as the *directory service entry (DSE)*.

Each object in the DIT must be unique within the LDAP structure. Therefore, you must use either a distinguished name (DN), which represents the object's full name as it fits within the DIT, or a relative distinguished name (RDN), which is a subset of the DN. For example, the DN identifying the user Lewellen in the trinity.org domain could be the following:

```
/O=Internet/DC=ORG/DC=trinity/CN=users/CN=Lewellen
```

where

- O represents the Organization
- DC represents the Domain Component
- CN represents the Common Name

The RDN for Lewellen in the previous example could be CN=Lewellen.

As you'd expect, the object-unique attributes are used in search operations when an application performs a query. There are three basic types of searches that can be performed on a DIT: string, numeric, and Boolean. Table 15-1 lists expressions for each of these types.

LDAP Version 3

Many improvements have been made to LDAP since its inception in 1994. Its current release, version 3, has gained much popularity and acceptance as one of the underlying support structures for the Internet and directory services. LDAP version 3 is described in RFCs 2251-2256.

The following is a list of improvements made to LDAP in version 3:

- Enhanced security
- Unicode and UTF-8 encoding support
- Multilingual support
- New commands to extend LDAP's functionality with other, proprietary systems
- Discovery enhancements for obtaining the schema and the DIT
- Load-balancing (queries can be passed off to other servers with less workloads)
- Partitioning of the DIT (e.g., domains partition the DIT)

Search Expression	Description
Approximate	Searches on variations on the specified query value
Equal to	Finds an exact match
Greater than	Greater than the string (alphabetically) or numeric value specified in the query
Greater than or equal to	A string or numeric value that matches or is greater than the specified query value
Less than	Less than the string (alphabetically) or numeric value specified in the query
Less than or equal to	A string or numeric value that matches or is less than the specified query value
Substring	All strings that contain the specified query value
And	Requires an exact match between the two specified query values
Or	Requires at least one match between the two values specified
Not	All other values other than what was specified

Table 15-1. *Possible Search Expressions*

Active Directory Concepts

Directory services are becoming increasingly vital to the stability, flexibility, and availability of your network environment. They provide it with consistency with regard to how you name, store, find, secure, and manage resources.

Although some may say it is late to the directory services game, AD is a full-scale, enterprise-class directory service for the Windows 2000 platform. It isn't simply an add-on to the operating system but rather a tightly integrated service. AD is intertwined with the rest of Windows 2000; management, TCP/IP related communications, security, and much more all support and rely on AD.

AD brings many advantages to your network environment, including:

- **Extensibility** AD comes with predefined objects and attributes for storing and managing a variety of information. However, if you feel that they don't adequately fit the needs of your environment, you can simply define more.

- **Supportability** Its very design helps minimize the number of directories that you need to support. Most, if not all, network-related objects can be centrally managed from AD. Reducing the number of directories you have to administer reduces cost and the amount of time needed to support a variety of different systems. Also, AD supports down-level client systems. Down-level clients view the domain as a Windows NT 4.0 domain (except in Native mode).

- **Standardization**   AD was built with open standards in mind. It's X.500 compatible and uses LDAP as its main communication protocol. Basing itself on open Internet standards allows it to communicate with other directories that conform to these same standards.

- **Scalability**   As mentioned earlier, AD allows you to add objects to its information store. In addition, AD is designed to accommodate different-sized network environments. It can support networks with relatively few objects as well as ones with millions of objects.

- **Flexibility**   AD can be stretched to support otherwise separate directories, and it can be molded to fit your operational needs.

- **Security**   Supporting open standards relates to security as well. AD's security is based on the Kerberos protocol for a more robust, secure environment. It surpasses the NTLM security mechanism in Windows NT environments.

The Active Directory Structure

Most of the AD structural components are new and unfamiliar, but there are some that you may feel comfortable with, depending on your background. No matter how much you know about Windows NT, networking, and programming, don't underestimate the learning curve for AD's new concepts and technologies.

Active Directory and the Windows 2000 Architecture

It's hard to imagine that a change in an operating system of this magnitude (30+ million lines of code!) didn't require a complete overhaul to Windows 2000's core services. Fortunately, Microsoft's planning the design for future enhancements has really paid off. Because Windows 2000 was built from a modular operating system (see Figure 15-1 for an illustration of the Windows NT architectural model), the development team could plug in additional components and enhance the original code as needed.

Figure 15-2 illustrates how AD fits within the Windows 2000 architectural model. You can see that it fits within the security subsystem. The reason that it's integrated with the security subsystem instead of being its own separate subsystem is because anytime a request is made to access a directory object, the process or user must be authenticated by the security subsystem. Then the process or user goes through an authorization process (validating permissions) performed by the security subsystem and security reference monitor. For more information on security, refer to Chapter 21.

Defining Key Active Directory Concepts

The key AD concepts may be a little confusing at first. To fully appreciate the new terms, technologies, concepts, and the like, you should also read Chapter 13 on TCP/IP

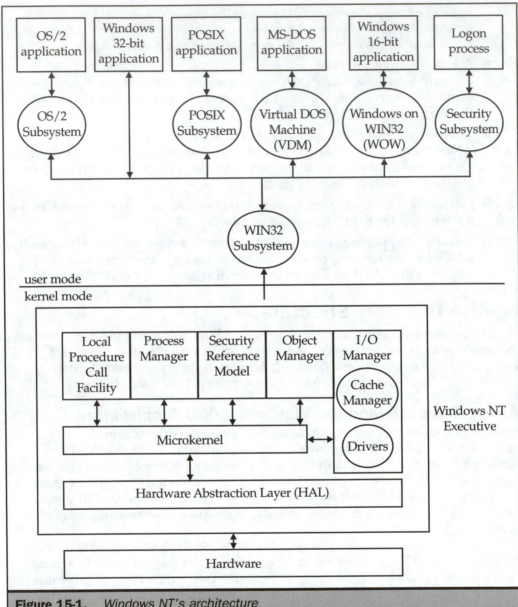

Figure 15-1. *Windows NT's architecture*

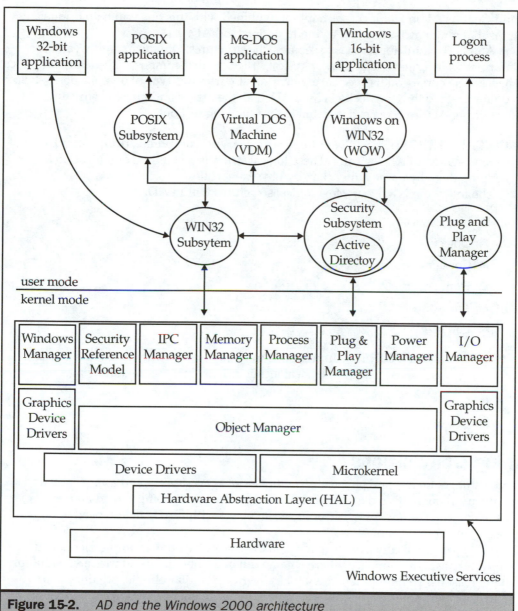

Figure 15-2. *AD and the Windows 2000 architecture*

and Chapter 14 on DNS. These chapters combined with this one will help bridge any gaps that you may have while trying to understand AD.

Another helpful approach is to separate the structures. Organizing this wealth of information in terms of logical and physical structures that compose AD greatly simplifies the learning curve you'll experience. Microsoft also uses this type of organization to help you understand the complexity behind AD. Both the logical and physical structures comprising AD are explained in detail in the following sections.

LOGICAL STRUCTURES   Resources, such as users, computers, printers, and so on, are represented in AD logically. These logical structures facilitate organization by grouping them by name rather than by physical location.

The following is a list of a few logical structures within AD:

- Namespace
- Objects
- Containers
- Domains
- Trees
- Forests

PHYSICAL STRUCTURES   In comparison to the logical structures, AD's physical structures are defined by their physical location. They include the following:

- Sites
- Domain controllers (DCs)

Naming Conventions

Everything—logical and physical structures—in AD is represented as an object and is given a name. This makes the directory service easier to comprehend and use. For instance, when you want to use or locate an object within AD, all you need to do is specify the object's name.

AD itself is actually a namespace (like the telephone book example mentioned earlier) that sets a boundary where a name can be resolved. Boundaries are useful for many reasons. To name a few, they logically group similar objects, organize your network environment, reduce storage space requirements needed to contain the information, and much more. Imagine trying to look up a person's phone number in a telephone directory for the entire world. What if that same telephone book wasn't organized by name or geographically? In that case, few would bother looking up the information; it would just be too difficult.

Since AD is represented by objects that are given names, these names must be unique. This doesn't mean that you're in trouble if you have two people with the same name in the same company. These two people are unique. As you will see below, AD guarantees that an object is unique within its boundaries.

Object Names

AD's support for many open Internet standards allows it to support a variety of name formats. These name formats also help differentiate each object name. Applications and users that need to access the directory service can use the following name formats:

- **DNS names**   AD domains are Domain Name System (DNS) names. This tight integration with DNS also sets up a namespace boundary (AD is a namespace boundary, as is DNS). These domain names are usually referred to by the DNS name. For example, smartonline.com is both the AD domain name and the DNS name. However, domains are also given a corresponding NetBIOS name for compatibility with down-level clients and NetBIOS-dependent applications. You can find out more information on DNS in Chapter 14.

- **HTTP URL**   The HTTP protocol can be used to locate domains or domain objects. For example, http://www.task-group.com locates the Web server within the task-group.com domain. You can also use it to locate other objects within a domain, such as a user, but this approach is not recommended due to the complexity of specifying the URL (e.g., http://osborne2000.osborne.com/User/OU=college/CN=ErinS).

- **Distinguished Name (DN)**   Remember that every object in AD is guaranteed to be unique. The DN is the primary reason for this. It is an X.500 naming convention that identifies not only the object but also the object's relative path in the hierarchy (and a long one at that). The information that this name alone carries is more than you'd ever likely encounter. Fortunately, you probably will never have to directly interface with the DN because it's meant to be used by directory service protocols such as LDAP. For example, LDAP uses the X.500 name CN=John Smith, OU=authors, O=Osborne, C=US to locate John Smith in AD.

- **Relative Distinguished Name (RDN)**   The RDN is an attribute of the DN and is therefore a part of the X.500 nomenclature. As a result, when the DN is created, you automatically get several RDNs.

- **LDAP URL**   An LDAP URL, such as LDAP://serverA.mycompany.com/CN=Users/CN=Kimberly, uses the X.500 name to locate an object.

- **Universal Naming Convention (UNC)**   Many of you are probably already familiar with locating resources by a UNC name, such as \\osborne2000\authors\book.doc. UNC names are used to refer to shared files, directories, and printers just as they were in Windows NT.

- **User Principal Name (UPN)**   UPN names are more people friendly than the other names mentioned above. They are comprised of the object's name (or a modified version of the name) and the DNS object name where the object

CONNECTING WITH
WINDOWS 2000

resides. The most common example of a UPN is an e-mail address such as kellyburke@us.medicineman.com. The UPN is also used to log onto a Windows 2000 domain. Yes, that means that you log on using your e-mail address.

■ **Globally Unique Identifier (GUID)** The GUID is one of those attributes that no one talks about but everyone has. It is a 128-bit number assigned to every object in AD and guaranteed to be unique. It's also guaranteed to stay permanently attached to that object for its lifetime no matter what happens. For instance, if the object moves to another domain, many attributes may change but the GUID won't. One useful application for this is that when a service or application retrieves an object's GUID and stores it, the object can always be referenced no matter where it goes or whether it is renamed.

Naming Contexts

The AD database stores all objects for a Windows 2000 environment. Whether you have a single domain, a tree of domains, or a forest of noncontiguous namespaces (multiple trees), the AD database is a single, uniform database. (Don't worry; these topics will be discussed in detail momentarily.) For instance, domains company.com and childcompany.com in a forest don't keep separate AD databases, although they are entirely different domains.

So how does AD keep up with or maintain the objects that are stored in the database? Does this mean that each DC stores all objects for every domain in the forest? This is where naming contexts come into play. Although the concept of naming contexts is not simple, it is critical to completely understanding AD. Naming contexts, which are essentially partitions or continuous subtrees in the directory, keep the objects for each domain separate. Each DC holds objects relating to the domain that it belongs to. For example, the DC for childcompany.com holds the portion of the AD database that pertains to childcompany.com. An easier way to remember this is to think of the AD database as a distributed database where each DC is responsible for maintaining the portion of the database relating to its domain.

In the AD, a DC always holds at least three naming contexts:

■ **Schema** The schema holds information relating to the domain that the DC is a member of and is responsible for (see the section "Schema," later in this chapter for more information on the schema).

■ **Configuration** This naming context contains the replication topology and related metadata. It helps to define units of replication.

■ **User naming contexts** User naming contexts are the subtrees that contain the actual objects in AD. Each DC stores at least one user-naming context, but it could hold several.

Information about all the domains, whether you're talking about a single domain or a forest of domains, needs to be replicated to other DCs to fulfill the multimaster functionality. The benefit to the naming context design is that the replication of information can be partitioned into separate, discrete units. You can then replicate information within a domain separately as well as keep the replicated information relevant to the entire tree or forest separate. Moreover, the domains can be unique and independent, and at the same time, be unified throughout the tree or forest.

Objects

An AD object is a rather easy concept to grasp because we're always dealing with an object of some sort. The keyboard you type on is an object, the picture on your wall is an object, and so on. Objects, including AD objects, are a set of *attributes* that collectively represent something real. The *attributes* are characteristics that make the object unique. For example, a user object has a name, e-mail address, mailing address, phone number, and so on, that make it different from another user object, computer, printer, and so on.

Microsoft has predefined a set of objects as well as attributes for each object type. It is meant as a guideline only. The objects and attributes, like many other concepts in AD, can be modified to adjust to your particular environment. However, many Windows 2000 network environments are probably more than likely going to be more than satisfied with what Microsoft has already defined.

Object Classes

Your network environment can contain a small number of objects or several million. Obviously, the more objects you have, the harder they would be to manage effectively without some organization. The object class helps you organize objects by likeness. For example, all users (user objects) fall under the object class Users. Since they are categorized in the same object class, they all have a certain set of attributes associated with them (for example, an e-mail address). Again, the objects within an object class must all be unique, although they have the same attribute category types. Figure 15-3 illustrates how two user objects can be different even though they still have the same attribute categories.

The object class unifies similar objects. When you create a particular object (for example, a user object), it automatically inherits properties from that class. From the original user object, each new user object may inherit attributes types such as first

First name: David
Last name: Brewster
E-mail: davidb@company.com

First name: Dean
Last name: Rogers
E-mail: deanr@company.com

Figure 15-3. *Two user objects with the same attribute types but different values for each attribute*

name, last name, e-mail address, mailing address, phone number, title, and so on. You can then specify values for each of these attributes.

Containers

A *container* is a special type of object within AD. The difference is that it can hold other objects, and it doesn't represent something real. For example, the Domain Controllers object, shown in Figure 15-4, doesn't represent something real in itself, but it does contain real entities (DCs).

By default, a domain contains the following containers:

■ **Built-in**   Contains group objects

■ **Computers**   Holds computer accounts from servers and client machines

■ **Domain Controllers**   Holds DCs for the domain, including Windows NT BDCs (while in mixed mode)

■ **Users**   Stores all user accounts including Windows 2000 groups

ORGANIZATIONAL UNITS   Another example of a container object is the organizational unit (OU). Like other container objects, the OU can contain other objects such as users, printers, groups, computers, other OUs, and much more (see Figure 15-5).

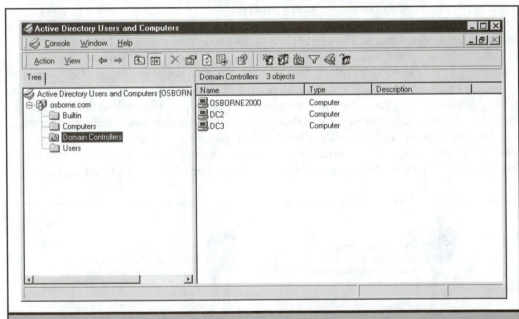

Figure 15-4.   *The Domain Controllers container*

Figure 15-5.   *An OU holding various objects*

However, an OU is unique and specialized in its role within AD. An OU organizes objects in a domain into logical administrative groups. In other words, it can be used to create a security boundary within a domain. These boundaries give you more control over the Windows 2000 environment by allowing you to delegate responsibilities and rights by assigning permissions to the OU.

> **Note**   *The OU is commonly represented as a circle within the triangular representation of a domain.*

OUs are also designed to be hierarchical (see Figure 15-6), meaning that you can not only contain other OUs in an OU but also can have OUs branching off from one another. This fosters more flexibility to fit the needs of your network environment. For example, remember in the former Windows NT environments where you had to create a resource domain to logically separate resources because of either geographic location or administrative delegation? Now, you have a simpler, more flexible option of tying those resources together in many different ways with an OU.

To create a new OU for your Windows 2000 network environment, do the following:

1. Start the Active Directory Users and Computers program from the Start | Programs | Administrative Tools menu.

2. In the left pane of the Active Directory Users and Computers window, as shown in Figure 15-7, click on the domain for which you want to create an OU.

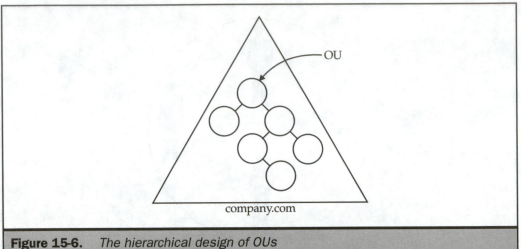

Figure 15-6.   *The hierarchical design of OUs*

3. Choose New | Organizational Unit from the Action menu.

4. In the New Object – Organizational Unit window (see Figure 15-8), type in the name of the OU that you want to create and then click OK.

At this point, you can configure the OU. For instance, you can add members to the group, delegate control of the OU, and much more.

Schema

The schema is essentially data about data (*metadata*). More specifically, the schema defines the contents of AD, its objects, and the attributes for objects. This includes the object class, described earlier, which is used to determine which attributes the object has.

Don't think of the schema as a rule base that's set in stone, because it's not. Actually, it's extensible. New classes and attributes can be added to extend the schema to fit the growing business needs.

 Don't attempt to modify the AD schema unless you're aware of how it will affect your environment. It's also highly recommended that you perform a full backup before proceeding to make changes.

The schema is an object too, and can be protected by access control lists (ACLs). Consequently, applications can read and use the schema. Also, when a change is made to the schema, those changes are replicated to the other DCs in the AD domain.

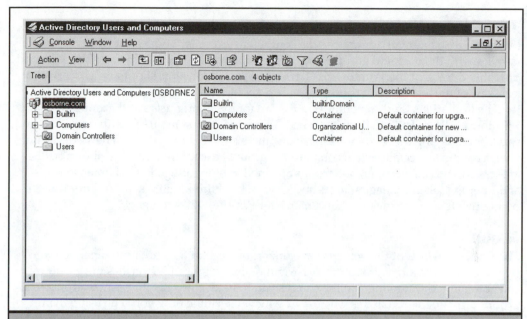

Figure 15-7.   *The Active Directory Users and Computers window*

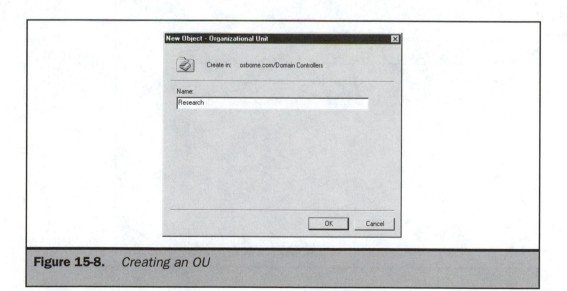

Figure 15-8.   *Creating an OU*

Users and Groups

Everyone who has ever administered a computer system (at home or at work) is probably familiar with the user and group concept. Those of you with a Windows NT background probably think that the Windows 2000 user and group concepts should be a breeze or at least one of the less difficult concepts to learn about with Windows 2000. Think again.

The limitations (and sometimes confusion) for managing users and groups in Windows NT have all but been abolished. Windows 2000 starts fresh with new ideas and ways of managing these concepts. Actually, there's really not that much new concerning user accounts (especially when compared to groups) except that more attributes can be associated with the account, but groups are another story altogether. Chapter 18 takes an in-depth look at managing users and groups, but I think that it's important to at least point out a few of the major enhancements for Windows 2000 here.

Groups

The first enhancement that groups have undergone is that they are now separated into two categories: security groups and distribution lists. Figure 15-9 verifies the group categorization by showing you the choices you'll make when creating a new group. The groups are categorized in this way because they determine how you'll be using them.

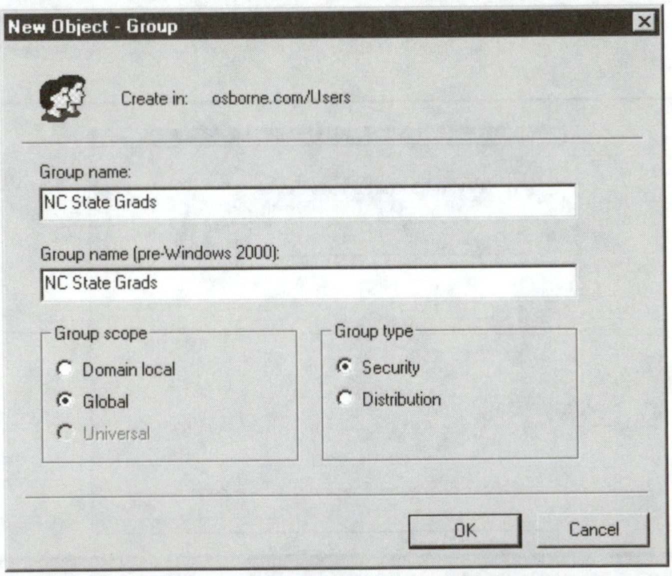

Figure 15-9. *Categorizing groups*

SECURITY GROUPS   The security group concept is similar to Windows NT groups in that you can assign permissions to them and you can nest some groups within others. This brings greater control and flexibility, but that's about it. A lot has changed from the Windows NT to Windows 2000 group implementation including, but not limited to, the following:

- **Nesting**   Throw away what you learned about nesting with Windows NT because the implementation is completely different in Windows 2000. There are some boundaries that you must adhere to (which groups can go where), but level of nesting is practically limitless.

- **Domain local group**   This is equivalent to the Windows NT local group. It can contain other groups (universal and global groups) and users, but their scope is limited to their domain. Because it contains only members of the particular domain, it isn't available in the global catalog (GC).

- **Global group**   A global group in Windows 2000 now has the ability to contain other global groups and users, but membership is limited to users until AD is switched to native mode. Also, membership is limited to the local domain, but the user can use a resource in another domain through ACL referencing. The global group appears in the GC, but it doesn't reveal its members.

- **Universal group**   If you want to contain members from anywhere in a tree or forest, this is the group for you. It becomes available only after you make the switch to native mode. The ACL used to check against for permissions to a particular resource can be a part of the ACL. This is another notable difference between a universal group and global group.

DISTRIBUTION LISTS   Up to now, there hasn't been a capability within the operating system to create distribution lists. Distribution lists are useful for a variety of different applications, the most common of which is for sending e-mails. The primary difference between security groups and distribution lists is that you can't assign permissions to a distribution list. An application must be AD aware before it can use them.

Domains

The domain concept in the AD namespace is similar to that in Windows NT 4.0, but the two do have their differences. Much like Windows NT 4.0 domains, AD domains are logical groupings or partitions of your network environment that establish security boundaries. All objects within the domain, such as users, computers, printers, and so on, become the essence of the domain. In this sense, domains can also be considered container objects.

As mentioned earlier, the AD domain, shown in Figure 15-10, is also different than its predecessor. The following is a list of some domain characteristics that are new concepts for the domain architecture:

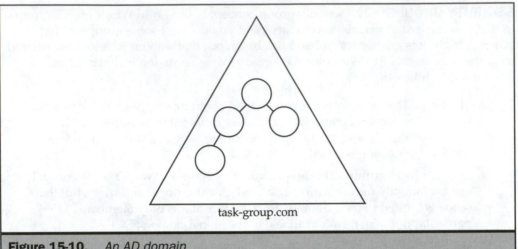

task-group.com

Figure 15-10. *An AD domain*

- **Namespace representation** The AD domain is tightly integrated with DNS (see Chapter 14 for more information on DNS). Therefore, AD domain names are also DNS namespaces. For example, task-group.com is the AD domain name as well as the DNS namespace.

- **Hierarchy** Since AD and DNS are so tightly integrated, the AD namespace inherits its hierarchical design. If a domain branches off of another domain, it is called a *child* domain, and it retains information about its parent domain namespace. In the previous example, a child domain, called *engineering*, would be represented as engineering.task-group.com as illustrated in Figure 15-11. This contrasts with the flat domains implemented in Windows NT 4.0.

- **Replication** A domain is also a boundary for replication. AD replicates information about the domain inside the domain to all DCs. It uses a multimaster replication scheme where all DCs are treated as equals (there is no one master copy). More information can be found on replication in the "Site Replication" section later in this chapter.

Domain Modes

AD domains essentially come in two flavors, mixed and native mode. The type of domain mode you use depends on many factors such as the following:

- Are you creating an AD domain for the first time?
- Are you upgrading a Windows NT domain?
- Are you adding a child domain to a mixed or native mode domain?

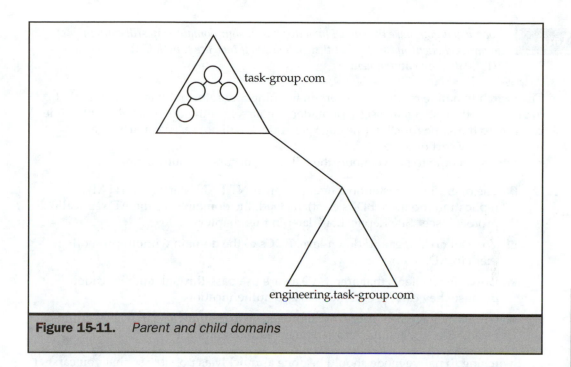

task-group.com

engineering.task-group.com

Figure 15-11.   *Parent and child domains*

By default, when you first create an AD domain, it is a mixed-mode domain, so it can support down-level clients and interact with Windows NT domain controllers (primary domain controllers, or PDCs; and backup domain controllers, or BDCs) that already exist in the domain.

Once you have established a mixed domain, you can begin considering whether or not to move to native mode. Native mode is a full-fledged Windows 2000 environment, and it brings several advantages to your network environment. Before you move to native mode, you must make sure that you have upgraded all Windows NT domain controllers and you aren't planning to add any. Any Windows NT domain controllers that existed in the domain will no longer be able to participate once you make the switch to native mode. Also, the domain controller, known as the *operations master* (similar to the PDC), is no longer the head honcho for the domain because it's now a peer with the other DCs.

DOMAIN MODE DIFFERENCES   Your domain is running in a mixed mode under the following conditions:

- The Windows NT 4 PDC is upgraded, but you haven't upgraded all of the BDCs

- The Windows NT 4 PDC and all BDCs are upgraded, but the native mode switch has not been turned on

Even when you make the switch to native mode, your domain may still contain down-level client machines, but they will act as if they are functioning in a Windows NT 4.0 domain environment.

The switch to native mode causes certain warning and informational messages that Windows 2000 systems will see as a matter of course, yet the down-level client, while reacting to the same function (message generator), will not receive a message indicating any sort of issue.

After switching to native mode, the following occurs to your domain:

- The operations master no longer performs NT LAN Manager (NTLM) replication (no more BDCs exist). Instead, the domain uses the AD replication protocol (see "Site Replication" later in this chapter).

- You can no longer add down-level BDCs to the domain without promoting them to AD.

- Down-level clients that aren't AD aware use pass-through authentication because they can't use Kerberos-based authentication.

- Group management is greatly improved. You can now use universal groups, nested groups, and full, cross-domain administration.

Switching to native mode should be done as quickly as possible so that you can get the increased manageability, functionality, security, and much more.

Before making the switch to native mode, test your domain's functionality to ensure that everything is operating smoothly. The switch is irreversible, so it is important that you are assured that everything is working properly. As soon as you are confident that they are, make the switch.

Switching to Native Mode

As explained earlier, native mode empowers your Windows 2000 network with full functionality. The downside, however, is that it's irreversible. If you need to revert back to mixed mode, you'll have to tear down everything that you've built so far and start from scratch.

TURNING ON NATIVE MODE   Now, the moment that you've been waiting for: switching to native mode. The actual process of changing the domain mode is easy, but as you are well aware, the preparation to get to this phase has been at the least challenging.

Double-check to make sure that you have upgraded all BDCs and have performed all the necessary testing because the switch is irreversible. If you decide you want to back out after the mode change, you'll have to destroy everything that you worked so diligently on.

To change to native mode, do the following:

1. On a DC, run the Active Directory Users and Computers located in Start |
   Programs | Administrative Tools menu.

2. Right-click the domain object, and then click Properties to display the domain
   object properties like the one shown in Figure 15-12.

3. Click the Change Mode button.

4. Restart the DC.

Trust Relationships

Trust relationships for Windows 2000 domains have been greatly improved upon from
the Windows NT trust relationship implementation. Basically, the implementation has
been simplified from an administrative point of view (comparatively speaking, it's
guaranteed to reduce your stress level).

Anytime a child domain is added, a trust relationship automatically joins the two
domains. The trust relationship that is established is a two-way, transitive trust made
possible through the Kerberos security protocol (see "Active Directory Security" later in
this chapter and Chapter 21 for more information on security-related issues). Although
Kerberos is new to Windows 2000, it has been an open standard for the industry. The

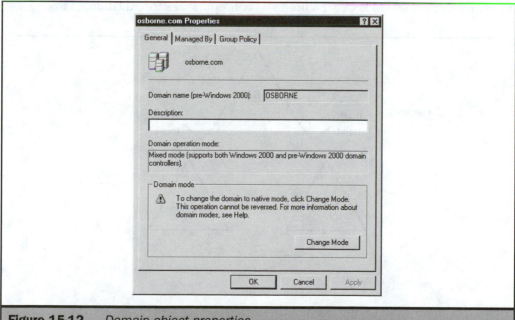

Figure 15-12.   *Domain object properties*

transitive trust means that if domain A trusts domain B and domain B trusts domain C, then domain A trusts domain C. If this is still a bit confusing, look at Figure 15-13 to get a visual representation. The inherited trust relationship that joined domains A and C is called an *implicit trust*. Implicit trusts are the result of transitivity and a domain's hierarchy.

Another benefit to Windows 2000 trust relationships is that by definition they reduce the number of trusts needed to bridge domains. In the example above, there are two two-way trusts, but in a Windows NT 4.0 environment, you'd need six trusts to get the same functionality. The number of trust relationships needed for *n* AD domains is *n*-1. This holds true for any AD domain configuration, including forest structures.

Trees

As mentioned earlier, domains can be joined together through trust relationships via the Kerberos security protocol. When these linked domains form a common namespace (for example., osborne.com and authors.osborne.com) and share a common schema, configuration, and global catalog (GC), the formation is known as a *tree*.

| Note | *Trees conform to the DNS naming standards just like a single domain does. In order to keep the namespace contiguous, a child domain adds its name to its parent domain name.* |

In the truest sense of the word, a tree can be single domain. However, it's more common (and easier to remember) to refer to a tree as more than one domain sharing the characteristics stated above. Figure 15-14 conceptualizes the AD domain tree.

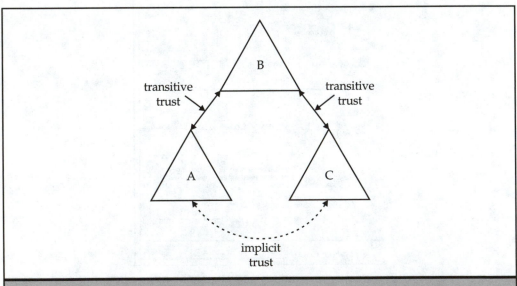

Figure 15-13.   *Transitive trust relationships*

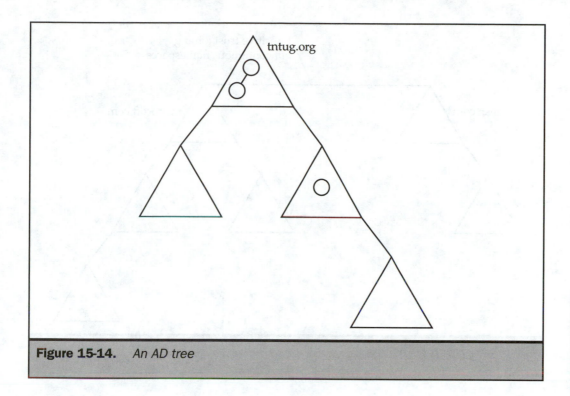

Figure 15-14.   *An AD tree*

Forests

Common sense tells you that a forest is a group of trees, and this is no different in AD. Forests build on the same principles of design as the tree did. They share a common schema, configuration, and GC. The key difference, however, is that forests link trees with different or noncontiguous namespaces.

Forests provide enough flexibility for those companies that have undergone a merger or acquisition. Moreover, companies that have completely disjointed business units that need to keep their namespaces separate, such as Time Warner and CNN or Microsoft and MSN, can benefit from using forests.

Communication between the trees in the forest is established via Kerberos trusts like the ones used between domains in a tree as shown in Figure 15-15. Each connection is a two-way transitive trust relationship that is established at the root of the AD domain tree (don't confuse the term *root domain* with the DNS meaning of root domain because they're not the same).

The communication that is established between the trees in the forest allows for each domain to be aware of the objects that are present throughout the forest. When a user in domain A wants to locate another user in domain B, the query to find the user uses the GC only because queries can only search the tree that it originated from and

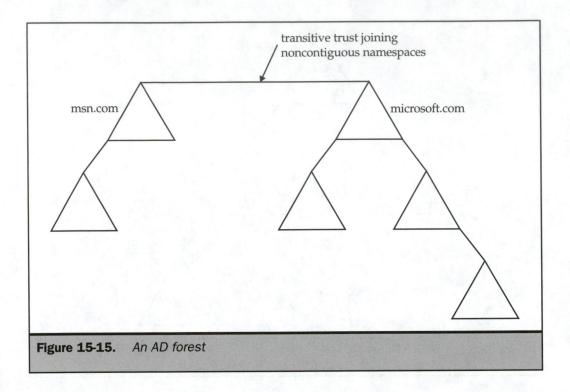

Figure 15-15.   *An AD forest*

the GC as illustrated in Figure 15-16. This design is intended to minimize security risks and provide the quickest response possible. Otherwise, depending on the size of the network environment, it could take a painfully long time just to find the user.

Although forests can be very useful for companies that must keep separate namespaces but also need to be tied together, most Windows 2000 network environments should try to avoid using them because of the increased design complexity and inherent limitations for performing searches. Always strive to keep the Windows 2000 AD environment as simple as possible. For instance, instead of creating multiple domains or multiple trees (forest), consider using OUs to separate business units, administrative boundaries, and the like.

Global Catalog

Your environment's one or more domains (or trees) represent partitions in the namespace. These domains contain only their own set of objects and nothing else. Take, for example, a tree with the company.com and marketing.company.com domains. Each domain contains information about them and this information is replicated within the domain. What's missing is that neither domain knows what objects are located within the other.

Now, since AD uses LDAP for searches, information about other domains in the same tree can be found through a referral method. For referrals, the LDAP search is

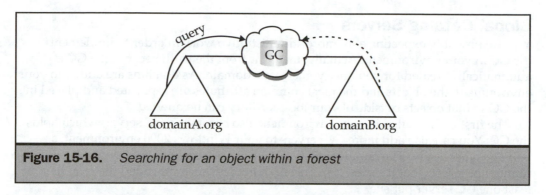

Figure 15-16.   *Searching for an object within a forest*

passed from domain to domain until the match is found. The referral method holds true only for a single tree because that's the defined maximum resolution. There are two issues to be concerned about with this type of search mechanism. First, referrals can lengthen the search time in a domain tree, especially in network environments where there are many objects. The second concern is that referrals don't stretch beyond a tree within a forest.

The GC bridges the information gap between all domains in a tree or forest, enabling users in one AD domain to locate objects in another AD domain. The GC stores a replica of every object from every domain in the tree or forest but contains only a few of the most common attributes for each object. The attributes that it keeps are the ones that you're most likely to use to find that object. For example, if you were to search for a user in another domain, you'd probably use the person's name or e-mail address rather than using an attribute such as their birthday. You wouldn't need to know too much about the user you were searching for, just an attribute. The GC boosts searches and allows you to search on a minimum amount of information.

> **Note**   *You can change the default setting of the number and type of attributes that are kept in the GC. If you do choose to change the default setting, keep in mind that adding attributes adds to AD replication and could slow down queries. Also, if you remove attributes, you are restricting the amount of information that clients can query. It's a balancing act; you must weigh the advantages and disadvantages for your environment.*

When and how exactly is the GC used? When a query (with a particular attribute) is made, the search begins in the local domain, and if the object isn't found, the GC is queried. From this point, three things can happen:

1. The object and attribute are not found, and the query fails. This indicates that whatever was searched for doesn't exist in the tree or forest.

2. The object is found, and the results are sent to the client that initiated the query.

3. The specified object is found in the GC, but the attribute needed by the query isn't (e.g., a person's birthday). The object's DN is returned, and a referral is made to the domain containing the object.

Global Catalog Servers

You are probably expecting a lot more administrative work in order to implement the GC in your environment. Actually, that's far from the truth because the GC is automatically created for you once you create a domain. As domains are added to your environment, the objects and the most common attributes are replicated and placed in the GC so that objects outside of your local territory can be queried.

The first DC installed in your environment also becomes a GC server, which holds the GC. You can also add more GC servers to your Windows 2000 environment, as you deem necessary. The number of GC servers in your environment depends on the number of objects that it stores. As a rule of thumb, it's recommended that you have at least one GC server per site.

Sites

For the first time in Window's history (Windows NT 3.*x* and 4.0), the concept of a site has been incorporated into the operating system. A *site* is a physical structure within Windows 2000 that brings awareness of the network environment's physical layout. More specifically, it is a collection of one or more "well-connected" TCP/IP subnets, as illustrated in Figure 15-17. It plays a critical role in determining the most effective authentication and replication traffic patterns and consequently influences overall network performance.

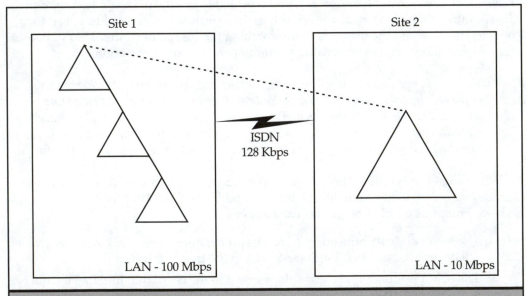

Figure 15-17.   *Two high-bandwidth sites connected via a WAN link*

A "well-connected" site, by Microsoft's standards, is defined as having high bandwidth (512 Kbps or higher).

Sites (physical structure) and domains (logical structure) don't always have to adhere to a 1:1 ratio. A single site can contain a single domain or span multiple domains.

A Site's Role in Authentication

AD authentication is based on Kerberos instead of NT LAN Manager (NTLM). One of Kerberos's improvements over NTLM is that client machines will try contacting the closest DC. This means the closest not necessarily in terms of physical location but rather in performance (high bandwidth and availability). The combination of the client's TCP/IP information (the subnet it's on) and Kerberos using site information helps the client find the nearest DC to use for authentication. As a result of a site's influence on authentication and the Kerberos security protocol, clients are able to log onto the domain much more quickly.

Site Replication

Replication of information has yet again undergone a complete transformation from Windows 2000's predecessor, Windows NT. AD introduces the concept that all DCs in a domain are equal and for the most part share in the responsibility of the domain. This means that all DCs have a complete, read/write copy of the AD database. Since all DCs can be updated, there must be a way to ensure that they all have an updated copy of the AD database. When a change is made (adding a user account, for example), it must be replicated to the other DCs to keep the domain synchronized.

Microsoft tries to strike a balance between when updates occur and when they are replicated. If they are updated immediately after the change occurs, a series of problems may result such as continuously high resource (processor, network, and so on) utilization among DCs and keeping up with which changes should rightfully be replicated. For instance, you wouldn't want to send a flurry of updates if the information has already been propagated. On the other hand, you don't want the information to become stale from sitting in one DC and not being replicated to the other DCs. Moreover, what happens if the same change occurs on two or more separate DCs?

Note *Some changes to the AD database are extremely time sensitive. For example, when you disable an account, you want to make sure that the change gets replicated immediately to prevent someone from gaining unauthorized access to your Windows 2000 environment. As a result, time-sensitive changes, like the one mentioned above, get immediate attention rather than waiting for the regular replication update.*

A site helps define when and how replication occurs within the domain because it defines the physical typology. For *intrasite* replication (between DCs in a site), the frequency of updates is higher and the information is uncompressed (see Figure 15-18). However, replication between sites (*intersite*) can be scheduled and compressed to save bandwidth on slower WAN links. Figure 15-19 helps you visualize both intrasite and intersite replication.

Note *For both intrasite and intersite replication, only the changes are replicated to the other DCs.*

Also, the Directory Replication Service (DRS) APIs, used to notify DCs of changes and replicate those changes, can use three types of communication methods, depending on whether it's for intrasite or intersite replication. Intrasite replication always uses remote procedure calls (RPCs), while intersite can choose between the Internet Protocol (IP), RPC, and the Simple Mail Transfer Protocol (SMTP).

KEEPING TRACK OF INTRASITE CHANGES   The question regarding how AD keeps track of changes being made on different DCs remains. Has this change already been made from another DC? If two identical changes have been made, which one gets replicated? These are just a couple of the questions you may be asking yourself, and they're all valid concerns.

Many directory services have adopted the use of time stamps to keep track of changes made to the directory. Time stamps require that all clocks on DCs be in synch with one another. However, using time stamps alone has severe limitations that can affect the consistency of the directory. It is a difficult, if not daunting, task to ensure that clocks on every DC are synchronized. Even if the DCs are managed well and timing is pretty well synchronized, you still run the risk of one of them losing the

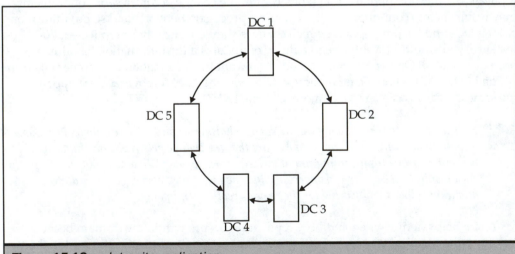

Figure 15-18.   *Intrasite replication*

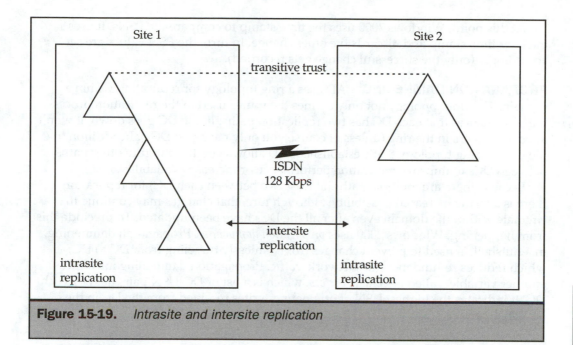

Figure 15-19.   *Intrasite and intersite replication*

correct time. Besides, isn't it enough work just to keep track of synchronizing replication, let alone time synchronization?

Instead, AD uses an Update Sequence Number (USN) for synchronization of updates between DCs. The USN is a 64-bit, unique number that increments by one for every change on a DC. In addition, each DC keeps a table of USNs from other DCs in the domain in order to keep track of the changes that occur. Increments are performed atomically, meaning that the increment either succeeds or fails. For example, if the server decides to crash on you during the USN increment, the USN fails to increment. The same applies when replication on a DC is interrupted or fails. The DC will notice the USN increment failed and will restart the replication process to synchronize with the rest of the domain.

There may also be situations where the same change occurs at two or more DCs. DC-A propagates the change and thinks that everything is updated on its end and it's only a matter of time when the others are updated. Meanwhile, the change hasn't yet reached DC-B, and it starts the replication process for the same change. When either DC-A or DC-B receives the other's change, a replication collision occurs. Replication collisions are detected by *Property Version Numbers (PSNs)*, which are similar to the USN but are specific to the property (attribute) for an object. The PSN is incremented only for the *originating write* (a write to a property at the DC responsible for making the change) and not for property changes that occurred because of replication (a change originating from another DC).

At this point, Windows 2000 uses the time stamp to compare the PSNs. It uses the later time stamp and discards the other change. In turn, the PSN values are set accordingly (only the successful change gets recorded).

PROPAGATION DAMPENING   AD uses a ring topology for replicating within a domain. The ring topology not only defines the routes used in the replication process, but also ensures that each DC has two replication paths. If one DC goes down, it won't affect the others in the ring (unless of course you only have two DCs). In addition to the default ring topology that's established, AD allows you to configure other paths between DCs to improve replication performance or increase availability.

Because there are multiple paths (at least two between each DC) for replication, there is also the increased possibility, although rare, that changes may continue to circulate within the domain even after all the DCs have been updated. To preclude this from happening, Windows 2000 uses *propagation dampening*. Propagation dampening, in a nutshell, is used to prevent changes from aimlessly traveling from DC to DC, which reduces redundancy and network traffic. Propagation dampening introduces another variable, called *up-to-date vectors*, which is a list of DC-USN pairs held by each DC. It indicates the highest USN of originating writes received from the DC in the DC-USN pair.

Domain Controllers

A domain controller (DC) is another AD physical structure that is defined as any Windows 2000 Server computer that is running Active Directory. In sharp contrast to the Windows NT single-master DC implementation (one PDC and any number of BDCs), each DC shares the responsibilities of the domain. They are considered peers, meaning that no single DC is authoritative over the other DCs in the Windows 2000 network environment.

DCs share domain-related responsibilities, such as authentication, storing, and maintaining the AD (which as you know by now involves a multitude of concepts), and much more. For instance, any change or modification (for example, adding an object) that is made to one DC is automatically replicated among the other DCs in the domain. There are a few situations, however, that require a single-master model instead of the normal multimaster model described earlier.

Single-Master Model

Many, but not all, situations follow the peer or multimaster model. An exception is the AD domain, which uses a *single-master model*, also referred to as a *Flexible Single Master Operation (FSMO)*. An FSMO completely avoids even the most remote possibility that there may be conflicting updates because a single DC is allowed to process updates. This parallels earlier versions of the operating system (Windows NT 3.51 and 4.0) where the PDC is responsible for processing all updates in a domain. In these rare cases where a single-master model is required, an *operations master* must be used to perform these actions. An operations master is a DC that assumes additional roles beyond those of its peers. There are five such FSMO operations:

- **Domain naming**   The operations master ensures that any changes to the domain namespace are unique to avoid conflicts. It is solely responsible for adding or removing a domain to or from the directory as well as any cross-references to domains in other, external directories.

- **Schema master**   The operations master is the only DC responsible for updating the directory schema. As soon as the update to the schema is complete, it is replicated to the other DCs in the directory.

- **Infrastructure**   This ensures domain object consistency throughout the domain (see Figure 15-20).

- **PDC**   This scenario applies if the domain is in mixed mode. It ensures compatibility for down-level clients by acting as if it were a PDC in a Windows NT environment (see Figure 15-21).

- **Relative ID (RID)**   This ensures the management and allocation of RIDs used in the creation of security identifiers (SIDs) as shown in Figure 15-22.

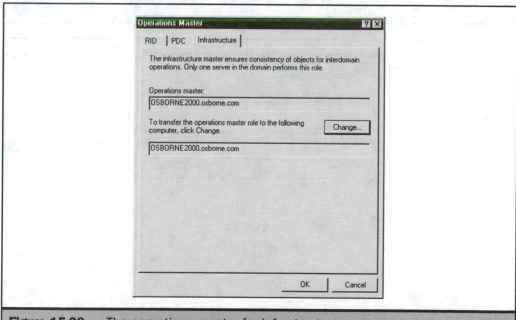

Figure 15-20.   *The operations master for Infrastructure support*

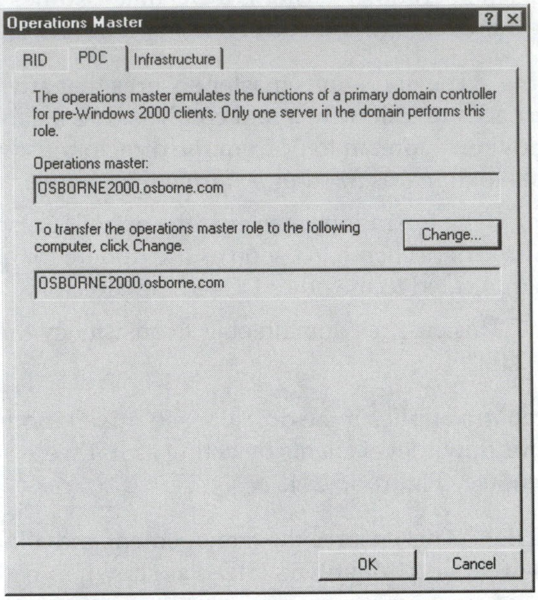

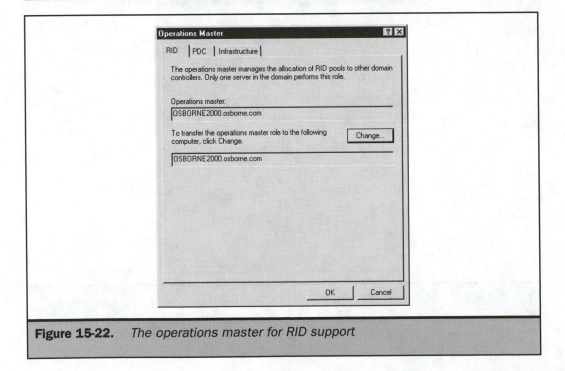

Figure 15-21. *The operations master for mixed-mode compatibility*

Figure 15-22. *The operations master for RID support*

Adding Another DC to a Domain

To provide better response time to users or add fault tolerance and availability to the domain, you can add an additional DC. The actual number of DCs that you need to add depends on many factors, such as the number of users the Windows 2000 network environment supports, the number of objects in the domain, the number of domains in your environment, and much more.

If you're upgrading a Windows NT 4.0 BDC, the Windows 2000 Server installation process automatically upgrades the server to DC status. When this is the case, you specify the AD domain you want to join. However, if you are starting from scratch (fresh Windows 2000 Server installation) or upgrading a Windows NT standalone server, you'll invoke the Active Directory Installation Wizard, DCPROMO, manually.

To add another DC to a domain, do the following:

1. Click Run from the Start menu and type **DCPROMO**. Then click OK.
2. Click Next to advance to the next screen, and then select Replica domain controller in existing domain.
3. Click Next and then type the DNS name of the domain you wish to replicate.
4. Click Next and then enter the name and password, with administrative privileges, in that domain.
5. Click Finish and allow for the machine to be restarted.

Once the machine is back online, it will serve as a DC for the domain you specified. For more information on installing AD, see the next section.

Installing Active Directory

The actual process of installing AD is much easier than the AD concepts you've been reading about. You have two possible scenarios for installing AD. The first is upgrading a Windows NT 4.0 PDC or BDC, and the second is installing AD on a stand-alone server. If you are upgrading a PDC or BDC, DCPROMO will run automatically. Otherwise, you need to manually invoke the DCPROMO by typing DCPROMO from the Run command dialog box, as shown in Figure 15-23.

 The new version of NTFS, NTFS 5, is required in order to install AD. If you haven't already converted to NTFS 5, do so now (see Chapter 20 for more information on file systems).

To install AD for the first time, start DCPROMO and do the following:

1. Go to the Domain Controller Type page and select Domain controller for a new domain.
2. Click Next and then select Create a new domain tree.

CONNECTING WITH WINDOWS 2000

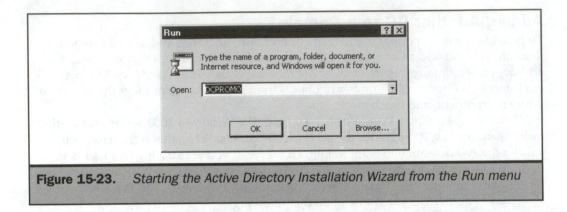

Figure 15-23. *Starting the Active Directory Installation Wizard from the Run menu*

3. Click Next, select Create a new forest of domain trees, and then click Next again to continue.

4. Enter the DNS name (e.g., company.com) that you chose during the design phase as shown in Figure 15-24. Click Next again to advance to the following screen. DCPROMO then verifies that the name is not already in use.

5. Windows 2000 then suggests a NetBIOS name based on the domain name you specified. It also gives you the opportunity to specify a NetBIOS name.

6. Click Next for the next three screens to accept the defaults for comparable NetBIOS name, AD database and log file paths, and System Volume path information (recommended).

7. You may see a pop-up warning message stating that it couldn't contact the DNS server. Don't worry about it; just click OK.

8. Select Yes to direct DCPROMO to configure your DNS and click Next.

9. Select Permissions compatible with pre-Windows 2000 servers if you have a Windows NT network in place. Otherwise, choose the second option.

10. Click Next to advance and then type and confirm the Administrator's password. Click Next twice to begin the promotion.

11. When the promotion is done, click Finish. A dialog box will prompt you to restart your machine to finalize the installation.

12. Select Restart Now to restart the machine.

The Active Directory Database

Using the Active Directory Installation Wizard to install AD automatically creates the AD database and associated log files. The actual size of the database varies depending on the size of your Windows 2000 network environment. It could be several megabytes in size or can scale well into the terabyte range. Unless otherwise specified during installation, the default path for the AD database is %Systemroot%\NTDS, as shown in Figure 15-25.

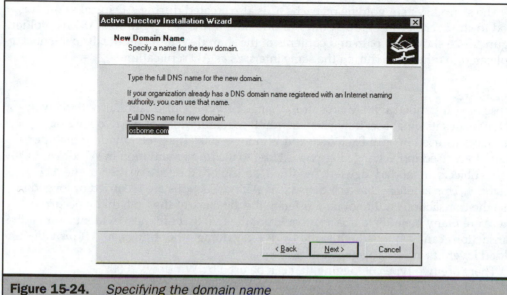

Figure 15-24.   *Specifying the domain name*

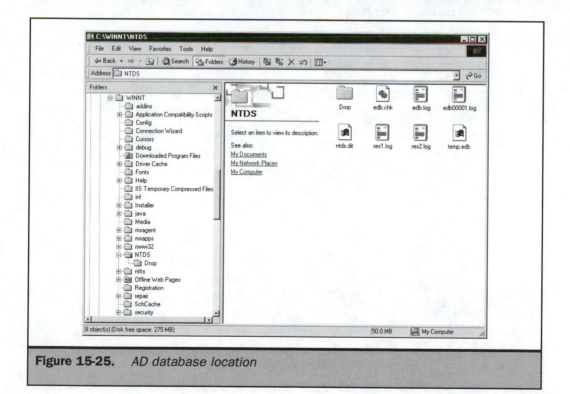

Figure 15-25.   *AD database location*

The shared system volume on each DC is also created during AD installation. It is used to store scripts and group policy information in the %Systemroot%\Sysvol folder. Figure 15-26 shows the path and contents of the shared system volume. Its contents are replicated to other DCs during the same intervals as AD replication.

Logging

Those of you familiar with Microsoft Exchange Server are also familiar with the way AD manages its database. In particular, you'll see similarities of the two logging mechanisms used in both Exchange and Windows 2000. It's pretty evident that the technology used in Exchange logging is close to the implementation in Windows 2000.

As objects are added, deleted, modified, and so on, they are written to the AD database. This is referred to as a *transaction*. All transactions are recorded or logged in case the transaction could not be written to the database at the time that it occurred. There are many benefits to this approach, but the two that are most evident are that the transactions can be queued while the DC is busy doing other things, and it provides an added layer of protection against data loss.

There are two types of logging that can be used by Windows 2000:

■ **Circular logging**   This type trades fault tolerance with disk space usage. It keeps the log file size down to a minimum by overwriting transactions that are no longer needed.

Figure 15-26.   *Shared system volume location and contents*

- **Sequential (noncircular)** This type provides the highest level of fault tolerance because it keeps the transactions instead of overwriting them. At specified intervals (every 12 hours), it truncates the logs and starts a new binary-format log file.

By default, AD uses sequential logging to provide additional insurance to the AD database. When all the transactions have been made to the AD database, AD keeps the log files for several hours before it discards them. This ensures that your hard disk doesn't start overflowing with old log files.

Installing the AD Client Software

The AD client software is network client software for Windows 9*x* down-level computers. It allows them to participate in the AD. By definition, the following operating systems are AD aware:

- Windows 2000 Server (member server) or Professional
- Computers running Windows 95 or Windows 98 that have installed the AD client software add-on

Note *Windows NT-based computers do not have AD client software, but they can participate on the network as if it were a Windows NT 4 domain.*

The Active Directory client is provided in the Clients\WIN9X folder on the Windows 2000 Server CD-ROM. To install the AD client software on a Windows 9*x* computer, do the following:

1. Install Internet Explorer 5.0 or higher.
2. Enable the Active Desktop.
3. Double click on the DSCLIENT.EXE file to initiate the Directory Service Client Setup Wizard.
4. Click Next twice and the wizard will begin installation.
5. Once the Directory Service Client Setup Wizard finishes, click Finish to restart the computer.
6. Windows 9*x* then asks you if you want to restart your machine. Click Yes.

Active Directory Security

Security is undoubtedly a paramount concern with computer systems. Systems hold a wealth of information that, in many cases, is priceless. I would argue that security implementations aren't just about protecting information against intentional and

CONNECTING WITH
WINDOWS 2000

accidental modification or deletion. They also involve ease of system use, flexibility, and system performance.

One of the most notable achievements of Windows 2000 security is its support for the Kerberos security protocol. For more information on security-related matters, refer to Chapter 21.

Kerberos

Kerberos support is an important enhancement to the Windows 2000 operating system. Specifically, Windows 2000 uses Kerberos version 5 security protocol for authentication, trust relationships, and much more. Kerberos is an open, standardized protocol supported not only by Windows 2000 but on a variety of other platforms including many UNIX flavors.

The benefits that Kerberos brings over NT LAN Manager (NTLM), Windows NT's security protocol, are enormous. For starters, Kerberos is more efficient and streamlined than NTLM. More importantly, it's a more secure protocol that's supported by the rest of the industry.

The Authentication Process

NTLM is notorious for redundancy. For instance, when a client first logs onto the domain, it gets authenticated. Then when the client requests access to a resource, such as a file, it asks the server holding the file and the server checks with a PDC or BDC to see if the client is allowed to use the file. The client is then given permission to use the file or is denied access. So far, there's no redundancy. But when the client tries to reestablish a connection to use the file, the process described above is repeated.

Kerberos, on the other hand, takes a different approach. When the client logs onto the domain, it communicates with the Kerberos Distribution Center (KDC). The KDC is the responsible party within Kerberos for managing authentication. It does so by distributing session tickets (STs), which are keys to use objects within AD. Think of an ST as a ticket for a movie; you can't see the movie unless you have a ticket (you can't sneak in either).

After the client logs into a Windows 2000 domain, it can request access to a file (or any other resource). The first time it does, it contacts the KDC for a session ticket to access the file. The client keeps this session ticket and can reuse it even when it tries to open the file again. It doesn't have to contact the KDC to get another session ticket. Instead, the client can communicate with the server that holds the file.

Active Directory Integration with DNS

As I've already mentioned, AD is tightly integrated with DNS. For example, AD domain names are, in fact, DNS names. Also, DNS is the default name resolution mechanism to locate and use resources (AD objects) within Windows 2000. More information on DNS can be found in Chapter 14.

AD can also be integrated with DNS by storing the DNS database. One of the primary reasons why you'd want to integrate the two services is to reduce the number of replication mechanisms within your Windows 2000 network environment.

 Storing the DNS database within the AD database is covered in-depth in the DNS chapter (Chapter 14). The next section serves more as an overview and is for your convenience.

Storing DNS Within the AD Database

Microsoft appears to be the first company that has successfully combined a directory service (AD) with DNS. DNS commonly stores the DNS database in ASCII text files on the primary DNS servers. Secondary DNS servers use the same information as the primary, but the files are read-only.

When you merge the two services, you're actually placing the DNS database within the AD structure. The combination is called an *Active Directory-integrated domain.* The benefits of using AD-integrated zones are enormous, including:

- It removes the single point of failure if you have multiple DCs and DNS servers. Updates can be made to more than just one DNS server for the zone.

- AD controls the replication intervals, and only the changes made to DNS are replicated instead of transferring the entire zone. This makes DNS replication faster and more efficient than standard zone transfers.

- You only have to deal with one replication technology. This makes DNS administration and management much simpler.

- AD sites can be used to manage the replication traffic on the LAN and WAN.

- It strengthens security. You can now use an access control list (ACL) to tighten security of the DNS database. You can also control access of zone objects as well as resource records.

- Zone information is automatically propagated to new DCs within that zone.

Changing the Zone Type to Active Directory

In order to take advantage of the benefits described above, you must change the zone type to AD-integrated status by the following method:

1. Open the DNS Manager from the Start | Programs | Administrative Tools menu.

2. Right-click on the primary zone you want to change to AD-integrated and select Properties.

3. Under the General tab, click the Change button.

4. Change the zone type from Standard Primary to Active Directory-integrated as shown in Figure 15-27.

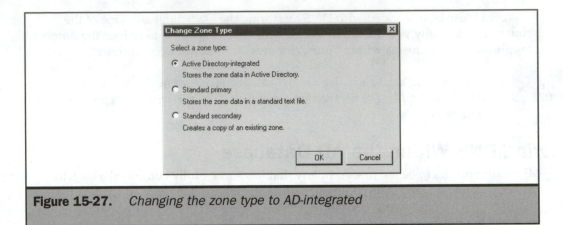

Figure 15-27.   *Changing the zone type to AD-integrated*

5. Click OK to close the Change Zone Type window.

6. Click OK to close the <Zone> Properties window.

7. Exit the DNS Manager.

Resource Kit Utilities

The Windows 2000 Resource Kit provides numerous utilities that help you manage, administer, and optimize the operating system. There are several utilities that are geared toward managing the AD. They include, but aren't limited to, the following:

■ **Active Directory Object Manager (MOVETREE)**   MoveTree is a command-line tool that allows administrators to move Active Directory objects, such as OUs and users between domains in a forest. These types of operations would be performed to support domain consolidation or organizational restructuring operations.

■ **DSASTAT**   This diagnostic tool compares and detects differences between naming contexts on DCs. It retrieves capacity statistics such as megabytes per server, objects per server, and megabytes per object class, and performs comparisons of attributes of replicated objects.

■ **Active Directory Administration Tool (LDP)**   LDP is a graphical tool that allows users to perform Lightweight Directory Access Protocol (LDAP) operations—such as connect, bind, search, modify, add, and delete—against any LDAP-compatible directory, such as Active Directory.

■ **Active Directory Access Control List Manager (DSACLS)**   This tool facilitates management of ACLs for directory services by enabling you to query and manipulate security attributes on AD objects.

■ **ACL Diagnostics (ACLDIAG)**   This command-line tool helps diagnose and troubleshoot problems with permissions on AD objects and also provides some simple clean-up functionality.

■ **Active Directory Replication Monitor (REPLMON)**   This tool enables administrators to view the low-level status of AD replication, force synchronization between DCs, view the topology in a graphical format, and monitor the status and performance of DC replication.

■ **ADSI Edit**   ADSI Edit is a low-level editor for AD. It uses the ADSI to provide a means to add, delete, and move objects within AD. The attributes of each object can be modified as well.

■ **Security Descriptor Check Utility (SDCHECK)**   This command-line tool displays the security descriptor for any object stored in AD. The security descriptor contains the ACLs defining the permissions that users have on AD objects. It also displays the object hierarchy and inheritance.

| Note | *Understanding Active Directory is key to effectively managing your Windows 2000 network environment. It is an invaluable, core service that affects most, if not all, of Windows 2000's functionality. AD defines your environment using objects and many other concepts, some of which are completely unfamiliar to you. This chapter is designed to reduce your learning curve with AD by examining AD concepts, installation issues, integration issues, and much more.* |

CONNECTING WITH
WINDOWS 2000

The Complete Reference

Windows 2000

Chapter 16

RRAS and VPNs

Routing and Remote Access (RRAS) has traditionally been an intriguing yet complicated technology for many. The Windows 2000 version of RRAS, although packed with new and enhanced features, simplifies installation, configuration, and management of its services. It overcomes the physical boundaries of your Windows 2000 network environment by enabling remote clients to connect and use resources on your network. It also is a means to connect network resources so that users can access resources on otherwise disjointed networks.

RRAS is a feature-rich service that includes support for sharing an Internet connection, dialing into the server, routing information from one network to another, protecting data through the use of a virtual private network (VPN), and more. This chapter gives you an overview of the technologies that RRAS offers and explains how to configure and manage solutions for your Windows 2000 network environment.

IP Routing Overview

Network environments are often segmented for a variety of reasons, including the following:

- The number of available IP addresses in a TCP/IP-based network environment
- Separation of administration and management
- Security
- Ownership of the network

Many routers, including a Windows 2000 router, can route TCP/IP, IPX, and AppleTalk. However, since Windows 2000 and the Internet rely on TCP/IP, the focus of this section is TCP/IP routing.

With TCP/IP, the IP address, combined with the subnet mask, defines a network address. The network address identifies the network where the device resides (see Figure 16-1). More information on TCP/IP can be found in Chapter 13. These networks, although disjointed, may require communication between them. This is where routing comes into the picture. *Routing* is the process of passing information across an internetwork boundary. The origination point is called the *source*, and the receiving end is the *destination*. An intermediary device (and sometimes multiple devices), usually a router, is responsible for passing the information from one network to another until the information reaches the intended recipient, as illustrated in Figure 16-2. For instance, when a computer on one network wants to send information to a computer located on a different network, it forwards the information to the router. The router then examines the packet and uses the destination address in the packet header to pass the information to the appropriate network.

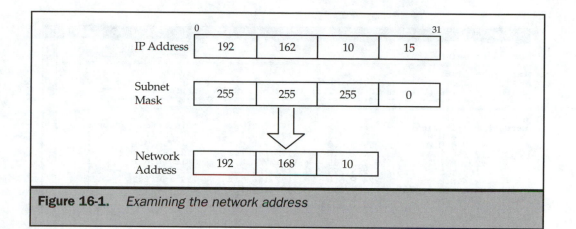

Figure 16-1.   *Examining the network address*

Note   *Routing is sometimes confused with bridging. The two technologies essentially take care of the same thing, passing information across an internetwork from source to destination, but the mechanisms used are quite different. Routing occurs at the network layer, while bridging occurs at the link layer in the OSI layer model. Operation at the different OSI layers affects how the information is processed and passed from source to destination.*

As I mentioned earlier, a router typically performs routing. However, Windows 2000's RRAS allows you to configure the server as a routing device as well. A router's function in life is to route packets from one network to the next. It does so by first determining the optimal routing paths using routing algorithms. Routing algorithms determine the shortest distance or the path of least resistance between a packet's source and its destination, as well as maintain routing tables, which host route information that can help optimize the transfer of information. Figure 16-3 shows a sample routing table that informs the router how it might send the packets of information.

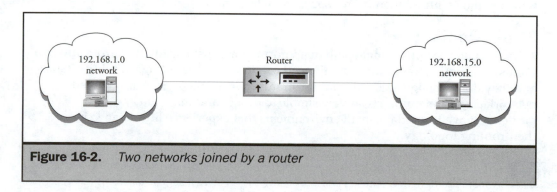

Figure 16-2.   *Two networks joined by a router*

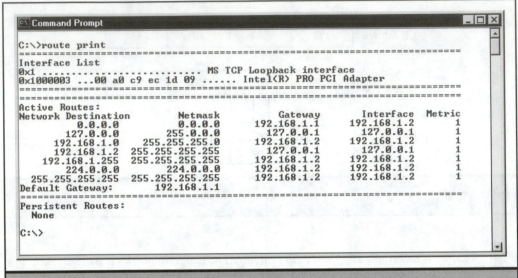

Figure 16-3. *Sample routing table*

Routers can also communicate with other routers to find the optimal paths for information being transferred from one network to another using a *router update message*. Employing router update messages allows routers to compare and update their routing tables with information about paths to other networks.

Routing Algorithms

Routers, and Windows 2000 servers configured as routers, typically use either static or dynamic routing algorithms, but demand-dial routing is also supported. All of these routing algorithms basically serve the same purpose but have different mechanisms in which to move information from a source to a destination.

Static Routing

A static route specifies a single path that information must use to travel from any two points. An administrator must identify and configure static routings in routing tables, and they don't change unless the administrator changes them. Statically routed network environments are relatively simple to design and maintain and are particularly well suited for small environments that experience little change in their routing topology.

Static routes are not necessarily persistent routes in Windows 2000. In other words, you must specify that a route is persistent using the –p switch so that when the server is restarted for any reason, the static route will stick to the routing table.

The major downfall of statically routed network environments is that they don't adapt to changing network conditions. For instance, if a router or link goes offline, the static routes wouldn't be able to reroute the packets to other routers in order to get to the intended destination. Also, when a network is added or removed from your environment, an administrator has to identify possible routing scenarios and configure them accordingly. Therefore, statically routed network environments, especially the ones undergoing constant change, aren't a viable routing choice for larger networks. The cost in administration alone should cause you to avoid using static routing for anything other than small environments.

As a general rule of thumb, use static routes only for the following conditions:

- Home or branch offices
- Network environments with a very small number of networks
- Connections that aren't going to change in the near future (for example, a router that is used as a last resort when the information can't be routed otherwise)

AUTO-STATIC ROUTING   Windows 2000 routers that use static routes can have their routing tables updated either manually or automatically. Automatically updating static routes is referred to as *auto-static* routing. Auto-static updates can be configured either through the RRAS interface, as shown in Figure 16-4, or by using the NETSH utility. This allows you to update Windows 2000 routers only at desired times to save connection costs and/or link bandwidth.

When you specify to have static routes updated, the router sends a request across an active connection to update all of the routes on the connection. The receiving router deletes any existing auto-static routes and then enters the new auto-static entries as static, persistent routes.

 Auto-static updates are supported only if you're using RIP for IP, RIP for IPX, and SAP for IPX.

Dynamic Routing

As the name implies, dynamic routing algorithms adapt to change in the network environment without manual intervention. Changes that are made are reflected almost instantaneously in the router. The following is a list of conditions for which dynamic routing is beneficial:

- A router or link goes down and the information must be rerouted.
- A router is added or removed in the internetwork.
- Large network environments that have many possible routing scenarios.
- Large network environments that frequently undergo changes in network topology.

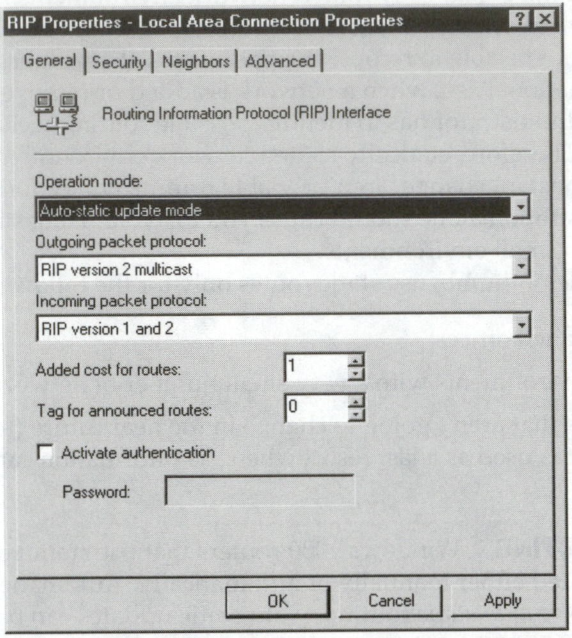

Figure 16-4. *Auto-static routing using the RRAS interface*

Dynamic routing algorithms are able to adapt, in real time, to changing conditions by communicating with other routers. When the router is notified that a network change has occurred, the router recalculates routes and notifies other routers. This allows all routers on the internetwork to be aware of the entire network topology even as it changes. Most routers today use dynamic routing algorithms and are well suited for any size network.

Demand-Dial Routing

The most common routing protocols (RIP, OSPF, etc.) that are used to communicate with other routers periodically send routing information to help adapt to dynamically changing network conditions. Generally speaking, this communication is an immense benefit for keeping track of changes so that information is routed through the path of least resistance. There are situations, however, when periodic router updates are less than desirable. For instance, you may be charged each time the link is activated.

To avoid these shortcomings, you can use *demand-dial routing*. Demand-dial routing activates a link only when information has to be passed through to the other side of the connection, which ultimately saves connection charges. Static routing or auto-static routing is used to keep the routers updated.

Routing Protocols

Routing protocols are a special type of protocol in that they keep track of the overall network topology in a routed network environment. They dynamically maintain information about other routers on the network and use this information to accurately predict the best route information should take.

Routing protocols use algorithms that can impact the router as well as influence how information is routed from one network to the next. Each routing protocol has characteristics that differentiate it from other routing protocols, but the primary goal for all of them is to provide simplicity, optimality, stability, and flexibility.

Routed vs. Routing Protocols

You've probably heard the terms "routed" and "routing protocols" being used interchangeably. For instance, you probably know that TCP/IP, IPX/SPX, etc., are routable protocols. Then, when you hear about routing protocols, you get confused on how the two types of protocols are different and how they are used. This mesh of terminology is quite common, but there is an important difference between the two.

Simply put, routing protocols route routed protocols such as TCP/IP, IPX/SPX, AppleTalk, and more. They are the missing link for getting information from one network to another. There are many routing protocols in use today including, but not limited to the following:

- Border Gateway Protocol (BGP)
- Enhanced Interior Gateway Routing Protocol (EIGRP)
- Exterior Gateway Protocol (EGP)
- Interior Gateway Routing Protocol (IGRP)
- Open Shortest Path First (OSPF)
- Routing Information Protocol (RIP)

Windows 2000's RRAS routers include built-in support for OSPF and RIP. In addition, RRAS can support third-party routing protocols, such as BGP, EIGRP, EGP, and IGRP, through its set of Application Programming Interfaces (APIs). The routing protocols that Windows 2000 supports are explained next.

RIP

RIP is a distance vector routing protocol that is relatively simple to use and configure. Distance vector routing protocols send router updates to adjacent routers only. RIP has been widely adopted by the industry and has been in use with TCP/IP networks for almost two decades. RIP is described in several RFCs, which are listed in Table 16-1.

CONNECTING WITH WINDOWS 2000

RFC	Description
1058	Routing Information Protocol
1721	RIP Version 2 Protocol Analysis
1722	RIP Version 2 Protocol Applicability Statement
1723	RIP Version 2 Carrying Additional Information

Table 16-1. *RFCs Associated with RIP*

As you can see from Table 16-1, there are two versions of RIP. Version 1 uses broadcast messaging while version 2 uses multicast messaging for router update messages. RIP dynamically maintains routing information by sending routing update messages to other routers using RIP on the internetwork every 30 seconds.

In addition to router update messages, RIP features several other mechanisms that fortify reliability and ensure that its routing tables are up-to-date. These include

- **Hop-count limit**   The trip between one router and another is considered a hop. RIP's hop-count limit limits the number of hops to a destination to 15. Destinations that require more than 15 hops are considered unreachable.

- **Hold-downs**   Hold-downs ensure that old, unroutable routes aren't used in the routing table.

- **Split horizons**   Split horizons prevent redundancy of routing update messages (routing loops) to the router from which the message was sent.

- **Poison reverse updates**   Poison reverse updates prevent routing loops on the internetwork.

Despite these features, RIP still has its limitations. It can become cumbersome in large enterprise networks because its router update messages tend to eat away at bandwidth. Also, information is considered unroutable after 15 hops, which may cause problems in such environments.

OSPF

The OSPF routing protocol was developed by the Internet Engineering Task Force (IETF) specifically for TCP/IP environments such as the Internet. It is an efficient yet complex routing protocol, and it maintains both link states and routing tables. As a link routing protocol, OSPF retains information from all other routers in the internetwork and uses this information to calculate the shortest path to each router. This is in contrast to distance vectoring protocols, mentioned earlier, which send router update messages only to adjacent routers.

OSPF was designed to overcome the limitations of other routing protocols, such as RIP. It is designed to scale without accruing large amounts of overhead. As a result, it meets the requirements for large enterprise internetworks. Here are the RFCs for the OSPF routing protocol:

RFC	Description
1247	OSPF
2328	OSPF Version 2

OSPF HIERARCHY   Another differentiating feature of OSPF is that it can operate hierarchically, as shown in the following illustration. Each OSPF router sends and receives routing information to all other routers in the *autonomous system (AS)*. An AS is a collection of routers (networks) that share a common routing strategy. Each AS can be divided into smaller groups called *areas*, which are essentially contiguous networks according to their network interfaces. Some routers may have multiple interfaces, and those that do can participate in more than one area. These routers are appropriately called *area border routers* (ABRs), and they are responsible for passing routing information from one area to another, which reduces routing traffic in the AS.

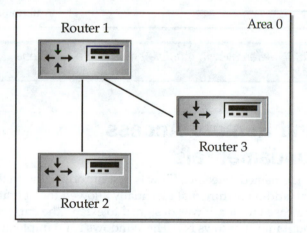

An AS containing multiple areas requires a *backbone* for structural and managerial support. The backbone connects ABRs and any networks that aren't totally contained in any specific area. Figure 16-5 shows an AS comprised of more than one area and a backbone. The backbone in is area 0.

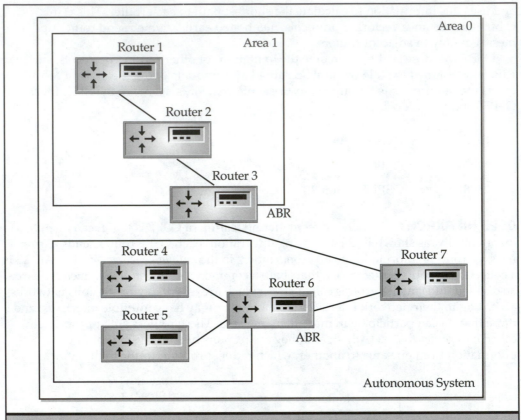

Figure 16-5.   *OSPF hierarchy with multiple areas and a backbone*

Routing and Remote Access Service Fundamentals

RRAS (formerly code-named "Steelhead") was first introduced with the Windows NT 4 Option Pack as an add-on feature that essentially allowed the operating system to serve as a software-based router. It was designed to extend the current implementation of RAS that was built into Windows NT. The Windows NT 4 implementation provided multiprotocol routing and enhanced enterprise networking. It enabled remote site connectivity (LAN to LAN, LAN to user, etc.) via a wide area network (WAN) or through a virtual private network (VPN) connection over a public network such as the Internet.

In Windows 2000, RRAS is no longer an add-on service. Instead, it is a single, unified service that combines the functionality of Windows NT's RAS and RRAS. It also improves upon the earlier implementations with an increased support for industry standards and furnishes usability enhancements that reduce administration costs. You can configure and manage an Internet Connection Server, a Remote Access Server, or a VPN Server, all from a single interface.

Although RRAS is a single service, it operates as a client/server service. A *client* is any entity that connects through the RRAS server service to access resources, while the server-side provides that connectivity. If you've used Windows NT versions of RAS or RRAS, you're probably already familiar with the concept of clients working from home or traveling using their modems to dial into an RRAS server. Windows 9*x* client machines configure a connection through Dial-Up Networking (DUN) to the RAS or RRAS server, and they're on their way. Other clients, such as Windows 3.1 and non-Microsoft operating systems, have other client-side software that allow them to connect remotely to resources through RAS or RRAS.

Windows 2000 changes the remote connectivity definition ever so slightly by extending the definition of a client. It's important to note that the most common (and supported) access methods from previous versions are still intact. Users can still connect using modems (see Figure 16-6), X.25 connections, virtual private networks (VPNs), and more. However, RRAS clients now include network-connected clients in home offices or small businesses when you configure Internet connection sharing in RRAS. Moreover, configuring the RRAS server as a VPN server extends the definition of a client to include a remote office.

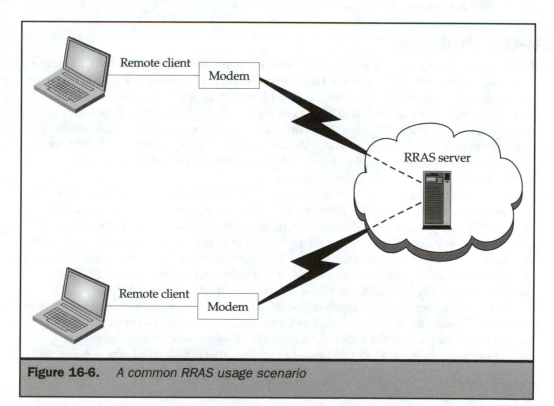

Figure 16-6.   *A common RRAS usage scenario*

Remote Connectivity vs. Remote Control

Before I go any further in this discussion of Windows 2000's RRAS, it would be useful for me to clear up a common misconception about remote connectivity and remote control. Remote connectivity is exactly what RRAS provides. It boils down to RRAS providing a network connection so that users can access resources—such as printers, network shares, and so on—remotely. It's also possible, but generally not recommended, to run applications over the wide area network (WAN) link. The reason to avoid running applications over the WAN link is that WAN links are typically slow connections. Depending on the size and type of application you're trying to run, you may find that it's excruciatingly slow.

With remote control, on the other hand, clients see a redirected screen output from the server exactly as it shows on the server's monitor. Every operation that is performed in the remote control session is actually being performed on the server end. Only the screen information is being sent across the connection. Remote control lets you, the client, feel as if you were right there on the server.

Windows 2000 does provide remote control operations as well, just not through RRAS. Instead, you use Terminal Server that comes bundled with the operating system. For more information on remote control and Terminal Server capabilities of Windows 2000, refer to Chapter 28.

Network Protocols

Language is fascinating because of its diversity. Even when you're speaking the same language with someone, there may be different dialects or accents that you'll interpret. Communicating (speaking, listening, etc.) with others in our native language is something that all of us do (some of us better than others) on a daily basis and is usually taken for granted. Only when you are trying to communicate with someone who can't speak your native language do things get difficult, and you probably resort to other forms of communication like hand gestures to get the other person to understand what you're trying to communicate.

Now, network protocols, such as TCP/IP, IPX/SPX, NetBEUI, and AppleTalk, are the basis for communication for computers whether they're on a LAN or connecting remotely. These protocols are different languages that computers use to talk with one another. The key difference is that if it's not set up to speak a certain language (protocol), it simply won't try, and it can't rely on hand gestures or other forms of communication to communicate with the other computer. So, if one computer speaks only TCP/IP and another speaks only IPX/SPX, the two won't be able to talk to each other.

The network protocols mentioned above are also used as a basis of communication for RRAS. It supports all of these network protocols for use with a variety of clients. What you decide to use not only must be loaded on both the client and server but, more importantly, the protocol or protocols should also match what you use in your Windows 2000 network environment. For example, allowing clients to dial-in using

NetBEUI while the rest of your network only uses TCP/IP wouldn't give clients the necessary access to the resources they need. In fact, they would be able to use only the resources that were provided on the RRAS server. Because most Windows 2000 services depend on TCP/IP, the TCP/IP protocol should be your first choice and possibly the only protocol that you use with RRAS.

TCP/IP

Windows 2000 has standardized on using the popular TCP/IP protocol. As you saw after reading about TCP/IP in Chapter 13, TCP/IP has rooted itself as the protocol of choice for Windows 2000 network environments and has become widely adopted by all companies on the Internet. There are many reasons why TCP/IP has become the de facto standard for networking and for Windows 2000. The most notable reasons are its routing capabilities, its flexibility, its reliability, and its scalability.

With TCP/IP-enabled RRAS, you must provide IP addresses to clients. Clients can either get an IP address directly from the RRAS server's static pool of addresses or they can use DHCP (described in Chapter 13) to get the necessary TCP/IP information.

RRAS can be configured to assign an IP address from a pool of one or more static IP addresses. Each subsequent client connecting through RRAS is assigned the next available IP address in the pool and is freed up only when the client disconnects.

Using RRAS to assign IP addresses to clients is recommended only for small environments that aren't using DHCP in the Windows 2000 network environment. The reason for this is twofold. First, the client is given a limited amount of information. You must manually configure other TCP/IP configuration parameters on the client side in order for it to effectively communicate with other machines and use resources on you network. In addition, you must ensure that each client is given a unique IP address so that there aren't any IP address conflicts on the network. As the number of clients connecting through RRAS increases, so does the amount of work you'll be doing to configure client TCP/IP configuration settings. The second reason is that when TCP/IP information changes, such as adding or changing a WINS or DNS server, that information is not propagated to the client. Each change in your network environment could potentially mean that you must reconfigure each client machine connecting through RRAS. Of course, you could write a script that would change TCP/IP configuration settings as they log onto the network through RRAS, but this is still much more difficult and time-consuming than using DHCP.

To overcome the limitations inherent with RRAS assigning an IP address to RRAS clients, you can use DHCP to dynamically assign them an IP address as well as other TCP/IP configuration parameters. The benefits are enormous, but it boils down to greater flexibility and control over your environment without placing more work on your already hectic schedule. DHCP can pass many TCP/IP configuration settings—an IP address, subnet mask, default gateway, DNS servers, WINS servers, and more—to the RRAS client upon connecting to the RRAS server. Also, if the network configuration changes (if you get a new default gateway, a new DNS server, etc.), then the change has to be made in only one place, the DHCP server.

CONNECTING WITH WINDOWS 2000

NAME RESOLUTION   Clients logging onto the Windows 2000 network through RRAS using TCP/IP also require a naming service or a method for name resolution. More specifically, in order to use resources on the network, they need name to IP address resolution and vice versa. For example, when a client wants to use a shared resource (such as a printer) on a computer named DR-K, it must use a service that translates the computer name to its corresponding IP address in order to connect to the computer.

There are five name resolution mechanisms that clients can use to locate and use resources:

- DNS
- WINS
- HOSTS
- LMHOSTS
- Broadcasts

These are covered in detail in Chapter 13.

IPX/SPX

Internetwork Packet Exchange/Sequenced Packet Exchange (IPX/SPX) is the protocol developed by Novell to be used on Novell NetWare networks, and it was derived from Xerox's Xerox Network Systems (XNS) protocol. Although its design is best suited for LAN environments, IPX/SPX is routable and can therefore be used in enterprise-wide internetworks and RRAS connections. IPX/SPX can use either of two routing protocols, RIP or NetWare Link Services Protocol (NLSP), to pass information to other routers.

Compared to TCP/IP, configuring and using the IPX/SPX protocol is a cakewalk. For starters, it doesn't rely on complex numbering systems that you need to configure to communicate, and it doesn't need to rely on other services for name resolution. In fact, very little configuration is needed once you install the protocol. This also makes IPX/SPX easy to install and use with RRAS.

Your first inclination may be to use this protocol for all your RRAS communications since it's relatively easy to install, configure, and maintain. Keep in mind, though, that you're already running TCP/IP in your Windows 2000 network, so your only compelling reason for using IPX/SPX is to support Novell NetWare connectivity. It is also important to point out that the IPX/SPX protocol broadcasts using the Service Advertisement Protocol (SAP) to identify resources on the network. Broadcasts, by definition, increase the amount of traffic generated on the network. As a result, think twice about supporting IPX/SPX with RRAS. Avoiding the use of this protocol helps you keep the number of protocols used in your network environment to a minimum and consequently reduces administration as well as traffic on the network.

IPX/SPX AND THE RRAS SERVER   As mentioned earlier, IPX/SPX is a rather simple protocol to support for RRAS, but it should be used only to support Novell NetWare connectivity. If your environment is heterogeneous (for example, if it contains both Novell NetWare and Windows 2000) and you have the protocol installed before you install and configure the RRAS server, the RRAS server will automatically provide support for clients using IPX/SPX.

After telling RRAS to use IPX/SPX, you can leave the default settings as they are and clients will be able to connect. You can also modify the settings to fit the needs of your environment. There are basically two parameters that you manipulate:

- Enable network access for remote clients and demand-dial connections
- IPX network number assignment

These options are explained next, in the section "IPX/SPX and the RRAS Client."

In the case where clients using IPX/SPX dial into RRAS and connect to Novell NetWare, the RRAS server is also a software-based router. It controls various types of traffic, such as RIP, SAP, and NetBIOS over IPX, between the RRAS server and the remote access client. The RRAS server (and client) also uses the PPP IPX Configuration Protocol (IPXCP) to configure the RRAS connection for IPX/SPX to allow RRAS clients to gain access to Novell NetWare file and print services and Windows Sockets (WinSock) applications over IPX.

IPX/SPX AND THE RRAS CLIENT   When remote clients connect through RRAS using IPX/SPX, the RRAS server provides the clients with an IPX network number so that it can effectively communicate with other computers on the IPX/SPX network. The IPX network number is generated either automatically by the RRAS server or from a static pool of network numbers configured by the administrator. You may notice that this is similar to the way TCP/IP passes its configuration information to remote clients.

The most efficient way of providing remote clients with an IPX network number is to let the RRAS server handle it for you. However, you can manually assign IPX network numbers if you want greater control of assignments for security and monitoring purposes. If you choose this option, you should be well versed in the IPX/SPX protocol, and you should carefully plan which IPX network numbers you'll use for the remote clients. As with TCP/IP, you must ensure that there are no duplicate IPX network numbers on the network to avoid potential connectivity problems.

NetBEUI

The NetBIOS Extended User Interface (NetBEUI) protocol was designed in the late 1980s as an extension to NetBIOS. NetBEUI is a relatively simple protocol that is best suited for small network environments only. In small network environments it provides quick response times when trying to locate services, but as the size of the network grows, performance diminishes because of the way it manages name resolution.

For many networks, NetBIOS is an integral part of the communication between computers and other network devices. Each device, whether a computer or printer, has a NetBIOS name associated with it. NetBEUI uses these NetBIOS names to locate resources on the network by broadcasting. So, when a computer wants to locate a printer, for example, it sends a broadcast out across the network to find the device attached to the NetBIOS name that it's looking for. As you can see, the more devices on the network using NetBEUI, the more traffic that will be clogging the network. A large number of broadcasts may even result in a broadcast storm, which can easily cripple a network. I have personally witnessed a 10,000-node network shut down due to a broadcast storm (no, I wasn't responsible for configuring the network). More information on NetBIOS name resolution can be found in Chapter 13.

One of the many innovations of Windows 2000 lets you stop relying on NetBIOS and related protocols. For example, Windows 2000 has standardized on TCP/IP and has the option to remove TCP/IP's dependency on NetBIOS. On the other hand, NetBEUI will always rely on NetBIOS and broadcasts to locate and use resources. Windows 2000 supports NetBEUI in LAN and WAN environments for compatibility reasons.

Use caution when you are contemplating whether or not to support NetBEUI with RRAS because bandwidth on WAN links is precious. You can't afford to waste bandwidth on broadcasts even when you have a considerable amount of throughput on a WAN link. Typically, NetBEUI is intended for small environments with very few RRAS connections.

AppleTalk

AppleTalk is the network protocol for Apple Macintosh computers and is supported in Windows 2000 RRAS. This network protocol dynamically assigns all devices (computers, printers, etc.) on the network a unique node number to distinguish them from other devices. It does so by the use of broadcasts.

Communication between computers and other network devices using AppleTalk relies on broadcasts, which is similar to a mass mailing. Every device speaking AppleTalk receives the message. When a successful name resolution occurs after a broadcast, the information is stored in the computer's AppleTalk Address Resolution Protocol (AARP) cache. The next time the computer needs name resolution, it checks its AARP cache before broadcasting.

Although your network may support Macintosh clients, you should configure RRAS to support AppleTalk only if some AppleTalk clients need to remotely connect to the Windows 2000 network.

Access Protocols

Access protocols, also known as encapsulation protocols, establish and control the transmission of information over a WAN link between the RRAS server and client. These protocols are vendor independent, which means that they foster communication between dissimilar vendor technologies and operating system platforms. As a result, many different types of clients (such as Macintosh, UNIX, etc.) can connect through RRAS.

Access protocols live and work in the data link layer of the OSI model while the network protocols, described above, operate at the network layer of the OSI model. The layer in which access protocols operate is the basis for their vendor independence. The primary responsibility of these protocols is to maintain the remote access session by providing compression, packetization of data, and error control. Some access protocols can also provide security by encrypting data before it is sent over the WAN link.

Point-to-Point Protocol (PPP)

PPP is one of the most common access protocols in use today and is the default for Windows 2000. It is actually a suite of standardized protocols, much like TCP/IP, that work together to provide a multitude of services used to establish and maintain point-to-point connections. PPP provides many features, including

- Encapsulation (tunneling) of data
- Compression of data
- Multiplexing (multilink) to combine two or more WAN links
- Reliability by using the High-Level Data Link Control (HDLC) protocol to configure framing of data
- Network configuration negotiation

PPP uses two other protocols, *Link Control Protocol (LCP)* and *Network Control Protocol (NCP)* to establish and maintain the point-to-point connections. LCP is primarily used to establish the connection and configure link parameters such as frame size. NCP, on the other hand, is primarily responsible for negotiating network configuration parameters, such as encapsulation and compression, for the network protocols (AppleTalk, TCP/IP, IPX/SPX, and NetBEUI) on the WAN link. Each network protocol has its own version of an NCP to be used. They are listed with their corresponding network protocol in Table 16-2.

NCP	Network Protocol
AppleTalk Control Protocol (ATCP)	AppleTalk
Internet Protocol Control Protocol (IPC)	TCP/IP
Internet Packet Exchange Control Protocol (IPXCP)	IPX/SPX
NetBEUI Control Protocol (NBTP)	NetBEUI

Table 16-2.   *NCPs and Corresponding Network Protocol*

As you might expect, PPP is defined in a series of RFCs. Table 16-3 lists the PPP RFCs, which can all be found at http://www.rfc-editor.org.

 PPP is the standard from which the PPTP and L2TP protocols were derived. These protocols are explained in the following sections.

Point-to-Point Tunneling Protocol (PPTP)

A popular remote access subject that has received a lot of attention in the past couple of years is virtual private networking (VPN), and PPTP started it all. More information on VPNs can be found later in this chapter. PPTP extends the PPP protocol by enhancing many of PPP's features such as security and multiprotocol support. PPTP can encapsulate TCP/IP, IPX/SPX, and NetBEUI protocols within PPP *datagrams*. Datagrams are associated with connectionless delivery methods that may or may not reach the intended recipient. PPTP is also a set of standardized protocols that work

RFC Number	Description
1549	Information regarding PPP in HDLC Framing
1552	Information regarding the PPP Internetwork Packet Exchange Control Protocol (IPXCP)
1334	Information regarding PPP Authentication Protocols
1332	Information regarding the PPP Internet Protocol Control Protocol (IPCP)
1661	Information regarding LCP
1990	Information regarding PPP Multilink Protocol
2125	Information regarding PPP Bandwidth Allocation Protocol (BAP) and PPP Bandwidth Allocation Control Protocol (BACP)
2097	The PPP NetBIOS Frames Control Protocol (NBFCP)
1962	The PPP Compression Control Protocol (CCP)
1570	PPP LCP Extensions
2284	PPP Extensible Authentication Protocol (EAP)

Table 16-3.   *PPP-related RFCs*

together to provide remote clients with a secure communications channel through a TCP/IP-based network, such as the Internet, to a private network.

 A PPTP connection is typically encrypted with either RC4 or DES 40-bit encryption schemes, but a 128-bit encryption version can also be obtained if it's kept within the United States.

Several practical implementations stem from PPTP connections. For example, while on the road, clients can establish a secure connection to their company through the Internet. This enables them to utilize resources on the company network without accruing long-distance phone costs. Another example is using PPTP connectivity to link various company sites securely and inexpensively, as in the configuration shown in Figure 16-7. As you can see from these examples, PPTP can be used with a dial-up connection, but it isn't required. All that is necessary is IP connectivity between two points.

EXTENSIBLE AUTHENTICATION PROTOCOL (EAP)   With help from EAP, security with PPTP connections is tightened. As the name implies, EAP is an authentication protocol that adds to and enhances authentication mechanisms with a PPTP connection. In particular, EAP brings to PPTP several authentication mechanisms including these:

- Token card authentication
- Public key authentication using smart cards and certificates
- One-time passwords

Depending on which implementation of EAP you use, the client, not the server, may be the only party obligated to prove its identity. However, with Windows 2000,

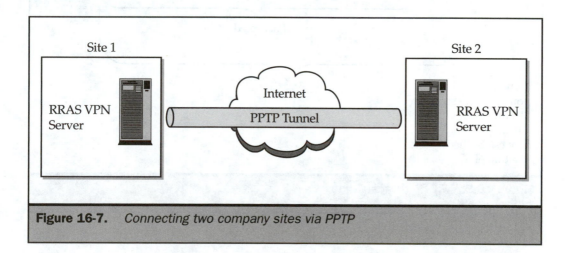

Figure 16-7.   *Connecting two company sites via PPTP*

both the client and server are obligated to prove to one another that they are who they say they are.

Layer Two Tunneling Protocol (L2TP)

L2TP promises to be the PPTP's replacement as the tunneling protocol of choice. It is supported by vendors such as Cisco, Microsoft, 3Com, and others. L2TP is based on PPTP and the Layer Two Forwarding (L2F) protocol. L2F was designed by Cisco and is a more robust tunneling protocol that supports the encapsulation of many more protocols than PPTP, including AppleTalk and SNA. This allows for a broader coverage of the operating system platforms that can be supported.

Like PPTP, L2TP can be used to create a secure, reliable communications channel between two endpoints, such as a remote client and server or site to site. It uses the Internet Protocol security (IPSec) for authentication and encryption to protect data traversing the connection. IPSec is covered in more detail later in this chapter. L2TP encapsulates PPP packets just like PPTP does in order to secure the connection. As you recall, PPP packets essentially encapsulate or wrap up network protocols (TCP/IP, IPX, etc.). Figure 16-8 illustrates how L2TP encapsulates the packets.

L2TP is frequently used for dial-up connections because its design is optimized for dial-up connections rather than site-to-site implementations. Moreover, the L2TP implementation in Windows 2000 is also designed primarily over IP networks, and it doesn't support native tunneling over X.25, Frame Relay, or ATM networks.

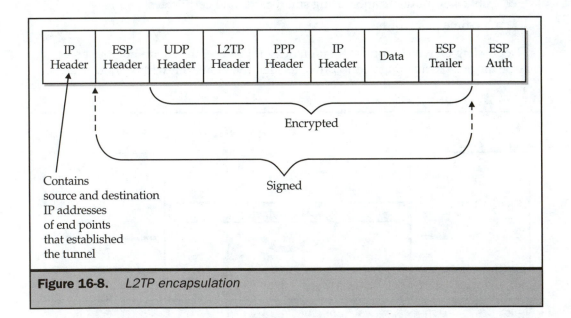

Figure 16-8. *L2TP encapsulation*

Serial Line Internet Protocol (SLIP)

SLIP is the oldest type of access protocol for point-to-point connections. It encapsulates network protocols so that they can be transmitted over the link, but it lacks many of the features of its protocols, including compression and error checking. As a result, SLIP does little to ensure the quality of data that is being transmitted and should therefore be used only as a last resort.

Windows 2000 supports SLIP only for backward compatibility with older systems that don't support the more robust PPP communications. SLIP is all but phased out as a means of point-to-point communications.

Access Methods

Now that we've discussed the various network and access protocols that RRAS supports, let's examine the methods that use the physical layer protocols for communication.

Analog Connections

The Public Switched Telephone Network (PSTN) is the standard telephone service that you're accustomed to using and is also known as the Plain Old Telephone System (POTS). POTS uses analog lines that were designed primarily for voice communications, but they are now also commonly used for data transmission. Modems allow you to transmit data over the analog system. Chances are that anywhere there is a telephone, you will be able to use a modem to make a remote connection to your own network. Because POTS was designed for voice communications, there are limitations on the rate at which data can be transmitted.

Modems convert digital signals to analog to be transmitted across the link and convert analog signals being received back to digital signals so that the computer can understand them. Generally speaking, modems are categorized by the standards they support (such as V.32, V.32bis, V.90) and the speed at which they send and receive data. Modems can operate at speeds up to 56 Kbps using the V.90 modulation standard. However, the Federal Communications Commission (FCC) power rules limit the ability to send data faster than 33.6 Kbps and receive data at 53 Kbps. The conversion, along with other factors such as noise that are inherent to POTS, chokes the amount of data that you can send and receive over the connection.

There are many vendors that supply modems, and Windows 2000 supports tons of them. This includes, for instance, most if not all of the major brands of modems, such as 3Com/US Robotics, and Hayes. However, to be on the safe side, you should verify that your modem is compatible. Check Microsoft's Hardware Compatibility List (HCL) at http://www.microsoft.com/HCL. After you install the modem, Windows 2000 is likely to detect it and install the appropriate drivers, because Windows 2000 fully supports Plug and Play.

ISDN

Integrated Services Digital Network (ISDN) is a digital version of the telephone system (POTS). It can transfer data at a rate much higher than the analog phone system because the line is much cleaner (higher clarity, less noise, etc.). Typically, phone lines transmit at up to 53 Kbps, with a 56 Kbps modem, whereas ISDN transmits data at either 64 or 128 Kbps depending on how many ISDN channels are used.

ISDN uses two B-channels for transferring data. Each channel operates at 64 Kbps. Therefore, operating with one B-channel allows you to transmit at 64 Kbps, and two channels boost speeds up to 128 Kbps through channel aggregation. ISDN also has a third channel, the D-channel, that isn't used for transmitting data but rather for overseeing and managing the two B-channels. The D-channel establishes the connection and controls data transfer such as signaling.

Two protocols are used with ISDN. They are Basic Rate Interface (BRI) and Primary Rate Interface (PRI). The type of protocol you use depends on how the phone company is providing the ISDN service to you. The most common ISDN protocol used is the BRI. It defaults to using two B-channels and a D-channel. PRI is a little less common because it uses a portion of a T1 data circuit. A T1 circuit (or line) is an aggregation of twenty-four 64 Kbps channels. When you use PRI, it can take three of those channels (two are used as B-channels and one as a D-channel).

Several years ago, ISDN was typically used for businesses because of its high price tag. However, ISDN is now becoming an affordable and widely available option for home use as well.

X.25

X.25 is a global standard developed in the 1970s for data communications over a telephone network or packet-switched networks (PSNs). Although X.25 implementations are gradually being replaced with other low-cost alternatives, it is often the best choice in underdeveloped areas around the world.

X.25 communications are very similar to telephone use or dial-up connections. A host calls another computer to request a connection, and if it's accepted, information can then be transferred. More specifically, data terminal equipment (DTE) connects to data circuit-terminating equipment (DCE) within a PSN.

In Windows 2000, network and dial-up connections support X.25 by using packet assemblers/disassemblers (PADs) and X.25 cards. RRAS clients may also use a modem to dial into a Windows 2000 Server using X.25, but the server must use an X.25 card to accept the call.

ADSL

Asymmetric Digital Subscriber Line (ADSL) is a new access method (and one of the most talked about) that has found its way into many small businesses and residential areas because of its relatively low cost and high bandwidth capabilities. ADSL provides high-speed data connections using the same copper phone lines that are used in POTS.

Although ADSL promises high bandwidth, the upstream (client-to-service) is slower than the downstream (service-to-client) data transfer rate. Typically, upstream transfer rates range from 64 Kbps to 256 Kbps, while downstream boasts an impressive 1.544 Mbps for data transmission. The downstream transfer rate is equivalent to a T1 line. There are also variations of ADSL, such as HDSL and VDSL, that claim substantially higher upstream and downstream transfer rates.

When you install an ADSL network adapter in Windows 2000, the adapter appears as either an Ethernet or a dial-up interface. The connection configuration depends on the interface it uses. For instance, if ADSL appears as an Ethernet interface, the connection operates just as it would with an Ethernet connection, but if it appears as a dial-up interface, ADSL uses *Asynchronous Transfer Mode (ATM)*.

ATM   ATM is a collection of technologies that provide robust, high-quality networking services for voice, video, and data. ATM uses very large-scale integration (VLSI) technology to segment data at high speeds into packets called *cells*. Each cell is 53 bytes in length and consists of 5 bytes of header information and 48 bytes of data, as shown in the illustration.

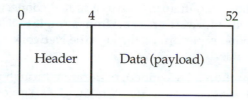

ATM is *connection oriented*, meaning that a path from source to destination is established before data is sent across the connection. This path is commonly referred to as a *virtual circuit (VC)*. Also, during the establishment of the connection, Quality of Service (QoS) parameters are negotiated to provide the highest level of accuracy and guarantee quality for the connection whether it's LAN or WAN based.

When comparing ATM with Ethernet or Token Ring, you'll notice many differing characteristics between the technologies, most notably these:

- **Connection oriented**   As mentioned above, ATM is connection oriented while Ethernet and Token Ring are connectionless oriented. Connectionless-oriented technologies do not establish a connection prior to sending data across the connection, but they do have other mechanisms within the upper-level, network protocols to ensure that data reaches the intended recipient.

- **Packets**   ATM packets are called *cells*, and each cell has a fixed length of 53 bytes. This is in contrast to Ethernet or Token Ring's variable packet length structure. Because the ATM cell is fixed in length, it's predictable. The network doesn't spend time determining where a particular cell begins or ends, and the overall transmission of the data is optimized.

Internet Connection Sharing

Internet Connection Sharing (ICS) is an invaluable service provided in Windows 2000. Basically, it allows you to share a dedicated or dial-up Internet connection with other machines in small office or home office (SOHO) environments. It also provides a low-cost alternative for the SOHO.

Traditionally, you were required to configure each machine in the SOHO with a registered IP address or a separate dial-up connection in order to get out onto the Internet. There are two inherent problems with this situation. First, registering IP addresses and buying addition equipment (routers, hubs, and so on) to connect the SOHO to the Internet is an expensive solution for this type of environment. Only larger environments could make this investment worthwhile. Also, creating separate dial-up connections requires additional expenses (phone lines, modems, and possibly several Internet accounts from your ISP) and your time, but more importantly, it patches up the problem rather than solving it. ICS removes these limitations by serving as a centralized, low-cost mechanism for connecting your environment to the Internet.

Following are two methods in which you can configure ICS:

- **Routed connection** Configuring ICS as a routed connection allows the server to act as a router that forwards packets from a single SOHO network to the Internet. This option is performed through the Network And Dial-Up Connections interface.

- **Translated connection** This option, performed through the RRAS management console, configures the Windows 2000 server again as a router that forwards packets from a network to the Internet. The difference between this option and the first one is that it can route packets from more than one IP address as well as service demand-dial connections.

Both methods perform network address translation (NAT), but it's more sophisticated in the translated connection because it can route more than one IP address. NAT hides the private IP address or addresses on the internal network behind one or more public IP addresses. For instance, your computer on the internal network has an IP address of 192.168.1.10 (private IP address), but when you jump onto the Internet, the server translates it into a public IP address. A public IP address is needed in order to use Internet resources such as the Web.

Securing RRAS

Securing remote access connections is key to successfully deploying remote access solutions. If you don't properly secure remote connections, you'll risk leaving your Windows 2000 network environment wide open. Windows 2000's RRAS provides many security features including encryption, authentication, callback, and caller ID, which help fortify your remote connections and consequently your network.

Authentication Methods

There are several authentication methods that you can use with remote connections. By default, RRAS uses MS-CHAP and MS-CHAPv2 authentication. Selected authentication methods are used in the following order:

1. Extensible Authentication Protocol (EAP)

2. Microsoft Challenge Handshake Authentication Protocol version 2 (MS-CHAPv2)

3. Microsoft Challenge Handshake Authentication Protocol (MS-CHAP)

4. Challenge Handshake Authentication Protocol (CHAP)

5. Shiva Password Authentication Protocol (SPAP)

6. Password Authentication Protocol (PAP)

7. Unauthenticated Access

These authentication methods, illustrated in Figure 16-9, can be found within the RRAS management console by selecting the appropriate server in the right console and selecting Properties. Then, under the Security tab, select the Authentication Methods button. To use any of the authentication methods, you simply check the box beside them.

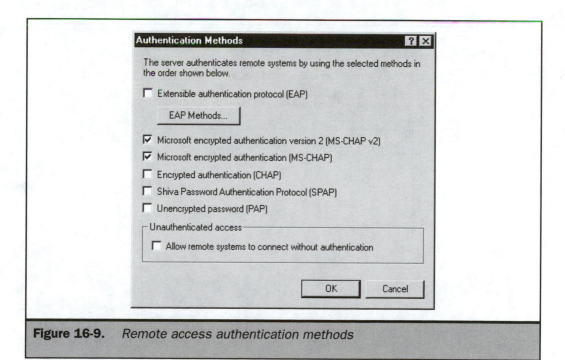

Figure 16-9.   *Remote access authentication methods*

EAP

EAP is an extension to PPP that allows an arbitrary authentication method to be
negotiated between the remote client and server. Once the link is established, the client
and server negotiate which EAP type of authentication mechanism will be used. These
options include EAP-MD5 CHAP, EAP-TLS, smart cards, and more. After a decision is
made, the client uses the selected authentication mechanism to gain access to the RRAS
server and network.

As the name implies, EAP is extensible, meaning that any number of EAP types
can be added at any time. To see which EAP methods you're currently using, do
the following:

1. Open the RRAS management console from the Start | Programs |
   Administrative Tools menu.

2. In the right console, right-click on a RRAS server and select Properties.

3. Under the Security tab, click the Authentication Methods button to display the
   Authentication Methods window.

4. Click the EAP Methods button to see the EAP methods that are currently
   installed, as shown in Figure 16-10.

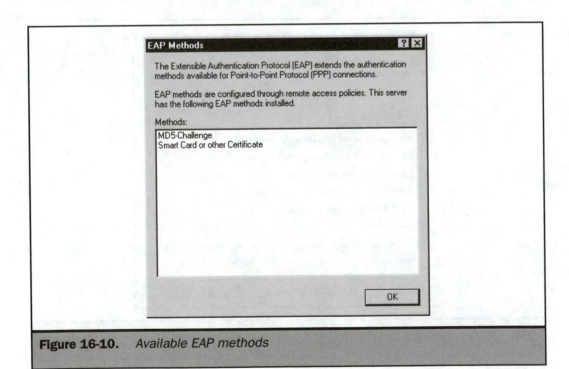

Figure 16-10. *Available EAP methods*

EAP METHODS   Windows 2000 can support any EAP method types (e.g., Smart Cards) as plug-ins, but it automatically provides the following two EAP methods:

- **EAP-MD5 CHAP**   EAP-Message Digest 5 CHAP is a required EAP method that retains many of the same attributes as CHAP but also sends the challenges and responses as EAP messages.

- **EAP-TLS**   The EAP-Transport Level Security method is certificate-based authentication. This method is required if you're using smart cards. EAP-TLS is currently the strongest type of authentication, and it requires that the RRAS server be a member of a domain. It provides mutual authentication (both client and server are authenticated), encryption, as well as secured private key exchange.

CHAP

CHAP is probably the most common authentication protocol in use today. Three versions of CHAP are supported by Windows 2000's RRAS:

- **CHAP**   As an industry standard, CHAP is a challenge-response authentication protocol that supports one-way encryption of responses to challenges. The authentication process uses three steps to completion. First, the server challenges the client to prove its identity. Then the client sends an encrypted CHAP message in response to the challenge. The server then verifies the response, and if it's correct, the client is granted access.

- **MS-CHAP**   MS-CHAP is a modified, proprietary version of CHAP. The major difference between MS-CHAP and CHAP in Windows 2000 is that the user's password is in a reversibly encrypted form.

- **MS-CHAPv2**   Version 2 of the MS-CHAP is a stronger, more secure authentication method than previous implementations. Some of the most notable differences are that it no longer supports NTLM (it can be used only with Windows 2000), it provides mutual authentication, and separate cryptographic keys are used for sending and receiving data.

SPAP

Shiva is an older, yet widely accepted, remote access solution. Clients using Shiva client software must be authenticated using SPAP. SPAP is a rather simple authentication method that encrypts passwords traveling across the link. This authentication option is supported by Windows 2000 only for Shiva clients that you may need to service.

PAP

PAP is actually a misnomer because it is the most insecure authentication method available today. Both the user name and password are sent across the link in clear text.

Anyone snooping the connection could easily grab and use the information to gain access to your network. As a result, using PAP for authentication is not advisable.

Unauthenticated Access

This option is pretty obvious so there's really no need to go into much depth about it. All that need be said is that you should never use this option unless you absolutely don't care about securing your environment. You're essentially opening access to anyone who wants to connect remotely.

Callback

Callback means just what the word implies. A remote client dials the RRAS server, and the client's credentials (username and password) are verified. Once the credentials are verified, the connection is dropped so that the RRAS server can call the remote client back. The number that the RRAS server calls can either be specified during the initial call or you can require that RRAS call a specific number. The latter of the two is the most secure method because it restricts remote connectivity locations. Another benefit of callback is to save on the remote client's connection charges.

Caller ID

Most, if not all, of you are already familiar with caller ID on your phone systems at home. Someone calls you, and his or her telephone number is displayed. This same functionality can be applied to remote access to offer heightened security.

Caller ID can be used to verify that a remote client that dials into RRAS is calling from a specified number. If the client isn't calling from the specified number, the connection is denied and dropped. Sometimes you may find that the phone company can't provide you with a caller's number because somewhere POTS isn't equipped to handle caller ID or the caller has blocked the number from being displayed. When the number can't be displayed, for whatever reason, the connection is denied.

Virtual Private Networking Fundamentals

VPNs are probably one of the most talked about, but surprisingly, one of the least understood, concepts relating to the Internet and remote access. VPNs have been around for years, but they haven't received a lot of attention until now. They have been supported by Microsoft since the Windows NT 4 implementation of RRAS and continue to be supported in Windows 2000's RRAS.

Part of the confusion stems from what the word "private" means. For instance, companies have long given their sites, such as branch offices, connectivity through dedicated leased lines. This is in fact a private network that has been extended to reach remote areas. This is also commonly referred to as a *carrier-based VPN*. The ISP (or phone company) sets up virtual circuits between sites. In this case, there are two types of virtual circuits, permanent virtual circuits (PVCs) and switched virtual circuits (SVCs), that provide private connectivity. The most common of these is the PVC.

The *Internet VPN*, will be the usage applied in this discussion. An Internet VPN is a means by which two computers or networks can communicate privately through an otherwise shared or public network such as the Internet. It is also an extension to your private network, but it doesn't require an ISP or phone company to place a separate, additional link to provide the connectivity, which can potentially save you tons of money. VPNs aren't limited to site-to-site connections. They also allow remote clients, such as road warriors and telecommuters, to connect securely to the company's network. For example, a remote client dials his or her local ISP (saving phone charges) and then establishes a VPN through the Internet to his or her company's network.

VPNs provide security and reliability to what would otherwise be an insecure connection through a public network. A VPN is basically composed of three technologies that when used together form the secure connection. They are *authentication, tunneling,* and *encryption.*

Authentication

The primary reason for authentication with VPNs is to have a method ensuring that the client and server are who they say they are before the VPN session is established. This doesn't necessarily imply that mutual authentication is required. Successful authentication is required before the tunnel can be established and data is transmitted, but the type of authentication used depends on the types of clients in your environment and your choice of authentication methods.

Any of the authentication methods described in the "Securing RRAS" section of this chapter can be used. The only drawback, though, is that if remote clients are down-level clients, they probably don't support the EAP authentication protocol. In fact, Windows NT and Windows 9x clients don't support it. When you're deciding which ones to use, keep in mind that it's important to provide the strongest level of authentication possible. This means using authentication protocols such as EAP, MS-CHAP, or MS-CHAPv2.

Tunneling

Tunneling is used to encapsulate network protocols (TCP/IP, IPX/SPX, AppleTalk, and NetBEUI) into an IP packet that can travel across the Internet. Yes, TCP/IP can travel across the Internet on its own, but then it wouldn't be a part of the tunnel or the VPN. Think of tunneling as a mole burrowing through the ground making a path from one site to the next.

Before the tunnel can be created, it must be verified that the two endpoints are who they say they are. Once they're authenticated, the tunnel is created and information between the two ends is sent, as illustrated in Figure 16-11. The two protocols that are responsible for creating the VPN tunnels in Windows 2000 are PPTP and L2TP, which were explained earlier. L2TP is an advancement over the PPTP tunneling protocol, and it uses the IPSec authentication and encryption protocol.

L2TP is available only in the Windows 2000 version of RRAS, and Windows 2000 clients are the only ones equipped to use it. Table 16-4 outlines which clients support the different tunneling protocols.

Encryption

The third major component of a VPN is encryption. Encryption is an extra precautionary measure that protects the data that is sent through the tunnel. Data is encrypted before it's encapsulated to reduce the risk that someone might tamper with it if the tunnel is breached.

Windows 2000 supports two encryption technologies, Microsoft Point-to-Point Encryption (MPPE) and IPSec. Both methods use an encryption key to encrypt and decrypt information at the sender and receiver ends. You can require that remote clients or sites use either method. If they don't use the encryption method you specify, you can configure RRAS to deny the connection.

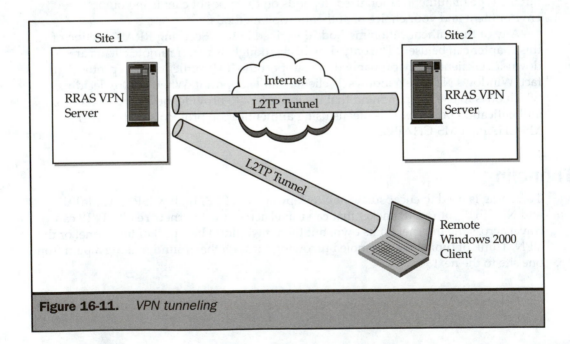

Figure 16-11.   *VPN tunneling*

VPN Client	Tunneling Protocols Supported
Windows 2000	PPTP, L2TP
Windows NT version 4	PPTP
Windows 98	PPTP
Windows 95	PPTP with Windows Dial-Up Networking 1.3

Table 16-4.   *Clients and the Tunneling Protocols They Support*

MPPE

MPPE can encrypt data in PPTP VPN connections. It supports the following encryption schemes:

- Standard 40-bit encryption
- Standard 56-bit encryption
- Strong 128-bit encryption for use only within the United States and Canada

To use MPPE, you must use either MS-CHAP or MS-CHAPv2 authentication protocols.

IPSec

Despite popular belief, IPSec is actually a collection of cryptography-based services and protocols. It provides authentication as well as encryption to a VPN connection that uses L2TP. However, L2TP still uses the authentication methods, such as EAP and MS-CHAP, described earlier.

IPSec, in Windows 2000 implementations, uses either Data Encryption Standard (DES) or Triple DES (3DES). DES uses 56-bit encryption key and can be used internationally. 3DES, on the other hand, uses two 56-bit encryption keys and is not for export outside the United States. The type of IPSec encryption used is determined by the *security association* (SA). An SA is set up between the two endpoints in the VPN, and it establishes the common security measures to be used.

VPN Implementation Considerations

Just because VPNs are one of the hottest technologies for remote access doesn't mean that a VPN is the right solution for you. Before you actually implement it as a solution in your Windows 2000 network environment, you need to consider the following:

- **Security**   Security concerns should be one of the major deciding factors that lead you to use a VPN solution. There are two questions that you should ask yourself. "Will a VPN be overkill for the type of information that I'm transmitting?" For instance, are you just sending nonconfidential email? The second question to ask is, "Is a VPN going to satisfy my security requirements?" Government agencies are often used in examples concerning security. The military, for instance, probably won't even consider using a VPN over a public network no matter how good the security it claims to provide.

■ **Budgetary Concerns** Initial and ongoing costs for setting up a VPN solution in your Windows 2000 network environment is miniscule compared to leased lines. A VPN clearly gives you the cost advantages because now sites and remote clients can connect to the company's network securely without additional charges such as connectivity hardware, phone costs, and so on. It's true that remote users could use an 800 number to dial in, but that doesn't totally solve the problem, and it's expensive.

■ **Throughput** Because VPNs require authentication and encryption, the rate at which data is transmitted is, by definition, going to be slower than without it. You can count on as little as 30 to as much as 50 percent degradation in performance using a VPN. You'll have to weigh the costs of throughput versus security.

These are just a few of the things you need to ponder before implementing a VPN solution. However, if you consider these three issues, you'll be prepared and more confident of your decision on whether or not to provide VPN capabilities to your Windows 2000 network.

Choosing a VPN Solution

There are basically two types of VPN solutions, dial-up VPN and site to site. A combination of the two can be categorized as a third type.

■ **Dial-up VPN** Typically, remote clients dial their local ISP and then "dial" the Windows 2000 VPN server to establish a VPN connection between the VPN server and remote client. This saves long-distance phone charges for the remote client and also saves money at the VPN server site because in many cases it can replace the need for large numbers of modems and other remote access devices for connectivity.

■ **Site to Site** The most commonly used VPN solution is the site-to-site implementation. In this scenario, you use two or more Windows 2000 VPN servers to establish a VPN between them. Communication is securely defined between the two sites. Users on either network can communicate with the other remote site.

■ **Combining Solutions** As the name implies, Windows 2000 environments that have both remote clients and sites can create a VPN solution to service both of them.

Installing RRAS

Installing RRAS is such an easy, straightforward topic that it may seem too obvious to mention. When you install Windows 2000 Server, RRAS is automatically installed for you but in a disabled state. This means that it's not taking up precious resources if you're not using it.

To start using RRAS, whether it's for remote access, routing, or setting up a VPN between sites, you first need to enable it.

Enabling RRAS

Your next step in getting RRAS up and running is almost as straightforward as installing it. Since it's disabled by default after you install Windows 2000 Server, you'll need to enable the service. Before doing so, you must have administrative privileges or be a member of the RAS and IAS Servers security group for the domain. To enable RRAS, do the following:

1. From the Start | Programs | Administrative Tools menu, select Routing And Remote Access to start the Routing And Remote Access snap-in manager shown in Figure 16-12.

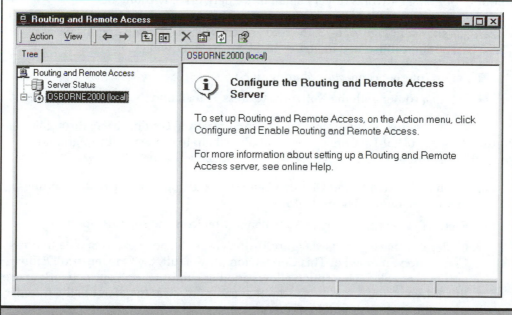

Figure 16-12. *The RRAS management console*

2. In the right pane, select the server you want to enable, and then click Configure And Enable Routing And Remote Access from the Action menu. At this point the Routing And Remote Access Server Setup Wizard appears, and you can begin configuring RRAS.

Next, you need to configure the functionality you want to use with RRAS.

Configuring RRAS

The Routing And Remote Access Server Setup Wizard abolishes much of the pain that you may have experienced with earlier versions of RAS or RRAS. This wizard holds your hand each step of the way whether you're configuring an Internet connection server, a remote access server, or configuring a VPN solution. It is important to note here that the following sections on configuring the server assume that you already have installed a modem or other devices used for remote connections.

Configuring an Internet Connection Server

Using RRAS to configure the server as an Internet Connection Server is a new feature within Windows 2000 that enables you to share a single Internet connection with other computers on the network. Sharing a single Internet connection is referred to as ICS. This feature is not intended, however, to be a solution for every network, but rather a solution for home networks or very small office network environments.

When you choose this option within the Routing And Remote Access Server Setup Wizard, as shown in Figure 16-13, the next screen will present two options for you. These two options, illustrated in Figure 16-14, are the following:

■ Set up Internet connection sharing (ICS)

■ Set up a router with the Network Address Translation (NAT) routing protocol

Choosing the first option immediately prompts you to configure ICS through Networking And Dial-Up Connections and offers help to guide you through that process. To configure ICS through Dial-Up Networking, do the following:

1. Open the Network And Dial-up Connections dialog from the Start | Settings menu as shown in Figure 16-15.

2. Right-click on the dial-up or VPN connection icon and select Properties.

3. Under the Sharing tab (see Figure 16-16), check the box next to Enable Internet Connection Sharing For This Connection. By default, the On-Demand Dialing option is enabled. This option allows another computer on your network to use this Internet connection (when another computer tries to get out to the Internet, the connection dials automatically).

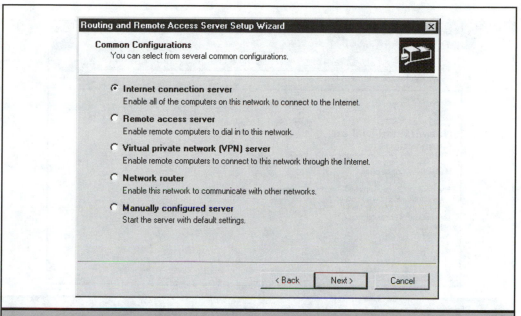

Figure 16-13.   *Choosing to configure an Internet Connection Server*

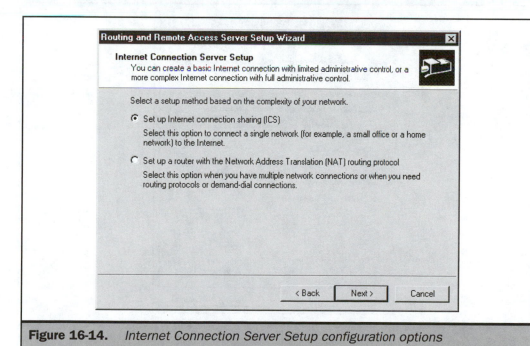

Figure 16-14.   *Internet Connection Server Setup configuration options*

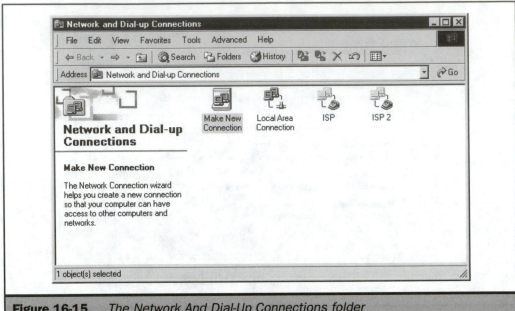

Figure 16-15.   *The Network And Dial-Up Connections folder*

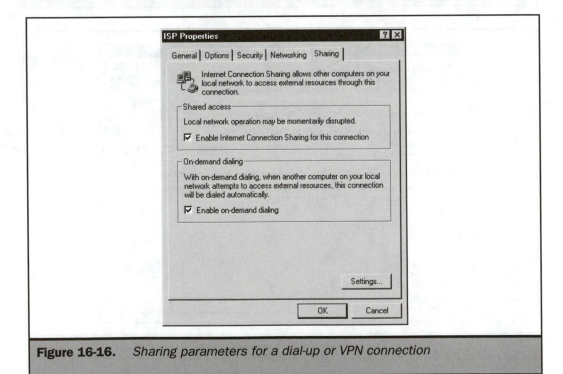

Figure 16-16.   *Sharing parameters for a dial-up or VPN connection*

4. Click OK. At this point, an informational dialog box appears, informing you that your network interface card's IP address will be set to 192.168.0.1 and recommending that you configure other computers on the same network to obtain an IP address automatically. Other computers on the network will use the same IP Class (Class B) address so that communication between computers is not lost. This is referred to as Plug and Play Networking (see Chapter 13 for more information).

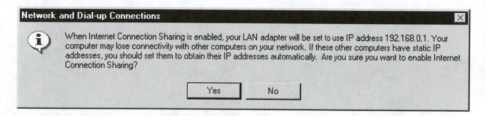

5. Click Yes.

Configuring an ICS Router Using NAT

The second option presented involves configuring Windows 2000 as an Internet Connection Server router using NAT connecting through a NIC. This option supports the following:

- Multiple public IP addresses
- Multiple SOHO interfaces
- Configurable IP address range for network clients

Note   *Use this option in an existing network with other domain controllers (DCs), DNS server, or DHCP servers.*

Here's how you can configure ICS on a Windows 2000 server as a router using NAT:

1. Open Routing And Remote Access from the Start | Programs | Administrative Tools menu.

2. From the Action menu, select Configure And Enable Routing And Remote Access. When the Routing And Remote Access Server Setup Wizard window pops up, click Next to continue.

3. Select Internet connection server and click Next.

4. Select Set Up A Router With The Network Address Translation (NAT) Routing Protocol, as shown in Figure 16-17, and then click Next.

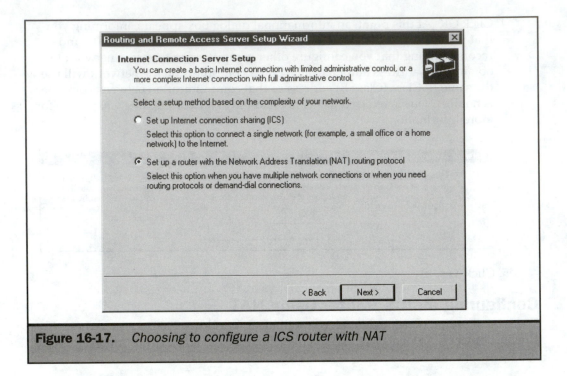

Figure 16-17.   *Choosing to configure a ICS router with NAT*

5. In the next window, choose one of two options: Use The Selected Internet Connection or Create A New Demand-Dial Internet Connection. After choosing the first option, you click Next and then on the next screen, click Finish. This example uses the latter option, which starts the Demand Dial Interface Wizard.

CREATING A DEMAND DIAL INTERFACE   The following describes how to configure a demand dial interface. (This continues the preceding instructions.)

6. As soon as the Demand Dial Interface Wizard starts, click Next to continue.

7. Specify the name of the interface and click Next.

8. The next window, shown in Figure 16-18, asks you to specify the connection type (modem or other adapter or use a VPN). Click Next to continue.

9. Specify the device from the list to be used and click Next.

10. Next, specify the protocols and security settings for the interface as illustrated in Figure 16-19. When you're finished, click Next to continue.

11. In the next window, specify the dial-out credentials. In particular, you'll specify the username, domain, and password that will be used to dial out. Click Next to continue.

12. Click Finish to complete the demand dial interface setup.

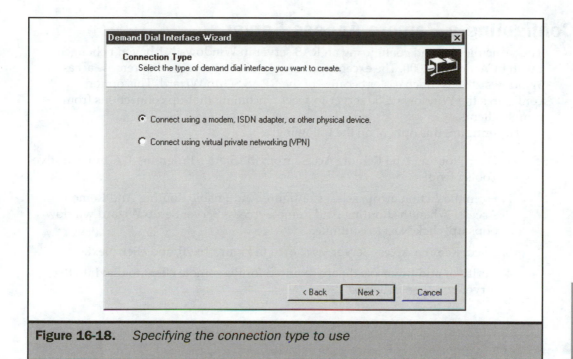

Figure 16-18. *Specifying the connection type to use*

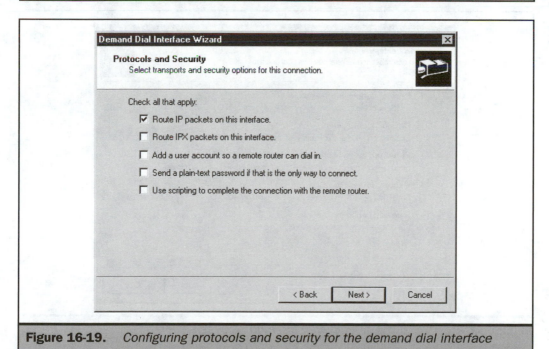

Figure 16-19. *Configuring protocols and security for the demand dial interface*

Configuring a Remote Access Server

The principles behind configuring an RAS server in Windows NT haven't changed much in Windows 2000. The exception, however, is that configuring remote access on Windows 2000 is much easier because of the RRAS Setup Wizard. This option configures the Windows 2000 server to accept incoming dial-up connections from remote clients.

To configure this option, do the following:

1. Open Routing And Remote Access from the Start | Programs | Administrative Tools menu.

2. From the Action menu, select Configure And Enable Routing And Remote Access. When the Routing And Remote Access Server Setup Wizard window pops up, click Next to continue.

3. Select Remote Access Server, as shown in Figure 16-20, and click Next.

4. Verify or add protocols tht are required for the remote client to dial into the server and then click next.

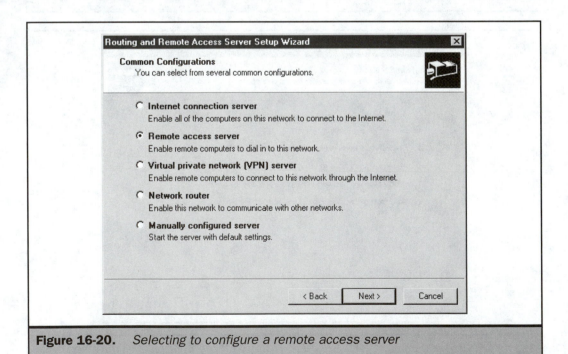

Figure 16-20.   *Selecting to configure a remote access server*

5. Next, choose how you'd like to assign IP addresses to remote clients. If you have a DHCP server in your network environment, this option is highly recommended. Otherwise, you must specify an IP address range.

6. Choose whether or not you want to configure a RADIUS server now (the default is no). If remote clients aren't going to use a VPN to connect, keeping the default is recommended.

7. Click Finish and you're done.

Configuring a VPN Server

By configuring RRAS as a VPN server, you are allowing remote clients to pass through a public network, such as the Internet, through an encrypted tunnel to your Windows 2000 network environment.

1. Open Routing And Remote Access from the Start | Programs | Administrative Tools menu.

2. From the Action menu, select Configure And Enable Routing And Remote Access. When the Routing And Remote Access Server Setup Wizard window pops up, click Next to continue.

3. Select Virtual Private Network (VPN) Server, as shown in Figure 16-21, and click Next.

CONNECTING WITH
WINDOWS 2000

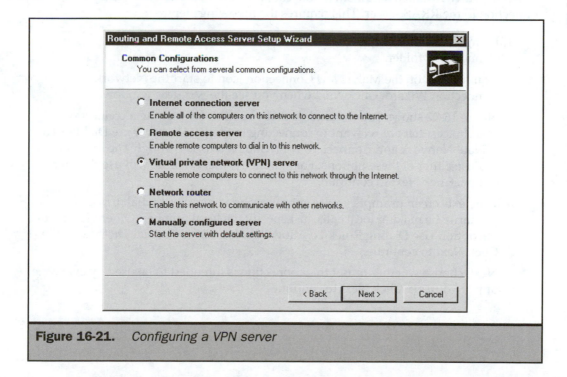

Figure 16-21.   *Configuring a VPN server*

4. Verify that the required protocols are installed on the server or add the appropriate protocols, and then click Next.

5. Select the appropriate connection to the Internet that will be used and click Next.

6. Choose how IP addresses are assigned to the client. If you have a DHCP server, you should use it. If you don't have DHCP, the VPN server will assign an IP address to the client from a range of IP addresses. Note that if you choose the latter option, you'll have to specify the range in the next step. Click Next to continue.

7. Assuming that you took the recommendation in Step 6, the next screen asks you if you want the VPN server to use a RADIUS server (this example keeps the default no). Click Next to continue.

8. Click Finish.

Configuring RRAS Clients

Configuring clients to connect remotely is a relatively simple procedure with Windows 2000. RRAS does support other client operating systems, including, but not limited to, Windows NT, Windows 9x, UNIX variants, Macintosh, and others connecting remotely, but the focus of this section is on Windows 2000 clients.

After you've installed a modem on the client, you're ready to configure a connection to the RRAS server. This requires the following steps:

1. From the Start | Settings menu, open the Network And Dial-Up Connections folder.

2. Double-click on the Make New Connection icon to start the Network Connection Wizard. Click Next when you see the wizard's window.

3. Figure 16-22 shows you the choices that you have for making a connection. The choices that are relevant to connecting to the RRAS server are Dial-Up To Private Network and Connect To A Private Network Through The Internet. Choose either of these options. For simplicity, this example will use the first option. Click Next to continue.

4. The next screen prompts you to supply a phone number to dial. If you'll primarily be making local calls, just specify the local number. Otherwise, check the option Use Dialing Rules To Allow Windows 2000 To Dial The Area Code. Click Next to continue.

5. Next, choose whether or not this connection is intended to be used by everyone or just yourself. Click Next to continue.

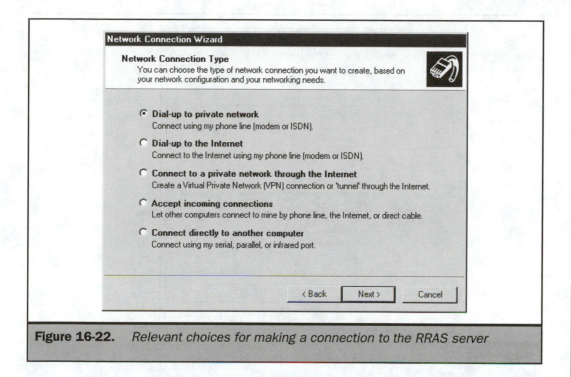

Figure 16-22.   *Relevant choices for making a connection to the RRAS server*

6. On the next screen, make sure that the Enable Internet Connection Sharing For This Connection Option is unchecked and then click Next. You don't want to enable this option.

7. Type in the name for the connection and then click Finish. You can optionally add a shortcut on the desktop for accessibility.

Specifying a Connection's Security Settings

At this point you're done unless you want to configure the connection's security. This is a good idea because the default setting for the client is to allow unsecured password validation.

1. Return to the Network And Dial-Up Connections folder, right-click on the connection you just finished configuring, and select Properties.

2. Under the Security tab you can choose your security options as shown in Figure 16-23. The best procedure here is to configure the client to use the security mechanisms used by the server. For example, a client should be told to use EAP if the server is using EAP. In this particular case, you would click the Advanced (Custom Settings) option, click on the Settings button, and click on Use Extensible Authentication Protocol (EAP) as illustrated in Figure 16-24.

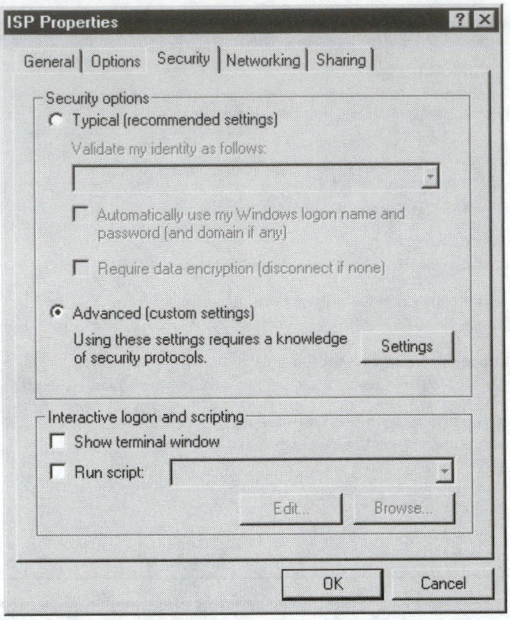

Figure 16-23. *A client's dial-up connection security properties*

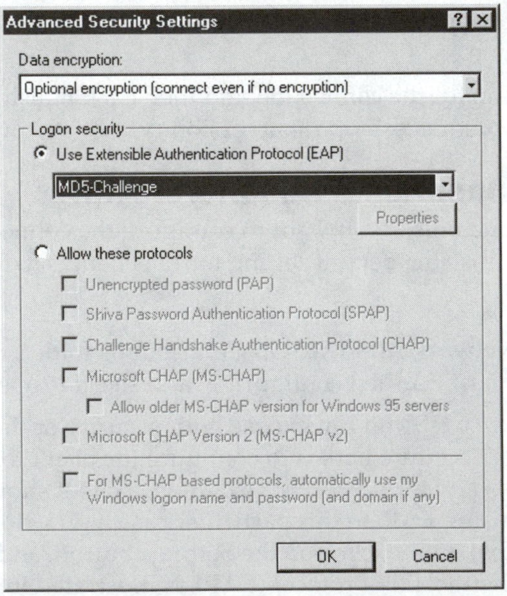

Figure 16-24. *Advanced security properties for a client*

Configuring Remote Access Policies

Remote access connections are granted access based on a user's account and remote access policies. Basically, a remote access policy defines the connection by imposing a set of conditions. Table 16-5 lists the most common remote access policies and provides a brief description of each.

When you're adding remote access policies, you aren't limited to using one per remote client. You can add as many as you'd like, but it's best to minimize the number of policies you use to keep the configuration as simple as possible.

To add a remote access policy, do the following:

1. Open Routing And Remote Access from the Start | Programs | Administrative Tools menu.

2. In the left pane of the console window, right-click on Remote Access Policies and select New Remote Access Policy. This displays the Add Remote Access Policy window as shown in Figure 16-25.

3. Specify a name for the policy and click Next.

4. Click the Add button to bring up the Select Attribute window as shown in Figure 16-26. After selecting the attribute, click the Add button.

5. Type in the parameter corresponding to the condition you're specifying. For example, for Caller-Station-Id, type in a phone number. It is important to note that the information you provide here depends on which condition you're trying to add. Click OK when done.

6. Repeat Steps 4 and 5 until you're done adding conditions. At that time, click Next to continue.

Policy Name	Policy Description
Called-Station-ID	Phone number dialed by user
Calling-Station-ID	Phone number from which call originated (caller ID)
Day-And-Time-Restrictions	Time periods and days of week during which user is allowed to connect
Framed-Protocol	The protocol to be used during the connection
Tunnel-Type	The tunneling protocols to be used during the connection
Windows-Groups	The Windows 2000 groups to which the user belongs

Table 16-5. *Common Remote Access Policies*

CONNECTING WITH
WINDOWS 2000

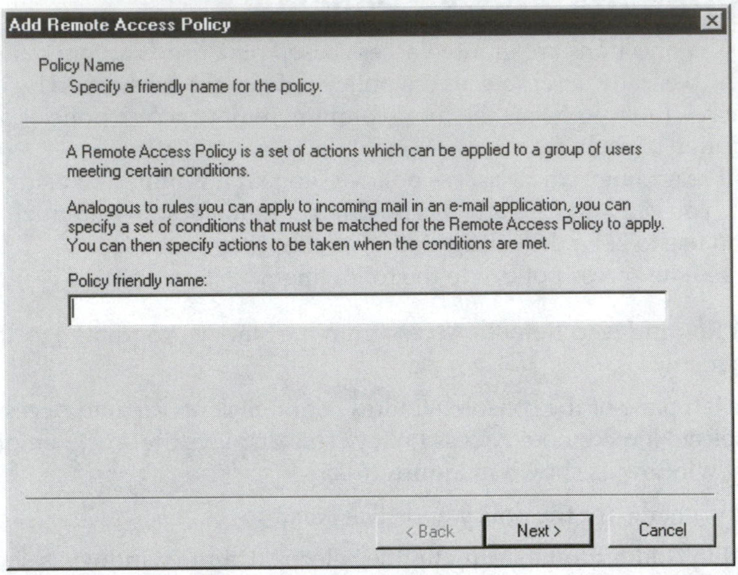

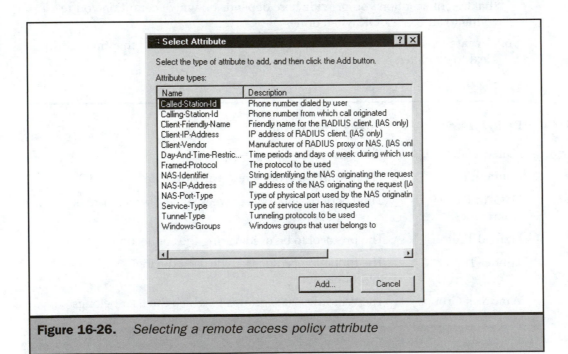

Figure 16-25. *Adding a remote access policy*

Figure 16-26. *Selecting a remote access policy attribute*

7. The next window in the wizard asks you if you want to grant or deny access to the user when the specified conditions are met. Choose either Grant or Deny and click Next.

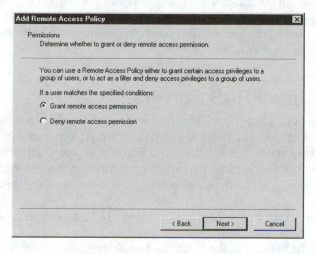

8. At this point, you can either edit the policy by clicking the Edit Profile button, or you can finish configuring the policy by clicking the Finish button.

Editing the remote access policy profile displays a number of different options. It allows you to configure dial-in constraints, IP, multilink, authentication, encryption, and other attributes settings. As you can see, remote access policies are extremely customizable to meet and exceed your environment's needs.

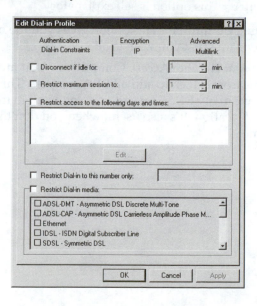

Managing and Troubleshooting RRAS

As with many services in Windows 2000, after you install and configure RRAS, you may need to periodically manage and troubleshoot it. For instance, you may want to reconfigure RRAS settings, add resources, monitor connections, and so on. Managing RRAS lets you customize its operation in your environment and allows you to keep up-to-date with its implementation.

Managing Multiple RRAS Servers

Managing a Windows 2000 network environment that has more than one RRAS server would get a bit overwhelming if you had to jump from machine to machine to manage them. By default, the Routing And Remote Access snap-in displays only the local computer in its server list. However, for simplicity and ease of use, you can add other RRAS servers to the snap-in so that you can manage them from a single location.

To add another server to the Routing And Remote Access snap-in, do the following:

1. Within the right pane of the Routing And Remote Access snap-in, right-click Server Status as shown in Figure 16-27.

2. Select Add Server from the Action menu to display the Add Server dialog box.

   At this point, you are given four options for locating and adding another RRAS server:

   - **This Computer**   This option is self explanatory.

   - **The Following Computer**   This option gives you the opportunity to specify the computer name that you wish to add.

   - **All Routing And Remote Access Computers**   You must specify the domain name from which to add all RRAS servers. This option is useful when you have many RRAS servers and you want to manage them all in one central location. It's also useful when you don't know the RRAS server's name.

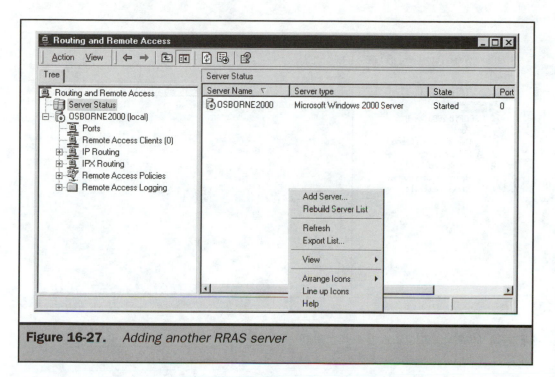

Figure 16-27. Adding another RRAS server

■ **Browse Active Directory (AD)** Use this option when you want to browse the directory service to find one or more RRAS servers in the domain or tree.

Monitoring Connections

A good habit to start practicing is periodically monitoring RRAS connections. The RRAS management console allows you to easily check the status of the service and any active connections. By doing so, you are able to get an accurate picture of RRAS in real time, and it's also an excellent way of troubleshooting any problems you may encounter. Checking server status is as simple as opening the RRAS management console and clicking on Server Status. The right console window, pictured in Figure 16-28, displays the status reports. In particular, it shows the following statistics:

■ The server name

■ The state of the RRAS service (started or stopped)

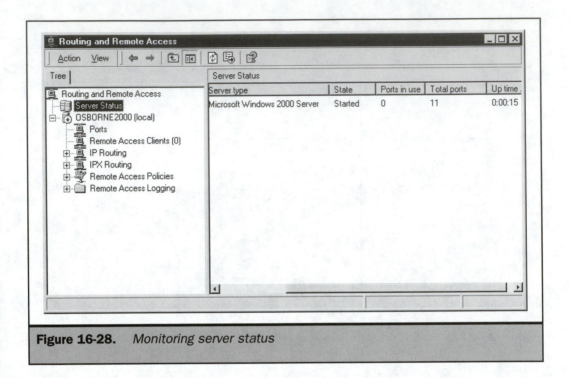

Figure 16-28.   *Monitoring server status*

- The total number of ports on the server
- The number of ports in use
- The amount of time that the server has been up since the RRAS service was last started

Viewing Routing Tables

Every Windows 2000 computer, with an installed network interface card (NIC), has a simple routing table created by default. You can view a computer's static routing entries in the routing table either through the Command Prompt or the RRAS interface.

To view the routing table from the Command Prompt, you simply type **route print**. You may also view the routing table using the RRAS interface by doing the following:

1. Open Routing And Remote Access from the Start | Programs | Administrative Tools menu.

2. In the left pane of the Routing And Remote Access window, expand the console tree to expose the Static Routes entry underneath either the IP Routing or IPX Routing subtrees.

3. Right-click Static Routes and select either Show IP Routing Table or Show IPX Routing Table to display the routing table.

Destination	Network mask	Gateway	Interface	Metric	Protocol	
0.0.0.0	0.0.0.0	192.168.1.1	Local Area C...	1	Network ma...	
127.0.0.0	255.0.0.0	127.0.0.1	Loopback	1	Local	
127.0.0.1	255.255.255.255	127.0.0.1	Loopback	1	Local	
192.168.1.0	255.255.255.0	192.168.1.2	Local Area C...	1	Local	
192.168.1.2	255.255.255.255	127.0.0.1	Loopback	1	Local	
224.0.0.0	240.0.0.0	192.168.1.2	Local Area C...	1	Local	
255.255.255.255	255.255.255.255	192.168.1.2	Local Area C...	1	Local	

OSBORNE2000 - IP Routing Table

Viewing the static routes in the routing table can be an extremely useful troubleshooting tool when you are presented with a possible routing problem. Examining the routing table helps you determine whether or not the server is properly sending or receiving routed information. This is especially useful when your network environment consists mainly of static routes.

Adding Static Routes

For small network environments such as a home office or small business, you may want or need to manually add a static route to the routing table to connect to another network. You can accomplish this in two ways, using the Route Add command at the Command Prompt (for example, route add 192.168.1.0 192.168.3.0) or through the RRAS interface. The easiest (and laziest) way to configure a static route is through the RRAS interface. Using the RRAS interface is recommended, especially if you're not familiar with the route command. Besides, you're less likely to make a syntax error or even worse, a configuration error.

To add a static route using the RRAS snap-in, do the following:

1. Open Routing And Remote Access from the Start | Programs | Administrative Tools menu.

2. In the left pane of the Routing And Remote Access, expand the console tree to expose the Static Routes entry underneath either the IP Routing or IPX Routing subtrees.

3. If you're adding a static route for IP routing, select New Static Route to display the Static Route window (see Figure 16-29). Otherwise, select New Route for a new static route for IPX (see Figure 16-30).

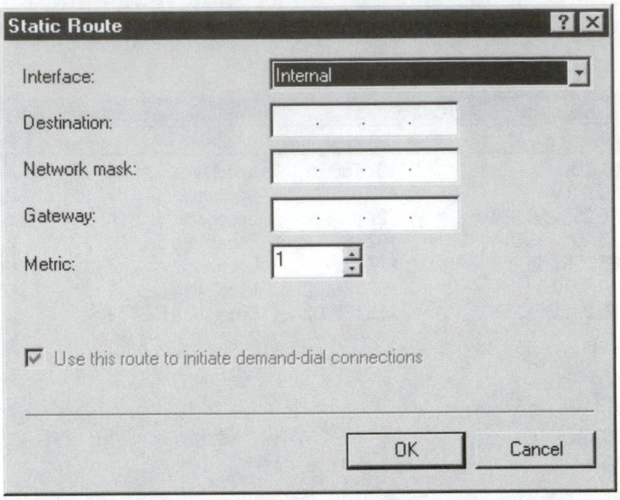

Figure 16-29. *Adding a new IP static route options*

4. Fill in the appropriate information for the following (for an IP static route):

■ **Interface**   The network interface to use to configure a static route.

■ **Destination**   The computer or router in which to route the information.

■ **Network Mask**   The network address that will use the route.

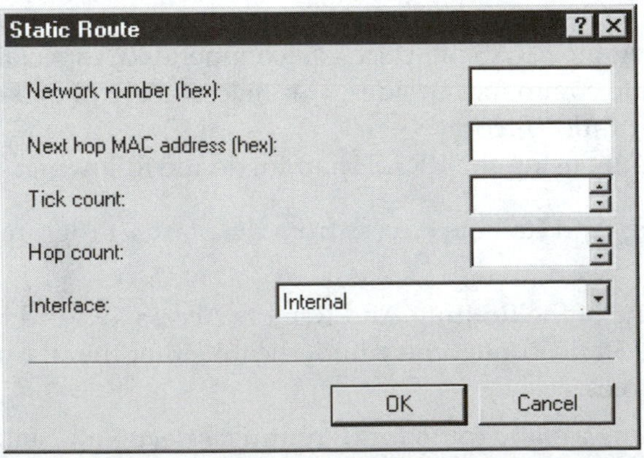

Figure 16-30. *Adding a new IPX route*

- **Gateway** An IP address that the packets must be sent to in order to get routed. This is typically the default gateway.

- **Metric** The number of hops to reach the destination.

5. Click OK.

Event Logging

Windows 2000 documents events that occur on the system, including those relating to the RRAS service. The events may be errors, warnings, or purely informational messages such as accounting logging. The messages can be viewed in the Windows 2000 system event log.

Reviewing the events in the system event log provides an invaluable means to keep track of the RRAS service and is especially useful when you need to troubleshoot a problem. Figure 16-31 shows you the various configurations for event logging. By default, RRAS records errors and warnings.

To modify the default logging parameters, do the following:

1. Open Routing And Remote Access from the Start | Programs | Administrative Tools menu.

2. In the left pane, right-click on the RRAS server and select Properties.

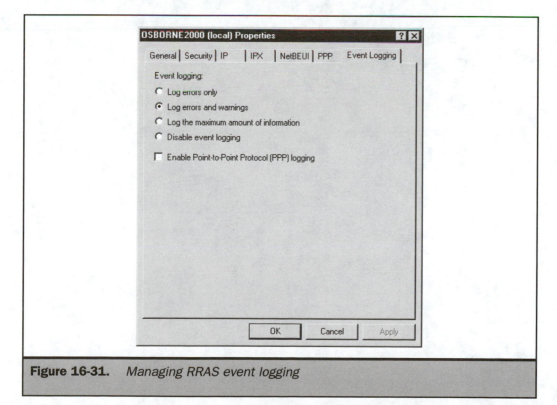

Figure 16-31. *Managing RRAS event logging*

3. Under the Event Logging tab, you can select how you'd like to log events, and you may even disable logging altogether for RRAS (not recommended).

Where Did My Options Go?

After reading this chapter, you may be wondering why you don't have some of the options described. In particular, you may notice that some dial-in options for user accounts in AD are unavailable. This occurs when AD is in mixed mode (refer to Chapter 15 for more information on AD modes of operation).

The following options are not available while you're running in mixed mode:

■ The ability to control access through remote access policy

■ Verifying a caller with Caller ID

■ Assigning a static IP address

■ Applying static routes

The Complete Reference

Chapter 17

Configuring Network Services

Throughout this book there have been discussions of a variety of network-related services such as DNS, DHCP, and WINS. This chapter focuses more on the client network-related services that are required for computers to operate with other computers in the Windows 2000 network. This includes how Windows 2000 clients operate with other Windows 2000 computers as well as how Windows 2000 computers communicate with non-Microsoft operating systems, such as Novell NetWare, Apple Macintosh, and UNIX. Windows 2000 packs a plethora of features and services for your networking environment that allow you to communicate and collaborate with a variety of other systems.

Windows 2000 Client Networking Service

Configuring Windows 2000 clients to connect to a Windows 2000 network requires two steps:

- Installing and configuring client software and one or more protocols on the client computer
- Creating a user account

This section discusses the Windows 2000 client software needed to communicate with other Windows 2000 computers.

Client for Microsoft Networks

Client for Microsoft Networks is a software component that allows a computer to access resources, such as file and print services, on a Microsoft network. When you install Windows 2000, it is installed automatically and is independent of the protocol that you choose to use. Also, Windows 2000 installs TCP/IP by default (see Chapter 13 for more information on TCP/IP).

Note *Client for Microsoft Networks is actually Server Message Blocks (SMBs) that ride on top of TCP/IP or any other protocol. SMB is a file and print service protocol that allows computers to transparently access resources located on remote computers.*

Client for Microsoft Networks, shown in Figure 17-1, uses a remote procedure call (RPC) to call services on other computers on the Windows 2000 network. An RPC is not a name resolution mechanism but rather a message-passing facility. By default, Windows 2000 uses the Windows Locator RPC, but it can also use the Distributed Computing Environment (DCE) Cell Directory Service.

Note *Client for Microsoft Networks is the equivalent of the Workstation service.*

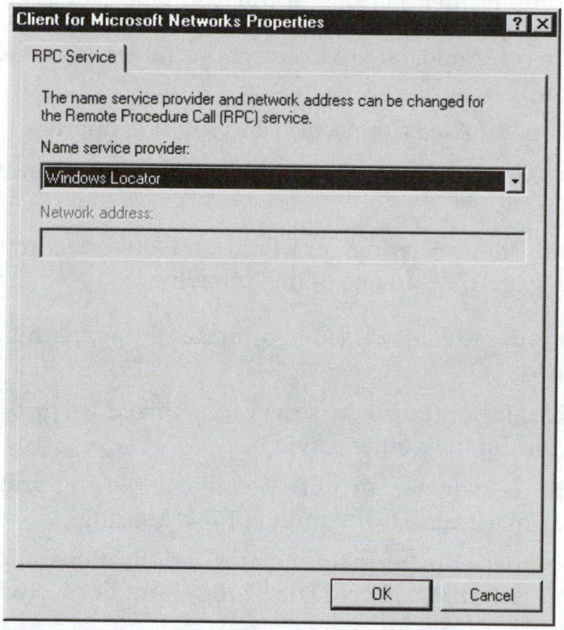

Figure 17-1.   *Client For Microsoft Networks Properties window*

File and Printer Sharing for Microsoft Networks

File and Printer Sharing for Microsoft Networks is a service component that complements the Client for Microsoft Networks service. It allows other computers on the Windows 2000 network to access any resources, files and printers, that you may be sharing, whereas the Client for Microsoft Networks service is used to access resources of other computers. By default, this service is installed and enabled on Windows 2000 computers.

> **Note**   *File and Printer Sharing for Microsoft Networks is the equivalent of the Server service.*

Configuring File and Printer Sharing for Microsoft Networks

There are a couple of configurable parameters for File and Printer Sharing for Microsoft Networks: optimization and the ability to make browser broadcasts to down-level clients.

To configure File and Printer Sharing for Microsoft Networks

1. Open the Network And Dial-Up Connections folder from the Start |
   Settings menu.

2. Right-click on Local Area Connection and select Properties.

3. Select File And Printer Sharing For Microsoft Networks, and click the
   Properties button.

4. In the File And Printer Sharing For Microsoft Networks Properties window,
   as shown in Figure 17-2, do one of the following:

   ■ Select Minimize Memory Used to optimize the server for a small number
     of clients.

   ■ Select Balance to optimize the server for a mixed usage of file and printer
     sharing in addition to other services.

   ■ To dedicate as many resources as possible to file and print server services,
     select Maximize Data Throughput For File Sharing.

   ■ To optimize server memory for network applications, such as Microsoft
     SQL Server, select Maximize Data Throughput For Network Applications.

5. Optionally, you can allow LAN Manager 2.*x* clients on your network to browse
   for shared resources on this computer by selecting Make Browser Broadcasts To
   LAN Manager 2.*x* Clients.

Browsing for Resources

Down-level clients use the browser service to announce themselves and their shared
resources on the network. Those of you familiar with Windows NT 4 will remember
double-clicking on the Network Neighborhood icon on the desktop and receiving
a list of computers within the domain or workgroup. This allowed you to easily find
computers and shared resources on the Windows NT network. The browser service
was responsible for this. It uses broadcasts at startup and at specified intervals to make
the announcements.

Although the idea for announcing a computer's existence and shared resources was
good, the initial implementation could potentially hinder network performance by
clogging the network with unnecessary broadcast messages. To minimize the browser
service's impact on the network, the concept of a *domain master browser* (DomMB) and
a *segment master browser* (SegMB) was used. The master browsers are responsible for
receiving announcements to help reduce clutter on the network as well as keeping an
accurate listing of the computers and shared resources. By definition, the Windows NT
4 primary domain controller (PDC) is the DomMB.

For Windows NT networks with multiple segments, the browser concept was
extended slightly with the SegMB. In this case, each segment would contain a SegMB
that is responsible for maintaining a browse list of the computers on the local segment.

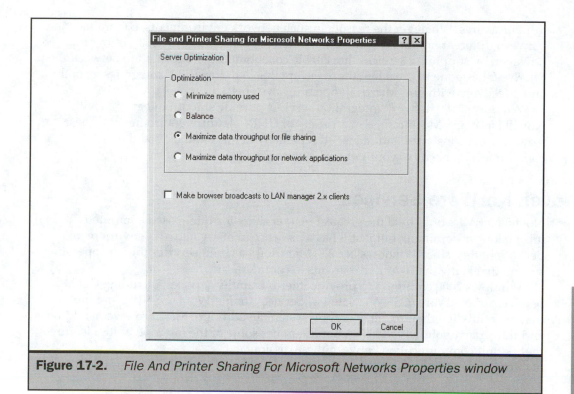

Figure 17-2. *File And Printer Sharing For Microsoft Networks Properties window*

Computers on that segment would query and obtain their browse list from the SegMB. The SegMB is also configured to forward the browse list to the DomMB and to request the domain browse list. The SegMB then combines the two lists and makes them available to its local clients.

In a Windows 2000 network environment, the browser service has been replaced by the Active Directory (AD) services. You may have the browser service running on Windows 2000, but it's only there for backward compatibility with down-level clients. When you upgrade all down-level clients to Windows 2000 and remove NetBIOS, the browser service will no longer be needed because you can rely solely on AD to locate and announce resources.

Network Integration Services

Many network environments (small to large enterprises) may have Windows 2000 systems operating with other non-Microsoft operating systems. There are probably many reasons why you may have a heterogeneous network environment including, but not limited to, different IT groups, expertise, or cost factors for replacing current infrastructures. Whatever the reason, in such network environments, communication between different operating systems is limited at best. Windows 2000 comes prepared, however, by supplying services that enable collaboration of information between them. Microsoft has gone to great lengths to ensure that Windows 2000 integrates smoothly and effectively with non-Microsoft operating systems.

Windows 2000 network integration services provide smooth integration with Novell NetWare, Macintosh, and a variety of UNIX platform environments. These services can be installed and managed separately to meet and exceed the communication needs of your network environment.

Novell NetWare Services

Novell NetWare once held the greatest market share for Intel-based computers. Today, it is no longer dominant, but it still has a presence in many network environments. Because of this, since Windows NT 3.5, Microsoft has built services into the operating system that allow the two environments to communicate.

Windows 2000 continues to provide interoperability services, including Client Services for NetWare (CSNW), Gateway Services for NetWare (GSNW), and more, that are built directly into the operating system. In addition, there are several add-on and third-party solutions. This section examines some of the interoperability features that permit communication between these dissimilar network environments.

The Fundamental Differences

The way in which Novell NetWare and Windows 2000 Server communicate with machines in their own environment is fundamentally different. Communication between the two systems requires additional services and/or multiple protocol stacks. NetWare clients typically use IPX/SPX (TCP/IP is also common with NetWare 5.0) and the Network Core Protocol (NCP) to function within their own environment, while Windows 2000 clients rely on SMBs. Both the NCP and SMB architectures are a means for the client to request services from a server, but they are incompatible with each other. This means that additional requirements are needed to bridge the communication barrier. From a Windows 2000 perspective, the two most widely used methods for bridging the communication barrier are to configure the clients with multiple protocols in conjunction with CSNW and to configure Windows 2000 Server as a NetWare gateway.

Table 17-1 offers an overview of the different types of services that can be used to connect the two network environments. The solution or solutions you employ greatly depend on what resources you want to access and the type of client needing access.

Client	Service Used	Resources That Can Be Accessed
Windows 2000	NWLink IPX/SPX/NetBIOS	Applications running on NetWare
Windows 2000	NWLink IPX/SPX/NetBIOS Client Services for NetWare Gateway Service for NetWare	File and print services on NetWare
NetWare client	NWLink IPX/SPX/NetBIOS Named Pipes Windows Sockets	IPX/SPX-compatible applications running on Windows 2000
NetWare client	NWLink IPX/SPX/NetBIOS	File and print services on Windows 2000 running File and Print Services for NetWare (FPNW) add-on

Table 17-1.   *Interoperability Options for Windows 2000 and NetWare Environments*

NWLink IPX/SPX/NetBIOS-Compatible Transport Protocol (NWLink)

Novell NetWare network environments commonly use the IPX/SPX protocol for network communications. Windows 2000 includes an IPX/SPX-compatible protocol called NWLink, which is the Windows 2000 implementation of the IPX/SPX protocol. NWLink allows Windows 2000 computers to communicate with computers running the IPX/SPX protocol. It supports WinSock and NetBIOS over IPX application programming interfaces (APIs).

INSTALLING NWLINK   The NWLink protocol is required for communication with NetWare environments as well as those using Client Service for NetWare (in Windows 2000 Professional) or Gateway (and Client) Services for NetWare (in Windows 2000 Server). Although it can be used in pure Windows 2000 environments, this is not recommended because TCP/IP should be the protocol of choice for all network environments, small and large.

Note   *If NWLink is not installed prior to installing the Client Service for NetWare or Gateway (and Client) Services for NetWare, Windows 2000 installs it automatically.*

To install NWLink, do the following:

1. Open the Network And Dial-Up Connections folder from the Start | Settings menu.

2. Right-click on Local Area Connection and select Properties.

3. Click Install.

4. Select Protocol and then click Add.

5. Select NWLink IPX/SPX/NetBIOS Compatible Transport Protocol, and click OK.

CONFIGURING NWLINK   After installation is complete, you'll want to configure three parameters for the NWLink protocol as shown in Figure 17-3. They are the following:

■ **Frame Type**   This parameter defines how data is formatted. By default, Windows 2000 detects the frame type for you.

■ **Network Number**   Network numbers are associated with the frame type. It is used to segment different frame types that may exist on the network. For example, every machine using a specific frame type will also use the same network number. This parameter is automatically detected by Windows 2000.

■ **Internal network number**   The internal network number is a hexadecimal identifier that is unique for each computer using NWLink.

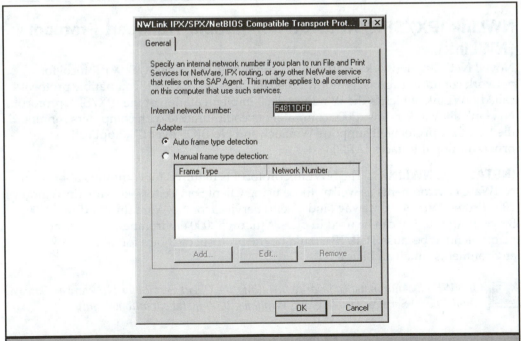

Figure 17-3.   *NWLink configuration parameters*

Client Service for NetWare

In addition to NWLink, the client must also install CSNW to access file and print resources on the NetWare network. CSNW, included in Windows 2000 Professional, provides the redirector services that NWLink lacks. You can use CSNW to connect to NetWare 2.*x* to 4.*x* servers for file and print services as well as to access Novell Directory Services (NDS) or bindery information. For example, clients communicating in a Windows 2000 network using the TCP/IP protocol must also use NWLink and CSNW in order to use file resources on NetWare servers. When a machine is configured with both sets of protocols and CSNW, clients directly access NetWare server resources. As a result of the direct access, there is no degradation in performance due to protocol translation.

> **Note**   *If the NetWare environment is running strictly TCP/IP, CSNW won't be useful because it only understands IPX/SPX and NetBEUI.*

If NWLink isn't installed prior to installing CSNW on Windows 2000 Professional, Windows 2000 automatically installs it. To install CSNW, do the following:

1. Open the Network And Dial-Up Connections folder from the Start | Settings menu.
2. Right-click on Local Area Connection and select Properties.
3. Click the Install button to display the Select Network Component Type window.
4. Select Client and click the Add button.
5. Select CSNW and click OK.

Gateway Services for NetWare

The second approach to gaining access to NetWare resources is configuring a Windows 2000 Server as a NetWare gateway. Installing GSNW drastically reduces the amount of administration needed for client access to NetWare servers. In fact, the only configuration needed is on the server; no additional configuration on clients is required. Clients can run only the client software for a Windows 2000 network without losing NetWare resources. The NetWare gateway translates any requests into IPX/SPX and NCP; they are then forwarded to the NetWare server. In addition, clients view NetWare resources as if they resided on the Windows 2000 Server because the Windows 2000 Server connects to NetWare Server's directory and shares it.

There is a common misconception associated with GSNW that is worth reviewing before planning to implement GSNW as a connectivity solution. The gateway is essentially one connection to NetWare resources. If many users will be accessing NetWare services on a regular basis through the gateway, performance may suffer because the single connection can quickly become congested with network. Moreover, extensive protocol translation at the gateway causes performance degradation. GSNW is designed for clients that only occasionally need access to NetWare resources. Table 17-2 lists some of the advantages and disadvantages of using GSNW.

Advantages	Disadvantages
No multiple protocol stacks on clients	May see performance degradation from protocol translation when a large number of users connect through the gateway simultaneously
Clients view NetWare resources in similar manner to that of Windows 2000 shares	Native NDS not supported; must use bindery-mode emulation for NetWare 4.x
Simplified administration	

Table 17-2. *Weighing the Costs of GSNW*

Before installing GSNW on a Windows 2000 Server, prepare the NetWare server to support the gateway. There is minimal setup required on the NetWare side, but you should proceed with caution because of security concerns. Perform the following tasks on NetWare before proceeding:

- Create a group named NTGATEWAY with the appropriate permissions for the resources that you want to access.

- Create a user account with the appropriate permissions for the resources that you want to access. If you're accessing a bindery resource or both NDS and bindery resources, use a bindery account. Otherwise, you can create a user account in NDS.

- Make the user account you just created be a member of the NTGATEWAY group.

Note *Any NetWare redirectors must be removed before installing GSNW. Also note that if the NWLink IPX/SPX Compatible Transport is not installed, GSNW installs it automatically during the service installation.*

To install GSNW, use the following steps:

1. Open the Network And Dial-Up Connections folder from the Start | Settings menu.

2. Right-click on Local Area Connection and select Properties.

3. Click the Install button to display the Select Network Component Type window.

4. Select Client and click the Add button.

5. Select GSNW and click OK.

6. At this point, GSNW prompts you to supply the appropriate NetWare information (for example, preferred server, or tree and context, and whether you'd like a login script to run). Once you have specified the information, Windows 2000 prompts you to reboot.

CONFIGURING THE NETWARE GATEWAY   The next step in creating a NetWare gateway is enabling the gateway, creating shares, and managing the permissions associated with the shares. All configurations mentioned above are done through the GSNW applet in the Control Panel (see Figure 17-4).

Figure 17-4.   *The GSNW applet in the Control Panel*

By default, GSNW is disabled. To enable it, do the following:

1. Open the Control Panel from the Start | Settings menu.

2. Double-click on the GSNW applet to display the Gateway Service For NetWare window.

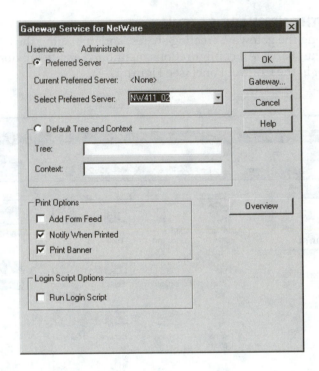

3. Specify either a Preferred Server (bindery server) or a Default Tree and Context (NDS tree).

4. Click the Gateway button to display the Configure Gateway dialog box.

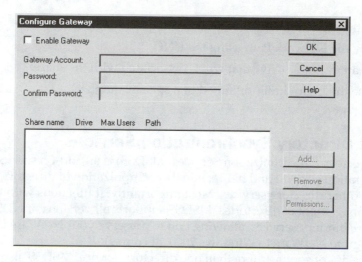

5. Check Enable Gateway, and then specify the Gateway Account and
its password.

   *You can select the Overview button to display help on creating and managing
the gateway.*

CONFIGURING GATEWAY RESOURCES   Once the gateway is enabled, you can
begin specifying resources that clients can connect to. To activate a gateway for a file
share, you can use the GSNW applet, and a printer share can be defined through the
Printers folder.

Use the following steps to create and manage shares:

1. In the Configure Gateway window, click the Add button to display the New
Share window.

2. Enter the name of the share that will be known to gateway users.

3. Specify the Network Path using the UNC.

4. Select an available drive that will be associated with the share.

5. Choose the User Limit (unlimited or a specific number).

6. Select OK.

Microsoft Directory Synchronization Services

Microsoft Directory Synchronization Services (MSDSS) is an add-on service that provides migration support and bidirectional synchronization of directory information with AD and other directory services. Most importantly, it functions with NDS for true enterprise management of directories. MSDSS supports all versions of NDS as well as older NetWare bindery services, allowing you to preserve your NetWare investment (until you migrate NetWare to Windows 2000, of course).

In the capacity of serving more than one directory service, MSDSS also serves as a metadirectory utility. Metadirectories glue various directory services into a unified, manageable service, while at the same time allowing the directory services to be managed separately as well. MSDSS can be configured and managed through its MMC snap-in. This allows you to easily manage shared information, such as user accounts, from a single interface.

File and Print Services for NetWare

To further aid in the integration of Windows 2000 and NetWare, Microsoft supplies another add-on product called File and Print Services for NetWare (FPNW), which can be purchased separately. This product is focused on interoperability for NetWare clients accessing a Windows 2000 network. FPNW allows a NetWare client to access file and print services on a Windows 2000 server. No configuration on the client is necessary because the client views the Windows 2000 server as a NetWare server. However, FPNW does not include the capability to manage permissions associated with the NetWare clients in the Windows 2000 network.

FPNW is an add-on for Windows 2000 that makes the server appear to NetWare clients as a NetWare server that supplies file and print services. This service is only intended for migrating from NetWare to Windows 2000, although it has been used only as a file and print services extension.

Macintosh Integration Services

Windows 2000 Server continues to foster interoperability between Intel-based PCs and the Macintosh platform with its Services for Macintosh (SFM), also known as AppleTalk network integration services. SFM is a collection of services that can be individually or collectively installed. They permit collaboration of information between the two different operating systems. SFM removes the barriers for file, print, and network services for client machines on either platform.

Network Integration

Integrating Macintosh and Intel-based computers isn't as simple as loading SFM on a Windows 2000 Server and expecting the two operating systems to talk to each other. You must also consider the network topologies that are being used primarily because of the different network hardware.

For Windows 2000, the most common network topology is Ethernet based, but it supports Token Ring, LocalTalk, FDDI, and ATM as well. Macintosh can also be equipped to use Ethernet but many still use LocalTalk (used in AppleTalk networking) because LocalTalk networking equipment is built into every Macintosh.

If everyone is using the same network media, such as Ethernet, then you're in luck. Otherwise, you'll need to take into consideration the number of Macintosh clients you have. The two most common scenarios are to install Ethernet adapters into all the Macintosh computers or install a LocalTalk adapter in the Windows 2000 Server that will run the SFM. There may be other scenarios such as some Macintosh computers using Token Ring, but the point is that there must be some common ground between them all. The single exception to this occurs when Macintosh computers only connect remotely through Windows 2000's Routing and Remote Access (RRAS). For more information on RRAS, refer to Chapter 16.

NETWORK PROTOCOLS   AppleTalk has traditionally been the standard network protocol enabling Macintosh computers to talk with one another. Although it's still in use today for many Macintosh LocalTalk networks, it is proprietary and used primarily with older Macintosh systems.

Much like every other operating system platform and the Internet, newer Macintosh systems have adopted TCP/IP as the protocol of choice. Those computers using TCP/IP support file sharing via Apple File Protocol (AFP) over TCP/IP.

As a result, Windows 2000 supports both AppleTalk and AFP over TCP/IP to ensure compatibility with all Macintosh systems. Since Windows 2000 relies on TCP/IP, you should standardize on the TCP/IP protocol on Macintosh systems that you're supporting if possible. Reducing the number of protocols supported in a network environment also reduces the total cost of administration.

If the AppleTalk and/or the AFP over TCP/IP protocols aren't installed before you install file or print services for the Macintosh, Windows 2000 installs them automatically for you. However, you can also install these protocols manually by doing the following:

1. From the Start | Settings menu, open the Network And Dial-Up Connections folder.

2. Right-click on Local Area Connection and then click Properties.

3. On the General tab, click the Install button.

4. In the Select Network Component Type window, click Protocol and then Add.

5. In the Select Network Protocol window, select the AppleTalk Protocol and then click OK.

APPLETALK ROUTING AND ZONES   Once you've installed AppleTalk, you'll want to enable AppleTalk routing and create a *zone*, which is similar to a workgroup in that it is a collection of computers. The zone also defines where the Macintosh clients will look to find Macintosh-accessible volumes and printers in the Windows 2000 environment. This is similar to the principles behind DNS zones (see Chapter 14) where a zone segments the network into manageable pieces. You can have one or more zones defined per segment.

By enabling AppleTalk routing, you're defining a network much as you do with TCP/IP (see Chapter 13). Each network is defined by a *network address range* where the number of numbers in the address range times 253 possible nodes per network address ($n \times 253$) defines how many devices you can have in the segment. A seed router is responsible for broadcasting routing information (such as seeding the network), such as network addresses, on the segment. A Windows 2000 Server with AppleTalk routing enabled serves as the seed router for Macintosh clients. If you have more than one NIC, you can seed more than one AppleTalk network. The actual number of networks you configure depends greatly on how many Macintosh clients you have, but it's generally a good idea to keep them to a minimum.

To configure a network adapter with a Macintosh zone, do the following:

1. From the Start | Programs | Administrative Tools menu, open the Routing And Remote Access Management Console.

2. Expand the RRAS server and right-click on AppleTalk Routing. Then select Enable AppleTalk Routing.

3. Select AppleTalk Routing in the left pane to display the connections that apply to AppleTalk Routing in the right pane.

4. Right-click on the connection (for example, Local Area Connection), and then click Properties.

5. Select the Enable Seed Routing On This Network check box, which then allows you to configure AppleTalk Routing parameters.

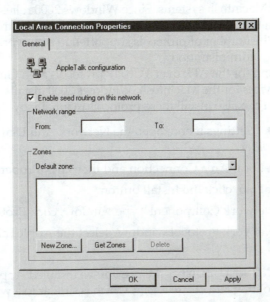

6. The first parameter that you'll configure is the Network range of numbers. The number you specify can be arbitrary as long as they're contiguous. Keep in mind that the number of AppleTalk nodes (such as computers, printers, etc.) that can be supported is 253 times the number of numbers in the network range. For example, a network range of 100 to 101 can support 506 (2 × 253) nodes.

7. If there aren't any default zones listed, you can either create a zone or get zones by pressing the New Zone or Get Zones button, respectively.

8. To create a new zone simply press the New Zone button (as I just mentioned) and type in the name of the zone in the Add New Zone dialog box.

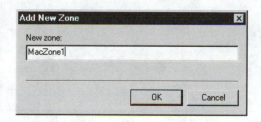

9. Click OK to create the zone.

10. Specify the default zone and click OK.

REMOTE ACCESS   In addition to supporting Macintosh clients on a local area network (LAN), Windows 2000's RRAS allows them to connect from remote locations using the AppleTalk Control Protocol (ATCP). ATCP dynamically configures a remote Macintosh client through a PPP link by negotiating various AppleTalk-based parameters, such as an AppleTalk network address. More information on ATCP can be found in RFC 1378. Once connected, Macintosh users can access Windows 2000 resources by using the Guest account or authenticating using the UAM.

To configure Windows 2000's RRAS to allow Macintosh clients remote access, do the following:

1. From the Start | Programs | Administrative Tools menu, open the Routing And Remote Access Management Console.

2. In the left pane, right-click on the RRAS server and select Properties.

3. Under the AppleTalk tab, select Enable AppleTalk Remote Access and click OK.

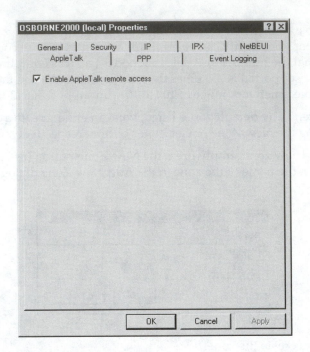

Authenticating Macintosh Clients

Macintosh clients are required to log on to the Windows 2000 network before they can use resources, such as file and printer services. However, the logon mechanism is slightly different than for Windows 2000 or down-level clients. Macintosh clients use their built-in user authentication module (UAM), which can be configured from their Chooser to log on to an AppleShare Server. However, when they log on to Windows 2000, they have other options as well. Windows 2000 supports the following UAM authentication methods:

- **Guest**   This allows Macintosh clients who don't have a user account and password to log on.

- **Client's AppleShare Authentication**   This prompts Macintosh clients for a username and password (which is sent as clear-text). It's important to note that Apple's built-in Random Number Exchange security method isn't supported by Windows 2000 because of the way Windows 2000 stores account information.

- **Microsoft UAM (MS UAM)**   When Macintosh clients log on to a Windows 2000 environment, they can optionally use Microsoft's UAM, which offers a higher degree of security than those mechanisms built into the Macintosh Chooser's UAM. There are two versions of Microsoft's UAM, version 1.0 and version 5.0. The later version comes bundled within Windows 2000 only.

Note   *MS UAM 5.0 requires that the client is running AppleShare Client 3.8 or greater or Mac OS 8.5 or greater. If not, the MS UAM 1.0 version is used.*

When you install File Services for Macintosh, Windows 2000 automatically creates a directory called Microsoft UAM Volume on an available NTFS partition. It shares this directory as a read-only Macintosh volume and also allows guests to access the directory shown in the following illustration. Macintosh clients connect to this share to get the MS UAM and install it on their computer. Once they have done so, they can log on securely using the MS UAM and connect to resources.

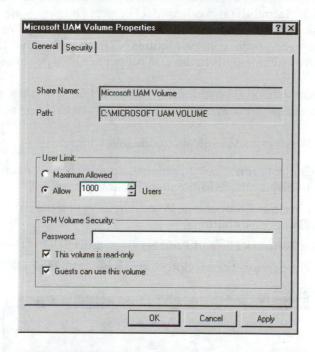

CONFIGURING MACINTOSH CLIENTS   If you tighten security by using MS UAM, you also need to configure Macintosh clients to install the MS UAM. To direct Macintosh clients to the authentication files located in the Microsoft UAM Volume, do the following:

1. On the Macintosh Apple menu, double-click Chooser.

2. Double-click the AppleShare icon, and then click the AppleTalk zone you configured on the Windows 2000 Server.

3. Select the name of the Windows 2000 Server, and click OK.

4. Click Guest and then OK.

5. Click the Microsoft UAM volume and then OK.

6. Close the Chooser dialog box.

7. Connect and select the Microsoft UAM volume.

8. On the Macintosh Desktop, double-click the Microsoft UAM volume to open it.

9. Double-click MS UAM Installer.

File Services for Macintosh

As noted earlier, for Macintosh users to access volume and file resources on the NT Server, at least one partition must be NTFS. This is because Macintosh files are significantly different from ones created on FAT or NTFS. Each file is composed of two components: the data fork and the resource fork. The data fork contains the data content while the resource fork contains the file type and creator information.

File Services for Macintosh (also called MacFile) lets you designate a directory that can be accessible to Macintosh as well as Windows 2000 users. For compatibility reasons, a Macintosh-accessible volume requires NTFS to ensure that filenames are set properly for the two environments to use and proper security permissions are invoked.

 CDFS (such as a CD-ROM drive) is also a supported file system that can be used for sharing between platforms. Permissions are read-only on CDFS drives.

To install File Services for Macintosh, do the following:

1. From the Control Panel (Start | Settings), double-click on Add/Remove Programs to display the Add/Remove Programs window.

2. Open the Windows Components Wizard by selecting the Add/Remove Windows Components button.

3. Select Other Network File and Print Services, and click the Details button.

4. Select the File Services For Macintosh check box, and click OK.

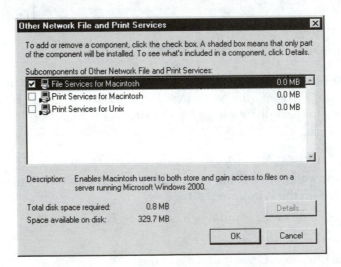

5. Click OK and then Next.

6. Click Finish to complete the installation.

The installation process is easy because Windows 2000 does most of the work for you. Some important installation issues the program takes care of are

■ When File Services for Macintosh and TCP/IP are installed, the Apple Filing Protocol (AFP) over TCP/IP is enabled automatically.

■ If the AppleTalk protocol is not installed before you attempt to install the service, it is installed automatically for you as it installs the services.

■ As mentioned earlier, the Microsoft User Authentication Module (UAM) Volume is created automatically.

There is a new way to configure and manage File Services for Macintosh. Instead of using the File Manager as you may have in Windows NT 4, you use the Shared Folders snap-in in the Microsoft Management Console (MMC) as illustrated in Figure 17-5. File Manager is no longer included with Windows 2000. If you do have it, it's because you've upgraded from Windows NT.

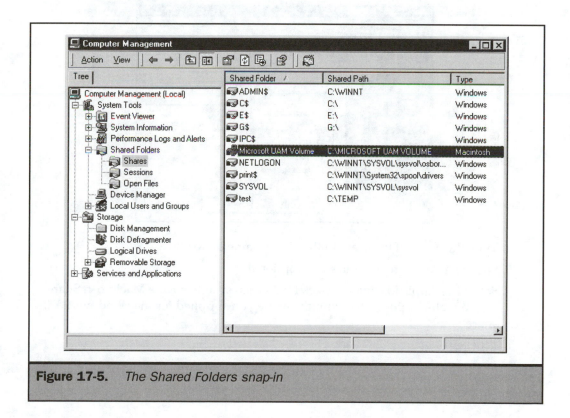

Figure 17-5.   *The Shared Folders snap-in*

A quick way of getting to the Shared Folders snap-in is to right-click on the My Computer desktop icon and select Manage.

CREATING OTHER MACINTOSH VOLUMES Besides the Microsoft UAM volume, other Macintosh-accessible volumes can be created to share files among Macintosh and Windows 2000 users. To create a Macintosh-accessible volume, do the following:

1. Open Computer Management from the Start | Programs | Administrative Tools menu, and expand Shared Folders (either double-click Shared Folders or click the + beside it).

2. Right-click on Shares, and then select New File Share.

3. In the Create Shared Folder window, as shown in the following illustration, type the drive and path to the folder you want to make Macintosh accessible in the Folder to share dialog box. You may optionally click the Browse button to find the appropriate folder.

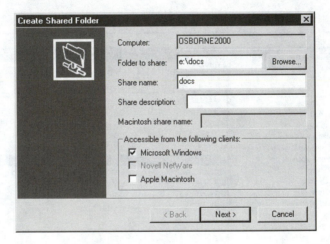

4. Type the name of the share in the Share Name dialog box.

5. Specify a description of the share (optional).

6. Select the Apple Macintosh check box. When you do so, the Macintosh Share Name dialog is populated with the name you supplied for the Windows 2000 share name.

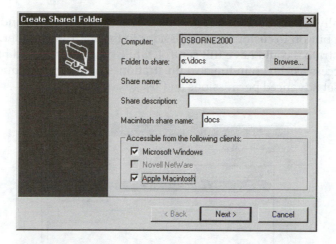

7. Click Next to start the Create Shared Folder Wizard.

8. The Create Shared Folder Wizard prompts you to set permissions for the shared folder. You have the following four options, as illustrated here:

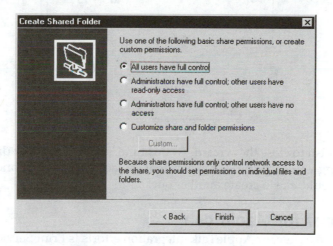

- All users have full control
- Administrators have full control; other users have read-only access
- Administrators have full control; other users have no access
- Customize share and folder permissions

9. Optionally, select Customize Share And Folder Permissions, and then click the Custom button to customize permissions to the share and folder. For example, administrators could have full control, while other users could have read and write access as shown in the next illustration. Choosing this option also allows you to set advanced permissions and usage auditing.

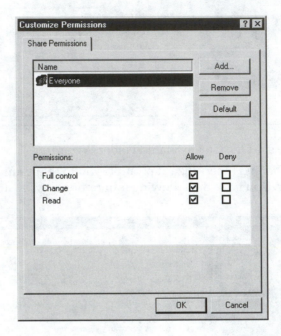

10. Click Finish to close the wizard. At this time, another window displays informing you of the type of clients that can access the folder and asks if you would like to create another one.

Print Services for Macintosh

The last service to ease your AppleTalk integration efforts is Print Services for Macintosh (also called MacPrint). It allows Macintosh users to print to print devices installed on a Windows 2000 Server as well as allowing Intel-based clients to print to AppleTalk PostScript printers. This service can be configured and managed within the Printers folder.

If you haven't already installed the AppleTalk protocol, it is installed automatically during the Print Services for Macintosh installation.

To install Print Services for Macintosh, do the following:

1. From the Control Panel (Start | Settings), double-click on Add/Remove Programs to display the Add/Remove Programs window.

2. Open the Windows Components Wizard by selecting the Add/Remove Windows Components button.

3. Select Other Network File and Print Services, and click the Details button.

4. Select the Print Services For Macintosh check box as illustrated in the next illustration, and click OK.

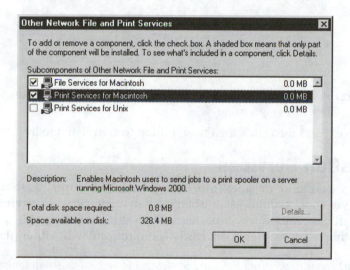

5. Click OK and then Next.

6. Click Finish to complete the installation.

CREATING A MACINTOSH-ACCESSIBLE PRINTER   Before Macintosh clients can use printers that are defined on Windows 2000, you must add and configure each printer to use AppleTalk. To create a printer, do the following:

1. Open the Printers folder from the Start | Settings menu.

2. In the Printers dialog box, double-click Add Printer to start the Add Printer Wizard.

3. Click Next to begin configuring a Macintosh-accessible printer.

4. Select Local printer. If the printer is directly attached, be sure to check Automatically Detect And Install My Plug And Play Printer check box to install the printer. Click Next to continue.

5. Click Create A New Port, and select AppleTalk Printing. Click Next to continue.

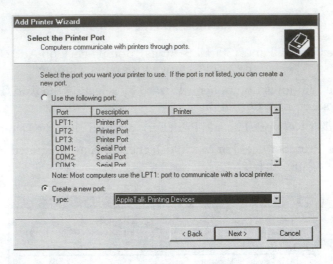

6. Expand the AppleTalk zone where the printer is located, and then select the printer. Click OK when done.

7. Click Next and then click the Finish button to complete the installation.

UNIX Integration Services

UNIX has been around for decades (much longer than Windows 2000 and earlier Windows NT versions) and has established itself in many network environments. As a result, Microsoft has realized the importance of fostering interoperability with UNIX so that clients of those environments can easily communicate with either platform.

Microsoft recently acquired Software Systems, Inc., which was renowned for its UNIX and Windows interoperability product line called INTERIX (formerly known as OPENNT). The product line offered users and developers a vast array of UNIX capabilities for Windows NT. Now, as a result of the acquisition, you can expect an even greater support of UNIX systems for Windows 2000 from a Microsoft add-on product. For more information, visit http://www.interix.com/.

Windows 2000 has a set of built-in components that enhance interoperability between the two environments, including file, printer, and network connectivity. Also, its Portable Operating System Interface for UNIX (POSIX) subsystem allows greater extensibility and development by third-party vendors. POSIX is an Institute of Electrical and Electronics Engineers (IEEE) standard that defines a set of operating-system services that make it easier to port services from one system to another.

POSIX

A set of IEEE portability standards has evolved ranging from POSIX.1 to POSIX.2. Windows 2000 uses the POSIX.1 compliant subsystem, meaning that it complies with the basic POSIX standards. These standards include case sensitivity and support for multiple filenames. Applications conforming to this standard can execute within the POSIX subsystem in their own protected memory space.

Print Services for UNIX

Print Services for UNIX gives Windows 2000 the ability to send and receive print jobs to and from UNIX clients and servers. The line printer remote (LPR) service is used for sending print jobs, while the line printer daemon (LPD) service is used to receive them. Another useful service that Windows 2000 provides with Print Services for UNIX is the line printer query (LPQ) service, which is similar to double-clicking on a printer icon within the Printers folder in that it can be used to retrieve information about an LPD print queue. For more information on printing and related services, refer to Chapter 12.

INSTALLING PRINT SERVICES FOR UNIX   Before you can start installing Print Services for UNIX, you need to have the TCP/IP protocol installed and configured. You've more than likely installed TCP/IP because it's Windows 2000's default protocol and it's the underlying protocol for Windows 2000 network environments. With TCP/IP installed, you're ready to install the printing service, using the following steps:

1. From the Control Panel (Start | Settings), double-click on Add/Remove Programs to display the Add/Remove Programs window.

2. Open the Windows Components Wizard by selecting the Add/Remove Windows Components button.

3. Select Other Network File And Print Services, and click the Details button.

4. Select the Print Services For UNIX check box as illustrated here, and click OK.

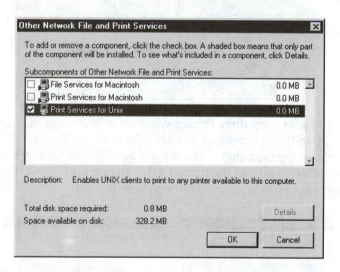

5. Click Next to begin the installation and choose Finish to complete it.

CREATING A UNIX-ACCESSIBLE PRINTER   After completing the installation of
UNIX print services, you can configure a printer within Windows 2000 to accept LPR
print jobs that are RFC 1179 compliant. Configuring a UNIX-accessible printer is
basically the same as configuring a local printer, except that you'll create a LPR port
that directs the print job.

To create a printer with a LPR port, do the following:

1. Open the Printers folder from the Start | Settings menu.

2. In the Printers dialog box, double-click Add Printer to start the Add Printer
   Wizard.

3. Click Next to begin configuring a UNIX-accessible printer.

4. Select Local printer. If the printer is directly attached, be sure to check
   Automatically Detect And Install My Plug And Play Printer check box to install
   the printer. Click Next to continue.

5. Select Create A New Port, select LPR Port, and then click Next.

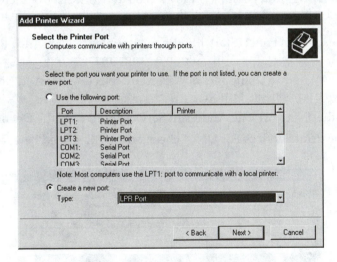

6. In the Add LPR Compatible Printer window, as shown in the following
   illustration. In the first field, enter either the host name or the IP address of the
   computer hosting the printer. The second field is a bit trickier because it asks
   you to provide a name of the printer as it's defined on the UNIX machine. You
   may also provide an IP address if the printer is directly attached to the network.

7. Click OK to continue so that Windows 2000 can try to communicate with the printer. If it's successful, you may be prompted to select the manufacturer and model of the printer. Click Next when you're done.

8. Choose an appropriate name for the printer and click Next.

9. Specify whether or not you want to share this printer (keep the default, which is yes), and click Next.

10. Enter a location description and any other comments, and click Next.

11. Select Yes to print a test page.

12. Click Finish to complete the installation.

Now that you've installed and configured the printer, it is ready to accept print jobs. Windows 2000 and down-level clients can connect to the printer using the Active Directory, or they can print using LPR commands as UNIX clients can. The LPR command syntax is as follows:

```
lpr -S server -P printer
```

For example, entering **lpr –s unix.mydomain.com –p sharedprinter c:\document.txt** would print document.txt on the printer SharedPrinter. More information on printing can be found in Chapter 12.

Network Connectivity

Fortunately, the Windows 2000 and UNIX platforms are in agreement about which underlying network protocol is most advantageous for network connectivity; it's TCP/IP. Also, the two platforms are in agreement that DNS is one of the most efficient mechanisms for name resolution and should therefore be used. However, which DNS solution you use is a completely different story. When you're investigating DNS integration issues, let me just give you some warning that you may find yourself in some rather heated religious battles. There's no need to rehash information on DNS platform issues, but do revisit Chapters 2 and 3 for preparation and installation issues as well as Chapter 14 on DNS for Windows 2000 before you delve into issues surrounding DNS. The DNS solution you choose greatly depends on your current infrastructure.

What rides on top of TCP/IP still remains fundamentally different for the different platforms—hence the need for interoperability services from the operating system developers as well as third-party vendors. Windows 2000 uses SMBs, while UNIX variants have standardized on the Network File System (NFS) to advertise services on their networks.

In order for clients on both sides to access file and other services, you will want to consider add-ons and/or third-party solutions. Microsoft has an add-on called Services for UNIX that gives you the ability to share resources, administer machines remotely, synchronize Windows 2000 and UNIX passwords, and much more. The choices you'll face when trying to integrate the two platforms are numerous, and you could probably write an entire book on the choices alone. Some of the more common choices that you may have to make and some possible vendors to seek solutions from appear in Table 17-3.

REMOTE ACCESS   Many people tend to think that remote access is about dialing into a server using PPP, virtual private networks (VPNs), and much more. It is true that both Windows 2000 and UNIX computers can use these technologies. The UNIX platform supports most, if not all, of the latest technologies associated with remote access. However, a common misperception is that the older Serial Line Internet Protocol (SLIP) is the only remote access method used on UNIX machines. This is not the case; in fact, the technology is rarely even used in legacy applications.

TELNET   Another popular remote access method for UNIX machines is Telnet. Telnet is a client/server service where Telnet on a client is used to connect to and log on to a server running the Telnet daemon. From a Telnet window, you can manage and configure just about anything that you have permission to use. The biggest drawback to Telnet is that it sends passwords across the network in plain text so that anyone sniffing the network can grab the password and use it to their advantage. For this reason, UNIX environment administrators who consider their data important usually implement some greater security measures like the use of Secure Shell (SSH) when they perform remote management and configuration.

Option	Vendors
Install NFS client software on Windows 2000 and down-level client computers	Microsoft: http://www.Microsoft.com HummingBird Communications: http://www.hummingbird.com FTP Software: http://www.ftp.com
Install SMB client software on UNIX clients and servers	SAMBA: http://samba.anu.edu.au/samba
Use application servers to share applications across both platforms	Microsoft: http://www.Microsoft.com NetManage: http://www.netmanage.com Citrix Systems: http://www.citrix.com

Table 17-3.   *Options for Integrating Windows 2000 and UNIX Environments*

Windows 2000 also has the capability of using Telnet for remote connectivity like its UNIX counterparts, as shown in Figure 17-6. The version that comes bundled within Windows 2000, however, is fundamentally different than previous Windows NT versions that you may be accustomed to using. Some of these differences include

■ **Telnet Server** Windows 2000 is now equipped with the ability to accept incoming Telnet connection requests. In earlier versions of the operating system, the Telnet service didn't provide this feature; you had to use third-party vendor Telnet servers. Windows 2000's Telnet server can be configured to use standard authentication methods (username and password) as well as domain user account information to grant access to the server.

Note *The Telnet server is not started automatically by default. You must start the Telnet server service from within the MMC Services snap-in or from the Command Prompt by typing* **net start tlntsvr***.*

■ **Security** Telnet can optionally use built-in security mechanisms that keep information from being sent across the link in plain text. Instead, the username and password are encrypted before they're sent.

■ **Logging** Logging is no longer an integrated feature, so you'll need to use Hyperterminal to first open a Telnet session so that you can log your session. You can also copy text from the Telnet session to another application, such as Notepad.

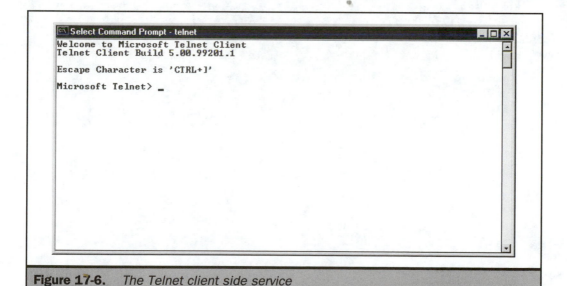

Figure 17-6. *The Telnet client side service*

Chapter 18

Managing Users

U ser accounts and groups form the cornerstone of security in Windows 2000. Accounts and groups let you grant permissions and rights to users on an individual or group basis. Integration in the Active Directory offers several new interesting administrative features in Windows 2000 not found in Windows NT. The new domain structure provided by the AD also adds a couple layers of complexity to understanding user management.

Understanding Groups and Accounts

Managing user accounts and groups is by far one of the most common, if not most important, system administration tasks in Windows 2000. Because accounts and groups are the means by which you protect both local and shared resources, a good understanding of accounts and groups is vital to any system administrator.

User Accounts

In any secure environment you need a method to identify and authenticate users. In nonsecure operating systems such as Windows 9*x*, anyone can create a new local account to log onto a computer. In order to protect local systems and network servers alike from unauthorized access, however, an operating system has to require that a user have a preexisting set of credentials before being permitted to access local and network resources. In Windows 2000, *user accounts* serve that purpose.

A user account provides a username and password that the person uses to log on to either the local computer or the domain. In addition, the user account, particularly in the Active Directory (AD), also serves to identify the user with data such as full name, e-mail address, phone number, department, and address. User accounts also serve as a means for granting permissions to a user, applying logon scripts, assigning profiles and home directories, and linking other working environment properties for the user.

Local Accounts

The first type of user account is a *local account*. Local accounts are created and stored in the local computer's security database. Local accounts are most often used in a workgroup environment to provide local logon capability for users of the local computer. However, local accounts also can be used to secure local resources that other users in the workgroup want to access. These other users connect to the resource across the LAN using a username and password stored on the computer where the resource resides (the account must have been granted permissions to the resource). As the number of workstations grows, however, local accounts and workgroups become impractical for controlling access to local resources. The answer is to switch to a domain environment and domain accounts.

Domain Accounts

A *domain account* resides on the domain controllers for a given domain. Rather than being localized to a specific computer, domain accounts offer privileges across the domain. Unless the domain account restricts him from doing so, the user can log on from any workstation in the domain. Once he's logged on, the domain account can grant him permissions to both local and shared network resources, depending on the permissions that are granted for each resource. In Windows 2000, domain accounts are stored and managed in the AD. The main advantage to using domain accounts is that they provide centralized administration and security.

Groups

Although you could grant permissions to users on a user-by-user basis, it would be a real pain to do it if you had more than a few users. Would you want to grant permissions to a network folder individually to 300 users? Probably not. You would much rather use groups.

A group, as the name implies, is a group of users. You don't put user accounts into groups, but instead, user accounts are assigned membership in groups. That distinction makes it clear that a user can belong to multiple groups. And groups can be *nested* in one another, with one group containing other groups. Groups come in four flavors depending on the type of logical network structure you're using.

| **Note** | *For the sake of simplicity, the rest of the chapter describes groups as containing user accounts and other groups. In reality, however, the groups don't actually contain anything. Instead, user accounts and groups are assigned membership in a group.* |

Local Groups

Local groups are most often used in workgroup environments and reside in a local computer's security database. Local groups can contain local user accounts and other local groups. You can use local groups to grant privileges to local resources to a group of users. Although you also can use local groups to grant permissions to local resources to other users in a workgroup across the LAN, it's impractical to do so with a large number of users.

Domain Groups

Just as you can create user accounts in a domain, you can create groups in a domain. A given domain group resides in only one domain, but its *scope* determines how the group is used. The scope determines the domain from which members can be added to the group, as well as the domain in which permissions and rights assigned to the group are valid. There are three domain group scopes: domain local, global, and universal. You use domain groups to grant permissions and rights across one or more domains. Each domain group is stored on the domain controllers for its domain.

DOMAIN LOCAL GROUPS   *Domain local groups* can contain user accounts, global groups, and universal groups from any domain, as well as domain local groups from the same domain. Domain local groups can belong to other domain local groups in the same domain, and are used to grant permissions only in the same domain. You can convert domain local groups to universal scope as long as the group doesn't contain any other domain local group.

GLOBAL GROUPS   *Global groups* can contain accounts and other global groups only from the domain in which the group resides. Global groups can belong to other global groups and are used to grant permissions in any domain (subject to trust relationships between the domains). You can convert a global group to universal scope only if the group doesn't contain any other group with global scope.

UNIVERSAL GROUPS   *Universal groups* can contain accounts from any domain, global groups from any domain, and universal groups from any domain. Universal groups can belong to any other universal group, and are used to grant permissions in any domain (also subject to trust relationships between domains). You can't convert a universal group to any other scope. Universal scope is supported only in Windows 2000 native mode domains.

NESTED GROUPS   You can nest one group inside another (make it a member of another group). Nesting groups enables you to consolidate group management, since changes to the "parent" group will affect those contained in it. Nested groups also can reduce replication time and traffic when changes occur that must be replicated to the other domain controllers in the domain.

Distribution Groups

Distribution groups are the second type of group in Windows 2000. Distribution groups are used for broadcasting e-mail and can't be used to grant permissions or apply security.

Overview of Authentication and Logon

Windows 2000 prompts for User name, Password, and Log on to <DomainName> when a user is logging onto a domain. In a workgroup, Windows 2000 prompts only for username and password. During logon, the user selects either a domain or the local computer from the Log On To drop-down list.

If the user chooses a domain in the drop-down list, Windows 2000 passes the logon request to the domain controller (DC) for the specified domain. The DC checks the information stored in the AD for the account. If the account and password are valid and the security settings allow that account to log on from that computer, the DC authorizes the logon. If the user instead specifies the local computer name in the Log On To drop-down box, Windows 2000 checks the local security database for a valid, matching account. The logon succeeds if the specified account is found.

Logon in Trusted Domains

In a trust relationship, the trusting domain trusts users and groups from the trusted domain. This enables users to log on in the trusting domain. When a user logs on to a trusting domain, she specifies the domain where her user account resides. Windows 2000 passes the logon request to the specified domain, which authenticates the logon request and grants logon if the account and domain relationship permits it.

Remote Logon

Remote authentication through Remote Access Services (RAS) enables a user to log on to a domain through a remote connection such as a dial-up account or dedicated WAN connection. Remote logon happens in much the same way as a local or local domain logon. The logon request is passed through the RAS server to the DC for the specified account's domain, which authenticates the request, passing the information to the RAS server to allow or deny logon.

Kerberos Authentication

As discussed in more depth in Chapter 21, Windows 2000 adds support for Kerberos authentication protocol. Kerberos defines the interaction between clients and a server-side authentication service called a Key Distribution Center (KDC). A KDC processes authentication requests and issues a Kerberos ticket to the client. The ticket grants client access to the requested resource (which could be any object, such as a folder, file, etc.). The client caches the ticket and can reuse it for future connections until it expires, at which time the client can request a new ticket. Kerberos is the primary authentication mechanism for domain authentication in Windows 2000. It replaces NTLM authentication in this regard.

Managing Accounts

Windows 2000 provides two different tools for managing user accounts. You use the Local Users And Groups branch of the Computer Management MMC snap-in to create local accounts and groups. In a domain you use the Active Directory Users and Computers MMC snap-in to create domain accounts in the AD. Regardless of which tool you use to create the account, you'll need to modify the account after creation to specify all the user account properties.

To use the Local Users And Groups branch of the Computer Management snap-in to create local accounts, right-click My Computer and choose Manage, or click Start | Programs | Administrative Tools | Computer Management.

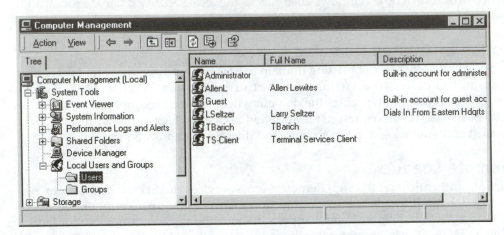

If you prefer, you can add the Local Users And Groups snap-in to any MMC console. Run the MMC, add the snap-in, and then save the console for later use. Save it in the Administrative Tools folder if you want it to appear in the Start menu.

To create domain accounts, open the Active Directory Users and Computers snap-in by clicking Start | Programs | Administrative Tools | Active Directory Users And Computers. Figure 18-1 shows the Active Directory Users And Computers snap-in.

Windows 2000 prevents you from running the Local Users And Groups snap-in on a domain controller.

Creating Accounts

When you create an account, whether local or domain, you specify general information about the user. When creating a local account, Windows 2000 prompts you for user data as shown in Figure 18-2.

- **User name**   This is the user's logon name. Use a naming scheme that provides consistency throughout your organization. For example, you might use first initial of the first name plus the last name. Or use first name plus the first few characters of the user's last name.

- **Full name**   This usually is the user's first name and surname. When you create a domain account, Windows 2000 builds this field for you from the First Name, Initials, and Last Name fields. Specify it manually for local accounts.

- **Description**   Use this optional description to further identify the user or users group, department, etc.

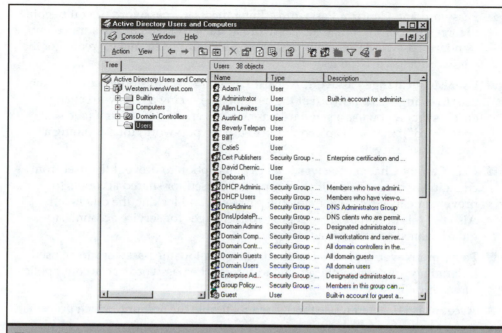

Figure 18-1.   *Use Active Directory Users And Computers to create domain user accounts*

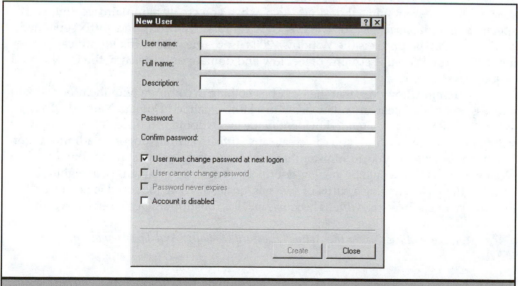

Figure 18-2.   *The New User dialog from Local Users And Groups*

- **Password and Confirm Password**   Enter the user's password. If you're going to force the user to change the password at the next logon, make sure you use a standard password (the word **password**, for example) or make a record of the password to give to the user.

- **User Must Change Password At Next Logon**   Select this option to force the user to change his password at the next logon. Forcing a password change ensures that if you use a standard password to create the account (such as "password"), the user can't continue to use the password, thus avoiding a potential security hole.

- **User Cannot Change Password**   Select this option to prevent the user from changing her password. Often, this option is used for shared accounts to prevent one user from changing the password and locking the others out. Also use this option to prevent password changes for service accounts, to guard against security breaches.

- **Password Never Expires**   Use this option to allow the password to be used indefinitely, or deselect this option to enforce the password age account policy (if one is defined).

- **Account Is Disabled**   Use this option to disable the account, which prevents it from being used.

When you create a domain account (see Figure 18-3), you can specify two logon names: one for logon from Windows 2000 systems and another when logging on from Windows NT or Windows 9*x* systems. You can specify the same name for consistency or specify a different name if desired. Also, when you create a domain account, you specify a *user principal name*, or UPN. A UPN comprises a prefix and suffix separated by the @ sign. The prefix is the Windows 2000 username. The suffix identifies the user's logon domain. With a username of joeblow and domain of ivens.com, the UPN would be joeblow@ivens.com.

Keep in mind, however, that the UPN has nothing in common with the user's e-mail address, nor does it bear any relationship to a Fully Qualified Domain Name (FQDN). While the UPN suffix is intended to identify the logon domain, it doesn't have to be a valid DNS domain. Instead, you can create any suffix to simplify logon or administration. For example, let's say you administer the domain support.westcoast.ivens.com. Poor old Joe Blow's UPN would be joeblow@support.westcoast.ivens.com. You might simplify things by creating a suffix of "wivens" instead. Then, Joe could log on using joeblow@wivens. In effect, wivens becomes an alias for support.westcoast.ivens.com.

Tip   *Add UPN aliases using the Active Directory Domains And Trusts snap-in.*

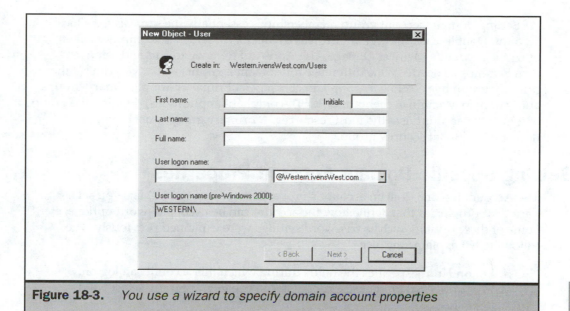

Figure 18-3.   *You use a wizard to specify domain account properties*

Managing General Account Properties

After you create an account, you can modify its properties to add other information about the user, or set additional properties such as password options, group membership, and logon hours. The property sheet for a local account comprises four tabs. The General tab lets you view and modify the same properties you use to create the account. One additional option, Account Is Locked Out, lets you unlock an account that has been locked through the effects of the security policy.

Several of the tabs for a domain account control general properties like account name, password, etc. The main difference from a local account is that you can specify considerably more information about the user, such as address, phone, e-mail address, and Web page. The properties on the General, Address, Telephones, and Organization tabs control general properties and are self-explanatory.

Managing Group Membership

After creating an account, you might need to modify group membership for the account. By default, local user accounts become members of the local Users group. Domain accounts become members of the Domain Users group. To modify membership for a local account, double-click the account in Local Users And Groups and then click the Member Of tab. Use Add And Remove Users as desired; then click OK or Apply.

Setting domain account group membership is essentially the same as for a local account. Double-click the account in Active Directory Users And Computers: then open the account's Member Of page. Use Add And Remove to add and remove memberships as needed. One difference for domain accounts is that you can set the primary group by selecting a group and clicking Set Primary Group. Primary groups apply only to Macintosh clients and POSIX-compliant applications, defining the group in which the account uses the most resources. A primary group must be either a universal or global security group.

Setting Specific Domain Account Properties

The Account tab of a domain account's properties (see Figure 18-4) lets you set a variety of properties that define how the account can be used, password options, etc. Some of these options such as password settings were explained previously. The following list explains the rest:

- **Logon Hours** specifies the hours during which this account can log on. Windows 2000 presents a dialog you can use to graphically select valid logon hours.

- **Log On To** defines the list of computers from which the account can log on. You can allow logon from all computers or restrict logon to a list of specific

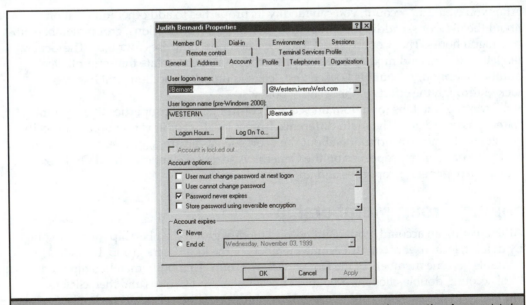

Figure 18-4. *You can set a variety of domain account properties on the Account tab*

computers. This is a useful security option for limiting logon location for the account, enabling you to keep users in their "own areas."

■ **Store Password Using Reversible Encryption** is used for Macintosh clients who need to store their passwords as encrypted clear text.

■ **Smart Card** is required for interactive logon specifies that the user must provide a smart card with a PIN (Personal Identification Number) to log on. This option requires a smart card reader connected to the logon computer.

■ **Account Is Trusted For Delegation** means the account has the ability to delegate administration of a portion of the domain namespace in the AD to another user, group, or organization.

■ **Account Is Sensitive And Cannot Be Delegated** prevents the account from being delegated for administration by another account.

■ **Use DES Encryption Types For This Account** requires Data Encryption Standard (DES) encryption to be used for the account. DES provides multiple levels of strong encryption for increased security.

■ **Do Not Require Kerberos Preauthentication** specifies that the account employs a different version of the Kerberos protocol that does not use Kerberos preauthentication.

■ **Account Expires** specifies if and when the account expires. An expired account can't be used to log on.

Configuring Profile Properties

Each account, whether local or domain, includes profile properties. User profiles enable a user's desktop settings and other interface and operating parameters to be retained from one session to another. The following few sections explain how to set user profile properties for an account. See the section "Managing User Profiles" later in this chapter for a detailed explanation of user profiles.

To set user profile properties, open the user's account properties and access the Profile tab. Figure 18-5 shows the Profile page for a domain account. The Profile page for a local account contains identical properties.

Specifying a Profile Path

The Profile Path field specifies the location of the account's Windows NT-style profile. The profile determines the account's operating environment settings at logon, although these settings can be overridden by group policy settings. Using this type of profile rather than group policy settings is most useful in a mixed environment where Windows NT workstations are present. In a homogenous Windows 2000 network, you can use group policies exclusively to apply user profile settings.

Note   *Refer to "Managing User Profiles" later in this chapter for more information.*

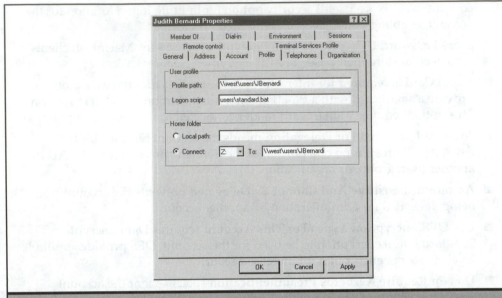

Figure 18-5.   *The Profile page defines the user's profile, logon script, and home folder*

Logon Script

Use the Logon script field to specify the name of a batch or command file (BAT or CMD), executable (EXE), or Windows Scripting Host script (VBScript or Jscript). The logon script executes automatically at logon and is most often used to set environment variables, map drives, or start background processes. The default path for scripts is the \%SystemRoot\System32\Repl\Import\Scripts folder on the local computer or the NETLOGON share on a domain controller within the domain. Specify a path relative to the default location. For example, use Scripts\Loguser.bat to specify a script named Loguser.bat in NETLOGON\Scripts.

Home Folder

Use the Home Folder group of controls to define the user's home folder at logon. Usually the home folder is where the user stores documents, but you can use any folder on the local computer or a network share. Select Local Path to specify a local folder and specify the desired path. Or click Connect and select an associated drive letter, and then specify a UNC pathname in the form \\server\share\folder in the To field.

A nice improvement in Windows 2000 over Windows NT is that you can specify a folder within a share, rather than specify a share. For example, you can create a single share called Users that contains several hundred folders, and reference each user's folder when needed in the profile settings. Under NT, you'd have to share each user's folder individually—a real pain.

Managing Groups

Windows 2000 includes a set of built-in and predefined groups to simplify management by providing a set of common groups you can use to grant permissions and control resource access. Table 18-1 lists the built-in groups. Built-in groups can't be deleted.

Table 18-2 lists the additional predefined groups in a domain environment. Note that the list of groups in a domain vary according to the services that are installed. These predefined groups can be deleted, although in most cases you won't want to do so.

You'll find that not only will you use the predefined groups, but you'll also create your own groups to handle specific circumstances such as accommodating departments of users. Use Local Users And Groups to create new local groups and assign membership in a group. Open Local Users And Groups, right-click Groups, and choose New Group. Specify a unique name for the new local group and click Add to add accounts to the group.

Use the Active Directory Users And Computers snap-in to create groups in a domain. Right-click at the level where you want the group created and choose New | Group. In the New Object—Group dialog (Figure 18-6), specify the following information:

- A unique name
- Pre-Windows 2000 group name (for Windows NT/9x users)

Group	Default Contents	Purpose
Account Operators	None	Administer domain user accounts and groups
Administrators	Domain Admins	Full control to administer system
Backup Operators	None	Back up files and folders
Guests	Domain Guests, Guest	Use but not configure system
Pre-Windows 2000 Compatible Access	None	For backward compatibility to allow read-only access for all domain users
Print Operators	None	Administer domain printers
Replicator	None	Supports file replication in a domain
Server Operators	None	Administer domain servers
Users	Authenticated Users	Use but not configure system

Table 18-1. *Built-in Local Groups*

Group	Type	Default Contents	Purpose
Cert Publishers	Global	None	Enterprise certification and renewal agents
DHCP Administrators	Domain Local	None	Administer DHCP server
DHCP Users	Domain Local	None	View-only access to DHCP server
DnsAdmins	Domain Local	None	Administer DNS namespace
DnsUpdateProxy	Global	None	Clients permitted dynamic DHCP update
Domain Admins	Global	Administrator	Administer the domain
Domain Computers	Global	Computers added to domain	Allow domain access by member computers
Domain Controllers	Global	Domain controllers in domain	Handle authentication and Active Directory replication
Domain Guests	Global	Guest account	Use but not configure computer in domain
Domain Users	Global	All domain accounts	Use but not configure computer in domain
Enterprise Admins	Universal	Administrator	Administer enterprise
Group Policy Creator Owners	Global	Administrator	Modify group policy for domain
Schema Admins	Universal	Administrator	Users can administer schema

Table 18-2.   *Predefined Groups for Domains*

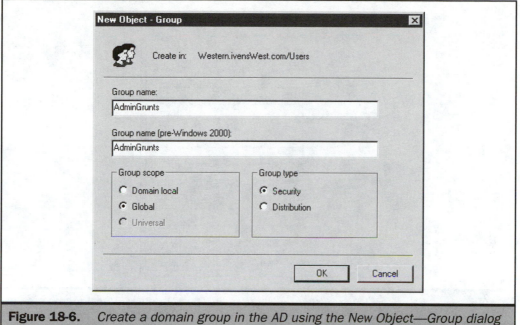

Figure 18-6. *Create a domain group in the AD using the New Object—Group dialog*

- Group scope (domain local, global, universal)
- Group type (security or distribution)

Click OK to create the group. After you create a group, open its properties and use its Members page to assign membership in the group. In addition to assigning membership in a group through its properties, you also can nest a group in another. As explained earlier, nested groups simplify administration and reduce AD replication. To nest a group, open its properties and access its Member Of tab. Click Add and select the other group(s) of which the current group will be a member.

The last of a group's Properties tabs, Managed By (see Figure 18-7), lets you specify which account is responsible for managing the group. Click Change and select a user account. The contact information for the user you select automatically appears in the Managed By page.

Understanding and Assigning Rights

User rights grant a user or group the authority to perform specific actions. Rights are different from permissions. Rights apply to systemwide objects and tasks, and permissions apply to specific objects such as files and printers. When a user logs on

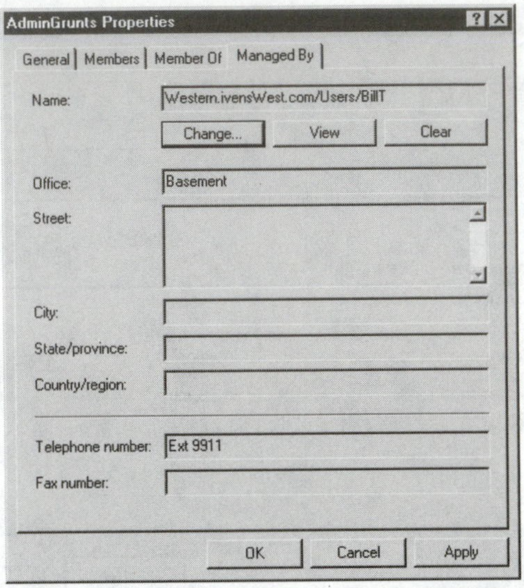

Figure 18-7. *Specify which account is responsible for managing a group*

with an account that has been granted a right directly to the account or implicitly through group membership, the user can perform the operation associated with that right. This section explains the types of rights, how they are used, and how to apply them.

Understanding Rights

There are two types of rights in Windows 2000: *privileges* and *logon rights*. Specific privileges are listed in Table 18-3 and logon rights are listed in Table 18-4. Some of the advanced user rights listed in the tables are only applicable within the framework of a custom application or Windows 2000 subsystem.

Some privileges/rights take precedence over permissions. Backup is a good example. Members of the Backup Operators group can perform backup operations on files even if the files' owners have set object permissions on them to deny access to all other users. The right to back up files and directories takes precedence over the files' permissions.

Although you can assign a right to an individual user, you should assign rights using groups instead, just as you do when granting permissions. This simplifies administration and makes it easier to determine who has which rights. If you need to grant a right to a single user, consider creating a group specifically for that purpose. You'll probably find that in the future you'll need to give other users the same right, and then you can just add those users to the group.

Right	Purpose
Act as part of the operating system	Lets the user act as trusted part of the operating system; granted automatically to certain subsystems.
Add workstations to domain	User can add workstations to domain, enabling domain logon from those workstations.
Back up files and directories	User can back up files and directories on computer; supersedes file and directory permissions. Does not enable user to view file or directory contents without explicit permission.
Bypass traverse checking	Lets user traverse directory trees, even if she lacks permission to traverse a specific directory; doesn't supersede ownership or permissions (can only traverse and not view or manipulate contents without specific permissions).
Change the system time	User can set computer's system clock.
Create a pagefile	Allows user to create a pagefile.
Create a token object	User can create security access tokens.
Create permanent shared objects	Enables user to create permanent shared objects such as device instances.
Debug programs	Allows user to debug programs.
Enable Trusted for Delegation on User and Computer Accounts	Lets user enable Trusted for Delegation on user and computer accounts.
Force shutdown from a remote system	Lets user force a system to shut down from a remote node (such as a dial-up connection).
Generate security audits	Allows user to generate security log entries.
Increase quotas	Enables user to increase object quotas.
Increase scheduling priority	Enables user to boost scheduling priority of a process.

Table 18-3.   *Common Windows 2000 Privileges*

Right	Purpose
Load and unload device drivers	Allows user to dynamically load and unload device drivers. Applies to domain controllers within a domain. Outside of a domain, applies only to computer on which right is assigned.
Lock pages in memory	User can lock pages in memory, preventing them from being paged to disk.
Manage auditing and security log	Enables user to manage auditing of files, directories, and other objects.
Modify firmware and environment values	Allows user to modify system environment variables.
Profile single process	Enables user to profile a process.
Profile system performance	Enables user to profile overall system performance.
Replace a process level token	Enables a user to modify a process' access token.
Restore files and directories	User can restore files previously backed up. Having backup permission does not give a user restore permission, and vice versa.
Shut down the system	Enables user to shut down the computer.
Take ownership of files or other objects	User can take ownership of files, directories, and printers. Applies to domain controllers within a domain. Outside of domain applies only to computer on which right is assigned.
Unlock a Laptop	User can unlock a laptop.

Table 18-3. *Common Windows 2000 Privileges* (Continued)

Assigning Rights

Use the Local Security Policy, Domain Security Policy, or Group Policy MMC snap-ins to assign rights, depending on the scope under which you want to apply the right. The process is essentially the same regardless of which tool you use. User rights fall under the Security Settings\Local Policies\User Rights Assignment branch of each snap-in. You can access the Local Security Policy snap-in from the Administrative Tools folder

Right	Purpose
Access this computer from network	Lets user connect to the computer from across the network.
Log on locally	User can log onto system locally. In most cases, you don't want users to have the right to log on locally to a server for security and performance reasons.
Log on as a batch job	Enables user to log onto system as a batch queue facility.
Log on as a service	Allow processes to register with the system as a service.
Deny Access to this Computer from the Network	Holder can deny the Access This Computer from the Network right.
Deny Logon as a Batch Job	Holder can deny the Log On as a Batch Job right.
Deny Logon as a Service	Holder can deny the Log On As a Service right.
Deny Local Logon	Holder can deny the Log On Locally right.

Table 18-4.   *Common Logon Rights*

(located on the Start menu). Once you've opened the tool you want to use to assign a right, you can see all the rights (see Figure 18-8).

Locate the right you want to work with and double-click it to view or modify its assignment. The right's Properties dialog box (see Figure 18-9) shows the user(s) and group(s) assigned the right, and in the case of a local policy, the effective policy enforced on the system as determined by group policies in the domain. Group policies generally override local policy settings. Select and deselect users or groups to grant and deny a right, respectively. Use Add to add new groups or users to the list, and assign rights as desired. Then click OK.

Using Group Policies

Group policies are a mechanism in Windows 2000 that enable you to assign security settings and other properties to users based on group membership or individual accounts. Group policies can effectively replace Windows NT user profiles to define, distribute, and control users' working environment in Windows 2000. However, you

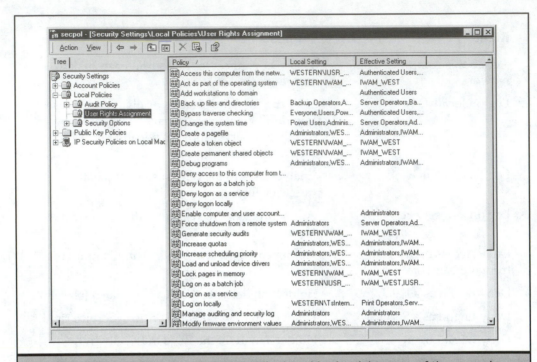

Figure 18-8. *All the current rights are displayed in the right pane of the console window*

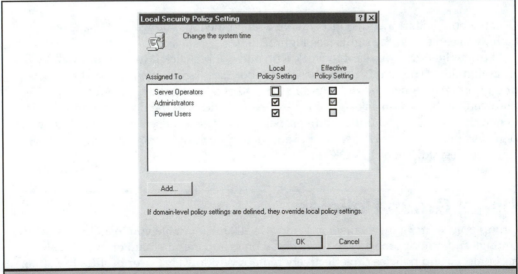

Figure 18-9. *Local security policy shows local and effective policy for a selected right*

can use group policies in conjunction with user profiles, which is useful in a mixed environment where Windows NT systems are present. Windows NT 4 system policies are disabled by default. Enable them through the group policy setting Disable System Policy (Use Group Policy Only) in Computer Configuration\Administrative Templates\System\Group Policy.

You'll find two types of group policies in Windows 2000: local and nonlocal. A single set of local policies exists on each computer and applies specifically to the local computer. Nonlocal policies are stored in the AD and apply to the site, domain, or organizational unit level where the group policy resides. If local and nonlocal policies conflict, nonlocal policies take precedence over local policies by default. Both apply when no conflict exists.

Understanding Policy Inheritance and Exclusion

Like permissions, policies can be *inherited*. This means that policies are passed down from parent container to child container within the AD. Inheritance follows a set of guidelines that determine how policies are inherited:

- Policies applied at the highest level pass down through successive levels (subject to restrictions described here).

- Explicit policy settings defined at a child container override policies defined by the parent container(s).

- Any settings that are not defined by the parent are not inherited by the child.

- Any settings disabled in the parent are inherited as disabled by the child.

- Settings that are configured at the parent but not at the child container are inherited by the child.

- Policy settings are inherited only if they are compatible. The child inherits the parent settings and applies additional, related settings when parent and child settings are compatible. The child doesn't inherit if settings are not compatible, but instead applies its own settings.

How Group Policies Are Applied

Windows 2000 uses a specific procedure to apply policy settings and the user profile:

1. The network and network-required services start during boot.

2. Windows 2000 obtains an ordered list of group policy objects, which depends on several factors including membership in a domain, location of the computer object in the AD, location of the User object in the AD, etc.

3. The computer policy is applied synchronously in this order: Windows NT 4 system policy, then group policies for local, site, domain, organizational unit, child organizational unit, etc. By default, the user interface is hidden while group policies are applied.

4. The startup scripts defined by the group policies execute.

5. User logon occurs, either through the user pressing CTRL-ALT-DEL or Windows 2000 automatically logging on the user, depending on how logon is configured.

6. After valid authentication, the user profile is loaded.

7. User policy is applied synchronously first by Windows NT 4 system policy and then by group policies for local, site, domain, organizational unit, child organizational unit, etc. By default, the user interface is hidden while user policies are applied.

8. Group policy-based logon scripts execute, followed by the user object script.

9. The user interface appears as defined by settings in the group policy and user profile.

Assigning Policies

You use the Group Policy MMC snap-in focused on the desired object (local computer, domain, organizational unit, etc.) to assign group polices. To manage the local policy, execute Gpedit.msc, located in the \%SystemRoot%\System32 folder. This opens the Group Policy snap-in focused on the local computer. To focus on another object, add the Group Policy snap-in to a console and when prompted, specify the focus for the object (local computer, default domain policy, and so forth).

Note *See Chapter 8 to learn how to add a snap-in to a console.*

Within the Group Policy snap-in you'll find two branches: Computer Configuration and User Configuration (see Figure 18-10). Computer Configuration defines computer-specific settings such as startup scripts, shutdown scripts, system services, the file system, and other settings that apply to the computer rather than individual users. The User Configuration branch defines settings that relate to users, such as logon scripts, and folder redirection. Both the Computer Configuration and User Configuration branches include their own Administrative Templates branch. This branch contains global settings that define how the group policies are applied and control general policy settings for printing, system configuration, and so on.

It isn't practical to discuss every group policy setting because there are just too many. Fortunately, most settings are self-explanatory to most system administrators familiar with Windows NT or Windows 2000. The latter includes an Explain property page for each policy that gives detailed information about the setting (see Figure 18-11).

The Setting column in the Group Policy snap-in shows the value of a setting. If the value indicates "Not Configured," the setting hasn't been set explicitly. Otherwise, the column shows either Enabled or Disabled, depending on how you've configured the setting. To view or modify a setting, simply double-click the setting to open its Properties

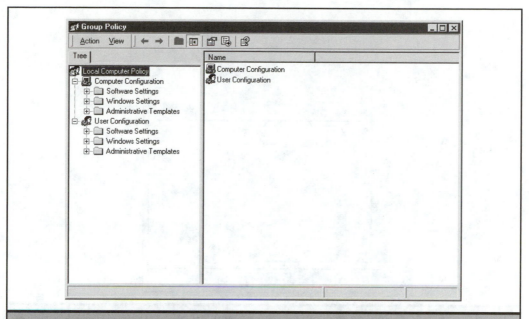

Figure 18-10. *The Group Policy snap-in focused on the default domain policy*

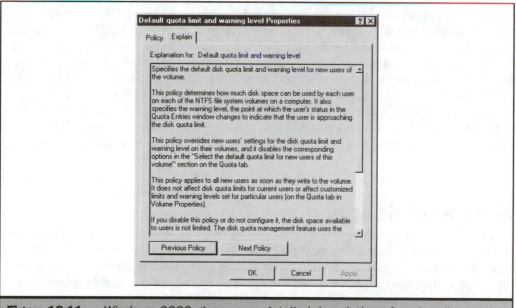

Figure 18-11. *Windows 2000 gives you a detailed description of each policy setting*

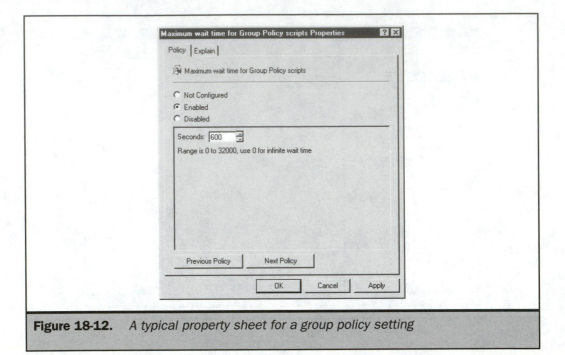

Figure 18-12.   *A typical property sheet for a group policy setting*

dialog box. In most cases, the dialog box comprises one or two tabs (perhaps more, depending on the setting). Figure 18-12 shows a typical Properties dialog box for a setting.

Configure a given setting by selecting Not Configured, Enabled, or Disabled, as needed. The additional options that Windows 2000 makes available for the setting depend entirely on the setting. In some cases, you can only set the status of the setting and not set additional options. Move to the Explain tab if you need a description of the setting.

Although it might take you a while to get through all of them, it's a good idea to browse through the group policy list to learn what they do. Through the rest of the chapter we'll cover some specific policy-defined properties like scripts and password policies.

Managing Scripts

Scripts are useful for performing actions automatically at system startup or shutdown, and at user logon or logoff. For example, you might use scripts to set environment variables, connect to network resources, or execute programs. A user's *object script* is the script you assign through the user's account properties as explained previously in the section "Configuring Profile Properties." A user's object script applies specifically to that user. You also can assign scripts through group policy to apply to the scope of users and groups to which the policy applies.

Creating and Storing Scripts

As mentioned previously, a script can be a batch file (BAT or CMD), executable (EXE), or script (VBScript or Jscript). You can use predefined scripts or create your own. To create your own script, create the batch file, executable, or script, and store it in the appropriate location. But where is that?

By default, the path to a user's object script is the NETLOGON share (the %SystemRoot%\System32\Repl\Import\Scripts folder) of the local computer when the user logs on locally in a workgroup. To manage multiple local scripts for users who log on locally, you'll need to create the folder, share it as NETLOGON, and place the scripts in the folder.

In Windows 2000 domains, however, the NETLOGON share points to \sysvol\ *DomainName*\Scripts on the domain controller. To distribute object scripts in a domain environment, place the scripts in the NETLOGON share of the domain controller. The scripts will be replicated to other domain controllers in the domain and be available for access by users regardless of their logon location (allowing for roaming users to have access to their scripts).

When you specify the path to a user's object script in his account's profile properties, make sure you specify a relative path to the script location. For example, if the user's script is %SystemRoot%*DomainName*\Scripts\Admins\Logme.bat, you'd specify Admins\Logme.bat in the user's account properties.

Logon and logoff scripts defined by the local group policy are stored by default locally in *systemroot*\Sytem32\GroupPolicy\Users\Scripts*type*, where *type* is either Logon or Logoff. Logon and logoff scripts defined by group policy in the domain are stored by default under *sysvol**domain*\Policies. Locally defined startup and shutdown scripts are stored by default in *systemroot*\System32\GroupPolicy\Machine\Scripts*type*, where *type* is either Startup or Shutdown. Scripts defined by group policy in the domain are stored by default under the *sysvol**domain*\Policies folder.

Assigning Scripts

To assign a user's object script, specify the script path in the user's account properties as explained previously in the section "Logon Scripts." Use the Group Policy snap-in focused on the desired location (local computer, default domain policy, etc.) to assign scripts through group policy. The following steps explain how:

1. Open the Group Policy snap-in and expand Computer Configuration\Windows Settings\Scripts for startup or shutdown scripts, or User Configuration\Windows Settings\Scripts for logon or logoff scripts.

2. In the right pane, double-click the type of script you want to assign to open the Scripts dialog.

3. Click Add to specify Script Name (name of script file) and Script Parameters, which are parameters passed to the script at execution. Click Browse if you want to browse for the script file.

4. Click OK to add the script; then add or remove other scripts as desired.

5. Click OK; then repeat the process for other script types.

6. Close the Group Policy snap-in when you've finished.

The Up and Down buttons on the Scripts page change the order in which scripts execute, although this has no effect unless you configure scripts for synchronous execution as explained in the next section.

Managing Script Execution

Group policy-defined scripts execute first, followed by the user's object script (if any). Policy-defined startup/shutdown scripts execute hidden from the user and synchronously, which means each must complete before the next executes. Execution is subject to a policy-defined timeout value (default = 600 seconds). All startup scripts must complete before the logon dialog appears.

Group policy-defined logon/logoff scripts execute hidden from the user and asynchronously (concurrently) by default. This means that the Explorer interface can appear before the script(s) complete execution. However, you can configure logon/logoff scripts to execute synchronously, requiring that each script complete before the next executes. This is useful typically only if one script relies on the tasks performed by the other. With synchronous execution, all scripts (including the user object script) must complete before the Explorer interface appears.

Use the settings in the User Configuration\Administrative Templates\System\ Logon/Logoff branch of the Group Policy snap-in to control script execution. These settings include the following:

- Run logon scripts synchronously.

- Run legacy logon scripts hidden.

- Run logon scripts visible.

- Run logoff scripts visible.

Settings in the Computer Configuration\Administrative Templates\System\Logon branch control startup and shutdown script execution. Here are some of them:

- Run logon scripts synchronously.

- Run startup scripts asynchronously.

- Run startup scripts visible.

- Run shutdown scripts visible.

- Maximum wait time for Group Policy scripts.

Environment Variables in Scripts

If you've done any batch programming you know that it's often useful to be able to read the value of environment variables within the batch file. The same is true for logon/logoff and startup/shutdown scripts. For example, you might want to set an environment variable to the name of the user's home directory server but use the same script to allow multiple users to map a home folder to a different server. You'd define a variable for the server within a policy-defined script, and then use that variable in the user's object script to map the local drive ID to the required network share.

Table 18-5 lists the reserved variables you can use in a logon script. These variables determine information about the user and environment at logon. You also can parse any environment variable on the system using %*variable*%, where *variable* is the environment variable name.

Environment variables are not just for use in scripts. You also can use them in user profile paths and home directory paths. For example, you might define %server% as the name of the desired server, and then use \\%server%\Users\%username% to map a local drive letter to the user's home folder on the server specified by %server%. If %server% resolved to DomSrv1, for example, and the user logged on as mary, the path would resolve to \\DomSrv1\Users\mary.

Variable	Function
%HOMEDRIVE%	User's local drive letter assigned to home folder
%HOMEPATH%	Full path to user's home folder
%OS%	Current operating system of logon workstation
%PROCESSOR_ARCHITECTURE%	Processor type of logon workstation (such as *x*86 for Intel)
%PROCESSOR_LEVEL%	Processor level of logon workstation
%USERDOMAIN%	Domain containing user's account
%USERNAME%	User's account (logon) name

Table 18-5.   *Logon Script Variables*

Setting Account and Password Policies

Account lockout and password settings in the local or group policy apply restrictions on passwords, how passwords are applied, account lockout, and other options that control user logon. Use the Group Policy snap-in to manage these settings.

Configuring the Password Policy

The password policy defines how passwords are handled. For example, you can age passwords so they expire and must be replaced, specify a minimum password length, and so on. Use the Computer Configuration\Windows Settings\Security Settings\Account Policies\Password Policy branch of the Group Policy snap in to set the following settings:

- **Enforce Password History**   Use this setting to retain the specified number of old passwords (range 0 to 24). Users are prevented from reusing a password that is still in the history list. Use a setting of 0 to disable password history.

- **Maximum Password Age**   Set the number of days to use the current password before requiring the user to change his password.

- **Minimum Password Age**   Set the minimum number of days the password must be used before it can be changed. A setting of 0 enables immediate password change.

- **Minimum Password Length**   This is the minimum number of characters required in password. A setting of 0 allows for no password, which poses a real security risk, so it isn't recommended. A higher value will increase security by making passwords harder to guess or crack.

- **Passwords Must Meet Complexity Requirements Of The Installed Password Filter**   Enabling this setting requires that the password meet criteria that include not containing the username in the password and containing three of the following: English uppercase letters, English lowercase letters, Westernized Arabic numerals, and non-alphanumeric characters (!, @, #, etc.). The default password filter is defined in the file Scecli.dll in *systemroot*\System32. You can modify the password filter by creating a different DLL, either by writing your own or using one from a third-party developer.

- **Store Password Using Reversible Encryption For All Users In The Domain**   Use this option to encrypt the password.

- **User Must Log On To Change The Password**   Enabling this option requires the user to first log on with the current password to be able to change the password. If you disable this setting the user is instead prompted to change passwords at logon.

Configuring the Account Lockout Policy

Keeping unauthorized users out of the system is obviously important to security. You can use the Account Lockout Policy settings to protect against password guessing or cracking attempts. Account lockout settings are defined in the Computer Configuration\Windows Settings\Security Settings\Account Policies\Account Lockout Policy branch of the Group Policy snap-in. The following list explains the settings:

- **Account Lockout Counter**   Use this setting to specify the number of invalid logon attempts that can occur before the account is locked out. The default value of 0 disables account lockout.

- **Account Lockout Duration**   This setting specifies the number of minutes the account will remain locked out. The default value is 30 minutes.

- **Reset Account Lockout Counter After**   Use this setting to specify the number of minutes after which the lockout counter is reset to 0. The default value is five minutes.

Managing User Profiles

As mentioned earlier in this chapter, a user profile enables a user's working environment settings (such as desktop configuration) to be retained from one logon session to another. User profiles are a means of providing a consistent interface regardless of where a user logs on, but the profiles also allow administrators to enforce specific user configurations. You can use group policies instead of profiles to achieve the same results, but profiles are still useful in mixed environments where Windows NT computers are present along with Windows 2000 systems. Because your transition to Windows 2000 will probably be a gradual one, we've included coverage of user profiles in this chapter.

Overview of Profiles

A user profile is a group of settings contained in a registry file and a set of folders and shortcuts, and those settings define a user's working environment. Windows 2000 builds the user's working environment through this user profile at logon. Typical user profile settings include desktop configuration and schemes, Control Panel settings, network printer connections, and so on. Profiles serve the following primary purposes:

- Provide a unique user interface configuration for each user, and allow that configuration to move with the user from workstation to workstation

- Enable users to retain a unique desktop even when sharing a single workstation

- Enable administrators to control the types of changes a user can make to the environment

Source	Settings
Windows Explorer	User-defined settings for Explorer
My Documents	User's My Documents folder
My Pictures	User's My Pictures folder
Favorites	User's Favorites folder
Mapped network drives	Network shares mapped to local drive IDs
My Network Places	User's My Network Places folder
Desktop contents	Items and shortcuts on user's desktop
Screen colors and fonts	User-specified desktop UI settings
Application data and registry hive	Application data and user-specified registry settings
Printer settings	Network printers and settings
Control Panel	User-specified changes made through Control Panel
Accessories	User-specified settings for Accessory programs
Windows 2000 applications	Per-user program settings
Help bookmarks	User-defined bookmarks in Help

Table 18-6.   *User Profile Contents*

Table 18-6 lists settings stored in a user profile.

There are three types of profiles: personal, mandatory, and default. A *personal profile* is one in which a user can change the profile from one logon session to another, subject to restrictions defined by the profile. Personal profiles are applied to users who need to be able to change their working environment and retain the changes for future logons.

Mandatory profiles are identical to personal profiles with one exception: the user can't carry changes from one logon session to another. The user can change certain aspects of the working environment (subject to restrictions in the profile), but those changes are lost when the user logs off. The only other difference between a personal profile and a mandatory profile is the file extension of the profile's registry file. Personal profiles use the .dat extension and mandatory profiles use the .man extension.

The *default profile* is used if the user has no other profile and becomes the user's saved profile upon logoff. Future logon sessions use this stored profile.

How Profiles Are Created and Stored

The registry file portion of a user profile is a cached copy of the HKEY_CURRENT_USER portion of the registry, stored as Ntuser.dat. A user-specific directory structure makes up the rest of the profile. Ntuser.dat defines the computer's hardware, installed software, and working environment settings. The directory structure and shortcuts therein determine the user's desktop and application environments. A local user profile is stored in the folder \Documents and Settings*user*, where *user* is the user's logon name.

At logon, Windows 2000 checks the user's account for a user profile path. If the path is valid and the profile exists, Windows 2000 uses the profile. If no profile is specified or the profile is inaccessible for some reason, Windows 2000 creates a profile folder for the user on the local computer, and then copies the contents of the Default User folder to the user's profile folder. Windows 2000 also uses the contents of the All Users folder to define the user's working environment. Any changes to the working environment are saved at logoff for the next session.

 See the section "Configuring Profile Properties" earlier in this chapter to learn how to assign a profile to a user.

Supporting Roaming Users

Roaming users are users who log onto the network from more than one computer. Roaming user profiles provide these users with a consistent working environment and interface that doesn't change from one logon session to the next. The only real difference between a personal or mandatory profile and a roaming profile is how the profile is accessed and where it is stored. The following sections explain.

New Roaming Profile

When you set up a user account, you specify the path to the user's profile. The profile must reside on a server accessible to the user at logon, regardless of logon location. To create a new roaming profile you can simply specify a network path in the user account properties and let Windows 2000 create the profile the first time the user logs on. Changes that the user makes during the session are stored in the profile for future logon sessions.

Preconfigured Roaming Profile

In cases where you don't want the default profile used to create the user's profile, you need to create a profile and place it in the user's profile location. The next time the user logs on that profile will be used to configure the user's working environment. You can't simply copy objects using Explorer to create the profile but instead must use a special function in Windows 2000 for copying profiles. The section "Copying Profiles" later in the chapter explains how to copy profiles.

Using Mandatory Profiles

Mandatory profiles restrict changes to a profile. To create a profile, allow the user to either create a new profile from the default or copy a preconfigured profile to the user's profile location. Then rename the registry file portion of the profile from Ntuser.dat to Ntuser.man. This simple extension change turns the personal profile into a mandatory profile.

Make sure the user doesn't have change access in the network share where the profile is stored. This would enable her to change the extension and convert the manual profile back to a personal profile.

Creating and Managing Profiles

Windows 2000 provides no special utility for creating user profiles. Instead, the profile is created automatically when the user logs on if no profile already exists. As the user makes changes to the working environment, those changes are written back to the registry, effectively updating the user's profile.

The only way to create a user profile is to log onto the target computer, modify the desktop and other environment settings as needed; then log off. Although you can create the profile on any computer and copy it to the desired location, bear in mind that hardware settings stored with the profile (such as display resolution and color depth) might not be applicable on another system. So you should create the profile on a system similar to the one the user will use most often. After you create the profile, log on as Administrator and copy the profile to the required server as explained in the next section.

Copying Profiles

As mentioned previously, you can't copy profiles simply by copying the registry file and folder structure from one place to another in Explorer. Instead, you have to use the System applet in the Control Panel to copy profiles. (Open the Control Panel and double-click System, or right-click My Computer and choose Properties.) Then move to the User Profiles tab (see Figure 18-13).

Select the profile you want to copy from the list, then click Copy To. Type the path to the folder where you want to copy the profile or click Browse to locate the folder. To specify which users and groups can use the profile, click Change. By default, only the user account under which the profile was created can use the profile. Click OK to copy the profile.

When you are logged on with a roaming profile, you can specify how Windows 2000 handles the profile. Open the System object and click the User Profiles tab; then click Change Type. In the resulting dialog, select Roaming profile to have

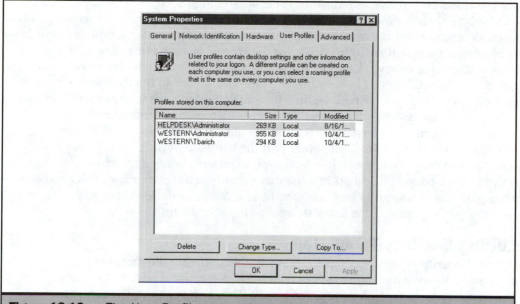

Figure 18-13.   *The User Profiles page shows all profiles created on the computer*

Windows 2000 download the profile from the server. Select Local profile to have
Windows 2000 use the copy of the roaming profile cached on the local computer.

Other Management Tools

A quick look through the Administrative Tools folder and the Control Panel will show
that Windows 2000 provides several MMC snap-ins for managing security. Two of the
most useful ones are the Security Templates and Security Configuration And Analysis
snap-ins. These are a subset of the Security Configuration Tool Set. You'll find discussion
of other snap-ins in the Tool Set in other chapters throughout this book. Or check online
at http://www.microsoft.com/windows for more information.

Security Templates Snap-In

Security templates simplify management of security settings. Windows 2000 provides
several templates as text files in the *systemroot*\\Security\\Templates folder. You can
use templates to define all security settings except IPSec (IP Security) and public key
policies. Security templates offer a quick and easy way to apply security settings for
various scenarios. Templates also serve as a baseline for analyzing security. Templates
are text files with a specific format (essentially, they are .inf files).

Windows 2000 provides templates for basic and high security in a domain, basic and high security for a workstation, basic and high security for member servers, and so forth. When you set up a new system, you can use the appropriate template to quickly apply the settings that are appropriate for the type of system. For example, if you were setting up a new workstation and wanted to apply a high degree of security, you'd use the predefined Hisecws.inf template, applying it to the computer's local or group policy. Once you've had the time to tweak your systems for optimum security, you can use that system's configurations to create your own custom templates.

It's important to understand that template files don't actually control security settings on a computer. Instead, you import the template into a computer or group policy object to apply settings. In effect, applying a template is a little like running a script in the Group Policy snap-in to modify security settings *en masse*. You also can use a template file as a security baseline when analyzing security for a computer or group policy object, comparing the template against the actual values.

Editing Security Templates

Use the Security Templates snap-in shown in the following illustration to view and edit security templates. Open an MMC session and add the Security Templates snap-in to the console; then save it. The snap-in shows the contents of %SystemRoot%\Security\Templates by default, but you can add paths to other folders to include their templates. Right-click Security Templates and choose New Template Search Path to add the folder as a new branch in the tree.

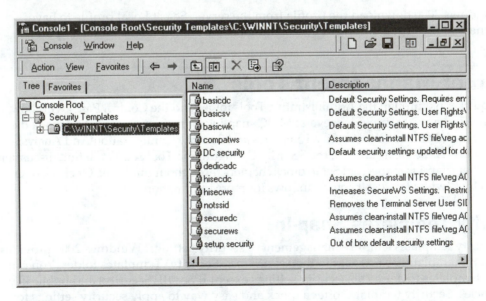

The structure of a template file is the same for all files. Expand a template and modify settings just as you would using the Group Policy editor to modify settings.

Double-click settings to view or change their values. When you're ready to save the template, right-click the template and choose Save to replace the existing file or Save As to create a new template file. Keep in mind as you're modifying templates, however, that you aren't actually modifying any "live" settings. You're just defining a group of settings in a text file. In this sense, the Security Templates snap-in is just a special-purpose text editor designed to handle the structure imposed on template files.

Creating a New Template

If you're a real glutton for punishment, or want to review and set every possible setting, you can create a new template by configuring all settings from scratch. Right-click the location in the tree where you want the new template stored and then choose New Template. Specify the template name and click OK. Modify the settings in the template and then save the changes. To view or change a template's description (comments), right-click the template and choose Set Description.

Applying Settings with a Template

Are you ready to apply settings using a template? You'll need the Security Configuration And Analysis snap-in, discussed in the next section.

Security Configuration And Analysis (SCA) Snap-In

The Security Configuration And Analysis snap-in (Figure 18-14) allows an administrator to analyze security settings for the local policy or group policy. You also can apply settings from one or more templates to the selected object. Finally, you can export settings from the selected object to a template file for use as a baseline or applying to another policy object.

In the SCA snap-in, you use a security database as a baseline configuration against which you analyze the current settings of the selected object. The database can also serve as the group of settings you apply to an object. You import one or more template files into the snap-in to create the database. You can merge multiple templates or overwrite settings with a single template depending on your requirements.

Use the SCA snap-in to analyze current system settings against those defined in the current database. The snap-in builds a side-by-side comparison that you can review for potential security problems. You can change individual settings or apply settings in the database to the system. If you prefer, you can open the Group Policy snap-in and make the changes there.

Defining the Database

Within the SCA snap-in, you can create a new database or open an existing one. You typically import one or more templates to create a new database, as follows:

1. Open the SCA snap-in, right-click Security Configuration And Analysis, and choose Open Database.

CONNECTING WITH
WINDOWS 2000

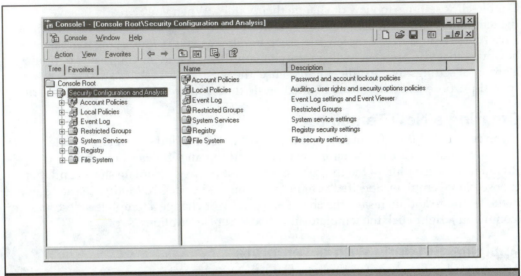

Figure 18-14.   *Use Security Configuration And Analysis to compare current settings against a database of settings that you define*

2. Specify a new database filename and click Open. The snap-in displays the Import Template dialog.

3. Choose a template to import into the database and click Open.

4. Right-click Security Configuration And Analysis again and choose Import Template if you want to merge another template. Choose another template, deselect the Clear option, and then click Open.

Analyzing the System

Once you define the baseline, you can analyze the system settings against the current database. Use these steps to perform the analysis:

1. Open or create the desired database.

2. Right-click Security Configuration And Analysis and choose Analyze Computer Now.

3. Specify the name of the file where you want errors logged and click OK. The snap-in analyzes the system settings against the database.

4. Expand the branches you're interested in and compare settings. A green check in the icon beside each setting indicates consistency (a match). A red "X" indicates inconsistency (mismatch). No icon indicates the attribute was not part of the database and therefore was not analyzed.

Configuring the System

You can use the SCA snap-in to apply security settings on a sort of global basis, applying all the settings in the database in one operation. To make individual changes, you would instead use the Group Policy snap-in. Follow these steps to apply all settings in the loaded database to the local system policy:

1. Open or create the desired database.

2. Analyze the system.

3. Make any desired changes to settings. Double-click a setting, select Define this policy in the database, and then specify the desired setting. This defines the setting in the database only, not the local setting.

4. When you've configured the database as desired, right-click Security Configuration And Analysis, choose Configure Computer Now, and click OK.

5. Specify the log file for error logging and click OK.

Exporting the Database

If you've spent a lot of time analyzing and configuring a system, you might want to export that system's settings for use elsewhere. Once you export the settings to a template, you can use the template to apply the settings to other systems with relatively little effort. Use these steps to export the current database to a security template file:

■ Configure the database settings as desired in the SCA snap-in.

■ Right-click Security Configuration And Analysis and choose Export Template.

■ Specify a filename and folder for the template INF file and click Save.

Chapter 19

Mobile Computing

Windows 2000 is the first version of Windows NT to have mobile computing support built in from the ground up. Many vendors, such as IBM and Digital, wrote special drivers to support their notebooks under Windows NT 4, but power management support from Microsoft was minimal.

Windows 2000 has inherent support for mobile computing devices through its support of systems based on the Advanced Configuration and Power Interface (ACPI), the successor standard to Advanced Power Management, used in older hardware.

Support for mobile computing in Windows 2000 goes far beyond power management, though. Windows 2000 Professional, the version used by notebook users, provides tools that assist the user in common mobile computing scenarios. It also has flexible facilities for connecting to networks and, in general, works to make the computing experience both on and off the network as seamless as possible.

Mobile Hardware Considerations

Very few notebook computers are shipped today without explicit support for Windows 98. In fact, the vast majority is shipped with Windows 98 preinstalled and configured. But you can't make any assumptions about support for Windows 2000 on a particular model of notebook, even from a top-tier vendor like IBM, Compaq, or Toshiba. The first thing you should do when shopping for a notebook on which to install Windows 2000 or deciding whether to install Windows 2000 on a notebook you already have is to check whether it is supported on your machine.

All large system vendors' Web pages describe the software, including operating systems, that they support on their hardware. You should also check the Windows Hardware Compatibility List (HCL) to see which products are supported on which systems.

The HCL is included on the Windows 2000 CD, but a better, more current version can be obtained at http://www.microsoft.com/hcl/. At this Web site you can see not only which systems support specific versions of Windows, but also whether there is driver support for particular peripheral devices, such as network adapters.

If a system is *not* listed as being supported, it may still work with Windows 2000, but you are taking the chance that it will not, and the system vendor and Microsoft may reasonably claim that you attempted an unsupported configuration. If you want to try anyway, take reasonable precautions such as backing up any data (which you should do even on a supported configuration), and leave time to test the system after you are done installing. Exercise all the hardware on the notebook that you will need, such as network and other PCMCIA adapters, Universal Serial Bus (USB) devices, and your modem. Also, check the Power Management applet (see the section "Power Management," later in this chapter) and test Windows 2000 both while plugged in and on battery to see that you are getting reasonable power management from the operating system.

Windows 2000 adds support for significant new classes of hardware into the operating system. The most important is ACPI, a hardware configuration and management standard that Windows 2000 uses for device management including power management. As we will discuss in Chapter 22, ACPI is at the heart of Windows 2000 hardware management and its support for Plug and Play.

Windows 2000 also supports USB, a new peripheral bus that is included in most new notebook computers. USB is particularly convenient for notebooks, because it allows devices to be attached on the fly, meaning that all USB devices are Plug and Play capable. USB devices also usually get their power from the system through the USB connection—one less power adapter for mobile users to carry.

Windows 2000 also supports docking stations and hot docking and undocking of the computer, allowing you to move your notebook computer from your desk to home to the train or anywhere else without rebooting; Windows will adjust to whatever devices are available.

Finally, many new notebooks support multiple batteries and newer "smart" batteries, and Windows 2000 has explicit support for these.

Hardware Profiles

A hardware profile tells Windows 2000 about different physical configurations of a particular computer, most often a mobile computer. If you're using a notebook and you plug into a variety of different hardware scenarios, you can make a different hardware profile for each scenario. When you arrive at a location, you don't have to reconfigure the system for the new combination of devices; instead, Windows 2000 selects from the available hardware profiles, boots to the one you select, and proceeds normally.

Create a Hardware Profile

To create a hardware profile, open the Control Panel System applet or right-click on My Computer and select Properties. Choose the Hardware tab and then click the Hardware Profiles button to open the Hardware Profiles dialog (see Figure 19-1).

You can't create a new profile explicitly, but you can copy an existing one, which is just as well since new profiles will likely resemble existing ones. You can tell Windows 2000 to list profiles when it boots and wait until you select from among them. Additionally, you can tell it to boot a specific profile after a certain number of seconds. To select which profile should be loaded automatically, use the up and down arrow buttons on the dialog box to move the profile to the top of the list.

Next you can enter the Device Manager, which you also access from the System applet, to enable and disable devices for the profile. In the hierarchical display of devices in the Device Manager, you can right-click on specific devices and select the Disable option if it is present. Some devices, such as modems, can be disabled, while others, such as disk drives, cannot.

Disabling a device in this way affects only the currently selected profile. If you want to change settings in a different profile, you need to boot the system into that profile and change settings there. Be careful about naming these profiles precisely so that you know which profile you are using and modifying.

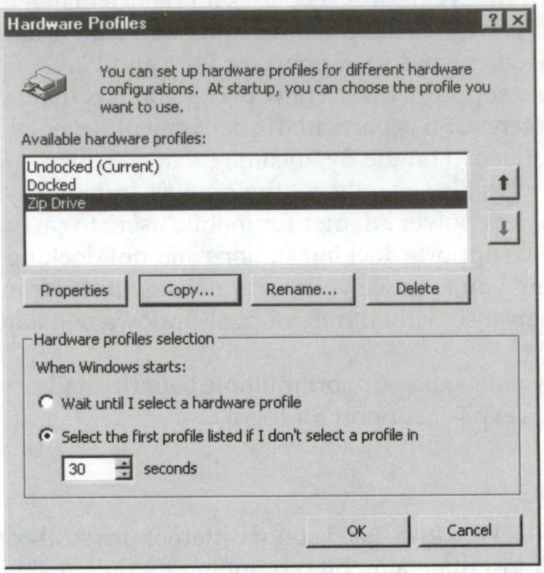

Figure 19-1. *You can make a unique hardware profile for each permutation and combination of devices the computer may contain*

For more control over disabling devices, open the Properties page for a particular device and select the General tab. At the bottom you'll see a Device Usage combo box with three options from which you can choose:

- Use this device (enable)
- Do not use this device in the current hardware profile (disable)
- Do not use this device in any hardware profiles (disable)

Docking Stations

One common use of hardware profiles is to support docking stations. A docking station is a device into which a notebook computer plugs, and which itself has connections to a full-size keyboard, mouse, network, and other standard ports such as you might find on a desktop computer.

Some docking stations are just passive connections to standard devices, and connecting to them is no different from manually plugging the individual devices in to the notebook computer. In this case, even though Windows 2000 supports Plug and Play, you may need to reboot to connect. Other devices support "hot docking," which allows you to connect and disconnect without rebooting the computer.

Power Management

Power management is obviously an important issue for mobile computers. Both the hardware and software support for power management have improved in recent years. Most power management tasks in Windows 2000 are performed in the Power Options Properties applet (Figure 19-2), which you can also load by right-clicking on the power icon in your tray (either a plug or a battery, depending on whether you are plugged in) and selecting Adjust Power Properties.

Power Schemes

You can use the Power Schemes page of this applet to control how long Windows 2000 will wait through a period of inactivity before turning off the monitor and hard disks in the system. You can create different sets of such rules for when the computer is plugged in and when it is running on batteries. You can save these settings and name them, so you can customize the power management behavior of the system for different circumstances. Windows 2000 comes with several typical configurations predefined. On the Power Schemes tab of the Power Options Properties dialog box, click on the combo box labeled Power Schemes to see a list of these schemes.

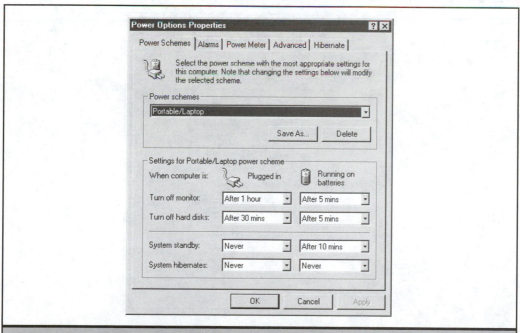

Figure 19-2. *Most power management is performed in the Power Options Properties applet*

In the Settings For Portable/Laptop Power Scheme section, you will find the individual timeout settings. You can set these devices to shut off in as little as one minute, as long as five hours, or never. As the predefined schemes indicate, it makes sense to have shorter timeout periods when running on battery than when plugged in.

System Standby is the time before Windows 2000 sets the system in Standby mode, a low-power mode in which the state of the notebook is maintained in memory, but all hardware shuts down except to maintain the memory. When you bring the system back from Standby mode, it recovers relatively quickly.

System Hibernates is the time before Windows 2000 sets the system in Hibernation mode, in which all memory is written to disk and the system shuts down completely. When you bring the system back from Hibernation mode, it can take several seconds because all the system RAM needs to be read from disk. The more RAM you have, the more memory has to be read back from disk.

Alarms

When you are running on battery power, by default Windows 2000 will warn you when the battery reaches 10 percent power. When it reaches 3 percent, Windows 2000 will warn you again and then put the system in Standby mode. You can adjust this behavior (see Figure 19-3).

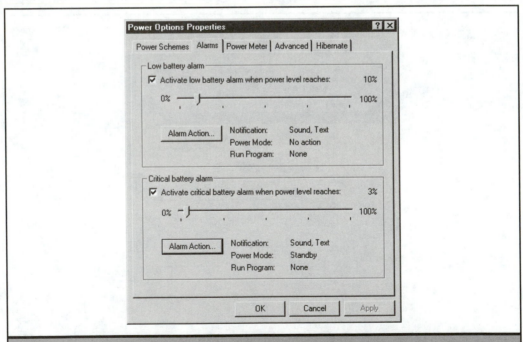

Figure 19-3.   *In the Alarms tab you can customize system behavior in low-power situations*

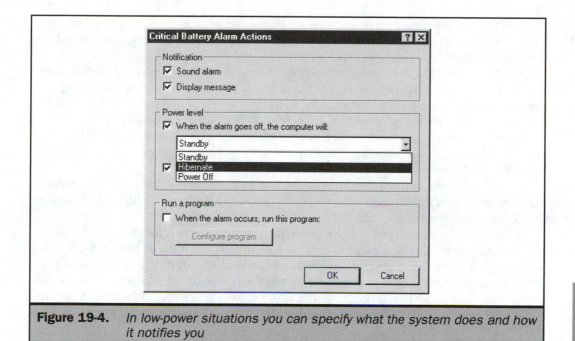

Figure 19-4.   *In low-power situations you can specify what the system does and how it notifies you*

In the Alarms tab of the Power Options Properties window, you can disable these alarms and change the threshold percentages at which they invoke. You can also change the behavior when the alarm goes off. Click Alarm Action in the Properties window to turn off the alarm sound and alarm message. In the Power Level section of the critical Battery Alarm Actions dialog that opens (Figure 19-4), you can tell the system to stand by, hibernate, or power off in this event. You can tell it to force a shutdown even if a program hangs during the process. Finally, you can run a specific program, although doing so in low power conditions can be dangerous.

Dial-Up Connections

As with Windows NT 4 and Windows 98, to have your computer dial out to another computer, you first need to create a new dial-up connection. The terminology for these operations has changed in Windows 2000. For example, there is no longer a Dial-Up Networking folder. Dial-up connections are just another type of network connection.

Creating a New Connection

The first thing you need to do is set up your modem or ISDN device. Refer to Chapter 7 for details on this procedure. To set up the dial-up connection, open the Control Panel and then the Network And Dial-Up Connections applet. A wizard begins.

Click Next on the first page, and you are presented with a series of options for different types of connections. Because you are dialing into an NT network, leave the default selection, Dial-Up To A Private Network, and click Next again.

Next, you provide the phone number of the server into which you are dialing. You may have to apply dialing rules in order to dial 9, 1, or other dialing prefixes, or to force the area code to be dialed if your location uses ten-digit dialing. See Chapter 7 for details. Enter the phone number of the server and click Next to proceed.

If you have sufficient rights, you'll see the Connection Availability page of the wizard. You can choose to set up this connection for your user only or for all users on the system. Make the appropriate selection and click Next.

In the last screen, you can name this connection to distinguish it from other connections you may have. You should choose a new name, such as "My server at work," and optionally check the box to create a shortcut to this connection on your desktop.

When you click Next, you see the Dial-Up/Logon dialog box for the new connection you just created. Your username will already be in the appropriate field, as will the phone number you supplied in the wizard and appropriate dial-up rules. You can change the username, if appropriate for your server account, and enter a password in the Password field. If you check the box labeled Save Password, Windows 2000 will remember your password the next time you attempt to connect on this connection.

The Properties Dialog

If, later on, you want to modify the settings for this dial-up connection, select Properties in the Connect <server name>dialog box. This will open a tabbed dialog box with the same title as your server connection.

The General Tab

The default tab on the properties dialog is General (Figure 19-5). Here you will find the modem or ISDN device you are using for the connection. If you have more than one such device, you can click on the device name, labeled Connect Using:, and choose a different device. To change the properties of this device, click Configure. See Chapter 7 for details on these settings. You can also change the phone number or dialing rules. If you select the Show Icon In Taskbar When Connected check box, then while you are connected an icon will appear on your taskbar that lets you obtain status about the connection or disconnect.

The Options Tab

In the Options tab, you can change many details of how Windows 2000 dials up the server (see Figure 19-6). If you select Display Progress While Connecting, you will see a progress indicator as you are dialing up the server and logging in. This is generally a useful option, so check it if it is not checked by default.

The Prompt For Name And Password, Certificate, Etc. option, which is selected by default, controls whether the username and password are requested in the login dialog. This should be selected by default, and you should leave it that way.

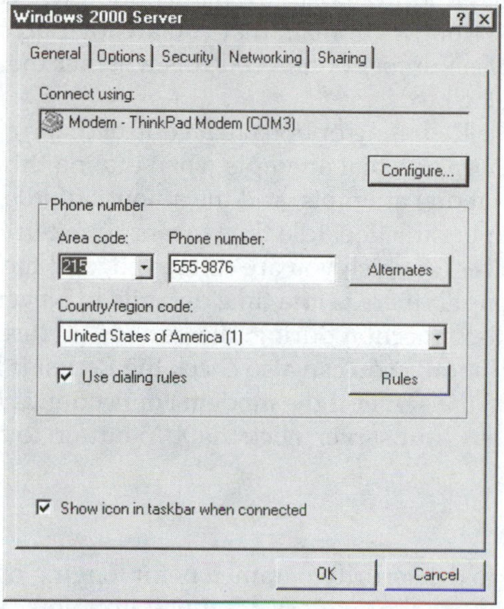

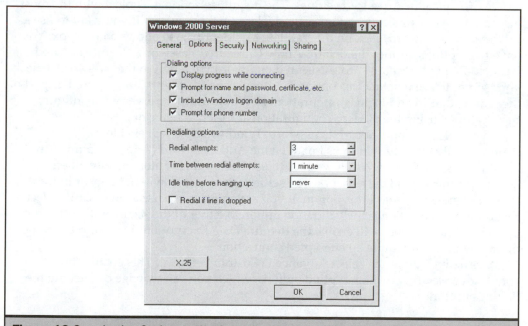

Figure 19-5.   *In the General tab of the Connection Properties dialog, you can change the modem and phone number parameters*

Figure 19-6.   *In the Options tab of the Connection Properties dialog, you can change parameters in the login dialog box*

Checking the Include Windows Logon Domain option will cause Windows 2000 to include the name of the Windows domain that you are logging into in the logon dialog.

The Prompt For Phone Number option controls whether the phone number appears in the logon dialog box.

The next section is the Redialing options that control dialing options for this server. You can change the number of redial attempts when dialing this particular server, the amount of time between redial attempts, and the amount of idle time the system should wait before dropping the line. Idle time means time during which you perform no operations on the server to which you are connected, and the option for disconnecting (hanging up) if there is idle time defaults to Never. You can enter a time if you want automatic disconnection during idle periods (in case you forget you're connected and go on vacation). You can also check the Redial If Line Is Dropped box to have the computer redial the server if the modem connection is lost. If you are using an X.25 network to connect to your server, click the X.25 button to adjust the settings for that connection.

The Security Tab

The Security tab relates to the security parameters for logging onto the network in your dial-up connection. If you are the network administrator, you can set the server side of this connection to require the user to enable certain of these options, such as a smart card or a secure connection.

In the Main Security Options portion of the Security tab (Figure 19-7), you have the choice of Typical or Advanced settings. The default selection is Typical with the most insecure type of connection, an unsecured (clear-text) password. If you want to use a more secure password, click on the Validate My Identity As Follows combo box. You have two options besides the default Allow Unsecured Password: Require Secured Password and Use Smart Card. A secured password will encrypt the password. Check your server to see whether this option, or other security options, are required as part of the remote dial-in and login configuration. In Windows 2000 Server you configure these settings using the modem configuration and Active Directory.

If you select Require Secured Password, Windows 2000 will enable the Automatically Use My Windows Login Name And Password (And Domain If Any) option, which will cause Windows 2000 to use these values automatically when authenticating you on the network. The settings you specify will not appear in the login scheme if you select this option. If you are equipped to use a smart card, select that option. If you change the validation option to either of the secure authentication options, Windows 2000 will enable the Require Data Encryption (Disconnect If None) option, which will require an encrypted connection.

Alternatively, you can select Advanced (Custom Settings). This enables fine control over security and encryption options, which you can manage by clicking the Settings button.

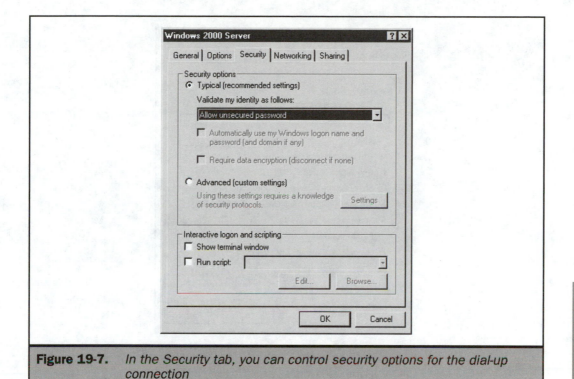

Figure 19-7. *In the Security tab, you can control security options for the dial-up connection*

In the Interactive Logon And Scripting section, you can tell Windows 2000 to open a terminal window to show you the details of the connection, and specify a script to run to control the logon process.

Select Advanced to enable the Settings button, which you can click to open the Advanced Security Settings dialog from which you can control specific security options (see Figure 19-8).

The first combo box controls, entitled Data Encryption, let you specify whether the encryption on the connection is disallowed, optional, or required.

The main Logon Security section of this dialog box has two options: Use Extensible Authentication Protocol (EAP) and Allow These Protocols. If you select EAP, Windows 2000 will enable two options: Smart Card Or Other Certificate (Encryption Enabled) and MD-5 Challenge. It is also possible to install third-party EAP providers that would then become available in this list. MD-5 is a standard password hashing scheme. Smart Card Or Other Certificate (Encryption Enabled) is helpful when you are using a digital certificate provided in a hardware smart card or in a file-based certificate. If you choose the certificate option, click the Properties button to specify the Certificate Authority and other options.

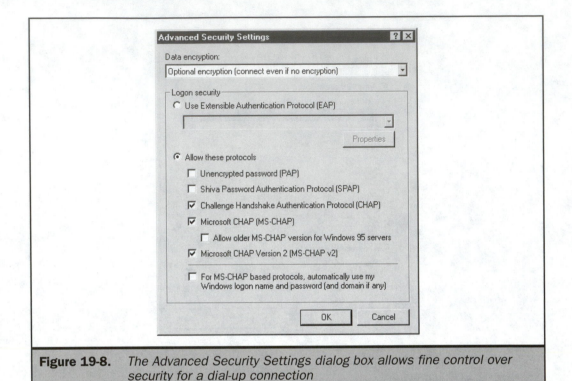

Figure 19-8. *The Advanced Security Settings dialog box allows fine control over security for a dial-up connection*

If you don't use EAP, you can select Allow These Protocols to pick specific authentication protocols that work with different servers and server configurations. You can also specify, if you are using MS-CHAP, that Windows 2000 should automatically use your default login name, password, and domain.

The Networking Tab

On the Networking tab (Figure 19-9), you will find two sets of options. In the first you specify whether you are dialing into a PPP (point-to-point protocol) or SLIP (Serial Line Interface Protocol) dial-up server. Most Windows-based servers are PPP servers; in fact, Windows 2000 Server will not support SLIP connections. SLIP is provided largely for older legacy, mostly UNIX, systems. If you have selected PPP and are having trouble connecting, press the Settings button on this window and you can modify some options that will help work with certain older PPP servers.

In the Components Checked Are Used By This Connection section of this dialog box, you can specify network protocols for use in this dial-up connection. See Chapter 13 for details on how to configure these settings.

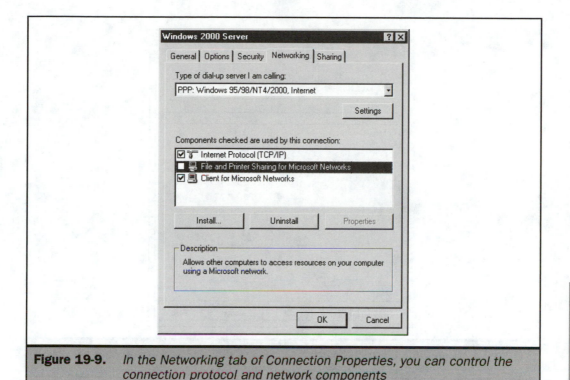

Figure 19-9.   *In the Networking tab of Connection Properties, you can control the connection protocol and network components*

The Internet Connection Sharing Tab

The Internet Connection Sharing section is designed to let other users on your network access Internet resources through your network connection. Since you are setting up a mobile computer to dial into a network, this option is not applicable.

Locations

If you use your modem on the road, you have to tell Windows 2000 about the different locations from which you are dialing. Using the Phone And Modem Options applet (Figure 19-10) in Control Panel (see Chapter 7 for more details), you can define these different locations.

Each location has a large number of options that go with it. The most obvious is the area code, which Windows needs to know in part so that it can tell if you are in the same area code as the number you are calling.

Choose New to create a new location definition. The Edit dialog box (Figure 19-11) is the same as the New dialog box, but values from an existing definition are included.

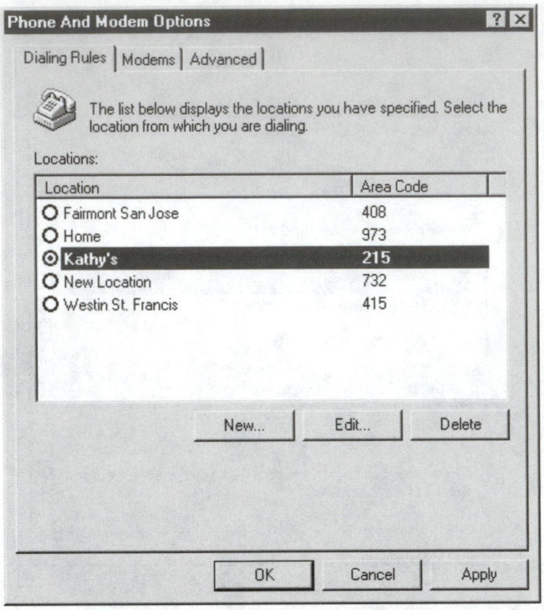

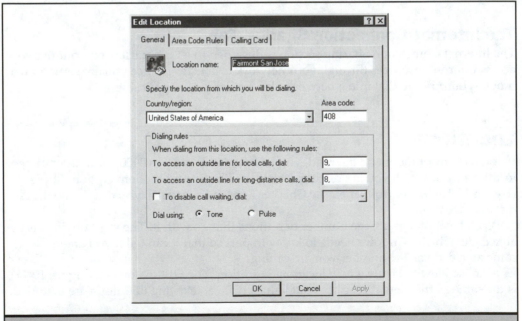

Figure 19-10.   *The Phone And Modem Options applet lets you define locations with area codes, dialing rules, and other localized options*

Figure 19-11.   *Each location can have a different access line, country, and call waiting options*

On the General tab of this dialog box you can give the location a memorable name (such as the name of the hotel or remote office at which you are working). If you are outside of your default country, you can specify which country you're in and the area code. Many offices and hotels require you to dial 9 or some other prefix to get an outside line, and you can specify different prefixes for local and long-distance. Finally, if your phone line has call waiting, you may want to disable it to prevent it from interfering with your data call. Windows makes it easy to include the code (usually *70) that disables call waiting.

Tip	*Windows figures out if you're making a long-distance call by checking your local area code against the area code you are calling. This isn't always accurate, as some long-distance numbers may be within your area code and some local calls may be in a different area code. C'est la vie; it's not perfect.*

The Area Code Rules tab of this dialog box is of increasing importance as many areas of the U.S. get new area codes and some areas get ten-digit dialing, where you must use the area code for all calls, even local ones.

The rules control, in precise detail, how to deal with different area codes and prefixes (usually known as *exchanges,* but Microsoft already uses that term for something else). For example, to tell Windows that a certain area uses ten-digit dialing, create a new area code rule. In the resulting dialog box (see Figure 19-12), enter the area code. If all phones in that area code must use ten-digit dialing, leave the default

CONNECTING WITH WINDOWS 2000

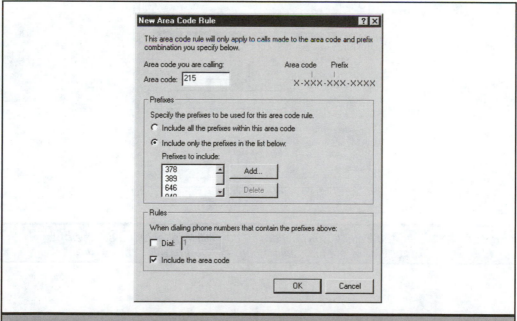

Figure 19-12.   *You can customize the circumstances under which Windows uses ten-digit dialing by creating area code rules*

selection of Include All The Prefixes In This Area Code. Otherwise, select the alternative option Include Only The Prefixes In The List Below and press Add to put prefixes in the list.

Once you have defined the numbers for which the rule applies, define the actual rules in the bottom section. You can specify that all calls to such numbers should be prefixed by 1 (or some other prefix), and that they should always use the area code, which implements ten-digit dialing.

Dialing via modem with a calling card used to be guesswork and luck. Windows has made it easy to use one of a large number of calling cards, even including the network access phone numbers into the definitions.

If you want to use a calling card, select the Calling Card tab in the Edit Location dialog (Figure 19-13). Scroll through the Card Types list until you find the appropriate entry. Enter your account number and, if needed, PIN in the fields below.

If you need to define a new calling card entry, perhaps for a private network, click New. In the tab that opens, enter the card type, account number, and PIN for the new card. In the tabs for Long Distance, International, and Local Calls, you can define the sequence of fields to dial and prompts to wait for.

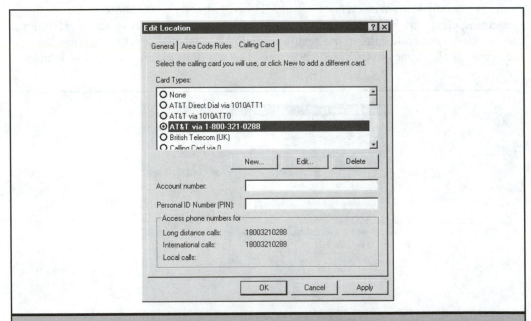

Figure 19-13.   *In the Calling Card page, you can tell Windows to use one of a number of popular calling cards or define rules for another*

Connecting

To dial into the server once you have your connection set up, click the Dial button in the logon dialog box. Windows 2000 will dial the server. Once the modem connects, your client will use the connection to attempt to log on to the server.

It may take a few seconds, because communicating over telephone lines is not as fast as communicating via network cable. Once the information has been sent from your computer to the server and the authentication processes are completed, Windows 2000 will log you onto the server.

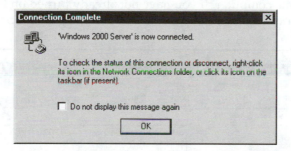

After you are connected, you will be able to access the network just as though you had connected over a local area network (see Figure 19-14). You can map network drives and, if supported by your connection, access the Internet through your dial-up server.

Some Windows' networking facilities won't work the same with dial-up connections as they do with LAN connections. For example, you won't see computers mapped in Computers Near Me or Entire Network. But you can use Explorer's Tools | Map Network Drive command or the command line Net Use command to map network drives on the server.

Right-click on the connection icon on your Desktop and select Status from the shortcut menu. In the Server Status dialog box, you'll see the speed of your connection and how much traffic has transpired. In the Details tab, you can see protocols you are using, as well as the IP addresses of your computer and the server to which you are connected.

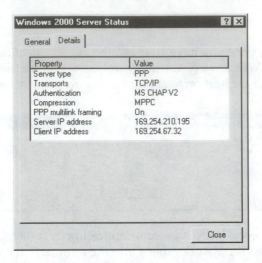

You can also connect to the network over your dial-up connection directly from your Windows 2000 logon screen, which you access when you press CTRL-ALT-DEL to restart or log onto the computer. If you have not already turned on Details in that login screen, do so and you will have an option to Log On Using Dial-Up Connection.

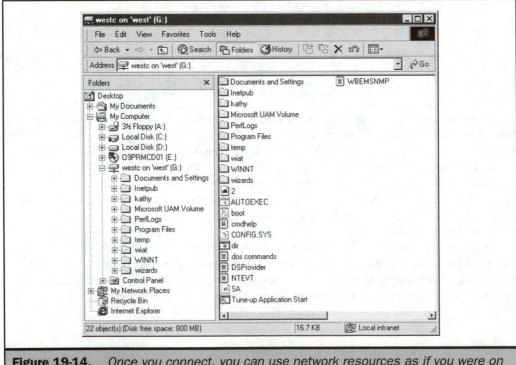

Figure 19-14.   *Once you connect, you can use network resources as if you were on the LAN*

If you want to disconnect from the network, right-click on the connection icon on your desktop and select Disconnect from the shortcut menu.

Using Resources Offline

Windows NT and Windows 95/98 had a little-used feature called the Briefcase, the goal of which was to let users define data to be used offline and then to synchronize the changes when connected again later on. Briefly put, the Briefcase was an inconvenient and obscure failure. In Windows 2000, Microsoft has finally done this job correctly.

Windows 2000 users can simply designate files or entire directory subtrees to be available while offline. When you are offline, you can then refer to them as if you were still online. For example, if the F: drive is a network drive on your system, you can mark files on it to be available offline (see Figure 19-15). When you are offline, you can still use those files on the F: drive as if you were connected.

Figure 19-15. *Windows 2000 Professional users can make a file available offline just by right-clicking and choosing a command*

Using Web Pages Offline

Users can also make Web pages available offline by right-clicking on an Internet shortcut and selecting Make Available Offline (Figure 19-16). This will work for Windows Internet shortcuts only, such as entries in your Links, Favorites, and shortcuts on the desktop; it won't work with normal links inside a Web page. A wizard walks you through the process. This feature replaces the Internet Explorer 4 subscriptions feature.

When you choose to take a Web page offline, Windows 2000 walks you through a wizard to determine which, if any, of the page's linked pages you also wish to take offline and what the schedule of updates will be.

The first decision you have to make is whether to download linked pages. Be very careful with this option. It's easy to underestimate the number of links on a typical Web page, how much data is in those links, and how long it will take to update it.

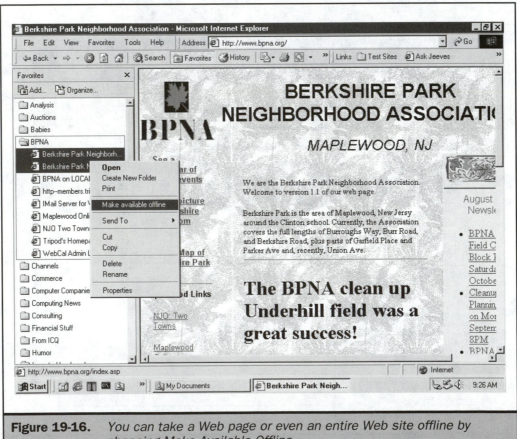

Figure 19-16. *You can take a Web page or even an entire Web site offline by choosing Make Available Offline*

You may be better off choosing specific links and making them available offline specifically, rather than choosing to take the data from all links on a home page.

Next, you define the schedule on which the offline version will be updated. The default is to update it when you choose to run the Synchronization utility (Tools | Synchronize in Internet Explorer). You can also define a timed schedule or use a previously defined schedule.

To create a new schedule, select I Would Like To create A New Schedule and click Next (Figure 19-17). This scheduling wizard allows you to specify that the update occur on increments of whole days at a specific time; for example, every one, two, or three days at 8:45A.M. But later on, you can go to the Synchronization applet's Settings dialog to edit this schedule item so that you have much better control over it.

After you have decided on a schedule, if the Web page requires a username and password, you can specify it. Then press Finish to complete. The Synchronization applet loads and copies the Web pages to a local folder on the mobile computer. (This folder is usually \winnt\Offline Web Pages.) Depending on how much data is on the pages you marked, this could take some time.

Offline files and folders are marked visually for offline use with little round-trip arrows in the bottom left corner, as shown in the following image.

Windows 2000 Professional users can synchronize files with any SMB-based server, such as Windows NT 4, Novell Netware, even Windows 95 and 98. But when you synchronize with Windows 2000 servers, the administrator gets special capabilities. For example, specific files and folders can be marked by the administrator as available but not available to be taken offline for security reasons. Unfortunately, these additional restrictions can be made globally only, to an entire share on the server and not to individual objects within it.

When you update files using the Synchronization Manager (see the section by that title following), only the files that have changed are transferred over the network, speeding up the process considerably. But individual applications can make the process even smarter. By writing to the Synchronization Manager Application Programming

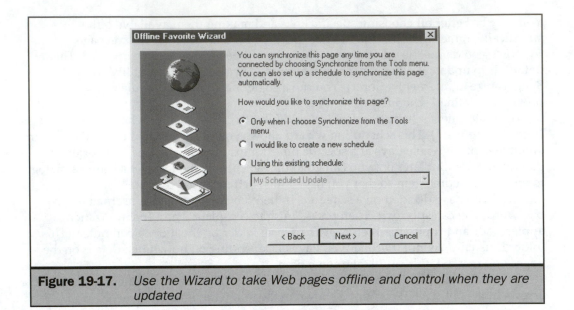

Figure 19-17.   *Use the Wizard to take Web pages offline and control when they are updated*

Interface, a program can tell the Synchronization Manager how to update only the portions of files that have been modified.

By default, certain files, generally database files, such as Access .mdb and dBase .dbf files, cannot be synchronized. If you attempt to synchronize them, you will receive error messages at the end of synchronization. You can modify this behavior in two ways, one in the registry on the client system and the other as an Active Directory Policy on the server.

The registry entry is in HKEY LOCAL MACHINE\Software\Microsoft\Windows\ CurrentVersion\NetCache key. Create a new string named ExcludeExtensions in the form "*.xxx *.yyy *.zzz", where xxx, yyy, and zzz are the extensions you want to exclude from synchronization. If you want to disable exclusion altogether, create an empty string. Unfortunately, you can create only a new exclusion list and the default one is not documented, so you cannot, in effect, remove a specific extension or extensions from the active exclusion list.

To create a new exclusion policy in Active Directory, enter the MMC and load the Group Policy snap-in. In the wizard that appears, select either the default Local computer or click Browse and select the object for which the policy will apply. Click Finish and then OK to exit the Add/Remove snap-in dialog.

Back in the MMC, expand the policy object to Computer Configuration\Administrative Templates\Network\Offline Files\Files Not Cached (Figure 19-18).

Right-click on Files Not Cached and select Properties. The Properties dialog box (Figure 19-19) provides a detailed explanation of the policy. In this environment the extensions should be separated not by spaces (as in the registry) but by semicolons. Of

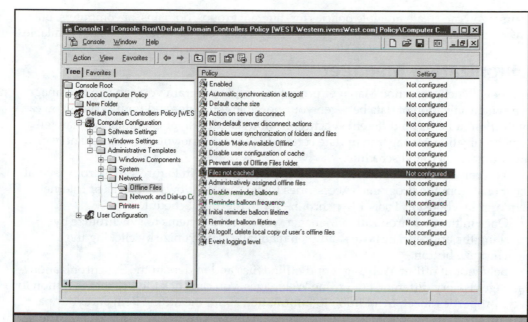

Figure 19-18. By creating an Active Directory policy, you can make synchronization exclusion lists for a domain, group, or computer

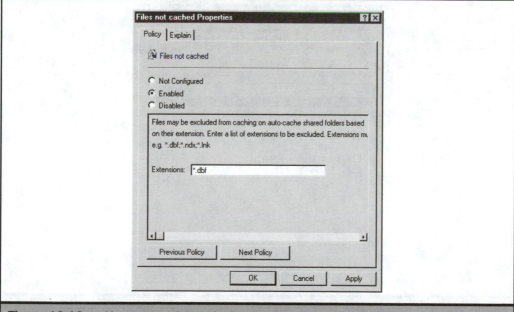

Figure 19-19. You create the exclusion list for the policy; multiple extensions should be separated by semicolons

course, you can create multiple policies for different groups, domains, or computers. But unfortunately, you still must create new exclusion lists, and the default list is not available.

Synchronization Manager

The new Synchronization Manager provides a single program you can use to manage the synchronization of data between your portable computer and your server. You can put different items on different synchronization schedules; for example, you can tell Synchronization Manager to update certain files every time you log onto the network, and others on a timed schedule.

You can access the Synchronization Manager (shown in Figure 19-20) from several locations: from the Programs\Accessories folder, via Windows Explorer or Internet Explorer by choosing Tools | Synchronize, or in the Task Scheduler.

Once in the Synchronization Manager, you can select items to synchronize by checking the appropriate boxes and then manually synchronize by clicking the Synchronize button.

Behavior of offline Web pages and offline files and folders in the Synchronization Manager is very different. For offline Web pages, you can click the Properties button to see a properties sheet. In addition to information about the offline item and your past synchronizations, you can modify the schedule for synchronizing it and change the behavior of synchronization.

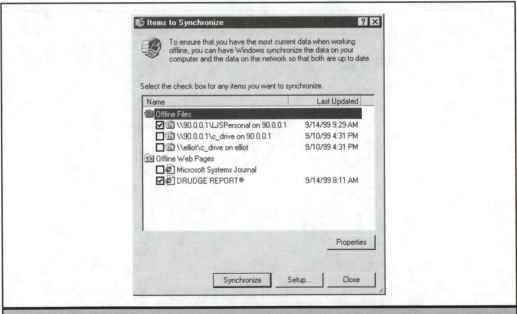

Figure 19-20.   *The Synchronization Manager can be used to synchronize all offline content, from network servers and the Internet, in one place*

Select the Schedule tab in the Offline Web Page Properties dialog. Here you can add a schedule for synchronizing this page alone. In this schedule you can set the page to synchronize on a daily basis only, meaning every one, two, three days, or so on, and at a particular time. You can also tell the Synchronization Manager to connect to the Internet at that time, if necessary.

Select the Download tab in the Offline Web Page Properties dialog. Here you can tell Synchronization Manager whether to follow links from the page and make the linked pages available offline as well. You can tell it not to follow links (such as advertisements) outside of the site of the page you took offline, and you can limit the amount of data, in kilobytes, that it should download. You can specify a username and password if required for the page, and have an e-mail sent if the page changes. If you click Advanced, you can tell Synchronization Manager whether to download images, audio files, ActiveX controls, and other rich content.

The Synchronization Settings dialog box (Figure 19-21) of the Synchronization Manager controls behavior for the whole program. You can set different behaviors for different network connections. You can also tell the Synchronization Manager to begin synchronizing when the system is idle or when you log on or log off. If you tell it to synchronize when the system is idle, you can control the amount of idle time necessary before synchronizing begins and whether the system should synchronize if running on battery power.

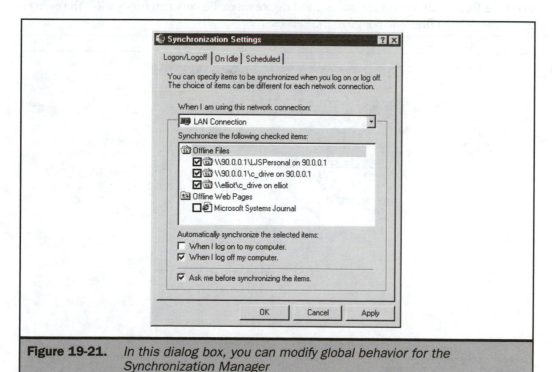

Figure 19-21.   *In this dialog box, you can modify global behavior for the Synchronization Manager*

If you click on the Scheduled tab of the Synchronization Settings dialog, you can view your current synchronization schedules. Create a new one by clicking Add to start a wizard. In the wizard, you can choose specific items to synchronize and a network connection to use. Then you can set the schedule for this synchronization, every day, on weekdays, or by some number of days (every two days, every three days, and so on), at a particular time of day. Then you can give the schedule a name and finish.

But if, on the Scheduled tab, you select one of the listed items and press the Edit button, you will find far greater flexibility in configuring the schedule and properties of synchronization. For example, you can schedule monthly and weekly, and you can tell the Synchronization Manager to repeat the task for some period of time as it executes (Figure 19-22). In the Settings tab of the Edit page, you can tell the Synchronization Manager to delete a task if its schedule is such that it will never again execute. You can also set an upper limit on its execution time, and adjust its behavior more precisely when running on batteries.

To remove an offline Web page from the Synchronization Manager list, select it, click Properties, and uncheck the Make This Page Available Offline option. Unfortunately, there is no way to remove a synchronization entry for a file or folder, although you can remove the local (offline) copies of the files. To do so, click Properties for the item; this will open an Explorer window with the Offline Files Folder. There you can sort by the location column, select the files for that synchronization, and delete them. Be very careful to select the correct files—the deleted files will not go to the Recycle Bin.

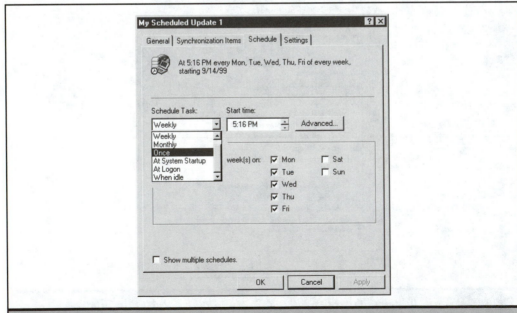

Figure 19-22.   *The Edit screen for schedules is much more powerful than the wizard that creates them*

Printing on the Road

When you're on the road with your portable computer, you probably want to print documents just as often as you do when you're back at the office. But very few of us carry around portable printers. You have a couple of options.

In Windows you can print to your printer back at the office, and Windows will defer the actual print job until it can once again communicate with the printer. Just go ahead and print the document. When you receive an error message that the printer is unavailable, click OK and ignore the error. When you connect to your printer back at the office, a message will appear saying that you have print jobs in the queue, asking if you want to print them.

But if you need hard copy then and there, the oldest trick in the traveling computer user's book is faxing the document to the hotel fax (or some other nearby fax machine). You can use Windows 2000's fax driver (see Chapter 7), or you may have access to fax services on the Internet.

The
Complete
Reference

Part IV

Inside Windows 2000

Chapter 20

File Systems

Y ou can choose among three file systems for disk partitions on a computer running Windows 2000: FAT, FAT32, and NTFS. This chapter discusses these file systems and also covers some of the file system features available in NTFS.

FAT and FAT32

The FAT (File Allocation Table) is a table of links that hold information about the data blocks that make up a file. The first FAT file system (which used 12-bit entries) was introduced with DOS. The first DOS version (1.0) didn't support subdirectories, and as DOS improved, the FAT file system was altered to handle the new features. For example, when DOS 4.0 was released, FAT entries were increased to 16 bits to handle partitions that were larger than 32MB.

The FAT is on the disk, along with a duplicate FAT, which is an effort to provide an element of fault tolerance (however, a damaged FAT is rarely successfully repaired). The system also contains a root directory section that has a fixed size, limiting the number of files that can be located in the root directory.

The FAT contains entries for filenames and file attributes such as the size, the attribute byte (an 8-bit entry for information such as hidden, read-only, etc.), last modification time/date (16-bit entries), and the starting allocation unit, which is a pointer to the file's entry in the FAT. If the file is not contiguous, there are FAT entries pointing to each block that contains an allocation unit for the file. This is called a *chain*. The last, or "end of file," entry contains the hexadecimal pattern FFFF, to indicate that it's the end of the chain. When the file is loaded or saved, the operating system uses the chain to track the location of the file fragments. As the chain grows longer (the disk is highly fragmented), performance suffers.

The files themselves are stored in clusters, the size of which depends on the size of the drive. Because the size of the FAT itself is fixed, the adjustments for handling large drives are made by changing the cluster size. The size of a cluster can be 2048 bytes, 4096 bytes, or 8192 bytes. The 16-bit length of the FAT entries limited the size of hard disks to 128MB (assuming a 2048-byte cluster). Theoretically, FAT could support a 512MB drive, but the cluster size would have to be 8192, which is highly inefficient. Starting with DOS 5.0, partitions up to 2GB were supported by creating separate FATs for each drive partition (up to four partitions).

FAT32, a table that held 32-bit entries, was introduced in Windows 95 OSR2. This new design brought a number of features to FAT file systems:

- The 32GB partition size limit was eliminated.

- The root directory isn't placed in a fixed position and can be relocated.

- There is no limit on the number of entries that can be placed on the root directory.

- The backup copies of the FAT actually work to resolve crashes.

- More important, FAT32 permits far more clusters on a disk by allowing 4096 bytes in a cluster, even for large drives.

NTFS

Windows 2000 Server introduced a new version of NTFS, called NTFS 5, that has built-in support for a variety of features that help you manage domains, user accounts, and security features. This is not the same NTFS system available in Windows NT 4. The features that NTFS 5 supports are part of the core design of Windows 2000, and include (but are not limited to), the following:

- **Active Directory**   Holds all the objects in the operating system, allowing and preventing access through permissions. See Chapter 15 to learn about the Active Directory.

- **Disk quotas**   Limits the use of disk space on a per-user or per-group basis. Chapter 27 has detailed information on disk quotas.

- **Encryption**   Automatic encryption and decryption of file data as files are written and read. See the section "Encrypting File System" later in this chapter.

- **Distributed File System**   Use a single directory tree to include multiple servers and shares. See the section "Distributed File System" later in this chapter.

- **Removable and Remote Storage**   Manage storage on remote disks. See Chapter 27 for information about using these features.

NTFS Master File Table (MFT)

Instead of a File Allocation Table, NTFS uses a special file called the Master File Table (MFT) to track all the files and directories on a volume. The size of the MFT is dynamic, and is automatically extended when necessary. The MFT is really an array of records, a database file of all the files on the system.

Each record in the MFT is usually fixed at 1K, and the first 16 records contain information about the volume. These volume-specific records are called the *metadata files*, which is the terminology used for overhead structures in the file system.

Normally, each record in the MFT corresponds to one file or directory in the file system. The record contains the file's attributes, including items such as read-only and archive flags, creation and last-accessed dates, the filename, and a security descriptor.

Note   *The filename in the record is usually two filenames: a long filename and a DOS-compatible filename (8.3).*

More important, and certainly far different from FAT, the file data is just another attribute of NTFS. There is a limit to the amount of data that can fit in the MFT record, and anything over that limit is replaced in the record with pointers to where the file data resides on the disk. The MFT record can hold about 750 bytes of file data (the actual amount depends on the number of attributes being stored in the MFT record). Small data files (under 750 bytes) can fit entirely within their MFT entries, providing incredibly good performance and no risk of fragmentation for those files.

There is at least one entry in the MFT for each file on the NTFS volume, including the MFT itself (which is a file) and other metadata files, such as the log file, the bad cluster map, and the root directory.

Of course, most files are not small enough to fit their data into their MFT entries, so the MFT stores their data on the disk. NTFS allocates files in units of clusters, which are referenced in two ways:

- Virtual Cluster Numbers (VCNs), from 0 through *n-1* where there are *n* clusters in the file.

- Logical Cluster Numbers (LCNs), which correspond to the clusters' numbers on the volume.

VCNs are the analog for file offsets requested by applications. An application knows the format of the data it uses in a file, and uses it to calculate a byte offset within the logical format of the file. When the application requests a read or write at that address of the file, NTFS divides that number by cluster size to determine the VCN to read or write.

LCNs are an index to the clusters on a volume, and when there is a need to read or write, NTFS uses an LCN to calculate an address on the disk. The calculation involves multiplying the LCN by the number of sectors per cluster, and then reading or writing sectors starting at that address on the disk. By associating VCNs with their LCN, NTFS associates a file's logical addressing with the physical locations on disk.

If any attribute (usually the file data attribute) doesn't fit in the MFT record, NTFS stores it in a new, separate set of clusters on the disk, called a *run* or an *extent*. As a matter of fact, other attributes besides the data attribute could become large enough to force new extents. For example, long filenames in Windows NT can be up to 255 characters that consume 2 bytes apiece (caused by the fact that filenames are stored in Unicode). An attribute that is stored within the MFT entry is called a *resident* attribute. When an attribute is forced out to an extent, it is called a *nonresident* attribute. This means that unless users consistently create extremely small files, the majority of the files on a volume have data that is a nonresident attribute.

When the extent needs to be enlarged (usually because a user adds data to a file), NTFS attempts to allocate physically contiguous clusters to the same extent. If there is no more contiguous space available, NTFS will allocate a new extent elsewhere on the disk, separating the file into two fragments. If the new extent also fails to provide enough contiguous space, the action is repeated. The data attribute header (kept within the MFT record) stores that information in the form of LCNs and run lengths, and NTFS uses the information to locate the extents.

In some cases, usually when the number of attributes is extremely large, NTFS may be forced to allocate an additional MFT entry for the file. If this occurs, NTFS creates an attribute called an *attribute list,* which acts as an index to all the attributes for the file. While this is an unusual situation, the presence of additional MFT entries can greatly slow the performance of operations on the affected files.

Directories are handled very much like files in NTFS. If a directory is small enough, the index to the files to which it points can fit in the MFT record. This information is an attribute, called the Index Root attribute.

If more entries are present than can fit in the MFT record, NTFS creates a new extent with a nonresident attribute called an *index buffer*. For those directories, the index buffers contain what is called a *b+ tree*, which is a data structure designed to minimize the number of comparisons needed to find a particular file entry. A b+ tree stores information (or indexes to information) in a sorted order. A request for a sorted list of the entries in a directory is satisfied quickly, because that is the order of storage in the index buffer. To find a particular entry, the lookup is quick because the trees tend to get wide rather than deep, which minimizes the number of accesses necessary to reach a particular point in the tree.

NTFS Fragmentation

Any rumors you've heard that NTFS prevents fragmentation are untrue. Windows NT and Windows 2000 are much smarter than earlier versions of Windows (and DOS) in allocating disk space to files, and as a result, systems are less prone to fragment files. However, NTFS is not immune to the forces that fragment individual files, and over time files on an NTFS volume will become fragmented. (Incidentally, a side effect of the operating system's efforts to prevent file fragmentation is fragmentation of the system's free space).

When you format a volume with NTFS, you have a choice of cluster size to use. Windows NT offers a default cluster size, based on the size of the volume, but if you have some knowledge about the way the volume is used, you can choose a cluster size that works better for that usage. However, you have to very careful if you opt to bypass the default size. Choosing a smaller cluster size will waste less space but is more likely to cause fragmentation. Larger cluster sizes are less likely to cause fragmentation but will waste more space.

Caution	*Choosing 512-byte clusters can be problematic, since the MFT consists of records that are always 1024 bytes. It is possible, with 512-byte clusters, to have individual MFT entries fragmented. This is not possible on larger sizes, which can hold more than one MFT entry with no waste.*

If a file or directory is contiguous, the cluster size doesn't matter, unless you choose to be upset about wasting a small amount of space. If you know that the volume will hold a very large number of small files, or if you know that almost all of the files will be very large, you have information you can use for a better cluster decision. Also, a very large absolute number of files (on the order of 100,000) will make fragmentation of the MFT more likely. In this case, a larger cluster size will limit the fragmentation in the MFT as it grows to accommodate the files.

It's important to note the distinctions between fragmentation at different levels of data storage. Individual applications, such as Microsoft Office, and database servers such as Oracle, have fragmentation issues within their own data storage. These issues are present regardless of the file system or operating system.

NTFS is not aware of the logical organization of user data. Wherever the file may exist on the disk, and whether or not the file is fragmented, the file system presents it to the application as a single contiguous area of storage. The application's view of the data in the file, however, has a logical structure. For mailing list software, a file is a group of first names, last names, addresses, and so forth. To NTFS, it is just a group of clusters of data.

Applications, in their own internal organization of data, may create gaps in the data, which effectively fragments the data. Like a file system, when you delete data in an application, it may not actually remove the data, but only mark it as deleted. The resulting gaps in the logical storage of data are known as *internal fragmentation*. To combat internal data fragmentation, some applications, such as Microsoft Access, provide utilities to compact the data in the file—in effect, a defragmentation of an internal file. Ironically, these compaction utilities frequently increase the level of fragmentation at the file system level, because they usually create an entirely new copy of the file, consuming large amounts of disk space in the process. Thus, regular defragmentation of your data files may exacerbate fragmentation of your file system.

Applications frequently create temporary files, which occupy space while the users works with the software, opening and saving files. The temporary files are deleted when the software is closed, leaving behind the empty allocated space. Data files may also have allocated but unused space as programs allocate space for their own organizational or performance reasons. Also, the individual files associated with an application can, over time, become physically dispersed across a disk. This type of fragmentation, known as *usage fragmentation*, is an especially difficult problem for a defragmentation program, because normal methods of fragmentation analysis may not identify it.

Fragmentation and defragmentation of directories work similarly to that of files. In fact, to NTFS, a directory is just a type of file, although directories have special types of attributes in their MFT records. While applications manage the contents of data files, NTFS manages the contents of directories, which are b+ trees that provide an indexed access to files contained in the directories.

Directories that hold program files don't grow or shrink much over their lifetimes. But user document directories, and the system's TEMP directory, change size quite a bit. As the number of files in a directory grows, NTFS can accommodate the growth by growing the directory storage. If the contents of the directory shrink, NTFS can also free up the unused space in the directory, but this doesn't always happen because it's a complicated maneuver. The directories that are most likely to grow and shrink are usually those that were created early in the system's configuration, such as My Documents and the TEMP directory. It is quite likely that the growth of these directories is noncontiguous. Because these directories are heavily used, their fragmentation has a real impact on the system's performance.

Speaking of performance, you should be aware that deeply nested directories may present an organizational convenience, but you're paying a performance penalty for them. When NTFS searches its b+ trees for data, it performs the search from the beginning for each level in the directory subtree. Therefore, performance may be better with flatter trees that have larger numbers of files in them than with deeper trees that have fewer files in each. Very deep subtrees can also create problems for applications that have limits to the number of characters in a complete file path (a limit of 255 characters is not unusual).

Note   *You can find information on using the Windows 2000 defragmentation program in Chapter 10.*

NTFS Compression

NTFS file compression is a built-in function of the file system. You can compress the data on an entire volume, in a specific directory, or in a specific file. To enable compression, open the Properties dialog box of a volume, directory, or file, and use the General tab as follows:

- For a volume, select the option Compress Drive To Save Disk Space. You are asked if you want to apply compression only to the root, or include all the folders.

- For a folder, click Advanced, and then select the option Compress Contents To Save Disk Space. You are asked if you also want to apply compression to subfolders.

- For a file, click Advanced, and then select the option Compress Contents To Save Disk Space.

When you view a compressed object's properties in My Computer or Windows Explorer, you see both sizes (see Figure 20-1).

Note   *Compression only works on volumes with 4K clusters or smaller.*

The NTFS compression scheme uses both VCNs and LCNs. In a file that has data stored in nonresident attributes or in extents, the data attribute contains mappings for the starting VCN and starting LCN in the extent, as well as the length in clusters. NTFS manipulates these cluster numbers to achieve compression, using one of two approaches: sparse storage or divided data.

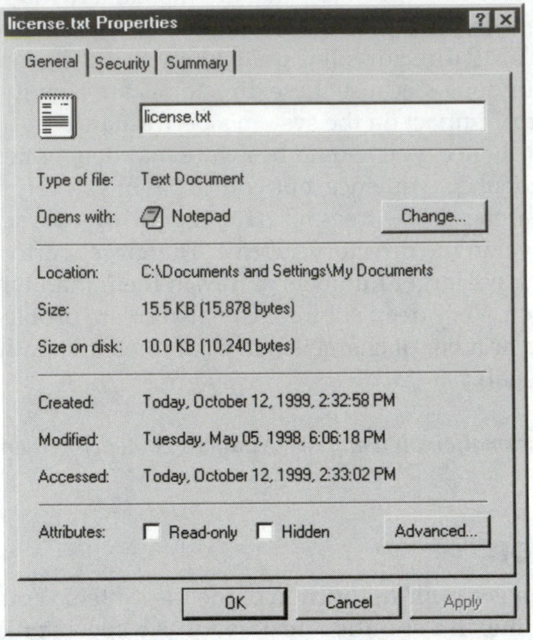

Figure 20-1. *Compressed file properties show the original and compressed sizes*

Sparse storage is a way to commit disk space so that null data blocks aren't stored on the disk. Sometimes, big files have large blocks of nulls (bytes of value 0). NTFS calls these files *sparse files,* and only stores the nonzero data. For example, you may have a 100-cluster file that contains real data in only the first 5 and last 5 clusters—the middle 90 clusters are all zeroes. NTFS can store two extents for this file, each of which is 5 clusters long. The first extent will have VCNs 0 through 4, and the second will have VCNs 95 through 99. NTFS infers that VCNs 5 through 94 are null, and do not need physical storage. If a program requests data in this space, NTFS simply fills the requesting program's buffer with nulls. When (or if) the application allocates real data (nonzero data) to this space, NTFS creates a new extent with the appropriate VCNs.

If a file is not predominately null, NTFS does not try to write the file data inside one extent; instead it divides the data into runs of 16 clusters each. In any particular extent, if compressing the data will save at least 1 cluster, NTFS stores the compressed data, resulting in 15 or fewer clusters. If the data cannot be effectively compressed (random data, for example, is generally not compressible), NTFS simply stores that entire extent as it normally would, without compression. In the MFT record for a compressed file, NTFS can see that there are missing VCNs in the runs, and knows that the file is compressed.

When data is stored in a compressed form, it is not possible to look up a specific byte by calculating the cluster in which it is stored. Instead, NTFS calculates in which 16 cluster run the address is located, decompresses the run back to 16 uncompressed clusters, and then calculates the offset into the file using valid virtual cluster numbers. To make this addressing scheme possible, NTFS ensures that all these runs begin with a virtual cluster number divisible by 16.

NTFS tries to write these runs in a single contiguous space, because the I/O system is already encountering enough added processing and management burden using compressed files without having to fragment individual extents. NTFS also tries to keep the individual, separate runs of the file contiguous, but this is a harder job. As a result, compressed files are more likely to be fragmented than noncompressed files.

> **Note** *NTFS compresses only the file's data attribute, not the metadata.*

Upgrading to NTFS

When you install Windows 2000 over an existing Windows NT 4 NTFS volume, the volume is automatically upgraded to the NTFS 5 file system. The upgrade is mandatory, and you have no control over the process. The file system upgrade is not a process that's spawned by Windows 2000 Setup; it is launched by the NTFS driver after installation is completed. All locally attached NTFS volumes are upgraded to the new version of the NTFS file system, including removable media. Windows NT 4 NTFS volumes that are removed or powered off during installation are upgraded automatically when the drives are next mounted. Any Windows NT 4 NTFS volumes that are not upgraded to NTFS 5 will not be mounted under Windows 2000.

> **Note** *If you want to dual boot between Windows NT 4 and Windows 2000, the NT 4 system must be at Service Pack 4 or better, and running NTFS. The new features supported by NTFS 5 change the data structure on disks, and the ntfs.sys file in SP4 (and higher) can handle the changes.*

When you upgrade over any Windows operating system that is not running NTFS, you are offered an option to convert the hard disk from FAT or FAT32 to NTFS during the text-based phase of Windows 2000 Setup. The screen displays the following message:

```
Upgrading to the Windows NT File System
Do you want Setup to upgrade your drive to NTFS?

Yes, Upgrade my drive
No, Do not upgrade my drive
```

- If you are installing Windows 2000 Server, the default selection is Yes.
- If you are installing Windows 2000 Professional, the default selection is No.

You can convert from FAT or FAT32 after you've installed Windows 2000 with the Convert.exe utility.

Deciding on a File System

Apart from domain controllers, which must run NTFS, you may want to decide on a file system instead of automatically installing NTFS 5. This is commonly an issue if you need to dual boot. This section presents some guidelines for making these decisions.

Choosing FAT or FAT32

There are some instances in which you may want to select FAT or FAT32 as the file system, and most of the time (if not always) this decision applies to workstations on which you are installing Windows 2000 Professional.

■ If you choose FAT, access to the computer and its files is available from every operating system: MS-DOS, any version of Windows, Windows NT, Windows 2000, and OS/2.

■ If you choose FAT32, access to the computer and its files is available through Windows 95 OSR2, Windows 98, and Windows 2000.

The truth is, if there's a grave problem with a workstation (it won't boot, or it boots with serious errors), it's much easier to get to the hard drive and its contents if you're running FAT.

Dual-Boot Considerations

Dual booting is commonly utilized if a computer needs to support applications that don't run in both of the operating systems installed on the machine. You can reboot the computer and choose the appropriate operating system to use a particular application. For workstations, I've seen dual booting used to allow multiple users to get to the operating system and applications needed by each specific user. However, before deciding on a dual-boot system, you must be aware of the compatibility issues between NTFS 5 and other file systems.

The primary rule to remember is that unlike previous versions of Windows NT, Windows 2000 must be installed on its own partition; selecting a new directory is not an option. This means that if your disk doesn't currently have two volumes, you must partition and format it, and then install the operating systems.

If you are dual booting between Windows NT 4 and Windows 2000, and want to use NTFS as the file system, Microsoft recommends upgrading Windows NT 4 to SP 4 or higher. However, I've found occasions when that didn't solve the potential problems of file access. I've found it better to dual boot between these operating systems using FAT partitions.

If you are dual booting between Windows NT 3.51 and Windows 2000, and you put the Windows 2000 installation on an NTFS partition, booting into NT 3.51 prevents you from seeing the Windows 2000 files. Again, in this situation I've found it better to dual boot with FAT partitions.

If you are dual booting between Windows 9x and Windows 2000, you must install both operating systems with FAT (or FAT32) in order to make sure the user has access to the Windows 2000 files when booting into Windows 9x.

You cannot dual boot between Windows 95 and Windows 98 (or triple boot between those two operating systems and Windows 2000). Windows 98 is an upgrade to Windows 95, and the last installed boot file wins, which means that one of those operating systems won't boot.

To dual boot between Windows 9x and Windows 2000, or between MS-DOS and Windows 2000, you must install the Windows 9x/MS-DOS system first.

To dual boot between OS/2 and Windows 2000, use FAT for both operating systems. The OS/2 HPFS file system and the Windows 2000 NTFS file system do not recognize each other. In fact, Windows 2000 doesn't support HPFS at all.

 I've run into one annoying problem with a Windows 98/Windows 2000 dual-boot workstation. The Windows 98 device configuration feature sometimes changes hardware settings, causing a problem with the device when booting into Windows 2000.

Encrypting File System (EFS)

Any computer that can be physically accessed is a potential target for data theft. Computers that hold sensitive data need special protection, and up to now, the solutions available in the operating system could be easily compromised. Windows 2000 includes an Encrypting File System (EFS) that provides file encryption capabilities for files stored on an NTFS volume.

EFS vs. Other Security Measures

Windows NT, UNIX, and other operating systems apply security based on a discretionary access control (DAC) system. DAC schemes let you protect sensitive data by restricting access to files and folders, which is useful and appropriate when multiple users have access to a computer. However, DAC depends on the operating system to protect the files, and any intruder who can bypass the OS can access files.

If a computer is formatted with the NTFS file system, booting with an MS-DOS floppy disk doesn't allow access to the files on the hard drive. Unfortunately, there are tools that permit access to those files. Furthermore, if an intruder can copy the files to a portable device (or upload them using software on a floppy disk), he or she can later load them onto an NTFS system. Breaking past the permissions to view the files is not difficult for a hacker.

I know of one company that insisted on BIOS boot passwords to protect data, which didn't work at all. There are a great many reasons not to use this scheme for security. Each computer's password must be unique (otherwise you've lost a large part of the point of this security measure), and the passwords must be maintained by an administrator in a database, a spreadsheet, a word processing document, or a large post-it note. There is no central administration tool for creating, changing, or administering boot passwords remotely—the work must be done at each computer. Eventually, administrators rebel, or at least complain. The final, fatal blow to this security measure was dealt when the employees arrived at work one morning to find that the hard drives from several computers had been removed! The intruder who walked away with the drives had no trouble getting to the file contents, because the data wasn't encrypted.

Security schemes that involve access permissions for files and folders offer only a limited level of security for file data. Those schemes are mainly employed to prevent unauthorized access to the system, to prevent malefactors from shutting down or impairing the network.

EFS, on the other hand, works with technology that is integrated with the file system, not just with the operating system. The EFS drivers run in operating system kernel mode.

Understanding EFS

EFS is based on public-key cryptography. Data is encrypted using a randomly generated file encryption key (FEK). Public key-based systems use a pair of keys: a private key and a public key. Only the user who owns the private key knows what that key is, while the public key is available to anyone who requests it. The user's public key encrypts FEKs, and the private key decrypts FEKs. NTFS stores a list of encrypted FEKs along with the encrypted file, using special EFS file attributes known as Data Decryption Fields (DDFs) and Data Recovery Fields (DRFs). This mechanism for storing keys is based on Windows 2000's CryptoAPI architecture, which stores users' public and private keys separately from the randomly generated FEK.

Note	*The CryptoAPI architecture is also employed for smart cards. Smart cards, which work with special smart-card readers attached to computers, are credit-card size devices that let users log onto Windows 2000 with a personal identification number (PIN). This device makes users' personal information (such as passwords and digital certificates) portable.*

The initial release of EFS supports only Data Encryption Standard (DES). Other encryption algorithms will probably be added in Service Pack releases for Windows 2000. The Data Encryption Standard is a popular data encryption procedure that uses a private key that is extremely difficult to break—there are more than 72 quadrillion possible encryption keys. (DES is also available for RAS logon password protection for Windows NT 4 systems.)

Also, the initial release of EFS does not permit file sharing for encrypted files. However, it's probable that developers will use the APIs to offer that capability, and that Microsoft will add it in the future.

Once a file is encrypted, all reads and writes to the file are decrypted and encrypted transparently to the user who encrypted the file. Any other user who tries to open the file sees an Access Denied error because the user does not posses a key to decrypt the file.

To see whether or not a file is encrypted, any user can check the file's Properties dialog box. In addition, the List view on Windows Explorer can be extended to display attributes, and an "E" in the attributes column indicates the file is encrypted.

EFS Components

There are four components to EFS: the EFS driver, the EFS File System Run Time Library, the EFS service, and the Win32 APIs.

The EFS driver runs on top of NTFS. It communicates with EFS service to request file encryption keys, DDFs, DRFs, and other key management services. It passes along the key management information to the EFS file system run-time library when a file has to be opened, read, or written.

The EFS File System Run Time Library (FSRTL) is a module of the EFS driver. FSRTL implements NTFS callouts to handle file system operations such as reads, writes, and opens on encrypted files and directories. It also handles the actual operations of encrypting and decrypting when file data is written to or read from disk.

The EFS driver and FSRTL are implemented as a single component, but they never communicate directly with each other. Each entity uses NTFS file control callouts to move information, because NTFS must be involved in all file operations. The particular tasks that use the NTFS file control mechanisms are writing the EFS attribute data (DDF and DRF) as file attributes, and sending the FEK (computed in the EFS service) to FSRTL, which in turn permits the FEK to be set up in the open file context. The open file context is what provides user-transparent encryption and decryption on writes and reads of file data.

The EFS service is part of the Windows 2000 security subsystem. The service communicates with the EFS driver using the existing LPC communication port between the Local Security Authority (LSA) and the kernel-mode security reference monitor. In user mode, it works with the CryptoAPI to provide file encryption keys and to generate the DDFs and DRFs. The EFS service also provides support for Win32 APIs (programming interfaces for encryption, decryption, recovery, backup, and restore).

 The Windows 2000 security subsystem enforces and replicates the EFS policy, which means that users can use file encryption when they're working offline.

The Win32 APIs provide programming interfaces for encrypting, decrypting, and recovering plaintext files. They also provide the interfaces for importing and exporting encrypted files (which do not have to be decrypted first). These APIs use a system DLL (%SystemRoot%\system32\advapi32.dll).

EFS Recovery Policy

EFS provides built-in data recovery support, and you cannot use file encryption unless your system is configured for a recovery key and a recovery agent. Recovery is needed to open encrypted files that were saved by employees who have left, or by employees who have lost their passwords.

EFS automatically configures a recovery policy that names the domain administrator account the recovery agent for the domain, and the local administrator the recovery agent for a computer. A self-signed certificate provides the authority for recovery. (For more information about certificates and security, read Chapter 21.)

Note	*Recovery works by using the file's randomly generated encryption key, not a user's private key. As a result, only the data that falls in the scope of influence of a recovery agent can be recovered by the agent; no other private information can be accidentally discovered.*

Domain administrators can use the Windows 2000 Directory Service delegation features to delegate the recovery agent function to other administrator accounts. The additional controls and the flexibility accrued from delegation makes the recovery process more efficient. EFS also supports multiple recovery agents, using multiple recovery key configurations, which provides redundancy.

You can tweak or reconfigure the default recovery policy. As with so many policies in Windows 2000, the recovery policy, which is actually named Encrypted Data Recovery Agents, is configured as part of Group Policy Objects (GPOs). The recovery agent GPOs can be assigned at different scopes, with the following rule: The policy defined at the closest scope to a given computer is the policy in effect on that computer.

To configure encryption recovery, open an MMC console and add the Group Policy Snap-in. Select the GPO (local or domain) and go to Encrypted Data Recovery Agents (\Computer Configuration\Windows Settings\Security Settings\Public Key Policies), seen in Figure 20-2.

To add recovery agents, right-click the Recovery Agents object in the right pane and follow the Add Recovery Agent wizard. The user(s) you choose must have the appropriate security certificates (see Chapter 21 for information on assigning security certificates in Windows 2000).

Using EFS

Files are encrypted by users, and further manipulation of an encrypted file is permitted for that user in an entirely transparent manner. You can encrypt files or folders on NTFS volumes (including volumes on remote computers), using the following guidelines:

- You cannot encrypt folders or files that are compressed.
- You cannot share encrypted files.
- You cannot encrypt system files.
- You cannot encrypt read-only files.

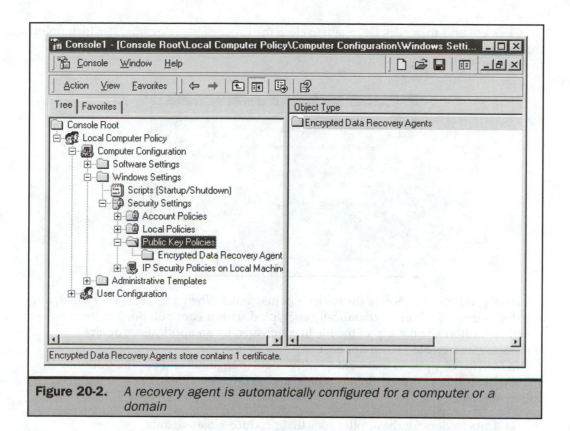

Figure 20-2. *A recovery agent is automatically configured for a computer or a domain*

To encrypt a file, right-click on its object in My Computer or Windows Explorer, and choose Properties from the shortcut menu. Click Advanced on the General tab and in the Advanced Attributes dialog box, select Encrypt Contents To Secure Data.

Click OK and then click OK again to close the Properties dialog box, at which point the system displays an Encryption Warning message that encourages you to encrypt the folder instead of just the file.

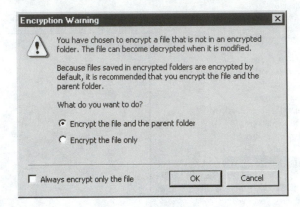

It's a good idea to encrypt the folder, not just a file. When a folder is encrypted, any file that is in the folder is automatically encrypted. This means you don't have to worry about any automatic backup of the file that's created by an application, or any temporary files created by an application.

In fact, for computers that hold sensitive data (personnel and payroll information, industrial secrets, company financial data, and so on), you should encrypt the following folders:

- Data folders for the applications that produce sensitive data
- My Documents
- System Temp folder

After a file is encrypted, the following rules apply:

- The file can only be opened by the user who encrypted it.
- Copying or moving the file to a non-NTFS volume eliminates the encryption.
- Use the copy/cut and paste commands to move a file into an encrypted folder and automatically encrypt that file—if you drag and drop the file, it is not automatically encrypted.

Distributed File System (Dfs)

The Distributed File System is not really a file system, but it acts enough like one to think of it as an ersatz file system ("I'm not a file system, but I play one on the screen"). Dfs provides a way to display a logical structure of a file system to users, where the components of the file system can be located anywhere on the network even though the structure looks like the tree of a drive. Dfs is installed automatically with Windows 2000 Server, and the Dfs service starts automatically at bootup.

 Microsoft's distributed file system is abbreviated as Dfs, not DFS, because DFS is the acronym for another distributed file system product, owned by Transarc Corporation. Transarc is a wholly owned subsidiary of IBM, and DFS is one of their enterprise computing products.

Dfs Advantages

Dfs provides an environment that lets users access information from wherever it's located to wherever it's needed, without forcing those users to understand, or navigate through, the complexities of the network. Users see a unified display of all the network resources that are available. Indeed, some administrators believe that system security is enhanced by the fact that users have no idea what servers are involved in providing resources, or where those servers are located.

With Dfs, users don't have to enter complicated UNCs to access resources on remote computers. The UNCs can become rather complicated when resources are on different sites or in different domains.

Dfs is easier to administer than mapped drives. Not only do you avoid the numerical limits of mapping, you achieve consistency. UserA, who might have mapped a resource to drive G:, and UserB, who might have mapped the same resource to drive F:, both access the resource by selecting a named resource.

Administrators, having named a resource, can change the point of origin for that named resource. If a server goes down, another server can be substituted. If a server is providing multiple shared resources, substituting another server for one of those resources is a load-balancing technique that's easy to administer. Changes made for either reason are transparent to users, who never know, and never have to adjust their program shortcuts.

Dfs Configuration Options

You can set up Dfs on a server as a stand-alone distributed file service or a domain-based service. A domain-based approach takes advantage of Active Directory, which provides automatic replication and fault tolerance. If you have multiple servers in a Windows 2000 domain, all of them (or as many as you care to include) can provide fault tolerance for Dfs, and you can be sure that the topology on the servers are matched. In addition, because the AD holds the information about links, the Dfs configuration data is written to the AD database instead of to a file, saving disk space and processing overhead for file lookups. (Some configuration information is also written to the registry.)

Note *If you configure Dfs on a Windows NT 4 server, you are restricted to the stand-alone Dfs configuration.*

In addition to the server components, there are Dfs client components that cache the referrals to Dfs links, making client access faster. (Administrators can configure the lifespan of the caches.) Client services for Dfs domain-wide implementation on Windows 2000 servers are available for Windows 9*x*, Windows NT 4 with SP3, and Windows 2000 Professional.

Setting Up the Dfs Root

Before you can make Dfs shares accessible to users, you must create a Dfs root object. This object is a container: it holds the links to shares and files that users access. To create a root object, choose Distributed File System from the Administrative Tools programs menu. This opens a Microsoft Management Console (MMC) with the Dfs object in the scope panel. To create a Dfs root, right-click on the Dfs object and choose New Dfs Root (or choose Action | New Dfs Root). This launches the New Dfs Root Wizard. Click Next to move past the introductory window, and then select either a Standalone or Domain type of Dfs root.

Standalone Dfs Root

If you're creating a standalone Dfs root, the next wizard window asks you to specify the server. The following wizard window prompts for a share on that server (see Figure 20-3).

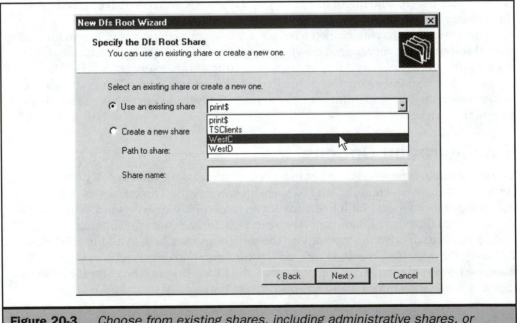

Figure 20-3.   *Choose from existing shares, including administrative shares, or create a new share*

A drop-down list displays all the shared folders on the server, or you can create a new share. There's no Browse function, so you must know the path to the folder for which you're creating the new share. If you enter a path to a folder that doesn't exist, the wizard will create the new folder and share it. Use the next wizard window to enter a descriptive comment about the share. You cannot create your own name for a stand-alone Dfs root; you must use the sharename. Click Finish to establish the Dfs root.

Domain-Based Dfs Root

If you're creating a domain-based Dfs root, the wizard asks you to select a domain (a list of available domains is displayed in the Trusting Domains text box). Then choose the server and the share. You can create a new share, or even create a new directory and share it. Next, specify a name for the Dfs root. You can use the name of the share, but it's not a requirement. The wizard presents a summary of the settings for the Dfs root. Click Finish (or go back to make any necessary corrections).

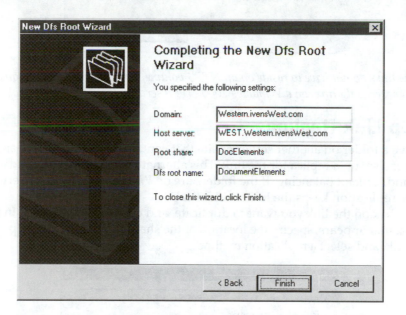

Replica Roots

For redundancy, set up the same root on another Windows 2000 NTFS server. The Replication Policy command appears on the root object's right-click menu so you can configure replication. See "Configuring Replication" later in this chapter.

Setting Up Dfs Links

To establish Dfs links in your Dfs root, open the Dfs MMC, right-click the appropriate root object, and choose New Dfs Link. Enter the name of the link, the folder it links to, and an optional comment. Also specify the duration for client caching, which is the amount of time client systems locally store the information about the link's location (after which they must select the link to refresh it). Repeat the process for other links you want to locate in this Dfs root.

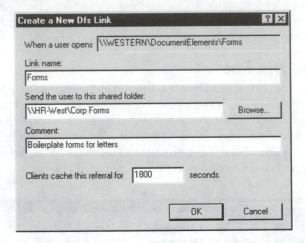

 The links do not have to reside on an NTFS volume, nor do they have to be on a server. However, only links on a Windows 2000 NTFS server are automatically replicated.

Setting Up Link Replicas

If you have a folder on another server or site that contains the same files as an existing link, you can set up a replica for the link. This alternate site provides redundancy for failover and/or load balancing. If the folders are on Windows 2000 NTFS servers, automatic replication keeps the folders identical.

Right-click on the link you want to duplicate, and choose New Replica. In the dialog box that appears, specify the location of the shared folder that is a replica of the original link, and select a replication method.

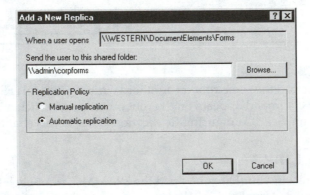

Managing Dfs

As you add links, you're building the hierarchical tree that users see. The tree looks as if it's a single network component, but it is, in fact, made up of folders from different servers and perhaps different sites.

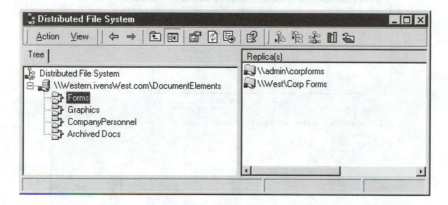

Use the Distributed File System console window to manage the objects in your Dfs tree. You can use the toolbar to delete a link, take a link offline, check the status of replication, remove a link from the namespace, add replicas, or set replication policy.

Keep an eye on the way contents change and tweak your links to maintain efficiency. If a link is busy and contents change frequently, shorten the cache timeout interval to make sure users get the latest version of any file they access. If contents don't change often (for example, a folder that holds boilerplate documents), lengthen the cache timeout to reduce network traffic.

Configuring Replication

To tweak or change the replication policy between root objects, or between link replicas, right-click the appropriate object in the tree and choose Replication Policy. Use the dialog box seen in Figure 20-4 to make changes in the policy.

- Select a share and choose Enable or Disable to determine whether the share participates in replication.

- Select a share and click Set Master to specify that the selected folder should initiate the first replication action. After replication occurs for the first time, the Set Master button is no longer available.

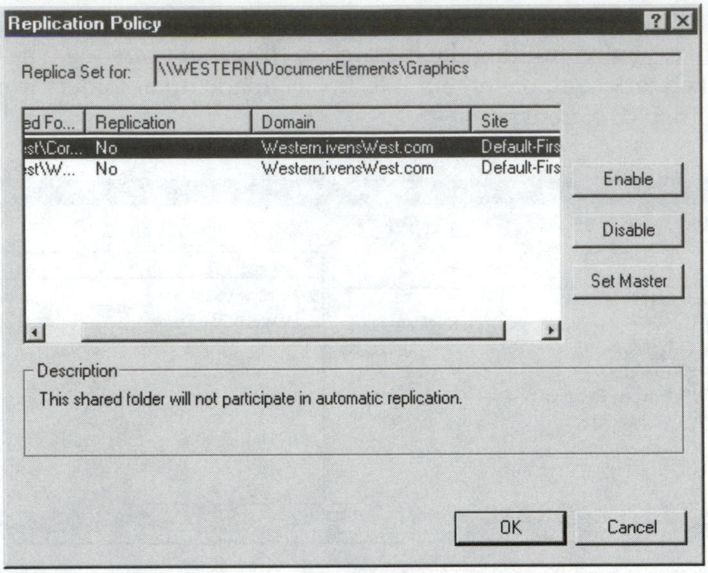

Figure 20-4. *If both folders are on Windows 2000 NTFS volumes, you can set automatic replication policies*

Chapter 21

Security

There's no doubt that the world economy has skyrocketed from the use of computers and technology. Whether you're buying gasoline with a credit card or using the Internet to purchase various commodities, you're in some fashion interacting with a computer. Computers are increasingly responsible for holding a wealth of information (personal, financial, corporate, and much more). As a result, security is of paramount concern for keeping sensitive, personal, financial, or mission-critical information safe and private.

One of the primary design goals for Windows 2000 was to provide the highest level of security for your environment. In fact, during the beta stages, Microsoft launched a Web site using a Windows 2000 server running IIS on the Internet and asked everyone to try and hack the server. It used only its internal security mechanisms to protect itself from intrusion. The purpose of this was to test Windows 2000's built-in security and uncover possible vulnerabilities. It withstood countless attacks, and it has been reported that the server was never actually penetrated. Now, Windows 2000 has an unprecedented level of security to protect your network environment.

Windows 2000 security infrastructure builds upon and strengthens the NT 4 security model. Many of the security schemes that were longed for in Windows NT make their debut in Windows 2000. This chapter is intended as an overview examining the security mechanisms used in Windows 2000 and the steps required for protecting your Windows 2000 environment. It also discusses other security measures that can be used beyond Windows 2000's built-in capabilities.

Security Fundamentals

Security is an extremely complex and intimidating subject for many. There are various security-related technologies directly integrated with Windows 2000 that you should at least be familiar with in order to safeguard your Windows 2000 environment. You also have a multitude of other choices that help protect your investment.

It's important to keep in mind that you'll never completely secure your Windows 2000 environment (or any other operating system environment), no matter which technologies you use. If someone really wants to get into the system, he or she will eventually find a way. The best thing you can do is strive to secure your systems to make unauthorized access as difficult as possible or at least not worth the hassle. The more effort you put into securing your environment, the less likely your information will be compromised, modified, or completely destroyed. Before you start deciding on how to secure your Windows 2000 environment, weigh the risks with the value of the information.

It's also true that you can have all the security technologies possible at your disposal, but they're only as good as your implementation of them. And if you don't implement them at all, you're leaving yourself vulnerable. Implementation includes making sure your users are aware of the security mechanisms in place and proper procedures that they must follow. With appropriate implementation of systemwide security and user awareness, you and your users can benefit from both worlds with a functional yet secure network environment.

Risk Assessment

An important issue to consider is the cost of securing your systems versus the value of the information. Your first thought may be to determine the monetary value of the information. This is a good place to start. How much would it cost you if the information was destroyed, altered, or stolen?

For some types of information it's extremely difficult, if not impossible, to determine a monetary value. For example, if you're responsible for securing a hospital's data, how would you calculate the value of patient records?

At the other extreme, you may consider that your information is not all that important. If this is the case, look at it in terms of what it would cost you to rebuild the infrastructure. Your time and effort shouldn't be compromised either.

It's important to secure your resources, and if you can at least strike a balance between the cost of securing the Windows 2000 environment and the value of the information, then you're heading in the right direction. Fortunately, Windows 2000 provides a variety of security mechanisms that enable you to create a solid security infrastructure without additional costs.

C2 Security Criteria

In addition to learning what a product claims to support, it's also a good idea to find out how it stands up to third-party standards measurement. Such measurements can gauge how well a product protects your network environment. This is similar to how benchmarks, such as the TPC-C and TPC-D, analyze a system's performance characteristics.

One of the most notable security certifications for the industry is the United States' *Trusted Computer System Evaluation Criteria*, also known as the Orange Book. The Orange Book outlines several government-rated security levels, the most popular of which is the C2 Security Level. C2 is used as a baseline security measurement that applies to operating systems on stand-alone PCs. That means that if your computer is connected to a network, it can't be C2 certified.

There are several other security levels for networked computers that are basically interpretations of the Orange Book levels. They include the Red and Blue Book interpretations.

The certification process is a strenuous and often lengthy one. Windows NT 4 has been evaluated at E3/F-C2 level and was certified in December of 1999. Windows 2000 was just starting the process at the time of this writing, but considering that it only strengthens the Windows NT security model, you can be sure that it will be successful in completing the evaluation.

New Security Features for Windows 2000

Throughout this book you've seen just how different Windows 2000 is from its previous Windows NT versions. Active Directory (AD) alone makes Windows 2000 radically different than Windows NT. Although you'd think that Windows 2000's security model is a complete overhaul, it really isn't. Windows 2000 actually builds on the Windows NT 4's security model.

It's also true that some of the security features of previous versions have been replaced with greater levels of protection. The most notable example is the replacement of NT LAN Manager (NTLM) authentication with the industry-standardized Kerberos.

The many new features that Windows 2000 introduces to help protect your Windows 2000 environment include:

- Encryption of data that is transmitted over the network
- Encryption of data that is stored on disk
- The use of Kerberos version 5 for authentication while also supporting multiple authentication methods for compatibility
- Kerberos transitive trust relationships
- Central storage of security policy and account information
- Automatic updating and synchronization of all security policy and account information across domain controllers (DCs)
- Access control for all objects in the AD
- Smart card support

Top Ten Security Measures

There are various steps you can take to secure your Windows 2000 environment, and they will vary according to environment. The ten suggestions that follow aren't the only ones that you should take; there are many others throughout this chapter.

1. Place servers in secure, locked rooms.
2. Keep up-to-date with service packs and hot fixes.
3. Keep current with the latest security technologies and concerns at Microsoft's Security Web site (http://www.microsoft.com/security/).
4. Use NTFS on all partitions, and encrypt sensitive data with EFS.
5. Use strong passwords.
6. Limit the number of users with administrator privileges.
7. Enable auditing (logon validations, security changes, etc.).
8. Keep abreast of group memberships.
9. Upgrade down-level clients to Windows 2000 to enable them to use Kerberos instead of NTLM authentication (Windows 9*x* and Windows NT computers can also use additional client software). This may also allow you to remove NetBIOS from your environment.

10. Secure remote connections by using Extensible authentication protocol (EAP), callback, caller ID, or virtual private networking (VPN) technologies. For more information on securing your remote connections, refer to Chapter 16.

Active Directory and Security Integration

AD is so tightly integrated with security that it's impossible to separate the two. If you look at Figure 15-2 in Chapter 15, you'll see that AD fits within the security subsystem rather than being its own independent subsystem. The advantages are enormous and will be explained throughout this chapter.

Windows 2000's security architecture has more flexibility than the Windows NT 4 model. In Windows NT 4, you were rather limited with the Security Accounts Manager (SAM). For example, trusts were established only one way, and the scope of assigning security rights was limited to a few levels. Now, however, you're dealing with a distributed service Active Directory (AD) that enables you to have much more diversified control over your network environment. You have new features such as organizational units (OUs) and delegated administration.

Objects and Their Contributions to Security

As you know, AD stores all Windows 2000 network objects and their associated attributes. These objects (users, groups, computers, printers, and other objects) are protected through the use of authentication and access control mechanisms.

Because of the integration of AD and security, you can control access to an object as a whole or down to the attribute level. For example, for the user account Jenna McMains, you can either allow access to all of her attributes or define a particular group (for example, HR) to be able to modify only certain attributes such as her address, department name, and e-mail address.

In addition, the integration also enables inheritance of security rights among most, if not all, objects. Inheritance is when an object receives similar properties from the object it was created. An analogy to this is you receiving similar characteristics (eye color, hair color, and so forth) from your parents.

Object Identity

Although all objects in the AD can be found using a distinguished name, they are also given other unique identities, the security identifier (SID) and globally unique identifier (GUID). These two unique identifiers are used internally by AD instead of by the object's name because, unlike an object name, SIDs and GUIDs never change.

SIDs and GUIDs are used when a process attempts to access a resource. Windows 2000 compares the process's SID or GUID with the resource's discretionary access control list (DACL). The DACL is also referred to simply as an ACL. If the two match, the process is allowed to use the resource.

SID　As in Windows NT 4, a Windows 2000 SID identifies a security principal (user, group, or machine account) within a domain. The domain is a boundary for the SID so it can't go outside to other domains.

The same limitations in the Windows NT 4 implementation still apply in Windows 2000. A SID is limited to a single domain, and duplicate SIDs can cause security-related problems in, for example, cloning computers.

SID HISTORY　If you did your homework and read Chapter 15 on AD, you'll recall that you can easily move objects from one domain to another. This is possible due to a new object attribute called SID History. A SID History keeps track of the domains in which the object has been a member.

Since it contains one or more SIDs for each domain in which the object has resided, any security rights from the older domain membership are still a part of the object. The object can transparently access resources that are now located on another domain to which it once belonged. This simplifies administration and helps bypass some of the limitations of the SID.

GUID　In addition to an object's distinguished name and SID, every object in AD has a GUID. A GUID is a 128-bit number that is guaranteed to be unique. It is similar to a SID, with a couple of major exceptions. First, administrators or the AD can never change a GUID itself. Also, a GUID stays permanently attached to the object for the duration of its life no matter where the object moves. In other words, the only boundary for the GUID is a Windows 2000 forest; it is guaranteed to be unique no matter how many domains in the tree or forest you have.

User and Group Accounts

User and group accounts, like other AD objects, can be protected with access rights. However, when they are combined with permissions of resources, they are either permitted or denied access to the resource.

The functionality behind user accounts hasn't changed from Windows NT 4 and probably never will. Users can still log onto a computer or domain and access resources. The difference is that the schema is modifiable, so that you can customize how many attributes a user account will use.

 It is highly recommended that you not modify the schema without thorough training and awareness of how the changes will affect your Windows 2000 network environment. Always make sure you have a complete and trustworthy backup in case something goes wrong.

There are numerous security-related configuration options to choose from for user accounts. For your convenience, here are a few.

- **Group membership**　This assigns which groups the user account is a member of (see Figure 21-1). You can also specify the primary group with which the user is affiliated.

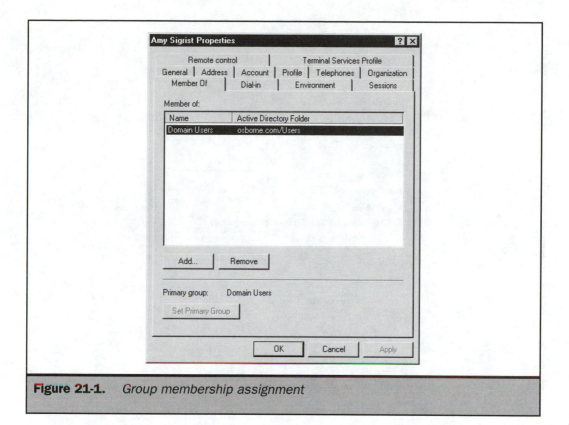

Figure 21-1.   *Group membership assignment*

- **Remote access dial-in or VPN permissions**   This gives you the option to allow or deny access for remote connections, and to set callback options as shown in Figure 21-2.

- **Logon hours**   This is used to specify the time of day in which the user can log on.

Groups

A group is a collection of user accounts that can be used to help simplify administration including configuring security options. For instance, instead of configuring several user accounts with the ability to log on after business hours, you can create a group, add the appropriate users, and then assign the rights in one fell swoop.

There are two types of groups: distribution and security. The primary difference between them is that you can't assign permissions to distribution groups.

You can assign permissions to security groups, and you can nest some groups within others for greater control and flexibility. The following are considered security groups:

- **Domain local group**   This group can contain other groups (universal and global groups) and users, but its scope is limited to its domain.

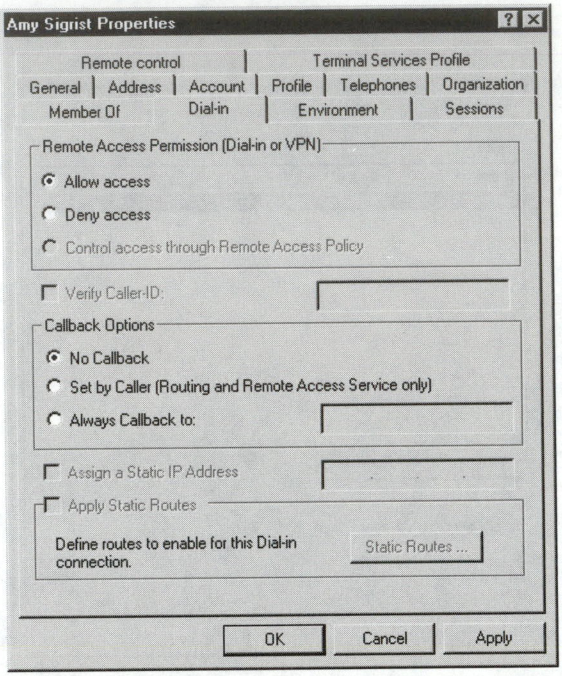

Figure 21-2. *Remote access security options*

■ **Global group** A global group can contain other global groups and users but only when the AD is in native mode. Also, membership is limited to the local domain, but the user can use a resource in another domain through ACL referencing.

■ **Universal group** This group becomes available only after you make the switch to native mode. It can contain members from anywhere in a Windows 2000 forest.

Account Rights

As an administrator, you can assign rights to user and group accounts that authorize them to perform certain actions such as backing up files or logging onto a machine locally. Don't confuse rights with permissions. Permissions apply to specific objects, whereas rights apply to specific actions.

From an administrative point of view, it's recommended that you define rights with groups rather than users. Using groups makes it easier to keep track of the rights that you assign, and it ensures that everyone that needs access has it.

There are two types of user rights: privileges and logon rights. Both can be managed through the Local Users And Groups snap-in for the Microsoft Management Console (MMC) for a member server or the Group Policy MMC snap-in for DCs.

PRIVILEGES   The following privileges can be assigned to a user or group:

- Act as part of the operating system
- Add workstations to domain
- Back up files and directories
- Bypass traverse checking
- Change the system time
- Create a page file
- Create a token object
- Create permanent shared objects
- Debug programs
- Enable computer and user accounts to be trusted for delegation
- Force shutdown from a remote system
- Generate security audits
- Increase quotas
- Increase scheduling priority
- Load and unload device drivers
- Lock pages in memory
- Manage auditing and security log
- Modify firmware environment values
- Profile single process
- Profile system performance
- Replace a process-level token
- Restore files and directories
- Shut down the system
- Take ownership of files or other objects
- Unlock a laptop

LOGON RIGHTS   The following list shows the logon rights that can be assigned to a user or group:

- Access this computer from network
- Log on locally

- Log on as a batch job
- Log on as a service
- Deny access to this computer from the network
- Deny logon as a batch job
- Deny logon as a service
- Deny local logon

Use Strong Passwords

Logon credentials (usernames and passwords) are usually one of the weakest security links in your Windows 2000 network environment and the first thing that hackers try to determine.

The username is an obvious target because it's the easiest to find. For one thing, most companies use some form of an employee's name. For example, the user Margaret Flanagan may well use margaret, margaretf, or mflanagan as her username. It's also very common for the user's e-mail address to also be the username (and we all have business cards with e-mail addresses on them, right?). The list can go on almost indefinitely, and unfortunately there's not too much you can do about hackers finding out your username.

Because usernames are easily discovered, it's imperative that you use strong passwords. Passwords aren't usually as vulnerable, but chances are a hacker will be able to determine it in no time. If the password isn't one of the common ones like birthdays, family members' names, or default passwords, the hacker can use various "dictionary attack" programs and other utilities to guess it.

To strengthen passwords, you need to set policies governing what is allowed. It's also important to have users understand the ramifications of weak passwords. The following is a list of guidelines that you should consider using:

- Passwords must be a minimum of six characters long.
- Passwords may not contain your username or any part of your full name.
- Passwords must be made up of characters from three of the following four classes shown in the following table.

Character Class	Example
Uppercase letters	A, B, C . . . Z
Lowercase letters	a, b, c . . . z
Numbers	0, 1 ,2, 3 . . . 9
Nonalphanumeric symbols	`~!@#$%^&*()=+,"<>.?\	[]{}

- Users should keep passwords secret (i.e., don't write them down or disclose them in any other way).

- Users should never reuse passwords.

- Exercise and enforce password rotation.

- Enforce account lockouts.

- Disable or remove unused user accounts.

Security Policies

Security policies (also known as security settings) give you yet another option to define security configuration parameters. They are applied through the use of Group Policy Objects (GPOs) enabling centralized management and control of security for your Windows 2000 network environment. For more information on Group Policies, refer to Chapter 18 and 25.

Windows 2000 computers have specific security areas where security policies can be applied through the GPO. The security areas that can be configured are the following:

- **Account Policies** This security area contains settings for password, account lockout, and Kerberos policies.

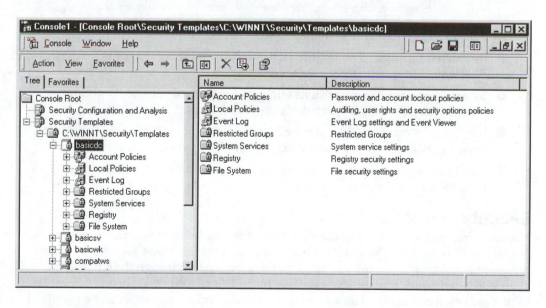

- **Local Policies** This area contains settings for auditing, user rights assignment, and security options.

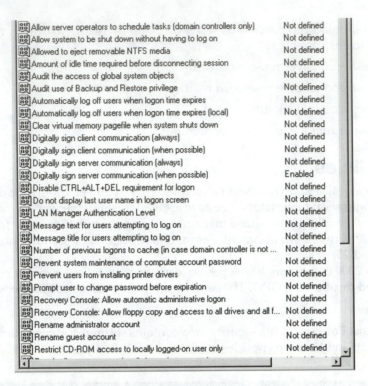

- **Event Log** This includes manageable Event Log settings.
- **Restricted Groups** The options here affect the membership of Windows 2000's built-in groups for the local computer.
- **System Services** These options allow you to control various configuration parameters on the local computer's system services.
- **Registry** Security settings for the local computer's registry include auditing keys, permissions to keys, and much more.
- **File System** This is used to configure security settings (permissions, etc.) for files, folders, and shares.

Security Templates

Microsoft has tried to make your life a little easier by predefining security templates that can be used to configure the security areas mentioned earlier. These security templates represent a collection of security settings that you can apply through the GPO.

Security templates are stored, by default, in the %SystemRoot%\Security\Templates folder, and each one is saved as a text-based .inf file. These templates can be managed using the Security Templates MMC snap-in. As you can see in Figure 21-3, there are several predefined security templates, and each one organizes security policies depending on the type of computer that it's being applied to. For instance, you probably wouldn't

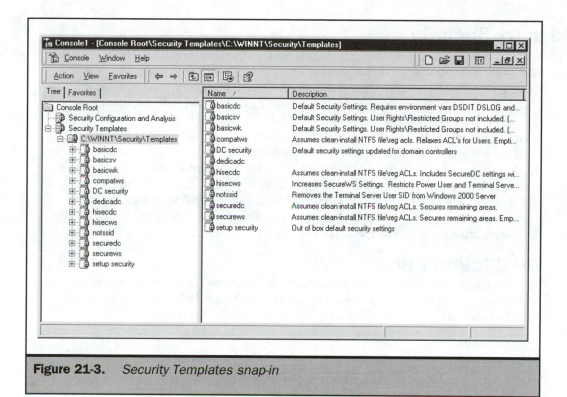

Figure 21-3.   *Security Templates snap-in*

want to apply one of the basic security templates to a DC, nor apply the DC security template to a Windows 2000 Professional client machine.

You're not limited to using the predefined security templates; you can easily create your own. Using the Security Template snap-in, simply right-click on the security templates path (for example, %SystemRoot%\Security\Templates) and select New Template. Once you give the template a name, Windows 2000 builds the default security areas for you. Then you can define each of the security areas of your choice.

Registry Security

The registry is a database containing static and dynamic information about your Windows 2000 computer. It is separated into a set of files found in the %SystemRoot%\System32\Config directory. Since the registry is comprised of these files, you are able to set access permissions just as you would with ordinary files, directories, or printers. If your system partition is using NTFS, you can modify the permissions on those files. By default, Administrators and the SYSTEM have Full Control, while Server Operators and Authenticated Users have List Folder Contents rights to these files as illustrated in Figure 21-4. For more information on setting file permissions, see the section "File and Share Security" later in this chapter.

The Registry Editor (REGEDT32.EXE) also has an internal security mechanism to prevent users from modifying the registry. The default security permissions for the Registry Editor are listed in Table 21-1.

The SECURITY Hive

The SECURITY hive contains all the security information for the local machine. This hive is not available for modification by default even to Administrators. Only the SYSTEM security context is allowed to make changes to this hive.

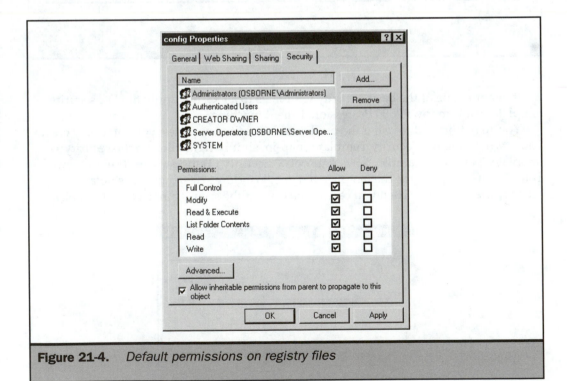

Figure 21-4. *Default permissions on registry files*

User or Group	Read Access	Full Control Access
Administrators	√	√
Everyone	√	
RESTRICTED	√	
SYSTEM	√	√

Table 21-1.   *Default Registry Security Permissions*

In order to modify this key, you must either log on as the SYSTEM security context or change the default Administrators settings. The easiest way to gain access to this hive is to change the default Administrators settings, by doing the following:

1. Start REGEDT32 by typing it on the Run menu or Command Prompt.

2. Open the HKEY_LOCAL_MACHINE window, and select the SECURITY hive.

3. From the Security menu, select Permissions to display the Permissions window as shown here.

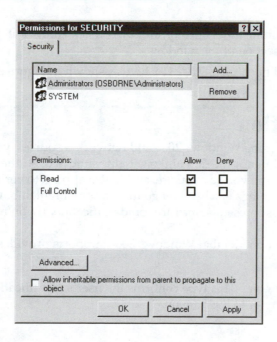

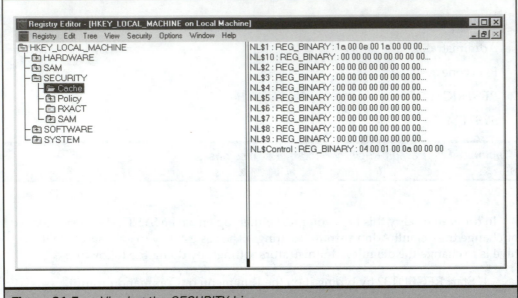

Figure 21-5. *Viewing the SECURITY hive*

4. Select the Administrators group, and then check Allow Full Control in the Permissions section of the window.

5. Click OK and open the SECURITY hive as shown in Figure 21-5.

Authentication

Before you can start using Windows 2000 and network resources, you must log on to either the local computer or the domain to get authenticated. Authentication is the process of verifying who you say you are, and it also applies to verifying an object's identity. An analogy to this is when you go to a bar or a nightclub. When you stand at the entrance, you must present some form of identification. If you're over 21, you're allowed in.

The authentication model that Windows 2000 supports provides two types of authentication:

- **Interactive logon** This type confirms the user's identification to the user's local computer or to the domain.

■ **Network authentication**   Network authentication refers to confirming the user's identification to any network resource or service that the user is attempting to access.

Windows 2000 includes three different protocols to support authentication, including NTLM, X.509 V3 public-key certificates for public-key infrastructure (PKI), and Kerberos version 5. Kerberos is used as the default authentication protocol for Windows 2000 clients as well as Windows 9x and Windows NT AD-aware clients.

> **Note**   *Windows 2000 uses either Kerberos or NTLM for interactive logon authentication. PKI is used strictly with network authentication.*

Down-level clients, such as Windows NT 3.x and 4.0 or Windows 9x (without the Directory Services client software) aren't AD or Kerberos aware. Therefore, the client determines which authentication protocol is to be used. For instance, when a user on Windows NT 4 tries to log on, it can authenticate only with NTLM because Windows NT 4 doesn't recognize the Kerberos protocol (without the Directory Services client software). The converse is true for network authentication as well. If the server holding the resource (resource server) isn't capable of understanding Kerberos, the client also must use NTLM.

NTLM

Windows NT systems have for years relied on NTLM for authentication. Now, NTLM is only supported for backward compatibility with down-level clients. It is used only in the following scenarios:

■ Down-level client computers logging onto Windows 2000 domains

■ Down-level client computers requesting resources from down-level servers

■ Down-level client computers requesting resources from Windows 2000 servers

■ Windows 2000 computers logging onto servers that are running Windows NT 4

■ Windows 2000 computers requesting resources in Windows NT 4 domains or resources on a Windows NT 4 computer in a Windows 2000 domain

> **Note**   *When you switch to native mode in Windows 2000, you're turning off NTLM authentication for good. NTLM is supported only in mixed mode, not native mode.*

The Logon Process

The logon process is also mandatory in Windows NT computers whether a user is accessing resources on the local machine or in a domain, but the process is different than for Windows 2000 computers.

The user must provide security credentials to gain access to resources. A user logging onto the local machine supplies a username and password, which are then validated by the machine's local SAM database. Logging on to a domain is much like logging on to the local machine, except that the domain controller validates the account instead of the local machine.

The user's request to log on to the domain is handled by either a PDC or one of the BDCs in the domain. In a Windows 2000 domain, the domain controllers (DCs) act as if they're either a PDC (a Windows 2000 Flexible Single Master Operation (FSMO) server or operations master) or most likely a BDC. It is essentially a race between the controllers to determine which processes the request. Typically, the BDC wins the race simply because it usually is not as busy as the PDC and can consequently respond to the request more quickly. The client machine accepts the first response, and the winner (PDC or BDC) begins processing the request. This process may involve loading user profiles, logon scripts, and drive mappings. Once a user is logged onto the domain, the user can access resources (with proper access permissions) within the domain. The NetLogon Service using NTLM performs this entire process.

NETLOGON SERVICE   The NetLogon Service has three responsibilities with regard to user authentication: discovery, secure channel setup, and pass-through authentication.

- **Discovery**   This process occurs during machine initialization. As the machine starts up, the NetLogon Service tries to locate a domain controller for the specified domain. More specifically, it looks for a machine that responds to the name *DOMAINNAME*<1C>. Domain controllers go through this process as well, except that they search for domain controllers in all trusted domains.

- **Secure channel setup**   A secure communications channel is established between an NT machine and the domain controller by a series of challenges that they issue to and from each other. This verifies the validity of machine accounts and ensures a secure channel between the two machines. This channel is then used to pass user identification information.

- **Pass-through authentication**   Pass-through authentication takes place when a user requests a service or attempts to connect to a resource where the user cannot be authenticated by a domain controller in the domain in which the user is logged on. The computer that is asked to provide a resource sends the user's request to the destination's domain controller for authentication. The same logon process occurs when a user with proper access privileges logs on to a domain controller, except that the user can log on to only the domain. Users cannot log on to a domain controller locally, because domain controllers do not store a local SAM database in addition to the domain SAM database.

Disadvantages of Using NTLM

As stated earlier, NTLM is used only for backward compatibility with down-level clients. There are several disadvantages to using NTLM (listed below), but most of them can be summed up into one disadvantage: it weakens Windows 2000's security model. The only way you can stop using NTLM authentication is to upgrade all down-level computers to Windows 2000, or at least install the Directory Service client software on Windows 9*x* and Windows NT computers and then switch to native mode.

The following is a list of disadvantages to using NTLM:

- NTLM doesn't support mutual authentication. This essentially means that a server can impersonate a network resource or service and trick the client into supplying secure information.

- The authentication process allows passwords to be transmitted across the network. Therefore, anyone using network sniffers can snoop and jeopardize security by grabbing passwords and other sensitive information.

- Trusts are nontransitive, hard to manage, and limited in scalability.

- NTLM is a slow authentication mechanism especially when compared to Kerberos.

- NTLM is a proprietary authentication protocol.

PKI

It's clear that Windows 2000 supports both NTLM and Kerberos authentication protocols for interactive logons. Users with accounts in the Windows 2000 domain or local computer can log on if they're given the proper access rights (i.e. they must be allowed to log on to the domain or local computer). But what happens if a user account doesn't exist on the local computer, domain, or trusted domain? Put simply, they're denied the ability to log on and are unable to use any resources.

Believe it or not, this is a growing problem for many companies mainly because of e-business or e-commerce. Whether it's business-to-business or business-to-customer, there must be methods in place that allow information to be securely transferred without having to create accounts in Windows 2000 computers or domains. Besides, would you really want to create user accounts for anyone coming in from the Internet?

Public-key security (PKI) can be used to solve these dilemmas. It enables the verification that sender and receiver are who they say they are, which then allows the data to be sent encrypted so as to discourage security breaches. If you've ever worked with secure Internet-based e-mail, such as the Pretty Good Privacy (PGP) or S/MIME, you'll see the similarities with PKI.

Public-Key Cryptography

Windows 2000's PKI uses public-key cryptography, which is the science of protecting data. Cryptographic algorithms combine data (*plaintext*) and an *encryption key* to generate encrypted data (*ciphertext*). It's virtually impossible to reverse engineer ciphertext. The only way to transform the data into something that is useable is to use a *decryption key*.

In PKI terminology, the keys mentioned above are two separate keys. The encryption key is called the *public key*, and the decryption key is called the *private key*. As their names imply, the public key is freely available to anyone who wishes to have it, and the private key is kept secret. It's also important to note here that each key serves a single purpose. In other words, the public key can't decrypt information, and the private key can't encrypt messages.

Certificates and the Certificate Authority

Both the public and private keys in PKI are stored in the certificate authority (CA). The CA is responsible for both issuing and signing certificates, which are digitally signed agreements that bind the value of the public key to a specific private key. The private key can represent a user or service.

Certificates typically hold the following information:

- The public key value
- The name of the user or service
- The certificate's validity period, which is the length of time the certificate is valid
- The CA's identifier information
- The digital signature

The CA acts as a liaison between the two entities that wish to exchange information securely. It verifies the validity of the digital certificate, so that you know you're communicating with the user or service you think you are. In Windows 2000, you create and manage certificates through Certificate Services (see "Installing Certificate Services" for more information).

With all this in mind, let's create a simple example to illustrate how public and private keys work. In this example, assume that Grant wants to send Andrew a secure message and that Windows 2000's Certificate Services has already created key pairs for each of them. Grant first writes the message and then encrypts it using Andrew's public key (which he freely obtained). The message is then sent to Andrew; upon receiving it, he uses his private key to decrypt the message and reads it. Figure 21-6 illustrates the process of sending a secure message via PKI.

In the simple example above, you should notice that neither Grant nor Andrew had to exchange passwords over the network. All they had to do was establish a trust with the CA.

| Note | *CAs trusting one another to form a certification hierarchy can extend the security infrastructure boundary beyond your imagination. If CAs trust each other, their users (or services) can trust each other.* |

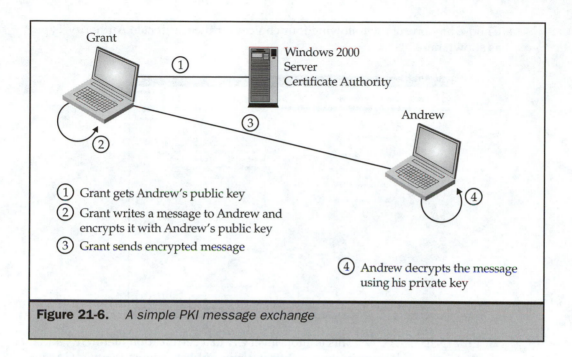

Figure 21-6. *A simple PKI message exchange*

Installing Certificate Services

Windows 2000 Certificate Services is required for using digital certificates. Before you install it, you should thoroughly plan how PKI will fit into your Windows 2000 network infrastructure. There are simply too many options and configurations to ignore.

To install Certificate Services, do the following:

1. Double-click Add/Remove Programs from the Control Panel.

2. Select Add/Remove Windows Components to display the Windows Components Wizard.

3. Check the Certificate Services check box. If you see a warning message, read it carefully before clicking Yes. Click Next to continue.

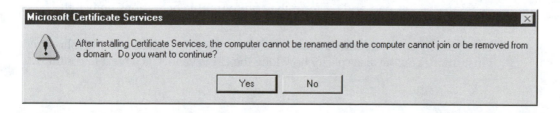

INSIDE
WINDOWS 2000

4. Choose any one of the following four choices for the Certificate Authority Type as shown here:

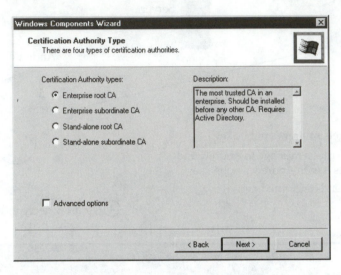

- **Enterprise root CA**   This is a top-level CA in a certification hierarchy, and it requires AD. It signs its own certificates and publishes them to other CAs in the enterprise through AD.

- **Enterprise subordinate CA**   This CA obtains its certificates from the Enterprise root CA and therefore requires AD.

- **Stand-alone root CA**   The primary difference between this CA and an Enterprise root CA is that it doesn't require AD, meaning that it doesn't have to be a part of the domain. However, it will use AD if it's installed on a DC.

- **Stand-alone subordinate CA**   This is similar to the Enterprise subordinate CA, but it doesn't require AD.

5. You can optionally select Advanced options to configure the Certificate Authority that you chose in Step 4. These options include key length, hash algorithms, and cryptographic service provider (CSP). The CSP is used to generate the key pair and perform the cryptographic operations on behalf of the CA.

6. Fill in the appropriate information to identify the CA as shown in the following illustration. You can also specify how long the CA is valid. Click Next to continue.

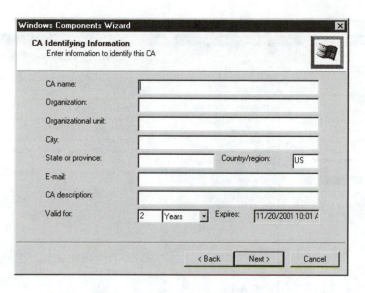

7. The next step is specifying where to store the configuration data, database, and log files. If you're unsure of where to store them, keep the defaults. Click Next to continue.

Note   *You may be prompted to stop the Internet Information Service (IIS) before proceeding. Make sure that you have your Windows 2000 installation files ready, too.*

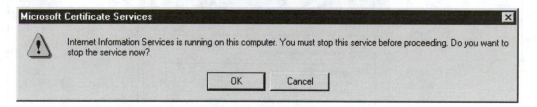

8. Click Finish to complete the installation.

After the installation is complete, you can use the Certificates or Certification Authority MMC snap-ins illustrated in Figure 21-7 to manage digital certificates (see Figure 21-8). Users and administrators can use the Certificates snap-in, but in order to use the Certification Authority, you must have administrative privileges.

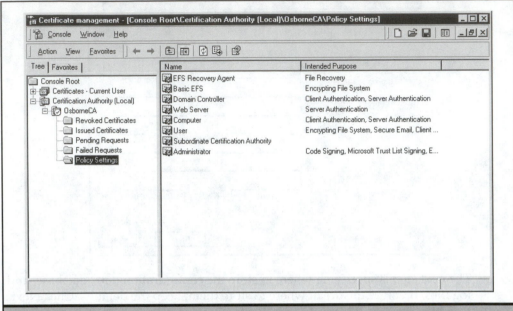

Figure 21-7.   *Certificates and Certification Authority MMC snap-ins*

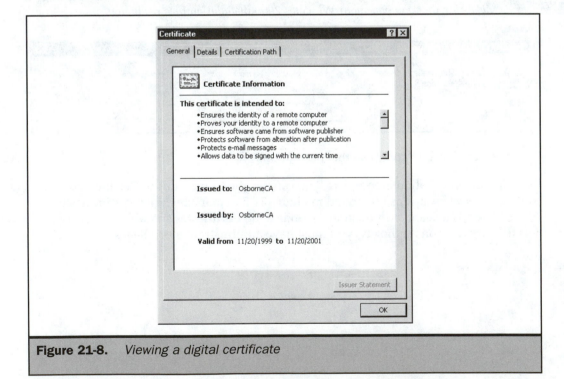

Figure 21-8.   *Viewing a digital certificate*

Kerberos

Kerberos is the default network authentication protocol used in Windows 2000. It's an industry standard developed by Massachusetts Institute of Technology (MIT) and is described in Request for Comments (RFC) 1510.

Many components rely on Kerberos for authentication, including logon authentication and trust relationships between domains. As an integral part of AD, Kerberos runs on each DC in a domain, and its client-side service runs on all Windows 2000 client computers. Down-level Windows 9x and Windows NT clients must install the Directory Services client software in order to take advantage of Kerberos.

Kerberos uses similar cryptography techniques as PKI, but the primary difference is that it uses private-key (also known as *shared-secret*) cryptography instead of public-key cryptography. In this scenario, a secret (the private key) is shared between the client and server. The client and server must prove that they know the shared secret. Both parties don't trust one another until they have proven to each other that they know the shared secret. This is called *mutual authentication*; they trust that the other is who they say they are.

The Authentication Process

A client using Kerberos first types in his or her user name and password and attempts to log on to the Windows 2000 domain. Behind the scenes, the password is *hashed*, which means that a number is generated using encryption and the user's password. The hash now becomes a *key*. The key is then bundled with other security identifying information before it's sent off as a request to the Kerberos Distribution Center (KDC).

The KDC is a service center on every DC that serves as a trusted intermediary between the client and server. Its primary purposes in life are the following:

- Provides session keys for mutual authentication
- Authenticates the client and server
- Grants tickets, which are essentially vouchers for a user's identity and other security-related information

When the KDC receives the request, it verifies that the user is who he or she claims to be by matching the key to its own master copy of the user's key. Once the user is verified, the KDC provides the user with an initial ticket called the *ticket-granting ticket (TGT)*, as illustrated in Figure 21-9.

The TGT is a special kind of ticket; it helps the user get other tickets. It is stored by the client (in the client's cache) and is used to get other tickets for authenticating with services and resources on the network. More specifically, when a user wants to use a network service or resource, the user's Kerberos client service presents the TGT to a DC, which in turn compares the TGT with the TGT that the KDC originally handed out. If the user has appropriate access privileges, the user is presented with a session

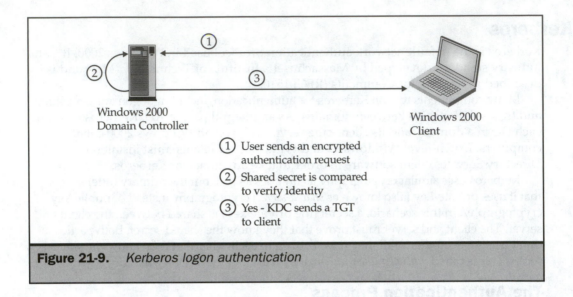

Figure 21-9.   *Kerberos logon authentication*

ticket (ST). This ST, when presented to the service or resource, enables the user to use the service or resource.

Kerberos Trust Relationships

In Chapter 15, Kerberos was described as the protocol responsible for establishing two-way, transitive trust relationships between domains. Since each domain has its own KDC, the way in which a user gains access to resources in other domains is changed slightly.

In the simplest scenario, you have two domains (consulting.ey.com and corp.ey.com) and a user in one domain trying to access a resource in the other domain. This user, named Kim, resides in consulting.ey.com, and let's assume that she's already been granted a TGT from her domain.

The KDC in her domain has no authority over the KDC in corp.ey.com, and it more than likely has no idea about the resource that she's trying to use. So, her KDC finds the KDC for corp.ey.com and passes a referral ticket to her. Her Kerberos client service then sends a request to obtain a TGT for the corp.ey.com domain. As soon as she receives the other TGT, she can use it to get an ST for the resource in corp.ey.com.

Smart Card Support

Windows 2000's support for smart cards further strengthens its commitment for high security standards. Smart cards replace traditional password authentication methods used with a stronger, more effective method. Smart card technology is comprised of a physical smart card, a personal identification number (PIN), and the smart card reader on a Windows 2000 computer. Smart cards can be viewed as basically high-tech, ATM bankcards.

Smart card support is an extension to the Kerberos authentication protocol. As explained earlier, Kerberos uses shared-secret cryptography, but the smart card implementation is a public-key extension much like the one used in PKI. A smart card contains both the public and private keys used to encrypt and decrypt. The private key is never shared (that is, only the user, not the KDC, has the key).

A user initiates the logon process by inserting the smart card into the smart card reader. Then the user types in a personal identification number (PIN). Windows 2000 uses the PIN to access the card, and all cryptographic operations are performed within the smart card. If the user types in the correct PIN and has the appropriate access rights, the user can log on to the system.

 Before you begin using smart cards, you must install a smart card reader as well as Certificate Services for Windows 2000. Refer to "Installing Certificate Services" earlier in this chapter for more information.

Access Control

Authentication of user accounts determines that a user who logs on to a Windows 2000 domain is who the user claims to be and that the user does indeed have an account either in the domain or in a domain that is trusted. After the user is authenticated, however, AD must provide an additional layer of security to determine which objects the authenticated user can view and use. This type of security is achieved through access control.

As with Windows NT and various other operating systems, Windows 2000 uses access control (also known as *authorization*) methods to allow or deny access to objects, such as files, shares, printers, and more. It authorizes access to these resource objects on a computer or on the network through the use of security descriptors, which are sets of information containing who can access the objects.

A security descriptor includes the following information for every securable object:

- **The objects owner**   This is the user who created the object and has privileges to change permissions on that object.

- **An Access Control List (ACL)**   The ACL is maintained by the object's owner (typically the Administrator account) and determines who can see the object and what actions can be performed on it. Windows 2000 enforces these permissions, which are set by the owner whenever a user or process requests to use the object. So if the user or process doesn't have the privilege to use the object, it's denied access.

- **Access Control Entry (ACE)**   An ACE is a single entry within the ACL.

■ **Auditing information**   Once enabled, you can monitor events that are triggered by specific user, group, or computer objects.

> **Note**   *Unlike Windows NT, Windows 2000's access control is very granular due to the object-oriented and distributed nature of AD. This means that you can configure access control security in greater detail and depth.*

Printer Security

After creating and then sharing a printer object, you can configure appropriate access to that printer. There are three basic levels of permissions (print, manage documents, and manage printers) for printers, but, as with many AD objects, you can assign permissions in greater detail if you wish.

By default, the Everyone group has access to print to the printer. This means that everyone, not just authenticated users, can print to this printer, and as a result this may or may not cause a security problem in your environment. It depends on how tightly you want to control access. For tighter control over printer access, you should remove the Everyone group and replace it with the Authenticated Users group to ensure that only those who log on to the domain have access. Also, administrators, print operators, and server operators on a domain controller have Manage Printer permission.

Table 21-2 lists the capabilities of the different permission levels.

Permission Capabilities	Print	Manage Documents	Manage Printer
Print documents	√	√	√
Pause, resume, restart, and cancel the user's own document	√	√	√
Connect to a printer	√	√	√
Control job settings for all documents		√	√
Pause, restart, and delete all documents		√	√
Share a printer			√
Change printer properties			√
Delete printers			√
Change printer permissions			√

Table 21-2.   *Printer Permissions and Capabilities*

To redefine printer permissions, do the following:

1. Open the Printers folder from the Start | Settings menu.

2. Right-click on the printer that you want to configure permissions for and select Properties.

3. Select the Security tab, and for each group you can define the appropriate permissions as shown here.

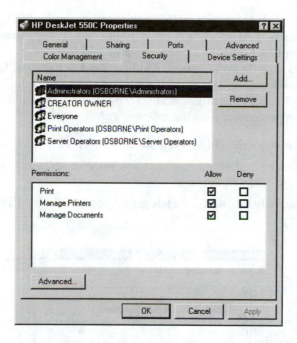

4. Optionally, you can add or remove groups by clicking the Add or Remove buttons, respectively.

File and Share Security

Giving access to files and folders can be split up into two ways. First, you can share a folder and assign specific share permissions to gain access. You can also establish access control on the files or folders themselves.

Both access control methods work in conjunction with one another. If you use both file and share access control methods, the more restrictive ACL takes precedence. For instance, if you set share permissions as read-only and the files have change control, then you'll only have read-only access. You benefit from the access control methods working nicely together because it restricts who has access to files on your system.

Note   *If you're using any other file system besides NTFS (for example, FAT, FAT32, CDFS, etc.), the only available access control method you can use is through shares.*

This section on file and share security only serves as an insight on how to secure your file system. If you want more information on file systems, refer to Chapter 20, which looks in-depth at each of the file systems supported by Windows 2000.

NTFS

For any system with data to protect, NTFS is the file system of choice (it's also required for many services such as AD). NTFS is the only file system supported by Windows 2000 that allows you to set permissions to files and folders.

File permissions include Full Control, Modify, Read & Execute, Read, and Write, while folder permissions adds one more permission to the list, which is List Folder Contents. Table 21-3 lists the permissions and the actions associated with them.

To configure file permissions do the following:

1. Open Windows Explorer from the Start | Programs | Accessories menu.

2. Select the files or a group of files that you want to set permissions for. Then right-click and select Properties.

3. Select the Security tab, and for each group you can define the appropriate permissions .

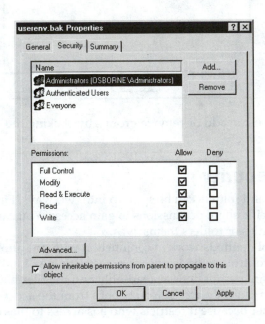

Action	Full Control	Modify	Read & Execute	Read	Write
Traverse Folder/Execute File	√	√	√		
List Folder/Read Data	√	√	√	√	
Read Attributes	√	√	√	√	
Read Extended Attributes	√	√	√	√	
Create Files/Write Data	√	√			√
Create Folders/Append Data	√	√			√
Write Attributes	√	√			√
Write Extended Attributes	√	√			√
Delete Subfolders and Files	√				
Delete	√	√			
Read Permissions	√	√	√	√	√
Change Permissions	√				
Take Ownership	√				
Synchronize	√	√	√	√	√

Table 21-3. *NTFS File and Folder Permission with Associated Actions*

4. Optionally, you can add or remove groups by clicking the Add or Remove buttons, respectively.

Note *The same steps can be applied when you're setting folder permissions. The differences are that you'll be choosing the folder instead of individual files and you'll have the ability to use the List Folder Contents permission.*

By default, Windows 2000 sets the Everyone group as having Full Control on file and folder permissions. Microsoft probably decided to set permissions this way for convenience rather than disregarding security concerns for files and folders. In order to beef up your file and folder security, you should remove the Everyone group and replace it with Authenticated Users. At a minimum, you should reduce the level of access that the Everyone group has.

EFS

The Encrypted File System (EFS) is an extra layer of protection against unauthorized access that allows you to encrypt files and folders on NTFS partitions using Data Encryption Standard (DES) 56-bit encryption. It is based on public-key cryptography, which is also used in PKI and Kerberos authentication.

EFS is tightly integrated with NTFS, meaning that files aren't just protected by the operating system's access control. So a hacker who is lucky enough to compromise NTFS permissions then has to break the encryption in order to use the files or folders. The applications for EFS are endless. It can be used to prevent intruders from using MS-DOS-based utilities that read NTFS partitions, discourage laptop theft, and much more.

 The initial release of EFS supports only DES encryption, but updates to Windows 2000 will most likely include updates for EFS. Keep in mind that the initial release only allows the person who encrypted the file to open it.

To encrypt a file or folder, do the following:

1. Open Windows Explorer from the Start | Programs | Accessories menu.
2. Select the files or folder that you want to encrypt. Then right-click and select Properties.
3. Under the General tab click the Advanced button.
4. In the Advanced Attributes window, select Encrypt Contents To Secure Data.

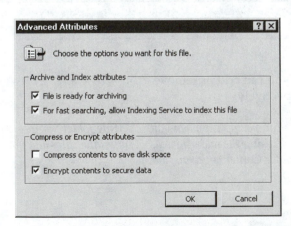

5. Click OK twice to close the Properties window. At this point, the Confirm Attribute Changes window appears and prompts you to decide how you'd like to apply the encryption change.

Share-Level Security

Share-level security enables you to control which users and processes can connect to the shared folder. What the user or process can do from there depends on the file and folder security you have defined. Share-level permissions include Full Control, Change, and Read access.

You can configure and manage shares either through the Windows Explorer or Shared Folders MMC snap-in (in this case using the Windows Explorer). To define share permissions, do the following:

1. Open Windows Explorer from the Start | Programs | Accessories menu.

2. Select the share that you want to set permissions for. Then right-click and select Properties.

3. Select the Sharing tab and click the Permissions button.

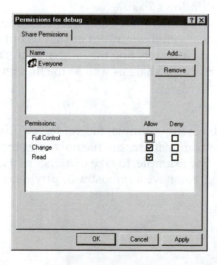

4. Configure the appropriate share permissions for groups or users.

5. You can optionally add or remove groups and users by using the Add and Remove buttons, respectively.

HIDDEN SHARES   In addition to shares that you can view from anywhere on the network, there are shares that are hidden. These shares are typically used for administrative purposes only and are denoted with the $ symbol. Table 21-4 lists the default hidden shares for Windows 2000.

You can create your own hidden shares for directories and printers by adding the $ to the end of the share name. Even though "out of sight is out of mind," you still are completely secure. Therefore, after creating the hidden share, make sure that you set the appropriate permissions to the share as well as the files and any subdirectories.

Ownership

The user that creates an object (for example, file, folder, or printer) is the object's owner. The owner and the administrator are the only ones that can change access permissions on the object. For example, to take ownership of a file or folder object, do the following (assuming you have administrator privileges):

Hidden Share	Path
Root of each partition	C:\, D:\, E:\, etc.
ADMIN$	%SystemRoot%
IPC$	
print$	%SystemRoot%\System32\spool\drivers

Table 21-4. *Windows 2000's Default Hidden Shares*

1. Open Windows Explorer from the Start | Programs | Accessories menu.
2. Locate the file or folder for which you want to take ownership.
3. Right-click the file or folder and then click Properties.
4. Select the Security tab and click the Advanced button.
5. Select the Owner tab and then click New Owner.
6. You can optionally take ownership on all of the subfolders by selecting Replace owner on subcontainers and objects.
7. Click OK.

It is also possible to transfer ownership of the object. This can only be done indirectly, meaning that you can grant another user the Take Ownership permission. You can't actually assign the ownership to another user.

Auditing

In addition to securing resources, it's critical to monitor security events. Auditing is an important, yet often overlooked, facet of security. The importance of auditing comes from the fact that it can record possible security problems or security-related events, provide evidence of security compromises, and ensure accountability.

There are numerous ways to audit a Windows 2000 system ranging from systemwide security events to monitoring security-related events for printers. How you can customize what to audit depends on the object that you're monitoring. All security-audited events can be viewed in the Security log within the Event Viewer.

The first and required step is to configure systemwide audit policies through the Local Computer Policy MMC snap-in or from the Group Policy snap-in for a DC. Once you've installed the snap-in, browse down the tree in the left pane (Computer Configuration | Windows Settings | Security Settings) and click on Audit Policy, as shown in Figure 21-10. In the right pane you'll see the following events that you can configure for auditing:

- Audit account logon events
- Audit account management
- Audit directory service access
- Audit logon events
- Audit object access
- Audit policy change
- Audit privilege use
- Audit process tracking
- Audit system events

These events can be audited for success or failure.

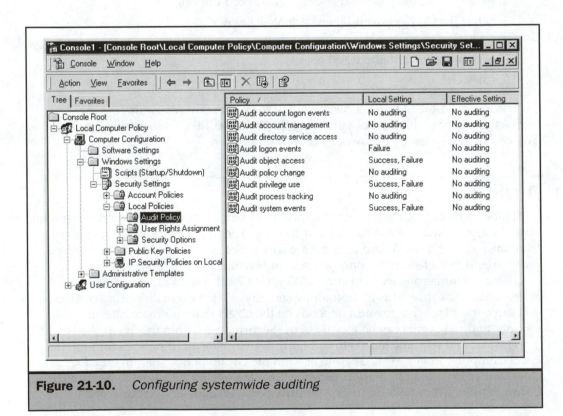

Figure 21-10. *Configuring systemwide auditing*

Auditing Files and Folders

Auditing files and folders allows you to monitor various security-related events for specific users or groups. For example, you can configure auditing to watch for Authenticated Users creating folders and Administrators changing permissions.

To perform audits on files or folders, do the following:

1. Open Windows Explorer from the Start | Programs | Accessories menu.

2. Right-click on the file or folder you wish to audit and select Properties.

3. Select the Security tab and then click the Advanced tab.

4. In the Access Control Settings window, select the Auditing button.

5. Click the Add button and then select a user, group, or computer to watch when accessing this file or folder. Click OK.

6. In the Auditing Entries window, specify the events that should be audited as shown in the next illustration. Click OK to close the window.

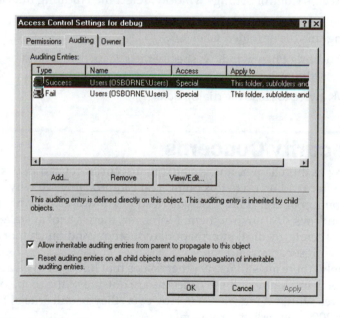

7. Click OK twice to exit completely.

Auditing Printers

You can audit printers to maintain tighter control and monitoring of your print processes. The major difference between auditing printers and other objects is what you are able to monitor.

The following printer events can be audited (successful or failed):

- Print
- Manage Printers
- Manage Documents
- Read Permissions
- Change Permissions
- Take Ownership

To perform audits on printers, do the following:

1. Open the Printers folder from the Start | Settings | Printers menu.

2. Right-click on the printer you wish to audit and select Properties.

3. Select the Security tab and then click the Advanced tab.

4. In the Access Control Settings window, select the Auditing button.

5. Click the Add button and then select a user, group, or computer to watch when accessing this file or folder. Click OK.

6. In the Auditing Entry window, specify the events that should be audited. Click OK to close the window.

7. Click OK twice to close the dialog box.

Other Security Concerns

In the beginning of this chapter, it was stated that security-related issues intimidate many people. After reading up to this point, you can probably see why: there's so much to learn on top of everything else you need to know about configuring and managing a Windows 2000 environment. Moreover, there's a lot at stake—financial costs, corporate secrets, medical information, reputation, and much more—when you're dealing with security concerns.

Unfortunately, there are still many other issues that have yet to be addressed when talking about security. Many of these concerns are outside of the scope of built-in security measures within Windows 2000. However, they're still crucial to protecting your Windows 2000 network environment.

Securely Connecting to the Internet

The Internet is one of the most common ways that hackers try to gain unauthorized access to your Windows 2000 network environment. From a security point of view, the Internet is untrustworthy in that you have no exercisable control over security measures being used. You do, however, have the ability to control what comes into and out of your network infrastructure.

No matter highly tightly you lock down your Windows 2000 network, if you don't guard the border, you'll create more vulnerability than you'd ever imagine. Millions of people would have the opportunity to take a crack at your security implementation. This is not to say that Windows 2000 is an insecure operating system, but rather that the more you protect the gateway to the Internet, the safer your network will be.

Firewalls and Proxies

Firewalls are blockades against unwanted intrusion that stand between your network and the rest of the world, as illustrated in Figure 21-11. On the other hand, proxy servers, such as Microsoft Proxy Server, have traditionally only provided performance enhancements (for example, network traffic caching) for your network but are now equipping themselves with firewall-class security mechanisms.

Different types of firewalls and proxies exist on the market, and you should research them in order to find out which one best suits your needs and budget. Many offer comparable features such as packet filtering, network address translation (NAT), support for a variety of protocols and security-related technologies, and the use of a

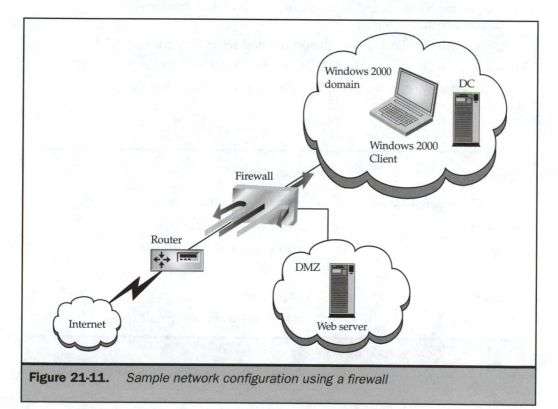

Figure 21-11.   *Sample network configuration using a firewall*

demilitarized zone (DMZ), and much more. Table 21-5 lists a variety of vendors that supply firewall security.

 A DMZ is created by the firewall to allow incoming Internet traffic in a controlled manner. For example, Web servers are typically placed in a DMZ and only allow Web-based traffic (for example, HTTP).

TCP/IP Filtering

Firewalls and/or proxies are highly recommended if you're connecting your network to the Internet, but some Windows 2000 environments just can't afford such solutions. A viable but less secure alternative is to use Windows 2000 to filter TCP/IP traffic coming in from the outside world.

TCP/IP filtering allows you to permit traffic coming into specific ports. These ports can be either TCP or UDP or both. Each service reserves a specific port number, and it also determines the port type (TCP, UDP, or both). Table 21-6 lists many TCP/IP related services and their associated ports and port types.

To enable TCP/IP filtering, do the following:

1. Open the Network and Dial-up Connections folder from the Start | Settings menu.

2. Right-click on Local Area Connections and select Properties.

3. Select the Internet Protocol (TCP/IP) and click the Properties button.

4. In the Internet Protocol (TCP/IP) Properties window, click the Advanced button.

Company	Web Site
CheckPoint Software	http://www.checkpoint.com
Borderware	http://www.border.com
Network-1	http://www.network-1.com
NetGuard	http://www.netguard.com
Raptor	http://www.raptor.com
Microsoft	http://www.microsoft.com/proxy/

Table 21-5. *Firewall and Proxy Vendors*

Port Number	Type	Name	Description
20	tcp,udp	ftp-data	File Transfer Protocol Data
21	tcp,udp	ftp	File Transfer Protocol Control
23	tcp,udp	telnet	Telnet
25	tcp,udp	smtp	Mail, Simple Mail Transport Protocol
67	tcp,udp	bootp	DHCP/BOOTP
68	tcp,udp	bootp	DHCP/BOOTP
69	tcp,udp	tftp	Trivial File Transfer Protocol
70	tcp,udp	gopher	Gopher
79	tcp,udp	finger	Finger
80	tcp,udp	www	HTTP, World Wide Web
110	tcp,udp	pop3	Post Office Protocol Version 3
119	tcp,udp	nntp	Network News Transfer Protocol
137	tcp,udp	netbios-ns	NetBIOS Name Serve
138	tcp,udp	netbios-dgm	NetBIOS Datagram Service
139	tcp,udp	netbios-ssn	NetBIOS Session Service
161	tcp,udp	snmp	Simple Network Management Protocol (SNMP)
162	tcp,udp	snmptrap	SNMP Trap

Table 21-6. *Several Reserved TCP/IP Ports*

INSIDE
WINDOWS 2000

5. In the Advanced TCP/IP Settings window, select the Options tab.

6. Select TCP/IP filtering and select Properties.

7. In the TCP/IP Filtering window, click Permit Only for TCP, UDP, or both. You'll notice that the Enable TCP/IP Filtering (All Adapters) check box is checked now. If you don't want filtering to be applied to all adapters, uncheck this option.

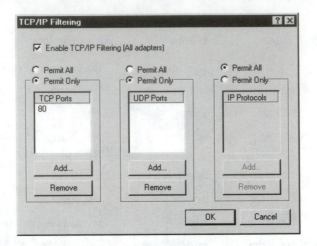

8. Click the Add button, and then type in the port number for the port type you selected. Click OK when done.

9. Click OK four times to completely exit.

The drawback to manually configuring TCP/IP filtering is that you have to know the specific ports that you'll need to permit. This is difficult even for those who are experienced with TCP/IP. So if you decide to use filtering, expect to spend a lot of time troubleshooting connectivity problems.

Remote Access

Successfully securing remote access connections into and away from your Windows 2000 network environment should be high priority. Improperly securing remote access connections can be devastating because it creates security holes that hackers can use to gain access to your network. Windows 2000's Routing and Remote Access (RRAS) includes many security features to help protect your network. These features include encryption, authentication, callback, VPN support, and much more.

Chapter 16 covers RRAS and RRAS security issues at length. For more information on securing remote access connections, consult Chapter 16.

Antivirus

Surprisingly, virus attacks have only received notable attention since the outbreak of the Michael Angelo virus a few years ago. Now, they're becoming increasingly widespread and even more damaging. For this reason, your security plan must include a third-party antivirus solution in order to protect against virus threats.

A virus is a piece of code that can self-replicate and is designed to affect your computer in some fashion without your knowledge or permission. The code could be malicious or benign, but in either case it's unwanted.

Types of and Effects from Viruses

There are several different types of viruses, including

- Master boot record and boot sector
- Trojan horses
- File infecting
- Stealth
- Polymorphic
- Macro
- Hoaxes

Unfortunately, the list goes on, and it's important that you protect your Windows 2000 network environment from them all. The effect of these viruses on your environment depends on the type of virus it is. For example, a Trojan horse is usually hidden within another program, and it can cause a considerable amount of damage (for example, corrupting all files on the hard disk) to the system it infects. Other viruses may just constantly display annoying messages on the screen.

Some common problems caused by viruses you may experience include, but aren't limited to:

- Boot failures
- Reduction in available system memory
- Slow system performance
- Changes to file time stamps
- Reduction in disk space

Virus Remedies

In order to prevent virus infections or to bring a system back to good health, you'll need help from an antivirus program. You can either buy a "shrink-wrapped" type of application or download shareware antivirus programs. The applications' features vary, but you should look for the types of viruses they detect and how they detect them. For example, some scan the hard disks, some stay resident in memory, and some allow you to schedule periodic scans. Table 21-7 lists a few companies that provide antivirus software.

Company	Web Site
Cheyenne Computer Associates	http://www.cheyenne.com
Dr. Solomon's Software	http://www.drsoloman.com
IBM	http://www.ibm.com
McAfee Associates	http://www.mcafee.com
Symantec	http://www.symantec.com

Table 21-7.   *Antivirus Software Companies*

Chapter 22

Systems
and Subsystems

Windows 2000, like Windows NT before it, is an advanced operating system designed from the ground up to support advanced features. All of its most sophisticated features, from symmetric multiprocessing support to asynchronous input and output to integrated security, are the result of the design of the kernel and associated low-level software.

Windows 95 and 98 may look a lot like Windows NT and Windows 2000, but internally they are very different. Because of the need to support as much existing software written for DOS and Windows 3.*x* as possible, Windows 9*x* is an inherently insecure operating system that can be brought crashing down by poorly written or malicious programs at almost any stage.

Windows NT and Windows 2000 are far more robust. The design of the operating system prevents most programs from causing harm to the system and to the other programs running on it. It also makes it possible for Windows 2000 to run different parts of your program on different processors, to continue running even as it waits for I/O to proceed, and to prevent it from accessing files to which it is not entitled.

The information in this chapter will help you, as an administrator, understand why applications behave the way they do. It will also be of interest to programmers who want to understand how their programs are functioning.

A good way to learn about how the core system services of Windows 2000 are operating on your computer is to use the Windows 2000 Resource Kit, which you can obtain from Microsoft. It contains many tools referenced in this chapter that show specific elements of the kernel, device drivers, and other core components of Windows 2000.

The more intrepid programmers among you may wish to examine the Windows 2000 Driver Development Kit (DDK), which contains the tools and information for writing programs that directly interface with the kernel and hardware. The DDK contains extensive documentation and tools from which you can learn about the inner workings of Windows 2000.

The Architecture of Windows 2000

To begin an understanding of the way the components of the operating system work, examine the diagram in Figure 22-1, which summarizes the architecture of the Windows 2000 operating system.

Superficially, the structure of this diagram hasn't changed much since the initial versions of it in 1992 when Microsoft first revealed Windows NT to the world. There are some new areas, including the Configuration Manager, Power Manager, and Plug and Play Manager. Another major difference is that some sections have moved from the upper (user mode) part of the diagram to the lower (kernel mode) part.

Programs running in kernel mode are privileged programs, which have full access to all data and resources in the computer. Most of these programs are the core of Windows 2000 and written by Microsoft, but device drivers also run in this area, and a poorly written device driver can bring down an entire Windows 2000 system.

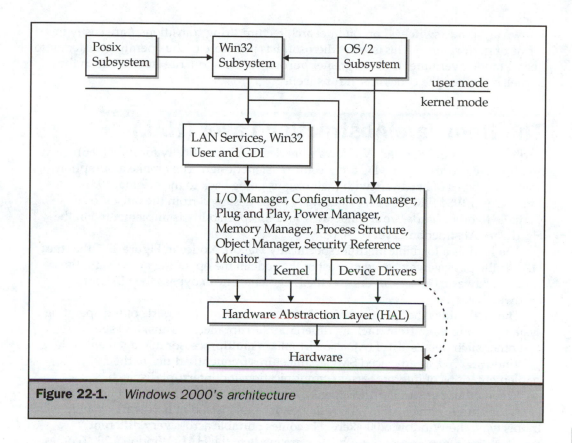

Figure 22-1. *Windows 2000's architecture*

Microsoft has gone to great lengths to improve the stability of device drivers in Windows 2000 and to increase accountability for driver authors. Early technical marketing for Windows NT spoke of its design as a "microkernel," a trendy concept in those days. The idea of a microkernel is that the kernel of the operating system should be as small as possible, and that operating system services should be run, if possible, as user mode programs. Structurally, NT resembled a microkernel in some ways because the services were defined modules outside of the formal kernel, but Microsoft always ran these programs in kernel mode. It's hard to call this a microkernel when so much code runs in kernel mode.

In the end, the decision of whether to run operating system services in user or kernel mode is a trade-off among performance, stability, and some other lesser issues (for example, it's easier to write and debug user mode programs). Microkernels theoretically make the system more stable but at a high performance cost, because calls to system services from applications (and from other system services) must pass through the microkernel, transitioning from user mode application to kernel mode to the user mode system service, and back around to the application. Such transitions, known as "mode switches" or, on Intel architecture, "ring transitions," are costly in terms of performance. This is why Microsoft has put more of the operating system into kernel mode over time. It puts a greater burden on them to write stable code in the kernel, but when the code runs, it runs well.

The Hardware Abstraction Layer (HAL)

Earlier versions of DOS and Windows were designed specifically for Intel (*x*86) architecture processors and PC architecture system design. They make assumptions of specific types of hardware with their origins going back to the original 1981 IBM PC and 1984 IBM PC-AT. Windows NT was designed from the outset to be portable to other hardware architectures, and this portability is implemented in the Hardware Abstraction Layer or HAL.

The HAL is a loadable module, specifically Hal.dll. Notice in Figure 22-1 that the HAL is the passageway between most of the code in the operating system and the actual hardware. Device drivers and the I/O manager can bypass the HAL for hardware access.

The HAL hides the specifics of hardware access from other parts of the operating system, freeing them from tracking different interrupt mechanisms, I/O specifics, and other such details. The HAL also virtualizes multiprocessor management code in Windows 2000, as advanced SMP architectures frequently differ in their implementations of interprocessor communication and interrupt dispatch.

When other parts of the operating system need to invoke these functions, they use HAL routines (or invoke third-party device drivers) instead of hardware-specific calls. In this way, the Windows 2000 kernel becomes portable across very different architectures when appropriate changes are made to the HAL. Windows 2000 comes with many HALs to support different architectures and decides at install time which HAL to install on the system as Hal.dll. OEM systems often come with custom-written preinstalled HALs to support their specific hardware.

The HAL routines are documented in the Windows 2000 DDK. Examples of these routines are HalGetAdapter, which device drivers can use to obtain information about specific adapters from the hardware and data structures through which they can access the adapter; and HalExamineMBR, which returns data from the master boot record (MBR) of a disk. If you want to learn more about the specifics of implementing a HAL, refer to the DDK.

The Kernel

Often the term "kernel" is used to refer to all the core system services, especially those that operate in kernel mode. There is some validity to this term, based on general computer science terminology, but Windows 2000 also has a more specific definition of "The Kernel."

The program, ntoskrnl.exe is what supplies many of the fundamental functions of modern computing to the rest of Windows 2000. The Kernel provides thread scheduling and dispatching, multiprocessor management, interrupt handling, and trap and exception handling, and it allocates objects used by other parts of the Executive. The *Executive* is the term for the collection of basic system services (such as I/O, cache manager, and so on), that are used by the operating system.

Nothing in Windows 2000 can work correctly without the Kernel functioning, so its performance and stability are crucial to Windows 2000's proper function. The memory in the Kernel is usually locked down so that it cannot be moved in memory or paged out to disk, and in Windows 2000 it is also write-protected using processor hardware features, so that other programs, even kernel mode programs, cannot accidentally overwrite it.

The functions in the Kernel illustrate how Windows 2000 maintains a powerful design while maximizing portability to different architectures. While the Kernel manages multiprocessor synchronization, it uses HAL routines to determine the specifics of processor organization and programming. The exact mechanisms of scheduling and dispatching of traps and interrupts also differ in different hardware architectures, so the Kernel uses the HAL to learn these details. In this way the Kernel remains portable, but can still work with the hardware in an optimal fashion.

The Kernel is the supplier of key system objects that are used by other system services, such as the Process and I/O Managers, to support applications. For example, it is the Kernel that supplies the base thread object used by the Process Manager to create processes. The policy for managing processes and threads is done by the Process Manager. These other services typically take the *kernel object* supplied to them by the Kernel and encapsulate it in a larger, more complex object, that allows for higher-level functionality and more detailed management.

There are different types of kernel objects. One, known as a *dispatcher object*, includes objects to control timers, threads, semaphores, and mutexes. *Control objects* include the kernel process object, the deferred procedure call (DPC) object, and interrupt objects. Dispatcher objects have a state that is set to either Signaled or Not-Signaled. Control objects do not.

System Services

The bulk of the Windows 2000 Executive is composed of a collection of system services. These are low-level routines that work through the kernel and HAL to talk to the hardware, and that use each other extensively.

The system services aren't programs you run in the conventional sense like databases or compilers. They *export* subroutines for the Windows subsystems, device drivers, and each other to use. They provide computing functionality in an abstract manner for programmers to use, usually indirectly through the Win32 subsystem.

Two of these services, the Plug and Play Manager and the Power Manager, are new in Windows 2000. These functions, to the extent they were available in Windows NT 4, were supplied by device drivers in a nonuniform manner. These new system services provide support for both Windows 2000-only drivers and WDM (Windows Driver Model) drivers.

Object Manager

Windows 2000 is an object-based system at its heart. The operating system components communicate by creating objects and passing them among each other and to applications. Device drivers follow these same protocols. This object-based structure facilitates both the portability of Windows 2000 between platforms and its extensibility from version to version. The existence of defined objects and interfaces to them allows Microsoft to make modifications in one system service without breaking the functionality in others.

The Object Manager provides routines that create and manage the lifetime of these objects. They ensure that an object still in use by one part of the operating system is not deleted by another. The Object Manager also helps components determine the access restrictions on a particular object.

Centralizing object management allows Windows 2000 to achieve many goals, including accounting for resource utilization by different processes and making rules for system object usage uniform throughout the system. It also isolates resource allocation in a way that is necessary for Windows 2000 to be certifiable as C2 security compliant.

The Object Manager maintains these generic services for object lifetime management, but the routines to create, open, and query services from an object are all implemented in each object for performance purposes. Generic services could have been written for these functions, as they are for user mode programs through the Component Object Model, but at the cost of processing overhead in performance-critical sections of the operating system.

The Object Manager manages two types of objects: kernel objects and executive objects. Kernel objects are implemented in the Kernel and used only within kernel mode, although access to them is often available through executive objects in which they are encapsulated. Executive objects are implemented in the various system services in the executive.

Objects of a particular type in the Executive and Kernel have certain types of data in common, such as security access information. In those cases, the Object Manager creates such object-type-specific information when the object type is created and stores it in an internal object called a *type object*.

A good example of an Executive object is an open file. Win32 programs that open files see them as file objects, created by the I/O Manager. Programs running in user mode in the protected subsystems such as Win32 typically make calls to those subsystems, and not directly into the Executive. The subsystems implement their own objects that usually are a veneer around Executive objects. Thus a file object in a Win32 program contains internal references to a file object in the I/O Manager.

The I/O Manager itself uses objects to communicate with other subsystems and device drivers. Each device in the I/O subsystem is a device object to it. When these objects communicate with device drivers, they do so through driver objects.

Security Reference Monitor

Security in Windows 2000 is complex and pervasive. The Security Reference Monitor (SRM) provides object-level security support routines for device drivers and system services, but a complete discussion of security in Windows 2000 involves numerous other components in the Win32 subsystem, network drivers, and file system drivers.

Most of the routines in the SRM are used by network transfer drivers to assign, remove, and check security privileges in a particular context.

Local Procedure Call

Local Procedure Calls (LPCs) are a fast interprocess message-passing facility available only to operating system services. User mode programs have a rich set of interprocess communication facilities through the Win32 subsystem, as well as the OS/2 and POSIX subsystems.

LPC is a generalized mechanism for communicating between processes within a single system. LPCs are used for a number of reasons, usually by server processes to communicate with client processes. While Win32 programs can't make direct LPC calls, Win32 processes do send LPC messages to the Win32 subsystem in certain circumstances.

Other user mode processes, such as the Session Manager (SMSS), which loads other user mode services, use LPCs to service requests. Another example is the WinLogon service, which manages interactive user session logons and logoffs, and uses LPCs to communicate with the local security authentication server process (LSASS). The SRM (see above) also uses LPCs to communicate with the LSASS.

User mode programs can initiate remote procedure calls (RPCs) that the operating system can transport to another system on the network to invoke on that system. If the target system turns out to be the local system, Windows 2000 invokes an LPC instead.

Processes use a special LPC object called a *port object* to communicate. The port object actually supports four types of ports that correspond to different modes of communication. Ports can be established by either the client or server, and can be named or unnamed. There can be only one unnamed port per client or server.

LPC also supports different methods based on the amount of data to be transferred. If there are fewer than 256 bytes, the data can be included in a buffer along with the message itself. Larger amounts can be passed through a shared memory area. Even larger amounts, which would be time-consuming to copy to a shared area, can be read from or written to a client's address space directly using LPC support functions.

Process Structure

The Windows 2000 Kernel works with threads, and threads are the basic unit of execution in the operating system. But programs consist of more than just threads and can create multiple threads in their context, so they are organized into what is known as a *process*.

In the Executive, processes are represented by a process object, created by the Executive. The Process Structure section of the Executive defines a number of routines that support the creation and management of threads in kernel mode. These are not the same routines that Win32 programs use to create and manage their own threads, but all user mode processes and threads are implemented through the use of embedded kernel mode objects managed by the Executive.

Process management, as with many other kernel mode functions, is handled partly in a large number of undocumented functions in the NT kernel, such as NtMapViewOfExecutableFile(), NtReadPEHeader(), and NtCreateInitialThread().

Process calls in the subsystems are implemented as wrappers around these calls and other kernel mode calls, to account for differences in process models of the subsystems. For example, the Windows 2000 POSIX subsystem implements a true fork capability, the traditional UNIX process-spawning feature, which creates a duplicate of the calling process. Win32 and OS/2 have no fork, although they use the same basic kernel mode calls to implement their own process models.

Windows 2000 also adds new functions in the Win32 subsystem for management of thread pools. Win32 has always provided a rich set of functions for managing individual threads, but it's common for developers, especially those writing server applications, to create groups of threads to service specific events. These developers usually have to write a lot of code to manage these pools, and this is complex programming. The new Thread Pool Components institutionalize a thread-pooling facility in the Win32 API that will be helpful to some of these programmers. The management of threads in the pool is made easier by changes in the Process Structure.

In addition to supporting user mode calls to implement processes and threads, the Process Structure routines support thread creation and management in other system component and device drivers. There are a variety of support routines to create, delete, and read the properties of such threads and processes, and some interesting additional support routines.

The PsSetCreateProcessNotifyRoutine and PsSetCreateThreadNotifyRoutine calls allow a driver to be notified when any process or thread is created. The PsSetLoadImageNotifyRoutine routine allows a driver to be notified when any image is loaded for execution. The latter would be a good hook for an antivirus program.

Job Objects

Windows 2000 adds a major new feature in the area of process management: job objects. *Job objects* are actually Win32 objects and exist in user space, but they are made possible by substantial changes in the kernel mode process structure.

Job objects allow Win32 programmers and administrators to gain considerable control over processes. A job object is a Win32 object that allows a programmer to group a series of processes together for certain administrative purposes. The programmer may also optionally say that any processes spawned by a process in the job should be part of the job.

Processes that are part of a job may have their lifetime and resource utilization limited by the operating system. For example, a process or group of processes may be given a maximum lifetime of some number of minutes, or may have their working set size (the amount of memory they consume) limited to a certain minimum or maximum size.

Job objects can also limit the number of processes another process can spawn, and set process priority class or processor affinity for the job globally. (*Affinity* is an expressed preference to run on a particular processor in a multiprocessor system. Individual threads can change their own affinity, but the job object controls affinity at a process level.) At any time, a program with sufficient privilege and access to the job object can terminate the entire job in one call.

Some processes spawn other processes and group them as one job object. New to Windows 2000 is the opportunity to end that multiple-process job object with one click, instead of manipulating each individual process in the job object. When you right-click the parent process you have the opportunity to end that process and all the other processes in the job object with the End Process Tree command, as shown in Figure 22-2.

Judicious use of job objects could prevent runaway programs in general and prevent memory leaks in applications from impeding overall system performance.

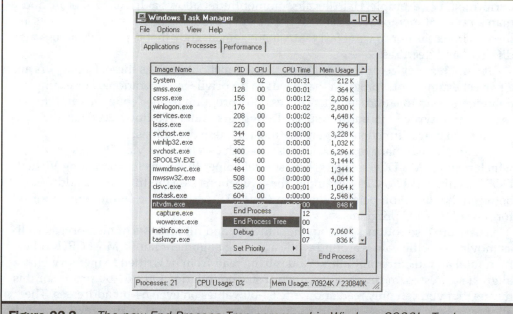

Figure 22-2. *The new End Process Tree command in Windows 2000's Task Manager is based on job objects*

Memory Manager

Memory management is another area where substantial improvements have been made since Windows NT 4, although many of them were first introduced in Windows NT 4 Enterprise Edition. Other memory management advances in Windows 2000 are purely matters involving the Win32 subsystem, not the kernel.

But there has always been a rich set of services available for kernel mode programs to manage memory and perform related operations. In the case of Windows 2000 there turns out to be a large number of related operations that kernel mode programs may wish to invoke.

Kernel mode programs, especially device drivers, frequently require that the memory they allocate be nonpaged, meaning that the virtual memory subsystem will not move it around in memory or swap it out to disk. These programs may need access to physical memory addresses; for example, if a network driver instructs a network adapter to read some number of bytes from the wire into memory, it needs to have a physical memory address, not one of Windows 2000's phony virtual addresses.

When a normal program gains an address to a variable in a protected operating system like Windows 2000, it usually is not dealing with a physical address but a virtual address. The processor knows how to use these virtual addresses to give access to actual physical addresses, but this isn't always adequate for kernel mode programs.

Device drivers and system services can use the memory management routines to convert addresses between the virtual and physical worlds and make memory paged or not. By using Hal routines, extremely low-level yet portable operations can be performed. For example, HalAllocateCommonBuffer allows a driver to allocate and map a range of memory accessible to both a device and the processor. This allows a device driver author to write fast DMA management code that is portable across very different architectures.

It's not just device drivers that need to use functions such as these. Debuggers are a perfect example of a program that needs to do privileged operations. For example, debuggers need to launch another process (the program being debugged) and then read from or write to its address space. Debuggers under Windows 2000 use the Memory Manager functions to perform most of these operations.

Programs that manage other processes—such as Virtual Device Drivers (VDDs), which manage MS-DOS sessions—use special helper functions for managing Virtual DOS Machines (VDMs). For example, these functions assist in translating addresses between the flat 32-bit pointers that Windows 2000 uses and the 16-bit segment:offset form used by DOS programs.

There are also routines for copying, moving, and filling areas of memory, as well as moving specific values around while avoiding alignment faults. Most CPUs other than Intel architecture only allow values to be read from or written to memory on aligned addresses, meaning on even word size boundaries. On a 64-bit processor this means that you can only read and write 64-bit values on even 64-bit addresses. The alignment-safe routines—such as RtlStoreUshort, which stores an unsigned short value at a specific address while avoiding alignment faults—will translate unaligned accesses into aligned ones if necessary.

Developers of performance-critical drivers may want at least parts of their programs not to page to disk, but it is possible to make a driver completely pagable when not in use. Using a series of Lock and Unlock routines, a driver can lock critical sections of code into memory and then release the locks when finished, allowing Windows to page them again and freeing up the physical memory. In fact, a driver can explicitly page out all of its code and data with a single call.

Like Win32 programs, kernel mode programs can create *file mappings*, known in the kernel as *section objects*. They can also manipulate the Win32 heaps, which are pools of memory from which programs allocate memory dynamically for their own use.

Heap management has improved in Windows 2000. In a busy system, programs can slow down because of contention for the Windows heap, which uses a single global lock to serialize access. In Windows 2000 the code inside this lock has been optimized to minimize the likelihood of contention.

Extended Addressing

There was a time, back in 1981, when Bill Gates could say that 640K was enough for everyone. Because it's a 32-bit operating system, Windows NT is limited to 4GB of memory space, only 2GB of which is available for applications, and even today that's enough for almost everyone. But there are some applications that benefit from even more memory, and it's inevitable that such amounts will become mainstream.

Beginning with Windows NT Server Enterprise Edition, Microsoft started playing tricks with memory and using special hardware features to allow access to 3GB, rather than the standard 2GB, of user space on conventional systems, and more than 4GB of total address space on Alpha and Intel Xeon processors. Windows 2000 supports these extensions and increases the limits in some cases.

The 2GB limit has its basis in Windows NT's portability to non-*x*86 processors. *x*86 CPUs use complex data structures to track those areas of memory that are owned by user mode and those owned by supervisor mode, but most RISC chips, including the Compaq Alpha, use the high bit of a 32-bit address to signify this mode. This reduces the effective addressing limit in either mode to 2GB. To make programs portable across implementations of NT, Microsoft carried the limitation to the *x*86 implementation as well. The increase in user space to 3GB on *x*86 systems with at least 4GB memory, known as the *4GB Tuning feature* or *4GT*, continues to work in Windows 2000.

There are other extended memory addressing schemes in different versions of Windows NT and Windows 2000, depending on the specifics of the situation. The Address Windowing Extensions (AWE) are the most significant. These allow applications on Xeon systems to address up to 63GB.

AWE is implemented in the Memory Manager and accessible in the Win32 API through three new APIs and the new MEM_PHYSICAL flag on VirtualAlloc. The new APIs are AllocateUserPhysicalPages, MapUserPhysicalPages, and FreeUserPhysicalPages. Applications may also use GlobalMemoryStatusEx to determine if there is physical RAM for the AWE to use. These APIs all work on all versions of Windows 2000.

AWE is a memory windowing system, not unlike the old Expanded Memory Specification of the mid-1980s. Only data, not code, can be stored above the 4GB line in memory.

AWE creates new compatibility requirements for devices and device drivers. In order to work in an AWE environment, and in order to get the appropriate logo from Microsoft, devices generally need to be 64-bit or Dual Address Cycle capable. See the Windows 2000 DDK and the Windows Driver and Hardware Development page (http://www.microsoft.com/HWDEV/) for more detail.

Choosing to employ the AWE is not a casual decision. Because programming considerations and restrictions when using it are very different than in conventional Win32 or NT kernel mode, only a small number of demanding applications should use it.

Memory protection is very strict in AWE. Only data can be mapped there. An area of memory may only be mapped into a single process, unlike with normal memory. Other restrictions on memory mapping usually employed for interprocess communication (IPC) exist, with the end result that AWE applications must move data into non-AWE memory in order to use it in interprocess communication. Because of the limits on IPC, AWE memory also cannot be used for storing temptingly large buffers, such as video data for streaming by a non-AWE server.

Microsoft claims that keeping the AWE API as simple as possible maximizes its portability and performance, and this is why advanced memory management features are unsupported in the AWE space. Even with these restrictions, there are clearly applications that benefit greatly from having as much physical memory space as possible. Very large databases can greatly improve performance by being able to increase the amount of data in memory. Large modeling applications, for meteorology or econometrics or chemical engineering, all can require huge amounts of data, and their performance is directly improved by increasing the amount of memory available to them.

Executive Support

The Executive actually encompasses many of the other kernel components discussed in this chapter, including process support, memory management, and so on. It includes a large number of documented and undocumented interfaces for kernel mode and user mode programs. In fact, once device drivers and most other kernel mode programs load, they are considered part of the Executive.

There are a large number of routines specifically labeled Executive Support Routines, and their domain is quite varied. They provide functions for device drivers and higher-level subsystems in the areas of memory and process management and resource management in a multiprocessor environment.

For example, kernel mode programs such as device drivers often need to gain exclusive access to a resource or to serialize access to a resource. Windows 2000 uses a device called a *spinlock* to gate access to a resource that only one program can hold at a time, which can be dangerous in a multiprocessor environment. The Executive support routines provide a variety of resource management routines that are "interlocked," meaning that they are synchronized using spinlocks in such a way as to be multiprocessor safe.

Many of the Executive support routines provide complex but common functions used by device drivers. For example, device drivers manage linked lists for their own resources, and historically have had to manage their own spinlocks or other synchronization methods for SMP environments. The Executive provides complex list management routines and guarantees them to be interlocked in a way that is portable across Windows 2000 environments.

Configuration Manager

Configuration Manager is tied into the new device management capabilities of Windows 2000. Configuration Manager, not surprisingly, manages the configuration of the system and Windows 2000's notion of what is installed. During initialization, Configuration Manager creates the hardware and current control set sections of the registry and populates part of them. Then device drivers can call routines exported by Configuration Manager to read and write registry entries relevant to their configuration.

Plug and Play Manager

Working closely with the Configuration Manager and kernel mode drivers (especially Windows Driver Model bus drivers), the Plug and Play Manager determines how to configure the system. The Plug and Play Manager performs a function similar to that of the HAL in that it virtualizes configuration access to hardware. It also provides the interface between user mode programs that manage Plug and Play devices and the hardware itself.

The Plug and Play Manager maintains a dynamic hierarchical tree of hardware that you can view through the Windows 2000 Device Manager (see Figure 22-3). When a device is added to or removed from the system, the Plug and Play Manager is notified by drivers, and it then calls the appropriate functions in the drivers and Configuration Manager in order to initialize the device properly and add it to the system configuration.

Power Manager

Power management in Windows NT 4 is an issue barely addressed by the operating system, and power policies of the system are under the control of third-party device drivers, with the result that support runs hot or cold, depending on the quality of the vendor's support software. Power management support is built into Windows 2000 and power policies are set by the Power Manager component of the Executive.

The Power Manager works with device drivers to control power management, which is actually done using I/O Request Packets (Power IRPs). Power Manager sends IRPs to drivers to read or change *power state*, which consists not only of power consumption data but also of available functionality, hardware latency, and ability to sleep or wake.

Power Manager can only set the power state of the system as a whole, as it is configured by the user in the Power Management applet. It is up to individual drivers to send appropriate IRPs to change their own individual states. The relationships of the

Figure 22-3.   *The Windows 2000 Device Manager is a visual display of the hierarchical display of the Plug and Play Manager's hardware configuration tree*

system to devices and power management policy are defined by the Advanced Configuration and Power Interface (ACPI). The Power Manager exports a series of routines to communicate with drivers.

System power states are named S0 through S5, and device power states are referred to as D0 through D3. The higher the number in either case, the more aggressive the power management. S0 and D0 are the states with the most functionality turned on and the least interruption by sleep. S5 and D3, on the other hand, have the lowest power, the quickest sleep, and the longest wake-up latency.

Having consistent policies and facilities makes it easier for vendors to implement correct and consistent functionality in systems and devices. The fact that Windows 98 also supports ACPI means that users and developers can expect consistent power policies between the two.

I/O Manager

The I/O Manager is arguably the most complex portion of the Windows 2000 Executive. Its basic function is to receive I/O requests from user mode and kernel mode programs and translate them into requests to lower-level drivers and from there to actual storage, from local drives to network drives.

Windows 2000 adds new storage mechanisms, such as FAT32 support, and new internal techniques, such as WDM Kernel Streaming. But the basic structure of the I/O Manager remains as it was in Windows NT 4.

It is the complex job of the I/O Manager to make I/O fast and reliable on both single and multiprocessor systems, and to do so in a way that meets the needs of different types of programs, including DOS, Win 3.1, OS/2, and NT Server applications. One way it does this is by separating support for the logical structure of the file system into a distinct set of drivers called *file system drivers*. We analyze file system drivers in a bit more detail in the "File Systems" and "Device Drivers" sections that follow.

The I/O Manager also provides the basic functionality for advanced IO techniques exposed in the Win32 subsystem. Among these are memory-mapped files, in which an application manipulates an area of memory, and the I/O Manager, together with the paging system, reads and writes data between the disk and that memory to give the application the illusion that the file is a large memory variable. High-bandwidth server applications can use I/O Completion Ports to perform asynchronous I/O, where different threads can create I/O requests while the application continues to perform other tasks. When the I/O request is completed, Windows 2000 wakes up the thread that services it.

Finally, the I/O Manager works closely with the security infrastructure of Windows 2000 to share access to I/O resources and restrict it where appropriate.

Programs in Windows 2000 never manipulate a file directly. They work with virtual files that might exist on any physical storage, from a floppy drive to a network-named pipe to a Web server. Most user mode programs call functions in their subsystem, such as Win32 or POSIX, to manipulate files, and the subsystems themselves translate these calls into calls to the I/O Manager. But the virtualization doesn't stop there: file system drivers manage the relationship between the request for a virtual file in Windows 2000's logical file system tree and the actual logical structure of the device on which the file resides. The file system driver, with the potential intervention by a filter driver, makes requests to the device drivers that control that device to perform the specific I/O. These device drivers themselves make use of driver support routines in the I/O Manager and elsewhere in the Executive to perform their own functions. Requests made by the I/O Manager may filter through the HAL and its I/O access routines before they reach physical I/O ports and registers.

File Systems

File systems in Windows 2000 have their own set of special device drivers called file system drivers. In fact, there is a second type of file system driver, a filter driver that allows software modification to be performed on an existing file system.

Windows 2000 includes file system support for the original FAT16 system that has its origins in DOS version 2, and adds support for the FAT32 system that Microsoft introduced in Windows 95 OEM service release 2. HPFS support is included to support the OS/2 subsystem, and CDFS support allows Windows 2000 to read CD-ROMs.

Other drivers, known as *network redirectors,* perform a function analogous to file system drivers by connecting to remote file systems, such as Novell NetWare servers, UNIX NFS servers, or other Windows NT and Windows 2000 systems using Microsoft's SMB/CIFS protocol. The new Distributed File System (Dfs) in Windows 2000 is another example of a file system type that exploits the already existing virtualization of storage in Windows 2000. All Dfs does is to create a virtual namespace consisting of local and remote storage, very much like the one that the I/O Manager presents to programs and subsystems.

Filter drivers are special intermediate drivers that intercept communications between two other software components, such as the I/O Manager and a file system driver, and modify the data being transacted. Filter drivers have been around for years and can be added by third parties. For example, some vendors have implemented Windows NT virus scanners as file system filters, because a filter has an opportunity to monitor data before it is read from or written to disk. The new Encrypted File System in Windows 2000 is another example of a file system filter; it encrypts data being written to disk and decrypts data being read from disk.

Finally, there is a class of intermediate-level drivers for managing generic types of devices, such as SCSI or other WDM drivers.

Device Drivers

Support for device drivers has changed considerably in Windows 2000 with the addition of Windows Driver Model. Many device drivers are now portable between Windows 98 and Windows 2000, and are much easier to write than native Windows NT drivers, many of which are still supported in Windows 2000.

The
Complete
Reference

Part V

Internet and Intranet Functionality

The
Complete
Reference

Chapter 23

Internet
Information Server 5

839

The Internet's popularity has grown to unimaginable levels in the past several years, providing companies and end users with more than just information, entertainment, and communication. One of the most popular of these Internet technologies is the World Wide Web (WWW) service.

Windows 2000 Server includes built-in Web service and related technology support through Internet Information Server (IIS). IIS provides an easy yet effective and efficient way to collaborate information via Web-based services.

Familiarizing Yourself with IIS

At first glance, IIS 5 doesn't appear to be radically different from earlier versions. However, when you take a look at what this new version of IIS has to offer, you'll be surprised at just how different it is. As an integral part of Windows 2000, it supports a greater number of Internet standards, clustering (with Windows 2000 Advanced Server), and much more.

Note	*For more information on clustering, refer to Chapter 26.*

Terminology

The purpose of this section is to familiarize you with some of the terminology used throughout this chapter. Although this section doesn't contain all the terminology for Web services and related technologies, it does include some important terms to help you understand the type of service that IIS provides.

- **Common Gateway Interface (CGI)**   This is an interface for services, such as database or messaging services, to communicate with the Web service. The CGI program or script can interact with a variety of services and can perform numerous operations (form handling between a database and Web service, for example).

- **File Transfer Protocol (FTP)**   This protocol within the TCP/IP suite of protocols is used to handle file transfers between local and remote computers.

- **Hypertext Markup Language (HTML)**   This is a formatting language used by the Web service. HTML files are plain text files with codes embedded in them indicating formatting, links, graphics, scripting languages to use, and more.

- **Hypertext Transfer Protocol (HTTP)**   This is a protocol used for communication between client Web browsers and the Web server.

- **Internet Server Application Programming Interface (ISAPI)**   ISAPI is similar to CGI in that it is an interface between services. However, instead of using external applications, ISAPI uses Dynamic Link Libraries (DLLs). This improves the performance of the interaction between the services.

■ **Uniform Resource Locator (URL)**   URLs are an addressing system used to locate information. A user types in a URL in a Web browser to request this information. A URL has the following format:

protocol://<computer_name or domain_name>:<port number>/document

It is important to note that some parameters are optional. For example, http://www.task-group.com/ is a URL that does not specify the port number or a specific document.

| Note | *The IIS documentation contains a large glossary of terminology that you can peruse.* |

New IIS 5 Features

With each new version of IIS comes a wealth of new and improved features that provide a robust and scalable architecture for Web, FTP, and other related Internet-technologies. Windows 2000's built-in IIS 5 is no exception.

For your convenience, Microsoft has organized these new features into several categories. They are listed here with their respective improvements:

■ **Security**

■ **Digest authentication**   In addition to the previously supported authentication mechanisms, Windows 2000 has added this secure and robust authentication mechanism that is especially designed for authenticating users across proxy servers and firewalls.

■ **Server-Gated Cryptography (SGC)**   SGC is an extension of the Secure Sockets Layer (SSL) technology that allows companies with export versions of IIS to use strong 128-bit encryption.

■ **Security wizards**   In order to simplify administration tasks, IIS provides wizards to help configure security settings on the server. They include the Web Server Certificate, Permissions, and Certificate Trust Lists (CTL) Wizards.

■ **Kerberos v5 compliance**   The integration of Kerberos with IIS allows you to pass authentication credentials among connected Windows 2000 computers.

■ **Certificate storage**   IIS certificate storage takes full advantage of the certificate services that are provided with Windows 2000's Certificate Server. It is now integrated with the Windows CryptoAPI storage. The Windows Certificate Manager provides a single point of entry that allows you to store, back up, and configure server certificates.

■ **FORTEZZA**   FORTEZZA, from the National Security Agency, is a family of products that enhance security standards. IIS now complies with this standard to provide bulletproof Web-based messaging.

- **Administration**

  - **Reliable restarts** In previous versions, you often had to restart the server in order to restart IIS services. To avoid this, Windows 2000 includes IIS Reliable Restart, which is a faster, easier, more flexible one-step restart process. The administrator can restart IIS through the Computer Management or Services Microsoft Management Console (MMC) snap-ins as well as by using the command line. Windows 2000 will also attempt to automatically restart the IIS services if the INETINFO process terminates unexpectedly. This promotes higher reliability and stability.

  - **Process accounting** When a server is hosting more than one Web site, it's often useful to know how each Web site affects the system's CPU utilization. Process accounting does just that; it provides information about how individual Web sites use the server's CPU resources.

  - **Process throttling** Process throttling allows you to limit the percentage of CPU utilization for individual Web sites.

- **Programmability**

  - **New Active Server Pages (ASP) features** ASP is a server-side scripting language that has been supported by previous versions of IIS. Improvements have been made to streamline performance and IIS scripts.

  - **Application protection** IIS increases reliability for your Web applications by either *pooling* processes or isolating them from other processes. Pooled processes run in a common memory space that is separate from memory areas where core IIS services are running.

  - **Active Directory (AD) support** IIS fully supports AD through **ADSI 2.0**. This gives you greater flexibility in configuring Web sites because you can create your own custom AD objects using ADSI.

- **Internet Standards**

  - **Web Distributed Authoring and Versioning (WebDAV)** WebDAV allows you to manage file and directory related properties of a Web site through a standard HTTP connection.

  - **FTP restart** If you've ever had to stop a download (or had one interrupted) when using FTP and then later want to resume downloading, you're probably well aware that you often have to start the download from scratch. Now you can resume it from where you left off.

  - **HTTP compression** HTTP compression combines compacting Web pages with caching of static files to gain speed at which users see the Web pages. Clients and servers that are compression enabled can utilize this feature.

Installing IIS

There are basically two installation scenarios regarding the installation of IIS. Both installations of IIS depend on whether you're installing Windows 2000 Server from scratch or upgrading to Windows 2000 Server.

If you're installing Windows 2000 Server from scratch, IIS is installed automatically and its services are running. You can immediately start configuring Web-based services.

If you're upgrading from a down-level server, Windows 2000 Server may or may not install IIS. The catch is that it will only install IIS during an upgrade if the server was already running a previous version of IIS.

IIS Installation Defaults

IIS is comprised of several components that constitute Internet-based services. The most familiar of these are Web site services and FTP. By default, Windows 2000's IIS installs the following components:

- Required IIS common files
- IIS documentation
- FTP Server
- FrontPage 2000 Server Extensions
- Internet Information Services snap-in
- Internet Services Manager (HTML)
- World Wide Web Server

There are other optional components, including the **Network News Transfer Protocol** (NNTP) service , the Simple Mail Transfer Protocol (SMTP) service, and the Visual InterDev RAD Remote Deployment Support. You can use the Add/ Remove Programs applet within the Control Panel to install IIS or add/remove IIS components as illustrated in Figure 23-1. If you're upgrading and you have these optional components installed and running before the upgrade, Windows 2000's IIS will install these services as well.

> **Note** *You probably don't want every Windows 2000 Server to have IIS running. In that case, you should save resources by uninstalling IIS or at a minimum prevent the IIS services from starting automatically.*

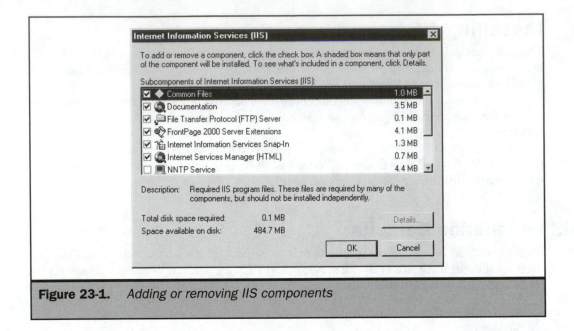

Figure 23-1. *Adding or removing IIS components*

Configuring IIS

After you complete the IIS installation process, including any optional components, you'll have a functioning IIS system. However, at this point, there isn't any content unless you've upgraded a Windows NT Server that previously housed IIS.

IIS can be configured and managed using the Internet Services Manager (ISM) locally or remotely using Terminal Server (see Chapter 28 for more information on Terminal Server) or through the ISM for HTML.

The ISM

The ISM is a management console that allows you to administer IIS services. The ISM comes in two flavors: a snap-in for the Microsoft Management Console (MMC) and a browser-based console. ISM delivers a single interface for managing and configuring

IIS. This includes everything from starting, stopping, and pausing IIS services to setting permissions. The only exception is that it can't create Web or FTP site content.

The ISM snap-in, shown in Figure 23-2, can be opened from the Start | Programs | Administrative Tools menu, while the browser-based console, shown in Figure 23-3, uses a Web browser to connect to the Windows 2000 Server running IIS. It's important to note that there is one major difference between the two flavors; the browser-based ISM doesn't start, stop, or pause IIS services. You must use the snap-in to perform such operations.

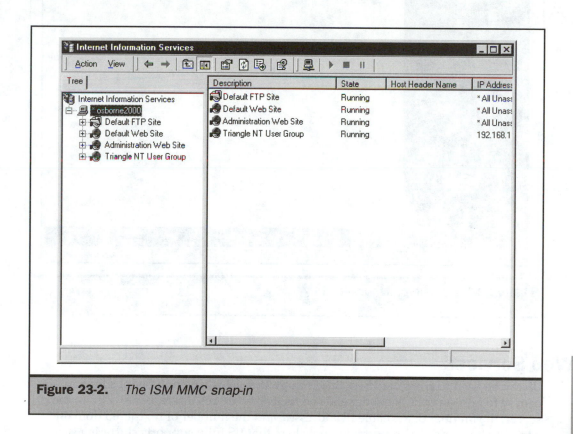

Figure 23-2.   *The ISM MMC snap-in*

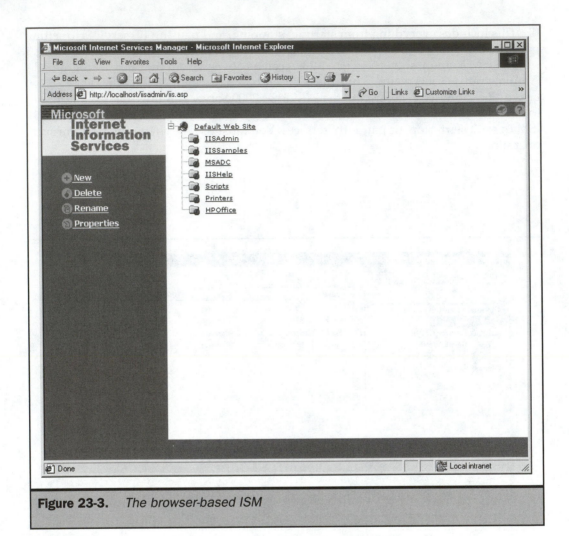

Figure 23-3. *The browser-based ISM*

Web Services

IIS can be used to create and host one or more Web sites. The number of sites you
choose to host on the system depends on the hardware resources, bandwidth to the
server, the number of available IP addresses, and the number of registered domain
names to host. It's also important to note here that IIS fully supports clustering services
that Windows 2000 Advanced Server and Datacenter Server offer. Windows 2000
Server doesn't have clustering services built into the operating system. For more
information on clustering services, refer to Chapter 26.

For each Web site that you configure for the Internet, you will need a registered domain name and an associated IP address. Typically, the Internet service provider (ISP) supplying you with Internet connectivity can assist you in obtaining public IP addresses and registering domain names.

Note   *If you only have one Web site domain registered but want to create another Web site, you can create a virtual directory (this is explained shortly) that allows you to use the public IP address and domain name. For example, let's say that your company (http://www.goodcompany.com) has decided to host a local, nonprofit organization's Web site, but finances for both sides are tight. A temporary workaround would be to create a virtual directory branching off of your company's Web site and place the nonprofit organization's Web site in that directory. Accessing the new Web site is like accessing a subdirectory (http://www.goodcompany.com/nonprofit/).*

Web sites can either be used internally on an intranet or can be made available for the world to see on the Internet. The first step is to create the site. Technically, you could build upon the default Web site, but I recommend that you start fresh.

To add a Web site, do the following:

1. Open ISM from the Start | Programs | Administrative Tools menu.

2. Right-click on Default Web Site in the left pane of the ISM, and select New | Site to start the Web Site Creation Wizard. Click Next to continue.

3. Type in the description of the Web site as shown in the following illustration, and then click Next.

4. Supply the IP address as well as the TCP port to use for the site. The Host Header dialog box can be optionally specified.

5. Specify the home directory for the site, or click the browse button to locate it. If you haven't already defined a home directory, do so now (otherwise you see an error message like the one in the next illustration). Also specify whether or not to allow anonymous access to the site. Click Next to continue.

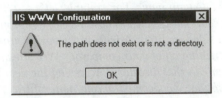

6. The next window in the wizard prompts you to set appropriate access permissions for the site. The defaults are Read and Run Scripts (Such As ASP), but you can also choose to permit execute, write, and browse permissions. Click Next to continue.

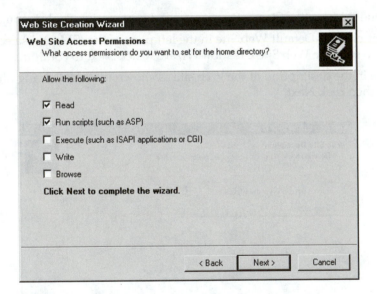

7. Click Finish.

Configuring a Web Site

There are various aspects of a Web site that you want to configure, and if you're hosting more than one Web site, you'll probably want to configure each one individually. Of course, how you configure the site depends largely on the site itself.

Sites automatically start by default when your computer restarts. In addition, individual Web site services can be stopped, started, and paused (still running but not accepting requests) using CD player-style buttons located on the button bar.

Configuration parameters can be found on the property pages for individual Web sites and are stored in a database called the metabase. To display the property pages, simply right-click on the Web site and select Properties. After displaying the property pages for a Web site, you'll notice that there are ten property page tabs. The most common, and typically the most relevant tabs, are discussed here.

WEB SITE PROPERTIES   Figure 23-4 shows the Web Site tab. It has three identifying characteristics: Web site identification, connections, and logging. First, it identifies the Web site's name, IP address, and TCP port number. You may also limit the number of simultaneous connections to this site as well as specify a connection timeout value. These two values combined allow you to keep response times within acceptable ranges. For example, suppose that after doing some testing, you discover that the Web site's performance degrades after 500 users connect simultaneously. As a result, you can limit the number of connections to 500.

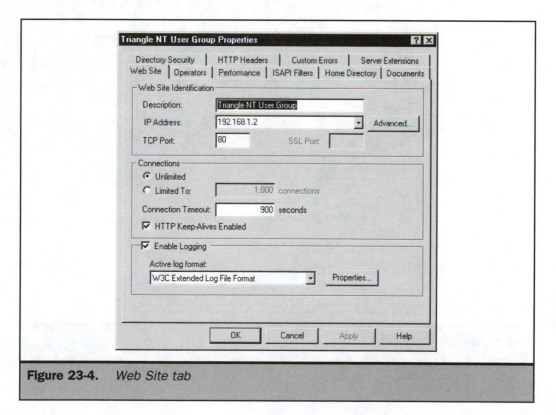

Figure 23-4.   *Web Site tab*

INTERNET AND INTRANET
FUNCTIONALITY

The final configuration setting on the Web Site tab is logging IIS events for this Web site. By default, IIS uses W3C Extended Log File Format and stores the log files in %SYSTEMROOT%\System32\LogFiles directory. By selecting the Properties button, you can customize log settings, such as location and more, as illustrated in Figure 23-5.

OPERATORS PROPERTIES The Operators tab, shown in Figure 23-6, allows you to grant limited privileges to other users who are or will be responsible for the operation of the Web site. The privileges are solely for the Web site rather than IIS.

Operators can change properties such as access permissions, logging, and content expiration. Because of their limited privileges, however, they can't change the following properties:

- Web site identification
- Performance characteristics
- Create or change virtual directories
- Application isolation

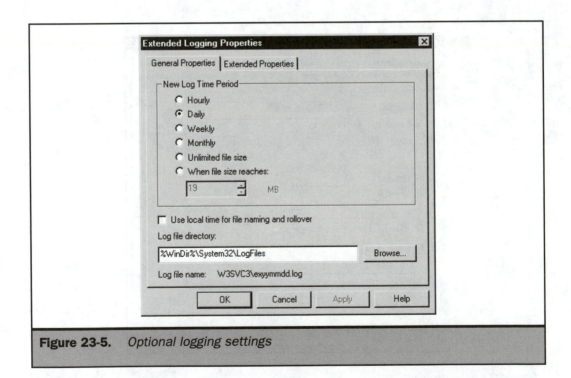

Figure 23-5. *Optional logging settings*

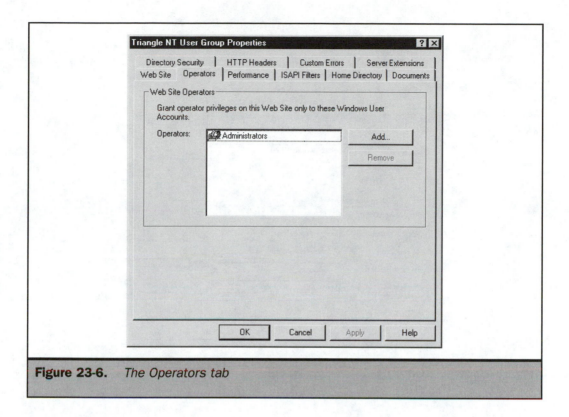

Figure 23-6. *The Operators tab*

PERFORMANCE PROPERTIES   In addition to limiting the number of connections (mentioned earlier), you can also configure each Web site's performance characteristics. In particular, you can tune your Web site according to the number of hits you expect per day, limit the available network bandwidth to the site, and set the maximum CPU usage this site can utilize.

HOME DIRECTORY PROPERTIES   A home directory is the topmost (root) directory for the Web site. A home directory is created, by default, for the default Web site, and it's required for all other sites that you create. Note that this directory is mapped to the Web site's domain name. For example, if your site's domain name is www.cadresys.com, and its home directory is C:\INETPUB\WWWROOT\CADRE, then when you connect to http://www.cadresys.com/, you're accessing files located in the home directory.

As you can see in Figure 23-7, you can choose one of three locations for your home directory: on the hard disk on the IIS server, in a shared directory on a remote computer, or as a redirection to another URL.

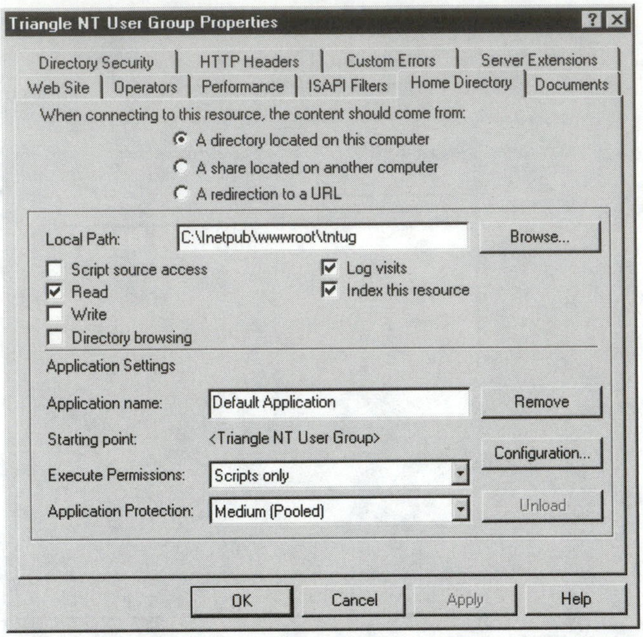

Figure 23-7. *Locating a Web site's home directory*

From this page, you can also configure access privileges to the home directory and provide application settings. Configuring the path's access privileges includes read, write, directory browsing, and so on. Application settings are similar in that you can decide the directory's execute permissions (none, scripts only, or scripts and executables) and the following application protection levels:

■ **Low (IIS process)** The process runs as a part of the IIS processes and in the same memory space.

■ **Medium (pooled)** By default, processes such as applications or scripts that are run from the Web site are pooled. This means that they run in a memory space that is separate from the rest of IIS (ensuring reliability of IIS), while simultaneously running in the same space as other processes specific for the Web site.

- **High (isolated)**   An isolated process runs in its own separate memory space. This provides the highest degree of reliability because the process is separated from IIS and other processes.

DIRECTORY SECURITY PROPERTIES   The Directory Security tab, shown in Figure 23-8, offers the following three distinct security configuration options:

- **Anonymous access and authentication control**   This level of control allows you to choose whether or not to have anonymous access and which account to use for the anonymous access. By default, IIS uses IUSR_<computer_name> for the anonymous account. If you don't allow anonymous access to the Web site, you can choose the authentication method to use (basic, clear text password authentication, digest authentication for Windows domain servers, or integrated Windows 2000 authentication).

- **IP address and domain name restrictions**   You can allow or deny access from a specific IP address or domain name. This is especially useful when you're creating an intranet Web site, because you can keep the outside world from viewing information on the site.

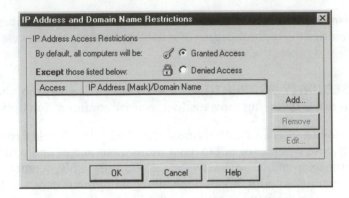

■ **Secure communications**   This option permits you to require certificates when
   trying to access this Web site. Selecting Secure communications invokes the IIS
   Certificate Wizard, which creates a certificate for the Web site or lets you obtain
   one from a Certificate Server in your Windows 2000 network environment.

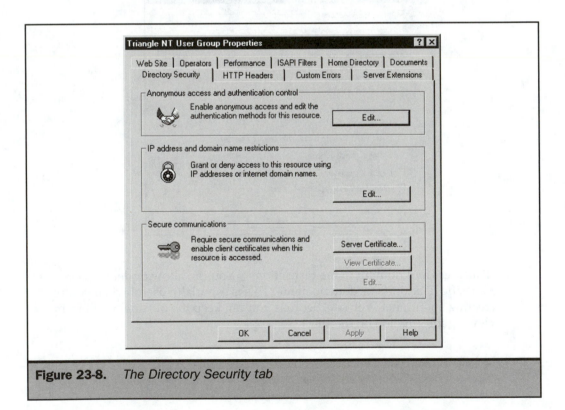

Figure 23-8.   *The Directory Security tab*

HTTP HEADERS PROPERTIES   The HTTP Headers tab, shown in Figure 23-9, is designed to help you manage the site's content. This doesn't mean that you can create Web pages from this interface. Instead, it gives you the ability to enable content expiration for time-sensitive data, assign ratings to the content you publish, and configure Multipurpose Internet Mail Extensions (MIME) mappings (a way for browsers to view multiple file formats).

Configuring a Virtual Directory

Virtual directories are a means to extend your home directory. By creating a virtual directory, you can publish Web pages from any directory that isn't contained within the home directory. The magic behind a virtual directory is that no matter where the actual files reside, it appears to client browsers as a subdirectory of the home directory.

Since the virtual directory can reside on a partition other than the one where the home directory is located as well as a remote computer, you need to give it an alias. Client browsers use the alias to access the Web pages in the directory.

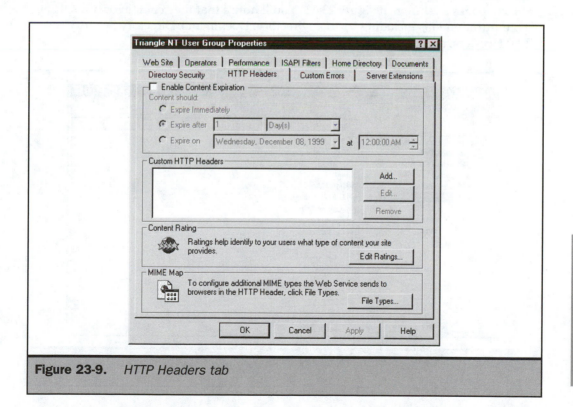

Figure 23-9.   *HTTP Headers tab*

For instance, Figure 23-10 shows the Triangle NT User Group (http://www.tntug.org) hosting a Microsoft Systems Management Server (SMS) special interest group (SIG) with a virtual directory. When client browsers access the SMS SIG site, it appears as if they're accessing a subdirectory of the Triangle NT User Group's Web site.

To create a virtual directory, do the following:

1. Open the ISM from the Start | Programs | Administrative Tools menu.

2. Right-click on your Web site in the left pane, and select New | Virtual Directory. When the Virtual Directory Creation Wizard opens, click Next to continue.

3. Specify the virtual directory's alias and click Next.

4. Enter the path to the directory containing the Web content, and click Next to continue.

5. Choose which access privileges you need for the virtual directory, and click Next to continue.

6. Click Finish

Like a Web site, you can use the property pages to configure the virtual directory. Right-click on the virtual directory you just created and select Properties to display the property pages as shown in Figure 23-11. You'll notice that they contain only a subset of configuration tabs including Virtual Directory, Documents, Directory Security, HTTP Headers, and Custom Errors.

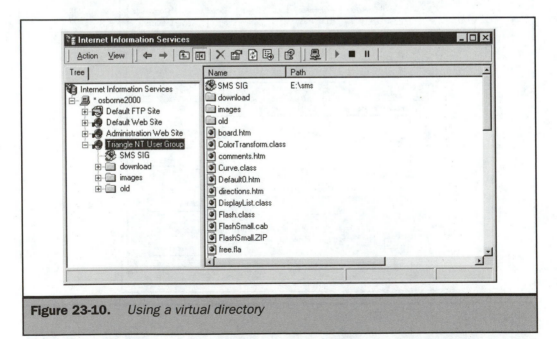

Figure 23-10.   *Using a virtual directory*

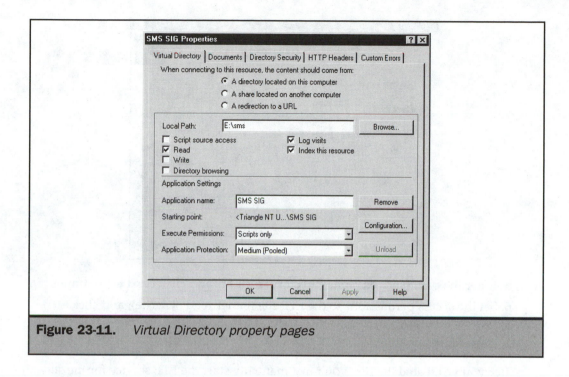

Figure 23-11.   *Virtual Directory property pages*

Creating an FTP Site

FTP is one of many utilities in the TCP/IP suite. It is basically used to upload and download files to and from remote computers on a TCP/IP network (such as the Internet). Therefore, FTP can be considered a client/server service where FTP clients can upload or download files to an FTP server service.

The FTP service, bundled within IIS, is installed by default. Once you create an FTP site, users can immediately begin using the FTP server—depending, of course, on the type of security you have set for the site.

To create an FTP site, do the following:

1. Open ISM from the Start | Programs | Administrative Tools menu.

2. Right-click on Default FTP Site in the left pane of the ISM, and select New | Site to start the FTP Site Creation Wizard. Click Next to continue.

3. Enter the name of the FTP site that users will use to connect to, and then click Next to continue.

4. From the drop-down box, select an IP address and then the TCP port to be used, as illustrated here. FTP defaults to using TCP port 21. Click Next to continue.

INTERNET AND INTRANET
FUNCTIONALITY

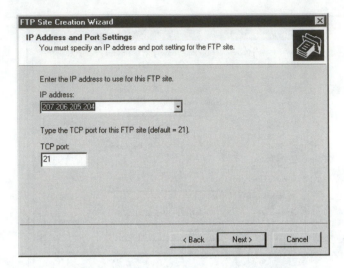

5. Enter the path (such as home directory) for FTP, and click Next to continue.

6. Set the access permissions to the FTP site (either read or write), and click Next to continue.

7. Click Finish.

After you've created the site, you must manually start the FTP service for the site by clicking on the play CD player-style button located on the ISM toolbar.

Configuring FTP

Configuring the FTP service is similar to configuring the Web service. You right-click on the FTP site and select Properties to display the property pages. These pages contain the various configuration parameters for each FTP site. There is only half the number of property pages for the FTP service that there were for the Web service.

FTP SITE PROPERTIES   The FTP Site tab, shown in Figure 23-12, gives you three configurable parameters: the FTP site's identification, connection, and logging settings. The identification settings are the same settings you specified when you created the site.

You can also view the FTP clients who are currently connected by clicking the Current Sessions button on the FTP Site tab.

The connection area on the FTP Site tab reflects the number of simultaneous connections that you allow and the time in which the connection will time out if it is idle. By default, the FTP service limits the number of simultaneous connections to 100,000, but you can also choose to have an unlimited number. Before you actually choose how many connections you'll allow, you must take into consideration the power behind the site. In other words, can the server adequately serve 1,000, 10,000, 100,000, or more simultaneous FTP clients, and are you supplying enough bandwidth to meet these needs?

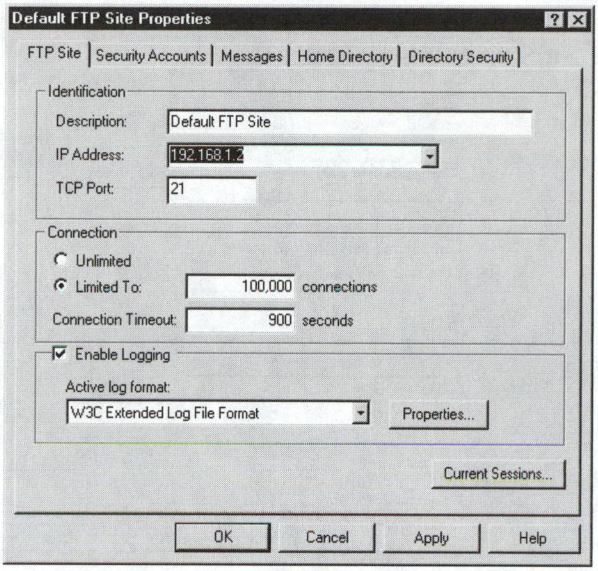

Figure 23-12.   *The FTP Site tab*

FTP logging settings are identical to the Web site logging settings. Refer to the "Web Site Properties" section earlier for more information on logging configurations.

SECURITY ACCOUNTS PROPERTIES   Security for the FTP service is very relaxed in comparison to other security technologies for IIS and Windows 2000. You can use either anonymous access or password security.

Anonymous access opens up the FTP site to anyone who can connect to the site. When an FTP client connects, he or she types in *anonymous* for the username and an e-mail address (or anything for that matter) for the password.

If you don't choose to use anonymous access, FTP clients must enter a valid username and password to gain access to the site. The username and password are sent in clear text, so you should be aware that this might cause security-related problems. Usernames and passwords can be compromised if someone were to capture network traffic coming into and away from the FTP site. As a rule of thumb, if you want to set up FTP, you should either allow anonymous connections create a special FTP account with limited privileges. The special FTP account's password should also be changed frequently. For more information on security and related technologies for Windows 2000, refer to Chapter 21.

The Security Accounts tab, shown in Figure 23-13, also gives you the option to choose which accounts have operator privileges for the FTP site. These users have limited administrative privileges for managing the specific FTP site only.

INTERNET AND INTRANET
FUNCTIONALITY

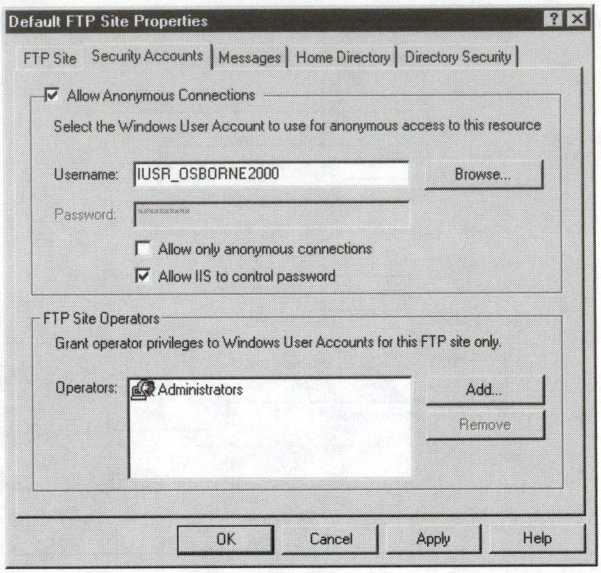

Figure 23-13. *The Security Accounts tab*

MESSAGES PROPERTIES   The Messages tab, shown in Figure 23-14, is unique to the FTP service. The messages that you enter on this tab are displayed to the FTP client. More specifically, the Welcome message greets users as they connect to the site, the Exit message displays when the user closes the connection, and the Maximum Connections message displays if the connection attempt was refused because the site's connection limit has been reached.

HOME DIRECTORY PROPERTIES   The Home Directory tab is similar to the same tab for the Web service. It shows the location of the FTP files and associated permissions. In addition, you can choose the directory listing style (MS-DOS or UNIX) on this tab.

DIRECTORY SECURITY PROPERTIES   The last property page for the FTP site service is the Directory Security tab. Use this tab to grant or deny access to certain IP addresses or IP address ranges. If you're unfamiliar with IP addressing, refer to Chapter 13.

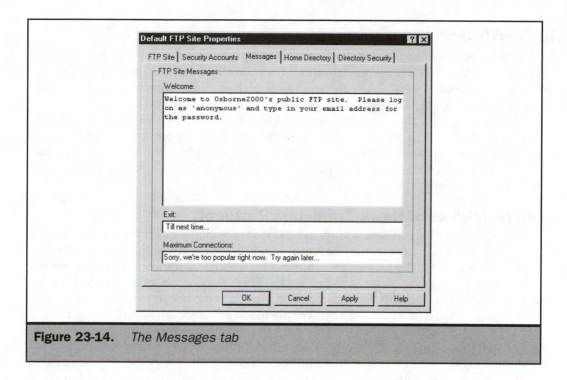

Figure 23-14.   *The Messages tab*

Optional IIS Components

The most commonly used IIS services (Web and FTP services) are installed by default. However, there are other optional components that can be installed for IIS. They include the following:

- **The SMTP Service**   The Simple Mail Transfer Protocol Service allows you to exchange e-mail messages over the Internet. SMTP is a TCP/IP protocol.

- **Visual InterDev RAD Remote Deployment Support**   This option is used to support Web applications that are built using Microsoft Visual InterDev. Visual InterDev is a development tool that allows you to rapidly create Web applications that enhance your Web site. For more information on Visual InterDev visit http://msdn.microsoft.com/vinterdev/.

- **The News Service (also known as the NNTP Service)**   This option allows you to host internal or Internet newsgroups for exchanging information.

The News Service

Newsgroups were one of the most popular communications mediums on the Internet long before the Web was used extensively. They were and still are a place to exchange ideas about almost every topic you could think of, including computer-related issues, job postings, social issues, recreation events, sciences, and much more.

Newsgroups are also a great place to find information on new products. Generally speaking, this isn't the type of information you'd get from the product's sales team (although you may see this, too). Instead, you can find out from others who are using the product what kind of experiences they've had with it, and use that information to avoid any problems.

NNTP (Network News Transport Protocol)

The driving force behind newsgroups is NNTP. It is responsible for the exchange of messages. Although the message exchange parallels dialog through e-mail, it is much more efficient especially for a large number of people. For instance, when you post a message, you only have to do so to the NNTP server rather than send an e-mail out to everyone that may want to read the message. Anyone who doesn't want to read your message doesn't have to; they can browse the message subjects without having to actually read the messages and thus get only the information they want.

NNTP message exchange can be categorized into two types, server-to-server and client-to-server. Server-to-server communication allows servers to exchange messages that they host. For example, you can configure an internal NNTP server to request message and newsgroup updates from another NNTP server located somewhere on the Internet. Since there are literally thousands of newsgroups, you can specify which ones you'd like to get updates from. On the other hand, the client-to-server model lets clients connect to the NNTP server to view newsgroups and exchange information. Clients use a newsgroup reader (from a Web browser or third-party product) to subscribe to different newsgroups. Once clients subscribe to a newsgroup, they can read the newsgroup's messages or post their own.

Installing the News Service

IIS provides an option to configure the server as newsgroup host using NNTP. You can create your own internal newsgroups, and you can configure the server to request newsgroups from an outside source.

In addition to satisfying the hardware requirements for Windows 2000 and the space needed to install the service, be aware that configuring Windows 2000 as a news server takes a considerable amount of disk space, especially when you request newsgroups from an Internet NNTP server. You can easily retrieve gigabytes worth of messages on a daily basis depending on the newsgroups you request.

To install the News Service, do the following:

1. Double-click on Add/Remove Programs from the Control Panel.

2. Select Add/Remove Windows Components in the Add/Remove Programs window.

3. Select Internet Information Services (IIS), and then click the Details button.

4. Check NNTP Service, as shown in the next illustration, and then click OK. Click Next to continue.

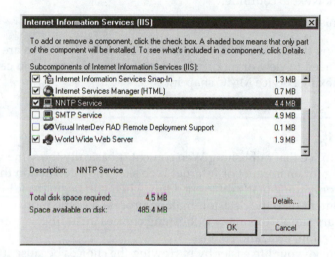

5. Click Finish.

The Indexing Service

In previous versions of IIS, you had to install Index Server separately in order to benefit from having Web-based documents indexed for search capabilities. In Windows 2000, it is now called the Indexing Service, and it is integrated into Windows 2000.

The Indexing Service builds an index of all the information on your site or sites. The information contained in the index can be from HTML pages as well as documents in many different formats, including Word and Excel. As HTML pages and documents are added or removed, the Indexing Service rebuilds the index automatically. When you create a query form on your Web site, users query for information contained on the site by querying the index created by the Indexing Service.

Installing Indexing Service

Installing the Indexing Service on an IIS server has been simplified due to its integration with Windows 2000. To install the service, do the following:

1. Open the Add/Remove Programs applet within the Control Panel.
2. Click Add/Remove Windows Components in the Add/Remove Programs window.
3. When the Windows Components Wizard appears, check Indexing Service and then click Next to continue.
4. Click Finish.

After installing the service, Web sites and the server's file system are automatically indexed. If you need to view or modify Indexing Service settings, you can do so through the Indexing Service MMC snap-in.

Publishing

It isn't difficult to see that publishing Web content is basically the same whether you're providing for an intranet or Internet Web site. The information that's displayed is probably the only thing that's different. Only when you begin deciding on how to publish Web content does the decision-making process become more complex and difficult. There are simply too many publishing choices including scripting languages, ASP, Flash animation, Java, and so on.

IIS doesn't make your life easier by narrowing the choices because it supports many, if not all, of the publishing standards. This section is designed to make you aware of some of the ways in which to publish content, but it doesn't by any means cover all possibilities. It does, however, highlight some of the more popular methods of publishing content.

Active Server Pages

ASP is a server-side execution environment that allows you to create dynamic and interactive Web sites. It combines standard HTML code with a variety of different scripts (for example, JavaScript, JScript, VBScript, and so on) and components (C++, Java, and others). In addition, it can customize the user's experience by creating browser-independent content. The content that is displayed to the user depends on the Web browser used and the functionality it supports.

ASP is Microsoft's answer to Common Gateway Interface (CGI) and Internet Server Application Programming Interface (ISAPI). It provides an easier, more flexible approach to publishing Web content. Also, from a performance point of view, ASP is much more efficient with resources than CGI or ISAPI.

Since its debut with IIS 3, ASP has continually been improved. With IIS 5, ASP once again has been enhanced with the following features:

- Program flow control
- Enhanced error handling
- Scriptless ASP
- Performance-enhanced objects
- Extensible Markup Language (XML) integration
- Windows script components
- New ways to determine browser capabilities
- ASP self-tuning for increased performance
- Encoded ASP scripts to hide and protect internal logic

WebDAV

Web Distributed Authoring and Versioning (WebDAV) is an extension to the HTTP 1.1 standard for publishing and managing Web resources. More specifically, WebDAV allows operators to access and manage file systems resources remotely over an HTTP connection. Many of the operations you're used to performing on files (for example, copying, moving, editing, deleting, and searching), while physically located at the server running IIS, can now be performed using Internet Explorer 5, a Microsoft Office 2000 application, or as a network connection using Windows 2000.

WebDAV is tightly integrated with Windows 2000's IIS, but it isn't enabled by default. You must first set up a WebDAV publishing directory using the IIS snap-in before you can begin reaping the benefits of WebDAV.

Creating a WebDAV Publishing Directory

To create a WebDAV publishing directory, do the following:

1. Using Windows Explorer (or other means), create a directory. You can create this anywhere you'd like except directly under the \Inetpub\wwwroot directory. The reason for this is that permissions are set differently under this directory by default than they are in other directories.

2. Create a virtual directory using the IIS snap-in that points to the directory you just created. If you're unfamiliar with creating a virtual directory, refer to "Configuring a Virtual Directory" earlier in this chapter.

3. Give Read, Write, and Browsing access permissions for the virtual directory.

Setting Write privileges to the WebDAV publishing directory doesn't automatically allow them to modify scripts in that directory. You must also grant Script source access for users to modify scripts.

FrontPage Server Extensions

Microsoft FrontPage Server Extensions offer an easy way for nonprogrammers to develop dynamic content, administer the Web site, and browse the Web site structure. They are tightly integrated with IIS and are installed by default. The extensions enable site operators to publish and manage Web content using Microsoft FrontPage 2000 or Visual InterDev, which are graphical authoring tools that can work directly with the content on IIS.

The FrontPage Server Extensions are a set of programs located on the Web server that are used to communicate with the FrontPage client. When the client connects to the Web site, all transactions are performed using standard HTTP.

Chapter 24

Managing Networks and Intranets with IIS

Windows 2000 has broken the division between the operating system and Web services by offering an unprecedented level of integration between the two technologies. With this integration comes greater continuity among otherwise disparate information systems. It also leads to an improvement in systems management by providing a common management platform.

We've been in the Information Age for a while now, but the way we are managing the information is just beginning to take shape. As bold a statement as this may seem, you can see that Web-related technologies—and how they are affecting our lives—are changing daily. The Web has become a common ground among the various operating system environments promoting information exchange where it was once impossible.

Web-Based Systems Management

Using IIS as a management platform has traditionally been an elusive topic for many. How can you use IIS to manage systems? What built-in features can be used to ease administrative burdens? Microsoft has gone to great lengths to tighten the integration of Web-based services and Windows 2000. The integration sheds light on how to administer and manage systems by bringing management capabilities into focus.

This section examines the technologies and techniques you can use to create a management platform using IIS. However, this is just the beginning. As you read through this chapter, you will begin to see just how extensive and customizable Web-based services can be with Windows 2000.

Administering IIS Remotely

Convenience should always be a factor when you're administering IIS. You shouldn't always have to be physically located at the IIS server in order to troubleshoot, make system changes, perform backups, and so forth. IIS gives you several options for managing its services through two interfaces:

- **IIS MMC snap-in**   Using the IIS MMC snap-in gives you complete functional control of IIS services. You can manage the local IIS services as well as other IIS servers (that is, use the snap-in to connect to a remote server). See Chapter 23 for more information on using the IIS MMC snap-in to manage IIS.

- **Internet Services Manager (HTML)**   This tool can be used from virtually anywhere (through the Internet, through a proxy server, and so on). It has limited capabilities when compared to the snap-in but is nonetheless an extremely useful way of administrating and managing the IIS services. Also, its functionality depends on how you connect to IIS. You can connect to individual Web sites (if you're hosting multiple Web sites), the Default Web Site (illustrated in Figure 24-1), or the Administration Web Site.

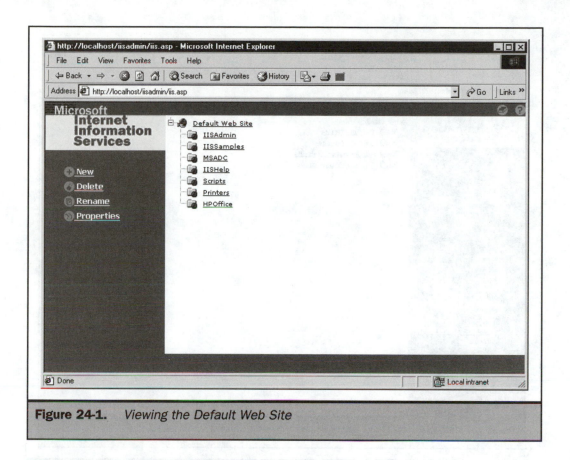

Figure 24-1.   *Viewing the Default Web Site*

The Administration Web Site

Internet Services Manager (HTML) can connect to a unique Web site called the Administration Web Site, shown in Figure 24-2, to access IIS properties. This site is installed by default during IIS installation to provide enhanced remote administration capabilities.

The first thing you'll notice about this site is how you connect to it. In addition to specifying the domain name or IP address of the IIS server, you must specify the TCP port to use to connect. This is because the Administration Web Site doesn't use the HTTP default port 80. Instead, a port number between 2,000 and 9,999 is randomly assigned. For example, the Administration Web Site in the example in Figure 24-2 is configured to use port 5281. In order to connect, the following syntax must be used:

http://*<localhost>:<port number>*

And as you can see in Figure 24-2, connection is made by typing http://localhost:5281. Note that the localhost and port number parameters will vary from environment to environment and that localhost can be a computer name, domain name, or an IP address.

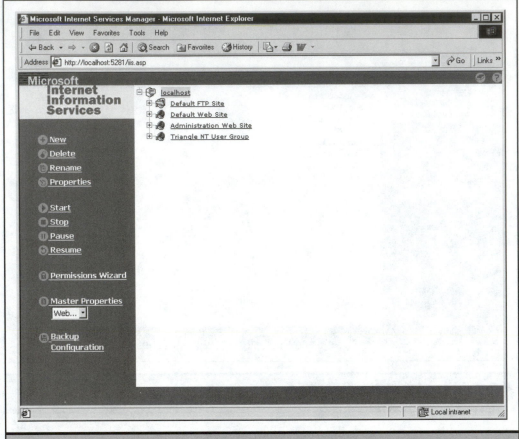

Figure 24-2. *Viewing the Administration Web Site*

The Administration Web Site allows you to administer and configure Web and FTP services for all sites hosted on the IIS server. From the Internet Services Manager (HTML) connected to the site, you can perform the following operations:

- Create a new site
- Delete a site
- Rename a specific site
- Control IIS services for a specific site
- Use the HTML-based Permissions Wizard, shown in the following illustration, to configure security settings for a site

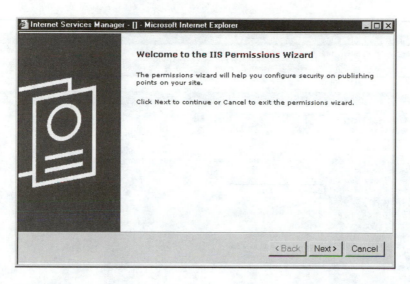

- Configure Master Properties, such as service, home directory, security, error messages, and so on for a site (see Figure 24-3)

- Back up configuration changes

Web-Based Enterprise Management (WBEM) Initiative

WBEM is a Distributed Management Task Force (DMTF) initiative that is designed to help unify enterprise management of information. It is comprised of sets of standards and technologies for exchanging information including, but not limited to, the Extensible Markup Language (XML), object-oriented schemas, and much more.

Note   *For more information on WBEM, visit http://www.dmtf.org/wbem/.*

Stemming from WBEM is an industry standard called the Common Information Model (CIM). CIM is an extensible object-oriented schema for managing systems, networks, applications, databases, and devices. Microsoft's version of the CIM is the Windows Management Instrumentation (WMI).

Windows Management Instrumentation

WMI is a WBEM-compliant version of CIM. It defines an interface to monitor and control system events relating to applications and hardware. Also, it helps organize and manage information from a single interface regardless of what type it is or where it came from. Therefore, administrators and developers can use WMI to access many system components, including the following:

- WMI for Windows Driver Model (WDM)

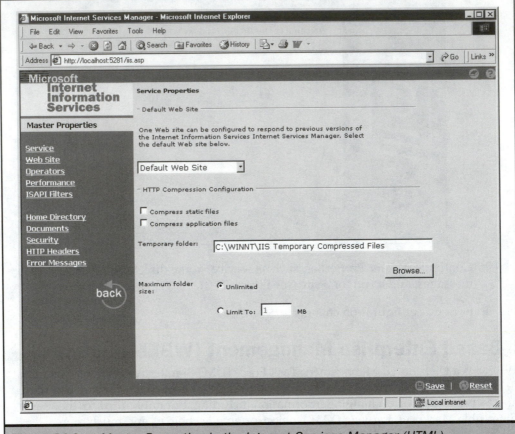

Figure 24-3. *Master Properties in the Internet Services Manager (HTML)*

- Registry
- Event logs
- Desktop Management Interface (DMI)
- Simple Network Management Protocol (SNMP)

So what does this all mean to systems management? First, it means that administrators and developers can create management tools, including those that are Web-based, without having to learn multiple application programming interfaces (APIs). The possibilities for these tools are endless; you can monitor events such as low disk space, SNMP traps, performance levels, and much more.

So, for example, if you wanted to listen for events in the Event Log, you could use the following Windows Scripting Host (WSH) script:

```
Set oCIM = GetObject("cim:")
for each NTEvent in oCIM.ExecNotificationQuery("SELECT * FROM
_InstanceCreationEvent WHERE TargetInstance ISA 'Win32_NTLogEvent'")
 WScript.Echo NTEvent.TargetInstance.Message
Next
```

Note *You can also use other scripting languages (VBScript, JScript, Perl, and others) to create Web-based management tools that interface with the WMI.*

IIS and Component Services

Combining IIS and Windows 2000's Component Services (COM) gives you yet another opportunity to create Web-based applications to manage Windows 2000 systems. IIS can use COM to control transactions, manage communications, and isolate processes between COM components.

One of the most useful COM-based services for management purposes is the Active Directory Service Interfaces (ADSI) directory service. ADSI allows you to develop Web applications that interact with AD from a single interface without knowing the underlying operational details. It's also important to note that you can use WSH, Windows 2000's internal scripting engine, to write scripts that interface with COM and IIS.

IIS and Internet Printing

Another powerful feature resulting from the integration of Web services and Windows 2000 is Internet printing. The Internet Printing Protocol (IPP) and IIS (or Peer Web Services, PWS, on Windows 2000 Professional) are used to host printers so that users can connect to printers over the Internet or intranet through a Web browser. IPP and IIS also allow you to view information about printers, such as printer name, status, location, number of print jobs, model, and any comments that are associated with the printer. Figure 24-4 shows information on the printer called HP through a Web browser connected to the localhost.

Note *You must use Internet Explorer version 4.0 or higher to connect to a printer.*

Table 24-1 lists the various ways you can connect to a printer using a Web browser.

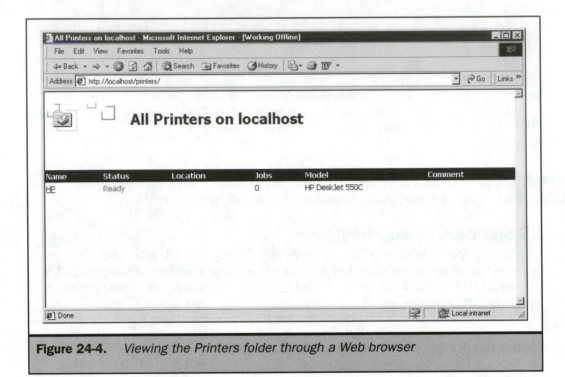

Figure 24-4. Viewing the Printers folder through a Web browser

Once you have established a connection to the printer through the Web browser, you can print as you normally would on a locally- or network-attached printer (see Figure 24-5). Windows 2000 automatically copies the printer driver to your local computer. Don't forget to bookmark it for later use!

Syntax	Example
http://*computer_name*/printers/	http://osborne2000/printers/
http://*computer_name*/*printer_name*	http://osborne2000/HP
http://*IP_address*/printers/	http://207.206.205.204/printers/
http://*IP_address*/*printer_name*	http://207.206.205.204/HP

Table 24-1. Various Ways to Connect to a Printer Using a Web Browser

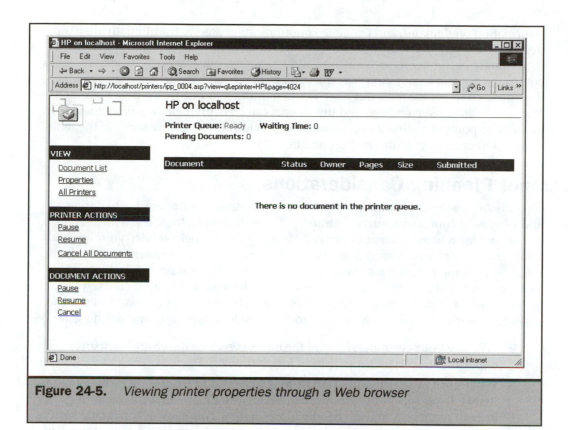

Figure 24-5.   *Viewing printer properties through a Web browser*

Building Familiarity with Intranets

An *intranet* is an Internet-technology-based solution that is controlled and accessed only within the business's infrastructure. It harnesses the power of the Internet yet is flexible enough to be tailored to suit the needs and goals of an organization. Intranets are not technically different than the Internet. However, they have far greater potential to redefine network computing and build corporate unity simply because they provide solutions-based corporate investments.

Intranets are dramatically affecting how businesses operate internally, and their functional role within a company is constantly transforming into greater possibilities. Intranets are already making headlines for the solutions they are providing today, and their applications are growing exponentially.

Intranets are quickly becoming a corporate necessity. They allow business needs and goals to be combined, provide an efficient and effective means to access information on demand, and promote communication among traditionally disparate departments/functional groups (such as R&D and Sales). Moreover, intranets are increasingly becoming a mechanism to allow seamless integration between Windows environments and legacy data. The question is, however, what technologies can be incorporated to get the most out of an existing intranet or one that is being planned? The possibilities seem endless, and the choices can be overwhelming. Nonetheless, it's possible to point out some useful services to provide and to review some of the tools required to expand your intranet capabilities.

Intranet Planning Considerations

As with any major integration project for your business, it is imperative to define and plan your company's intranet strategy. This is true even for those who already have some form of an intranet in place. A design plan will help service your internal customers better by providing a more reliable, structured environment to stimulate collaboration and enhance functionality and productivity. It is not advisable to assemble an intranet without such planning, because you will more than likely be faced with a massive reengineering project instead of providing quality service to your customers. Typical concerns you should consider addressing and defining are

- **Who are your customers?**   Will the intranet service the entire company, departments, certain geographical locations, etc.?

- **What kind of information will be available and to whom?**   The information that is displayed on the intranet can be anything that you wish, including, but not limited to, general product information, company events, trade secrets, and so on. Also, you can be very selective as to who can see different types of information.

- **How is information routinely exchanged?**   Intranets can contain static or dynamic information through Web page forms, forums, newsgroups, and much more. You must decide on how to effectively provide the information.

- **What organizational communication weaknesses can an intranet strengthen?**   In other words, are some of your business processes lacking efficiency? Do you feel as though some things just fall into a black hole and are forgotten? Note that while intranets aren't cure-alls, they can help reduce lag times and mistakes.

- **Who will manage the intranet?**   This typically depends on how your current infrastructure operates. Some environments may administer and manage the intranet centrally or by department, while others may have a mix of centralized and decentralized levels of responsibility.

- **What tools will be used to access and/or manipulate existing data?**   There are many tools to choose from for managing the intranet and the information it provides. Microsoft has several products that can be integrated with IIS, including FrontPage 2000, Windows DNA, JScript, Visual InterDev, and much more.

■ **Should clients be allowed to install IIS or other types of personal Web servers?** I've often seen environments where users were allowed to create their own personal Web servers. As an alternative, I would recommend that if users want to create home pages and the like, give them the ability to do so on the intranet rather than allow them to create their own IIS server.

Once you have a well-formulated definition of what your intranet will be used for and who it will be used by, you can begin designing your intranet infrastructure.

Intranet Tools

The software market is flooded with various applications used to help you create, manage, and enhance your intranet. Since intranets are based on Internet technologies, almost every application "designed for Internet usage" can be used with intranets. Consequently, this presents us with an overwhelming number of choices to develop the perfect intranet. Personally, I find that the abundance of intranet tools a mixed blessing. The overpopulated market can often present an exhausting amount of choices, yet, on the other hand, it spawns growth and development of technologies through competition.

There are several categories of Internet/intranet applications. There are server applications, HTML editors, graphic editors, development tools, among others. The categories that will be the most beneficial for your customers as well as your intranet strategy depend on the type of functionality that you're trying to bring to your intranet.

Searching for Information

Wouldn't it be fantastic to add a valuable service to your customers and forget about it? Well, one of the best services you can provide within your intranet is the ability to search for information on your intranet. Comprehensive indexing of documents scattered about your network drastically reduces the time a customer may take to find the information they need to be more effective in the workplace.

Windows 2000's Indexing Service is one of the fastest, most self-sufficient indexing/searching tools available. The service builds and maintains catalogs of the contents stored on the local or remote hard drives. As new documents are added or deleted, the Indexing Service automatically redefines its master index so that when a user searches for a particular subject or keyword they are provided with an up-to-date result. Working with the service is simplified to save a tremendous amount of your time to make a reliable, hassle-free service for you and your customers.

You're probably most familiar with searching using the Indexing Service from the Search function located on the Start menu. However, this useful feature can also be used through a Web interface so that users can enter search terms to locate information on the intranet.

The Indexing Service is disabled and set to manual startup by default, so you'll need to change both of these parameters before you can offer searching capabilities for the intranet. For more information on the Indexing Service, see Chapter 23.

411   Another key searching capability that gives your customers quick access to a wealth of information is directory assistance. While employee phone lists are probably generated internally with the assistance of AD, you have to rely on other sources for nationally published telephone numbers and addresses. You can provide this information in a variety of ways including links to Web sites that specialize in this type of service (for example, http://www.555-1212.com, shown in Figure 24-6, or http://people.yahoo.com), from internal contact databases, or from phonebook software packages.

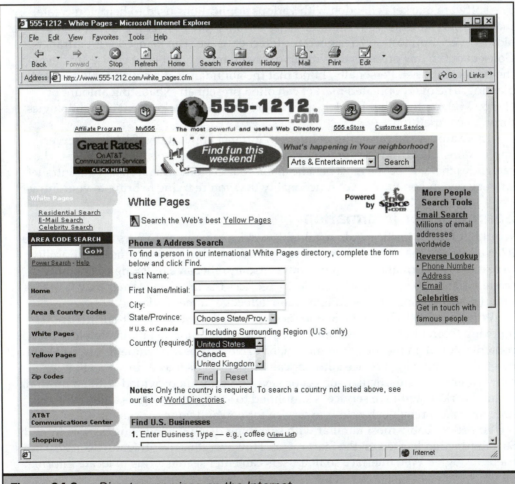

Figure 24-6.   *Directory services on the Internet*

Most of the CD-ROM phone books that publish white and yellow page listings are packaged in six or more CDs. In order to share the database information, you would either have to configure a CD-ROM drive array or copy the entire contents of the CDs to a hard drive (hard drive space is getting cheaper by the minute). Many products however, such as PhoneDisc PowerFinder, from Digital Directory Assistance, are also available and contain this type of information on a single DVD.

With a minimum amount of effort, you can allow your customers to use the directory assistance database for phone number or address lookups, address verifications, and demographic information. Everyone can benefit especially departments such as sales and marketing that are most likely to call directory assistance. The company benefits not only from employees being able to get information more efficiently but also from the cost savings generated from not having to rely on the phone company's directory assistance. Calling directory assistance can cost companies thousands of dollars annually.

MAPS The same principle of searching for names, addresses, and telephone numbers can be expanded to using mapping programs and services. You can include links to map services located on the Internet (for example, http://maps.yahoo.com) or you can use CD-ROM or DVD software programs to provide mapping services through the intranet.

Real-Time Applications

Another popular topic for intranets today is providing real-time communications between PCs and legacy host and peer systems. Many companies have valuable information stored on mainframes, AS/400s, and other legacy systems and need an efficient and effective way to exchange information with PC systems such as Windows 2000. PC clients that need information on an IBM host system, such as the 3090 mainframe, use a 3270 emulation, while PC clients that need access to peer systems, such as the IBM AS/400, need a 5250 emulation. Traditional emulation packages are often limited in the scope of operations that can be performed through either the 3270 or 5250 sessions and do not provide any user interface enhancements over the DOS-style interface. The connection to the host or peer system mimics the terminal services offered by Windows 2000 in that all processing is done on the server and it seems as if the user is physically located on the server.

The first intranet applications to attempt legacy system communications were crude at best. They offered relatively little enhancement or advantage over the software packages that were already providing reliable communication between PCs and legacy systems. The best intranet applications providing access to legacy systems use ActiveX and Java for secure, reliable, and graphical communication.

Many companies have developed viable solutions that bring legacy data and applications to the PC desktop through the Web. Some products provide a SNA-to-HTML conversion while others, such as Client/Server Technology's Jacada or OpenConnect Systems' OC://Webconnect, use Java technology for a more secure and flexible SNA-to-Web integration. OC://Webconnect delivers one of the most functional solutions to access legacy data and applications through any Java-enabled Web browser. Besides its ability to provide 3270, 5250, and VT200 emulation, OC://Webconnect's

most notable feature is its multi-tiered approach to security. It uses a number of user authentication techniques at the server and SNA host, RSA encryption during the transfer, and finally enhanced SNA session security. OC://Webconnect also has a companion, OpenVista (see Figure 24-7), which is an integrated development environment that transforms the dull, character-based sessions into a clearer, more functional graphical user interface. The companies mentioned above and their respective products for legacy system integration with intranets is located in Table 24-2.

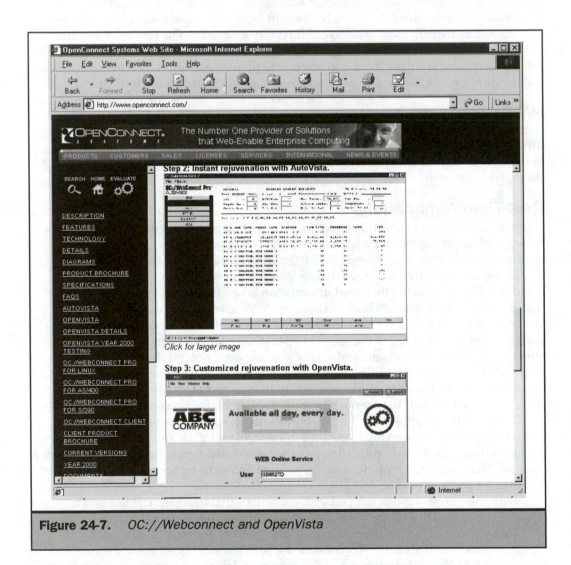

Figure 24-7. *OC://Webconnect and OpenVista*

Product	Company	Web Site
OC://WebConnect 2.5 and OpenVista	OpenConnect Systems	http://www.oc.com
Jacada	Client/Server Technology	http://www.cst.com

Table 24-2. *Legacy System Integration Products*

NetMeeting

The use of audio and video on an intranet can provide an affordable and compelling solution to corporate communications. Microsoft's NetMeeting is a perfect example of a real-time communications package that should be strongly considered as part of your intranet site. NetMeeting has many sharp features that are designed to enhance multimedia communication and collaboration for Internet and intranet usage. NetMeeting, illustrated in Figure 24-8, is bundled with Windows 2000. It includes voice communications with support for international conferencing standards, multi-user application sharing, whiteboard collaboration, chat capabilities, and more.

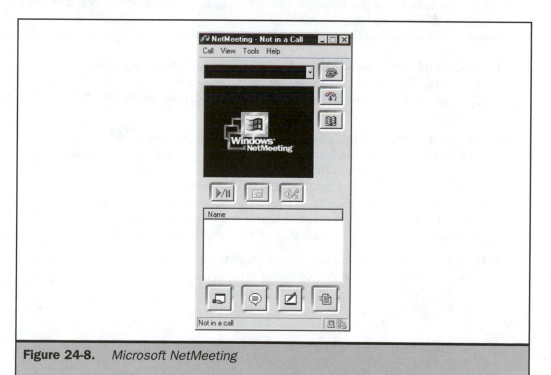

Figure 24-8. *Microsoft NetMeeting*

Its ability to use the Internet, as well as your intranet, instead of traditional phone lines for long distance communication will undoubtedly save an organization a great deal of money in phone costs. With the proper hardware support, you can even transform ordinary conferencing calls into virtual meetings. Moreover, employees that have long daily commutes can save time and money by still being able to attend virtual meetings, collaborate on proposals, and the like without ever leaving home. NetMeeting's whiteboard is another tool used for collaboration efforts. It is a window or a page that can appear on many computers and allows all participants to make and see those changes in real-time. Other possible applications extending from NetMeeting are document collaboration, training, and technical support.

Windows Media Services

As I mentioned earlier, application possibilities for multimedia services on the Internet and intranet is exploding and compression and network bandwidths are continuously improving to give greater support for the increasing demands from multimedia. Multimedia is being used for educational services, company news and events, publicity, e-business, and more.

Windows 2000's Windows Media Services provides the server service and necessary tools to create and deliver multimedia for your Windows 2000 environment. It supports a wide range of streaming media bandwidths (from 3Kbps to over 3Mbps) for a variety of multimedia applications.

Three notable features of Media Services are the following:

- **Synchronization capabilities**   Multimedia presentations can be synchronized using scripts (VBScript, Javascript, ActiveX, Java, and so on) so that there is a greater level of control among the various audio, text, image, and video elements.

- **Multicast support**   Media Services' server-based streaming video tames the bandwidth requirements associated with streaming media by using buffering and IP multicasting techniques. IP multicasting is a type of broadcasting without the limitations or disadvantages of IP broadcasting. It can transmit data to hundreds, if not thousands, of users simultaneously without causing as big a performance hit as IP broadcasting and it can even cross router boundaries. It does so by segmenting a set amount of bandwidth for all clients.

- **Digital Rights Management**   This management scheme protects multimedia content from piracy by incorporating the authentication and authorization capabilities of Windows 2000. Specifically, it uses license keys that aren't transferable to grant access. In addition, these keys can be set to expire after a specified amount of time. You can think of Digital Rights Management as a pay-per-view service (although you don't have to pay).

Since Windows Media Services are not installed by default with IIS or Windows 2000, you'll need to install it using the Add/Remove Programs applet within the Control Panel. Once you've installed it, you can configure and manage it through the Windows Media Administrator as shown in Figure 24-9.

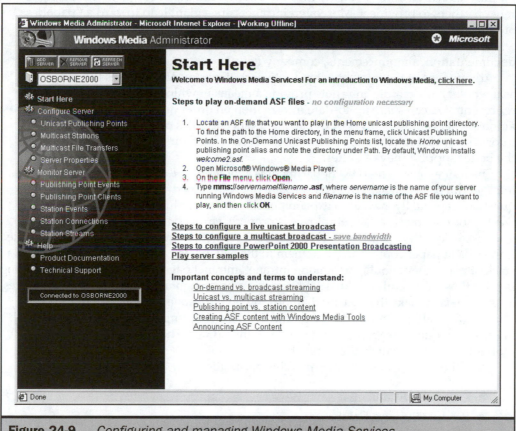

Figure 24-9.   *Configuring and managing Windows Media Services*

Other Intranet Applications

The tools that I have mentioned barely scratch the surface concerning the provision of services to your customers. This is only the beginning of what intranets can do for you and it is only meant to stir ideas for creating an intranet for your Windows 2000 network infrastructure. There are many more applications that can be applied to your intranet to make communication more cost effective and productive.

First, and foremost, the establishment of an intranet will undoubtedly reduce company costs. It saves employees time by steering them away from having to micromanage themselves and enables them to concentrate on the task at hand. Employees will be able to quickly find the information they need without having to rely on others to provide it. Moreover, intranets are a giant leap toward a "paperless" organization. Paperless communication drastically reduces company costs associated with printed materials such as policies, procedures, enrollment forms, product documentation, announcements, company newsletters, and the like.

Advantages of the intranet extend into each department as well as the company as a whole. For example, intranets provide a means in which each customer service representative can share up-to-date information on order or billing status from or among other representatives or departments such as sales or shipping. The more information customer service representatives have on their customers and accounts, the better support they can offer.

The human resources (HR) department is another prime candidate in which an intranet can be beneficial. HR personnel are often swamped with answering the same questions repeatedly, having to explain policies and procedures that seem to change weekly, or making sure each employee is properly enrolled in different plans. It is just as easy to place those stacks of HR forms and information on the intranet as it is to make hundreds of paper copies and place them in the hall. In fact, anywhere a company sees a stack of paper they should be thinking intranet. Intranet pages can also be a great holding pen for those frequently asked HR questions. Some thought must be put into these pages, as the goal is to make them easier than picking up the phone and calling HR directly. Your intranet HR pages can also be interactive, allowing employees to modify personal addresses, request vacations, or amend tax withholdings. They could even adjust and monitor their 401k plan on the intranet.

The following is a list of other possible applications for intranets:

- Product Information
- Product Support Databases
- Software Libraries
- Policies and Procedures
- Catalogs of Services and Products
- Information on Competitors
- Employee Recognition for Achievements

- Project Information
- Registration for Company Events
- Employee Information
- Historical Company Information
- Job Openings
- Strategic Goals of the Company
- Email

As you can see, the application of the intranet is limited only by your own imagination.

Intranet Security

Security is paramount, especially with the increasing reliance on the Internet and intranets for information. The Internet/intranet craze has made many companies more aware that their information is invaluable and has caused them to focus on securing themselves from outsiders. Many, however, have overlooked securing their assets internally even when they knowingly increase accessibility to information through an intranet. Don't be so naïve as to believe that simply blocking security breaches from the outside is enough protection. Many attacks come from employees who usually have some knowledge of what to look for or what to destroy.

As a general rule of thumb, protect your intranet investment as if it were exposed to the outside world. Make use of the security measures that are inherent to Windows 2000. For instance, configure the intranet to grant access only to internal IP addresses and use authentication and certificates to verify identities.

Of course, every network is not, and cannot be, completely secure. The point is, however, to incorporate as much security as possible to discourage people inside and outside the company from attempting to gain illegal access. One of the most advantageous solutions to secure an intranet is installation of a firewall in addition to Windows 2000's built-in security measures. Access control, authentication, encryption, network address translation, and auditing are standard components that most firewalls provide to protect against intrusion. I also highly recommend that you review Chapter 21 on Windows 2000 security before you build the intranet infrastructure.

INTERNET AND INTRANET
FUNCTIONALITY

The
Complete
Reference

Part VI

Enterprise Components

The
Complete
Reference

Chapter 25

Configuration
Management

For small environments, managing several desktop computers as well as a few servers, at most, while not trivial by any means, isn't always all that difficult either. However, as the network environment grows, so does the complexity of managing users and computers. Take the amount of work that you do to configure and support a single computer and then imagine what it would be like multiplied by hundreds, if not thousands, of times. Administrators face the continuing dilemma of managing their network environments, and it's easy to see why many are intimidated at just the thought of supporting medium to large network environments. Sheer network environment size can make even the simplest desktop configurations seem complex and terrifying to support.

Group Policy Management

In Windows NT 4, the System Policy Editor was used to specify user and computer configurations. Despite its shortcomings (discussed below), many network environments used it simply because there weren't many viable alternatives. If you're at all familiar with the System Policy Editor for Windows NT 4, you'll gladly welcome Windows 2000's answer to this tool: the Group Policy.

Group Policy is much more than an extension of the System Policy Editor; think of it as a System Policy Editor on steroids. It offers your environment a way to centrally manage computers and users. In addition, its ties with the Active Directory (AD) allow you to delegate its administrative responsibilities for tighter control over the environment without the additional administrative burden.

Note   *For more information on AD, refer to Chapter 15.*

More specifically, the Group Policy allows administrators to set or declare policies affecting users' experience and environment configurations. There are many aspects that can be controlled with a Group Policy including, but not limited to, the following:

- Security configuration settings
- Scripts—logon, logoff, startup, and shutdown scripts
- Software installation
- Folder redirection
- Registry modifications
- Customize desktop environments on a per-user or per-computer basis
- Desktop lockdowns

Group Policy management is a Catch 22. With its enormous functionality and flexibility comes a potentially more complex and dangerous management tool. If you're not careful, Group Policies could wreak havoc in your Windows 2000 environment. For instance, two extreme examples are that you could prevent all users from logging onto the domain, or you could leave security wide open, allowing anyone to gain unauthorized access to anything in your environment.

Comparing System Policies and Group Policies

Windows NT introduced System Policies, which were essentially registry configuration settings contained within a policy file (*.pol). These configuration settings were written to either the user or computer portion of the registry.

As already stated, Windows NT 4's System Policy Editor has many limitations especially compared to Windows 2000's Group Policy. The following is a list of some of the most notable differences between these two management tools:

- **Administrative control**   The System Policy Editor represents a flat structure much like the Windows NT 4 domain models it serves. Group Policy, on the other hand, is hierarchical in nature because of its integration with AD. The hierarchical structure of a Group Policy permits granular control over who's managing the policies.

- **Security**   Microsoft has admitted that security is more relaxed with System Policies especially when compared to Group Policies. System Policies were limited to locking down a desktop, and there wasn't any enforcement of the policy other than the registry modification. In contrast, the local system and the AD enforce a Group Policy. It doesn't rely solely on the applied registry configuration settings for security.

- **Flexibility**   A Group Policy has the flexibility to be applied to the local computer, an AD site, an AD domain, or an organizational unit (OU). In addition, security groups can be used alongside Group Policies to further control the environment. Unfortunately, a System Policy could only be dispersed on a domain-wide basis, offering little flexibility to control a user's experience or environment.

- **Persistence**   When a System Policy makes registry modifications, the changes stick until either the policy or the registry modifications are reversed. Microsoft has affectionately coined this as *tattooing*. This causes a lot of frustration and headaches on the part of the administrator because when another user logs into the same system, any registry settings that have been changed still apply even though the new user doesn't have the same restrictions. This no longer applies with a Group Policy. Any registry changes are cleaned up after the user logs off of the computer. If another user logs on, the Group Policy that user is under is the only policy that gets applied.

- **Registry modifications**   Group Policies inherit the System Policies' abilities to make modifications to the registry. In addition to these modification abilities, Group Policies can also change keys that are in binary data format. This extends the Group Policy's functionality by being able to modify more registry keys than its predecessor.

As you can see, the Group Policy brings more control, flexibility, and security to a network environment than System Policies could ever hope to bring. Remember, though, that with the advantages that a Group Policy brings, it also is more complex and potentially more dangerous. You must take the greatest care in setting Group Policies to avoid inadvertently changing a setting that could affect your Windows 2000 environment.

 Group Policies don't provide client support for Windows NT or Windows 9x computers; they only support Windows 2000 computers. Therefore, you'll have to resort to using the System Policy Editor for these down-level clients.

Group Policy Objects

Group Policies are comprised of Group Policy Objects (GPOs), which are (like almost everything in Windows 2000) AD objects. GPOs give you control over your environment's desktops, servers, users, and more. They contain configuration setting information and can be applied to or associated with a domain, site, or OU. A GPO is somewhat similar to the system policy file, yet it can contain files and other AD objects.

 There are literally hundreds of GPOs that you can use with Windows 2000. For a complete listing and description of all of the available GPOs for Windows 2000, visit http://www.admin911.com. You'll find other valuable updates to this book, as well as vast amounts of information on administering network environments on this site.

Inside GPOs

Configuration settings that you specify for a GPO are stored in two locations: the Group Policy Container (GPC) and the Group Policy Template (GPT). Every GPO that you define has a corresponding GPC and GPT.

GROUP POLICY CONTAINER   The GPC is an AD object that contains a variety of information for the GPO. Typically, the information stored in the GPC is small in size and doesn't change frequently. In particular, the GPC contains the following information:

■ **Version information**   Because there are two components to a GPO (the GPC and GPT), the information contained within each of them must be synchronized. Version information ensures that the information in the GPC is in synch with GPT information.

■ **Status information**   You have the option of disabling a GPO. For instance, when you're creating a new GPO, it's always a good practice to disable it until it is complete so that any users or computers that are targeted by this GPO won't be affected until you're finished.

■ **Class Store information**   Class Store information is used for application deployment purposes, including assignment and publishing.

As an AD object, a GPC is naturally stored within the AD. To view the GPCs for your domain, do the following:

1. Open the Active directory Users And Computers snap-in, located in Start | Programs | Administrative Tools.

2. Select Advanced Features from the View menu.

3. Drill down from the Active Directory Users And Computers snap-in to the System container and then to the Policies extension (Active Directory Users and Computers | System | Policies) as shown in Figure 25-1. You'll see the GPCs in the right pane.

When you create a GPO and consequently the GPC, the GPC is given a globally unique ID (GUID). A GUID is assigned to all AD objects. This is a 128-bit number that is guaranteed to be unique with the domain, tree, or forest structure. One of the

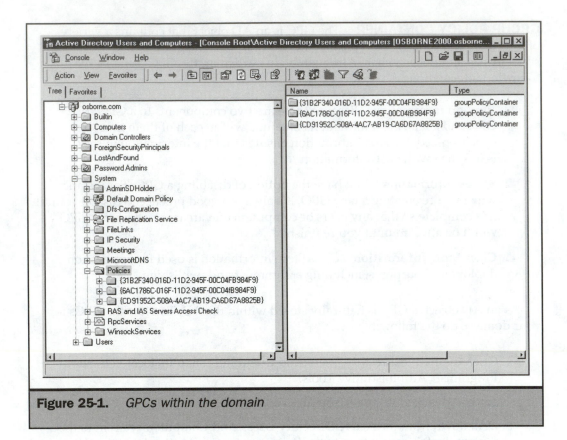

Figure 25-1. *GPCs within the domain*

advantages of assigning a GUID to the GPC is being able to allow a GPO to cross domain boundaries and still be unique. This means that you can apply a GPO to any user or computer within the forest; you're not limited to just domain assignments.

GROUP POLICY TEMPLATE   The GPT is a directory structure, located within the %SYSTEMROOT%\SYSVOL\sysvol\<*domain_name*>\Policies folder (see Figure 25-2) on domain controllers (DCs), that contains information for all policy, script, and application deployment. It is important to note that the information contained within the Sysvol shared/folder is replicated throughout the domain's DCs.

Under the Policies folder, you'll notice several other folders and a single file. As you work with GPOs, additional folders may be created within the USER and

ENTERPRISE
COMPONENTS

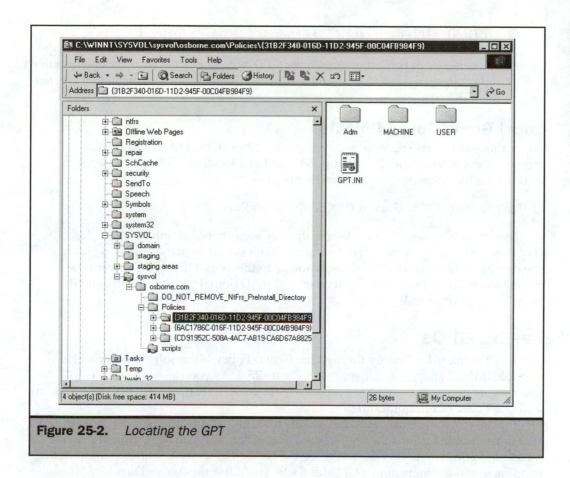

Figure 25-2. *Locating the GPT*

MACHINE folders, depending on the Group Policies that you set. They can include the following:

- **ADM**   Contains all the .ADM files for the GPT. These files are administrative templates that can be applied to the GPO.

- **USER**   This folder can contain a variety of user-related information including the Registry.pol file (that contains HKEY_CURRENT_USER registry settings to be used) and other subfolders (Applications, Documents & Settings, Scripts, and other folders).

- **MACHINE**   This folder can contain a variety of user-related information including the Registry.pol file (that contains HKEY_LOCAL_MACHINE registry settings to be used) and other subfolders.

■ **GPT.INI** This file is created at the root of each GPT folder. It stores information containing which client-side extensions of the Group Policy snap-in contain user or computer data in the GPO, whether or not the user or computer data is in a disabled state, and the version number of the extension that created the GPO.

Local Group Policy Objects

So far this section has concentrated on explaining how GPOs fit within the AD. However, every Windows 2000 computer also has a localized GPO that resides only on the local computer. It is stored within the

%SYSTEMROOT%\System32\ GroupPolicy folder

The local GPO is configured to contain only security policy information. Also, it can only be managed locally, meaning you can't expect to manage it along with the domain, site, or OU GPOs. The advantage to this is that if you don't want the Windows 2000 computer to be a member of the AD domain, you can still benefit from using a GPO locally.

Managing GPOs

GPOs are managed primarily through the Group Policy Microsoft Management Console (MMC) snap-in as illustrated in Figure 25-3. As you can see from the illustration, policies are managed separately for computers (Computers Configuration) and users (User Configuration).

The other way you can manage GPOs is through the directory service snap-in that is applicable for how the GPO is used. For instance, if you are trying to manage a GPO for a domain or an OU, you'd use the Active Directory Users and Computers snap-in; if you are managing a GPO for a site, you'd use the Active Directory Sites and Services snap-in.

Managing an Existing GPO

If you're a bit confused about managing GPOs, don't worry. Let's see what management options are available when managing an existing GPO. For simplicity, this discussion will focus on managing a GPO for a domain. Start by opening the Active Directory Users and Computers snap-in, and then right-click on the domain. Select Properties, and in the Domain Properties window, select the Group Policy tab as illustrated in Figure 25-4.

At this point, you'll see the GPOs that pertain to the domain as well as several options for managing a GPO. Microsoft highly recommends that you leave the Default Domain Policy as it is. Although it's always a good idea to lessen complexity by minimizing the number of GPOs that you're managing, it's better to create a new GPO rather than changing the configuration of the Default Domain Policy. If you follow this guideline, you'll save yourself a lot of headaches trying to troubleshoot problems caused by a misconfigured setting.

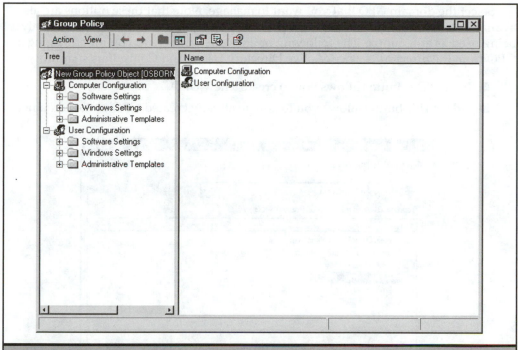

Figure 25-3.   *The Group Policy MMC snap-in*

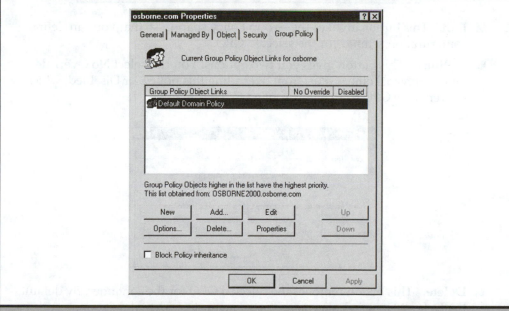

Figure 25-4.   *GPO management options from a directory service snap-in*

Select the domain GPO that you want to manage. Note that these options are also available to you if you are managing a site or OU GPO, and the domain GPO is only being used as an example. The following options are available to you for managing a GPO from the directory service (Active Directory Users And Computers snap-in):

- **New** This button allows you to create a new GPO.

- **Add** This button allows you to add an already created GPO to the container.

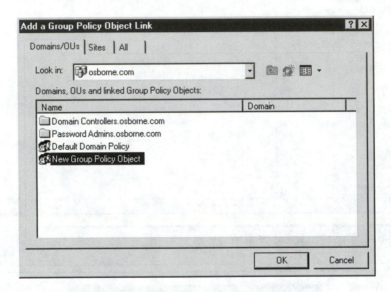

- **Edit** This button invokes the Group Policy snap-in so that you can define configuration settings for the selected GPO.

- **Options** This button gives you two options. You can select No Override, which prevents other GPOs from overriding this policy, or Disabled, which prevents the GPO from being applied to the container.

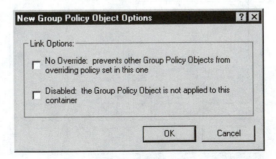

- **Delete** This button removes the selected GPO for the container. By default, the Default Domain Policy is protected against accidental deletion.

■ **Properties**   This button allows you to configure numerous options for the GPO including disabling Computer Configuration or User Configuration settings and Security assignments.

   You can also find other containers that use the GPO from the Links tab located within the GPO Properties.

■ **Block Policy Inheritance**   This option lets you prevent a child GPO from inheriting policy properties from its parent GPO. For example, you block inheritance to an OU-based GPO that needs unique configuration settings.

Creating a GPO

Creating a GPO is essentially a two-step process. You'll first create the GPO using one of the directory service snap-ins (Active Directory Users and Computers, or Active Directory Sites and Services). The snap-in you choose depends on which container you want the GPO to apply to. For example, to create a GPO and apply it to a site, you would use the Active Directory Sites and Services snap-in. The next step is defining the configuration settings of the GPO.

   It can be very useful to create your own console settings combining the Active Directory Users and Computers and Active Directory Sites and Services snap-ins. This way you can more easily manage all the GPOs in your environment. To do so, simply start the MMC and add these two snap-ins. Once you have done so, select Save As from the Console menu. The next time you need to use these two snap-ins, you can immediately access them from the Start | Programs | Administrative Tools menu.

To create a GPO, do the following:

1. Start the directory service snap-in (either Active Directory Users and Computers or Active Directory Sites and Services).
2. Right-click on the container that you want to create the GPO in, and select Properties.

3. Click New to create a new GPO. Note that you may also click Add to add an existing GPO to the container.

4. Type the name of the GPO, and then hit ENTER as shown in Figure 25-5.

5. Select the newly created GPO, and then click the Options button.

6. Disable the GPO. Temporarily disabling the GPO while you're defining it is highly recommended. When you're finished defining the GPO, you'll enable it so that it is applied to the container.

7. Select the new GPO, and click the Edit button to invoke the Group Policy snap-in.

8. Define the GPO's Software Settings, Windows Settings, and/or Administrative Templates for the Computer Configuration and/or the User Configuration nodes.

9. Close the Group Policy snap-in.

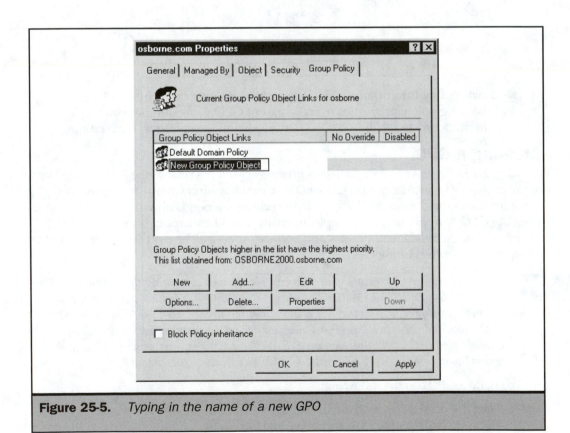

Figure 25-5.   *Typing in the name of a new GPO*

10. Select the Properties button and then the Security tab, as shown in Figure 25-6, to filter which groups and users will have the GPO applied to them. See the section called "Filtering" later in this chapter for more information.

11. Click OK.

12. Click the Options button once again and enable the GPO.

Inheritance and Precedence

Inheritance means that an object retains characteristics or properties of its parent object. This holds true for the AD as well as Group Policies. Group Policies also affect all users and computers in the AD container by default.

Group Policies are processed in a specific order. The first GPO that is processed is the local GPO. Then the container objects (site, domain, and OU) are processed. An easy way to remember the order of precedence is using the acronym LSDOU (that is, local, site, domain, and then OU).

The order of inheritance and precedence allows Windows 2000 to evaluate the Group Policy first on the local computer and then from the AD container that is

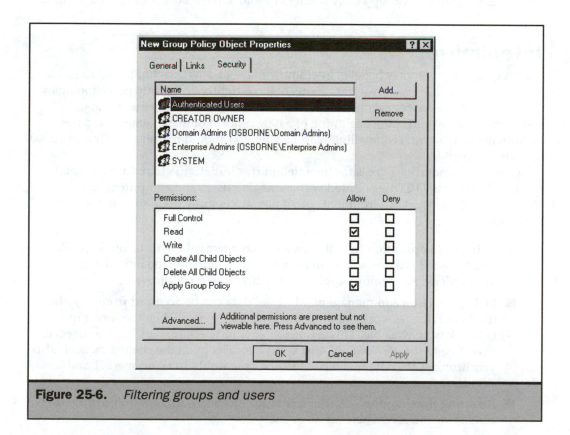

Figure 25-6. *Filtering groups and users*

farthest away from the user or computer object. This allows the GPO in the AD container that is closest to the user or computer object to override any conflicting settings in higher AD containers.

Inheritance and precedence are extremely important concepts to master. They are vital to the flexibility and manageability of your environment. Although, at first glance, these concepts may seem elementary, they can become very complex as you add and mix GPOs in your Windows 2000 environment. As a rule of thumb, you should keep the implementation of GPOs as simple as possible to avoid any confusion that might stem from inheritance and precedence issues.

FILTERING   As mentioned earlier, GPOs affect only users and computers for a given AD container. However, you can filter a GPO's scope by defining security settings with security groups and the Apply Group Policy setting. This causes Windows 2000 to bypass processing GPOs for security groups that aren't allowed to use the Apply Group Policy setting.

By default, the Authenticated Users security group processes the GPO. If you don't want a particular group to process a GPO, you can specify the security group and either deny the Apply Group Policy setting or remove the Allow setting for this right.

Intellimirror

Contrary to what you may believe, Intellimirror is not a single technology, nor is it a single service within Windows 2000. Instead, it is a tightly knit group of technologies that drastically improves user and computer configuration management. This innovation clearly marks the beginning of a new concept of management, and it is definitely one of several compelling reasons why you should migrate to Windows 2000 as soon as possible.

One of the underlying goals for the Intellimirror initiative is to reduce the Total Cost of Ownership (TCO) associated with managing users and computers in a Windows 2000 network environment, and it has successfully done so. Intellimirror offers the following core features:

- **Software/Application installation and management**   This technology allows you to install Windows 2000 and applications remotely, repair damaged installations, and remove applications with little or no intervention.

- **Data protection and management**   User data can be accessed from anywhere (that is, on the network or on the local machine), even when the server or network is unavailable. This is due to folder redirection, which forces users to save data to the network but also keeps a local copy in the client's cache. It also synchronizes the data much like the Briefcase utility in Windows NT and Windows 9x computers.

- **Roaming user support**   A user's data, applications, and environment settings can follow the user wherever he or she goes.

These features can be used separately or in conjunction with one another. Many of Intellimirror's features have been examined in chapters throughout this book. Therefore this section focuses on software/application installation and management core features, specifically using the Windows Installer for application management.

Intellimirror and Application Management

Installing and maintaining applications on a few client computers hasn't been much of a problem. We can definitely credit Microsoft for ease of use. However, this doesn't hold true when you're faced with supporting many computers, and it becomes extremely challenging when you're supporting hundreds, if not thousands, of computers in your network environment. Some of the most common challenges are the following:

- Application variations on where to install binary files (DLLs, EXEs, etc.)
- Applications requiring administrative access to the file system and/or the registry
- Managing paths where shared components (DLLs, data, etc.) reside
- Shared component conflicts (that is, applications using the same shared component but require different versions)
- Updating applications

The problems that I've mentioned above are compounded when you bring a computer's location into the picture. How do you provide application support when computers are spread across various geographic locations? Also, how do you accommodate users who need access to certain applications and data no matter where they are (that is, how do you mirror the user's experience on any computer regardless of the location)?

Before Windows 2000, you either had to invest in Microsoft's Systems Management Server (SMS) or third-party utilities to iron out some, but not all, of these challenges. I know from personal experience that these solutions took care of many of these administrative burdens, but they were limited in scope. Moreover, many of them strained network resources.

Intellimirror features only work with Windows 2000 computers because down-level computers (for example, Windows NT and Windows 9x) lack the features needed to support it. This is true even when down-level clients are running the AD client software.

Fortunately, Intellimirror solves many of the administration issues that you face today. As an integral part of Windows 2000, it leverages AD, Group Policy, and the Windows Installer to provide a complete application installation and management solution.

Windows Installer

Formerly known as the Microsoft Installer (MSI), the Windows Installer is a group of services, formatting standards (such as MSI files), and application programming interfaces (APIs) that, when used in conjunction with AD and Group Policies, allows you to effectively install, maintain, and advertise applications on Windows 2000 systems. It can perform a variety of tasks including:

- Support and simplify on-demand installation of applications as well as unattended installation
- Diagnose and repair applications
- Prevent shared application information conflicts (for example, DLL inconsistencies)
- Restore configurations after installation failure
- Remove applications

Note *One of several functions of the Windows Installer APIs is to keep information on applications regarding whether or not they are in an installed, uninstalled, or damaged state.*

AD basically serves as the repository for application information that you make available to your user population. It hosts the standardized formatting for application information. Its container objects and security groups also help define the users and computer to be affected.

On the other hand, Group Policy (explained earlier in this chapter) helps to advertise the applications. Using a GPO, you can either publish or assign (see "Publishing and Assigning Applications" later in this chapter for more information) applications to an individual or collective groups. A GPO is applied to an AD container (site, domain, or OU), but, with the help of defined security groups and users, it can be customized to be applied only to specific groups or users.

One of the primary responsibilities of the Windows Installer service is to perform the actual install and maintenance of the published or assigned application on a Windows 2000 computer. Anytime an application needs to be installed, updated, repaired, or removed, the service performs the necessary operations. It runs as the Local System service account by default so that it can handle any security-related problems such as writing to the system's registry (that is, applications typically require that you have proper rights to modify the HKEY_LOCAL_MACHINE key and sometimes the HKEY_CURRENT_USER key).

The end result is that when users log onto any Windows 2000 computer, applications are always available to them with little or no intervention on their part. In addition, the application is always functional as well as up-to-date with the implementations that everyone else in the Windows 2000 network environment is using.

MSI Structure

The Windows Installer uses MSI files containing application information for installation and maintenance purposes. MSI files aren't simply the setup files that you're used to; instead, they pack a variety of information into a relational database file structure including, but not limited to, the following:

- Install and uninstall information
- Instructions for upgrading an application
- Any customized features that are to be included in the install
- Registry settings
- Whether an application places an icon in the user's Start menu or on the desktop

As a relational database file, the MSI file contains tables that are interrelated. Table 25-1 lists and briefly describes the tables that are common within an MSI file.

Microsoft has gone to great lengths defining the format of MSI files in order to provide consistency among vendors and is adhering to these standards for its own products. You can expect to see an MSI file for every Microsoft product. As for

Group	Description
Core table	Describes the fundamental features and components of the application and installer package
File table	Contains the files (for example, cabinet files) associated with the application
Registry table	Contains the registry entries required by the application
System table	Tracks the tables and columns of the installation database
Locator table	Used to search the registry, installer configuration data, directory tree, or .ini files
Program installation	Holds properties, bitmaps, shortcuts, and other elements needed for the application installation
Installation procedure	Manages the application installation

Table 25-1. *Tables Contained in an MSI File*

third-party vendors, an increasing number of them support this format. In fact, any application that has received certification from the Windows Logo Program (http://msdn.microsoft.com/winlogo/) is required to have an MSI file. Typically, a product's MSI file can be found on the root of the installation media (for example, CD-ROM).

LEGACY AND CUSTOMIZED APPLICATIONS   Many environments have legacy and customized applications that don't conform to Microsoft's MSI standard. Luckily, you can still use the Windows Installer to install these applications, but you'll have more work ahead of you. Plus, some of the Windows Installer's feature benefits don't apply, including:

- Install on-demand (for both full installations and feature installs)
- Protection against installation failures
- Ability to repair or remove applications

There are three options available that enable you to use the Windows Installer, upgrade the application to a Windows 2000 certified version, create a ZAP file, or use a third-party utility to create an MSI file. The first choice is pretty obvious, but often it isn't an option due to the vendor, it was developed in-house, or is a result of budget constraints.

The second choice involves creating a plain-text file with the .zap extension. ZAP files are similar to .ini files that describe how to install the application and denote application properties. You should place the application's installation files in its own directory and then share the directory before you create the ZAP file. After you create the ZAP file, save it in the network share that you created for the application.

Note	*Managing ZAP files is similar to publishing (see "Publishing and Assigning Applications," later in this chapter) because the application appears only in the Add/Remove Programs in the Control Panel. It isn't installed automatically, so no icon appears on the user's Start menu or desktop.*

The following is a sample ZAP file:

```
; ZAP file for AppX
; Semicolons (;) represent comments that aren't read by the Windows Installer.
[Application]
FriendlyName = "AppX"
SetupCommand = "\\server_name\share_name\setup.exe"
; The DisplayVersion parameter is optional
DisplayVersion = 4.2
; The Publisher parameter is optional
Publisher = Company.com
```

The last option is to purchase a third-party utility, such as the ones listed in Table 25-2, to package the application's installation files into an MSI file.

CUSTOMIZING AND PREPARING THE MSI FILE   It's often necessary to tailor an application's installation to fit individual needs. For example, when installing Microsoft Office 2000, it isn't necessary to load everything that it offers; you can choose to customize the installation to install only the features you need on the computer. The same principle can be applied when you're working with the Windows Installer; you can customize how the application is installed. However, you don't want to customize MSI files; instead, you work with *transform files* (that is, .mst files).

Transform files allow you to control the installation. You create them to transform or change the application's default installation procedures. For instance, you can choose which features are to be installed (as you may have done with MS Office 2000), modify application paths, direct the application to run from a server, and much more.

Note	*It is recommended to place transform files (that is, .mst files) in the same folder as the MSI package that they customize.*

Once you have the MSI files and any MST files, you need to prepare for their usage. This means creating a software distribution site, which essentially is creating a folder somewhere on the server and sharing it, and then configuring the security permissions on the share and folder with Administrators having Full Control and the Everyone group having Read-only access. After doing this, place the MSI and MST files within the software distribution site. It's important to note here that you may want to consider using the distributed file system (DFS) to manage where the files actually reside and where they are accessed.

Publishing and Assigning Applications

Using Group Policy management alongside the Windows Installer, you have two options for managing an application's life cycle. You either publish or assign

Product Name	Company
InstallShield	InstallShield Software Corporation
InstallManager	WISE Solutions, Inc.
WinINSTALL	Veritas Software Corporation

Table 25-2.   *Vendors that Develop MSI Files*

applications using Software Settings | Software Installation within the Group Policy snap-in like the one illustrated in Figure 25-7.

Publishing can be thought of as advertising an application within the AD. Published applications are available to users within an AD container (site, domain, OU) that the GPO applies. The applications aren't installed automatically. Users must use the Add/Remove Programs applet within the Control Panel to install a published application. Publishing an application can be used for several circumstances, but the two most notable are the following:

- Legacy or customize applications that must rely on ZAP files to be used with the Windows Installer
- Giving users the option to install a supported but not required application

Assigning applications is a bit more interesting than publishing because it contributes to the user's experience in your Windows 2000 network environment. Assignment is used when an application is required, or mandatory, and you can assign an application to either a user or a computer.

When you assign an application to a user, the application's icon appears in the user's Start menu or on the desktop regardless of the computer that the user logs onto.

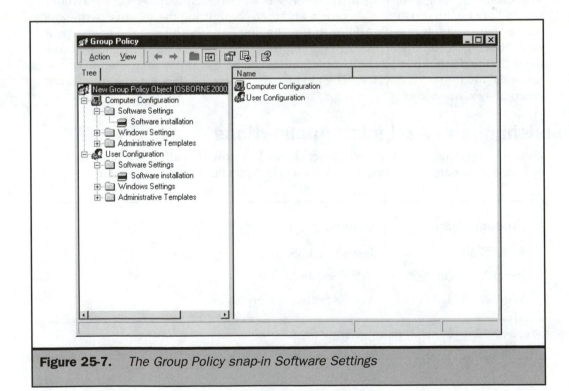

Figure 25-7.   *The Group Policy snap-in Software Settings*

As the user invokes the application (that is, by using the icon on the Start menu or desktop, through file association, and so on), the system checks to see whether or not the application is already installed. If not, the Windows Installer reads the registry to determine the location of the MSI file and then starts the installation process. Once the install is complete, the application opens. Also, if the user tries to remove the shortcut icon or the installation, it magically reappears (actually, the application's assignment status prevents the user from removing the application).

| Note | *Assigned applications (for both user- and computer-assigned applications) get installed only when the user needs or wants to use the application. The installation doesn't require any intervention on the part of the user.* |

The other assignment option is assigning an application to a computer. In this case, the application is installed the next time the computer is started or rebooted. All users who log on to that computer can access the application. This is very useful when specific applications are required for certain computers. For example, the computer that acts as the print server for the printer that holds the company checks probably runs accounting software (or at least the accounts payable module) regardless of who logs on. And, a computer that has a modem and Internet access is a good candidate for an antivirus application.

Configuring a Published or Assigned Application

Once you have an MSI file and have decided on whether to publish or assign the application, you're ready to configure it for your environment. Although this stepwise procedure doesn't go through possible configuration, it does illustrate the most common and most important steps to familiarize you with the process. This procedure assumes that you have already created a software distribution site on your network. If you haven't, refer to the "Customizing and Preparing the MSI File" section earlier in this chapter.

To publish or assign an application, do the following:

1. Start a directory service MMC snap-in (either the Active Directory Users and Computers, or Active Directory Sites and Services snap-in). The one you choose depends on the GPO that you're trying to work with. This example uses a GPO that is applied to a domain, and thus the Active Directory Users and Computers snap-in.

2. Select a domain (or other AD container that the GPO is applied to), and right-click on it to select Properties.

3. Click the Group Policy tab.

4. Choose a GPO, and then click the Edit button.

5. Expand either the Computer Configuration or User Configuration node by clicking on the plus sign (+) beside it. If you're planning on publishing a document, remember that you can't publish to a computer.

6. Expand Software Settings by clicking on the plus sign (+) beside it. Now for this example let's expand the Software Settings node under User Configuration.

7. Right-click on Software Installation, and select New | Package.

8. Locate the MSI file in the software distribution site and open it. You may get a warning message indicating that the location can't be verified. If you do and you're confident of the location, click Yes.

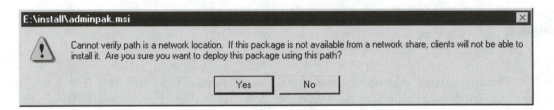

9. In the Deploy Software window, choose either Published, Assigned, or Advanced Published Or Assigned. Note that the Advanced feature automatically brings up the properties for the application to be deployed.

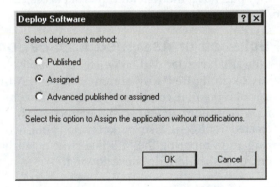

10. You can now view the Published or Assigned application in the right pane of the Group Policy window as illustrated in Figure 25-8.

If you didn't choose the Advanced Published or the Assigned option, you can display those options later by right-clicking on the MSI deployment package within the Group Policy window and selecting Properties.

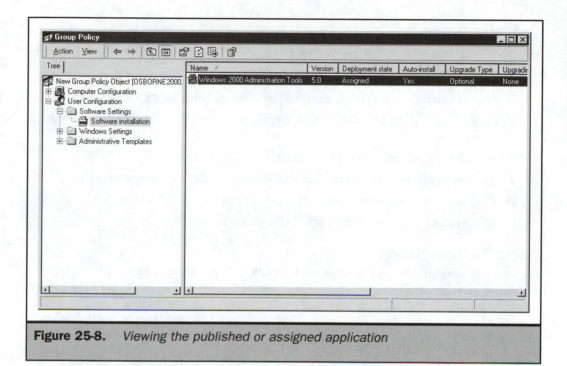

Figure 25-8.   *Viewing the published or assigned application*

Security Configuration and Analysis

Windows 2000 offers the Security Configuration And Analysis tool to give
administrators a method of insuring system security on a computer. You can use
Security Configuration And Analysis to analyze security and configure security (to
overcome problems discovered in the analysis). This is not a one-time task, because
security is dynamic as folders and files are created and secured. Plan to use the
Security Configuration And Analysis tool on a regular basis.

Security Configuration and Analysis Architecture

The Security Configuration Tool Set is a set of snap-ins for MMC that gives
administrators a mechanism for analyzing and configuring security. Although the
Security Analysis And Configuration tool is used locally to secure a computer, you can
import and export your saved configurations to expand your security designs across
the enterprise. One of the big advantages of this tool is its centralized approach,
replacing multiple dialogs in Windows NT to accomplish the same tasks. Because the
tool deals with local files and folders security, it's used on volumes formatted with
NTFS. In addition to the snap-in, there's a command line program, secedit.exe, that you
can use for quick access to many tasks.

Security Areas

The Security Analysis And Configuration tool works with the following security areas:

- **Account Policies**   Password policies, account lockout policies, and Kerberos settings
- **Local Policies**   User rights, auditing, and security options in the registry
- **Event Log**   Setting for the system, application, security and directory service event logs
- **Restricted Groups**   Policies connected to group membership
- **System Services**   Access control and startup modes for system services
- **Registry**   Access control settings of registry keys
- **File System**   Access control settings for folders and files

Security Templates

The security configurations are based on templates. These are text files with an .inf extension that specify each type of configuration option in its own section of the file. The information in the .inf files is parsed by the Security Configuration And Analysis engine. Windows 2000 ships with several preconfigured security templates that you can use as provided, or you can modify via the Security And Configuration Analysis snap-in in MMC.

The security templates are located in %SystemRoot%\Security\Templates. For Windows 2000 computers that are not domain controllers, the following templates are available:

basicdc.inf	ocfiless.inf
basicsv.inf	ocfilesw.inf
basicwk.inf	securedc.inf
compatws.inf	securews.inf
hisecdc.inf	setup security.inf
hisecws.inf	

DCs have two additional templates:

dc security.inf

notssid.inf

The template named setup security.inf is used during setup of a clean install of Windows 2000. The other templates represent varying degrees of security for Windows

2000 computers (the specific security features in the templates differ). For example, hisecdc.inf and hisecws.inf are high-security templates for a DC or a workstation.

When you configure a computer with a template, the settings in that template become the configuration settings for that computer until you change the settings or import a different template.

Security Database

The templates used by Security Configuration And Analysis are contained in a database. It's actually a data store rather than a database in the traditional sense, because it's a container. The database holds a security template or multiple security templates (multiple security templates are another misnomer; you really end up with one security template, a *composite* template that contains settings from merged multiple templates).

Setting Up the Database

To configure security, you must create a database and import at least one template into the database. Security Configuration And Analysis is an MMC snap-in, and you can use an existing MMC console, or open a new console to accomplish this.

Choose Console | Add Remove Snap-in, and then click Add in the Add/Remove Snap-in dialog. Select Security Configuration And Analysis from the list of snap-ins, and click Add; then close the dialogs to return to the MMC console. Save the console.

Create a Working Database

The template you use is contained in a database (called a *personal database*), and you must open a database in order to use the Security Configuration And Analysis tool. The first time you use this tool, you'll have to create a database and populate it with a template; thereafter you'll just have to open this database.

To create a database, right-click the Security Configuration And Analysis item in the console and choose Open Database from the shortcut menu to display the Open Database dialog box, which has no listings to choose from.

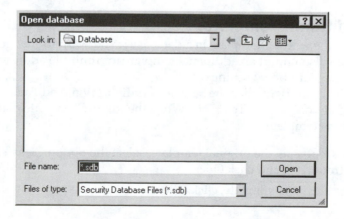

The default folder for the Open Database dialog box is not the system database folder, %SystemRoot%\Security\Database. Instead, the default folder is C:\Documents and Settings\<current user name>\My Documents\Security\Database. This feature is user linked.

Name the new database, and click Open to load it.

Import a Template

In order to use the database, you must populate it with a template. When you open the newly created database, a list of the templates available on this computer (stored in %SystemRoot%\Security\Templates) appears.

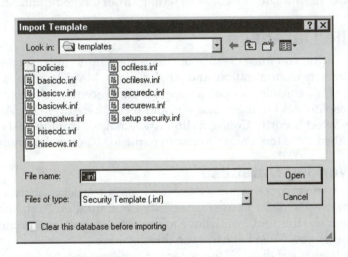

Select the appropriate template and click Open. The template is imported, and now you can use it to configure system security. Each time you want to modify settings, open this database.

Import Additional Templates

You can replace the existing template in a database if you want to change the basic settings. You can also import an additional template (or multiple additional templates) if you want to gain additional settings.

To accomplish this, right-click the Security Configuration And Analysis object in the console and choose Import Template. When the Import Template dialog box appears, select the template.

- If you're replacing the original template, select the option Clear The Database Before Importing and click Open.
- If you're adding a template, click Open.

Create Additional Databases

It's possible to create multiple databases, importing a different template into each. For example, you may want very tight security for a computer that's available to multiple users a great deal of the time. Perhaps the computer is in a kiosk, or available for general use by a group of employees. When the computer is appropriated by a user who must work with files or folders that are unavailable under tight security, however, loading a database with a different template might be more efficient than giving the user administrator permissions.

If you choose this route, you'll need to load the appropriate database before the user type changes. This means you'll have to log on with administrative rights and use the Security Configuration And Analysis console each time the machine changes user types.

Configure and Analyze the System

Now that you have a database and the template it contains, you can configure the computer to match the settings you've imported. Depending on the template you selected, a varying number of computer settings are affected. Less stringent templates make fewer changes to the computer's configuration. This means that after you configure the system, there may be a number of settings that aren't applied, because the template doesn't use them.

Configure the System

To configure the system for the template you imported, right-click on Security Configuration And Analysis in the console and choose Configure Computer Now. Confirm (or change) the location of the log file and click OK. The Security Configuration And Analysis engine configures the computer to match the template you selected.

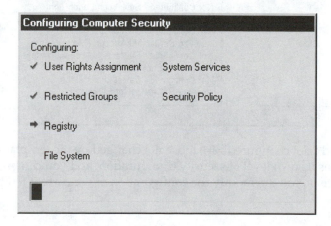

The template becomes the base configuration for security for this computer. You can modify individual settings, but before doing so, you should perform an analysis of the system's settings compared to the template.

Analyze the System

The analysis engine examines the system's security settings for all the security areas included in the currently loaded template. The values found in the system are compared to the base configuration of the template, and the results are written to a log file.

To begin the analysis, right-click the Security Configuration And Analysis object in the console and choose Analyze Computer Now. Confirm or change the location of the log file and click OK.

View the Log

You can see the log by right-clicking the Security Configuration And Analysis object in the console and choosing View Log File. The log appears in the right pane of the console.

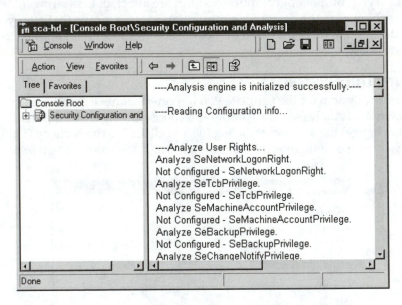

Items marked "not configured" are those not changed by the template you imported. Each template has its own level of security configuration, and you can import a new, stronger template or you can modify the configuration of the current template.

Modifying Configuration Settings

You can change the settings for individual items in the template. It's important to realize that when you make changes to any policy settings, you are only changing the template in the currently loaded database. There are two important ramifications to that statement:

- The original template is not changed; only the copy you imported to your database is altered.

- No changes are made to the computer's settings, only to the template, until you right-click the Security Configuration And Analysis object in the console and choose Configure Computer Now.

To make changes, expand the Security Configuration And Analysis item in the console to see the categories, expand the category you want to modify, and select the setting you want to modify.

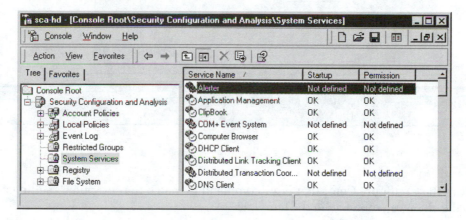

Double-click the setting you want to modify to open a dialog that displays the choices for the setting. Different types of settings offer different choices. For instance, if you're working with services, you can change when and how services launch. Figure 25-9 shows the policy setting for the Windows 2000 Alerter service.

Policy settings that are not set by the template in the current database are grayed out because the selection to define the policy is not checked. To add the setting to the current policy, select the check box that allows you to define the policy, and then configure the setting(s).

Policy settings that are set by the templates in the current database are marked as such (the check box has a check mark), and a selection is preconfigured. Change the selection to match your needs.

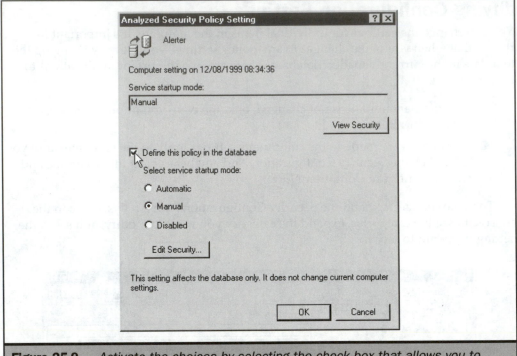

Figure 25-9.   *Activate the choices by selecting the check box that allows you to define the policy*

Run the Configure Computer Now command to match the computer's settings with the changes you made in the template.

Security Configuration And Analysis vs. Group Policy

The settings you establish with the Security Configuration And Analysis tool have less precedence than (and are overwritten by) Group Policy settings, whether those settings originate locally from an OU, or from a domain.

Therefore, it's best to use the Security Configuration And Analysis tool only for those settings not covered by Group Policies, such as security settings for local folders and files, settings for local services, and settings for local registry keys.

Exporting Templates

When you have a composite template (multiple imported templates), or when you've changed a template by altering some of the settings, you can export the template so that it can be used on other computers. This saves you all the work of importing clean templates and reconfiguring them. To accomplish this, right-click the Security Configuration And Analysis object in the console and choose Export Template.

The Export Template To dialog box defaults to the original location of the templates that were automatically installed on this computer, %SystemRoot%\Security\ Templates. If you're planning to use the template around the network, it's probably a good idea to export it to a server share that's accessible from any computer on the network. Don't forget to give the template a unique, descriptive name.

Windows Script Host

Windows Script Host (WSH) is an engine you can use to run interactive or noninteractive scripts. WSH comes in two flavors: a Windows version (wscript.exe) and a command-line version (cscript.exe). Because it's an engine, the only task you need to perform in WSH is property setting. That means you establish the environment under which a script runs, and WSH controls your script according to the settings you decree.

WSH Object Model

WSH is a language-independent scripting host for 32-bit Windows platforms that acts as a controller of ActiveX scripting engines, and supports VBScript and Jscript files by reading and passing script file contents to the registered script engine. The scripting engine uses file extensions (for example, .vbs and .js) to identify the script, maintaining its own map of extension-to- programmatic ID (ProgID) relationships. This means the scriptwriter doesn't need to be familiar with the ProgID of the various script engines, because the script host itself maintains information about the relationships, and then uses the Windows association model to launch the right engine when a user runs a script.

The WSH object model provides two types of ActiveX interfaces:

■ **Script execution**   For script execution, WSH provides the properties and processes that are responsible for the execution of the script. WSH provides the object interfaces that permit scripts to manipulate the host as needed, send on-screen messages to the user, and perform basic programming/ scripting functions.

■ **Helper functions**   Helper functions are the methods for accomplishing
additional actions as needed by the script, such as setting environment
variables (including registry changes), mapping drives, accessing resources,
and so on.

The power of WSH is extremely robust, and you can write scripts using any
ActiveX controls that provide automation interfaces for tasks.

In addition to taking advantage of the ActiveX scripting architecture (without the
need to worry about HTML SCRIPT tags), WSH works with the lean, mean scripts that
are MS-DOS batch files (such as simple logon scripts).

*Microsoft has a collection of sample scripts you can use to familiarize yourself
with the way WSH works at http://www.microsoft.com/scripting/windowshost/
docs/samples/default.htm. Be aware that Microsoft moves Web pages constantly, so
this link may not work the day you try it and you'll have to invoke a search on the
Microsoft site.*

Wscript.exe

Wscript.exe is the Windows-based version of WSH. Use WScript.exe to run scripts in
Windows with any of the following actions:

■ Double-click the script file object in My Computer or Windows Explorer.

■ Enter the script path and full name at the Run command on the Start menu.

■ Enter **WScript.exe**, followed by the script path and full name, at the
Run command.

*The Windows 2000 documentation says that unlike previous incarnations of WSH,
you don't have to enter the file extension when invoking a WSH-run script under
Windows 2000. This is apparently an erroneous statement. I "bugged" it, but at the
time of this writing it wasn't fixed. Therefore, enter the extension of your script file to
make sure it runs.*

The reason the first two choices work is the association between WSH and the
script file. If that association isn't established, Windows presents the Open With dialog
box so you can select the association. Choose WScript and select Always Use This
Program To Open This File to register WScript as the default application for all files
having the same extension as the one you double-clicked.

You can set specific behavior properties for any script. Right-click the script file and choose Properties from the shortcut menu. Move to the Script tab, shown in Figure 25-10 with the default settings applied, to customize the way the script behaves.

■ To set a time limit for the script's execution, select the option Stop Script After Specified Number Of Seconds and enter a value in the spin box. You can specify up to 32,767 seconds.

■ To eliminate the use of a logo when the script is executed in a command console, deselect that option.

When you make changes to the default properties, the system creates a second file for the script, a Script Host Control file that has the extension .wsh. Both files must

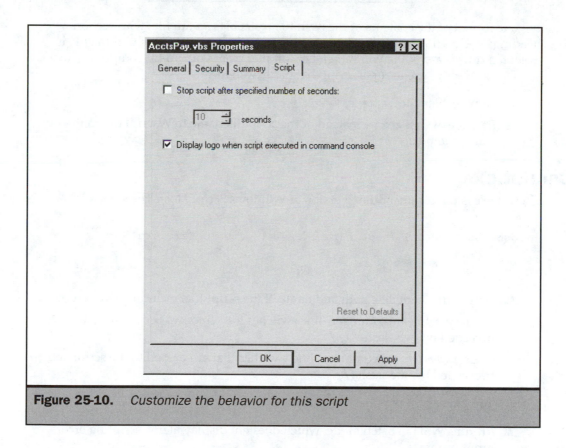

Figure 25-10.   *Customize the behavior for this script*

ENTERPRISE
COMPONENTS

exist to run the script. The .wsh file contains a pointer to the script, along with the changed properties.

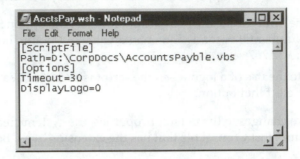

The format of the contents of the .wsh file resembles an .ini file, with section headings enclosed in brackets. The behavior is similar to a .pif file in that the file is executed (this is assuming you remember .pif files from your 16-bit computing days).

To use Wscript.exe to run a script that has a .wsh file:

■ Double-click the .wsh file.

■ Pass the .wsh filename instead of the script filename to Wscript.exe in the Run command box.

Cscript.exe

Cscript.exe is the command-line version of Windows Script Host. The syntax is

```
cscript [Script] [host parameters] [script parameters]
```

where:

■ *Script* is the complete path and name of the script file, including extension.

■ *host parameters* are command-line switches for Windows Script Host, and are preceded by two slashes (/ /).

■ *script parameters* are command-line switches that are passed to the script and are proceeded by one slash (/).

The following host parameters are available:

■ **//B** runs WSH in batch mode, which does not display alerts, scripting errors, or input prompts.

■ **//D** turns on the debugger.

■ **//E:***engine* names the scripting language used to run the script.

- **//H:cscript** registers Cscript.exe as the default application for running scripts.

- **//H:wscript** registers Wscript.exe as the default application for running scripts (this is the default if no specification is made).

- **//I** runs the script in interactive mode, which displays alerts, scripting errors, and input prompts (this is the default).

- **//Logo** displays the logo at run time (this is the default).

- **//Nologo** does not display the logo at run time.

- **//S** saves the current options for the current user.

- **//T:***nnnnn* specifies the maximum time the script can run (*nnnnn* is entered as seconds).

- **//X** opens the script in the debugger.

Writing scripts and using Windows Script Host adds power to your administrative arsenal of tools and tricks. For detailed information on scripting in Windows 2000, read *Scripting Windows 2000* by Jeffrey Honeyman, MCSE (Osborne/McGraw-Hill, 2000),

Windows Management Instrumentation

Windows Management Instrumentation (WMI) is the Microsoft implementation of Web-Based Enterprise Management (WBEM), an industrywide initiative to develop technology that helps administrators manage enterprise environments. WMI is totally WBEM compliant and has built-in support for the Common Information Model (CIM).

  CIM is the data model that describes the objects in a management environment. It's an extensible object-oriented schema for managing systems, networks, applications, databases, and devices.

WMI Architecture

WMI isn't a program, it's an "initiative." Working within the Windows platform, it extends the power of an administrator who needs to monitor, control, and analyze software, hardware, networks, users, and policies. Using the WMI functions, administrators can understand (and alter) what is currently happening, and determine what has already happened, to software applications, hardware components, and networks.

The *Object Repository* is a CIM-compliant database of object definitions. The *CIM Object Manager* handles the collection and manipulation of the objects in the repository. In addition, the CIM Object Manager also gathers information from the WMI providers. The *WMI providers* are intermediaries between the components of the operating system and applications that access those components. (For instance, there's a registry provider that is responsible for eliciting information from the registry.) The WMI Control is used to modify configuration settings.

All of these functions act on Windows 2000 management tools that have been WMI-enabled, including tools for the following:

- Logical Drives
- System Properties
- System Information

The capabilities of the WMI Control for modifying configuration settings go beyond those management tools and can manage user and group permissions

The WMI Control

The WMI Control is a tool you can use to configure WMI settings (a host of configuration options) for a local or remote computer. To launch the WMI Control tool, open the Run menu item and enter **wmimgmt.msc**. When the WMI console opens, the WMI Control (Local) object is in the console pane.

If you want to work on a remote computer, right-click the WMI Control object and choose Connect To Another Computer. In the Change Managed Computer dialog box, enter the name of the computer you want to use as the target of your configuration efforts. Notice that there's no Browse button; you must know the computer name.

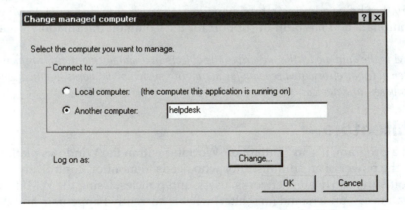

If you don't have the appropriate permissions, click the Change button to enter a username and password for a user who has sufficient rights on the target computer.

WMI Logon ? X

☐ Log on as current user

User name: judyb

Password: ×××××××

OK   Cancel

When you're connected to the target computer, the object in the console pane changes to WMI Control (*ComputerName*). You can now begin to use the WMI Control tool.

Configure Permissions for WMI Tools

WMI has its own security, and users must be authorized to connect to WMI. The WMI security is actually another layer of security, over and above the security provided by the operating system. WMI security is checked when a user logs onto WMI services.

WMI security is separate from the operating system security, so you won't interfere with the basic security configuration you've already established for users and groups. WMI permissions are configured via the WMI Control console.

Note   *By default, any user who is a member of the Administrators group already has full control of WMI services.*

To configure WMI security, right-click the WMI Control object in the console pane and choose Properties. Then select the Security tab (see Figure 25-11).

Expand the objects to select the namespace for which you want to allow access to selected users and groups. Then click the Security button to open the Security dialog box for the selected namespace. As you can see in Figure 25-12, it looks like the Windows 2000 Security dialog box, and you can add or remove users and groups, or use the Advanced button to set granular permissions for a selected user or group.

Enable WMI Error Logging

Error logging is a way to track, and therefore attempt to troubleshoot, WMI problems. You can enable error logging and configure it to report everything that happens or only those events that trigger an error. To set up WMI Error Logging, right-click the WMI

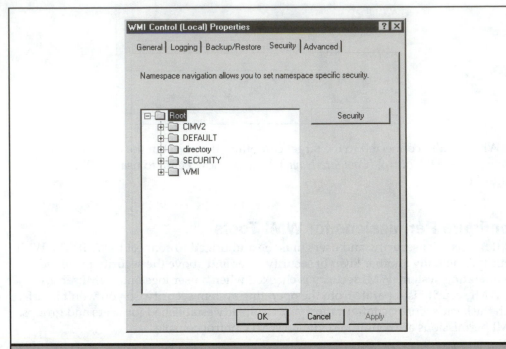

Figure 25-11. *Expand the Root object to see the namespaces in which you can change WMI security*

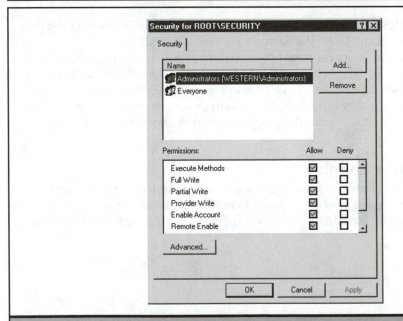

Figure 25-12. *Add or modify user and group permissions for WMI as necessary*

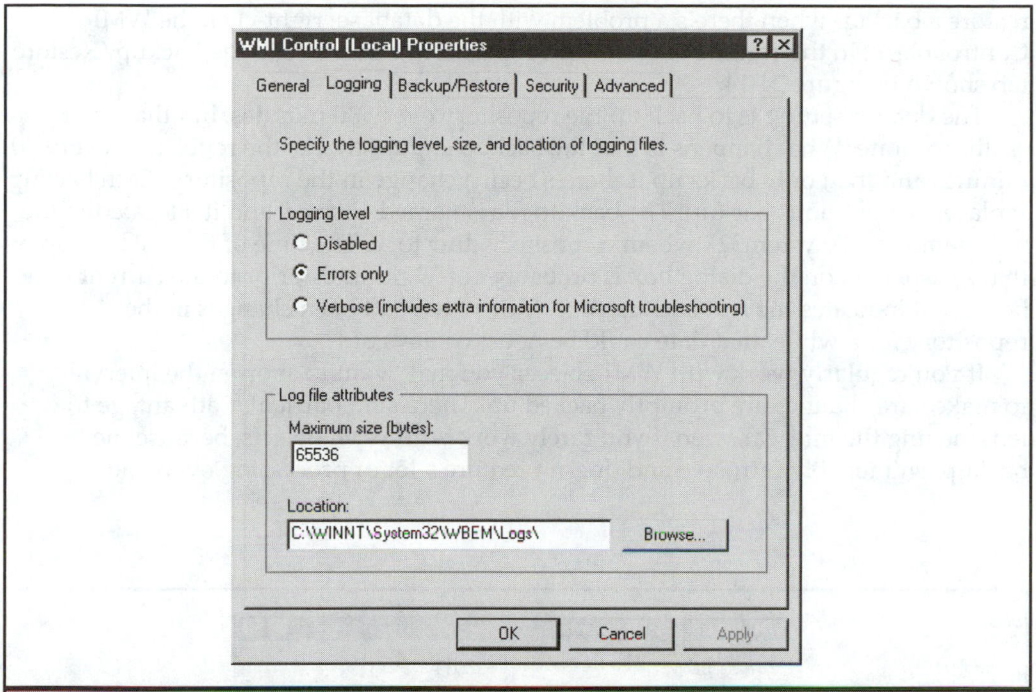

Figure 25-13.   *Enable and configure WMI logging in the Logging tab of the WMI Control Properties dialog*

Control object in the console pane and choose Properties. Then select the Logging tab shown in Figure 25-13.

- Choose Errors Only to report errors that occur with WMI.
- Choose Verbose to report all actions.

Verbose logging can impair performance, so only choose that option if you need to see everything that occurs in order to investigate a recurring problem.

Note   *Log files are kept for all of WMI, and for each WMI-enabled provider.*

If the log reaches the maximum size you've specified, the log file is renamed from filename.log to filename.lo_, and then a new log file is begun. When the new file reaches the maximum size, filename.lo_ is deleted, the new file is renamed to filename.lo_, and a new log file is started.

Configure Backup for the WMI Repository

WMI's CIM-compliant object repository is its database of objects, and it's backed up whenever there's a change to the database. To configure the backup parameters, or to restore a backup when there's a problem with the database, right-click the WMI Control object in the console and choose Properties. Then move to the Backup/Restore tab shown in Figure 24-14.

The default setting is to back up the repository every 30 minutes, but that's not really accurate. What happens is that the backup engine checks the repository every 30 minutes and then only backs up if there's been a change in the repository. Each backup replaces the previous backup. The backup file is named cim.rec, and it's located in the %SystemRoot%\system32\.wbem\repository directory. The time of the last backup that's displayed on the dialog box is probably not 30 minutes prior to the current time, because it indicates the real backup time. If there haven't been changes in the repository for a while, that date could be hours or days old.

If you regularly work with WMI objects, you may want to shorten the interval to make sure changes are promptly backed up. There's no particular advantage to lengthening the interval, even if you rarely work with WMI objects, because the backup isn't terribly intrusive and doesn't require a lot of processing overhead.

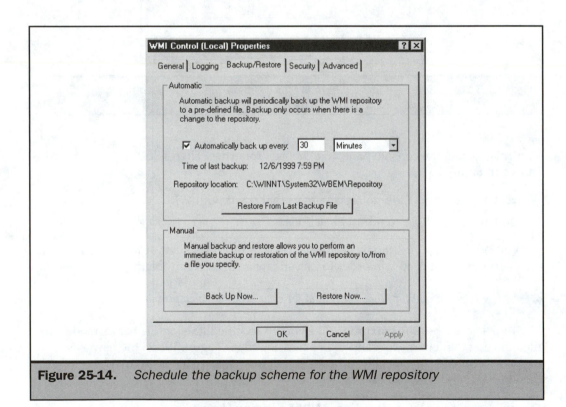

Figure 25-14.   *Schedule the backup scheme for the WMI repository*

You can manually back up the repository by clicking Back Up Now. This is advantageous under either (or both) of the following circumstances:

■ You're planning to make changes to objects in the repository and don't want to wait for the next scheduled backup.

■ You want to take advantage of the fact that you can specify a different filename for the backup file, which provides an additional copy.

To restore the repository from the last regularly scheduled backup, click Restore From Last Backup File. To restore from the last manual backup, click Restore Now.

Configure WMI Scripting Settings

Use the Advanced tab of the WMI Control dialog box to change the scripting namespace for WMI. By default, the namespace is root\cimv2. Click Change to browse for a namespace to use for any object that isn't already attached to a full namespace path.

Using WMI to Measure Performance

You can use WMI instead of the registry to collect data about resources. To use a performance monitor under WMI, enter **perfmon.exe /wmi** in the Run command. The Performance console that appears looks the same as that launched when you open it without WMI (see Figure 25-15).

The difference between using Perfmon normally and using it under WMI is in the way Windows interacts with the console. Under WMI, a group of DLLs (called *Performance Data Helper DLLs*) act as an intermediary between WMI and the

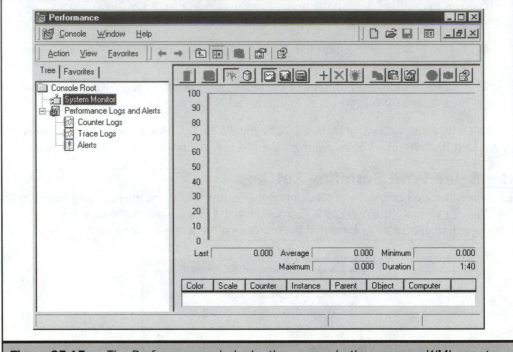

Figure 25-15. *The Perfmon console looks the same whether you use WMI or not*

performance tool being used. The DLLs format data and make any necessary calculations to translate information into the format needed by WMI.

You use the counters as you normally would; the fact that WMI is calling for the information and collecting the information is transparent.

Using the Logical Drives Tool

Logical Drives is a WMI tool you can use to manage local or mapped remote drives. You can use the Internet or your company intranet to perform tasks against remote drives. To open the Computer Management console shown in Figure 25-16, right-click My Computer and choose Manage.

To use a remote computer, right-click the Computer Management object in the console pane and choose Connect To Another Computer. Then specify the computer you want to target.

Select the Logical Drives object in the console to view the drives attached to the currently selected computer. Select the drive you want to manage, and right-click on its object. Choose Properties to open the drive's Properties dialog box.

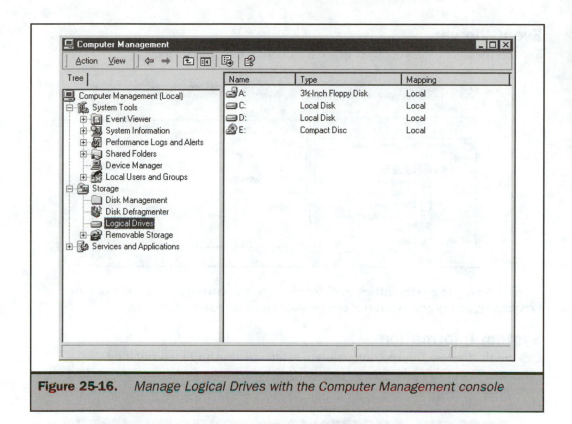

Figure 25-16.   *Manage Logical Drives with the Computer Management console*

On the General tab, in addition to viewing information about the drive (size, free space, file system), you can create or modify the Volume Label. On the Security tab, you can perform the following tasks:

- Set access permissions
- Set ownership
- Set audit entries
- Set special permissions

Using the System Tools

To use the WMI System tools, open the Computer Management console as described in the previous section, and select a remote computer if you're not working on the local system. Then select the System Tools node in the console tree. You can use any of the six tools, as described in this section.

Event Viewer

Expand the Event Viewer object to see the existing Event View logs.

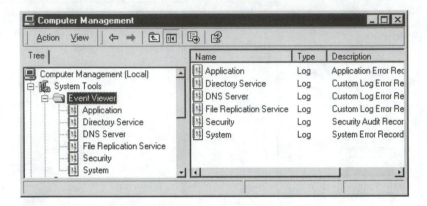

Select a log to see its entries, and double-click any entry you want to examine. Frequently, errors and warnings can provide clues to system problems.

System Information

Expand the System Information object to begin viewing and manipulating the components of this node. (Your component list may differ from mine, depending on software installation.)

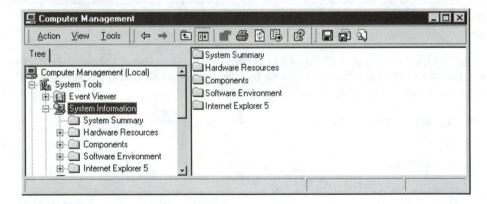

- **System Summary** displays basic information about the computer and operating system.

- **Hardware Resources** expands to provide information about the various types of resources in the system. This is the place to look for hardware conflicts or components that aren't working.

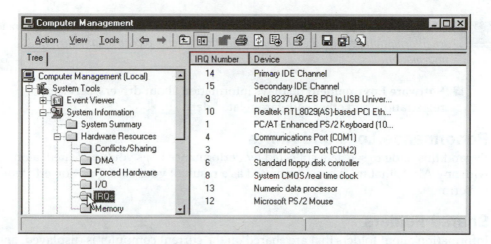

■ **Components** expands to let you examine the system devices. As shown in Figure 25-17, you can view information about any device on the system.

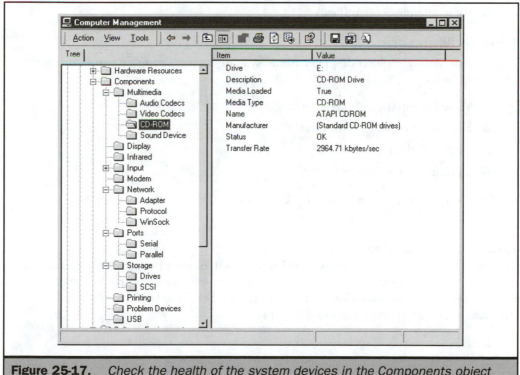

Figure 25-17.   *Check the health of the system devices in the Components object*

When you select an object from the Components node, it takes a few seconds before you see information because the system queries the target device to obtain current information.

- **Software Environment** displays information about drivers, services, registration, and other software-related data.

Performance Logs and Alerts

Expand this node to see data collected by Performance Logs you've created, along with any Alerts that have been generated as a result of your configuration efforts in Perfmon.

Shared Folders

Information about folders that are shared on the current computer is displayed, and you can perform the following tasks:

- Set permissions for shares
- View and disconnect users
- View and close open files

Device Manager

The Device Manager object displays all the system devices, and you can perform the following tasks:

- View information about each device
- Configure properties for devices
- Uninstall devices
- Update device drivers

Detailed information on using this powerful tool is available in Chapter 7, in the section "Device Manager."

Local Users and Groups

For computers running Windows 2000 Professional, or member servers, you can use this object to manage the users and groups on the current computer. This object cannot be accessed on a Windows 2000 domain controller. See Chapter 18 for detailed information on managing users and groups.

The Complete Reference

Chapter 26

Clustering

Microsoft has long seen clustering as the solution to any real or perceived Windows NT/Windows 2000 scalability problems. From their roots in the Wolfpack Project at Microsoft, clusters are beginning to mature into an important part of any enterprise Windows 2000 implementation. This chapter examines Microsoft's latest cluster offerings and describes how they can be used to scale and extend Windows 2000.

A *cluster* can most easily be defined as a group of individual servers that work together as a single system. Software and clients see the cluster as a single entity, and the cluster is managed as a single unit. Clustering is used to ensure high availability for mission-critical applications, manageability for 24/7 implementations, and scalability for large enterprise solutions.

Clustering is available on both the Windows 2000 Advanced Server and the Data Center Server. Two major clustering technologies are available from Microsoft, and they can be employed individually or at the same time:

■ **Network Load Balancing clusters** provide scalability for server-based applications by distributing client requests across the multiple servers in the cluster.

■ **Server clusters** ensure system availability by enabling failover technology from one node to another. The cluster software automatically moves processes and resources of the failed system to the remaining systems in the cluster.

Network Load Balancing Clusters

Network Load Balancing is a software solution used by Microsoft Windows clustering to scale the performance of server-based programs by distributing client requests among the multiple servers within the cluster. Usually, load balancing is established for applications such as high-end databases, client/server applications, or Web-based applications.

> **Note** *Windows 2000 Network Load Balancing is the replacement for Windows Load Balancing Service (WLBS) in Windows NT 4. However, you'll find that references to the original WLBS aren't entirely gone—for example, the command-line management program is still wlbs.exe.*

Load Balancing Advantages

Using Network Load Balancing, clusters of up to 32 hosts can be created over which client requests can be distributed. The main advantage of Network Load Balancing is higher performance; however, it has other important advantages in the form of availability and scalability.

Availability

Beyond high performance, Network Load Balancing offers significant high-availability capabilities for enterprise systems. The cluster software can automatically reallocate the distribution of client requests in the event of server failure. To accomplish this, the cluster and the individual servers within the cluster monitor the health of each other. Multicast or broadcast messages are exchanged among the servers, and between each server and the cluster.

If the status of a server or servers within the cluster changes, the remaining servers exchange messages to determine the current state of the cluster, and then launch a process called *convergence* to stabilize the cluster. The server with the highest host priority is then designated as the *default host*, and that server handles all of the network traffic while the system reallocates the distribution of client requests.

Note	*Client requests that are directed to a specific server as a result of port rules might not be reassigned to the default host. See the section "Port Rules" later in this chapter.*

In the case of an additional host being added to the cluster, this same convergence process permits the new host to receive its share of traffic. Expansion of the cluster in this way is completed transparently to both clients and programs. In addition, if a server is taken offline for maintenance, the convergence process will make sure that cluster operations are not interrupted. This allows for impressive amounts of uptime and availability.

Scalability

Two levels of scalability are achieved with Network Load Balancing:

- **Scalable activity**   Additional users and traffic are managed smoothly by the constant distribution of requests to give all clients equal access to the application or service.

- **Scalable system**   Additional components (servers or processors) can be added to the cluster. Network Load Balancing is further enhanced by the fact that it uses commodity products, which drives the price down to reasonable levels.

Managability

Administration of Network Load Balancing is efficient because the cluster is managed as a single unit from a single control point (which can be remote). Administrators can use any Windows 2000 computer on the network to manage the cluster, using shell commands and scripts to start, stop, and manage the behavior of a Network Load Balancing cluster. In addition, the ability to take individual systems offline allows for easier maintenance and upgrades.

Load-Balancing Architecture

Network Load Balancing runs as a Windows 2000 networking driver, and the operations of the driver are transparent to the TCP/IP stack. All computers in the cluster can be addressed by the cluster IP address. However, each computer also maintains its own unique, dedicated IP address. Client requests are distributed throughout the cluster in the form of TCP/IP traffic across the hosts. Each host can be configured with a specific load percentage, or the load can be distributed equally among all the hosts.

Hardware and Protocols

Network Load Balancing is built to provide clustering support for TCP/IP-based server programs. This, of course, requires TCP/IP to be installed in order to use this feature. The version of Network Load Balancing in Windows 2000 operates on FDDI or Ethernet-based LANs within the cluster.

Network Load Balancing performance is enhanced if there are two network adapters installed in a host. In this case, Network Load Balancing uses one network adapter for the client-to-cluster traffic, and the other for all other network traffic. (However, multiple network adapters are not a requirement.)

Network Load Balancing enables all of the hosts on a single subnet to detect incoming network traffic for the primary IP address of the cluster. The Network Load Balancing driver provides a filter between each host's cluster adapter driver and the TCP/IP stack. The filter permits a portion of the incoming network traffic to be received by the host.

Note   *For multihomed hosts, the additional IP addresses are also detected.*

Incoming client requests are mapped to cluster hosts via a distributed algorithm. When a packet arrives, every host performs the mapping simultaneously. This allows a quick determination of which host should handle the packet. This simultaneous filtering algorithm is more efficient for packet handling than are programs that use centralized load-balancing programs. Centralized filtering involves the modification and retransmission of packets, which can add latency. As a result of this simultaneous filtering, Network Load Balancing can provide a high aggregate bandwidth.

Network Load Balancing controls the distribution on a per-connection basis for TCP, and a per-datagram basis for UDP, by filtering the incoming traffic before anything gets to the TCP/IP protocol software. Only the TCP and UDP protocols within TCP/IP are handled, and all controls are applied on a per-port basis.

Note   *Some point-to-point TCP/IP programs, most notably Ping, will produce duplicate responses when targeting the cluster IP address. To avoid this, use the specific IP address for each host.*

Network Load Balancing can be configured to handle the cluster traffic more precisely using features such as port rules or affinity. See the section "Installing and Configuring Network Load Balancing" later in this chapter for more information.

Application Configuration

There are several ways to configure applications on a Network Load Balancing cluster. The cluster can be configured in such a way that a copy of a server-based program runs on every host; or the application can be run on one host, sending all client requests to that host instead of distributing the load throughout the cluster. This decision will depend on the type of application. For instance, applications that require centralization, such as Exchange Server 5.5, are far easier to maintain if they're on a single host. In addition, writes to a database can be sent to a dedicated database server within the system. If databases are load balanced in a cluster, updates to the contents of the data files have to be synchronized by being merged offline at regular intervals. Most of the time, however, mission-critical databases are deployed in a server cluster environment instead of a Network Load Balancing environment (see "Server Clusters" later in this chapter).

Pure Network Load Balancing is best suited for noncentralized data storage, or for applications that don't accept data from clients accessing the server. Web sites are an ideal candidate for Network Load Balancing because it is easy to provide each host with a current copy of the pages (which are usually static) to make sure that high-volume traffic is handled with ease and speed. For Web clients who need access to a database, the Web servers can direct the requests to a database server. Other good candidates for Network Load Balancing are the following:

- HTTP, HTTPS, FTP, TFTP, and SMTP over TCP/IP
- HTTP over SSL—port 443
- FTP—port 21, port 20, ports 1024–65, and port 535
- SMTP—port 25
- Terminal Services—port 3389
- Web servers (such as Microsoft Internet Information Services)—port 80
- Web servers using round-robin DNS
- Virtual private network servers
- Streaming media servers

Software applications can be deployed on a Network Load Balancing cluster as long as multiple instances of the application can run simultaneously without error or harm.

Understanding Application Servers and Stateful Connections

There are two kinds of client-host connections for application servers, and they're usually described with the term *stateful connection*.

- **Interclient state** is the state where updates are synchronized with transactions performed for other clients. An example is the update of the inventory on an e-commerce site after the sale of goods to a client connection.

- **Intraclient state** is the state that's maintained for a specific client throughout a session, such as the sale of products (usually involving a shopping cart process) at an e-commerce site. In fact, at most e-commerce sites, the shopping cart process can span multiple separate connections from the same client.

Network Load Balancing works best when it is used to provide scalability for stateless front-end services (Microsoft Internet Information Services is an example), even if those front-end services access a shared back-end database server.

Network Load Balancing should never be used with interclient stateful connections. The applications that use this stateful connection type aren't designed to permit multiple instances of connections that access a shared database and simultaneously synchronize updates.

Network Load Balancing can be used to scale intraclient state applications, even within a session that spans multiple connections. With client affinity enabled, Network Load Balancing directs all TCP connections to the same cluster host, which permits the session state to be maintained in host memory. (Client/server applications that embed the state within cookies or send it to a back-end database don't require client affinity.)

Installing and Configuring Network Load Balancing

Network Load Balancing is a service bound to a NIC, so the installation process is the same as adding any other service to the adapter. Configuration parameters are established through the Network Load Balancing Properties dialog box, and the settings are written to the registry.

In addition, after the service has been installed, the TCP/IP protocol for the Network Load Balancing NIC must be configured in order to make the settings consistent.

Installing the Network Load Balancing Service

The first step in installing the Network Load Balancing Service is to open the Control Panel and then the Network And Dial-Up Connections applet. Right-click the Local Area Connection on which you want to run Network Load Balancing, and choose Properties. (If the computer has multiple NICs, there's a Local Area Connection icon for each one.)

In the Properties dialog box, Network Load Balancing is listed as a component. If there is no check mark in the check box, click the check box to place one in it as shown in Figure 26-1.

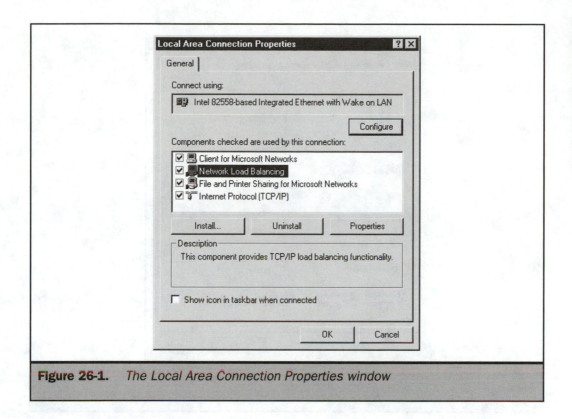

Figure 26-1.   *The Local Area Connection Properties window*

> **Note**   *If Network Load Balancing isn't listed on the Properties dialog (which usually means it was specifically uninstalled), click the Install button and choose Service as the type of network component. Then click Add and install Network Load Balancing.*

With the Network Load Balancing selection highlighted, choose Properties to open the Network Load Balancing Properties dialog box, which has three tabs: Cluster Parameters, Host Parameters, and Port Rules.

Setting Cluster Parameters for Network Load Balancing

The Cluster Parameters tab, shown in Figure 26-2, has options that apply to the entire cluster. Configure the cluster parameters for each host in the cluster, using the guidelines discussed in this section.

PRIMARY IP ADDRESS   Enter the cluster's primary IP address, using standard Internet dotted notation. The address is a virtual IP address because it's the one that's used for the cluster as a whole. You must use this same address for all the hosts in the cluster.

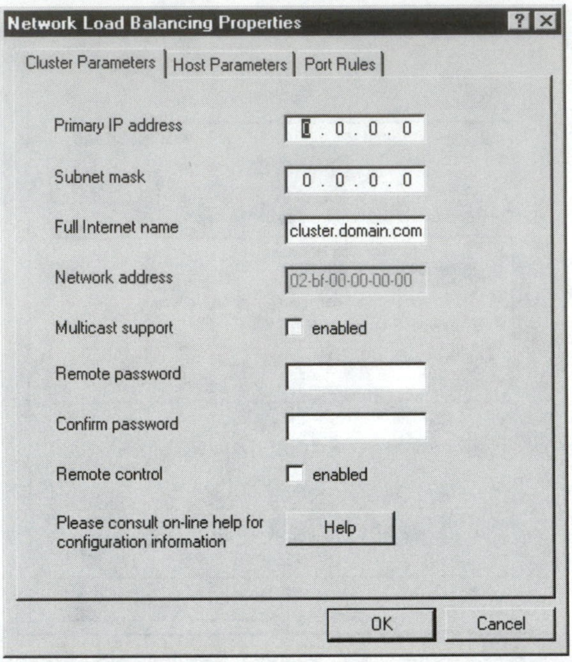

Figure 26-2.   *The Cluster Parameters tab*

SUBNET MASK   Enter the subnet mask, which is the one for the IP address you just entered (for instance, 255.255.255.0).

CLUSTER'S FULL INTERNET NAME   Enter the cluster's full Internet name, for example, cluster.grant.com. This name is applied to the cluster as a whole, and should be the same for all the hosts in the cluster. The name must also be resolvable to the cluster's primary IP address through a DNS server or the Hosts file.

CLUSTER'S NETWORK ADDRESS   Network Load Balancing automatically generates the network address (MAC address) for the NIC that will handle client-to-cluster traffic, based on the cluster's primary IP address. Network Load Balancing uses a locally administered address that is also a multicast MAC address, assuming multicast support is enabled.

MULTICAST SUPPORT   Specify multicast or unicast mode. In most cases, multicast mode should be enabled, as it is more efficient. If multicast mode is enabled, a multicast MAC address is used for cluster operations. Network Load Balancing changes the cluster MAC address that belongs to the cluster adapter into a multicast address. This means that the cluster's primary IP address will resolve to this multicast address as part of the ARP protocol. In addition, the adapter can use its original, built-in MAC address (which is disabled in unicast mode).

If clients are accessing a cluster operating in multicast mode via a router, the router must accept an ARP reply that has one MAC address in the payload of the ARP structure but appears to arrive from a station with another MAC address (as seen in the Ethernet header). Additionally, the router must be able to accept an ARP reply that has a multicast MAC address in the payload of the ARP structure. If the router cannot meet these requirements, a static ARP entry can be created in the router to support the resolution of unicast IP addresses to multicast MAC addresses.

In unicast mode, Network Load Balancing forces the driver that belongs to the cluster adapter to override the unique, built-in network address for the NIC so that its MAC address becomes the cluster's MAC address.

If the NIC does not permit changes to the MAC address, you'll have to replace the NIC with one that does. This is a hardware requirement for Network Load Balancing in unicast mode.

In unicast mode, two NICs should always be used, dedicating one to client-to-cluster traffic and one to cluster-to-cluster traffic. This will keep the performance level of the cluster at a usable level.

Note   *You cannot mix multicast and unicast mode in a Network Load Balancing cluster.*

REMOTE PASSWORD   A remote password may be used to access the cluster from a remote Windows 2000 machine. This password is used for authentication by the Wlbs.exe cluster control program (it is not used when controlling the cluster operations from the cluster host). Remote operations from Wlbs.exe require the /passw parameter on the command line, along with the password, to perform control operations on the cluster.

Note   *To eliminate the need for a password, clear both the Remote Password and Confirm Password fields.*

If remote control is enabled, it is important to secure the cluster because it is possible for intruders to take advantage of the environment through the remote control ports. Use a firewall to control access to the Network Load Balancing UDP control ports (the ports that receive the remote-control commands). By default, these are ports 1717 and 2504 at the cluster IP address.

Host Parameters

The Host Parameters tab of the Network Load Balancing Properties dialog box offers options that apply to the host in question. This section presents guidelines for configuring this (and every other) host computer in the cluster. Figure 26-3 shows the available Host Parameters configuration options.

PRIORITY (UNIQUE HOST ID)   The priority ID is this host's priority for handling default network traffic for TCP and UDP ports that are not specifically configured in the Port Rules tab (covered in the next section). The priority is unique to this host, and is used for convergence.

The value can range between 1 and X, where X is the maximum number of hosts. The highest priority is 1, and higher numbers indicate lower priorities. Each host in the cluster must have a unique priority ID.

If a host within the cluster fails, the convergence process must know which of the remaining hosts can handle the traffic for the offline host. The host with the highest priority will be selected, and if that host fails, the host with the highest priority among the remaining hosts steps in. This system provides some fault tolerance for the Network Load Balancing cluster.

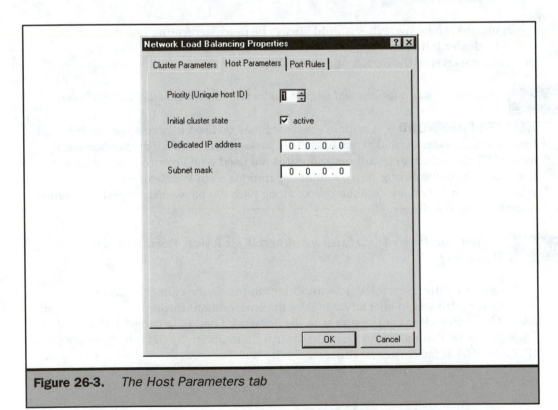

Figure 26-3.   *The Host Parameters tab*

Keep records about the priority that is assigned for each host. If a new host is added to the cluster that has a conflicted priority, the new host will not be able to join the cluster (the Windows event log reports the problem).

INITIAL CLUSTER STATE The Initial State parameter determines whether Network Load Balancing should start when the operating system loads on this host. If this option is selected (by clicking the check box), Network Load Balancing starts each time Windows 2000 boots. If the box is unchecked, then hosts can join and leave the cluster via Network Load Balancing command-line controls. See the section "Cluster Commands" later in this chapter. This is useful if there are other services that need to be loaded on the host (usually manually) before bringing the host into the cluster.

DEDICATED IP ADDRESS The dedicated IP address is this host's unique IP address, and it's used for network traffic that's unrelated to the cluster. Enter the address in standard Internet dotted notation. This IP address will be used to address each host individually, so it must be unique. Most of the time it's easiest to use the original IP address, because that's unique to the host. Enter the dedicated IP address and subnet mask as a static IP address.

| Note | *The dedicated IP Address cannot be a DHCP address.* |

Port Rules

Port rules allow Network Load Balancing clusters to be easily configured and controlled. Port rules help determine the way the cluster traffic is handled for each port. The method by which a port handles network traffic is referred to as its *filtering mode*. The Port Rules tab, illustrated in Figure 26-4, is used to create, edit, and remove a port rule.

Creating a port rule is accomplished by specifying a set of configuration parameters that define the filtering mode. Each rule contains the following parameters:

- The TCP or UDP port range to which the rule is applied
- The protocols for which the rule applies (TCP, UDP, or both)
- The filtering mode that determines the way the cluster handles traffic for the port range and protocols you're configuring
- Optionally, a selection for client affinity

The number and type of rules that are created on one host must be duplicated on every other host in the cluster. If a host attempts to join the cluster without being configured with identical port rules, the host will not be accepted as a member of the cluster.

This section presents the guidelines for using the Port Rules tab to create a port rule.

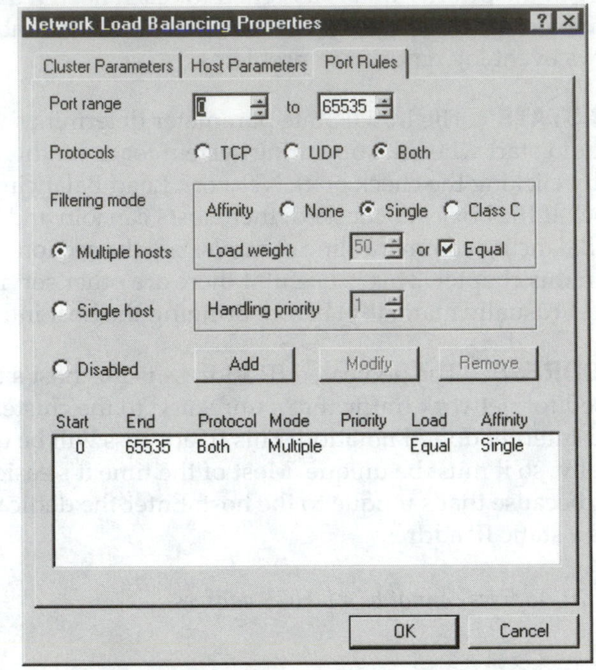

Figure 26-4. *The Port Rules tab*

PORT RANGE Specify the TCP/UDP port range that the port rule covers. Any port numbers in the range 0 to 65,535 are supported, and the default range is 1 to 65,535. To add a single port, enter the same starting and ending port number.

PROTOCOLS Select the specific TCP/IP protocol that the port rule covers (TCP, UDP, or both). The network traffic for the protocol that is named here will be the only traffic that is affected by this rule. All other traffic will be handled using the default filtering mode.

FILTERING MODE To specify that multiple hosts in the cluster will handle network traffic for this port rule, the Multiple Hosts option must be selected. By distributing the load among multiple hosts, there will be a distinct fault tolerance gain as well as scaled performance. The filter mode also allows the option of deciding whether the load should be distributed equally among the hosts in the cluster, or whether a specific host should handle a specific percentage of the load.

Select Single Host to specify that network traffic for the port rule should be handled by a single host in the cluster, according to a priority that is set. This priority overrides the host priority ID for this port's traffic.

Select Disabled to specify that the network traffic for this port rule should be blocked. This is a simple way to build a firewall to prevent network access to a specific range of ports.

AFFINITY   *Client affinity* is the redirection of multiple client requests from a specific client to a specific cluster host, instead of sending each individual request from the same client to the cluster for a load-balanced response. Network Load Balancing uses the IP addresses to link the client and host. Affinity can be turned on and configured in the Port Rules tab.

Select None to specify that Network Load Balancing should not direct multiple requests from the same client to the same cluster host.

Select Single (the default setting) to specify that multiple requests from the same client IP address should be directed to the same cluster host. Affinity has a negative effect on performance, but under certain circumstances this is outweighed by the efficiency provided to the client making the multiple requests. For example, if each request from a client is connected to a cookie, keeping the client at the same host is more efficient.

Class C affinity provides affinity for a group instead of a single-client IP address. Selecting this option directs multiple requests from the same TCP/IP Class C address range to the same host. With this configuration, clients that use multiple proxy servers are treated in the same manner that individual client IP addresses are handled under Single affinity. When a client who is accessing the cluster through multiple proxy servers makes multiple requests, each request appears to originate from a different computer. If all of the client's proxy servers are located within the same Class C address range (usually a safe assumption), enabling the Class C option means that client sessions are handled is a similar manner as they are in Single affinity.

LOAD WEIGHT   In the Multiple Hosts filtering mode, the Load Weight parameter can be used to specify the percentage of traffic a host should handle for the associated port rule. To prevent the host from receiving network traffic, specify zero. To specify a percentage, use a value between 1 and 100.

As each host is configured, the total of the individual Load Weight parameters does not have to add up to 100 percent. The actual traffic load is computed dynamically, using the host's load weight specification divided by the total of the cluster's load. Insistence on a constant value of 100 percent for all load weights would not work because hosts occasionally enter or leave the cluster.

EQUAL LOAD DISTRIBUTION   The Equal Load Distribution option is used to specify that a host participates in equally balanced traffic in multiple-host filtering mode for the associated port rule.

HANDLING PRIORITY The Handling Priority is used if single-host filtering mode is utilized, and it specifies the host's priority level for traffic for this port rule. The host with the highest handling priority for a rule will handle all of the traffic for that rule. Enter a value between 1 and X, where X is the number of hosts. Each host must have a unique value for this parameter. The value 1 is the highest priority.

Configuring TCP/IP for Network Load Balancing

The TCP/IP properties for the NIC that is used for Network Load Balancing must also be configured during setup of Network Load Balancing. The following entries must be the same in both the Network Load Balancing configuration and the TCP/IP configuration:

- Dedicated IP address (must be static)
- Cluster IP address

Managing Network Load Balancing Hosts

Network Load Balancing is designed to allow the adding of hosts to a cluster, the removing of a host from a cluster for maintenance, and the reconfiguration of rules and parameters without interrupting the work of the entire cluster. In addition to managing the hosts, there are command-lines tools for managing the cluster itself. This section covers some of the management options that are useful for controlling Network Load Balancing.

Modifying Host Parameters

When Network Load Balancing starts, the Network Load Balancing driver reads all configuration parameters and checks for the following:

- Are all parameters valid?
- Are all parameters consistent throughout the cluster?

If a problem exists, Network Load Balancing does not start cluster operations. Any errors are reported in the Windows 2000 event log.

If a new host joins the cluster while the cluster is operational, it exchanges information about its parameter values with all the other hosts in the cluster. If any of the following problems are found, the new host is not permitted to handle cluster traffic:

- Duplicate host priorities
- Different number of port rules
- Inconsistent port rule

The solution is to remove the host from the cluster (using the command **wlbs stop**). Then use the Network Load Balancing Properties dialog box to correct the problem.

To reconfigure the cluster, simply modify the rules and update the parameters for each host, one at a time. First, remove a host from the cluster, change the parameters, and then return the host to the cluster. During this process, the other hosts in the cluster will detect the inconsistencies that are created and keep the cluster traffic moving. The effect is as follows:

- If a new rule is added, it will not take effect until all the hosts in the cluster have had the same rule added.

- If a rule is modified, the rule is not put into effect until the same change is made on all the other hosts. In this way, all rules are always consistent throughout the cluster.

Error Handling for Host Problems

When a problem is detected, Network Load Balancing is very good at automatically recovering. It reports all problems by writing to the Windows error log. In fact, Network Load Balancing reports all activities, even those that aren't problems to the same log. Following are the error types that are written to the error log, along with their common causes:

- **Information**   Normal events such as driver startup, completion of convergence, and other usual cluster control actions.

- **Caution**   Abnormal occurrences that do not stop cluster operations, such as configuration problems or limited driver resources.

- **Error**   Major problems that usually require immediate attention, such as widespread configuration problems, serious inconsistencies, or execution errors.

When the configuration of a host is changed and the host attempts to join the cluster, an error will be produced in the error log. Until the same change is made on all hosts, an error will be written to the error log. If an administrator has not made an accompanying change, it usually means the cluster operations were somehow disrupted. In that instance, each host should be stopped and check for errors. To view the event log record, use the command **wlbs display**.

Managing the Network Load Balancing Cluster

After Network Load Balancing has been installed and configured, its operations can be controlled (and parameter settings modified) with the Network Load Balancing control program, wlbs.exe. This program can be found in the %SystemRoot%\System32 folder.

Wlbs.exe can be used from cluster hosts or from any remote Windows 2000 computer that can access the cluster over a LAN or WAN. Wlbs.exe is a shell-based program, which allows administrators to write and execute command-line scripts to simplify administration.

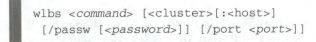 **Note**   *Wlbs.exe cannot be used to modify the parameters of a host from a remote computer.*

The syntax for wlbs.exe is

```
wlbs <command> [<cluster>[:<host>]
  [/passw [<password>]] [/port <port>]]
```

where:

- *command* is one of the supported commands (listed next) and the following parameters are used when accessing a cluster from a remote computer:
- **cluster** is the cluster primary IP address.
- **host** is the IP address of a host in the cluster (if omitted, all hosts).
- **/passw** *<password>* is the password for remote access.
- **/port** *<port>* is the cluster's remote-control UDP port.

Commands:

- **ip2mac** *<cluster>* converts cluster IP to cluster MAC address
- **reload** reloads parameters from the registry.
- **query** queries to see which hosts are currently part of the cluster.
- **display** displays configuration parameters, current status, and recent event log messages.
- **suspend** suspends control of cluster operations.
- **resume** resumes control of cluster operations.
- **start** starts cluster operations.
- **stop** stops cluster operations.
- **drainstop** ends all existing connections and stops cluster operations.
- **enable** *<port>* | **all** enables traffic for *<port>* rule or ALL ports.
- **disable** *<port>* | **all** disables ALL traffic for <port> rule or ALL ports.
- **drain** <port> | **all** disables NEW traffic for <port> rule or ALL ports.

Server Clusters

The second component in Windows Clustering is *server clusters*. The goal behind server clusters differs slightly than that of Network Load Balancing. Server cluster functionality focuses more on providing high availability, scalability, and manageability to your Windows 2000 network environment, whereas Network Load Balancing works primarily on providing high reliability and performance.

Server Cluster Architecture

Like Network Load Balancing, a server cluster is a group of computers that work together as a single entity. Windows 2000 Advanced Server supports two computers in a server cluster while Windows 2000 Datacenter Server supports four computers. In a server cluster, each computer in the server cluster is called a *node*, and each node is equally responsible for maintaining server and application availability. In addition, every node is attached to one or more storage devices. These storage devices are used to share data and applications between two or more nodes.

Server clusters offer centralized management of the systems. Since server clusters work as a single entity, so should the management software work as if it were managing a single system. This streamlines the process of accessing and managing server clusters so that you can work more effectively and efficiently.

Failover and Failback

Server clusters provide high availability by ensuring that applications and nodes are constantly accessible. If a node or application were to go offline (that is, planned or unplanned downtime), another node in the server cluster would immediately take over the responsibilities. This process is known as *failover*.

FAILOVER   Failover is one of the many features of server clusters that differentiate it from Network Load Balancing. Failover occurs when either an application or a node experiences a failure. For instance, when a hardware resource on a node causes the system to crash, the other node in the server cluster domain immediately takes control.

It first takes ownership of the failed node's resources. Dependent resources are taken offline before the resources on which they depend are taken offline. The Cluster Service does this by using the Resource Monitor to communicate with the resource DLL that manages the resource (see below for more information on Resource Monitor). If the resource can't be contacted or brought offline gracefully, it is terminated abruptly. Once the resources are offline, the recovery node then begins to take ownership of the resources, assumes the IP address of the downed node, and finally automatically starts providing the services of the downed node to clients (that is, brings the resources and services back online).

Application failure, although a very similar process, goes through a slightly different procedure from that of node failure. After detecting the application failure, the node can first try to restart the application. If it's unsuccessful, the node initiates failover so that the other node in the server cluster starts the application.

There are two very important things to remember concerning failover:

■ Failover is only truly useful if the node recovering the application or an entire node can adequately service the additional workload. Since unplanned failures are rarely, if ever, predictable, you should equip all nodes so that they can easily accommodate workloads failed over to it.

■ The failover process is entirely customizable. You can use the Cluster Administrator to define policies and procedures for failover. For example, you can define application dependencies—whether or not an application failure invokes application restart on the same node—and failback policies.

FAILBACK   After failover, a recovery node (or nodes) is hosting services from a node or application that has gone offline. You should only consider this failover solution as a temporary one because, generally speaking, resources are more strained. As a result, you should try to get the application or node back online as soon as possible.

The mechanism for restoring the original configuration is called *failback*. Failback is essentially failover in reverse. It automatically balances the workload when the application or node becomes available again (that is, gets online).

Server Cluster Operation Modes

There are two basic operation modes for Windows 2000 server clusters within your network environment. These modes are not to be confused with the clustering scenarios that clustering can provide to your environment. Rather, they are the underlying mechanisms that allow server clusters to be versatile in your environment.

The two operation modes supported by Windows 2000 server clusters are the following:

■ **Active/active clustering**   *Active/active clustering* is the most productive and efficient operational mode that you can use. In this mode, all nodes are operating under workloads (they're services clients), and they're able to provide recovery services for any application or node that goes offline. The benefit is that hardware resources are used more efficiently. In other words, resources aren't wasted by sitting idle and waiting for an application or node to go offline.

■ **Active/passive clustering**   *Active/passive clustering* is used to provide the highest level of availability, stability, and performance. In this mode, one node is actively providing services while the other is sitting idle waiting for the active application or node to go offline. Although this mode provides the highest level of security for your Windows 2000 server cluster, the downside is that you are wasting valuable resources.

Hardware Components

Hardware components that are required by the server cluster is another differentiating factor between server clusters and Network Load Balancing. Simply put, there are heavier resource requirements needed to support the functionality of server clusters (that is, failover, failback, and active/active clustering). The following sections detail the fundamental hardware components needed to create and support a server cluster.

NODES As mentioned earlier, a server cluster is comprised of two or more individual computer systems (nodes) that work as a single entity. Client computers see and use server clusters as a single resource.

Before a server can become a node and participate in the server cluster, it must meet the following prerequisites:

■ The server must be running Windows 2000 Advanced Server or Datacenter Server.

■ The server must have the Cluster Service installed and running.

■ It must be attached to one or more shared storage mediums. See "Shared Storage Devices" later in this chapter for more information.

■ It must become a member of a server cluster domain. The server cluster domain is a logical, collective grouping of servers that work together as a server cluster. The server cluster domain name is used for management purposes as well as by clients to access the resource entity.

Once the prerequisites have been met, the server can actively participate with other members of a server cluster. The nodes, by definition, retain the following properties:

■ Since every node in the server cluster is attached to one or more shared storage devices, each of them shares the data stored on those devices.

■ Each node detects the presence of other nodes in the server cluster through an interconnect. An *interconnect* is typically a high-speed connection that is attached to each node. Nodes don't have to have a separate interconnect apart from their network interface card (NIC) that connects them with the rest of the Windows 2000 network environment. However, a separate interconnect is highly recommended.

Note *Nodes participating in a server cluster can also detect when nodes are joining or leaving the server cluster. This detection ability is also responsible for detecting both system and application failures.*

A node's participation within the server cluster can fluctuate. Table 26-1 lists the five possible operational states for a node. A node can only be in one state at a time.

State	Description
Down	The node isn't operational within the server cluster. This can be due to a system or application failure as well as planned maintenance.
Joining	The node is becoming a member of the server cluster domain.
Paused	Shared resources are tied up so the node is temporarily waiting on resources to be freed.
Up	The node is active and operational within the server cluster.
Unknown	The node's state of operation can't be determined.

Table 26-1.   *Node Operational States*

SHARED STORAGE DEVICES   All nodes participating in a server cluster share one or more storage devices like the one illustrated in Figure 26-5. These storage devices use a shared SCSI bus to connect to two or more nodes in the server cluster. Windows 2000 Advanced Server and Datacenter Server can support a wide range of SCSI hardware manufacturers, but it is highly recommend that you consult the hardware compatibility list (HCL) before you attempt to create a server cluster. You'll save yourself a huge amount of time if you make sure that the SCSI devices are operating properly before you add other elements into the picture.

The storage devices themselves store any data that the nodes will need to share. They also store all of the server cluster's configuration and resource information. Only one node can take temporary ownership of the data contained in the shared storage device or devices. This prevents these resources from conflicting.

> **Note**   *For additional fault tolerance, you should use Redundant Array of Independent Disks (RAID) 5. RAID 5 stripes data among three or more disks in the array and keeps parity information to improve performance and reduce the risk of losing data due to disk subsystem failures.*

INTERCONNECTS   An interconnect is the physical medium used for server cluster communications. It can either be the NIC that is also used for communication with the rest of the network (that is, NIC used to receive incoming client requests) or another NIC that is dedicated to serving server cluster communications only. For improved performance and redundancy, typical configurations use a dedicated NIC for cluster communication and a second NIC for communicating with the rest of the network.

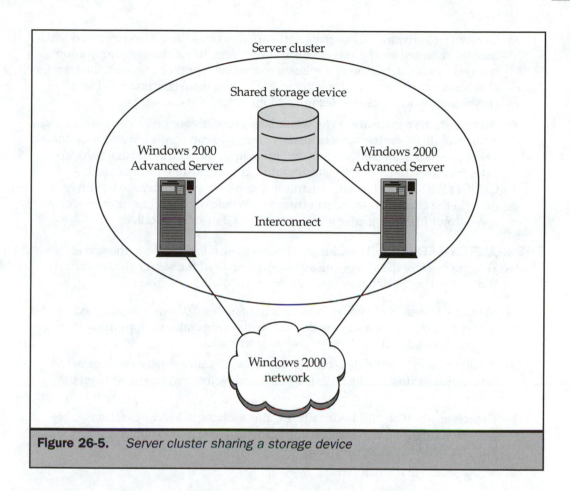

Figure 26-5.   *Server cluster sharing a storage device*

Two NICs in each node isn't a requirement, but it's the recommended configuration. The reasoning is rather straightforward. First, network traffic that is generated between two nodes won't be negatively affected by other traffic circulating the network. Most importantly, however, you're reducing the number of single points of failure in the server cluster. Isn't this one of the primary reasons why you're using server clusters in the first place?

Clusnet.sys, the cluster network driver, runs on each node and manages the server cluster communications. The server cluster communications includes, but isn't limited to, routing messages such as *heartbeats*, which are periodic messages that are used to detect communication failures between nodes and node status information.

Software Components

Several software components make up server clusters. These can be broken down into two categories:

- **Clustering software**   Clustering software describes the software components that are required for the server cluster to operate. It enables communication between nodes, detection of application or node operational status, the transfer of resource operations, and much more. The two main components for clustering software are the Resource Monitor and the Cluster Service.

- **Administrative software**   The administrative software gives you control and manageability over the server cluster so that you can configure and monitor it. There are two main components that are within the administrative software category: the Cluster Administrator and a command-line utility called CLUSTER.EXE. Cluster Administrator doesn't necessary have to be run on a node in the cluster; it can be run from any Windows 2000 computer as well as a Windows NT 4 computer with Service Pack 3 or later installed.

THE CLUSTER SERVICE   The Cluster Service runs on each node in the server cluster. It is the heart of the server cluster controlling all of the server cluster activity. More specifically, the Cluster Service controls the following activities:

- Manages all server cluster objects including nodes (for example, the node that it is installed on), shared storage devices, and configuration information (for example, a node's IP address or computer name).

- Facilitates and coordinates communication with other cluster services in the server cluster domain, including when a node joins or is removed from the server cluster.

- Detects application and node failures, and initiates failover operations. This may include trying to restart an application as well as distributing workloads to another node in the server cluster.

- Manages event notification.

THE RESOURCE MONITOR   Any physical or logical component, most of which were mentioned above, within a server cluster is considered a resource by the Cluster Service. In order to increase the manageability aspects of the server cluster, a Resource Monitor is used to aid in the communication between the Cluster Service and the server cluster resources.

Resource Monitors are various software components that basically serve as a liaison between the Cluster Service and server cluster resources. It allows these resources to run separately from each other and the Cluster Service. The separation of resources, including the Cluster Service and Resource Monitors, promotes reliability, availability, and scalability for the server cluster. For instance, if a resource fails, it doesn't affect the operability of the Cluster Service. Also, the Resource Monitor is used to watch over the Cluster Service, so that if it fails, the Resource Monitor can respond by taking all of the node's resources offline.

For the most part, the Resource Monitor doesn't invoke any server cluster operations. The exceptions to the rule are for gathering status reports from the Cluster Service or resources, and when the Cluster Service fails, it brings all of the node's resources offline. When the Resource Monitor communicates with a resource, it's actually communicating with the resource's *resource DLL*. The resource DLL can be viewed as the interface to the resource. Take, for example, a resource where an event has occurred. The resource DLL must report this event to the Cluster Service. This is when the Resource Monitor steps in; it essentially takes the message and makes sure that the Cluster Service is notified.

THE CLUSTER ADMINISTRATOR   Cluster Administrator is the primary tool that you'll use to administer and configure server cluster objects such as nodes, groups, and other resources. It's installed by default on every node in the cluster, but it can also be installed on any Windows 2000 or Windows NT 4 with Service Pack 3 or higher computer. This allows you to manage the server cluster without having to actually be physically located at one of the nodes.

THE COMMAND-LINE CLUSTER UTILITY   Cluster.exe gives you the ability to manage the cluster from the Command prompt (see Figure 26-6) or from a script. Scripts can call cluster.exe and automate management of the server cluster. The utility can be run from any Windows 2000 or Windows NT 4 with Service Pack 3 or higher computer in your Windows 2000 network environment.

Before you begin using this utility, there are some important syntax rules that you must abide by, including the following:

- Use quotation marks around all names that contain spaces and special characters.

- For Boolean values (True and False), specify 1 (one) for True and 0 (zero) for False.

- If you don't specify a server cluster name or use a period (.), it is assumed that you are working from and specifying the local server cluster.

- Cluster.exe processes options from left to right, and if an option fails, the command will stop executing at the failed option.

- Use double quotation marks (") in a string that has two consecutive double quotation marks (" ").

The syntax that you use for cluster.exe depends on what you're trying to manage. Table 26-2 shows you the various properties that you can manage as well as their corresponding basic syntax.

Note   *To display the options for any of the basic syntax definitions in Table 26-2, you can use either the /? or /help option.*

```
Command Prompt                                                    _ □ ×

C:\>cluster /?
The syntax of this command is:

CLUSTER /LIST[:domain-name]
CLUSTER [[/CLUSTER:]cluster-name] <options>

<options> =
  /PROP[ERTIES] [<prop-list>]
  /PRIV[PROPERTIES] [<prop-list>]
  /PROP[ERTIES][:propname[,propname ...] /USEDEFAULT]
  /PRIV[PROPERTIES][:propname[,propname ...] /USEDEFAULT]
  /REN[AME]:cluster-name
  /VER[SION]
  /QUORUM[RESOURCE][:resource-name] [/PATH:path] [/MAXLOGSIZE:max-size-kbytes]
  /SETFAIL[UREACTIONS][:node-name[,node-name ...]]
  /REG[ADMIN]EXT:admin-extension-dll[,admin-extension-dll ...]
  /UNREG[ADMIN]EXT:admin-extension-dll[,admin-extension-dll ...]
  NODE [node-name] node-command
  GROUP [group-name] group-command
  RES[OURCE] [resource-name] resource-command
  <RESOURCETYPE|RESTYPE> [resourcetype-name] resourcetype-command
  NET[WORK] [network-name] network-command
  NETINT[ERFACE] [interface-name] interface-command

<prop-list> =
  name=value[,value ...][:<format>] [name=value[,value ...][:<format>] ...]

<format> =
  BINARY|DWORD|STR[ING]|EXPANDSTR[ING]|MULTISTR[ING]|SECURITY|ULARGE

CLUSTER /?
CLUSTER /HELP

C:\>_
```

Figure 26-6.   *Cluster.exe used from the command prompt*

Property	Basic Syntax
Cluster	**cluster [[/cluster:]***cluster name] /*option
Cluster node	**cluster [[/cluster:]***cluster name]* **node** *node name /*option
Cluster group	**cluster [[/cluster:]***cluster name]* **group** *group name /*option
Cluster network	**cluster [[/cluster:]***cluster name]* **network** *network name /*option
Cluster netinterface	**cluster [[/cluster:]***cluster name]* **netinterface /node:** *node name* **/network:** *network name /option*
Cluster resource	**cluster [[/cluster:]***cluster name]* **resource** *resource name /*option
Cluster resourcetype	**cluster [[/cluster:]***cluster name]* **resourcetype** *resource type display name /*option

Table 26-2.   *Properties and Corresponding Syntax That Can Be Managed Using cluster.exe*

Using Server Clusters in Your Environment

Planning how server clusters will fit into your Windows 2000 network environment is a crucial step that you must take before the implementation phase. Unfortunately, planning is all too often not given enough consideration. However, if you take the time to consider a server cluster's functional roles, your environment will benefit immensely.

There are several predefined, implementation variations that you can choose from. What you choose depends on the following:

- *What are you trying to support?* File and print services, Web services, and applications are just a few of the things that you can have server clusters support. What you choose has a tremendous impact on the model that you'll follow.

- *What level of high availability, scalability, reliability, and performance do you need?* The models that Microsoft presents vary slightly in the type of services that it offers. In other words, one model may offer the highest degree of availability while not offering much in terms of scalability.

- *What, if any, budget constraints do you have?* Budget considerations can vary widely. Some environments are rightfully budget conscious; others don't have to worry much about finances. Financial considerations do influence the model that you'll choose to follow.

This section presents the configuration models that Microsoft suggests you consider. For simplicity, here the number of nodes in each model will be limited to two. Keep the questions above in mind while you're reviewing each of the models to see which one is more appropriate for your Windows 2000 network environment.

Hot Spare Cluster Model

The "hot spare" cluster model, illustrated in Figure 26-7, is also called the active/passive model because not all the hardware resources are being used simultaneously. As a result, this model provides the highest level of availability for your Windows 2000 network environment.

In this model, only one node in the server cluster services all requests for resources. The other node sits patiently idle until the active node fails. Think of the hot spare or passive node as a dedicated backup.

Typically, the passive node uses the same hardware configuration as the active node. This is so that if a failure does occur, the passive node can quickly take its place and provide the same level of service under similar workloads.

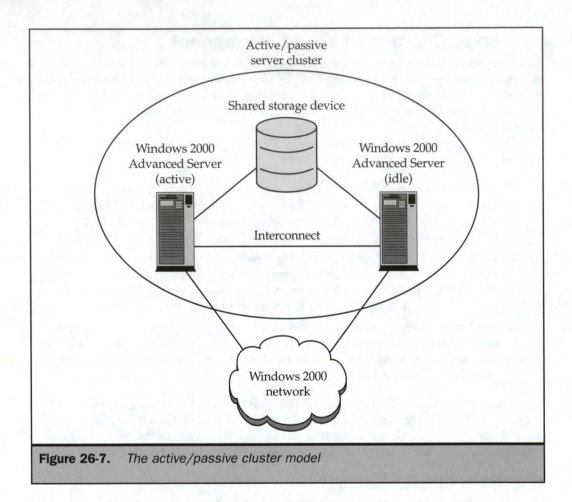

Figure 26-7. *The active/passive cluster model*

The primary advantage to this model is that it provides the highest level of availability without sacrificing performance degradations. However, it is only recommended for your most critical applications and services. Also, you must be willing to spend the extra expenses to have a node sit idle for much of the duration of its life.

Active/Active Cluster Model

The active/active cluster model represents two nodes in a server cluster that are working simultaneously. Each node is responsible for its own server cluster resources until a failover occurs. If a failover does occur, the surviving node assumes the resources of the failed node.

This model, shown in Figure 26-8, insures the same level of high availability as the "hot spare" cluster model. However, performance can be compromised depending on

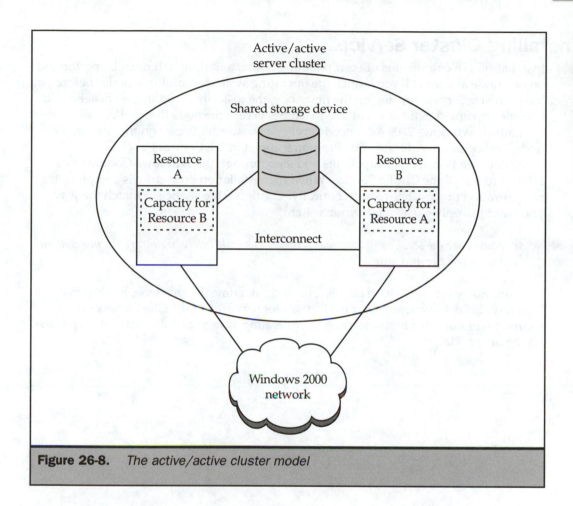

Figure 26-8.   *The active/active cluster model*

the type of resource being assumed and the surviving node's capacity to handle the additional workload when the other node fails. For this reason, it is key that you size each node to adequately handle workloads for all resources.

Server Cluster and Network Load Balancing Model

This server cluster model is a hybrid of the other two models that combines the best of both. It essentially takes the active/active model and enables Network Load Balancing to increase reliability and performance. For example, both nodes in the server cluster handle requests for each resource, and if one node fails, the other takes over.

The advantages to this model are enormous. It provides high availability, reliability, scalability, and performance. If a failover does occur, the performance hit that is experienced depends on the capacity of the remaining node.

Installing Cluster Service

Installation is a culmination of your planning efforts and design. It must be performed on one node at a time. If you launch the operating system on multiple nodes before you have Cluster Service running on the first node, the disks involved in the cluster could become corrupted. Shut down all the machines except the node that you're installing.

Launch Windows 2000 Advanced Server or Datacenter Server on the first target node, and open the Add/Remove Programs applet in the Control Panel. Click Add/Remove Windows Components and step through the Windows Components Wizard to install the Cluster Service. When the installation procedure is complete, the configuration process begins automatically. Configure the service to match the way you want to apply clustering to your system.

Note   *Make sure the service runs without error on this node before beginning the installation process on the next node.*

Continue your installation efforts, one node at a time. In each case, be sure that Windows 2000 Advanced Server (or Datacenter Server) and the Cluster Service are running without error before starting the operating system and the installation process on the next node.

The Complete Reference

Chapter 27

Advanced Disk Management

W indows 2000 provides tools to help you manage users and resources. You can
control disk space usage by assigning disk quotas to users, manipulate remote
storage volumes, and manage removable storage (typically backup targets).

Disk Quotas

Disk quotas provide a method of managing the amount of disk space users can fill.
You can limit the amount of disk space available to each user, which is a double-edged
sword. On one side, it's a marvelous tool for preventing disk usage from growing so
large that you have to keep purchasing drives. On the other side, you're going to spend
more time dealing with user complaints and requests for special favors.

Your philosophical approach to disk quotas can take either of two forms:

- **Strict quotas**—where users cannot exceed the allowable disk space

- **Loose quotas**—which permits users to exceed their quotas but tracks usage so
  you can decide which users to approach about reducing disk usage

The loose quotas choice has another approach you might want to consider, which
is what I call the quota-on/quota-off information-gathering paradigm. That sounds
more complicated than it is, so I'll explain. When you impose quotas, you can get quick
quota reports quite easily. If disk space isn't an immediate and drastic problem, you
can use those reports to speak to certain users (the disk hogs) about their disk usage.
Then turn off quotas. The next time you want to track disk usage, turn quotas on again
to get the quick reports and repeat the conversations (probably with the same users).
The advantage to this is you don't have to run a volume full-time with quotas applied
(quotas require some overhead).

Requirements for Disk Quotas

The following conditions must exist if you want to apply disk quotas on a volume:

- The volume must be formatted as NTFS version 5. (NTFS version 4 volumes
  are upgraded automatically by Windows 2000 Setup to NTFS version 5.)

- To administer quotas, you must be a member of the administrators group on
  the computer where the volume resides (disk quotas can be administered for
  both local and remote volumes).

- Volumes must be shared from the volume's root directory.

| Tip | *If you're not sure of the file system, a quick way to check is to open the Properties dialog box for a volume. The file system is displayed on the General tab, and there's a Quota tab on NTFS 5 volumes. On a remote volume, if you don't see the Quota tab, you don't have administrative permissions for that remote computer.* |

File Compression and Disk Quotas

File compression doesn't count. If a user has a quota of 5MB of disk space, that space is filled when 5MB of files have been written to the volume. If file compression is in effect and therefore the 5MB of files occupy 3MB of disk space, it doesn't matter—the user has reached the 5MB limit. If you use file compression, you might want to make this fact very clear to users to avoid any arguments about the definition of a megabyte of disk space.

Volume Structures and Disk Quotas

Quotas are applied to a volume, whether the volume is part of a drive that has multiple volumes or the volume spans multiple physical disks.

The folder structure of a volume plays no part in the quotas. Users are free to write to as many folders as they wish (and have access to), and only the total space used on the volume is calculated for the quota. Users who move files from one folder to another on the same volume don't change their space usage. However, users who copy files to a different folder on the same volume double their space usage. This works because quotas track file ownership on the volume.

Upgrading Issues

Because quotas track file ownership, you could have some potential problems with existing files if you've upgraded to NTFS 5.

If you upgraded to Windows 2000 and NTFS 5 from a volume running Windows NT 4 using NTFS 4, the file ownership field tracked by NTFS 4 works perfectly with NTFS 5.

However, if you upgraded to Windows 2000 and NTFS 5 from a FAT or FAT32 volume, there is no ownership information on files. After the volume is converted to NTFS 5, all files are owned by the administrator. This presents no particular problem to the administrator because disk quotas aren't typically applied to the administrator. However, the user files that were on the volume at the time of conversion don't count against user quotas. When a user accesses or modifies a file, the ownership doesn't change. If you don't have a lot of users, or you have a lot of spare time, you could probably change the ownership of each file to reflect its user, but that seems rather excessive.

Planning Default Quotas

When you set quotas, start with a default quota for each volume, and then adjust individual user quotas as needed. It's far more efficient to set a tight (low) default quota and then adjust specific users upwards instead of the other way around. You can also adjust the default quota when necessary.

Some users require more space than others. For instance, the graphics department creates files that are much larger than those created by the word processing department. The ideal situation is to assign volumes for user types (if you have enough disks and volumes to do so). The volume for the graphics department would require a much higher default quota than the volume for the clerical department.

Tip   *Never let users outside of the administrators group install software on volumes that have quotas. The ownership counts against the user's quota (and most applications are far larger than any quota), but quotas don't apply to administrators.*

You may decide to make default quotas small if you're not using strict quota rules; that is, you will not stop users from writing to a volume when they exceed their quotas (although you may choose to contact users who exceed their quotas). In that case, you're really using quotas to track disk usage as a preventive measure, in a "kinder and gentler" manner than applying strict enforcement (using the quota limit as a psychological deterrent).

Enabling and Applying Quotas

To begin working with quotas on a volume, right-click the volume in My Computer and choose Properties from the shortcut menu. In the Properties dialog box, move to the Quota tab.

Enable Disk Quotas

To enable quotas, select the Enable quota management check box. This action makes the other choices on the tab available, as seen in Figure 27-1.

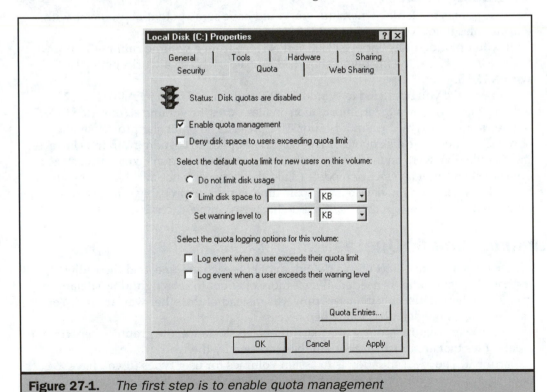

Figure 27-1.   *The first step is to enable quota management*

Set Default Quotas

You can set two values for quotas:

- **Disk quota limit**—which is the amount of disk space a user is permitted to use
- **Disk quota warning level**—which is the point at which you feel users are getting close enough to the disk quota limit to receive a warning

To enter the quotas, select Limit Disk Space To and enter a number. Then choose the measurement unit from the drop-down list in the measurement box. The measurement units displayed in the drop-down list are created dynamically, and they depend on the size of the volume for which you are enabling quotas. If the volume is less than 1GB, the drop-down list includes only KB and MB. If the volume is larger than 1GB, the drop-down list includes all the available units of measurement. There may be some measurement units that are unfamiliar to you:

- **TB** is terabyte, which is 1000 gigabytes.
- **PB** is petabyte, which is approximately a thousand terabytes (2 to the 50th power bytes).
- **EB** is exabyte, which is billion gigabytes (2 to the 60th power bytes). Some people refer to an exabyte as a quintillion bytes (1,152,921,504,606,846,976 bytes).

Deny Access When Quota Is Reached

Select Deny Disk Space To Users Exceeding Quota Limit if you want to prevent users from writing to the volume when their allotted disk space is filled. Users will have to clear out files to make room for new ones. The error message the user sees depends on the software, but most programs report that the disk is full.

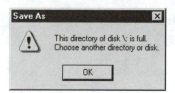

Set Logging Options

You can opt to write an event to the Event Viewer when a user exceeds the quota level, the warning level, or both. The events are written to the System Log of the Event Viewer. They are Information events, and the event type is Disk Event.

Viewing the event isn't terribly helpful. The information includes the user S.I.D instead of the logon name, and the description of the event is "A user hit their quota limit on Volume X" or "A user hit their quota threshold on Volume X". There's no particular advantage to enabling this option; it just fills up the Event Viewer.

Set Individual Quota Entries

There may be users who should have quotas that are either larger or smaller than the default limit you specified. And there may be users who should not have any limits imposed at all. To customize quota entries for users, click Quota Entries to open the Quota Entries dialog box.

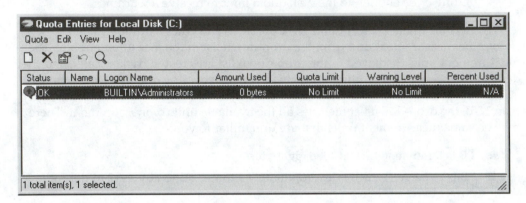

By default, the administrators group is listed and has no limits. To add specific quota entries, choose Quota | New Quota Entry and select users from the Select Users dialog box and then click OK. You can select multiple users as long as all your selections are to receive the same quota limits. When you've completed your selections, click OK to apply the quotas. Set a quota that differs from the default, or turn off quotas for the selected users.

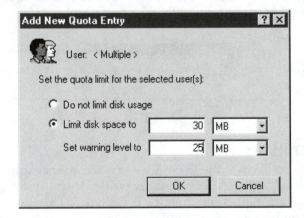

Technically, you can select groups as well as users when you're assigning quota entries. However, it's difficult to remove them, and removing a user from the quota entries list is not uncommon (users leave or are transferred to other departments or branches).

After you've completed all your configurations for establishing disk quotas, click OK on the Quota tab. The system displays a message explaining that the volume will be scanned to update the disk usage information.

When the scan is completed, open the Quota Entries window to see the current status of user disk quotas.

Status	Name	Logon Name	Amount Used	Quota Limit	Warning Level	Percent Used
⚠ Warning	Allen L...	WESTERN\AllenL	27.77 MB	30 MB	25 MB	92
🚫 Above ...	Tom B...	TBarich@Western.ivensWe...	59.69 MB	30 MB	25 MB	198
⊕ OK		BUILTIN\Administrators	1.2 GB	No Limit	No Limit	N/A
⊕ OK		NT AUTHORITY\SYSTEM	883.4 KB	No Limit	No Limit	N/A

Quota Entries for Local Disk (C:)
Quota Edit View Help
4 total item(s), 1 selected.

- Click on a column heading to sort the list by that column's contents (click again to change the sort order).

- Double-click a listing to edit the quota limits.

- Select a listing and press DEL to remove the entry.

Deleting User Quota Entries

You can't remove a quota tracking entry for a user account until all the files owned by that user have been deleted from the volume, moved to another volume, or have had their ownership transferred to another user. You can perform those tasks during the user quota entry deletion process, so that requirement is not overly onerous.

To delete a user from quota entries, open the volume's Properties dialog box and move to the Quotas tab. Then click Quota Entries to open the Quota Entries window.

ENTERPRISE COMPONENTS

Select the user you want to remove from the list and press DEL. The system asks you to confirm that you want to delete the user listing; click Yes.

The Disk Quota dialog box opens, displaying all the files on the volume that belong to the user you're deleting. Select a file, multiple files, or all the files and then take one of these actions:

- Delete the files (you're asked to confirm the deletion).

- Take ownership (the files immediately disappear from the list; no confirmation dialog box appears).

- Move the files to another volume (which can be on another computer on the network).

If you don't reassign or remove the files, you cannot delete the user. Incidentally, without disk quotas, the operating system doesn't care whether the owner of a file (or lots of files and folders) has disappeared from the system. In fact, it happens all the time.

Note *You are not deleting the user; you are merely deleting the user account from quota tracking.*

Quota Reports

After the system is scanned, and at any time thereafter, you can check the status of user disk quotas by opening the volume's Properties dialog box and moving to the Quota tab. Click Quota Entries to see the disk space status of the users who access this volume. The status column's icon is a quick indicator of a user's quota level:

- An UpArrow in a white circle indicates the user is below the warning level.

- An exclamation point in a yellow triangle indicates the user is over the warning level but below the limit.

- An exclamation point in a red circle indicates the user has reached the limit.

The first time you open the Quota Entries window to view disk space usage, the system does a lookup on each user, resolving the S.I.D. to the username. That process takes a bit of time. The list of resolved names is saved to a file, and thereafter the file is loaded so there's no delay in the display of usernames and statistics. However, that file is outdated if you add users, so you must press F5 to refresh the list.

You can create reports in a host of software applications, using any of several methods. Start by selecting the users you want to include in your report. Your selection actually includes more than the highlighted listings; it also automatically includes the title bar of the window and the column headings.

- Use the clipboard to copy the selection into a software application. Whether you paste the clipboard contents into a word processor or a spreadsheet, the listings and the column headings are positioned appropriately (using a table in a word processor).

- Open the appropriate software application, and drag the selection to the software window. Again, everything is laid out correctly.

Moving Quota Entries to Another Volume

Suppose a user transfers to another location in the company, or for some other reason is going to use another volume for file services. You can move his or her quota entries to the new volume (it's like a haunting). The following events characterize a transfer of quota entries:

- The files on the source volume are not transferred.

- The quota levels on the source volume are not removed (the user now has quota levels on two volumes).

There are three methods for transferring a user's quota entries records between volumes:

- Open the Quota Entries window for both volumes, and drag the information between volumes.

- Export the information from the source volume to the target volume.

- Export the information from the source volume to a file; then import the file to the target volume.

The Export and Import commands are on the Quota menu. The import/export file has no extension (don't add one), and the format of the file is proprietary to the Quota feature. Microsoft says the extension is hidden, even if you have folders configured to display hidden extensions, but I've examined the file with all sorts of utilities, and I think there's just no extension.

Remote Storage Service

The Remote Storage Service (RSS) is a way to extend disk space on a server without adding hard disks. RSS keeps an eye on the amount of free space available on a server volume, and automatically moves infrequently accessed files (the criteria for determining "infrequently " is set by an administrator) to a tape when disk usage reaches a level determined by the administrator. When a user needs one of the transferred files, it's fetched from the tape. A placeholder for the file remains on the server, which points to the remote file. Remote Storage runs as a service on a Windows

2000 Server and uses the Removable Storage Manager (RSM) to access the tapes (RSM is discussed later in the "Removable Storage Management" section of this chapter). RSS is administered via a MMC snap-in.

Remote Storage data storage is a two-level hierarchy. The upper level, called *local storage,* includes the NTFS volumes of the server running RSS. The lower level, called *remote storage,* is on the tape drive (or robotic tape library) that is connected to the server computer.

Quick Overview of RSS

Before you start configuring and using RSS, it's a good idea to understand the guidelines and limitations.

- RSS runs only volumes on Windows 2000 Server with NTFS 5. Do not use RSS on a Windows 2000 Advanced Server installation that is configured for clustering. Remote storage does not failover to other nodes.

- Disk quotas are unaffected by the actions of RSS. When files are transferred, even though no disk space is actually used, the logical size and the date/time (created, last modified, last accessed) attributes of the file remain unchanged.

- RSS supports all SCSI class 4 mm, 8 mm, and DLT tapes. QIC tapes and optical disk media are not supported. Exabyte 8200 tapes do not work properly and are not recommended.

- The media type you specify during installation cannot be changed later.

- You can reconfigure your settings for RSS, but you can't start over if you want to change the basic configuration. (In fact, you can't get the RSS wizard to run again after you've initially installed the service on a drive.)

- File management on an RSS-managed volume must be approached with care. Renaming and deleting files, or moving files to other RSS-managed volumes, interferes with the matchup on the remote media.

- Administrative permissions are required to configure the RSS settings, but normal user permissions apply to the files.

- Remote Storage has its own media pool for tapes, and you must be sure you have a sufficient number of tapes in that pool. You cannot use tapes from another service's media pool for RSS. (See the discussion on media pools later in this chapter.)

Installing RSS

Installing RSS is a two-step process: install the component, and then install the service. RSS is not installed by default when you install the operating system, so if you didn't select it during setup, you must use the Add/Remove Windows Components section

ENTERPRISE
COMPONENTS

of the Add/Remove Programs applet in Control Panel to add it. You install the service by launching the RSS wizard, which can be accessed in any of the following locations:

- Remote Storage menu item on the Administrative Tools menu
- Remote Storage snap-in in the MMC
- Administrative tools folder in Control Panel

Click Next on the wizard introductory window to launch a search for your tape system. Then continue with the wizard to configure RSS services, which includes the following tasks:

- Select the volumes you want to manage.
- Set the free-space level for managed volumes.
- Set the criteria for copying files to tape.
- Select the type of tape to use.
- Set the automatic file-copy schedule.
- Specify the number of media copies.

 If the wizard cannot find a tape drive, the service installation halts. Check the connection and configuration of your tape drive and try again.

Tweaking RSS Settings

The settings you establish in the wizard during setup of RSS are for all managed volumes. If you have more than one managed volume, you may want to create different settings for each. Even if you're managing only one volume, you may find you need to make changes as you gain experience with RSS. This section covers some guidelines.

To change settings, open the Remote Storage console by choosing Remote Storage from the Administrative Tools menu. When the Remote Storage console opens, expand the console tree to find the object you want to modify.

File Copy Schedule

You can modify the file copy schedule in the Remote Storage console. Right-click the Remote Storage object, and choose Change Schedule from the shortcut menu. In the File Copy Schedule dialog box, make the changes you require. (Remember that you can create multiple schedules.) The schedules you create are transferred to your Scheduled Tasks folder, which you can open if you want to monitor the status of your RSS copies.

Copy Files Manually

You may find there are times you want to copy files to remote storage before the next scheduled automatic copy process. To accomplish this, open the Remote Storage console and select the Managed Volumes object in the console tree. In the right pane, right-click the volume and choose All Tasks | Copy Files to Remote Storage.

Free Space Settings

To modify the settings for free space on the managed volume, select the Managed Volumes object in the Remote Storage console. In the right pane, right-click the volume and choose Settings from the shortcut menu. On the Settings tab, use the arrows in the Desired Free Space section to change the value. When the available space on the volume falls below your setting, RSS removed cached data from files that have been copied to the tape.

Create Free Space Manually

If you need to free up space on the volume immediately, you can do so in the Remote Storage console. Select the Managed Volumes object in the console tree, and then right-click the volume in the right pane. Select All Tasks | Create Free Space from the shortcut menu. All cached data from files that have been copied to tape is removed. (If the cached data from local files had already been removed through the normal RSS procedures, you won't gain any additional space.)

Remember that the more cached data you remove from the volume, the more recall activity your users must wait for if they need those files.

File Selection Criteria

You can alter the file selection criteria you set in the RSS wizard at any time in the RS console. There are two reasons to do this:

- Your current criteria do not produce enough free space on the volume.

- Your current criteria are too aggressive, and your users are complaining that too many files are fetched by recalling them from the tape.

Select the Managed Volumes option in the console tree. Right-click the volume in the right pane, and choose Settings from the shortcut menu. You can change the file size value or the last accessed value. In addition, you can set exclusion and inclusion rules by right-clicking the volume in the RS console and choosing Include/Exclude Rules.

Remote Storage predefines some file inclusion and exclusion rules, and some of them can't be changed (which means neither the rule nor its priority can be changed). You can, however, create a new rule by clicking Add. Any rule you write can be edited.

The order of rules (called the rule *priority*) is important, because the first rule that matches a file is used, even if rules that fall later in line also match that file. To change the priority of a rule, select it and use the arrows to move it up or down on the list (raising or lowering the priority).

Media Copies

The tape (or tape collection) that receives the files from local storage is called the *media master set*. If you have the hardware to support it (additional removable drives), RSS can create copies of the media master, which are called the *media copy set*. You can automatically create up to three media copy sets. To accomplish this, right-click the Remote Storage object in the RSS console and choose Properties. Move to the Media Copies tab and change the value.

To synchronize the media copy set, right-click the Media object and select Synchronize Media Copies from the shortcut menu. A wizard walks you through the process. You can only synchronize one media copy set at a time. During synchronization, files can't be recalled or managed.

You should prepare sufficient tapes for your media copies in the Remote Storage media pool. However, after using all available media in the Remote Storage media pool, RSS will use media in the Free media pool.

If you reduce the number of media copies, the media is not deallocated. To deallocate the media, you must first delete the media copies. To accomplish this, select the Media object in the console tree. Then right-click one of the displayed media in the right pane and choose Media Copies. On the Media Copies tab, click Delete Copy X, where X is Copy 1, Copy 2, or Copy 3.

If the media master set becomes corrupted (or disappears), you can re-create it using a media copy. To accomplish this, select the Media object in the console tree, and then right-click a media listing and choose Properties. Move to the Recovery tab and select Re-Create Master. Follow the instructions to complete the task.

Validate Stored Files

It's important to make sure that the files on the managed volume point to the right data on the remote media. The validation process checks those links and also updates the statistics for the volume. To configure validation, select Managed Volumes in the console tree. In the right pane, right-click the volume and choose All Tasks | Validate Files from the shortcut menu.

Using the Files Managed by RSS

RSS works by reacting to two different configuration settings: the file selection criteria for copying files to tape, and the amount of free space you mandate for the managed volume.

When a file meets the criteria, it's copied to remote storage. The original data is still stored on the managed volume, and the data is referred to as *cached* data. The difference between cached data and standard file data is a technicality, merely signifying that a file has been copied to the remote media. The file continues to occupy the same amount of disk space. If a user needs the file, it's opened from the volume, and the user doesn't know that the data is considered to be cached. As time goes by, and additional files meet the criteria due to their aging, those files are added to the list of files that are copied to the remote tape and cached locally.

When the free space on the managed volume dips below the size you specified in your configuration setting, RSS removes the cached data from a sufficient number of files to provide the disk space you configured. The file's object remains on the volume, but the file uses no disk space.

When a user wants to use a file that has no cached data on the volume, the process is called a file *recall*. The file is opened by selecting its listing on the volume in the usual way (from an application, My Computer, or Windows Explorer). However, in order to display the data to the user, the file must be fetched from the remote tape. This takes more time than opening a file directly from the volume. In fact, it can take as long as five minutes to open a file.

■ When a Windows 2000 computer views the volume with Windows Explorer, the icon for an offline file changes to denote that the file is archived. Legacy Windows systems, including NT 4, do not see the icon.

When a Windows 2000 user opens an archived file, a message appears on the screen stating that the file is being recalled from offline storage. Legacy clients do not receive a message and therefore don't know they have to wait a long time for the file (which can cause some problems if you don't explain what's going on). If a user or application recalls a second file within ten seconds, it's called a *runaway recall*. You can limit the number of runaway recalls a user or application can perform. To set the limit, right-click Remote Storage in the console tree and choose Properties from the shortcut menu. Move to the Recall Limit tab and specify a maximum number of successive recalls.

If you're running virus-checking software or indexing, these applications read files, and those read actions count as recalls. The Findfast tool that is installed by default with Microsoft Office is a classic example. Either stop using the tools or raise the recall limit.

Tip *You can use the Exempt check box to exclude administrators from the recall limit.*

Don't delete, move, or modify files that are involved in the RSS copy process. The RSS database will lose track of them. The use of these files should be limited to viewing and printing. If file data needs to be changed, save the file with a new filename.

RSS Backups

Your backup software should back up the following RSS files:

■ Files cached on the managed volumes

■ The Remote Storage database and other RSS program data files in the %SystemRoot%\System32\RemoteStorage folder

By default, backup software doesn't back up the tapes used by RSS. However, the media copy set is a full backup of the RSS-managed files. On a regular basis (in fact, on a daily basis), move a media copy set from the Remote Storage media pool into the Backup media pool. Each time you move a tape from the RS media pool into the Backup media pool, move the previous day's tape back to the RS media pool. This ensures that a restore operation will restore your RSS environment.

RSS Database

The RSS database is located in the SystemRoot%\System32\RemoteStorage folder, along with the RSS program tools. In addition, a copy of the database is placed on each tape as data is migrated from the managed volume to the tape set.

When a user accesses a file managed by RSS, the database on the volume is used to locate the file. If the user receives an error message indicating that the file can't be found, it could mean the database is damaged.

The most reliable method of replacing a corrupt database is to restore the last database that was migrated to tape. This requires a number of steps, which I'll go over in this section.

You must stop the RSS services, which is accomplished in the Computer Management snap-in. To open the snap-in, choose Computer Management from the Administrative Tools menu. In the console tree, expand Services And Applications and then select Services (see Figure 27-2). Scroll through the listing, and stop the following services by right-clicking on their listings and choosing Stop from the shortcut menu:

- Remote Storage Engine
- Remote Storage File
- Remote Storage Media

Use Removable Storage Manager (RSM) to open the media pools, moving to the Import pool. Find the most recent tape used by RSS to store migrated files. By default, RSS media names are RS-X-N, where X is the machine name and N is an incremented number. Obviously, the media name with the highest number has the most recent copy of the database.

 For more information on RSM, see the section "Removable Storage Manager" later in this chapter.

Use RSM to move this media into the NTbackup media pool. The NTbackup media pool is created the first time you use Windows 2000 Backup (NTbackup.exe). Then use Windows 2000 Backup to catalog the tape so you can find the most recent copy of the RSS database in %SystemRoot%\System32\RemoteStorage (it's the subfolder with the most recent date).

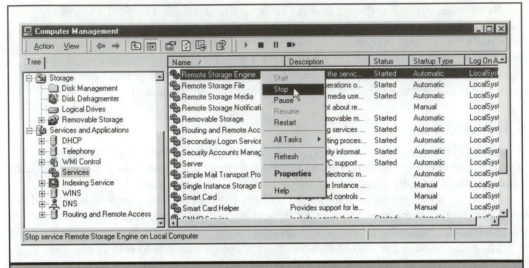

Figure 27-2. *You must stop the RSS service before you can restore its files*

> **Note** *For information on using Windows 2000 Backup, see Chapter 10.*

Using the Restore program in Windows 2000 Backup, choose this subfolder and be sure you select All File under the subfolder. In the Restore Files To box, select Alternate Location, and then select the drive that contains the %SystemRoot% folder. This ensures that the database is restored to the correct volume (which may not be the managed volume—the default restore operation would be to restore the database to the managed volume).

After the restore process has finished, open a command prompt at %SystemRoot%\system32\RemoteStorage\engdb. Empty this folder by moving its files to another folder. Enter the following command from the engdb subfolder: **Rstore %SystemRoot%\System32\RemoteStorage\engdb.bak**. (Rstore.exe is a utility that is installed when you install RSS, and it is located in %SystemRoot%\ System32.)

Now you can restart the services you stopped in the Computer Management console. Then open the Remote Services console and make sure everything is correct. In fact, it's a good idea to recall a file to test the database. Also, use RSM to move the tape back to the Remote Storage media pool.

Removing RSS

If you decide to discontinue volume management with RSS, you must take a few preliminary steps before removing the feature. First, make sure you have enough room on the volume to recall all the data that's stored offline. If this step requires moving files to another volume, change your settings to avoid additional copies, and go through the steps to perform a manual copy to the offline tape. Then validate the files on the volume to update the statistics (explained earlier in this chapter).

Open the Remote Storage console, and select the Managed Volumes object in the console tree. Then right-click the volume in the right pane, and select Remove from the shortcut menu. Go through the Remove Volume Management wizard to complete the process. During the process you are given the option to recall all the copied data from storage, which you should do.

Removable Storage Management

Removable Storage Management (RSM) tracks and manages removable media (tapes and discs) and hardware (drives, changers, and jukeboxes). To manage the media, RSM labels and catalogs the tapes and discs. Managing the hardware involves controlling the slots and doors to access and remove the media. RSM doesn't work alone; it is the media management arm for applications and features that interact with removable media, such as Backup and Remote Storage.

 To use CDs with RSM, the discs must be rewritable and must be formatted with the CDFS file system. Optical media can be formatted with FAT, FAT32, or NTFS.

RSM cannot support more than one computer-removable media connection. All applications that use removable media must run on the same computer that connects to the removable media library. Within the context of RSM, the word "library" means a data storage system that consists of removable media and the hardware that reads and writes to that media. There are two library types: robotic libraries, which are automated multiple-drive devices; and stand-alone libraries, which are manually loaded single-drive devices.

Note *In Windows 2000, your ATAPI CD-ROM changer has only a single drive letter assigned. The Removable Storage Manager mounts, dismounts, and manages all the removable media.*

Configuring Removable Storage

Removable Storage is part of the Computer Management console (choose Computer Management from the Administrative Tools menu). In the Computer Management console, expand the Storage object, and then expand the Removable Storage object.

In addition, there's a preconfigured common console for RSM, named ntmsmgr.msc in %SystemRoot%\System32. Create a desktop or taskbar shortcut to this MMC file to make it easier to work with RSM (see Figure 27-3).

You can view or set the configuration properties for the RSM components by selecting the appropriate object in the console tree. You'll find you spend most of your time working with media (moving media in and out of media pools or ascertaining the state of media) or library management. In the following sections, I'll define and discuss the library and media elements you'll manage in RSM.

Libraries

A *library* is the combination of media and the device used to read and write to that media. There are two types of libraries: robotic and stand-alone. Technically, you could say there's a third library, the offline library. RSM tracks offline media when the media is not contained in a library. The media could be anywhere—in your desk, on a shelf, or in your lunch box. RSM tracks offline media, so we can say that all media that's currently offline is part of the offline library.

Robotic Libraries

Robotic libraries are automated drives that can hold multiple physical media (tapes or discs). Sometimes these devices are called *changers* or *jukeboxes.* There's usually

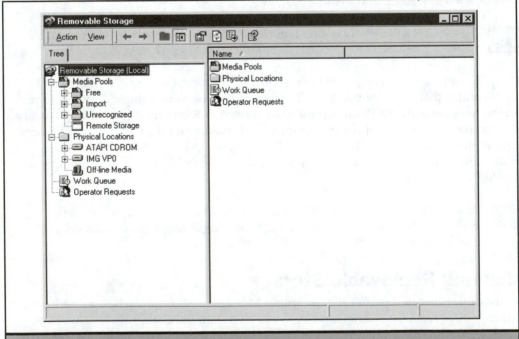

Figure 27-3. *Manage Removable Storage from the Computer Management console*

a robotic subsystem (sometimes called *drive bays*) that move the media in and out of slots. The slots can be storage slots (the media is parked when not being accessed) or drive slots (the media is the active target). Some robotic libraries have additional hardware components such as doors, cleaning cartridges, bar-code readers, and inject/eject ports. Those additional components are also managed by RSM.

Stand-Alone Libraries

Stand-alone libraries are single-drive units that are not automated. The drive holds a single tape or a single CD disc, and the media must be inserted manually.

Library Inventories

On a robotic library, you can perform an inventory to ensure that all media in the library is accounted for. There are two inventory types:

- **Fast Inventory**—checks for changes in the state of each slot (from full to empty and vice versa).

- **Full Inventory**—which identifies each piece of media. If the media is bar-coded, the inventory reads the bar codes. If the media is not bar-coded, the inventory process reads the on-media identifier (which can take a long time).

To set the default inventory type, expand the Physical Locations object in the Removable Storage console. Right-click the library object, and set the Inventory type (the choices are Fast, Full, and None).

To perform the inventory, right-click the library object and select Inventory from the shortcut menu. The inventory results are displayed in the right pane.

Media Pools

All media belongs to a *media pool.* A media pool is a collection of media that share certain attributes, including media type and management policies. Media pools have a hierarchical structure that starts with the media pool class. There are two classes: Application and System.

- **Application** media pools are created by software applications for the purpose of grouping and tracking media. In Windows 2000, Backup and Remote Storage each maintain an application media pool.

- **System** media pools are created and managed by RSM, and include the following pools:

    - Unrecognized
    - Free
    - Import

Note *Media can be moved from one media pool to another, and that job is always managed by RSM.*

Unrecognized Media Pools

Unrecognized media pools hold media that RSM doesn't recognize. This is usually because the media is totally blank and has not yet received an ID from RSM (which occurs when you insert the media in the library). However, media that has an ID that RSM is unable to read or understand also becomes part of the unrecognized media pool. Media in the unrecognized pools is not listed in the RSM database and is therefore not available to applications.

Free Media Pools

Free media pools hold media that are not currently being used by applications. The media is available for use by any application that needs it. It's assumed that any data on the media is not needed, usually because the data is an old backup and would not be useful for a restore procedure.

You can configure RSM to have applications draw media from the Free media pool automatically, whenever an application runs out of media in its own pool. If you don't configure automatic draws from the Free pool, you must move media manually into the application pool when it's needed.

Import Media Pools

Import media pools contain media that is recognized as a valid media type, but has not been used by RSM. Typically, media lands in the Import pool when it is brought to an RSM system from a different RSM system within the organization. You can move media from an Import pool into a Free pool or an application pool.

A media pool can contain one of the following types of elements: media or other media pools.

A media pool cannot contain both media and other pools; it is either a single structure or a hierarchical structure. For example, the Free pool could contain media pools for each type of media.

A library can include media from various media pools, and a single media pool can work with multiple libraries.

Media Identification

In order to track media and keep its inventory records, RSM identifies each unit of media. There are two identification methods: on-media identifiers and bar codes.

On-Media Identification

On-media identifiers are recorded electronically the first time the media is inserted into a library. The identifier has two parts:

- **The label type**—which identifies the format used to record data. The format is dependent on the type of media.
- **The label ID**—which is a unique identifier for the specific disc or tape.

Bar Code Identification

If your library supports bar codes, RSM can identify media from the bar codes you supply. Media that use bar codes also receive on-media IDs, and RSM can use either method to identify the tape or disc. Bar codes are easier because you don't have to mount the media in the drive in order to identify it.

Media Formats

RSM uses a *Media Label Library (MLL)* to manage on-media identifiers. An MLL is a DLL that's used to interpret the format of a media label that was written by an application. RSM supports FAT, NTFS, and CDFS for disk media, and MTF (Microsoft Tape Format) for tape media. RSM can discern which application wrote the media label by checking the registered MLLs. Developers who distribute applications that use another media format must provide MLLs.

Media States

The media state is the current operational status of a tape or disc. RSM uses the on-media identifier or the bar code to ascertain the current state. Media states are determined on two levels: physical state and side state.

The *physical* state identifies the current status regarding the media's location and physical use. There are five possible physical states, described in Table 27-1.

The *side* state is the status of the side(s) where data is stored. Every type of media has either one or two sides. For example, magnetic-optical disks have two sides, while tape has a single side. RSM tracks the sides of media, as described in Table 27-2.

An allocation maximum is set by an administrator to control the number of times an application can allocate and deallocate the media. RSM checks the count each time

Physical State	Description
Idle	The media is offline, either in a storage slot (in a robotic device) or physically absent (stored).
In Use	RSM is currently moving the media.
Loaded	The media is mounted in a drive and is available for reading or writing data.
Mounted	The media is in a drive but not yet available for reading or writing data.
Unloaded	The media has been dismounted and is waiting for someone to physically remove it.

Table 27-1. *Possible Physical States of Removable Media*

Side State	Description
Allocated	The side is reserved by an application and is not available to any other application.
Available	The side is available for use by an application.
Completed	The side is full.
Decommissioned	The side is not available because it has reached its allocation maximum (see note on allocation maximum).
Imported	The side's label type is recognized. The label ID is not recognized.
Incompatible	The media type is not compatible with the library and should be removed.
Reserved	The side is only available to a specific application. This state applies to two-sided media where one side is allocated.
Unprepared	The side is in a Free media pool and has not yet received a free media label.
Unrecognized	RSM does not recognize the side's label type and ID.

Table 27-2.   *Description of Side States*

a side is deallocated, and when the maximum is reached, the side is decommissioned. This feature lets administrators prevent media from being used beyond their normal useful life (especially important with tape).

Managing Media Pools

You use the Computer Management console to manage media pools. You can create a pool, delete a pool, and move media between pools.

Create and Configure a Media Pool

You can create a media pool for an application, either as a new top-level pool or within an existing application pool (but not within the system pools, Free, Import, or Unrecognized).

- To create a top-level media pool, right-click the Media Pools object in the console tree and select Create Media Pool from the shortcut menu.

- To create a media pool within an existing pool, right-click the existing pool and select Create Media Pool from the shortcut menu.

Configure the new media pool in the Create a New Media Pool Properties dialog box seen in Figure 27-4.

Use these guidelines to configure the General tab of the media pool's properties:

- Enter a name for the new media pool.

- Enter a description (optional).

- In the Media information section, configure the media pool to hold other media pools, or to hold media.

- Enter the media type if the pool contains media.

- Select allocation/deallocation/reallocation options as follows:

  - Automatically draw media from a Free pool when this media pool runs out of media. Don't select this option if you prefer to move media from a Free pool to this pool manually (using the RSM console).

  - Automatically return media to a Free pool when the media is no longer needed by an application. Don't select this option if you prefer to move the media to the Free pool manually.

  - Limit the number of times the media can be allocated by other media pools.

Use the Security tab to give permissions to users and groups to manipulate this media pool.

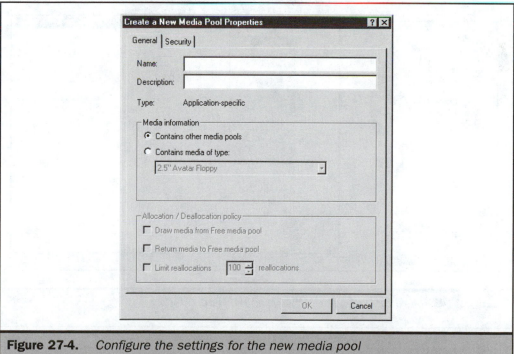

Figure 27-4.   *Configure the settings for the new media pool*

Delete a Media Pool

You can remove an application media pool from the Removable Storage console. Expand the console tree to see the media pools, and then right-click the media pool you want to remove and choose Delete from the shortcut menu. You're asked to confirm your action.

Managing Media

You need to move media between media pools, allocate and deallocate media, and perform other tasks related to keeping RSM well supplied with media.

Preparing Media

New media must be prepared for RSM, which means it must receive an ID so RSM can track it. To prepare media, insert the media into its drive and open the Removable Storage console. Expand Physical Locations, expand the applicable library, and select the Media object for the library (see Figure 27-5). In the right pane, right-click the media and choose Prepare from the shortcut menu.

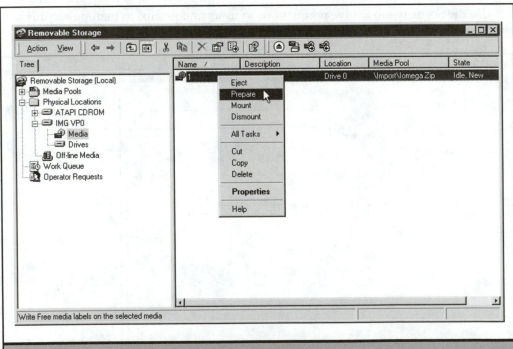

Figure 27-5.   *Prepare media for RSM management*

You are asked to confirm the preparation. Preparation has three effects:

- Any data on the media is destroyed.
- The media receives an identification label.
- The media is moved to the Free media pool.

Moving Media to Another Media Pool

You can drag media from one media pool to another in the Removable Storage console. If either the source or target media pool is in a hierarchy, expand the parent media pool in the console tree. Select the source media pool in the console tree, and drag the media from the right pane of the source media pool object to the target media pool in the console tree (see Figure 27-6).

| **Note** | *When you create and configure media pools, if you don't set the option to draw media from and return media to the Free media pool, you must use this manual method of moving the media.* |

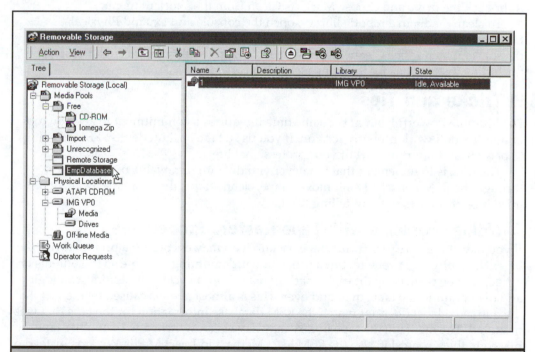

Figure 27-6. *Moving media from the Free pool to an application pool requires only a drag-and-drop operation*

Ejecting Media

Eject media from the RSM console so the RSM program knows that the media is removed from the library. The method you use differs between stand-alone libraries and robotic libraries.

- If the media is in a stand-alone library, expand the Physical Locations object. Right-click the library object and choose Eject from the shortcut menu.

- If the media is in a robotic library, expand Physical Locations, and then expand the library. Right-click the library's media object, and choose Eject from the shortcut menu. Then follow the steps in the Media Eject Wizard.

Cleaning Media

RSM keeps records on media-cleaning procedures, so you should use the RSM console when you perform a cleaning operation. The steps you use in the console differ between a stand-alone library and a robotic library.

To clean media in a stand-alone library, manually insert the cleaning cartridge. Then, to notify RSM, open the console and expand Physical Locations, expand the appropriate library, and select the drive object for the library. In the right pane, right-click the drive and choose Mark As Clean from the shortcut menu.

To clean media in a robotic library, open the console and expand Physical Locations. Right-click the appropriate library, and choose Cleaner Management from the shortcut menu. The Cleaner Management Wizard walks you through the steps (including instructions for inserting a cleaning cartridge).

RSM Tricks and Tips

RSM is quite powerful, but at the same time it requires a commitment to keep on top of it or it won't work properly for you. If you use a tape backup device, RSM is going to become an important part of your professional life.

The trick is to remember that whatever you do with removable media, do it through the RSM console. Don't move a tape, clean a tape, throw a tape away, or introduce new tapes without telling RSM.

Avoiding Problems with Tape Restore Procedures

If you have to restore files from a tape backup, you may encounter a problem with the tape. Not a physical problem, but a problem with mounting the tape so its contents or catalog can be read. Sometimes, NTbackup may show a cycle of mounting, cataloging, and dismounting the tape, over and over. This is almost always caused by the fact that the on-media label does not match the RSM database information for the tape that was mounted. The media in the tape library may have been switched with another tape, or placed in the wrong slot. Use the RSM Eject Media and Inject Media Wizards instead of manually removing and replacing media. This permits RSM to keep track of the media.

If it's too late to heed my advice, and the tape you need for a restore is endlessly cycling, here's the fix: cancel the restore and perform a full inventory of the library.

To accomplish this, use these steps:

1. Open the RSM console, and expand the Physical Locations object.

2. Right-click the appropriate library, and choose Properties from the shortcut menu.

3. Specify an inventory method of Full and click OK.

4. Right-click the library once again, and choose Inventory from the shortcut menu.

RSM performs a full inventory by identifying each piece of media (you can keep an eye on progress in the Work queue). After the inventory, RSM should be able to recognize the tape and mount it correctly.

Understanding the Work Queue

RSM can't multitask; it works sequentially, plugging away at one task at a time. If your tape unit has multiple drives and you want RSM to prepare two tapes, it will finish the first tape before beginning the second, even though both tapes are equally accessible.

You can keep an eye on the progress of multiple jobs by viewing the RSM Work Queue. To get there, open the RSM console, expand the Physical Locations object, and select the Work Queue object. The right-pane displays the tasks and their status (see Figure 27-7).

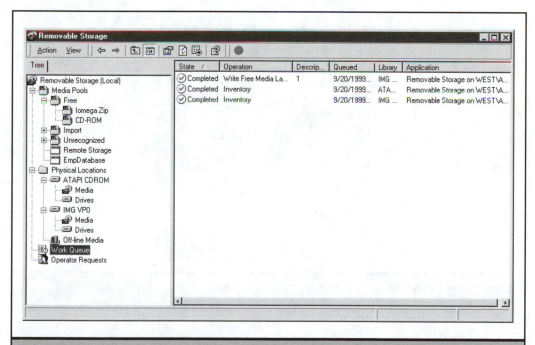

Figure 27-7. *The Work Queue shows RSM has completed all my jobs*

Configuring the RSM Console Window

You can personalize the appearance of the RSM console window and the detail pane (the right pane). To change the way the RSM console window looks, choose View | Customize from the console window toolbar. The Customize View dialog box seen in Figure 27-8 appears, and you can select or deselect the elements you want to appear in the console window.

When you select an object in the console tree and that object displays information in the right pane, the information is presented in columnar form. (Of course, the column headings differ according to the type of information being displayed.) You can sort the display, and you can also add and remove columns.

To sort the display, click on the column heading you want to use for the sort scheme. Click again to reverse the sort order. The column heading being used displays an etched arrow, and the direction of the arrow indicates the sort order.

To modify the columns, in the console tree right-click the object for which you want to customize the right-pane display. Choose View | Choose Columns from the shortcut menu to open the Modify Columns dialog box. This dialog box displays both the

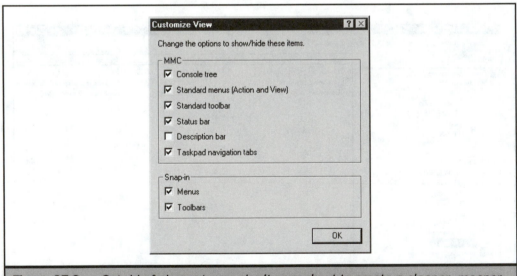

Figure 27-8. *Get rid of elements you don't care about to create a cleaner, meaner window*

columns that are currently displayed and those that aren't currently displayed (called Hidden columns). The column headings are specific to the object you selected in the console tree. For example, here's the Modify Columns dialog box for the right-pane display of an application media pool.

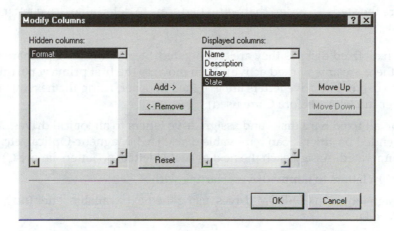

- To add a column, select it in the Hidden columns list and click Add.
- To remove a column, select it in the Displayed columns list and click Remove.
- To change the order of columns, select a column and use the Move Up and Move Down buttons. The top-to-bottom listing is translated to a left-to-right listing in the console window.

Disk Management and Drive Letter Assignments

Drive letter assignments are handled differently in Windows 2000 than they were in previous incarnations of Windows. For instance, if you have an ATAPI CD-ROM changer, it is assigned a single drive letter. The Removable Storage Manager mounts, dismounts, and manages all its media. In Windows NT 4.0, such a device has a separate drive letter for each piece of media the device is capable of managing, and as you call for each drive letter, the media is swapped automatically.

In Windows 2000, drive letters are assigned to volumes by the Mount Manager (MountMgr) program. When a drive letter is assigned to a volume, that drive letter is reserved for that volume in the MountMgr database (which is in the registry).

When you perform a Windows 2000 upgrade from Windows NT, the existing drive letter assignments are exported to the Win_nt.~bt\Migrate.inf file so that the text-mode setup process can read and import the information into the MountMgr database.

Basic Disk Drive Letter Assignments

During a fresh Windows 2000 installation, MountMgr follows a procedure for assigning letters and then continues to use that procedure for volumes or drives that are added to the system.

Here are the steps, in order, that Setup performs to determine drive letter assignments:

1. Scan all fixed disks as they are enumerated. Start with active primary partitions (if there are any marked active). Then move to the first primary partition on each drive. The drive letters are assigned in order, using the next available letter (no letters before C are used).

2. Scan all fixed hard disks and assign drive letters to all logical drives in an extended partition. Scan removable disks (JAZ, Magnetic-Optical, etc.), as enumerated. Assign each the next available letter (no letters before C).

3. Assign letters to floppy drives, starting with A.

4. Assign letters to CD-ROM drives, using the next available letter (no letters before D).

There is an exception to this scheme. Legacy Fault Tolerant Sets on basic disks record their last-used drive letter in a private region on the physical disk. During installation of Windows 2000, these drive letters are noted and given priority during the drive assignment process. Therefore, legacy FT-sets are assigned drive letters before any other drive letters are assigned to other basic disk partition.

Assigned drive letters are persistent, and should remain as is unless a volume is deleted or manually changed using Disk Management. An exception occurs if a volume (removable disk) is offline, and a new volume is brought online. The new volume may receive the offline volume's drive letter. To keep your drive letter assignments intact, keep existing volumes online when you introduce new volumes.

Dynamic Disk Drive Letter Assignments

Logical Disk Manager (LDM) tracks the last drive letter assigned to a dynamic volume in its configuration database. This database is located in a 1MB private region at the end of each dynamic disk. When MountMgr is assigning letters to dynamic volumes, the LDM is queried to see if it has a "suggested drive letter," based on the information in its configuration database.

MountMgr assigns drive letters to dynamic volumes using the following guidelines:

■ If the MountMgr database in the registry already has a drive letter recorded for the volume, the volume gets that drive letter.

■ If the MountMgr database does not contain a drive letter for the volume, MountMgr asks LDM for a "suggested" drive letter. LDM checks its configuration database and if a recorded drive letter is found, that letter is suggested to MountMgr.

■ If this suggested drive letter is available, it is assigned to the volume and recorded in the MountMgr database so it can be used during the next mount.

■ If the suggested drive letter is already used, the volume is assigned the next available drive letter.

■ If LDM does not have a suggested drive letter, the volume is assigned the next available letter.

The
Complete
Reference

Chapter 28

Terminal Services

All versions of Windows 2000 Server include Terminal Services, and the program is now a component of the operating system. The advantages to this approach are meaningful.

- Updates to the operating system automatically update Terminal Services.
- Terminal Services can use the features built into Windows 2000.

This chapter presents an overview of Terminal Services, and isn't intended as a complete set of guidelines for installing and using this component. Because Terminal Services is now part of the operating system, and because I think this can be an effective way to get real use from legacy hardware, it seems worthwhile to present the information in this book. In fact, you may want to experiment with Terminal Services (now that you don't have to purchase it as a separate program).

Terminal Services includes two different install modes: Remote Administration and Application Server. You select the mode when you install the Terminal Services component.

Remote Administration Mode

Remote Administration mode installs the Terminal Services components that are needed to provide remote access to a network. This gives you, as an administrator, a powerful, easy-to-use way to administer any Windows 2000-based server over a TCP/IP connection. The remote administration powers are the same as those you invoke when you are administering servers from a workstation on the LAN (assuming you're logged in as an administrator). Using Remote Administration mode, you can use any built-in Windows 2000 management tool. You can manage forests and trees, mixed domains (Windows 2000 and NT), and clusters.

Limitations of Remote Administration Mode

Terminal Services permit only two concurrent Remote Administration connections, and only system administrators can use a connection. Users cannot inadvertently (or deliberately) use Remote Administrator mode to gain access to administrative resources. No licensing is required for the two Remote Administration connections (see the section "Licenses" later in this chapter). Two connections are permitted so you can collaborate with another administrator, but Remote Administration mode does not support multiuser computing or multiple administrators running different tasks concurrently.

Tip *Another reason for permitting two connections is recovery, in case there's a problem and a lost connection before logging off.*

Advantages of Remote Administration Mode

Remote Administration mode omits installation of the application-sharing components, which means there's very little overhead when you're running the program. Therefore, you can install Remote Administration mode on servers that are already performing important functions. In fact, there's so little impact on the server that there's no reason not to enable it on all the servers in a forest. Or you can install Remote Administration on a limited number of servers (the domain controllers would be a logical decision). Then you can administer other servers across your domain using the standard Windows 2000 LAN-based management tools. Terminal Services can even be used to administer clustered Windows 2000 servers.

Installing Remote Administration Mode

You install Terminal Services Remote Administration directly on the server you want to use for Terminal Services. You can use any server in your system, and you can install Terminal Services on multiple servers if you wish. To install Remote Administration Mode, follow these steps:

1. Open the Add/Remove Programs applet in the Control Panel of the server you want to use for Terminal Services.

2. Click Add/Remove Windows Components and start the Add/Remove Components wizard. (If the wizard pauses, click next, but most of the time the wizard moves right to the Windows Components window.)

3. Scroll through the component list to find Terminal Services and select it.

4. Click Details to see the Terminal Services component selection window.

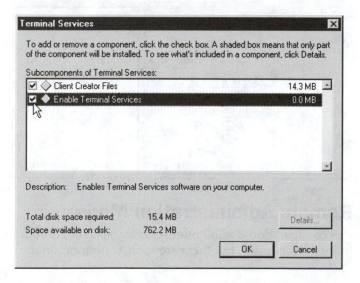

5. Click both selections (Client Creator Files and Enable Terminal Services) to add check marks.

6. Click OK to return to the Windows Components window.

7. Click Next.

8. Select Remote administration mode and click Next. (If your Windows 2000 installation is not from a network share point, you're asked to insert the Windows 2000 CD-ROM.)

9. Click Finish after the files are copied.

10. Close the Add/Remove Programs applet.

You must restart the server. After bootup, there are a couple of additions to your server:

■ The Administrative Tools menu includes three new items: Terminal Services Client Creator, Terminal Services Configuration, and Terminal Services Manager.

■ A new directory, %SystemRoot%\system32\clients\tsclient, contains subdirectories for Terminal Services clients. See the section "Clients" later in this chapter for information about client services for Terminal Services.

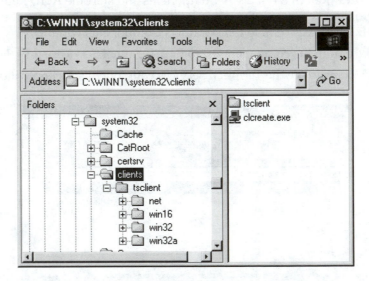

Configuring Remote Administration Mode

Terminal Services configuration doesn't offer separate, specific configuration options for Remote Administration mode, but there are some configuration settings for

Terminal Services that are preset as a result of installing this mode. To see the configuration options, display the Administrative Tools menu and choose Terminal Services Configuration. An MMC opens with the Terminal Services Configuration snap-in loaded.

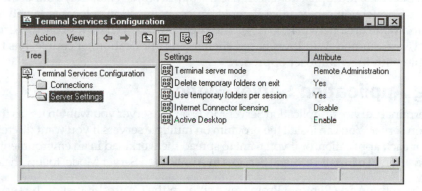

The two settings options in the console tree are Connections settings and Server Settings. The Connections settings are discussed in the section "Clients" later in this chapter. For Server Settings, you can make changes by right-clicking the appropriate setting and choosing Properties.

- **Terminal Server Mode** cannot be changed unless you return to the Add/Remove Programs applet in Control Panel and reinstall Terminal Services in Application Server mode.

- **Delete Temporary Folders On Exit** defaults to Yes, which is usually preferable. Terminal Server creates a discrete temporary folder for each new session, and any temporary files accumulated during the session are located in that folder. There's rarely a reason to save temporary files, but if you think you need to, change the setting to No.

- **Use Temporary Folders Per Session** defaults to Yes, and it really means a new folder for temporary files is created for each new session. If you opt to save the temporary folders, you can use this setting to determine whether Terminal Services creates a new folder for each session or continues to use the existing folder.

- **Internet Connector Licensing** is disabled by default and should not be changed for Remote Administration mode, which requires no Terminal Services License. See the section "Licenses" later in this chapter.

- **Active Desktop** is enabled by default. You should think about disabling Active Desktop for your Remote Administration sessions to reduce the overhead. The Active Desktop uses more resources than the classic Windows desktop, and generally isn't necessary for administrative tasks.

Application Server Mode

In Application Server mode, applications are run and managed from the server, saving deployment, maintenance, and upgrade tasks. When an application is deployed via Terminal Services, multiple clients can use the application when they connect to the server. Connection can be via a Remote Access connection, a local area network (LAN), or a wide area network (WAN). The clients can be Windows-based, Windows CE-based, or even non–Windows-based clients. The application, of course, has to be compatible with this multiuser approach.

Installing Application Server Mode

Install Terminal Services Application Server Mode on the server you want to use as the application server. You can install the program on multiple servers if you want discrete servers for each application, or if you want to spread the workload in an environment with a lot of busy users. To install Terminal Services in Application Server Mode, follow these steps:

1. Open the Add/Remove Programs applet in the Control Panel of the server you want to use for Terminal Services.

2. Click Add/Remove Windows Components and start the Add/Remove Components Wizard. (If the wizard pauses, click next; remember, most of the time the wizard moves right to the Windows Components window.)

3. Scroll through the component list to find Terminal Services and select it.

4. Click Details to see the Terminal Services component selection window.

5. Click both selections (Client Creator Files and Enable Terminal Services) to add check marks.

6. Click OK to return to the Windows Components window.

7. Select Terminal Services Licensing to place a check mark in the check box.

8. Click Next.

9. Select Application server and click Next

10. In the Terminal Services Licensing setup screen, select Your Entire Enterprise, or Your Domain Or Workgroup, and leave the Install License Server Database At This Location as it is. (See the section "Licenses" later in this chapter to learn how to use the Licensing feature.)

11. Click Finish after the files are copied (you will need your Windows 2000 Server CD if you didn't install the operating system from a network share).

12. Close the Add/Remove Programs applet.

You must restart the server. After bootup, there are a couple of additions to your server:

■ The Administrative Tools menu includes four new items: Terminal Services Client Creator, Terminal Services Configuration, Terminal Services Manager, and Terminal Services Licensing.

■ A new directory, %SystemRoot%\system32\clients\tsclient, contains subdirectories for Terminal Services clients. See the section "Clients" later in this chapter for information about client services for Terminal Services.

Configuring Application Server Mode

To configure Terminal Services, choose Terminal Services Configuration from the Administrative Tools menu to open the Terminal Services Configuration console. The two settings options in the console tree are Connections settings and Server Settings. The Connections settings are discussed in the section "Clients" later in this chapter. For Server Settings, you can make changes by right-clicking the appropriate setting and choosing Properties.

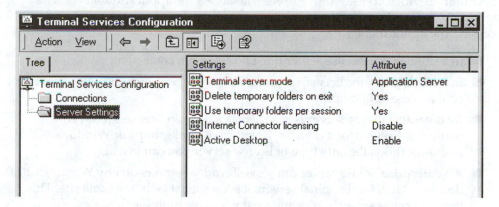

■ **Terminal Server Mode** cannot be changed unless you return to the Add/Remove Programs applet in Control Panel and reinstall Terminal Services in Remote Administration mode.

■ **Delete Temporary Folders On Exit** defaults to Yes, which is usually preferable. Terminal Server creates a discrete temporary folder for each new session, and any temporary files accumulated during the session are located in that folder. There's rarely a reason to save temporary files, but if you think you need to, change the setting to No.

■ **Use Temporary Folders Per Session** defaults to Yes, and it really means a new folder for temporary files is created for each new session. If you opt to save the temporary folders, you can use this setting to determine whether

Terminal Server creates a new folder for each session or continues to use the existing folder.

- **Internet Connector Licensing** is disabled by default, but you can enable this option if you have anonymous users (not employees) who have a reason to access this Terminal Services server. This is useful for companies that provide access to databases or software to contractors and vendors, or for kiosks. This requires a special license (see the section "Licenses" later in this chapter).

- **Active Desktop** is enabled by default. You should think about disabling Active Desktop for your Remote Administration sessions to reduce the overhead. The Active Desktop uses more resources than the classic Windows desktop, and generally isn't necessary for administrative tasks.

Licenses

When you run Terminal Services in Application Server mode, you must have a license server that provides licenses for the users who access the application server. The application server(s) contact the license server to issue licenses to users who are accessing the application(s).

- In a domain, the license server must be a domain controller.

- In a workgroup, the license server can be any server, including the server that contains the application.

- By default, a license server is installed as a domain license server, which maintains licenses for a domain. If you have workgroups or Windows NT 4.0 domains, this is the only type of license server you can install.

- An enterprise license server can serve Terminal servers on any Windows 2000 domain. All of the Terminal servers it serves must be in the same site. This type of license server is appropriate if you have multiple domains.

You have 90 days after purchasing Windows 2000 to install a license server. During that time, your Terminal server will admit a client in an unlicensed state. After the grace period, the Terminal server will refuse unlicensed clients.

The license server gets its licenses from Microsoft, and you start the process by activating the license server, which automatically launches the process of obtaining licenses. You can use the Internet, the Web, a telephone, or a fax to get the license information from Microsoft. The difference between the Internet and the Web is that Internet licensing takes place from the computer that is acting as the license server, and the Web licensing takes place from any other computer on the network that can connect to the Microsoft licensing site.

When you activate a license server, Microsoft links the server to a digital certificate that validates the identity (and ownership) of the server. The license server uses this certificate to receive more licenses for your Terminal Services servers, if you need to increase the number of licenses.

Choose Terminal Services Licensing from the Administrative Tools menu to open the Terminal Services Licensing dialog box. The server on which you installed Terminal Services is listed with an Activation Status of Not Activated.

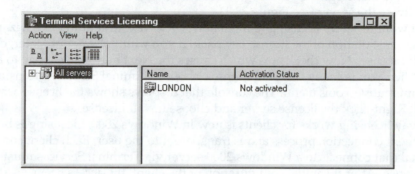

The quickest way to activate the license server and to access the Microsoft Clearinghouse is to install the license server on a computer that has Internet access. Otherwise, you'll have some manual data entry to perform to transfer the information you receive.

To activate a license server and obtain licenses, in the Terminal Services Licensing console, expand the servers, right-click the license server you want to activate, and choose Activate Server. The Licensing Wizard launches, which you step through by making choices and clicking Next. Start by specifying the method you want to use to contact Microsoft.

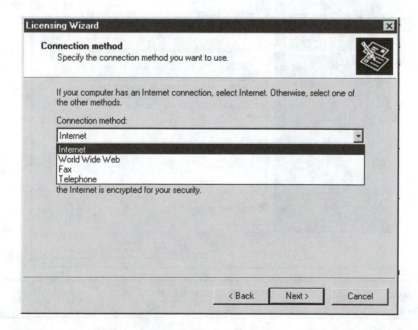

Continue to step through the wizard, and when you have finished, Microsoft will send you a Personal Identification Number (PIN) for the license server. The PIN arrives via e-mail if you use the Internet or Web connection (immediately; it's an automatic reply), or over the telephone or fax if you use either of those connections. Enter the PIN to activate the server (see Figure 28-1).

If you want to set up licensing immediately, click Next to continue the wizard through the installation of the license key pack. If you want to wait until later, clear the Install Licenses Now check box, which causes the Next button to change to a Finish button. When you're ready to install licenses, choose Terminal Services Licensing from the Administrative Tools menu. The console that displays shows the license server as activated. Right-click the license server and choose Install Licenses.

The way licensing works for clients is new in Windows 2000. Licensing is built into the client connection process and is transparent to the user. Each client computer or terminal that connects to a Windows 2000 server via Terminal Services must have a valid license. After the initial configuration of the client, the access license is stored locally at the client and is presented to the Terminal server every time the client connects.

Note   *When the number of clients requesting licenses from a license server exceeds the number of licenses you have installed, a notification is issued in the form of an event in the system log of the Event Viewer. You can repeat the licensing installation procedure to purchase more licenses.*

Figure 28-1.   *You can set up licenses now or later*

There are two additional, optional licenses available for Terminal Services:

■ Internet Connector License

■ Work at Home Client Access License

The Internet Connector License is used instead of the client access licenses and can be purchased as an add-on license. It allows up to 200 concurrent users to connect anonymously to a Terminal server over the Internet. This is useful if you want Internet users to have access to company Windows-based software without rewriting the applications as Web applications. The users who access a Terminal server with this license cannot be employees of your company.

The Work at Home Client Access License is available for employees who need home-based access to the Windows 2000 desktop and 32-bit Windows-based applications at the company. The license is available through the Microsoft Volume licensing program. You can purchase a Work at Home License for each regular Client Access License you purchased for corporate employee use.

Clients

Client access software must be installed before client computers or terminals can access the server. You can use the Terminal Services Client Creator, or let client machines connect to the client software on the server running Terminal Services.

Using the Client Creator

The Client Creator creates installation disks for 16-bit and 32-bit Windows desktops. The number of disks varies, depending on the platform:

■ Windows 16-bit clients take four floppy disks

■ Windows 32-bit Intel clients take two floppy disks

■ Windows 32-bit Alpha clients take two floppy disks

Take these steps to create the disks:

1. Choose Terminal Server Client Creator from the Administrative Tools menu.

2. Click on the appropriate client.

3. Specify the floppy drive (usually A:).

4. Select the Format disks check box.

5. Click OK to create the disk.

6. Insert a disk into the drive and click OK.

7. Click Yes to confirm the creation of the disk and then Yes to confirm the erasure of any existing data.

8. Continue to insert disks and select Yes until the disks are created.

The disks are used at the client computers to set up the client software. Log on to a client computer as an administrator and open Run from the Start menu. Put the first floppy disk into drive A and enter **a:\setup**; then click OK. Follow the prompts to install the software.

Using the Server-Based Client Files

After the installation of Terminal Services on a Windows 2000 Server, the %SystemRoot%\system32\clients\tsclient\net directory contains subdirectories that hold the software needed to set up Windows-based 16-bit and 32-bit client machines. You should create a share for the directory so users can find it easily, and access the appropriate subdirectory. (The share permissions need only include Read.) Then notify users where to find the client software so they can travel to the appropriate subdirectory and open Setup.exe. The client subdirectories are

- Win16 for 16-bit clients
- Win32 for Intel 32-bit clients
- Win32a for Alpha 32-bit clients

Note *During setup, you are asked whether you want the client software to be accessible to all users of the computer or just the currently logged-on user. If you are logged on as administrator, select all users. Otherwise, make a choice depending upon your own preference.*

Logging On

After the client software is installed, the Programs menu includes a Terminal Services Client menu item with two items on its submenu:

- Client Connection Manager, for creating a profile for future connections
- Terminal Services Client, for logging onto the Terminal Services server

Using the Client Connection Manager

To create a profile for connecting to the Terminal Services server, choose Client Connection Manager from the Terminal Services Client submenu. Choose File | New Connection to launch the Client Connection Manager Wizard shown in Figure 28-2. Then configure your connection profile as follows:

1. On the Create A Connection page, enter a friendly connection name (such as **TS connection** or **Bob's TS**). In the Server name or IP address, enter the name of the Terminal server, or the server IP address.

2. On the Automatic Logon page, enter logon information if you want to enable automatic logons at the client. This is useful for kiosk-based applications, but not a good idea on a standard network computer. It's a good idea to click Next without filling out the page.

3. On the Screen Options page, select the screen size you want for your client window. If you select full screen, the client window will obscure your local window. Because you'll be using software from the server, that's fine, and when you log off, you're returned to your original computer window. Choose a resolution for the screen.

4. On the Connections Properties page, select the compression and caching options you want to use if you're connecting over a slow link (caching writes to the local machine).

5. On the Starting A Program page, you can opt to start a program automatically when a Terminal Services session is established.

6. On the Icon And Program Group page, select an icon and program group settings.

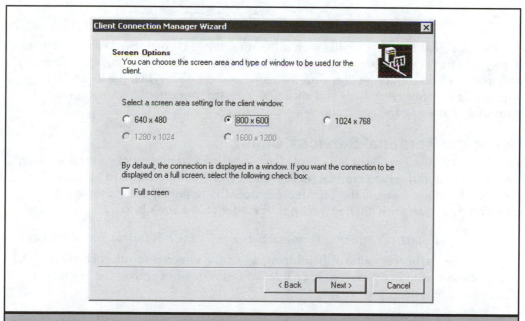

Figure 28-2. *Supposedly, 640×480 speeds things up, but any reduction in speed seems to be negligible when using higher resolutions*

When you finish, a preconfigured connection exists in the Client Connection list on the Start menu.

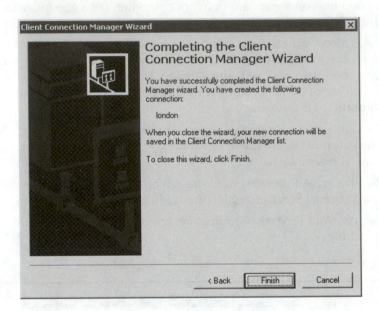

You can create another profile with different settings if you wish. When you want to log onto the Terminal server, choose Start | Programs | Terminal Services Client and then click on the connection with the name you created. When the logon box appears, enter your credentials and click OK. You are connected to the server, and you can begin using the applications installed there.

Using the Terminal Services Client

The Terminal Services Client is a simple logon routine that you must go through each time you want to use the Terminal server. Using the Client Connection Manager obviates these steps, so use the Terminal Services Client only if there's some reason you want to log on with different settings or credentials. Here's how:

1. Choose Start | Programs | Terminal Services Client | Terminal Services Client.

2. Enter the Server name or IP address, select the screen resolution you want, and choose whether you want to enable data compression or to cache bitmaps to the client disk.

3. Click Connect.

Log on and go to work.

CE Handheld Clients

A special installation method is needed for the Terminal Services client for Windows CE Handheld PC Professional Edition v3.0-based devices. The installation has to be geared to the desktop synchronization tools that are used to install applications on these devices. To use the Terminal Services client, you must have a Windows CE Handheld PC Professional Edition v.3.0-based device, the Windows CE desktop synchronization software installed on a desktop machine, connectivity between the desktop host and the Windows CE-based device, and network connectivity (via net cable, wireless, or cellular) to the Terminal server. More information is available in the Terminal Services help files on your Windows 2000 Server.

Managing Terminal Server

Administrators can configure the way client connections interact with the Terminal server, and can control activity as it occurs. There is a great deal of administrative power in this program.

Configuring Connection Properties

You can configure and control the connections to the server in the Terminal Services Configuration console. Open the console by choosing Terminal Services Configuration from the Administrative Tools menu. Select the Connections object in the tree to display the installed connections in the right pane. Unless you have installed third-party connections (see the section "Citrix" later in this chapter), only the Microsoft connection is listed.

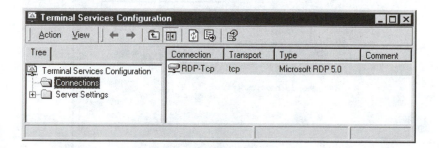

Right-click the connection you want to work with, and choose the appropriate command:

- Choose All Tasks | Disable Connection to make this connection unavailable.
- Choose All Tasks | Rename Connection to give this connection a new name.
- Choose Delete to remove the connection.
- Choose Properties to display the connection's Properties dialog box.

The connections Properties dialog box offers a wide range of options for configuring the connection. It's beyond the scope of this overview discussion to enumerate all the detailed controls you have, but a summary examination is appropriate.

General Tab

Use the General tab (see Figure 28-3) to enter a descriptive comment for this connection and to select an encryption level from the drop-down list. All the available encryption levels use standard RSA RC4 encryption.

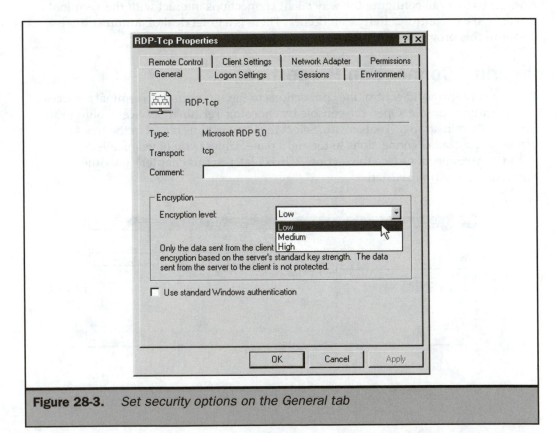

Figure 28-3.   *Set security options on the General tab*

- Choose **Low** to encrypt data sent from the client to the server with either a 40-bit or 56-bit key. The 56-bit key is applied for Windows2000 clients, and a 40-bit key is applied for legacy Windows clients. Low encryption is input-only, and is generally used to protect sensitive data, such as user passwords.

- Choose **Medium** to encrypt data sent in both directions, using the same 40-bit or 56-bit keys.

- Choose **High** (only if you are located in the United States or Canada) to encrypt data in both directions using strong 128-bit encryption.

Select the Use Standard Windows Authentication check box to direct Terminal Services to use the standard Windows authentication if there is a third-party authentication package installed on the server.

Logon Settings Tab

You can use the fields in the Logon Settings tab (see Figure 28-4) to direct Terminal Services to accept logon information (name and password) from the client, or insist that all logons be performed with logon information you enter in this tab.

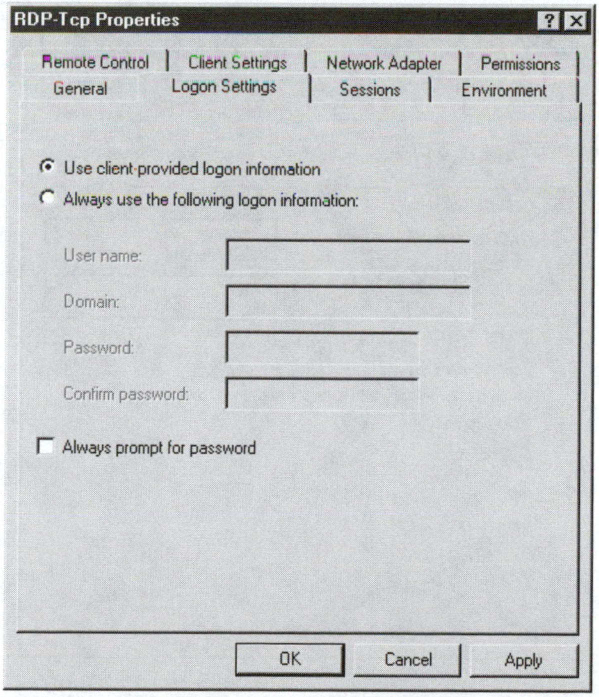

Figure 28-4. *Terminal Services can accept client-configured logon information or information specified by the administrator*

The user information that's provided by the client is the data that was entered and configured during the connection setup at the client machine. You can also use the Logon Settings tab to specify that the system will always prompt for a password, even if the configuration options indicate a cached password.

Sessions Tab

Use the Sessions tab (see Figure 28-5) to set disconnection options. By default, the user options control sessions, but you should make changes to invoke administrative controls over these settings.

In case the terminology is confusing, here's the difference between *disconnect* and *end*:

- **Disconnect** closes the connection between the client and the server so data cannot be sent. The session continues to exist, and the client can resume by reconnecting. Temporary folders and files remain on the server, and a license is in use.

- **End** deletes the session. Temporary folders and files are removed from the server (unless you configured the system to hold onto them). The client must log on all over again.

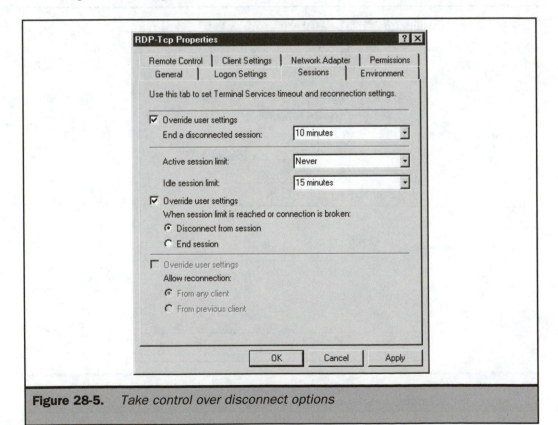

Figure 28-5. *Take control over disconnect options*

Environment Tab

Use the Environment tab (see Figure 28-6) to set the environment for all users who log on to this Terminal server. This is a way to apply a consistent environment for the server, but it only works well if the user community is homogenous. For example, controlling the software environment works if all users who log on to this server use the same application (perhaps your accounting package).

Remember that the option to launch an application upon connection is also available in the user configuration settings, and the data you enter in this tab overrides any options set at the client end.

The option to disable wallpaper is selected by default and should not be changed, because wallpaper is an unnecessary decorative item that you shouldn't permit to use bandwidth.

Remote Control Tab

Use the Remote Control tab (see Figure 28-7) to establish administrative control levels over client sessions. The level of control you have in Terminal Services is quite extensive.

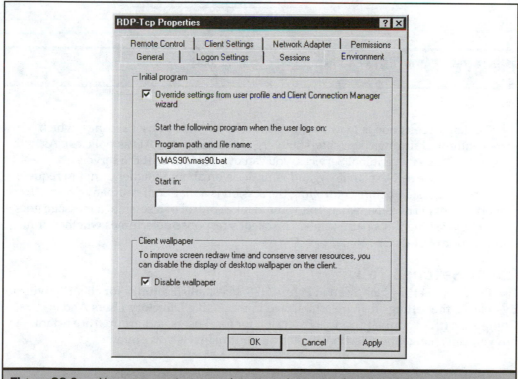

Figure 28-6.   *You can create a consistent environment for all users*

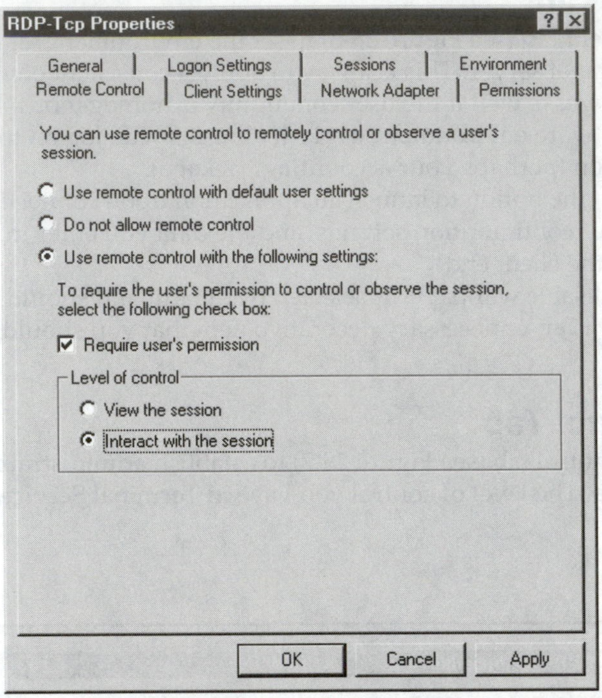

Figure 28-7.   *You can view or control a client session*

The default selection is to use remote control with default user settings, which were configured during client setup (and are contained in the AD as policies). As with all client settings in Terminal Services, you can override them at the server.

The fields are self-explanatory, and your decision about whether or not to request a client's permission before controlling the session is a matter of company policy. If you opt to get permission, when you want to take control of a session, a message goes to the client asking if it's permissible. The client's response determines whether or not you get control of the session.

Client Settings Tab

Use the Client Settings tab, seen in Figure 28-8, to establish settings for client activities. By default, the settings that are established in the Active Directory Users And Computers (the Terminal Services Extension for local users and groups) are extant, but you can change the selections to suit the control levels you prefer.

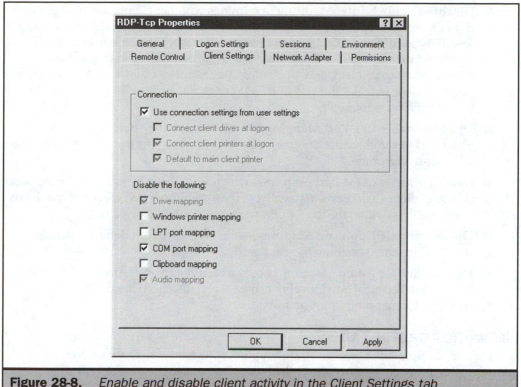

Figure 28-8. *Enable and disable client activity in the Client Settings tab*

Here are the explanations for the choices on this tab:

- **Connect Client Drives At Logon** is available only if you've installed the Citrix ICA-based Terminal Services client software. Selecting this option means client-configured drive mappings are automatically connected at logon.

- **Connect Client Printers At Logon**, which is selected by default, automatically reconnects mapped local printers at logon.

- **Default To Main Client Printer**, which is selected by default, automatically sends print jobs to the client's default printer.

- **Disable/Enable Drive Mapping** is only available if you've installed the Citrix ICA-based Terminal Services client software. This option controls whether or not clients can map drives. By default, mapping is disabled.

■ **Disable/Enable Printer Mapping** determines whether clients can map printers. If you select this option (disable), clients cannot map printers. If you also clear (enable) the LPT and COM port mappings, clients will be able to create and install printers manually. If you clear the check box to enable this activity, clients can map printers, and all printer queues are reconnected at logon. Unless you also clear (enable) the LPT and COM port mappings, clients will not be able to create printers manually.

■ **Disable/Enable LPT Port Mapping**, which is enabled by default, means that LPT ports at the client are automatically mapped for printing and are available when creating printers.

■ **Disable/Enable COM Port Mapping**, which is disabled by default, determines whether client COM ports are available for mapping. If you clear the check box to enable this option, the local COM ports are available for printers.

■ **Disable/Enable Clipboard Mapping**, which is enabled by default, specifies whether the client can map the clipboard.

■ **Disable/Enable Audio Mapping** is only available if you've installed the Citrix ICA-based Terminal Services client software. If disabled (the default selection), client audio mapping is not permitted.

Network Adapter Tab

If there are multiple NICs on the computer, you can use this tab to select one, or configure Terminal Services to use all the NICs. This is also the place to specify whether you permit unlimited connections to the Terminal server or want to set a maximum number of connections. Setting a maximum improves performance for the users that connect to the server. If you do opt for a maximum, be sure to set tighter restrictions on the Sessions tab so that idle users don't occupy a connection that another user is waiting for.

Permissions Tab

This is a standard Windows 2000 Permissions dialog box in which you grant permissions to access the server.

Terminal Services Manager

You can keep an eye on the condition of the Terminal Services server with the Terminal Services Manager. Open this console by selecting Terminal Services Manager from the Administrative Tools menu. You can view the current state of sessions, users, and processes.

Support for Citrix MetaFrame

Microsoft supports third-party software for Terminal Services, which enhance the application's feature set. The most popular of these is MetaFrame from Citrix (http://www.citrix.com). The Citrix ICA (Independent Computer Architecture) is a server-based technology that separates an application's logic from its user interface and allows 100 percent application execution from the server.

To learn more about running Terminal Services with Citrix MetaFrame, read *Citrix: The Official Guide to Windows Terminal Services & Metaframe* by Steve Kaplan and Marc Mangus (Osborne/McGraw-Hill, 2000).

The
Complete
Reference

Part VII

Appendix

Appendix

Windows 2000
Version Differences

Microsoft has expanded the packaging for Windows 2000, and most noteworthy are the number of varieties of Server. The differences among Server offerings aren't enormous, but it's important to understand them in order to deploy the versions that match your needs and your applications.

Windows 2000 Professional

The workstation component of a Windows 2000 network is Windows 2000 Professional. It's obvious that the operating system's parentage is in the NT kernel, because the logon, security, and user management features are based on Windows NT.

It's equally obvious that Microsoft took a lot of the best design features from Windows 98 and inserted them in Windows 2000 Professional. Plug and Play, hardware and driver configuration management utilities (such as Device Manager, which all of us longed for in NT), multimonitor support, and the power management features are welcome additions to the Windows 2000 client.

There's a great deal more hardware support than existed in Windows NT, and you'll find it amazingly easy to install scanners, cameras, and parallel-port peripherals such as Zip drives. In addition, Windows 2000 Professional supports two-way symmetrical multiprocessing.

For mobile users, Windows 2000 Professional works better than Windows NT, due to the robust power management features.

Windows 2000 Professional is available in two versions: Upgrade Version and Full Version. See the section "Upgrading to Windows 2000" later in this appendix.

Windows 2000 Server

Microsoft is offering three versions of Windows 2000 Server, all of which have a great many services that were not available in Windows NT. Some of the new features contained in all versions include the following:

- **Active Directory**, an enterprise-class directory service that is scalable and configurable.

- **Asynchronous Transfer Mode (ATM)**, which transports multiple types of traffic across LANs and WANs simultaneously. (It requires hardware that supports the feature-look for NICs that offload processing from the CPU to the NIC.)

- **Certificate Services**, which provide the ability to deploy your own public key infrastructure. This means you can use smart cards, Secure Sockets Layer (SSL) security, and issue your own X509 V3 certificates.

- **Disk Quotas**, which let you monitor and limit user disk space on NTFS volumes.

- **Dynamic DHCP**, which works with the Active Directory and DNS on IP networks. This relieves administrators of the need to assign and track static IP addresses.

- **Encrypting File System (EFS)**, which adds new access controls you can use to enhance file security. EFS is an integrated system service.

- **Group Policies**, which provide a way to define permissions and settings across the enterprise. This feature works as an integral part of the Active Directory.

- **Indexing Service**, which gives users a powerful tool for finding information across the network.

- **Internet Authentication Service (IAS)**, which provides a way to manage dial-in or VPN users, including authentication, authorization and auditing. (It's also known as RADIUS.)

- **Internet Connection Sharing**, with which you can share an Internet connection throughout the network.

- **Lightweight Directory Access Protocol (LDAP)**, which is the primary access protocol for Active Directory.

- **Message Queuing**, integrated into the operating system, which lets applications run across networks and the Internet, across disparate platforms.

- **Microsoft Management Console (MMC)**, which provides a single interface for managing all the objects in the system.

- **Network Address Translation (NAT)**, which translates private internal addresses to public external addresses. This means you can use unregistered addresses internally, and protect your internal network from external systems. (NAT is the support technology behind Internet Connection Sharing.)

- **Quality of Service (QOS)**, which lets you control the bandwidth used by applications.

- **Removable and Remote Storage Services**, which provide management controls over removable media and remote media.

Windows 2000 Server

Windows 2000 Server, the standard server product, supports up to four-way processing and up to 4GB of memory. Suitable for small-to-medium size businesses, this version contains all the components needed to run a variety of applications and business ventures, in addition to a wide range of new administrative components.

For small businesses, Standard Server works perfectly as a domain controller, and if the number of users is small enough (less than 50), the DC can also house the Active Directory and DNS services.

For large organizations that may be deploying more powerful versions of Windows 2000 Server throughout the enterprise, Standard Server is an economical way to take care of a number of functions, such as file and print services, Terminal Servers, and other services, especially in small remote locations or departments.

Windows 2000 Server is available in two versions: Upgrade Version and Full Version. See the section "Upgrading to Windows 2000" later in this appendix.

Windows 2000 Advanced Server

Replacing Windows NT Server Enterprise Edition, Advanced Server supports up to eight-way processing and 8GB memory. Designed for large enterprise services, this version is a good choice for database-intensive environments.

Advanced Server is the choice if you require clustering and load balancing services, which are built into this version. These features make it easier to ensure scalability and availability, both in terms of application and data access, and also for failover.

Windows 2000 Advanced Server is available in two versions: Upgrade Version and Full Version. See the section "Upgrading to Windows 2000" later in this appendix.

Windows 2000 Datacenter Server

Datacenter Server has been described as the most powerful and functional server operating system ever offered by Microsoft. It supports up to 32-way SMP and up to 64GB of physical memory.

Note *Datacenter Server natively provides up to 16-way SMP, but some OEM installations scale to 32-way.*

Providing both clustering and load balancing services as standard features, this product has been optimized for large projects, such as data warehouses and large-scale simulations in science and engineering. Datacenter Server is designed to support access by 10,000 simultaneous users without degradation. This version of Server also supports Media Services, which let you deliver streaming multimedia to users on the Internet and on your intranet.

Organizations that are upgrading from Windows NT should look at Datacenter Server with a view toward consolidating existing servers. ISPs and organizations that host Web sites will find Datacenter Server appropriate for their massive transactional processing needs.

Datacenter Server is sold only as a Retail version; there is no Upgrade version.

Upgrading to Windows 2000

You can upgrade previous versions of Windows to Windows 2000 with two restrictions:

- You cannot upgrade Windows 3.*x*.
- You cannot upgrade Windows NT versions earlier than 3.51.

The available upgrade paths from previous versions of Windows to Windows 2000 are described in Table A-1.

After you have deployed Windows 2000, you cannot upgrade a workstation to a server, and you cannot upgrade Server to Advanced Server or Datacenter Server. You can, however, upgrade Advanced Server to Datacenter Server.

AppCenter

During the beta test phase of Windows 2000, distributed services for COM+ were removed from the base operating system and built into a new product called AppCenter, sometimes called AppCenter Server. This product is *not* another version of Windows 2000 Server.

AppCenter is designed to help administrators manage sites. It supports some of the scalability issues facing large and growing organizations. Its most important use, however, is letting administrators manage a farm of servers (usually all the servers in a site) as though all the servers in the farm were a single entity.

Deploying applications, upgrades, updates, and service packs across a site via AppCenter is far easier and more manageable than it would be through standard deployment measures. The underlying built-in failover protection is obvious, and should be a motivation for large companies to consider this product. Additionally, the product is optimized for Web content.

In effect, AppCenter builds a single application image, with all of its attendant details (such as security settings, database connection information, performance tuning settings, and so forth). Administrators can deploy, manage, and tweak all the servers in the farm from this central location.

Adding and removing servers from the farm is a simple matter of clicking the appropriate choices in a GUI management utility.

AppCenter can gather all the performance data across the cluster into one console, so the performance of an application distributed across the farm can be examined. If needed, the administrator can drill down into an individual server to examine the performance statistics there.

You can think of AppCenter as WLBS on steroids.

Current Version	Prof. Retail	Prof. Upgrade	Srv. Retail	Srv. Upgrade	Adv Srv. Retail	Adv. Srv. Upgrade	Data-center
Windows 9x	X	X					
Windows NT 3.51 Workstation	X	X					
Windows NT 4 Workstation	X	X					
Windows NT 3.51 Server			X	X	X		
Windows NT 4 Server			X	X	X		
Windows NT 4 Terminal Server			X	X	X		
Windows NT 4 Enterprise Edition					X	X	X

Table -1. *Available Upgrade Paths to Windows 2000*

Index

D

S